Trekking in
NEPAL

Trekking in

NEPAL

A Traveler's Guide

7th Edition

Stephen Bezruchka

Foreword by Sir Edmund Hillary

**THE
MOUNTAINEERS**

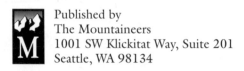

Published by
The Mountaineers
1001 SW Klickitat Way, Suite 201
Seattle, WA 98134

First edition, 1972.; second edition, 1974; third edition, 1976; all by Sahayogi Press,
    Kathmandu, Nepal.
Fourth edition, 1981; fifth edition, 1985; sixth edition, 1991, published in the
    United States, by The Mountaineers, Seattle, Washington.
Seventh edition: first printing 1997, second printing 1998, revised 1999.

Published simultaneously in Great Britain by Cordee, 3a DeMontfort Street,
Leicester, England, LE1 7HD

Manufactured in Canada

Edited by Dana Fos
Maps by Nick Gregoric
All photographs by the author, unless otherwise noted
Cover design by Betty Watson
Layout by Jennifer Shontz
Book design by The Mountaineers Books
Cover photograph: *Samagaon* Gomba *behind Mansalu.* Photo by Pat Morrow.
Frontispiece: *The author's wife and daughter, on the trail from Namche Bazaar to
    Thami, approach a* chorten, *keeping it on the right.*

Library of Congress Cataloging-in-Publication Data
Bezruchka, Stephen.
    Trekking in Nepal: a traveler's guide / Stephen Bezruchka. — 7th
ed.
        p.   cm.
    Includes bibliographical references and index.
    ISBN 0-89886-535-2
    1. Hiking—Nepal—Guidebooks. 2. Nepal—Guidebooks.
GV199.44.N46B49 1997
915.49604—dc21   97-21915
                                                                CIP

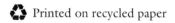

Table of Contents

Foreword by Sir Edmund Hillary 7

Preface 9

SECTION I: PREPARING TO TREK

Background 14

How to Use This Book 18

Chapter 1: **Trekking Styles and Destinations** 20

Chapter 2: **Preparations** 43

Chapter 3: **Interacting with Nepal** 72

Chapter 4: **Health and Health Care** 105

SECTION II: THE ROUTES

Following the Route Descriptions 145

Chapter 5: **North of Pokhara** 164

Chapter 6: **Solu-Khumbu (The Everest Region)** 212

Chapter 7: **Langtang, Gosainkund, and Helambu** 248

Chapter 8: **Eastern Nepal** 278

Chapter 9: **Western Nepal** 323

APPENDICES

Appendix A: **Addresses** 356

Appendix B: **Further Reading** 362

Appendix C: **Nepali Language Introduction** 369

Glossary 372

Index 375

Mount Everest was first climbed by Sir Edmund Hillary and Tenzing Norgay on May 29, 1953.

Foreword

Stephen Bezruchka's book has proved a resounding success. Many of the trekkers I see each year in the Himalaya carry a much-used copy as a guide and friend.

Since 1976 when I first wrote a foreword to *A Guide to Trekking in Nepal*, I have seen many changes in the country—both good and bad. Population pressure has relentlessly increased and the growth of tourism has been quite remarkable. Many of the walking tracks and campsites are cleaner now as trekking agencies make greater efforts to tidy up behind them. But in the mountains the climbing expeditions still leave piles of rubbish around. There has been a determined effort to increase reforestation but the steep hillsides are frequently barren and scarred with great slips carrying soil down into the flooded rivers.

But despite the devastation Nepal is still very beautiful. The mountains are as superb as ever and the people just as friendly. Trekking in Nepal is an experience never to be forgotten. Those of us who have been around a long time can see the changes but the newcomer sees only the drama and the beauty. Perhaps it is better that way. We must desperately battle for environmental protection but not lose our ability to absorb the remaining beauty of the mountains and the valleys. It is the responsibility of all of us to encourage reforestation and make a determined effort to leave the country at least as tidy as we found it—or maybe a little bit better.

Sir Edmund Hillary

These Kham Magar *girls near Dhorpatan wear banded cigarette wrappers in their ear lobes to make them look more Buddha-like.*

Preface

Nepal is on the map for the adventure traveler, and even the casual tourist. Adventure used to be for the elite or crazy, but now "adventures" are undertaken by ordinary people in economically rich countries—perhaps a disease of the complex, modern, postindustrial society.

Trekking in its various styles is an increasingly popular activity, with over 80,000 participants in Nepal annually. Especially along the popular routes, there have been many changes over the span of almost thirty years that I have been fortunate to be involved with Nepal.

Trekking is so popular because of the landforms in this remarkably varied country and because of the nature of the Nepali spirit. What can be done to enhance the experience of both the visitor and the Nepali host? Clearly it is understanding on both sides that is necessary. With the remarkable quality of Nepali tolerance, there is little that needs to be said about that aspect. But for the visitor, there is much to be learned about the way of Nepal if you want to be respected by your hosts. That is the purpose of this book. Whether you are going with an agency, organizing your own portered trip, or going it alone, this book will help you have an experience that is remarkable, memorable, and close to the heart of Nepal. For even though you might surmise that the larger numbers of tourists will dilute the hospitality of the Nepali people, the opposite is true. The more you are sensitive to the ways of Nepal, the more intimate and wonderful your experience. This will set you apart from the others.

My purpose in writing this guidebook is to provide visitors with the information they need to be culturally appropriate and environmentally sensitive guests in this remarkable country and to keep them on the correct trails. Some tourists who come to Nepal want to be served in ways they can't in their own country because they can't afford it. Such tourism is neocolonial imperialism and, although you can't entirely escape elements of it in your travels, I try to show you ways to get beyond this mode. It is still possible to have the same wonderful, intimate experience with Nepali people today that I had almost thirty years ago. Today there are options that make it easier to not have this opportunity. This book will help you avoid these options if you wish a different experience than suggested by the glossy adventure travel brochures. In this atypical guidebook, I try to provide various insights to the riches of this perhaps most diverse spectrum of peoples and terrain in the world. I pose mentally stimulating questions, many that are unanswerable, as well as present information about what is seen, heard, or smelled.

I have also written a booklet on the Nepali language. It is sold separately in a pocket-size version, together with a language tape, to help you study the *baasaa* before you go and to learn it as you trek. There is no more important advice I can give you to enjoy Nepal than to study Nepali and use it in the country. Nothing else will as easily set you apart from the other trekkers.

Many people have helped me in updating this edition. Thanks go to Line Antonsen, Robin Biellik, Rupert Blum, Gunter Boch, Cherie Bremer-Kamp, Bruce and Ellen Campbell, Susan Clark, Norm Coleman, Mary Ann Davis, Don and Aiko Diehl, Thiley Lama Domaray, Ed Earl, Jim and Isabel Foster, Lori Green, Roger Hoehfurtner, Eric and Ingred Holzman, Inu K.C., Liesl Messerschmidt K.C., Patricia

Knox, Wendy Brewer Lama, Steve LeClerq, Jim Litch, Eugene Marguilis, Tom Manery, Julie Nassif, John Peirce, Edmund Potter Rachel Rosen, David Schensted, Surendra Sharma, Ang Rita Sherpa, Kazi Sambu Sherpa, Lhakpa Norbu Sherpa, David Shlim, Tenzing Tamang, Jean Thomas, Kay Timms, Eric Wolf, and Laura Ziemer. Thanks to *Himal* Magazine for permission to reprint the climbing totem on page 30. My wife, Mary Anne Mercer, facilitated this edition in countless ways. My porters continue to teach me most of what I know about Nepal. I am especially grateful to Chandra Pal Rai. The production staff at The Mountaineers has been very helpful. Thank you all.

This guidebook, faced with a landform that is constantly changing, is bound to be out of date in some places and in error in others. Over the years, many trekkers have sent information to me, and this has resulted in substantial improvements to the book. Please keep the comments and letters coming.

I have been involved with writing this guidebook for almost thirty years. At some point in the future, I hope to find an enthusiastic, younger trekker to pass the flame to. If you are under thirty, have walked much of Nepal, speak Nepali, have an on-going relationship with it, love the country, and wish to help others do so by helping me keep this guidebook up to date, please write me care of the publisher.

A Note about Safety

Safety is an important concern in all outdoor activities. No guidebook can alert you to every hazard or anticipate the limitations of every reader. Therefore, the descriptions of roads, trails, routes, and natural features in this book are not representations that a particular place or excursion will be safe for your party. When you follow any of the routes described in this book, you assume responsibility for your own safety. Under normal conditions, such excursions require the usual attention to traffic, road and trail conditions, altitude, weather, terrain, the capabilities of your party, and other factors. Keeping informed on current conditions and exercising common sense are the keys to a safe, enjoyable outing.

Political conditions may add to the risks of travel in Nepal in ways that this book cannot predict. When you travel, you assume this risk, and should keep informed of political developments that may make safe travel difficult or impossible.

The Mountaineers

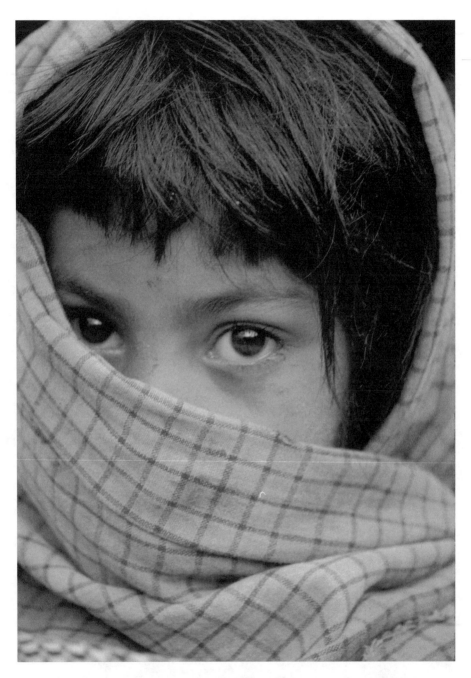

Nepal is there to change you, not for you to change it. Lose yourself in its soul. Make your footprints with care and awareness of the precarious balance around you. Take souvenirs in your heart and spirit, not in your pockets. Nepal is not only a place on the map, but an experience, a way of life from which we all can learn.

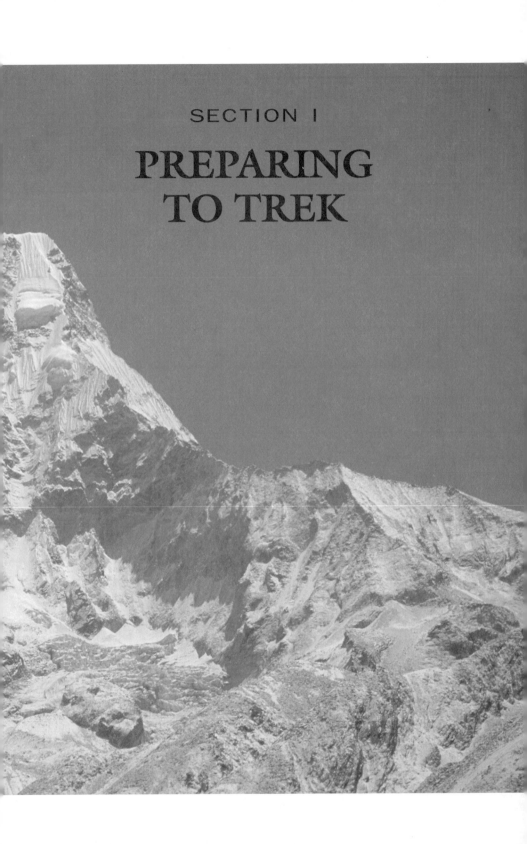

SECTION I

PREPARING TO TREK

Background

A hundred divine epochs would not suffice to describe all the marvels of the Himalaya.

Sanskrit proverb

What kind of experience will you have in Nepal? Think of waking up early one morning and directing your gaze to the north. It is quite cloudy, but for some reason you lift up your eyes. There it is—the triangular rock-and-snow face of Machhapuchhre, glistening in the sun through a hole in the clouds. But it is not even 23,000 ft (7000 m) high! How could it look so big? Or you are walking along the trail when you suddenly hear, "Good morning, sir," spoken in perfect English. You turn around, astonished, to see an ordinary-looking Nepali. Yes, the speaker is a Gurkha soldier, retired from the British Army. The two of you pass many miles talking together. Or it is the day's end and you are resting after the walk, looking at a Western book or magazine that you carry. Soon you are surrounded by children who gaze intently at the pictures. You want to tell them that the world those pictures represent is not better than theirs. Or it is spring and you have toiled to get far above the valley. The rhododendrons make the mountains look like a paradise. The blooms are red in many places, yet the colors can be light, and even beautifully white. Every day there will be many times like these when you will forget the miles you have yet to go, the vertical feet yet to climb, the load on your back. And you will vow to return.

Nepal is a land of unparalleled variety. Imagine a rectangle, 500 by 150 mi (800 by 240 km), divided lengthwise into three strips. The northernmost strip is the Himalaya, meaning "abode of snow," and includes eight of the ten highest mountains in the world. The Himalayan region is sparsely settled by people who speak languages of the Tibeto-Burman family and practice Tibetan Buddhism. The southernmost region, called the Tarai, is an extension of the Gangetic plain of northern India, containing jungles with elephants, rhinoceroses, and tigers. These inhabitants contrast markedly with the yaks and snow leopards less than 100 mi (160 km) to the north. This area is populated by people who speak Indo-European languages and practice Hinduism. Between the two outer strips lies an interface of hills and valleys. The inhabitants speak languages of both the Tibeto-Burman and Indo-European families and generally practice Hinduism with many Buddhist, animistic, and shamanic influences. This "religion of the hills" defies categorization. This middle region, the hills, is the unexpected treasure of Nepal.

Climatically, the country has subtropical, temperate, and alpine regions, determined by elevation. It contains examples of most of the vegetation zones of the world.

The country known as Nepal is a conglomeration of as many very different ethnic groups, languages, and cultures as it is biogeographic regions. This hostile terrain was settled by peoples fleeing invaders from all directions. They found solace in remote valleys and eventually became incorporated into myriad small kingdoms, until one, Gorkha, led by Prithvinarayan Shah, politically unified the country in the 1760s. For over a hundred years, until 1951, Nepal was ruled by a sequence of hereditary prime ministers, the Ranas. During this period Nepal was essentially cut off from outside influences. Because of its forbidding mountains to the north and

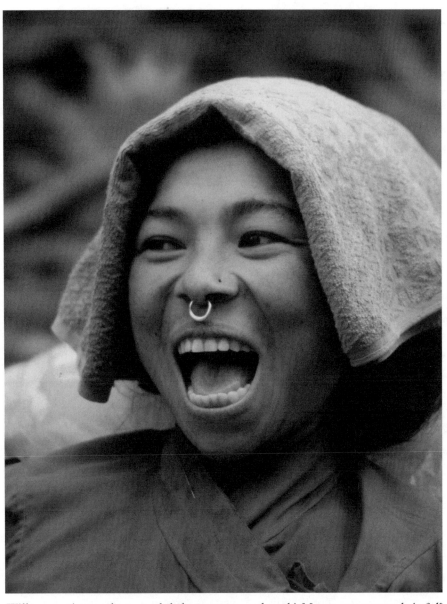

Will your actions and presence help keep women, such as this Magar, *spontaneously joyful?*

Overleaf: *Trekkers under Ama Dablang, between Pangboche and Phortse, after a fresh snowfall*

deadly malaria endemic in the Tarai to the south, Nepal was never successfully invaded by a major power. After an attempt at democracy in 1959, which threatened the status quo, political parties were outlawed; the country was said to be ruled by a system of participatory councils, but real power was vested in the king and his personally chosen secretariat.

In early 1990, popular support for democracy again surfaced. The movement never had grassroots support throughout the country but was led by students and the educated in the large cities. Supported by the quest for democracy throughout the world at that time, and the threat of more uprisings, the *jana andolan* was able to overthrow the monarchical rule with the loss of no more than several hundred lives. In November 1990 a new constitution was adopted, with the king as a constitutional monarch and head of the army but with real power vested in a popularly elected parliament. There have been several elections, at the national and local levels. As in many third world countries, poverty has recently increased, a direct result of so-called "development." In 1990, few believed that so little would have been accomplished in the first nine years of democracy. One factor is that systems of patronage and corruption that date back at least to the century of Rana rule have been maintained in the political mechanism. Nepali society and politics have changed little during this century. But the mood of the country has regressed from optimism to disappointment to frustration to cynicism.

The economy is one of subsistence agriculture. Nepal has most of the statistical characteristics of the world's poorest countries in terms of per capita gross domestic product, literacy, and infant mortality. The high rate of population growth—doubling time is about thirty years—outstrips food production. Another serious problem is deforestation, especially in the Tarai, where after malaria was controlled forests were cut to clear land for agricultural use to feed the increasing population. Nepal's population is over 21 million, growing at over 2% a year.

Nepal, closed to foreigners and foreign influence until 1951, did not officially open its doors to tourists until a few years later. But by 1995, over 350,000 tourists were visiting the country each year, and a massive amount of foreign aid was pushing Nepal on the road to "development." Major contributors of aid have been India, Japan, Germany, France, China, and the United States. Having observed this process over twenty-five years, I see development along Western European and North American lines as basically exploitive, but this is hidden by euphemisms. Most aid is tied; it requires purchasing products and services from the donor countries, and much funding pays expatriate salaries for work Nepalis could do themselves. Few projects benefit the disadvantaged. Only 10% of development assistance is said to reach the poor. Much of the funding leaks, finding its ways into the pockets of the *nouveaux riches*—it has been estimated that anywhere between 10 to over 50% of flows get lost. A look at the burgeoning wealth of the middle class in Kathmandu, where homes cost more than in U.S. cities, attests to this. Thanks to structural adjustment policies carried out as a condition of receiving World Bank and International Monetary Fund loans, which resulted in devaluation of the rupee, foreigners receive excellent value for their hard currency in Nepal, while the poor there suffer more. One could remark that countries that have had modern "development" are worse off than countries that haven't. Look at Korea, Taiwan, Japan, and China as examples of Asian miracles. They escaped the development process.

On the basis of outside advice and funding, Nepal has set aside the largest percentage of any country's land as national parks, a process begun in 1973. Although the concept supposedly creates a haven for touristic needs, it has conflicted with resident people who have sometimes been resettled far from their homeland with disastrous results. Discord between the needs of local peoples, with their increasing numbers, and those of businesses that cater to the tourism industry will continue.

Nepal's greatest economic resource is said to be the hydroelectric potential of its vast rivers fed by the Himalaya. Attempts at massive international development of this treasure have been thwarted so far, but numerous small projects electrify parts of the country. India would like to control this asset and use it to power the billion people sitting south. An unrecognized major asset is the self-respect (*ijat*) of the hill peasant, who was never subjugated by an external power. He or she works hard and, if away from the development mainstream, does not dwell on being economically poor. Only near the imbroglio of progress do you find people monetarily much wealthier talking about how poor they are. "Development" teaches poverty.

In spite of this, many outsiders (myself included) and Nepalis are strongly committed to trying to improve the situation in Nepal. Many work at grassroots levels and in organizations making significant changes. These efforts should not distract us from looking at the big picture, recognizing the powerful forces at work, and trying to change them.

As a typical visitor, isolated from problems of the world, your trek is an opportunity to come face to face with the inequities and dilemmas of the consequences of development. You may choose to shut the door and never venture forth again, or assuage your guilt and "help" some individuals or look at the big picture and then work for global change and an end to the hegemony of the powerful, within nations and among nations. Or you may effect some combination of these responses.

With an understanding of these harsh realities for the bulk of Nepali people, I hope to provide you with information to travel within this amazing land and to limit your perpetration of the bad effects of "development." This land of contrasts beckons those who are willing to travel, as the Nepalis do, on foot. Walking is the only means of reaching most destinations, because Nepal still has the fewest miles of roads in proportion to area of population of any country in the world. The trails that trekkers use are the public transportation and communication routes for the local people.

Trekking, as described here, means travel by foot for many days. The term originated from a Dutch word for travel and came to be an Afrikaans word meaning a migration by oxcart. Trekking routes pass through rural, sparsely settled areas, the homeland of the Nepali people, and travel is by foot, not oxcart. During a trek, travelers can spend nights in recently constructed, simple hotels, or they can camp by themselves or stay in the homes of local people, an option little used by tourists but still the most hospitable form of travel available. They can eat either local food or food they have brought with them. Most of Nepal is not wilderness as the term is understood in the West. Visitors need to be cognizant of the local values and culture, a subject expanded upon in chapter 3.

Trekking is a very healthy activity, although not without its hazards. It is strenuous and burns calories, and many overweight people shed their excess load along the trail. And everyone feels his or her muscles strengthen and firm up. To be sure, there are perils and lower standards of hygiene. Furthermore, modern health care is not available in the hill and mountain areas. But when sensible precautions are taken, few get seriously sick in Nepal. To the contrary, most people find it physically and spiritually enlightening.

How to Use This Book

> *But in the end, guidebooks, like textbooks, are no substitute for the real world. They tell you what to expect from an endeavour—travel—in which the greatest pleasure is the unexpected.*
> Thomas Swick, travel editor,
> *Fort Lauderdale Sun-Sentinel*

Before trekking in Nepal, some basic decisions need to be made early. Chapter 1 outlines the most important ones, namely, how, where, and when to trek. This chapter also contains a summary of treks that will give you an idea of the best trek for you. If you go with an agency headquartered outside Nepal, most of your arrangements will be made with them. If you decide to go on your own, or with a Nepali agency, then more preparations are needed, including the obvious one of getting to Nepal. Flights to Kathmandu are usually heavily booked during the major tourist seasons, so the sooner you start this process the better. If you plan to go with a Nepali agency, you should contact them soon, too. It helps to try to work with several and choose one that fits your needs and seems responsible. A list of trekking agencies is given in Appendix A.

Questions to Ponder: Nepal— A Part of the Himalayan Mosaic?

Peoples of the Himalayan region live in all the ways that human beings have devised to survive on the earth: as hunters and gatherers, nomadic herdsmen, shifting slash and burn cultivators, settled agriculturalists, petty traders, and industrial entrepreneurs. They live in felt tents, thatched huts, brick houses, and stucco palaces. Over forty million people live across the terrain dominated by the world's highest mountain range. This frontier region is predominantly rural. Transport and communication are particularly difficult, and the ethnic groups are astoundingly diverse. Isolation and countless migrations have led to myriad forms of social and cultural adaptation. There are Muslims, Hindus, and Buddhists, but many peoples also retain their own separate ethnic identity and worship. This one thousand, five hundred mile long region is the homeland for what is arguably the most diverse spectrum of peoples in the world.
Todd T. Lewis and Theodore Riccardi, Jr.,
The Himalayas: A Syllabus of the Region's History, Anthropology, and Religion

If you have traveled in other mountain areas of the Himalaya, how do your experiences there compare with those in Nepal? If you have been to Tibet, how do you relate to the Tibetans there compared with those in Nepal? Is there a distinct Nepali character, a Nepali spirit, or is it just a part of a larger Himalayan mosaic?

Chapter 2 discusses the logistics of preparing for a Nepali trek, whereas chapter 3 introduces Nepali customs that will help the trekker prepare for an enjoyable and rich experience. Chapter 4, on health, both physical and mental, discusses what you need to know before and during your trek. You should obtain the language tape and pocket reference that accompany this book and begin to learn the Nepali language. At your leisure look at the routes in Section II. Numerous side bars are scattered through the book to help enhance your understanding of the country and to tease your intellect and sharpen your powers of observation. The subjects are indexed. Most likely, on your return home, it will no longer be difficult to understand why this tiny country has had such a profound impact on foreigners.

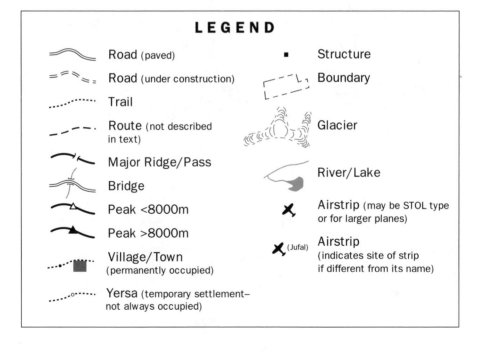

LEGEND

Road (paved)

Road (under construction)

Trail

Route (not described in text)

Major Ridge/Pass

Bridge

Peak <8000m

Peak >8000m

Village/Town (permanently occupied)

Yersa (temporary settlement– not always occupied)

■ Structure

Boundary

Glacier

River/Lake

Airstrip (may be STOL type or for larger planes)

(Jufal) Airstrip (indicates site of strip if different from its name)

1 Trekking Styles and Destinations

It's the richest banquet imaginable. For anyone with an appetite for fantastic legends, a thirst for color (especially red), and a general craving for utter theological wonder, visiting Nepal is a case study in all-you-can-eat.

Jeff Greenwald, *Shopping for Buddhas*

Trekking Styles and Related Activities

There are three basic approaches to trekking, but within each there are many variations as well as some related activities that can be enjoyed during treks. The style you choose depends on your budget, time available, and personal preferences. The areas you wish to visit dictate certain choices. Finally, your choice depends on what you want from your trek.

TREKKING WITHOUT A GUIDE

Trekking without a guide, also known as the "live on the land" approach, is very popular among budget-conscious travelers. Along the popular trails, enterprising Nepalis have established hotels and lodges that provide rooms for trekkers and offer international menus. Villagers are very likely to run after you or at least shout if you take the wrong turn on a trail. It is easy for people to travel without a guide, carrying their own small loads. Along the popular routes, your main human contacts usually are with other, similar-minded trekkers. Local porters can usually be hired anywhere along a trek. If you have porters, they can keep you on the right trails. This is a good way to learn Nepali, especially if traveling off the popular routes. Daily costs, on the popular routes, not including any porters, can average U.S.$5–$10 per person, depending on the amounts spent on food and accommodation. For those traveling on the popular routes north of Pokhara, to and within Everest, or north of Kathmandu, this is perfectly feasible and enjoyable.

Disadvantages of this mode of travel can include spending time in Kathmandu organizing affairs, getting lost occasionally—especially when traveling off the standard routes—and being limited in the areas you can travel to. The more trekkers in the party, the less interaction there will be with the local people, and the less intimate your experience with Nepal will be. Two trekkers are probably the limit for a close interaction with the people, unless most participants speak Nepali.

Trekkers who choose to travel without a guide are more likely to be disappointed in meeting some of their expectations than those who have their treks catered through a professional agency, although most people manage quite well. Trekkers who arrange travel with an agency to popular areas often remark they could have done it on their own and plan to next time. The advantage of trekking without a guide is that learning to deal without the cultural props you grew up with can be a very educational and enlightening experience. Attempting to view the world through Nepali eyes may be the best lesson trekking in Nepal has to offer.

TREKKING WITH A GUIDE

Trekking with a guide can mean arranging and outfitting a large trek just as a professional agency would do, or it might mean simply hiring a guide to accompany a small group. A guide can keep the party on the correct trails and may sometimes cook, carry a load, or attend to other chores. Many guides are quite knowledgeable and can be a valuable resource to explain things seen, and not seen. Porters—that is, people hired strictly for load-carrying—can be taken on along the trail when necessary or hired in Kathmandu before starting a trek. The guide can take care of this. Parties may camp all the way; or they may eat and sleep in hotels and camp only where necessary. Camping is a good way for older people and those wishing less uncertainty about the quality of food and accommodation to travel, providing they bring along enough equipment and food for comfort. Many trekkers hire a guide for themselves if alone or for their small party and travel using lodges and restaurants for accommodation and food. They enjoy the association with the guide and the company of other trekkers.

Recognize that if you have a staff of more than, say, four, it is unlikely that fast times can be made over long distances. The larger the party, the more likely that it will move at the customary pace for specific treks (see "Guides and Porters," in chapter 2).

A guide can be hired either privately (sometimes at specific points along a trek for difficult portions), asking at the hotel in Kathmandu or out in the hills, or through a trekking agency. The agency can also make other arrangements, such as organizing air and bus travel and providing equipment and porters. With the large number of agencies competing for business, they try to accommodate to desired trekking arrangements that are less than a completely organized trek.

Parties wishing more of a spirit of adventure—and a savings on wages—can hire an inexperienced guide. Such a person may be an older porter for treks and mountaineering expeditions or a youngster eager to break into the business. Such people can be excellent and will often do much more than guide—they can cook, carry, and help in other ways. On my first trek in Nepal in 1969, I hired Nima Thundu, a young inexperienced Sherpa. We both learned a great deal and enjoyed ourselves immensely. He went on to start the first company producing trekking food.

In hiring a guide, one of the benefits may be a visit to the family's home. This is worth a considerable detour. Oftentimes, trekkers discover it to be the highlight of their visit, especially if this takes place after the bulk of the journey. They experience wonderful hospitality and continue to maintain a rewarding friendship with this individual and his or her family after they leave the country.

The advantage of trekking with a guide is that it allows considerable flexibility in the choice of route, diversions, and scheduling. There is also a greater opportunity for interacting with the local people encountered en route, especially if the party is small. However, arranging all this after arriving in Nepal can be time-consuming, frustrating, and somewhat difficult. It can be helpful to seek the assistance of a local trekking agency.

Trekking in a modest style is a good means of getting money into the hands of people in the hills of Nepal, because the villagers, who provide food, run the inns, and work as porters, benefit directly. This is a true form of economic assistance, with less chance of leakage compared to international aid projects. Costs for this style are considerably less than for professionally arranged treks and depend on the number of assistants hired.

TREKKING WITH A PROFESSIONAL AGENCY

Mountain Travel, founded in 1965 by the late Himalayan veteran Lt. Col. James Roberts, was the first trekking agency. Hundreds operate within Nepal today. There are no standards—the industry is unregulated.

Many trekking agencies and organizations based in other countries operate treks for groups to various regions of Nepal. Glossy brochures present many superlatives. There are many special interest treks these days, focusing on areas such as art, health matters, natural history, and religion. Other treks cater to people with disabilities. Itineraries tend to take trekkers to less visited areas, an added attraction. The actual treks are subcontracted by one of the trekking agency operators in Nepal. Information about such agencies can be obtained from travel agents in your own country. There can be no congruence in the names of such agencies—for example, Gonzo Treks based in Truth or Consequences, New Mexico, may not operate through Gonzo Treks in Kathmandu. You can deal directly with the Nepali agency from home beforehand and thereby have more of your money go directly to services in Nepal. A list of those that have operated for some time is provided in Appendix A. You can write or fax several and organize a trek through one that appeals. Be specific and clear in your correspondence, asking questions and stating your needs in a point-wise fashion. This should include dates, routes, equipment, food, staff, and so forth. Include plenty of information about your party, such as ages and experience. Some trekkers wait until they arrive in Nepal, visit various agencies, and shop around to see what can be organized for them at short notice. For one or two trekkers not planning a route far off the beaten path, this can work out fine. Some have done this in a day, but plan on 2 or 3, especially during peak times.

This mode of travel is expensive but offers a degree of luxury that is not available in the others. Treks are organized for both large (ten to fifteen) and small (one to two) groups and are usually conducted by Sherpa guides called Sirdars, who can be famous for their mountaineering exploits on Himalayan expeditions. The guides speak sufficient English to allay fears of language difficulties. A large retinue of porters ensures that nothing essential to the comfort and well-being of trekkers is left behind. The parties usually camp in tents near villages and skilled cooks prepare fine meals. Trekkers camping in cold, high places, however, will not be as warm as those who stay in lodges where some heat source exists. The parties often have someone with medical expertise along, and emergencies can usually be handled more quickly than in noncommercial groups. There is also no need to spend time planning for all these arrangements in Kathmandu. Trekking with an agency also means there is a company to complain to if there are problems, something that is important to some visitors. Complaints are usually responded to better when made to an agency in your own country.

Agency trek parties usually have to stick to a predetermined route and schedule, so there is less leeway for interesting diversions or layovers. The maximum distance covered a day is usually limited by how far a laden porter can go. Members of large parties generally keep together. Trekkers in these professionally organized parties are usually rather insulated from the local people encountered en route. Participants tend to relate exclusively to one another, to the guides, and to other employees of the trek. In small groups where you don't know the other travelers beforehand, personality clashes and acrimony can develop.

Certain areas, such as the regions around Kangchenjunga, Mustang, Humla, and Dolpo, are only open to trekkers going through an agency. This is said to be an attempt by the government to lessen the environmental impact.

If going with an agency, ask how many rest days are built into the schedule at high altitude. Also ask how flexible the schedule is should a member of the party develop altitude illness. Be aware that most of the serious cases of altitude illness develop among group trekkers, because these parties try to stick to a predetermined schedule, and peer pressure pushes people beyond their limits. If the party will sleep above 14,000 ft (4270 m), do they carry oxygen, and do they have a Gamow Bag™? (For details, see "Altitude Illness," in chapter 4.) What is the name of their liability insurance company and the amount of insurance it carries? The standard is at least $1 million. Has the staff had wilderness medical care training?

Ask the prospective outfitter for references so you can talk to the people who have taken the trip you are interested in. Much of the experience is leader-dependent, so talk to people who have been with that leader. Talk to him or her directly and get a sense of what your experience with that person will be like. Question background, wilderness and medical skills, language ability, and so forth. Going with a leader who has particular expertise in your area of interests would be an important factor in choosing a trek with an agency. These days, to save costs, many agencies use a local leader, and contacting that person from home may be more difficult. Find out about the subcontractor and exactly what is included in the price. Oftentimes extra expenses are tacked on later. Determine your responsibilities. With some discount agencies, you have to do your share. Ask whether or not the agency screens the clients for potential health problems and level of physical fitness or just for the size of their pocketbook.

Ask whether all the cooking, including meals for the porters, is done on kerosene. Ask whether porters are provided with sufficient equipment so they don't need to huddle around fires at night to keep warm. Inspect the porters' equipment to verify. Given the scarcity of firewood in Nepal, it is necessary for the trekker going with an agency to choose one that minimizes its impact on the environment. Ask how they handle garbage. Do they carry out nonburnables? Has the staff attended the KEEP workshop on responsible trekking, as attested to by a certificate?

Some agencies offer teahouse/trekker lodge-style treks. In these, accommodation and food are contracted out to the various establishments en route. This results in a cheaper trek, compared to the traditional camping style. A guide is along to take care of logistics and interpret features about the countryside. This mode is suitable for small groups heading for the popular trails.

With increasing competition among the many agencies operating today in Nepal, you can negotiate partial arrangements with an agency. This could include as little as getting permits and arranging a guide, or perhaps porters.

The costs, exclusive of airfares and charters, run from about U.S.$20 to over U.S.$100 per person per day and vary according to the length of the trek and the number of people in the party. This kind of travel is especially suited for those who have neither the time nor the desire to make their own arrangements but wish to enjoy the scenery of the country. In contrast to people who prefer other styles of trekking, those who embark on this type of trek are paying for comfort and security.

Some people argue that an agency trek is preferable because your food is carried from Kathmandu and does not deplete local resources. Similarly, when the trekkers' food is prepared on kerosene stoves, there is less pressure on local wood resources. On such treks, however, all of the food for the porters is purchased along the route, and some food for trekkers may be purchased locally, as well. The argument that Sirdars for trekking groups will get the best prices for local foods does not hold up. When the primary concern is that the trek go well, cooks and Sirdars pay high prices for food items. As a consequence, the price for villagers goes up too. Porters almost always use local wood, and for big treks there are many more porters than trekkers. So the net impact of such travel is found to be less environmentally and economically friendly than small-scale treks.

Much of the money to support an agency trek leaves Nepal to pay for imported food and equipment. There is little sharing of profits with the locals. An estimated 67% of Nepal's dollar earnings from tourism is spent to import goods and services required by visitors. I don't mean to discourage travel with agency treks. It is best to decide what your hopes, needs, and means are and to travel accordingly.

CHOOSING A TREKKING STYLE

It is basically true that "anybody" can trek in Nepal—if they try to match level of experience to the difficulty of the journey. Given the tremendous travel expense, time commitment, and, for many, a once-in-a-lifetime opportunity, ambition can easily outstrip ability. Trekking in the Himalaya was once considered at the high end of the spectrum of walking, backpacking, and mountaineering. Often, mountaineers experienced in ranges such as the Alps, Rockies, or Sierra become "mere" trekkers in the Himalaya, where routes carry them thousands of feet above the summits of their home ranges.

But these days, less experienced hikers elect to undertake harder treks. Walking in the mountains is a skill that requires training and experience. The number of tourists who have fallen from trails (fatal and nonfatal) is up dramatically. Inexperienced hikers have become incapacitated by severe musculoskeletal problems that could have been prevented by adequate training.

Trekking should be regarded as an expedition: you are often far from any form of outside help. Unless you are experienced and confident of your self-sufficiency skills, first treks should be on established tourist trails that offer a minimum of difficulty and no dangerous passes. The scenery in Nepal is no less exotic because other outsiders have seen it before you. As your experience, skills, and confidence grow, you can plan more challenging, isolated, and adventurous treks.

Agency trekkers predominate in the Annapurna and Everest regions, while a greater percentage of independent trekkers travel to the Langtang area, according to 1995 statistics. Some 56% of trekkers signed on with an agency, with higher than average percentages for those from Australia, France, Germany, Japan, and the United States, in contrast to the British, for those sending large numbers to Nepal. Among countries sending small numbers, Canadians, Danish, Israelis, Swedes, and Swiss tended to go individually.

There is a laudable worldwide movement afoot to promote what is variably known as "ecotourism," "alternative tourism," "discerning tourism," "gentle tourism," or "tourism with insight." Advocates try to promote travel that is consistent with local needs and attempt to maintain local cultural values and remain environmentally sensitive. Agencies may advertise such travel, but it can certainly be done outside of an organized trek—and done better.

> **More Time Than Money.** If you crave adventure, have plenty of time but limited money, want to adapt your schedule to circumstances, and want to interact with local people as much as possible, then organize your own trek.

> **More Money Than Time.** An organized trek with one of the well-known agencies may be for you if you have a limited amount of time yet want to cover a major route and can accept limitations in flexibility. An agency trek

may be an attractive option if you enjoy the idea of camping in Nepal with food prepared to familiar tastes and with all arrangements made for you. One disadvantage of such treks is the relative lack of close contact with the local people. Others may not like the colonial relationship between the "membars" and the staff.

Of course, the dichotomy is not quite so cut and dried. Many agencies allow some flexibility in scheduling, and with increasing competition they try to adapt treks to your needs.

Another "decision tree" for the first-time trekker to Nepal is the following: If you are on a tight budget, basically go trekking on a popular route and stay in local inns. If you enjoy carrying a pack, then don't hire a porter—but if you don't want to carry anything heavier than a day pack, hire a local porter. Those with more funds, and perhaps more anxiety about doing it themselves, often hire a guide and porters, usually through an agency in Kathmandu, and stay in local hotels.

If you have more money to spend and have your own group, organize a trek through an agency, and stay in tents. If you don't have a group and are willing to travel with strangers, join an organized group through one of the agencies in Kathmandu. Those with a lot of money and wanting as few hassles as possible should join an organized trek from their home country.

TREKKING ALONE

Trekking alone—that is, without other foreign companions—is the best way to get to know Nepal. Those trekking alone would be wise to hire a guide or a porter, especially on trails with few foreigners. If traveling alone along the popular trails without a porter, you will find it easy to meet up with similar-minded people and travel together. It is also easy to meet and join up with other trekkers in Kathmandu. People advertise for trekking partners on bulletin boards in tourist-frequented places there.

Women especially should not travel alone but should try to find a female guide or porter. Nepalis find it difficult to understand why foreigners, especially women, would travel alone—indeed, Nepali women wouldn't. Local people may consider a woman walking alone to be a witch or person of low morals. The Chhetri Sisters Guest House at the lake in Pokhara has a reputation for finding women porters for female trekkers. Take time and ask around. You should be able to find someone suitable, not necessarily English-speaking, which will be an opportunity to learn some Nepali. The same caution applies to men, although sometimes one may see a Nepali man traveling alone. On a trek in which I went with three porters, Tupi Pasang, a yak herder, remarked to me, "You must be a poor man in your country; you're traveling alone and with few porters or supplies."

There have been instances of attacks on trekkers, usually those who are alone in remote areas. I can no longer state that you are perfectly safe from human harm in Nepal, but if you follow the principles outlined in chapter 3 and are sensitive to your hosts, you should have no problems. Travel in Nepal is certainly safer than in almost every other country, including your homeland.

TREKKING WITH YOUR FAMILY

Children need not be left at home in order for the adults of a family to enjoy a trek in Nepal. Certainly a trek with children will be different from one without children, but it need not be any less enjoyable or memorable. In fact, children can be real icebreakers in an alien land; they provide a common link with which the local people can identify.

When I first came to Nepal in 1969, no one trekked with children except occasional expatriates working there; now you often see families along the popular trails. The Nepali village people are open and friendly, and the sight of a trekking family will interest them. While you eat, they will often care for the child, holding, comforting, and playing with him or her. Although a small child may initially be overwhelmed by the interest of outsiders, an exciting cultural exchange can be encouraged if the child becomes accustomed to the local people. Flexibility in the itinerary is particularly important if the family hopes to achieve this communication. Many of the difficulties encountered in trekking with children in Nepal can be overcome if the family tries some overnight trips near home. In fact, I would not recommend that a family attempt trekking in Nepal if they have not done overnight hikes together at home. In chapter 4 there is an important section on health care for children. It should be read concurrently with this section.

It is best not to travel with very young children, perhaps those under five years of age, unless parents have prior trekking experience in Nepal. If a child is over five, it is advisable to have more than one child along for companionship. Families who wish to trek independently of an agency will find it easiest to take one of the popular routes where lodges cater to trekkers.

Don't assume that treks must be modest in scope. One family with children aged four and six trekked with another family with a child of six. They covered almost 500 mi (800 km) in 55 days, from Pokhara to Baitadi in the extreme western part

My son Michael never lacked attention in Nepal. (Mary Lynn Hanley)

of Nepal. This trek was more ambitious than most people would choose to undertake with children of that age, but for them it was a wonderful, unforgettable experience. The two families, by carrying moderate packs themselves (30 to 50 lb, 13 to 23 kg) and living off the land insofar as possible, were able to get by with only two porters. They never carried any of the children except across streams or rickety bridges. The pace was slower than that of normal adults, but they compensated for this by increased attention to peripheral activities, such as photography and bird-watching. The children thrived on the physical exercise. They received a lot of personalized attention from their parents and were constantly stimulated by new sights and activities. At the end of the day, they had little energy left and usually fell asleep soon after dinner.

It may not be inappropriate to consider taking older children out of school for a trek. Understanding school officials will probably agree that what the children learn on the trip far outweighs any loss in classroom learning. You can bring materials to home school during the time away. I did this with my daughter, Maia, and when she returned she was ahead of her class! Parents can help children keep journals of their activities and adventures, which will aid them with their writing and provide fascinating memories of the trip, a resource for later use.

Younger children need not be left at home. Infants can trek, though I would recommend that only breast-fed infants be taken. One trekking family with a two-year-old found it most convenient that the child was still breast feeding. In Nepal children nurse at their mother's breasts until they are quite old. Certainly this is the most sanitary method of feeding, and it has many other health benefits.

There are many practical ideas to consider to make your family trek both fun and full of pleasant memories. These are discussed in chapter 3.

TREKKING WITH DISABILITIES

There is increased recognition of the benefits of outdoor activities for those with physical and mental disabilities who face different challenges from the rest of us. Quadriplegics, amputees, the blind, the hearing-impaired, and many others have enjoyed travel off the road in Nepal. Such people should have had some experience in their home country first in order to adapt equipment and procedures. Many of the agencies will be helpful in fine-tuning the adaptations for Nepal. While some risks are increased by trekking in Nepal, the benefits may be greater, especially in terms of increased self-esteem and broadened perspectives. Nepali society is very tolerant of people with disabilities, as such individuals have always been accepted into the fabric of daily life.

Two quadriplegics who recently undertook a 3-day trek north of Pokhara came back with very positive impressions. The trekking agent prepared special *Doko* to carry the individuals and organized three porters per person who switched off on steep ascents while much longer stretches were covered on more moderate terrain. Local attitudes and those of the staff were not patronizing and were fully supportive.

Individuals with chronic medical problems or caducity can undertake treks providing they understand the lack of access to modern medical facilities. Seniors on popular treks can undertake short daily distances, interspersed with frequent rests, and have all the duffel carried by porters. Although many such individuals travel with agencies, there is no reason why you couldn't do it independently and stay in people's homes, rather than in lodges, the book's theme for ensuring an intimate experience in Nepal.

TREKKING IN THE MONSOON

> *In Nepal all paths and bridges are liable to disappear or change at no notice due to monsoons, act of Gods, etc.*
>
> note on trekking map, 1972

Although many consider it out of the question, the joys of trekking during the rainy season have been discovered by a select few "Nepalophiles." There are several reasons to consider joining these eccentrics. Many people can come to Nepal only during the Western summer holidays, which correspond to the monsoon. Some want to trek when popular trails are not packed with foreigners, or they are interested in the plant and animal life that is most spectacular at this time. It is undeniably a most beautiful time of the year. Everything is lush and green. The clouds perform dramatically and periodically part to reveal the splendor of spectacular vistas. Mist-shrouded mountain views during the monsoon are unforgettable. The high country is alive with activity as people pasture their animals on the lush upper slopes.

Transplanting rice in the monsoon is hard women's work.

During the monsoon, Nepal is much like it was years ago, except that now there are better bridges, portable radios, more supplies available, and children who may remember to beg when they see you. You can plan your route to get either behind (north of) the Himalaya (north of Pokhara), or to the far west (RaRa), or into the Himalaya (Khumbu) to experience less rainfall. See the climatological data in "Weather," in the following section.

There are problems, however. Everything tends to get soaked. Trails are often very muddy, always wet, and sometimes treacherously slippery. It is always hot and muggy at low altitudes, although more comfortable higher up. Distant views are clouded most of the time. Bridges may wash out, necessitating time-consuming and difficult detours. What may have been a trickle in the dry season becomes a deep, fast torrent in the monsoon. Travel often involves fording rivers. At times you may have to wait a day or two for the water level to drop enough for a safe ford. To make matters worse, leeches populate the forests at higher elevations (see the "Animal Bites" section, chapter 4), while mosquitoes abound at lower elevations.

Yet, just as you can adjust to trekking in Nepal during the dry season, so you can adapt to the monsoon. Certain items of equipment are essential: a waterproof cover for your pack, sheets of plastic for the porter loads, an umbrella, ski poles, and footwear with good traction, preferably new (not worn) waffle-soled running shoes, cross-training shoes, or boots with flexible Vibram™ soles. Light skirts for women, preferably with a hem about calf length, and shorts for men are the most practical clothing. Most waterproof rain parkas and cagoules are not very useful—if you do not get wet from the outside, you will soak in sweat from the inside. Gear made from Gore-Tex™-like fabrics, which breathe yet are waterproof if kept clean, are suitable for the higher altitudes. Gore-Tex™ jackets with underarm zippers allow considerable ventilation, as do such pants with side zippers. Pile clothing or garments of synthetic, downlike material are useful in the wet high altitudes.

In planning a monsoon trek, do not plan on covering too much distance in a short time. It is hard to equal dry-season trekking times. Many of the trails will be different during the monsoon. Drier ridges are usually taken instead of the flooded valley bottoms. Take time to enjoy village life, to sample the fruits and vegetables in season, and to enjoy the prodigious plant life. And do not tell too many people how much you enjoyed it!

MOUNTAINEERING

Besides the many expeditionary peaks, the highest mountains, there are eighteen minor peaks, called "trekking summits," that can be climbed by trekkers if they get the proper permits. The fact that they are called trekking summits in no way implies that they are trivial. Some are difficult and dangerous, and some have only had a few ascents. These high-altitude tourist summits are not suitable for trekkers who do not have substantial experience in alpine climbing. In a recent tragedy, eleven people (ten clients and a Sherpa) were killed on one such climb when a climber presumably slipped on a steep icy slope and dominoed the rest. Poor judgment and technique accounted for the disaster, the largest number to die in a single climbing accident in the Himalaya. Further information on these climbs can be obtained from Bill O'Connor's book *The Trekking Peaks of Nepal,* mountaineering journals, trekking agencies, and the climbing community.

To attempt one of these peaks, apply to the Nepal Mountaineering Association (NMA), GPO Box 1435, Naxal, Nag Pokhari, Kathmandu, Nepal (phone 411525, fax 416278). Fees, payable at the time of application, are nonrefundable. Climbers can apply after they arrive in Nepal. There are specific regulations to follow. Although it is not necessary to use a trekking agency, most climbers do.

The trekking peaks, grouped according to the area and using the term *Himal,* which means "range," are the following:

Khumbu Himal
Imja Tse (Island Peak) (6160 m)
Khongma Tse (Mehra Peak) (5820 m)
Kusum Kanguru (6367 m)
Kwangde (6011 m)
Lobuje (Lobuche) East (6119 m)
Pokalde (5806 m)

Manang Himal
Chulu East (6584 m)
Pisang (6091 m)
Chulu West (6419 m)

Rolwaling Himal
Pharchamo (6187 m)
Ramdung (5925 m)

Langtang Himal
Naya Kanga (5844 m)
Mera Peak (6476 m)

Ganesh Himal
Paldor Peak (5928 m)

Annapurna Himal
Hiunchuli (6331 m)
Mardi Himal (5555 m)
Singu Chuli (Fluted Peak) (6501 m)
Tharpu Chuli (Tent Peak) (5500 m)

Foreign
travel
agent

Local
trekking
agent

Sardar

High
altitude
porter

Lowland
porter

THE CLIMBING TOTEM

If you have been to Kala Pattar and other high-altitude trekking destinations in Nepal and are looking for new "summits," are trekking peaks for you? If you are not a mountaineer, by and large the answer is no. Although some are not technically difficult, they do involve mountaineering skills, unlike almost all the treks described in this book, which require just walking. Considerable familiarity with climbing on rock, ice, and snow and ice, camping on snow, and the understanding of objective hazards is necessary.

Where and When to Trek

In choosing a trek, consider the following: the time available, the strength and ability of the members of the party, and the desires of the trekkers. Certain treks offer majestic mountain scenery, others a glimpse of hill life in Nepal, and still others spectacular floral displays. Routes can be linked to provide many different experiences. Some entail entering potentially dangerous mountain terrain. Finally, the time of year is very important, as certain treks are difficult if not impossible during heavy snowfalls. Some trekkers are very uncomfortable in the pre-monsoon heat. Read the introduction to each region for a sense of the area.

With the increased popularity of trekking, lodges abound in places to which travel occurs where there are no villages and when no Nepalis would be there. This is outside of normal transhumance seasonality. Recognize that in such areas as the high regions of Khumbu and north of Pokhara, or Kathmandu, you will have less opportunity to sample Nepali life as it was, and still is, under the influence of normal routines. The most popular times to trek in decreasing order are October, November, March, April, December, February, January, September, May, August, June, July.

In making a choice, understand that the first few days of a trek get you used to the rhythm. I feel little is gained by the neophyte Nepal visitor who is out for just a couple of days. People do undertake such brief treks, but I suggest you aim for at least a week on the trail for starters.

WEATHER

The usual trekking season lasts from October to May. In October and November the skies are generally clear with outstanding views. Occasional short storms may dump considerable snow at high altitudes, and above 10,000 ft (3050 m) the temperature often goes below freezing at night. This is the most popular time for trekking. Although the monsoon is unually over by the beginning of October, sometimes it has dragged on for much of the month.

December and January are the coldest months, but there is little snowfall. Excellent clear views at altitude are common, although haze more commonly sits in valleys than it used to. Temperatures constantly plunge below freezing at night above 10,000 ft (3050 m) and below 0°F (-18°C) at altitudes above 14,000 ft (4300 m). Some inhabitants of the northern Himalayan region head south for the winter at this time. It can be a hauntingly beautiful time of the year to trek.

February and March bring warmer weather but more frequent storms and considerable snowfall at higher altitudes. Birds and flowers, especially rhododendrons, are seen at the lower altitudes. Toward the end of March, haze—caused by dust from the plains of India—and smoke from local fires often obscure distant views. In addition, it becomes much warmer in the regions below 3000 ft (1000 m).

April and May are less suitable for trekking because of the heat—sometimes 100°F (38°C)—at altitudes below 3000 ft (1000 m). Also, the haze mars distant views of the peaks. During these months, however, you encounter many species of plant and animal life not seen at other times. As the season progresses, the magnificent rhododendrons bloom at higher and higher altitudes until the flowers reach treeline. Occasional premonsoon storms clear the haze and cool the atmosphere for a few days. While temperatures below freezing can be encountered above 12,000 ft (3600 m), it becomes warm below 8000 ft (2500 m) and almost oppressive below 3000 ft (1000 m).

Heavy snowfalls, especially during January, February, and March, limit travel on passes, such as Thorung La, Trashi Labsta, Cho La in Khumbu, Laurebina La near Gosainkund, the high route from Pokhara to Jumla, and Ganja La.

Trekking in the monsoon (June to the end of September) can be undertaken by the keen or experienced. Rain, mist, and fog can be expected almost daily, but clouds part occasionally to give spectacular views of the mountains. The flora are usually at their most colorful. Leeches abound in midelevation forests.

CLIMATOLOGICAL DATA FOR SELECTED TREKKING TOWNS

(First line: Precipitation [mm]. Second line: Temperature—Max/Min [°C])

Town (Altitude [meters/feet])	Jan.	Feb.	March	April	May	June	July	Aug.	Sept.	Oct.	Nov.	Dec.
Kathmandu	18	11	33	54	83	270	383	338	160	62	7	2
(1336/4383)	19/2	21/3	25/7	28/10	30/14	29/18	28/19	28/19	27/17	27/12	23/7	20/2
Trisuli	20	23	29	57	90	319	463	474	265	107	14	5
(541/1775)	22/7	25/8	30/13	34/17	33/19	33/21	32/20	32/20	31/18	30/15	27/12	23/8
Langtang												
(3500/11,483)	2/-11	3/-10	8/-6	14/-2	17/2	18/7	19/9	18/8	16/7	15/2	9/-8	8/-10
Pokhara	26	25	50	87	292	569	809	705	581	224	19	1
(827/2713)	19/6	21/8	26/12	30/15	30/18	29/20	29/21	29/21	28/20	26/17	23/11	20/7
Lumle	28	45	52	194	318	902	1522	1339	932	294	23	2
(1615/5300)	13/5	14/6	19/10	22/13	22/14	23/17	22/17	23/17	21/16	20/14	16/9	13/6
Marpha	14	13	27	22	26	44	63	58	45	58	7	2
(2667/8750)	10/-1	12/0	15/3	18/5	19/7	21/11	21/12	21/12	20/11	17/7	14/2	12/0
Jomosom	20	18	23	15	11	17	41	54	35	37	2	2
(2713/8900)	12/-3	13/-1	16/2	20/4	23/7	25/12	25/14	25/14	23/11	19/5	15/1	13/-2
Chame	3	71	72	—	50	106	182	145	65	59	8	24
(2615/8580)	9/-3	13/1	14/1	20/7	19/6	21/11	21/10	21/10	19/10	17/6	14/1	11/-3
Jumla	32	40	43	27	40	70	162	173	92	39	1	4
(2329/7640)	11/-2	13/-3	17/0	22/3	24/6	24/13	23/15	24/15	23/12	24/6	19/-4	15/-5
Jiri	18	20	47	71	139	381	599	605	337	93	15	3
(1905/6250)	13/0	15/1	19/4	22/8	22/12	23/16	23/17	23/17	22/15	20/10	17/4	14/1
Namche Bazaar	26	23	34	26	41	140	243	243	165	78	9	39
(3446/11,300)	7/-8	6/-6	9/-3	12/1	14/4	15/6	16/8	16/8	15/6	12/2	9/3	7/-6
Tengboche	13	24	23	25	29	95	280	265	140	72	9	2
(3867/12,887)	4/-9	5/-9	9/-6	12/-4	14/-1	14/3	14/5	14/4	13/2	12/-2	8/-7	6/-7
Taplejung	15	32	55	111	243	335	448	400	271	82	14	4
(1783/5850)	14/4	15/6	19/9	22/2	23/14	24/17	24/18	24/17	23/16	22/13	18/8	15/5
Ilam	10	8	18	62	139	321	463	280	215	81	8	2
(1300/4265)	16/9	18/10	23/14	25/16	25/17	25/18	25/18	25/19	25/17	25/16	21/12	18/8

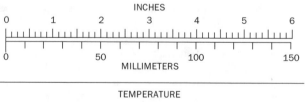

INCHES

MILLIMETERS

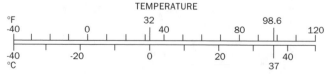

TEMPERATURE

Mountain weather is highly unpredictable. Classic signs of a storm approaching, such as a cirrus-clouded sky or a fall in barometric pressure, can be misleading. Occasionally, unexpected heavy storms can wreak havoc. In October 1987, November 1995, and October 1996, surprise storms dumped several feet of snow in all the high areas, resulting in some trekker deaths.

The table on page 32 gives precipitation and maximum and minimum temperatures for various trekking locations. You can estimate temperatures for other nearby locations by a simple formula. For a rise of 100 m the temperature falls 0.65°C, or for a rise of 1000 ft it falls 3.5°F. Metric units are used; conversion scales are given below the table.

Climate

Nepal has a monsoon climate. The heavy rains of the monsoon, originating in the Bay of Bengal, occur from June to September and begin in the eastern parts—two to three weeks can separate the onset of the monsoon in the east from that in the west. More rain falls in the east, which is closer to the moisture source. At high altitudes, above about 20,000 ft (6000 m), there is snow rather than rain. In addition, a less well-defined winter monsoon occurs from December to the end of March. This precipitation takes the form of snow at altitudes above about 8000 ft (2440 m).

The monsoon is caused by the movement of moist air north and west from the Bay of Bengal. As the moist air rises, it cools and condenses as rain. This precipitation falls on the southern side of the main Himalayan range. Generally, there is less precipitation at higher altitudes, because the clouds have already released much moisture at the lower altitudes. When the resulting dry air mass crosses the Himalaya, it has very little moisture left to deposit on the northern sides. A rain screen thus exists on the north sides of the Himalaya, producing the xerophytic conditions in Dolpo and Mustang.

The winter rains enable Nepalis to grow a second crop at lower altitudes. Generally, crops are grown up to the altitude at which clouds hang during the monsoon, as the clouds limit the amount of sun available. Local factors are immensely important in determining the rainfall and climate. Rain falling on north and west faces evaporates less, and more rain falls on steeper slopes, so there tends to be greater variety in the flora in these areas. Shady areas also have a more varied vegetation. While trekking, observe the changes in vegetation on different terrain, and try to predict local climatic factors that produce them.

WHERE TO GO

First-time trekkers on one of the popular routes are often surprised to discover that travel in Nepal is neither a wilderness experience like they are used to back home nor, increasingly, a stark cross-cultural experience. The Ministry of Tourism and other agencies are working hard to create food and accommodation standards that suit tourist tastes. The Nepal of legend is there but not on the popular trails—at least not without effort to find it.

Observing interactions between trekkers along the trails, I sometimes find disdain that someone else is here to enjoy this exotic area. They don't want to be one of a hundred trekkers in Lobuche in early November. Others delight in meeting travelers encountered everywhere on the trek. Use the information in this book to choose a route and a time when you won't meet many other trekkers if this is your inclination. On a popular route, if you want to find an experience out of the ordinary, hang around in less popular sites, hire a local guide (not one from Kathmandu), and stay in people's homes rather than in lodges.

North of Pokhara

The area north of Pokhara is the most popular with trekkers, seeing over 47,000 people in 1995. The mountain scenery is as spectacular as any in Nepal. The many different ethnic groups encountered are as interesting, if not as famous, as the Sherpas of Khumbu. Some of the areas provide perhaps the finest native cuisine in rural Nepal and acceptable tourist accommodation. Those searching for the best food along the trails of Nepal will find it up the Kali Gandaki. The area is most suitable for those traveling without guides or porters. Most of the treks in this region traverse through many different ecological zones. They begin with the customary terraces of the hills, encounter rain and deciduous and pine forests, pass through arid desertlike country similar to the Tibetan plateau, and even reach alpine areas. Remarkable transitions through different areas, each with its customary animal life, can be made in a week or less.

The most famous trek follows a trade route from Pokhara to the Kali Gandaki river and up it goes through one of the deepest gorges in the world—that between Annapurna and Dhaulagiri, to Jomosom, the administrative center of the Mustang District. The region above the narrowest portion is called Khola, the ancestral home of the *Thakali.* This route stays below 10,000 ft (3048 m) and is not very strenuous. Ten days is the minimum time for a round-trip to Jomosom. Most parties prefer to take two weeks and travel up to Muktinath (12,460 ft, 3798 m), an ancient pilgrimage site a day beyond Jomosom. The quickest and least strenuous way to enjoy this area is to fly to Jomosom and walk to Baglung. You can then board a bus back to Pokhara or Kathmandu. The whole trip would take a week or even less.

Annapurna Sanctuary, the basin southwest of Annapurna that is the source of the Modi Khola, is a fine objective for those who wish to trek only a short time, yet include a trip into alpine country. The *Gurung* villages en route are particularly colorful. Ten days is the minimum time.

Manang, the region north and east of the Annapurna massif, is a third worthwhile objective north of Pokhara. The people of the villages of Manang are traders and, many of them, world travelers. Beyond the villages a high pass, Thorung La, leads over to Muktinath, allowing a complete circuit of the Annapurna massif without backtracking. You can travel across Thorung La during the popular season without bringing food or shelter. It is best crossed from Manang to Thak Khola in order to allow enough time for acclimatization. Combining Manang and Thak Khola in a circuit covers more than 150 mi (240 km) and requires almost three weeks. The Thorung La pass usually cannot be crossed from December to March because of winter conditions.

Annapurna Conservation Area (2660 sq km), lying north of Pokhara, includes the Himalayan biogeographical divide, the Kali Gandaki valley. The conservation area therefore supports species from both the eastern and western Himalaya, as well as flora and fauna typical of the trans-Himalayan zone. A total of 441 bird species has been recorded. A wide variety of mammals occur, including the lesser panda, snow leopard, Himalayan musk deer, and bharal.

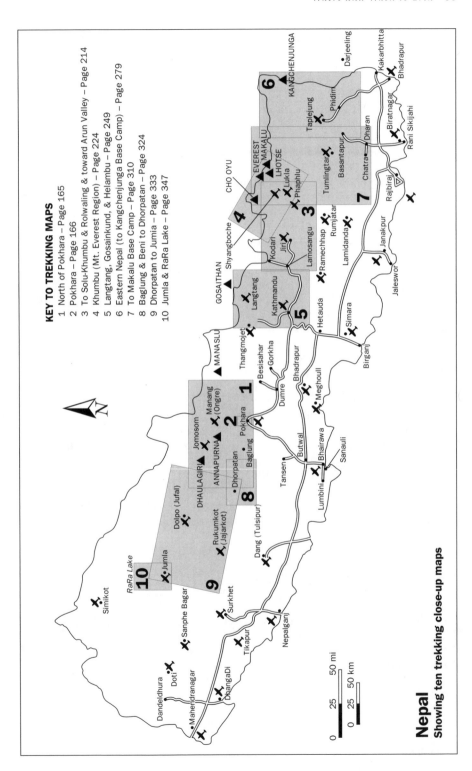

KEY TO TREKKING MAPS

1 North of Pokhara – Page 165
2 Pokhara – Page 166
3 To Solu-Khumbu & Rolwaling & toward Arun Valley – Page 214
4 Khumbu (Mt. Everest Region) – Page 224
5 Langtang, Gosainkund, & Helambu – Page 249
6 Eastern Nepal (to Kangchenjunga Base Camp) – Page 279
7 To Makalu Base Camp – Page 310
8 Baglung & Beni to Dhorpatan – Page 324
9 Dhorpatan to Jumla – Page 333
10 Jumla & RaRa Lake – Page 347

Nepal
Showing ten trekking close-up maps

Lomanthang, the fabled hidden kingdom of Mustang north of Kagbeni, has been opened up to limited agency treks for those willing to pay the high fees. The area is stark, desertlike, and very beautiful.

Solu–Khumbu

Solu–Khumbu, the district south and west of Mount Everest, is populated by Sherpas, an ethnic group that has achieved fame from exploits of its men on mountaineering expeditions. Khumbu, the northern half of this region, includes the highest mountain in the world and three other 8000-m (26,247-ft) summits, all part of Sagarmatha National Park.

The attractions are the majestic mountains, the villages in the high mountain valleys, the associated monasteries, and the legendary inhabitants. The area is the second-most popular trekking area in Nepal. Actually, fewer people a year visit Khumbu (about 14,900 in 1995) than crowd into small areas of well-known European and North American mountain parks in a weekend! Cuisine ranks second below the Annapurna region.

Choices in travel to and from Khumbu include walking from Jiri near Kathmandu, or flying from Kathmandu to Lukla, an airstrip located 1 to 2 days south of Namche Bazaar, the entrance to Khumbu, or directly to Shyangboche in Khumbu. Trekkers who land at high altitudes such as at Lukla and, even worse, at Shyangboche and venture into the rarefied altitudes are at greater risk of altitude illness. It is preferable to walk to Khumbu and to fly out.

Two weeks is the minimum time I would recommend spending in Khumbu if your goal is the foot of Everest. If you walk from Jiri and fly back, the entire trip takes three to four weeks. Walking to and from Khumbu makes that part of the trip almost two weeks. Many trekkers find the walk to Khumbu from Jiri better than the destination itself. Ethnic groups encountered along the way include the Hindu castes, *Tamang, Jirel,* and *Rai.* Those with less time fly in and stay in the lower villages of Khumbu. Other approaches to Khumbu on foot include walking to Rolwaling, either from Barabise on the Kathmandu–Kodari road or from Charikot on the Lamosangu–Jiri road, and crossing Trashi Labsta Pass (described in chapter 7). Another attractive route is to walk to or from the southeast and the Arun drainage (noted in chapter 8). Also, you can enter and leave from the Tarai.

Sagarmatha National Park (1148 sq km), a World Heritage Site, is situated in the Solu–Khumbu District in the northeast. The park is an easy place to see high-altitude species, such as Himalayan monal and Tibetan snow cock.

Langtang, Gosainkund, and Helambu

The trekking most accessible to Kathmandu is in Helambu, Gosainkund, and Langtang, all north of the capital city. The region is the third most popular trekking area, seeing over 8000 people in 1995. Helambu is typical of hill Nepal near Kathmandu, with Yolmo (Sherpa) populations higher up, *Tamang* lower down, and Hindu castes in the valleys. The lake at Gosainkund is a holy pilgrimage site, while Langtang is an alpine valley nestled in the Himalaya, and both are the site of Langtang National Park (1710 sq km), which contains a wide range of habitats, from subtropical to alpine. It is especially important for upper temperate and subalpine species, such as pheasants. Mammals include the red panda, Himalayan musk deer, and Himalayan tahr. In spring there is a rich variety of butterflies and flowers. Trails link the three regions, and as many can be visited as time and conditions permit. The minimum time for a brief visit is a week. Two weeks would allow you to combine two of the regions, and in three weeks you could enjoy the entire area. Food and lodging are available except for the Ganja La crossing linking Langtang and Helambu, which requires mountaineering skills and self-sufficiency. The Gosainkund–Helambu link involves a moderate pass with facilities available during the popular season. Accommodation and cuisine rank behind those of the two most popular areas.

Eastern Nepal

The region around Kangchenjunga is open for treks organized through an approved agency. Trekkers will encounter the Hindu castes, *Tamang, Rai,* and *Limbu* as well as *BhoTiya,* some of whom call themselves Sherpa and others *Wallungi.* There are few trekker lodges or tea shops, many difficult trail sections, and pristine forests. Over 660 trekkers went there in 1995.

Three weeks to a month is an appropriate time to get to and explore either the North Kangchenjunga Base Camp or the south, or even both. The walk in and out has much to offer, and a circuit of sorts can be made to avoid much backtracking. The "grand tour" encircling Kangchenjunga done by Freshfield's party in 1899 (he sneaked into forbidden Nepal from Sikkim and India) is currently not allowed either, and the chances of escaping detection are nil. The description here begins by flying to Tumlingtar on the Arun Khola from Kathmandu, because that is currently the easiest predictable access. At Taplejung there is an airstrip that puts the trekker even closer to Kangchenjunga, but there are few flights from Kathmandu, and these are often canceled. There are also flights there from Biratnagar at present. It is much harder to get out of Taplejung by air.

The other major access is by road, usually from Kathmandu. The long journey is not as formidable as it used to be, on account of regular, almost pleasant, night bus service from Kathmandu to Dharan, Biratnagar, or Ithari (on the East–West Highway, at the junction to Dharan). Seats can be reserved, and it is even possible to get enough leg room for my 6-ft 5-in. (196-cm) frame! Once in Dharan, another bus can be taken to Basantapur and foot travel begun there. I describe the route in the opposite direction from Taplejung to Basantapur, as an exit from Kangchenjunga. There is a road almost completed to Taplejung, near the Kangchenjunga area from Ilam. When regular service is available, it will shorten the hill portion of the trek if the trekker wishes.

How future road construction will affect trekker choices is unclear. I continue to recommend the route as described here, because it traverses interesting eastern hills, which are generally more wealthy and better developed than in western Nepal. Reaching the ridge that Gupha Pokhari sits on and walking along it is an idyllic walk in itself, affording views of the massive Kangchenjunga Range, as well as the entire Everest, Lhotse, and Makalu group. Where else can you gaze upon five (Cho Oyu is there, too) of the world's fourteen 8000-m peaks all at the same time?

Another way to get to Khumbu from the east, this one (unlike the exit over the Trashi Labsta) suitable for all trekkers, is the walk from Tumlingtar to Karikhola. It takes about 5 days and is best done during the winter when there is little haze from the plains of India to obscure the view and the weather in the lowlands is coolest at this time.

Makalu-Barun National Park (1400 sq km), an extension of Sagarmatha National Park, lies to the east in the Arun Valley watershed. It is one of Nepal's newest and is visited by perhaps 500 trekkers a year. I describe ascending the Arun Khola from Tumlingtar to reach the Makalu Base Camp in the upper Barun Khola valley. Ethnic groups encountered include the Hindu castes, *Tamang, Rai,* and Sherpa. Once

Beneath the immense South Face of Makalu

you leave Tashigaon, the last inhabited place where food can be obtained, it takes about 5 days to reach the base camp, so food and porters are necessary. The sense of leaving hill Nepal on the crest of a ridge from Tashigaon and crossing a high pass to enter a valley of sacred and majestic wild mountains is unparalleled in Nepal. This valley is clothed in dense forests hardly touched by people and is rich in wild-life. Two new bird species for Nepal have been found there in recent years, the slaty-bellied tesia and spotted wren-babbler. A brief description of routes through the area south of the park is outlined for trekkers eager to explore less traveled trails.

Western Nepal

Generally, the part of Nepal west of the Kali Gandaki river is not often visited by trekkers. Facilities are few and distances are great. Very few roads are suitable for launching treks, and air transportation is more difficult. Food is sometimes impossible to obtain. Except for the treks near the Dhaulagiri Range, few trails provide views of spectacular mountains. In fact, Dhaulagiri is the only 8000-m peak in Nepal west of the Kali Gandaki. The feeling of being right in the mountains, as in Khumbu, is rare here. The country is very rugged and, in the northern reaches, has a feeling of openness. The farther west you go, the less contact the people have had with Westerners.

One trekker destination is a circuit from Jumla to RaRa Lake, Nepal's largest and the site of a national park (106 sq km) that is dominated by magnificent conifer-ous forests. Jumla is reached by scheduled planes from Kathmandu, but it is easier to get from Jumla to Nepalganj and then to take a scheduled flight or bus from there back to Kathmandu. Food and shelter must be carried on the week-long circuit. Finding the way can be a challenge, so those on their first trek in Nepal should hire a guide if they are not on a professionally organized trek. Few trekkers visit this region, even now. Ethnic groups encountered on this trek include *BhoTiya, Thakuri,* and the Hindu castes. Like the rest of western Nepal, RaRa Lake National Park is relatively species-poor compared to the east. However, because the west is under-recorded, a visit should prove exciting, as there is a good chance of finding something new. RaRa also provides opportunities to see some western Nepal bird specialties, such as the cheer pheasant and white-throated tit. The lake is a popular staging point for migrating waterbirds overflying the Himalaya. Grasslands bordering the lake are full of colorful flowers in spring and summer.

History of Nepal: Before the Gorkha Conquest

The Himalaya has always been viewed, it seems, as a safe haven for immigrants and refugees. One large movement of peoples into Nepal dates from the twelfth to fifteenth centuries C.E. (A.D. *sic*), when many Hindus—particularly of Rajput origins—fled the Indian plains during the Mughal invasion. Some refugees settled in the Kathmandu Valley, but great numbers remained more rural, populating the lower valleys and hills all across the land. The *PahAARi* people of the adjacent India hills (Kumaon and Garhwal, just west of Nepal) are culturally, physically, and linguistically the "cousin-brothers" of the Nepali caste hillspeople who date from this refugee invasion.

The refugee arrivals were mostly *Brahman* (priest caste) and *Chhetri* (warrior caste, known as *Kshatriya* in India), along with low-caste craftspeople and menial laborers. They encountered a local population of *Khas* people and many ethnic groups, with whom they intermixed to various degrees—linguistically, economically, religiously, and socially. The caste Hindu migrants brought certain strong social and cultural traditions—a status hierarchy, language, religion, and a rice- and cattle-based economy that, blended with the local lifestyle and world view, formed what is today's unique Nepali national culture.

Nepali history until the Gorkha Conquest of the eighteenth century C.E. is one of petty principalities. These small hill kingdoms fell into two groups—the *baaisi raja*, or twenty-two kingdoms, of western Nepal, and the *chaubisi raja*, or twenty-four kingdoms, of central Nepal (between the Kali Gandaki and the Trisuli Rivers). Many treks of central and western Nepal pass through these former kingdoms, and if you are observant you can see remnants of fortresses (*koT*) on many of the higher hilltops. The most famous fortress, now a sacred temple site, is the "Gorkha Darbar" (Gorkha palace) above Gorkha Bazaar in central Nepal. Others are found in high places along the Marsyangdi River trail (e.g., Lamjung Darbar, just west of Besisahar), near Pokhara (Kingdom of Kaski), and along the Kali Gandaki just north of Beni (Rakhu). The famous Malla Kingdom of far west Nepal encompassed parts of western Tibet and was so strong that it influenced political events as far east as the upper Kali Gandaki valley. The west Nepal Mallas (not to be confused with the later Malla rulers of Kathmandu's three city-states) ruled from about the twelfth to fourteenth centuries C.E. (A.D. *sic*). They were apparently related to the *Khas* people, an ancient group whose presence as a power in the region had profound effects on all of Nepal's subsequent social history. They ruled simultaneously with the arrival of the migrant Rajputs. The fighting forces for these Nepali kingdoms were conscripted from local ethnic populations, such as the *Magar* and the *Gurung*.

It should be noted that various kingdoms of western Tibet, Ladakh, and Kashmir also had influence on northern Nepali affairs, particularly in the region of Jumla (far northwest) and Mustang (north central). Many Tibetan fortresses (*dzong*) may be seen in the northern border areas. The history of these regions is only now beginning to be rediscovered by scholars. The ancient alliances and influences of these many principalities, Nepali and Tibetan, are still felt in the internal political workings of the present-day kingdom of Nepal. And the silent and empty ruins speak to a rich and yet little-studied feudal past—part of its untapped sociohistorical and archaeological heritage.

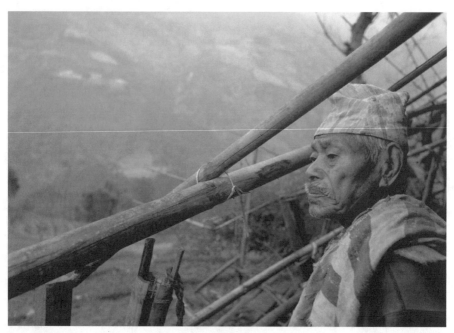

Retired Gurkha soldiers, such as Major Nanda Bir Rai of Tamku, have been agents of significant change upon their return home.

A classic strenuous trek from Pokhara to Jumla crosses several high passes and visits Shey Phoksumdo National Park (3555 sq km). This largest of Nepal's protected areas lies mainly in the trans-Himalayan region in the northwest. Birds are typical of those in the Tibetan plateau and include Tibetan partridge and Hume's ground jay. The snow leopard and bharal occur. Regulations stipulate that treks through Dolpo must be organized through a trekking agency and that food and fuel must be carried. There are no hotels such as those around Annapurna or through Khumbu that cater to the trekker. It is a difficult, rewarding journey through one of the most remote areas of Nepal. You pass through the Dhorpatan Hunting Reserve (1325 sq km), where there is controlled hunting of the blue sheep population by foreign trophy chasers. The forests are mainly temperate and subalpine and are dominated by conifers. There is a good population of the cheer pheasant, and the satyr tragopan also occurs. Ethnic groups met along the way include *Magar, Chantel, Tarali,* and *BhoTiya.*

In general, if this is your first visit to Nepal, choose one of the other treks unless you have some specific reason for wanting to trek in western Nepal. On the other hand, if you are a veteran trekker and are looking for new, exciting, interesting experiences, go west.

Other Treks

All of Nepal is now open for trekking, although most high areas such as Mustang, Humla, Mugu, and Dolpo require organizing your journey through a trekking agency and are not described here except for the trek through lower Dolpo. Areas worth exploring include the hills below Ganesh Himal, the Hongu Basin, and around

Dhaulagiri. I find many areas that aren't visually spectacular and famous at least as enjoyable as those that are. I have tried to include descriptions of some of these.

Consider linking several treks. Some wanderers head from Kathmandu to Khumbu, then to Makalu, and on to Kangchenjunga. You could essentially traverse all the Himalaya in Nepal. Before doing some of the more remote, less popular treks, do one of the standard ones.

Summary of Treks

DIFFICULTY
Easiest
Pokhara to Jomosom
Moderate
Helambu

Jumla to RaRa Lake circuit

Langtang

Kangchenjunga Base Camp

Gosainkund

North of Pokhara to Jomosom

Rolwaling Valley
More Difficult
Pokhara to Jumla, through Dolpo

High-altitude wanderings north of Pokhara, in Khumbu, and beyond Rolwaling

High passes such as Ganja La, Trashi Labsta, and Thorung La

Makalu Base Camp

TIME
Shortest (a Few Days)
Flying to Lukla, Hongde, or Jomosom, walking a day or two without altitude gain, and flying back

Initial part of almost any trek (starting out and returning after a day or two)

Gosainkund

Helambu

Khumbu—flying in and out, but not going to the Everest Base Camp or Kala Pattar

Langtang

Pokhara to Ghandruk circuit

Pokhara to GhoRepani circuit

Flying to Jomosom and walking to Baglung or Birethanti

RaRa Lake circuit
Two Weeks or More
Combining two or three areas north of Kathmandu

Khumbu—flying in and out and visiting the Everest Base Camp and Kala Pattar

To Manang and back from Pokhara

To the Kangchenjunga Base Camp, flying (or driving) to Taplejung Rolwaling

To Thak Khola heading north from Pokhara and returning the same way
Three Weeks or More
North of Pokhara with a lot of side trips or the Annapurna circuit

Khumbu with plenty of side trips or walking from Kathmandu and back

To the Makalu Base Camp

Pokhara to Jumla

FEATURES

Most Spectacular Mountain Scenery

Annapurna circuit

Khumbu

Upper Langtang Valley

Manang

Side trips north of Pokhara, such as Annapurna Sanctuary, the Annapurna Base Camp, the Dhaulagiri Icefall, Tilicho Tal, or Dhampus Pass

Kangchenjunga Base Camp

Makalu Base Camp

Upper Rolwaling Valley

Good Springtime Introduction to Flora, Especially Rhododendrons

Eastern Nepal (Kangchenjunga or the Makalu Base Camp)

Dhorpatan circuit

Gosainkund, Helambu, and Langtang

Rolwaling

Solu–Khumbu

New Adventures

Trek during monsoon season—even in areas you have visited before

Go on a far west or far east trek

Rewalk a trek you did ten or more years ago

Trek with few if any other trekkers on a less popular route

Take your family (spouse, parents, or children)

Don't go with an agency if you have done so previously

Don't hire any guides or porters who speak English

Focus on a specific interest, such as flowers, birding, local crafts, photography, or architecture

Go on a pilgrimage at the time Nepalis visit pilgrimage sites

Climb a trekking peak if you have the requisite mountaineering experience

History of Nepal: The Gorkha Conquest

The small central hill kingdom of Gorkha eventually became the most famous under its eighteenth-century leader Prithvinarayan Shah. His grandiose plans were to unify the Himalaya into one great mountain state. In the 1760s he laid siege to the Malla *Newar* city-states of Kathmandu-PaaTan and BhatgAAU (Bhaktapur) and ultimately went on to control a vast territory, from Bhutan on the east to Kashmir on the west, parts of southern Tibet on the north, and territories of the British East India Company on the south. By the early 1800s, however, this Gorkha conquest was halted by the British, and the Gorkha domain was cut back to approximately its present boundaries. The British were so impressed with the fighting abilities of the Gorkha hillspeople, however, that they chose not to subjugate the kingdom. Instead, they allowed it to remain independent and a source of the warriors of Gorkha, whom they called Gurkhas, for the British Army. The present Shah kings of Nepal are the direct descendants of Prithvinarayan Shah of Gorkha.

2   Preparations

All obstacles are blessings of the guru.
a BhoTiya saying

Remember this saying when in Nepal, for, despite all your careful preparations, some "serendipitous accident" may occur. The message in this chapter is "be prepared" but, most of all, be prepared to be flexible and to make the best of all circumstances. Trekking in Nepal, like any other activity, is usually more successful if the participants are ready and if they have some idea of what to expect.

Once you decide to go to Nepal and have a departure date in mind, book an airline ticket. Flights to Nepal are heavily booked in autumn and spring, so if you are going independently plan ahead. Inquire with consolidator travel agencies for the lowest fares.

Visas and Permits

Visas for travel to Nepal can be obtained from one of the Nepali Embassies and Consular Services in eighteen countries throughout the world. The visas are valid for up to one month. Two passport-size photographs are necessary for the application, and travelers should bring a dozen or so to Nepal for use in formalities.

Visas valid for 15 or 30 days only are issued at entry points to Nepal. The common entry points are (1) Kathmandu, for those arriving by air, (2) Kodari, along the Nepal–Tibet border (open only to those in organized groups; you can often join a group through a travel agent in Kathmandu), (3) Birgunj across from Raxaul, India, on the main road from India to Kathmandu, and (4) Sunauli across from Nautanwa, India, near the town of Bhairawa on the road from India to Pokhara. Other border points with India, less used by tourists, are DhangaDi, Jaleswor, Kakarbhitta, Koilabas, Mahendranagar, Nepalganj, and Rani Sikijahi. Travelers coming by road need a *carnet de passage* for their vehicles. There is also bus service on the main roads.

Nepali Embassies and Consular Services are located in Nedjands, Sydney, and Victoria, Australia; Dacca, Bangladesh; Antwerp, Belgium; Toronto, Canada; Beijing and Lhasa, People's Republic of China; Copenhagen, Denmark; Cairo, Egypt; London, England; Erottaja, Finland; Paris, France; Bonn, Germany; Hong Kong; New Delhi and Calcutta, India; Rome, Italy; Tokyo, Japan; Beirut, Lebanon; Yangoon, Myanmar; Amsterdam, The Netherlands; Islamabad, Pakistan; Manila, Philippines; Moscow, Russia; Riyadh, Saudi Arabia; Barcelona, Spain; Colombo, Sri Lanka; Stockholm, Sweden; Geneva and Zurich, Switzerland; Bangkok, Thailand; and Washington, D.C., New York, Chicago, Tiffin (Ohio), Dallas, and San Francisco, United States. There may be honorary consuls in other locations from time to time.

As this book was going to press in mid-1999, it has been reported that the government will abolish trekking permit requirements for treks to Everest, Langtang, and the Annapurna regions. For other regions, permits are still required and you will most likely need to go through a trekking agency to obtain one of those. Check with agencies and web sites for the latest information.

Economics of National Parks

Data from 1988 suggest that $27 million of tourist expenditure in Nepal was attributed to protected areas, at a time when the costs of managing the parks were less than $5 million and direct fees collected from the visitors were less than $1 million. Most of the revenue goes to foreigners. Because so little of the value of tourism is captured at the national or local levels, Nepalis feel these protected areas are of inconsequential value. Hence, there is little support for increased spending on park management. Of the moneys trekkers spend that stay within the parks, most go only to lodge owners. More needs to be done to optimize charges and make local benefits from the protected areas be in line with local costs, which will help local people recognize the value of these assets.

Trekking permits were issued at the Central Immigration Office of the Home Ministry, His Majesty's Government (HMG), at Baneshwor in Kathmandu (all areas), and in Pokhara near the airport (for treks north and west of Pokhara). A visa extension is issued first and then a trekking permit. Separate charges are levied for both. The restricted areas such as Kangchenjunga, Manaslu, Mustang, and Dolpo have higher charges and require the use of a trekking agency. The places that you are permitted to go are stated on the permit and are standardized for the popular treks. In applying, state the northernmost town in each major valley as well as names of towns with police check posts. Two passport-size photographs are required. Bring a supply of passport photographs with you to Nepal and a negative to print more if necessary. If you forget, there are several shops supplying instant passport photos near the Immigration Department in Kathmandu.

In the past, the trekking permit was presented at police check posts along the route and annotated. What role police check posts will have with the new regulations regarding permits is unclear. With the increasing number of incidents occuring to trekkers, it is advisable to check in at police posts en route in case you end up missing or being sought in an emergency.

The limit for tourist visas is five months in any calendar year. Those wishing extended stays have been known to arrange their first five months to end in late December and then leave for a nearby country and return in early January. Extensions can usually be granted only in Kathmandu or Pokhara, though occasionally it may be possible to obtain one-week extensions at a police post. Visas and trekking permits can usually be obtained the same day if you apply early. All government offices are closed on Saturday, the weekly holiday, and on other frequent holidays.

The final necessary formality is to register in Kathmandu with your embassy or consulate or register at the Himalayan Rescue Association near the immigration office. If there is no consulate, find out which country, if any, represents your country in Nepal. This can be determined from the state department or corresponding institution in your own country. The essential information needed by the consulate is your name, a contact number back home, your passport number, and itinerary. Bring the phone numbers of the appropriate individual to contact if help is needed while on trek. The many benefits of this process include making it easier to carry out a rescue and to contact you if there is a family emergency.

National Parks and Conservation Areas

Eight areas of Nepal have been designated national parks. This is the highest percentage of any country. They include, from west to east, Khaptad Royal Bardiya, RaRa, Shey Phoksumdo, Royal Chitwan, Langtang, Sagarmatha (Everest), Makalu-Barun National Parks, and Kangchenjunga. Foreigners must pay a fee, obtain a park permit at the entrance or in Kathmandu, and follow the regulations. Buying wood from locals or taking it from the forests is illegal in the parks. All travelers are required to carry nonwood stoves and fuel. The flora and fauna are protected. Violators can be arrested and fined.

In addition to national parks, there are wildlife reserves and conservation areas, alternatives to designating an area as a national park. Trekkers visiting the Annapurna Conservation Area Project (ACAP) pay a fee to the King Mahendra Trust for Nature Conservation at the time they obtain their trekking permit. The funds collected are spent on sustainable development projects for the residents of the region, as well as the conservation of natural resources in an attempt to balance the effects of trekking tourism with development for its residents. The ACAP has improved the trails in the area, built toilets and garbage pits, organized litter collection in the Annapurna Sanctuary, standardized menus and set prices at lodges, and has produced useful publications. They have also produced a Minimum Impact Code for trekkers to help preserve the experience visitors have here for future generations. Their headquarters and visitors center are in Ghandruk. Unlike the situation with national parks, where the entrance fee goes into the general government treasury, the fee you pay to visit this region is spent on local community development.

Protected Areas

Nepal has an extensive protected-area system, which now covers 13.8% of the country. The country's Department of National Parks and Wildlife Conservation (DNPWC) is aiming to protect representative samples of the country's ecosystems. The majority of these are well represented.

The task of protecting such a large proportion of the country is formidable. Many protected areas are remote and are only accessible by air or on foot. The rugged terrain of the Himalayan-protected areas makes coverage problematical. Nepal has a national conservation strategy that aims to strike a balance between the needs of people and those of nature—which are ultimately the same. Practicing conservation education in a country where most of the population lives in widely dispersed small villages is very difficult.

The King Mahendra Trust for Nature Conservation is responsible for managing the Annapurna Conservation Area. The measures the trust is taking are both innovative and successful. The aim is to balance the needs of the local people, trekkers, and the natural environment. The trust, established in 1982, is a nongovernmental, nonprofit, independent organization. It aims to conserve and manage natural resources in order to improve the quality of life of the Nepali people.

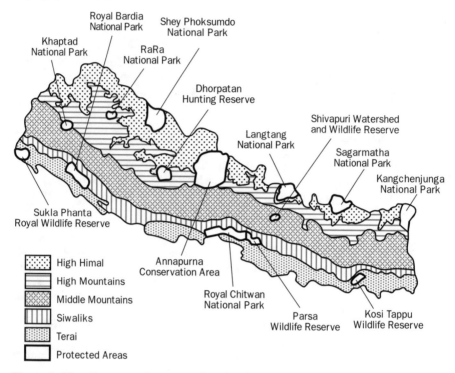

Figure 1. Nepal's protected areas and main physiographic zones.

PROTECTED AREAS NOT COVERED IN THIS BOOK INCLUDE THE FOLLOWING.

ROYAL CHITWAN NATIONAL PARK AND PARSA WILDLIFE RESERVE

Chitwan (932 sq km), the first park in Nepal, was established in 1973 and lies in the central lowlands. Parsa (499 sq km) is adjacent to Chitwan and was designated in 1984. Together they comprise sal and riverine forests and grasslands and extend into the Siwalik Hills, which are forested with chir pine and sal. Chitwan is famous for its large mammals, which include tiger, leopard, Indian rhinoceros, and gaur. Bird species recorded at Chitwan total 489, a larger number than in any of Nepal's other protected areas. The park also supports a larger number of nationally threatened birds than the others.

KHAPTAD NATIONAL PARK

Khaptad (225 sq km) is an isolated massif reaching 3100 m; it lies in far western Nepal south of the main Himalayan chain. Beautiful oak and rhododendron forests cover the slopes, and the rolling plateau on top consists of coniferous forests interspersed with grasslands. There is an interesting variety of bird species present, including the satyr tragopan pheasant and great parrotbill. The meadows are covered in a mass of flowers in spring and summer. Khaptad is nationally renowned for its medicinal herbs.

ROYAL BARDIA NATIONAL PARK

Bardia (968 sq km) is situated in midwestern Nepal. It extends from the lowlands, which contain sal and riverine forests and grasslands, into the Siwalik Hills, which are covered in chir pine and stunted sal. Mammals include tiger, swamp deer, and the recently introduced Indian rhinoceros. The park is rich in lowland forest; birds include some western specialties, such as the white-naped woodpecker.

ROYAL SUKLA PHANTA WILDLIFE RESERVE

Sukla Phanta (155 sq km) lies in the lowlands of the extreme southwest and consists of sal forests and extensive grasslands (*phanta* means "grassland"). The reserve is important for grassland wildlife, notably its large herd of swamp deer, the threatened hispid hare, Bengal florican, and swamp francolin. Except for a wildlife camp operating on the outskirts, there are few facilities for visitors at present.

Maps

Maps are to trekkers what tomatoes are to Bloody Marys. The maps in this book, drawn to scale, showing the towns and trails described in the text, help the reader visualize the route descriptions. Except for major ridge features and drainage systems, little else is depicted. For those wishing to explore further, acquire a larger map.

Himalaya Kartographisches Institute produces maps of most popular trekking areas, usually on a scale of 1:125,000. Their trail depiction is fair for the popular routes. Locally produced, adequate maps are available at bookstores in Nepal. Trails, towns, and some contours are shown on most of them, drawn by people who haven't trekked, so accuracy is sometimes limited. Titles in the "Latest Trekking Map" series include *Dhankuta to Kangchenjunga, Mt. Everest, Makalu and Arun Valley; Dolpo (Jumla to Jomosom); Jomosom to Jumla and Surkhet; Jomosom to Mustang; Jumla to Api and Saipal Himal; Kathmandu, Helambu, Langtang, Gosainkund; Kathmandu to Manaslu, Ganesh Himal; Kathmandu to Pokhara; Khumbu Himal; Lamosangu to Mt. Everest and Solu Khumbu; Pokhara to Dhorpatan Tansen Circuit; Pokhara to Jomosom, Manang;* and *Pokhara to Round Dhaulagiri Himal.* The series "Nepal Maps for Extreme and Soft Trekking," covering popular treks in scales close to 1:120,000, is available in Nepal. The *Kangchenjunga, Annapurna,* and *Dhaulagiri* sheets map areas better than other available sources.

Excellent topographic maps (1:50,000 [1 in. = 0.8 mi]) of many trekking areas are published by Kartographische Anstalt Freytag-Berndt und Artaria, Vienna, Austria. The *Tamba Kosi–Likhu Khola Nepal* sheet covers about 5 days of the hill portion of the trek to Khumbu. The *Shorong/Hinku* sheet covers the next portion to just below Namche Bazaar. The *Khumbu Himal Nepal* sheet covers the region from Namche Bazaar north. The *Lapchi Kang Nepal* and *Rolwaling Himal (Gaurishankar) Nepal* sheets cover the trek from the Kathmandu–Kodari road to Rolwaling and beyond. The *Dudh Kosi* sheet covers the southern part of Solu. The *Helambu–Langtang* sheet covers the appropriate area north of Kathmandu on the 1:100,000 scale, as does the *Annapurna* map for treks north of Pokhara. In this text, they are often referred to as the Schneider maps after the original cartographer.

A map titled *Mount Everest,* of both the north and south sides of the mountain, was published by the National Geographic Society in November 1988. On a scale of 1:50,000, it has details not present on the *Khumbu Himal* sheet of the Austrian series and is helpful for trekkers heading from Pangboche on up. Order it (#20033) from the National Geographic Society, Box 2806, Washington, D.C. 20013. It is often available for sale in Kathmandu.

The King Mahendra Trust for Nature Conservation has published a topographical map, *Annapurna Conservation Area,* on a scale of 1:125,000, available in Kathmandu. A map covering Langtang and Gosainkund on a scale of 1:50,000 in two sheets, titled *Langthang Himal,* published by Alpenvereinskarte of the Austrian Alpine Club, can be ordered from the European sources below, as it is currently hard to find in Kathmandu. Get it if planning to explore the upper Langtang valley or cross Ganja La. Geo Buch's catalog (below) lists all the 1:50,000 sheets of the Nepal Land Systems maps. A new series of maps on a scale of 1:50,000 is being produced by HMG with Finnish aid. In Kathmandu they are available from the "Maps of Nepal" shop (listed below) east of the Everest Hotel. They may also be ordered from Cordee and Aree Greul, listed below. These may be helpful for those undertaking less popular treks. Eastern Nepal is currently available. Expect western areas shortly.

Map sellers handling many of the maps (including those published in Nepal) are:

Adventurous Traveler Bookstore, P.O. Box 1468, Williston, VT 05495, USA, 1-800-282-3963, (802) 860-6776, fax: 1-800-677-1821 or (802) 860-6667, e-mail: books@atbook.com;

Aree Greul, Am Goldsteinpark 28, D-60529 Frankfurt a/M, Germany, fax: 49-69-666-18-17, email: greulmountain@compuserve.com

Chessler Books, P.O. Box 399, Kittredge, CO 80457, USA, 1-800-654-8502, (303) 670-0093, fax: (303) 670-9727

Cordee Outdoor Books & Maps, 3a DeMontfort Street, Leicester LE1 7HD, England, fax: 44-116-247-1176

Geo Buch, Rosental 6, D-80331 München, Germany, fax 49-89-26-3713

Edward Stanford Limited, 12-14 Long Acre, London WC2E 9LP, England, fax: 44-171-836-0189

S. M. Trading Centre, Maps of Nepal, P. O. Box 4782, Kathmandu, 977-1-492304, fax c/o 977-1-227058, email c/o ankur@mos.com.np.

Travel Books & Language Center Inc., 4931 Cordell Ave., Bethesda, MD 20814, USA, 1-800-220-2665, (301) 951-8533, fax: (301) 951-8546, e-mail: travelbks@aol.com

Equipment

Camping and mountaineering equipment used by Sherpas, other trekkers, and climbers on Himalayan expeditions is often available for sale or rent in Kathmandu, Pokhara, and Namche Bazaar and some other towns in the hills. Much of it is new gear unused on expeditions. While much of it is designed for climbing, a lot of equipment is suitable for trekking as well. Prices vary from cheap to outrageous, and the quality is not uniform. Some trekkers sell their equipment after their treks by means of notices in restaurants and hotels. Packs, jackets, and many other items are locally manufactured (not under license), complete with a foreign label. Such gear might last one trek. Some people are able to pick up everything they need in the city, but it is safer to come at least minimally prepared.

If you don't own items such as good down sleeping bags, jackets, foam pads, and packs, or if you have other travel plans that make it difficult to bring your own equipment, plan to rent. I would not advise renting footwear, so do bring your own shoes and boots, first wearing them at home to break them in before they "break you" on the trail. When renting equipment, don't leave your passport as collateral—you may need it. Cash, either Nepali rupees or hard currency (U.S. dollars, etc.), is usually left as a deposit. Sometimes a guide well known to the shopkeeper can vouch for your return of the gear. Such trust in Nepal may surprise you.

Equipment can be rented in Kathmandu, Pokhara, or in popular high-altitude destinations such as Namche Bazaar, Kyangjin Gomba, Jomosom, and Manang. In remote places, you can outfit your party for excursions where there are no lodges by renting tents, sleeping bags, and cooking and climbing gear. Inspect any equipment carefully before you trust it for a prolonged period in the high country.

FOOTWEAR

Comfortable footwear is a must. Look for good traction, shock absorbency, waterproofness, breathability, good foot and ankle support, light weight, durability, and a separate, perhaps shock-absorbent, insole. A variety of good and bad designs appear in trekking stores in Kathmandu.

Running shoes, cross-trainers, and the like are popular and quite suitable below the snowline. But make sure they provide adequate traction. Models with good shock-absorbing heels are excellent for downhill travel. This type of footwear is not suitable for snow. If you plan to cross high passes, take along substantial boots for snow and cold or face serious frostbite. Substantial leather and fabric hiking boots with shock-absorbing heels are good for the hills—if they are strong enough to last. Individuals prone to ankle sprains should always wear boots that go over the ankle and provide support. Those troubled with knee problems, especially when going downhill, should wear boots or shoes with beefed-up shock-absorbing heels. Trekkers carrying a heavy pack are better off with a more substantial boot. For high-altitude treks, take two pairs, a light, flexible pair and a more substantial pair for rugged terrain. For the substantial pair, make sure there is enough room to comfortably accommodate an extra pair of socks for the cold regions. Bring spare insoles. In snow or wet weather, appropriate waterproofing material is needed. Try the footwear out at home on terrain similar, if in lesser scale, to that in Nepal.

I also find rubber sandals with Velcro™-attached straps that do not come between the toes, ideal to change into at the end of the day. They can also be used for some limited trail walking and are unexcelled for wading streams. I wear wool socks over a light, thin pair of synthetic socks.

If boots or shoes are irritating your feet, determine what the problem is. Does the foot move relative to the shoe or boot and create friction? If so, try using the laces in a creative way to decrease the movement. Try lacing loosely to the instep, and then tying a knot and lacing tightly the rest of the way, especially for downhills. Boots with locking lace hooks make this easier. On some boots, avoiding some of the first lacing holes and lacing diagonally may prevent painful infolding of the leather. Try adding padding, such as moleskin, in layers to the area where friction is occurring to redistribute the stresses. If your footwear has removable insoles, carry a spare pair and change them frequently. Bring spare laces or nylon cord.

Once you have a well-fitting, comfortable shoe, the secret of foot care is in the socks. The outer pair, which should be soft and woolen to absorb the moisture, should be changed frequently. Avoid thick outer socks made of synthetic material (acrylic or nylon) because they do not absorb sweat well and often lead to blisters. Wick dry socks are preferred by some. Synthetic socks as thin inners worn under heavier outers allow the feet and the inner socks to slip around inside the outer socks, decreasing stress and preventing blisters. (For prevention and care of blisters, see chapter 4.) A plastic bag over the inner sock may prevent the inside of the boot from getting wet from sweat and help keep feet warm in cold, snowy conditions. If forced to use inadequate footwear in unexpected snowy conditions, use of this vapor-barrier technique may save toes. Change socks twice a day or more, keeping a pair drying outside the pack, if you are having trouble with your feet. Take enough pairs, say four to six, for the journey. In the high snowy regions, gaiters are useful in keeping snow out of boot tops.

CLOTHING

Loose trousers for men, long skirts for women, and shirts with pockets are good basic garments. To understand why skirts are *de rigueur* for women, see the "Dress" section in chapter 3.

Wool clothing is traditionally chosen for the cold because it feels warm when wet. Long thermal underwear is needed at higher altitudes, especially during the winter months. Synthetic fabrics such as polypropylene keep moisture away from the skin and are more comfortable than wool when the wearer sweats. Wool over such garments adds warmth. A down jacket is a light, efficient alternative to a sweater, but down is useless when wet. Synthetic, fiber-insulated clothing works well in wet weather and also dries quickly. A pile jacket with underarm zippers that allow me to remove my arms from the sleeves while walking is the ultimate insulator. If you tend to overheat, modify a garment to provide this.

Down pants or synthetic pile pants for sitting around in the cool high campsites are also good. Most important is a windproof outer pant inside drafty lodges and in the high country. I carry a Gore-Tex™ outer pant with leg zippers that can be put on over existing pants. Women can wear this under a skirt. Garments that can be easily put on over existing clothing are the most versatile. A layered system with polypropylene underwear, pile pants, and jacket, covered with a Gore-Tex™ jacket and zippered pants, provides versatility for almost all conditions. Wear the underwear and the Gore-Tex™ outer wear for active situations, adding the pile in severe cold. It takes practice to adjust clothing, donning and doffing it when necessary to keep from overheating and then freezing in your sweat, or from getting too cold when you stop.

A hat, especially a balaclava, is important on cold days because considerable heat can be lost from the scalp because of its particularly good blood supply. A visor to shade the eyes from the sun is an ideal addition. Dark glasses or goggles are also essential at high altitudes, especially on snow. Such eye protection should have eye shields to prevent light from coming in from the sides. They should absorb all ultraviolet light and at least 90% of visible light. If you or someone else is stuck on snow without them, jury-rig a pair by poking little holes in paper or cloth and wrapping it around the eyes. Long hair combed over the eyes can also help. If you wear eyeglasses or contact lenses, bring a spare pair and a copy of the refraction prescription. Consider bringing disposable contact lenses to solve the problem of cleaning them in Nepal.

Mittens are better than gloves for cold weather. Fingerless gloves, or ones made of thin silk or synthetic material, are good for operating cameras or attending to other intricate details in the snow. Thermolactyl™ mitts (not gloves) are thin enough to allow fine touch for various tasks. Finally, for snow or winds up high, a waterproof or at least wind-resistant outer mitt is necessary. An unexpected snowfall, falling and getting mittens wet, and numerous other situations can result in finger and toe loss from frostbite. If you are stuck, and inadequately equipped, use spare socks as mittens, and cover them with plastic bags or stuff sacks, to save digits.

It is difficult to stay dry while walking in rainy weather. Those wearing water-proof garments tend to sweat inside them. Gore-Tex™ jackets and pants with zippered areas under the arms and down the legs are preferable, because they have better ventilation. In the 100% humidity of an intense rainfall, no clothing can breathe, so you will get wet from the inside no matter what. In those circumstances, light clothes and an umbrella or loose-fitting poncho may be the best compromise. Trekkers often use umbrellas for shade in the hot sun as well as for excretory privacy.

Men should bring shorts for the hot, low altitudes. A bathing suit can be useful and modesty should prevail at all times.

You may feel chilly in the morning, when it could be well below freezing, yet sweat later in the day, as you exercise in the sun. The climatological data in Chapter 2 should help you plan what to bring.

SLEEPING GEAR

A down or synthetic-fiber mummy sleeping bag is usually necessary for comfort at temperatures below freezing. A bag with a full zipper is more versatile because it is comfortable at cool, high altitudes and in warm, low country. A washable sleeping bag liner solves some hygiene problems, and the liner alone may be all you'll need during the monsoon season at low altitudes. Trekkers not spending time in the cold heights may bring a bag that is too thick and hence too warm. Unfortunately, sleeping bags do not have removable layers of insulation. Many lodges have quilts, comforters, and blankets, but you can't count on their presence. Some trekkers do manage without a sleeping bag, but I wouldn't advise this on high-altitude routes.

An air pad or foam pad helps provide a comfortable night's sleep. I find the Thermarest™ pad by Cascade Designs to be the most comfortable and durable. The short models, extending from the knees to the shoulders, weigh little and are sufficient. Some people carry inflatable pillows. If you do, bring a repair kit. A sheet of plastic under the sleeping assembly helps keep equipment clean and dry and stops dampness from coming up from the ground, especially in minimal high-altitude situations. In lodges along the popular trekking trails, you usually get a mattress and a pillow to sleep on, but not everywhere, especially in high locations like Phedi below Thorung Pass.

The lightest, most versatile combination for all but the highest elevations is a light rectangular sleeping bag with a full zipper and a removable bottom sheet with slots for an air mattress or pad. The combination bottom sheet, zipped to the top bag, makes a light comfortable bed for two, especially when the air bed or pad is installed. The unzipped bag, with sheet attached, can be used as a blanket for two in the warmer zones. The bottom sheet can be zipped to make a single cool cloth bag for low elevations. This cloth bag can be installed in the regular sleeping bag as a liner for individual use up high. Wearing plenty of clothing in this case can make it suitable at higher elevations, if you choose a bag size large enough.

SHELTER

Your route and preferred style dictate whether you need a tent. If you prefer to camp, or desire privacy where there aren't trekker lodges, a tent is necessary, as it is at high altitudes if there is no shelter. Generally, having one large enough to house other people such as porters in an emergency is best. Check out the erection instructions, and practice before you depart.

PACKS

Many well-designed packs are available. Choose one that will store items requiring easy access in pockets and can expand capacity when necessary. Carry a spare plastic buckle for the waistband, in case you step on the buckle and break it. Equipment and supplies that the porters carry can be packed in sturdy, bright-colored duffel bags, preferably ones that can be locked. Belt or fanny packs, worn in front, can keep needed items easily accessible.

While I understand the "carry it all yourself" philosophy, it makes little sense to burden yourself down like a pack animal and then wear yourself out carrying the load. There may be little for you to enjoy except the feeling that you did it. By hiring porters, you ease your load and provide employment.

COOKING GEAR

For those organizing their own cooking kits, gear is available in Kathmandu. Regulations require that all trekkers and their porters, cooks, and guides be self-sufficient in the national parks. Trekkers should use kerosene stoves at all times, especially in the high-altitude areas. One group, crossing Thorung La after a heavy snowfall on the last day of November, was wise in bringing a kerosene stove. They were able to melt snow and have a hot drink up high. On the same day there, another unprepared trekker sustained serious frostbite. So even if you are eating in lodges, carrying a kerosene stove can be a life-saver in the high country as well as provide a tasty cup of tea!

Kerosene is the only fuel available in the hills. There are depots available so you can periodically replenish supply, including at the entrance to national parks and at Chomrong below the Annapurna Sanctuary. The MSR Whisper Lite Internationale™ Stove, which can simmer, is light and reliable and, with the Trillium™ stove base, can be effectively used on snow. Be sure to carry appropriate spare parts (MSR produces maintenance kits for their stoves) and a funnel containing a wool filter. The impure kerosene available usually clogs up most stoves, so periodic cleaning of the fuel jet becomes necessary. Become familiar with the stove's operation before you leave.

MISCELLANEOUS

A medical kit is essential (see chapter 4).

Take enough stuff sacks to store all your gear so it is easier to keep track of your goods. Light, zippered, nylon bags in various colors can be used to store small items. They can be packed in a duffel bag or a porter's *Doko* ("basket"). A sturdy, zippered duffel bag that locks is ideal for a porter to carry. Get a heavy nylon or canvas model—light nylon wears too quickly. Another lockable piece of luggage in which to store your extra gear at your hotel when you trek is a good idea. The small combination locks are easiest to use. A bright-colored bag makes it easy to spot from afar and can help locate your porter. On long treks during the monsoon, I use large plastic garbage bags (brought from home) to protect the contents of those duffel bags that don't need to be unpacked too often. Small plastic bags inside stuff sacks are useful for other gear in the monsoon.

An ingenious device, the Thermarester™ converts a sleeping pad into a comfortable

This craftsman uses a wooden lathe powered by water falling off an irrigation ditch onto a turbine to make a wooden yogurt container.

seat, especially useful for those staying in tents, or in Nepali homes where they are floor-bound, and want to read or write for hours. Another version, by Crazy Creek, is a stand-alone model.

Consider what might break down and carry appropriate spare parts and repair tools. A sewing kit is indispensable, as is a sewing awl for heavier items. Epoxy glue can repair most things if used discriminately. A flexible contact cement, such as Barge™ cement, is useful on boots. A pair of pliers can be good to have; the combination wrench, pliers, and screwdriver originally made for ski troops is ideal. A pocket knife with a few gadgets on it will also come in handy. Nylon (parachute) cord is always useful, especially for shoe laces.

Ski poles, ice axes, walking sticks, and the like are favorites, especially with older European trekkers. The telescopic ski poles adjust to various lengths and collapse to a small size. People customarily use them for steep descents to shift weight from the lower body to the upper, thus easing the impact on their knees and hips and possibly lessening fatigue. They help maintain balance on difficult trails. Consider rigging a carabiner and sling to each pack strap to attach to the wrist loops of collapsed poles to secure them when you want to photograph or not bother having to hold them. A jury-rigged ¼-in.-by-20-screw head on the ski pole handle provides a monopod for your camera. For most trekkers I advise carrying them, using them occasionally on difficult stretches. They may prevent stumbles leading to injurious falls. Constant use of ski poles wastes energy and tires the arms and shoulders. As well, your sense of balance relaxes, and in precarious situations where you can't use poles, or on easy terrain without them, this could be dangerous. In difficult, extremely steep situations, you are better off holding onto the rock for support and balance. Ski poles are ideal for crossing streams on ice-covered rocks, for snow drifts on high passes, on slippery monsoon trails, on slippery moraines, and on icy trails after snowfalls. Those with severely arthritic hips or knees find them useful on descent. As a slight assist, one pole is adequate, but people with disabilities should use two, kept close to the body. Practice before relying on them. An ice ax is advisable for steep snow or glacier travel but only if you know how to use this potentially lethal weapon.

Bring several handkerchiefs for colds and upper respiratory infections, or learn to blow your nose Nepali style. The use of toilet paper for nose blowing creates insolvable disposal problems. Petrolatum jelly is good for cold-weather chapping. Tampons for women should be the variety that can be inserted without an applicator that then must be discarded.

A water bottle of at least 1-quart (liter) capacity should be carried for each person in the party. Visit your local hospital emergency department and pick up a few empty one-liter plastic bottles that were used to hold irrigation fluids. Water bags may be useful to trekking parties who have to carry water a distance to their site. Consider one of the lightweight stainless-steel vacuum bottles to carry hot drinks in cold high places. Some trekkers find a wide-mouth "pee bottle" useful in a cold tent or lodge at night. Take biodegradable soap in a container, a washcloth or towel, and a toothbrush. Take a small flashlight or torch—the plastic kind is warmer to handle in cold weather. I like a headlamp with a low-wattage bulb and a lithium battery, so I can read and write at night. I also carry a spare battery and have a makeshift rig to power my tape recorder from this if all else fails. Battery and bulb life can be over 100 hours. Carry spares. D- and AA-cell batteries are about the only kind obtainable outside of Kathmandu, and AAs can't be found everywhere, though some other sizes may appear in popular trekking areas. Bring long-lasting lithium batteries from home to power your devices, rather than depend on frequently replacing the other kinds and having to take the spent cells back to your home country for proper disposal. I bring interlocking folding toilet paper from home, the kind that you find in public washrooms and buy from sanitary supply houses. Consider earplugs for noisy hotels and especially for flying in the noisy Russian helicopters. A combination lock can secure hotel room doors without keys and allow several people to enter independently. Such locks can also be used for duffel bags and pack pockets.

It is wise to have at least one compass in the party for high mountain travel. Magnetic declination in Nepal is less than 2 or 3 degrees west in most places and can be overlooked for most map work. GPS (Global Positioning System) technology has yet to be used by trekkers in Nepal. A pair of binoculars, an altimeter, and a thermometer can be helpful. For those wishing to have a convenient multipurpose instrument, there are now several watches that combine an altimeter with the time keeper.

Trekkers wearing contact lenses are advised that the risks of infectious complications are probably greater than at home. Bring plenty of sterilizing/disinfecting solutions, and don't exceed advised recommended wearing times. Use boiled water for cleansing when water is called for. At the first sign of any problems, remove the lenses and wear glasses. Use the treatment for conjunctivitis outlined in chapter 4. Disposable extended-wear contact lenses are probably the best for a trek.

Insects are not usually a problem in the high country, but those trekkers traveling extensively in the lowlands during the warmer months or during the monsoon should use mosquito netting while sleeping and insect repellents (the ones with DEET or N,N-diethyl-meta-toluamide are the best) while traveling. Insecticide sprays and powders (those containing pyrethrins or permethrin are safest) may help in the sleeping bag and be applied to the netting. Some people attract bed bugs and other critters that wreak havoc in the night especially in some lodges. Repellents, nets, and insecticides help.

Consider taking a tape recorder to capture the local music and other sounds of Nepal. You might consider using a dictation recorder, for your voice impressions as you walk. I now do this for trail descriptions and use an "office holder," the OR Possum Pocket, for my pack strap that carries the recorder, notebook, pencil, and altimeter in separate pockets. It is a great way to carry a small camera or binoculars as well. A separate microphone for the recorder greatly improves sound quality.

If you are a musician who plays a portable instrument, consider bringing it along. A harmonica, recorder, or flute can help break the ice in a village and elicit "good vibrations." Consider other social and entertainment skills that you may have that you could share with special people in Nepal. Perhaps you juggle, or can play games with string, or perform magic tricks.

Most trekkers carry reading matter and writing materials. Years later, rereading a journal kept on a trek can be very rewarding. Bring a picture book about your country to show to special Nepali people you encounter. Rural Nepali folk

Flint and steel is preferred to matches by many: the monsoon rains don't affect it, it is always available, and costs nothing.

especially appreciate looking at pictures of farm scenes, horses, cows, sheep, goats, and produce. Assemble a small photo album of family and farm-related activities. Viewing this will be a special gift to share. Obtain the language tape and book. And bring this book, an essential item. If its weight seems too great, remove the trail descriptions that don't apply to your trek.

Trekkers who might visit monasteries en route should acquire some *kata,* or ceremonial scarves, to present to lamas, or otherwise adorn sacred objects. Fine silk ones can be purchased in Kathmandu, but you can often get simple cotton ones at the monastery by asking another monk.

For the rare situation in which you may have to deal with the bureaucracy in rural Nepal, especially off the main trekking routes, a supply of business cards and letterhead stationary can be valuable. Rubber stamps and, especially, embossed seals can also help get things done.

For anything absolutely indispensable, that you could not replace on the trail, consider taking a spare. You might also bring items to barter or trade on your trek. Warm clothes, booties, almost any kind of clothing, including designer labels, are valuable currency, particularly along the well-trekked trails. See chapter 3 for gift suggestions and appropriate circumstances.

For many reasons, including some important ones to be discussed later, be reasonable in what you bring and keep most of it packed until needed. Trekkers who carry their own equipment often find they return having lugged many nonemergency items they never used. Often they end up leaving things along the way. Review your equipment list, and pare it down beforehand.

Photography in Nepal

"Photography is a magical process that has given Sahibs all over the world the chance to rest under the guise of business," states Ed Cronin. Inexperienced photographers should bring a small, simple 35-mm point-and-shoot camera. An instant picture or self-developing camera may make you popular with some people, but I would be cautious in its use. If you use an instant camera, everybody will approach you for their photograph. A chest pack to hold the camera and several lenses keeps my equipment close at hand. E-6 and C-41 processing is available in Kathmandu. Bring necessary spare batteries (lithium is best) to power the modern camera, for none will be available in the hills.

Jim Elzinga once remarked that if you are walking along a trail in Nepal with a camera, lose your step, and fall, and in the process accidentally trip the camera shutter, you will get a good photograph. It does take a little more work, a lot more if you want top images, but Nepal is very photogenic. Problems in getting good results stem from the immense scale of the terrain, contrasty light, and poorly lit interiors. In Nepal the range of light intensities in bright sun makes good results almost impossible except in the early morning or late in the day. So for best results restrict your photography to the oblique filtered light close to sunrise and sunset.

The video revolution has come to Nepal, too. A video camera can enable you to capture many scenes and events that you experience. It can also serve as a kind of diary. The major problem is that most cameras run on rechargeable battery packs, and there is less opportunity to restore them outside of Kathmandu and big centers with electricity, which averages 220 volts/50 cycle in Nepal. Carry extra charged battery packs. Entrepreneurs in areas with electricity may sometimes be able to charge your batteries for a fee. Be aware that North American equipment conforms to a

Pat Morrow waits for the best light on the West Face of Dhaulagiri at sunset.

different standard than that found in Asia (PAL), which is not the same as that in Europe. Hence, you won't be able to play your tapes recorded on equipment purchased in one area on playback units and monitors used in another. Bringing such equipment through customs in Nepal can be problematic. They may ask you to pay fees and to assure them you will take it with you on departure.

Food

In lodges catering to trekkers, an international menu of greatly varying quality is available. Where possible, stick to the local foods, *daal bhaat tarkaari,* which is more energy efficient to prepare and uses local resources. Noodles carried in from the road have become more commonplace in shops and inns throughout much of the country as a fast food. The quick-cooking variety is called Maggi, RaRa, or WaiWai, depending on the brand penetration. In a pinch you can eat the noodles uncooked. The expeditionary trekker, organizing food to cook along the way, can find considerable variety in Kathmandu, where many Western processed and packaged foods are now available in the new shopping areas such as the Bluebird Supermarket near the Blue Star Hotel, set up mainly to cater to the new Nepali middle class. Other big cities, such as Pokhara, will have processed foods. Dehydrated foods produced in Kathmandu, suitable for trekking and mountaineering expeditions, are available. These foods are of good quality, are quite reasonably priced, and require less fuel to cook than many other foods.

The type of food available in the hills varies depending on the place and the season. Weekly markets, a great source of supplies in addition to being entertaining, are often found in the hills. Staples and occasional processed foods are available. Foods taken on mountaineering expeditions find their way into shops in the appropriate areas—for instance, around Namche Bazaar, north of Pokhara and near Langtang. The variety and quality vary greatly. Cooked meals available at inns, lodges, and hotels are described in the next chapter.

Although the metric system has been introduced and is the legal standard, the traditional system of measure given here is still used in distant locales. The metric measures used in the hills have variable standards. The Nepali beer bottle, holding about 700 milliliters, is often passed off as a liter. Volume is traditionally measured in *maanaa*. One *maanaa* equals 20 ounces or 2½ cups (0.7 liter). Eight *maanaa* equal a *paathi*. Be sure to bring containers with you on a trek to carry the foods you might buy. Small cloth bags with plastic liners are ideal.

You may want to bring items from home that aren't usually available in Nepal—drink mixes, instant soup mixes, freeze-dried meats, vegetables, mustard powder, and desserts.

Note that few meat items are mentioned. Most Westerners are used to meals centered around meat, but this was not traditionally so in Nepal, and is even changing in the West for health reasons. Along trekking and main travel routes, meat, chicken, goat, or buffalo is often available at extra cost. For more on nutrition, see chapter 4.

Guides and Porters

Porters are the culture of Nepal.
Bill O'Connor,
The Trekking Peaks of Nepal

The trekker who does not travel with porters is missing out on the perfect opportunity to get to know the people of this country. If you are traveling on an agency-organized trek, you should read most of this section for general information and to understand your responsibility for their safety.

Sherpas are an ethnic group living in the shadow of Everest who have become famous for their exploits on mountaineering expeditions. The term *Sherpa*, as commonly used by Nepalis, does not stand for a specific job description but for a group of people who originally migrated from eastern Tibet and settled in the Solu–Khumbu region of Nepal. They have often been employed by trekkers as guides (sirdars), cooks, and porters, though it is rare for any Sherpa to porter these days. But the term Sherpa, especially when used by foreigners, and sometimes by Nepalis, at times refers to anyone of any ethnic group who does those tasks. Don't use the word in this way even though it is becoming established. It is like calling any businessman in New York a Jew.

On the popular routes north of Pokhara, Langtang, Helambu, and Khumbu, you can do fine without a guide or sirdar. People trekking in Nepal for the first time, especially off the popular routes, will generally have fewer problems if they have a guide or sirdar. This is especially true for a group of people who are planning to hire a number of porters for a long trek they have organized themselves. Send the sirdar to the starting point a day or two ahead to hire the needed porters and make other arrangements. It is best to recognize one person in the group of trekkers as the leader and have the Sirdar deal with him or her. The rate of pay for guides, porters, and so forth varies depending on where they are hired (rates are highest in Kathmandu, on the side of a high-altitude pass, and in western Nepal), where you are going (more is expected when you will go up high, be on snow, etc.), the time of year (rates are higher in times when there is plenty of trekking or village work), the experience and language capabilities of the guide, and whether the trekker provides food (they usually do for sirdars). Find out the current rates for sirdars and porters from other trekkers, and inquire at trekking stores and agencies. It is wise to ask several people to get a good estimate. For a small group of, say, two trekkers and two porters, eating locally, it is more efficient to have the Sirdars and porters eat with the trekkers than it is to hire porters and expect them to cook separately. You may want to set a limit for the daily cost of the food, so you don't incur large bills for alcohol and snacks. This should be increased up high and in remote areas where everything is much more expensive.

Porter Loads

Porter loads in one study found youngsters carrying 135% of their body mass, peaking for those in their twenties just shy of 160%. Even those in their sixties were carrying 116%. One forty-seven-year-old carried 228% of his body weight!

Talk to your hotel manager about getting a guide. Send word out that you are looking for people. Except in peak season, you may soon be inundated with offers. Take your time in the hiring process. Do not immediately hire the first person who approaches you. Trust your impressions of people, and talk to several to find those you can get along with. I prefer to hire porters who have not worked mostly for trekking groups and who dress in simple clothes.

Guides sometimes demand excessive amounts of equipment and I would seek another person in this circumstance. Experienced Sirdars do not carry loads and usually do not cook either; they confine their activities to guiding, hiring porters, and attending to various logistical matters. Most guides speak some English, and some speak varying degrees of French, German, Japanese, and other languages. Be aware that if you ask someone to arrange hiring porters at a site, the porter may have to pay a percentage of the wages to the "agent." Patronage is an old concept in Nepal. Sometimes younger people with little experience or knowledge of English, who are nevertheless enthusiastic and quite capable, can be hired for less. Such people are, in a way, more desirable, especially for the trekker who wants as few assistants as possible and wants to learn some Nepali. Sometimes these workers may carry a porter's load and do some cooking in addition to guiding.

In the Annapurna Conservation Area region and in Sagarmatha National Park, a requirement that guides (sirdars) be hired from recognized trekking agencies may be enforced. This is sometimes monitored at police check posts, where a guide might be asked to produce a letter from an agency. Trekkers who have hired independent guides might do well to be processed apart from their guides at check posts and to state that they are their own guides, if this regulation appears to be enforced. Alternatively, if you have hired a guide with the help of a trekking agency, then be sure to have a letter stating his connection with that company.

The guide will make many decisions about routes and stops for the night. His choices may be dictated by personal factors, such as where he has friends or other business to do. Trekkers may find that they did not visit areas they had wished to, for poorly understood reasons. It is important to read the trail descriptions and decide for yourself.

For a large party not eating locally, a cook and perhaps a helper are needed, in addition to the porters, who are hired strictly for load carrying. The guide can usually suggest a cook. Porters are also hired by the guide, or by you if you do not have a guide. It is often possible to make a contract with a porter to carry the load a certain distance, an arrangement that may work out to be cheaper than a daily wage. Porters usually carry their own food. Guides and porters can be hired through trekking agencies in Kathmandu, in other areas at airstrips, restaurants, and hotels frequented by foreigners, or at staging areas for treks. Lodge owners can be a big help. Some trekkers prefer to bring reliable people with them from Kathmandu. Porters hired locally may be Sherpas or Tibetans in Khumbu, Tibetans in Pokhara, *Gurung* north of Pokhara, *Tamang* in Kathmandu, or people of other ethnic groups, depending on the area. I find the Hindu caste porters less satisfactory than the hill ethnic groups. Others have found this true for guides as well. Women as well as men can be good porters; a few women have become guides. One agency in Pokhara, Lakeside, Himalayan Sherpa Trekking, provides all women guides and porters for women trekkers. Uneducated women from the hills find portering opens up economic opportunities in spite of the physiologic difficulties with large loads and sexual harassment that occurs. For a family trekking with young children, women porters may help care for and play with the kids. Some porters on the large treks prefer the companionship of their friends to that of the trekkers. Look for porters who might enjoy close contact with trekkers.

If you hire a porter or guide from a trekking agency and pay the agency the salary, be aware that a substantial part of that pay will go to the agency, as overhead. Trekkers on organized treks are sometimes surprised to discover how little salary their staff make. Inquire from the porters, and compare the wage scales with the land costs you paid. Sometimes women porters and guides have been taken advantage of by disreputable agencies and not paid. Check on this if you have any doubts, and use whatever means you can to get them their salary. The legal system characteristically supports employers rather than laborers. Some trekkers concerned with the inequitable distribution of the funds they paid for their trek have on future treks arranged a flat fee with the agency to obtain the porters and then paid the porters themselves.

Portering in Nepal takes place for four reasons: (1) to replenish a family's domestic supplies including water, firewood, and staples, (2) to stock shops of hill merchants, (3) to bring in materials for development projects, and (4) to support tourist groups.

Porters carry their loads—usually around 65 lb (30 kg)—by means of a tumpline or *naamlo*, a band going around the load and around the forehead. You might need only to put the load in a sack or duffel bag, hopefully one that you can lock. Or porters use a *Doko,* a conical basket available for a few rupees throughout much of Nepal. Anything can be carried in it, and an outer wrapping of plastic can keep the load dry when it rains. Items carried by porters receive rough treatment, and it is best to carry fragile items yourself. Even if you give your porters a modern pack to carry, some may disregard the straps and waist belt in favor of a tumpline, which supports the weight from their foreheads. This may be the most efficient and comfortable way to carry a heavy load. Try a tumpline with your pack and gradually increase the weight it supports.

All transportation costs such as bus or plane fares to the actual beginning of the trek are the responsibility of the trekker. In addition, if the trek does not leave an employee at his home or point of hiring, you are obligated to pay for his return,

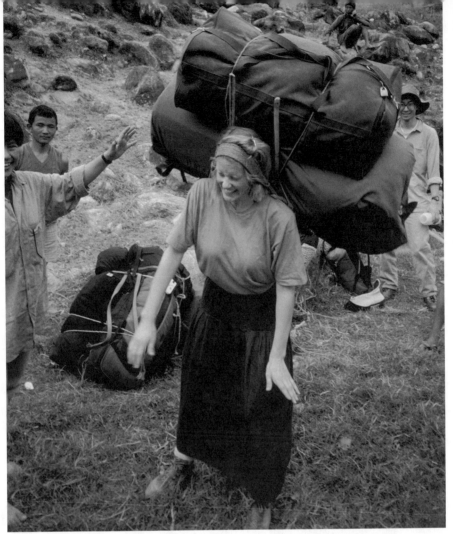

Try lifting a porter's load to get a better sense of the art of portering using a tumpline.

usually at half the daily rate. Travel is faster on the return trip, so the number of days the journey will take should be agreed upon in advance.

Large groups organized by trekking agencies commonly follow day-to-day itineraries or "camps," stopping at agreed-upon points. Porters hired for such routes may insist that you pay them the daily rate for the usual stages—a fixed sum for the distance to be covered—instead of the days you actually walk. In such circumstances I would advise trying to find other porters who are more flexible, because it is often likely that a small, fit group will cover ground faster than at the camp rate. Sometimes you may not be able to get around paying the camp rate, but because this amount often does not include pay for the return journey, it may work out to be similar to a daily rate.

Do not give an unknown guide a large advance, perhaps 2 or 3 days' wages at the most. Even if your guide is looking after the porters, you should, at the start of a trip, make the wages clear with them yourself to avoid possible misunderstandings later. An advance of 2 or 3 days' wages may be paid to the porters so that they can purchase needed items. Have the guide keep an account book. Also, do not loan your guide or porters money in contrived circumstances if you expect to get it back. If you feel insecure about your potential guide, ask for references and try to verify them. There are stories of guides whose primary purpose is to embezzle their clients. This is unlikely with guides who come from agencies or reliable sources.

Portering in the Past

In the past when there was more respect for portering, *chautaaraa* and other aids for the porter were built and maintained but these are languishing now. Historically, portering was used by the state to extract value from villages that didn't produce a taxable surplus. *Tamang* near Kathmandu served as porters in the service of central elites and were guarded from recruitment to the *Gurkhas*.

When you hire porters and guides, you are taking responsibility for them. If they get sick or injured, see to it that they get suitable medical attention. Many lowland porters have never been on snow or in below-freezing temperatures. They may not be aware of conditions in the places you want to take them. They depend on you to look after them. Provide them with footwear, clothes, bedding, and shelter if necessary. Equipment for porters can be rented in many towns along popular routes. Make sure the porters understand that the equipment is a loan, not a gift. Bring old clothes and out-of-style hiking gear from home to loan or give to your porters who don't have enough. (Take inventory at home—you will be surprised at what you have that you will never use.) If you go through a trekking agency, give such equipment directly to the needy porters rather than to the staff of the company.

The following scene is all too common. The trekker is in his tent, comfortable and warm in his down sleeping bag sitting on a thick foam pad. His down jacket and pants are stuffed in the corner. Outside, huddled together by some rocks used as a windbreak, his wet, shivering porters do not sleep a wink all night. The sahib wonders why they are so slow the next day.

If you have a guide, it is his responsibility to see to the needs of the porters, but this does not relieve you of responsibility. Time and time again, porters have died needlessly on high passes in storms after they were abandoned by guides. In a storm, it is wise to sit low and wait it out rather than to cross a pass to keep on schedule. Take charge and safeguard the party.

If you have a group of porters and feel that they are taking too many rests, check to see that their loads are not too heavy. Sometimes, rather than staying with them, shadowing them, it may turn out to be more efficient to agree on a destination for lunch or that evening, and walk independently of them, especially after a trusting relationship has developed. You might also travel ahead and arrange to have food cooked for them at a hotel or *bhaTTi*. Then it is ready when they arrive.

Recognize that as outside wealth has come to Nepal, portering, never a job with status, has become even more menial. People who work as porters do so to supplement their families' income. Porters are treated disrespectfully by status-conscious Nepalis as a rule. By rising above this, the trekker can gain friends and learn much about Nepal. Those who have traveled in the Karakorum will know that the Balti porters there have tried to gain a measure of control over their labor. Some may resent their strikes and disputes but these acts are a resistance against domination.

What does this mean for Nepali porters and our relationship with them?

There are good ways to share your satisfaction with porters on the trip and to show your appreciation for their efforts at its end. English lessons are much valued. You could buy some appropriate language materials in Kathmandu or bring them from home. Good gifts include used clothing, pocket knives, pencils, crayons, paper notebooks, sewing needles, and strong thread.

Do not overlook the possibility of using nonhuman animals to carry loads. This is especially feasible in Khumbu and other northern regions. I have used a yak and a *zopkio*—the sterile male offspring of a cow mated with a yak. These animals are remarkably sure-footed, the *zopkio* has a much better disposition than the yak, which requires pulling and pushing at times, but the yak can withstand more cold than the *zopkio*. In some areas horses can be used. Animal use depends on the availability of fodder, so high passes such as the Jangla would not be feasible during the late fall and winter but quite appropriate in the monsoon. Sometimes a person whom you may want to hire as a porter will carry nothing but use a pack animal. In this case, the person is paid as a porter, or two, depending on the load carried by the animal. Be sure that the arrangement is clear beforehand.

SLEEPING COOLIE

On his back a fifty-pound load
spine bent double
six miles straight up in the January snow,
hungry griefs!
naked bones,
two rupees worth of life in his body
to challenge the mountain.

Cloth cap black with sweat
and worn to shreds,
body swarming with lice and fleas,
mind dulled.
It's like sulphur, but how tough
this human frame.

The bird of his heart panting,
sweat and breath.
On the cliff his hut, kids trembling:

No greens to eat; his wife combs the woods
for weeds and nettles.
Beneath the snow peak

of this more than human hero's mountain,
conquering nature, with a hoard of pearls—
the sweat on his forehead—
and above only the lid of night
bright with stars:
in this night he is rich with sleep.

Laxmiprasad Devkota, 1958
(1909–1959), Nepal's foremost poet

Air Travel

The anthropologist Ralph Beals once wrote that as an effective agent of change, one road is worth a thousand schools. The same might be said for one STOL (short-take-off-and-landing) airstrip.
James Fisher, *Sherpas*

Flying in Nepal is exciting, for the pilots are skilled at landing in remote airstrips and fly in seemingly impossible monsoon weather without benefit of IFR beacons. The old adage that they don't fly when there are clouds because "the clouds have rocks in them" doesn't seem to hold these days, especially where the route is reasonable. Their safety record is enviable.

Small STOL (Short-Take-Off-and-Landing) aircraft provide service to small airstrips in many parts of Nepal. Helicopters can also provide service to trekking sites. There is increasing helicopter access to other places in the hills, not just airstrips but district centers. Many of these sites are not popular with trekkers but can be useful for jumping off. Flights and charters are arranged in Kathmandu through the offices of Royal Nepal Airlines (RNAC) or any of the private airlines, Asian Airlines, Buddha Air, Cosmic Air, Dynasty Aviation, Fishtail, Garud Air, Gorkha Airways, Karmali Air, Lumbini Airways, Manakamana Airways, Necon Airways, and Yeti Airways.

Trekking and travel agencies in Kathmandu can take care of many of the hassles dealing with domestic flights and with international carriers even if you don't arrange a trek with them. There are fewer hassles with air travel within Nepal for trekkers in the last few years as more carriers compete for tourist traffic. Some suggestions for further minimizing hassles with flights in Nepal include making sure you have a return reservation back home before you arrive in Nepal. If you do, then once you arrive, reconfirm it in person at that airline's office, and get the ticket so stamped. Otherwise, make sure you book a flight back before you leave on your trek.

Local flights must be paid for in hard currency. If you haven't asked a local agency to book a flight for you, queue up at the airline's office. If you have a return ticket to Kathmandu or some other destination in Nepal, when you arrive at the remote location, take time to reconfirm at the airline's local station, and see that your name is on the passenger list. If your flight is bumped, then patiently go daily to the office and try to make arrangements to get back. Be aware that each flight has seats reserved for government officials. Travelers with legitimate, documentable reasons can sometimes get clearance from government officials such as the Chief District Officer (CDO) to be issued these seats. This process is begun by writing a letter (on letterhead if possible) explaining the reason to the responsible official.

Many flights to remote areas leave from hubs such as Biratnagar, Dharan (for helicopters), Pokhara, or Nepalganj, and transportation from Kathmandu must be arranged. Once there, getting to the airport from your hotel in town can be problematic, so scout out the options the day before, and arrange something. Baggage allowance is usually limited to 15 kg per person; excess baggage charges then apply to anything over that. Sometimes everything, including carry-on, is weighed, especially on flights into high-altitude areas. Comply with these regulations so the plane is not overloaded. Crashes have resulted by people's insistence to carry everything!

Trekking parties are cautioned not to wave at low-flying helicopters, as this is an invitation to be rescued. Such activity has confused rescue pilots trying to locate the stricken party.

Buses, Trucks, and Cars

A fast approach by plane robs the journey of anticipation; a slow approach by road always begins with the hope of a pleasant trip, and continues with the hope of simply reaching the destination.
George Schaller, *Stones of Silence*

In the 1970s studies showed road building in Nepal to have a net negative effect on economic development. This is now forgotten and there is a frenzy of road building, with little budgeted for maintenance. New roads will increase the popularity of other areas for trekking, though it may take a few years after completion for the word to get out. Roads are planned to Jumla, to Num, just completed to Taplejung, and perhaps someday there will be a road to Namche Bazaar. This is in addition to the current spur roads to Jiri, Gorkha, Syabrubensi, Besisahar, and Baglung and the major access roads to Kathmandu, Kodari, and Pokhara, as well as the network in the Tarai. Landslides and washouts will continue to make getting there problematic, and perhaps the old trails will still be useful. Any road described in this book may not be motorable at the time you access it or you may have to walk across a slide to board a different vehicle on the other side.

Private bus companies provide service over Nepal's main roads. The routes most often used by trekkers are Kathmandu to Jiri for treks east; Kathmandu to Dhunche and Syabrubensi for treks north; Kathmandu to Pokhara and Baglung for treks north of Pokhara; and Kathmandu to Nepalganj for western treks. Use of feeder roads, such as from Pokhara to Baglung, and Dumre to Besisahar, or Dharan to Basantapur, are also popular. There are several categories of bus service, with no uniform standard. Tourist buses make few if any stops and have reserved seats. Tickets for them can be purchased from the various travel and trekking agencies, and they may leave from Tridevimarga near the Immigration Office or other convenient sites. But for local buses go to the bus parks in Kathmandu, east of Ratna Park (for Jiri), and near Baleju (Naya Bas Park) for Dhunche, Syabrubensi, Pokhara, Baglung, Hille, and the Tarai. Go there a day early to buy tickets, though arriving beforehand can often get you on the bus. By buying a ticket early, you can choose a seat close to the front of the bus and, if you are tall like me, try to get one with legroom. Consider buying two seats to be less crammed. On the day of departure, get there early enough to find your bus and be prepared for contingencies.

Mini-buses are more expensive and use smaller vehicles. Local buses are crammed full with people smoking cigarettes or vomiting, goats, chickens, and luggage. Stopping often, they take forever. Riding on these buses often taxes the trekker as much as two weeks' walk with a pack. Riding on top of buses is currently prohibited close to police check posts. Most trekkers are willing to put up with the slow, pitching buses in order to save time. Riding closer to the front and not eating a big meal before boarding is advised. There are night bus services between Kathmandu and many points in the Tarai. This odyssey begins in the late afternoon, and you arrive bedraggled in the morning. Observing the culture of bus driving, with the different personnel required, is a fascinating diversion for the weary rider. Expect any bus ride outside of the Kathmandu Valley to take most of a day.

Trekkers may sometimes be able to purchase rides on trucks transporting goods; this may even be preferable to the crowded buses. If you find yourself in the back of a pitching truck, try to get your center of gravity as low and forward as you can. In dusty situations, ride as high and far forward as you can. In trucks or buses, try to get seats up close to the driver. Vehicles often charge extra from trekkers for transporting their equipment. It may be more convenient for a large party wishing to transport all its gear, porters, and trekkers to the start of a trek to hire taxis, four-wheel-drive, or other private vehicles. It can also be easier for small groups or individuals. Trekking agencies usually make these arrangements and provide pickup services. Otherwise, look near the main office of the Nepal Bank Limited just off New Road in Kathmandu.

A high incidence of road accidents commonly accompany road development in the third world; Nepal is no exception. Roads are narrow, often made narrower by washouts, and without the substantial restraining barriers seen at home. Vehicles are often overloaded, repairs jury-rigged, brakes a fantasy, and drivers fatigued, with alcohol compounding the problem. Speeds along the roads are increasing in spite of more frequent accidents for all the newer vehicles are capable of rapidly plunging into obstacles. So your risk of accidents in road travel in Nepal is substantial, perhaps comparable to the risk of serious altitude illness or greater. If a road accident occurs, emergency medical service and definitive care are limited at best. Your greatest risk of injury in Nepal while not trekking, is from motor vehicle accidents. Avoid travel at night if possible. Get off a vehicle if you feel a driver is behaving unsafely. Take number 11 where possible (*eghaara nambarle*), referring to the symbol of using two legs in Nepal.

At road heads, I advise you to sleep as far from the bus staging area as possible. Otherwise, you may spend much of the night listening to the mating calls of these beasts.

Jewelry

Jewelry and other body decoration is another fascinating aspect of Nepali culture that attracts the attention of visitors. As in most societies, jewelry is used for decoration; for women, it used to be their inalienable property and their dowry. Currently, with seasonal economic hardship men take it to pawn in the winter, hopefully to get it back in the spring.

Such decoration shows affluence, with little individuality or idiosyncratic expression. At festivals and weddings, however, it is appropriate and necessary to wear all one has, for Nepal is very much a public culture.

Wearing jewelry is "auspicious" for women, who wear it at their ears, neck, and wrists. The religious implications are many. To honor is to adorn: men, their wives and daughters; hosts, their guests, with *kata* (scarves) and *maalaa* (flowers); and devotees, their gods, with red powder, *kata*, *maalaa*, and real jewelry; and *stupa* and mountain passes, with prayer flags and flowers.

Many styles are borrowed freely from adjacent groups. Occasional indicators of ethnicity are found: *Newar* never pierce noses; caste Hindus always do; only Sherpas and other *BhoTiya* wear striped aprons and the big silver hook clasps to hold them.

Jewelry is almost always handmade by a goldsmith. The metal is paid for by weight, with a small fee for craftsmanship.

Money

Individual trekkers should take 10-, 20-, and 50-rupee (*rupiyAA*) notes. For a group paying bills together, 100- and 500-rupee notes are also convenient. A rupee is equal to less than 2 cents (U.S.) at the 1996 exchange rate. It is easiest to exchange currency at banks in Kathmandu and Pokhara. While banks do have branches in most of the district centers and a few towns, exchanging foreign currency at them can be time-consuming and difficult, if not impossible, but as always Nepali bureaucracy is fascinating. Credit cards are unknown in the rural areas! Some facilities in Kathmandu take them presently, and at least several banks will issue traveler's checks against a Visa or Mastercard. The exchange rate for this may be quite unfavorable. There is an American Express office in Kathmandu. If money has to be sent to you in Nepal, the most versatile way for U.S. citizens may be to have it sent to the State Department in Washington, D.C. They will send a transmittal letter to the Embassy allowing disbursement of U.S. cash.

Hard currency (U.S. dollars, etc.) is necessary for purchasing air tickets, as well as for paying for trekking permits to certain areas. Bring some hard cash and traveler's checks in small denominations to Nepal, especially if not trekking with a foreign-based agency. Carry some U.S. cash with you while trekking if your route takes you by an airstrip and you might decide to fly out unexpectedly.

Jewelers in the village work on the ground with their hands and feet turning out beautiful adornments. Consider having something made for you.

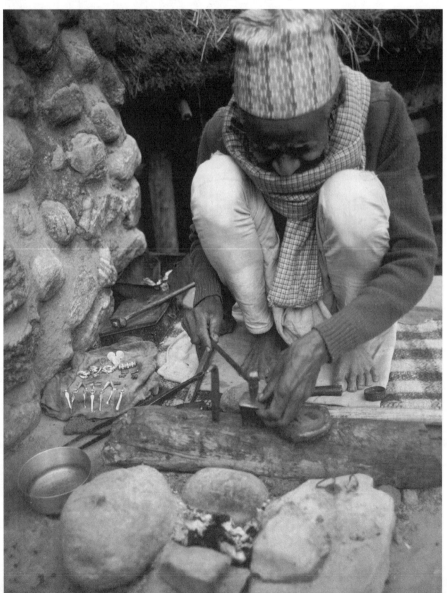

Some trekkers barter clothes and equipment for Nepali crafts, meals, and lodging. Western goods can also be exchanged for cash at times. The local people like to obtain useful foreign goods in this way. I usually travel with minimal gear that is difficult to replace in Nepal and do most of my commerce with cash. Some who are in Nepal for short periods of time exchange, sell, or give away much of their clothing and equipment toward the end of their trek.

It is best to take new currency on your trek. Exchange worn, tattered notes for crisp new ones in Kathmandu. People in the hills may refuse a ragged, torn note. If everything has been arranged by a prepaid trekking company, little money is needed. If you are traveling without porters or guides and eating food locally, U.S.$5–$10 per person per day takes care of the necessities. In the Annapurna region, and Khumbu where there are more sophisticated hotels, you can spend a great deal more. Carry enough funds for contingencies. You get incredible value for the money spent in Nepal. Don't lose that perspective. The scale of porter wages I paid in 1969 ($1.50 then in 1969 dollars), is comparable to that paid in 1996 U.S. dollars ($2–$4 in 1996 dollars). We have IMF structural adjustment to thank for that. It hurts Nepal's poor, but benefits us.

The prices throughout this book are based on 1997 rates. Although you may well find the prices higher when you reach Nepal, you'll at least have some idea of what to expect.

Communication within Nepal

CALLING HOME

Calling home was once restricted to an interminable process at one office in Kathmandu, but now service from many district centers is available. There are VHF links powered by solar cells in many remote areas for you to call home. Ask for the location of these and bring considerable cash for the charges you might incur. You can't call collect.

ELECTRONIC MAIL

The Internet has come to Nepal, and there are several private operators where you can send and receive electronic mail at varying prices based on document size. Look near the Immigration Office for these agencies and consider using them, but don't ask anyone to send you a photograph or other bytey document. Fax sending and receiving facilities abound, and this provides another way to communicate. Trekkers with access to the World Wide Web will find postings relating to trekking in Nepal, both from commercial operators and from individuals relating their experiences and giving advice.

ADDRESSES FOR RECEIVING SNAIL MAIL IN NEPAL

The best, in order of preference, are (1) a friend living in Nepal, (2) your trekking agency, if you have one, (3) your embassy, (4) American Express, if you use their traveler's checks, and (5) Post Restante (General Delivery, Kathmandu, Nepal).

Equipment List

In the following equipment list, **R** indicates items you may be able to rent in Nepal, and **P** indicates items you can hope to purchase in Nepal, though you may not be able to count on the quality.

R	P	

ESSENTIAL FOR ALL TREKKERS

R	P	
		walking shoes, well broken in, and spare insoles if appropriate
	x	socks: several pairs of heavy wool outer socks and a few pairs of nylon inner socks
	x	skirts: midcalf to above the ankle for women
	x	pants: baggy ones are best (for women, only between settlements)
	x	shirts, blouses, T-shirts
	x	unmentionables (underwear and the like)
	x	hat with wide brim (or visor)
x	x	sleeping bag adequate for temperatures encountered (may be provided by some trekking agencies)
		repair kit to deal with all your gear
	x	water-purification materials (see chapter 4)
	x	water bottle; at least 1-liter capacity per person
x	x	backpack with outside pockets to handle smaller items
	x	nylon stuff sacks for organizing equipment
	x	medical kit (see chapter 4)
	x	flashlight (torch) with spare lithium batteries and bulbs (consider headlamp)
	x	handkerchief
	x	toiletries (soap, washcloth, towel, toothbrush and paste, dental floss, comb, shampoos)
		trekking permit
	x	this book
		verified phone numbers for your embassy or consulate, trekking agency (home number of managing director), and helicopter services, to use in case of needing a rescue
	x	*Nepali for Trekkers* (book and tape)
	x	rupees in a variety of denominations
		U.S. dollars, enough for an air ticket fare if your route takes you near airstrips and plans change so you want to fly out
	x	pen or pencil, ink, paper (letterhead if possible), envelopes (to write an emergency message should the need arise), and business cards
	x	pocket knife, perhaps with can opener and scissors
	x	plastic bags: several sizes with rubber bands or twist ties
	x	nylon line (parachute cord), elastic bands
	x	blister materials (see chapter 4)
	x	feminine hygiene materials (imported varieties now available at supermarkets in Kathmandu)
		plastic trowel to bury feces
	x	matches or cigarette lighter for toilet paper
	x	sunglasses
		spare eyeglasses or contact lenses if you wear them
	x	umbrella if traveling in warm sunny lowlands or in the monsoon
		smiles

R P

FOR TREKS TO COLD, SNOWY, AND HIGH PLACES

x   wool or pile hat; balaclava
x   x   wool sweaters or pile or down jacket
x   x   wool or pile pants
x   long underwear of polypropylene or wool
x   x   mitts (possibly gloves) with water-resistant shell and warm, light inner lining
        for dexterity
x   x   windproof outer garments, pants, and jacket
x   x   boots, well broken in and waterproofed
x   gaiters to keep snow out of boots
x   x   ice ax, rope, and crampons for glacier travel
x   glacier goggles with spares, including enough for Nepali employees
x   sunscreen; zinc oxide for lips

IF TREKKING WITH AN AGENCY (CHECK WITH THE MANAGER REGARDING ITEMS IN THE OTHER CATEGORIES)

x   duffel bag (sturdy, zippered, lockable with all your gear stowed inside) to give
        to your porter
        phone numbers of the agency, including the home phone of the managing director

IF TREKKING INDEPENDENTLY AND RELYING ON LODGES

x   toilet paper
x   makeshift shelter (plastic sheeting or bivouac shelter)
x   air mattress or foam pad (optional)
x   plastic ground sheet (especially if up high)
x   some food for contingencies

IF TREKKING INDEPENDENTLY AND CAMPING/COOKING FOOD (OCCASIONALLY)

x   x   tent
x   toilet paper
x   sturdy duffel bags, zippered and lockable, for gear
x   x   kerosene stove
x   fuel containers, fuel filter
x   x   nesting pots
x   cups, plates, spoons
x   scouring pad
x   alcohol in a plastic container (for priming stove if your model requires this)
x   x   shelter, warm clothing, and cooking facilities for your employees if you will be
        in remote areas
x   food, packed appropriately
x   water bag for carrying large quantities from a distant source

MONSOON TREKS

        running shoes with new waffle soles
x   umbrella
x   x   collapsible ski poles
x   waterproof (Gore-Tex™) jacket with underarm zips, or a rain poncho or cape
        (latter now made in Kathmandu and good value)

R P

x	waterproof rain chaps or pants (optional)
x	large, heavy-duty plastic bags and several smaller ones
x	plastic sheeting for covering porters' loads and other uses
	insect repellent, permethrin spray
	patience
	adaptability

OPTIONAL GEAR

x	specialty food items
x	bathing suit
x	shorts for men
	shaving paraphernalia for men (battery-operated or safety razor)
	altimeter
	compass
	thermometer
x	watch with a chronograph and alarm (possibly an altimeter)
x	binoculars
x	spotting telescope and tripod
x	maps
	star chart
	ear plugs (for sleeping despite barking dogs or in noisy Russian helicopters)
x	headlamp
	vacuum bottle
	candle lantern
x	candles
x	reading material
x	journal, diary, or pocket notebook to record observations
x	stationery, air letters, post cards, stamps
x	English-language learning materials to use with porters (buy in Kathmandu)
x	*kata* or ceremonial scarf to give to a lama or adorn sacred object
	a picture book or post cards about your country or favorite activities
	a picture book of farms, farm activities, and animals
	photographs of your family, friends, and activities
x	photographic equipment, film, appropriate spare lithium batteries
x	tape recorder, external microphone, lithium batteries, blank tapes
x	prerecorded tapes
x	headphones
x	language tape and book
	musical instrument
	games
x	belt bag or fanny pack for easy access to selected items while walking
x	collapsible ski poles

This bamboo comb removes lice nits, and ghiu *(used as hair oil) suffocates the critters, part of hygiene for Nepalis.*

3   Interacting with Nepal

Madam, this is Nepal. In America you can be a bird in a gilded cage.
Here the bird is free. And for that there is a price.

A Nepali to an inconvenienced and
angry trekker

This chapter provides not only basic information on day-to-day trekking, but also food for thought on how to help preserve the character of trekking in Nepal. This type of tourism is now being called "tourism with insight," "alternative tourism," or "eco-trekking," among other things. I am pleased to see Nepali organizations now espousing the cross-cultural attitudes first presented in this book in 1976.

Trekking Life, Food, and Accommodation

ROUTINE

Variables such as the type of trek, the size of the party, and the area visited all affect the way you organize your daily trekking activities. Those traveling in areas where there are plenty of trekker-oriented hotels can structure the day much as they wish. Trekkers employing Nepali assistants are advised to adhere to a schedule compatible with their employees. Those on an organized camping trek follow a personalized daily routine, usually with hot tea served in your tent before you get up. Breakfast follows, then you hike till around midday, eat lunch prepared by an advance cook team, then continue till the evening stop. Trekkers traveling in areas where there are few foreigners and who wish to eat local food must adhere to the local schedules.

Though local schedules vary depending on the area and the village, the following general outline gives you some idea of what to expect. In the hills, Nepali people get up around sunrise, sometimes have a brief snack, then work until the midmorning meal around 10:00 A.M. Work then continues until the late afternoon and is followed by the second meal of the day. A snack immediately preceding this meal is not uncommon. Because activities coincide with period of daylight, people tend to go to sleep soon after sunset. In the mountains, people wait until it warms up a little before engaging in much activity. They generally eat three meals a day.

LODGES AND HOTELS

Tourist lodges are located mostly north of Pokhara, north of Kathmandu, and to and in Khumbu. There generally you find private and dormitory rooms with beds or sleeping platforms, covered with foam or cotton mattresses. Cotton mattress covers and pillow cases are provided, but these are not renewed after each traveler spends a night. The walls between private rooms are thin, so vocal privacy is rare. Noisy parties can be disruptive. There is usually a central dining area, sometimes with an electric light or a bright kerosene lantern and often a wood stove for warmth. To date, trekkers are not segregated, so nonsmokers have to put up with fuming travelers. There is a latrine outside, often locked and sometimes a flush toilet, but usually a pit. Some toilets will have a container in which to put used toilet paper, instead of down the hole to keep the system from clogging. Toilet paper is almost never provided. You can expect hot water for washing and often a hot shower in a simple setup, all of which are usually charged for separately. Some lodges offer massages for aching limbs, which are not the sex-tour variety found in other countries. In high-altitude settings, the facilities will be more spartan, and private rooms may not be available, just a central sleeping area off the kitchen. Floors and walls may be built of sod blocks carved from the alpine meadows nearby.

The term *lodge* tends to mean a place to eat and spend the night, as does hotel, but terminology is not standardized. You can always sleep in a hotel or tea shop though the amenities may be very spartan.

In some areas north of Pokhara or in Khumbu, there are luxurious facilities with corresponding prices. Lodges may sometimes cater only to clientele with a specific travel agency; however, if bookings have been low, you may be accommodated.

I make no effort to evaluate the quality of the services of the lodges. Guide Michelin standards, reliability, and ratings can't be counted on in rural Nepal. Nor can I guarantee lodges will function when mentioned in the text. These are usually open only during trekker season. Ask before proceeding to high areas, especially if in off-season times.

These modern lodges provide attractive accommodations and a chance to interact with other trekkers.

There is an increasing tendency, especially in the national parks, to cook on kerosene in these lodges. In other places, mudded-in wood stoves are norm and electric hot plates may be found. Kitchen facilities are usually wanting, and hoteliers, in spite of their lengthy menus, may only have one or two stoves to cook on for everybody. Fast food hasn't yet arrived in rural Nepal; the closest approximation is fast-cooking noodles. It makes sense to adjust your order to what is already being cooked, rather than have each person order a separate item. International menus have become commonplace in many lodges, with the quality of the food varying enormously from place to place and from time to time. Some trekkers in lodges complain when all the items they order are not served piping hot all together. If this applies to you, reread the epigraph. Prices in lodges are fixed; there is no bargaining except possibly in off-season times.

Seek out less popular lodges, or *bhaTTi* ("traditional inns") rather than patronizing the most frequented places. Such redistribution of income will have a significant economic impact in the area. At a popular trekking stop, you may find everyone staying there, not necessarily because it is the best, but because everyone else is there or it was mentioned in a book. Avoid this herd mentality.

Lodge owners along the popular trekking routes are especially eager to please tourists. By asking about toilets and rubbish disposal, segregation of smokers, use of kerosene, and hygiene, a trekker can influence future directions for the lodges. Compliment lodge people for the many things they do well.

People's Homes

In North America and other travel destinations, bed and breakfasts (B&Bs) have become popular, partly because they allow the visitor a more homey atmosphere and a chance to get to know a family. Almost any home in Nepal is a B&B and offers the trekker a chance to intimately experience Nepali life. Small parties, up to four or five including porters and guides, can ask in villages, even if lodges exist, to be fed and put up overnight in a home. I have been doing this for twenty-seven years and find Nepalis in popular trekking towns today delighted to participate in the tourist economy by offering food and lodging this way. Porters and guides find the experience enjoyable too for they get an opportunity to experience other cultures in the mosaic of Nepal. If you speak a little Nepali, you will face little difficulty arranging this. If you don't, try to use a few phrases, or advise your guide or porter to enquire for you. I cannot more strongly support any other activity associated with trekking. This is as fun, adventurous, and memorable as it gets.

Once you or your guide has established that you will stay in someone's home, remove your shoes, bend forward so you don't hit your head, and enter. In the dim light, you will be offered a place to sit near the fire, usually on a mat of some kind. Take this place, smile and wait for some food or drink to be prepared. Don't take the space closest to the fire in a Sherpa or *BhoTiya* home unless that has been offered, for that is the place of honor. Talk about your travels. Relax. Some discussion may ensue about what you eat. Ask that you eat the same food as the rest of the family. If you are with other trekkers, limit the closed interactions between you and show interest in the people and place you are in. Play with children, compliment the family, and tell them a little about yourself. Food will appear and you will have an opportunity to eat simple, wholesome, tasty fare. Usually you will wash your hands outside first. Don't worry about getting sick from this. You won't die if you have a loose movement, you've probably had a few already while being cautious. Satiated, bring out your photo album and share a little of yourself and country. If asked what your gear or items in your country cost, tell them you don't remember, it was purchased so long ago. Eventually, make sleeping arrangements, usually on the floor with the rest of the family, or on benches along the walls. Morning will bring a new experience. When it is time to leave, ask how much to pay. Sometimes this will be left up to you, so pay appropriately. You may not want to stay in lodges often after this. Staying in this traditional way provides a great window on rural Nepali life that has been described as Chaucerian or biblical. I urge you to take the opportunity to share this kind of experience. I stay in such a fashion whenever I can and began doing so long before I gained facility with Nepali.

Camping and Using Shelters

If camping and stopping to cook your own food along the trail during the day, expect to take 2 hours. Setting up camp with an agency trek in the evening takes 30 minutes, and breaking it the next morning takes an hour. Trekkers on trips organized through an agency will tend to have customary meals at the usual times. Lunch is usually prepared by the cooking staff, who then go on ahead. The staff sets up and breaks camps, and makes sure that the trekker keeps to the correct trail.

Trekkers traveling in the high country on less foreigner–frequented trails may stay at *goTh,* temporary shelters used by shepherds. Some are quite substantial structures, whereas others are only four walls or just the frames for the walls. When the shepherds bring their animals up to graze during the hot monsoon months, they bring bamboo mats or yak wool roofs to cover the frames. *Yersa* in Khumbu are groups of *goTh* used by those who pasture yak and sheep. If there is any doubt about whether these shelters will be available or if privacy is desired, it is best to carry a tent.

Those camping will find a variety of sites. Organized treks will have these all arranged. Your tents will be set up and ready when you arrive. In the morning, a hot cup of tea or coffee will be at your tent entrance, and warm wash water usually follows. On your own, look near villages for campsites on terraces that are harvested or in fallow or use school yards. Make a donation to a responsible person of the school for upkeep and supplies. Clearings in the forest, monastery courtyards, and dharmsala (resting houses for native travelers) are other sites. Popular trekking areas will have designated fee camping sites near lodges. In western Nepal, where there are flat-roofed houses, you can often pitch your tent on a roof! Be sure to obtain permission to use people's land. Finding water may be difficult. Ridges and hillsides may lack water, especially before the monsoon. Trek descriptions in later chapters indicate where I know water to be a problem.

In all these situations, keep track of your equipment and supplies and, when you leave, check that nothing is left behind. In lodges, look under the bed and in the corners of the room and dining area for your belongings. At the first and last days of a trek, you may be more careless and leave stuff behind.

FOOD

Try to eat the local diet, *daal bhaat,* which consists of a large quantity of rice with a lentillike soup poured over it. There are usually some cooked vegetables available, and occasionally you may be able to get an egg or some meat. Unlimited quantities of *bhaat* (rice) are included in the meal, but the *daal* (lentils) and vegetables are rationed. In some trekking areas, the number of additional helpings is rationed. The usual custom is to have it prepared fresh, and oftentimes the quantities are misjudged so you can't get more rice. I find it very tasty and not at all disgusting as is often portrayed to foreigners. Sometimes, away from the popular trekking areas, rice is not available, and you may eat *saatu, dherdo,* or *piTho,* terms for roasted flour (corn, millet, or wheat) made into a thick paste by adding boiling water. Eat it with a spicy sauce and vegetables if available. Many trekkers on organized treks ask the cooks to prepare this tasty menu.

Tea with milk and sugar is the traditional beverage along the trade routes in the hills. Lodge owners will make it without the additives, or with lemon or ginger. In the north, Tibetan salt-butter tea (*solja*) is common, a hearty broth. You can also ask for boiling water or hot water. If the kettle has been sitting on the stove at a rolling boil or if the water comes from a vacuum bottle used to make tea, it is pretty safe. I find this a good way to replenish fluids in homes and lodges in cold high places, when I get sick of sweet tea and *solja* is not available.

Local alcoholic drinks include *chang* (Tibetan) or *jAAR* (Nepali) for the beer leeched from a fermented mash of corn, rice, millet, or barley; *rakshi* (Nepali) or *aara* (Tibetan) for a distilled version of the above mash; and *tOmba* (Nepali) for drink sucked through a bamboo straw by pouring boiled water over a bamboo canister of fermented millet mash. These are inexpensive and tastes vary widely; *tOmba* is only

Consider staying in someone's home to have potatoes, Sherpa style.

found in the east and may be the safest brew. Alas, modernization has brought potent commercial distilled products, which are relatively less expensive, and beer, which has become the rich man's drink, though little is consumed by locals outside of Kathmandu. There is no consistent widespread terminology for these commercial products, with the exception of *biyar*.

In Khumbu as in most mountain areas, the traditional diet can be mostly potatoes. They are made into a stew (*shakpa*) or pancakes (*riki kur*) or mashed and served with a spicy sauce (*riltok sen*), but most often they are boiled and eaten after peeling the skin off. Other features of the Sherpa diet, also common to other *BhoTiya*, are *thukpa*, a noodle soup, and *tsampa* (roasted barley flour). *Tsampa* is eaten either as a watery porridge (*chamdur*), made by pouring tea over it and mixing it with a finger, or as a drier form (*pak*) poured into the tea. You will be given a half-filled bowl of Tibetan tea and the flour in a separate container, usually with a spoon. Add some, then mix with a finger, adding more, to knead it with all your fingers in the bowl and produce a thick dried plug (*pak*). Eat pieces with some stewed vegetables. This is a common early morning startup.

Quick cooking noodles are becoming a staple in Nepal for a fast-food trail snack. You won't find it in most people's homes, however. When traveling in remote high country, carry some snacks such as biscuits, quick cooking noodles (which can be eaten uncooked), or nuts, to tide you over stretches without facilities. Do not eat huge meals for lunch or you may experience heartburn, especially as you tighten your pack's waistband and begin the uphill climb.

Trekking with Children

Resourceful families who have ventured into the wilderness or taken foreign trips with their children will have a good idea of what to do. The following is a synthesis of practical advice. Like almost everything in life as a parent, there are new challenges, new insights, and many tales to tell to friends back home afterwards.

Families with younger children have carried them in a back- or front-style pack carrier. A back carrier with an elevator seat is probably best. Other families hire a porter, the best being a woman—a Sherpani or hill Nepali. It will be difficult to hire just one woman. Two together could porter and help take care of the child. Most such women have children themselves and enjoy singing and playing with the child. They usually prefer carrying the child in a *Doko,* the conical wicker basket, using a tumpline. A foam pad for the inside and an umbrella attached to the basket rim for shade keep the child comfortable. It is not unreasonable to carry a child up to 44 lb (22 kg) in this manner. Some children, especially active ones, may not tolerate being carried in a basket by a stranger. The method you choose depends on your personal preferences. Certainly carrying your own child can contribute to an important relationship with him or her.

Children in diapers need not be a problem. Use cloth diapers, which either you or the porters wash. It is not a chore that a porter can be expected to do, but an arrangement can be worked out beforehand. Your porter will probably prefer to wash the diapers away from town and out of sight of the villagers. Try to avoid pollution of streams when washing diapers by using a separate pan and scattering the wash water. Bring a string for a clothesline, soap, and clothespins. Drying diapers is difficult in the monsoon. In fact, it is probably not advisable to trek with young children at that time. Nepali children never use diapers as we know them. A few disposable diapers may come in handy in case of diarrhea, even for a toilet-trained child. Disposable diapers are not available in Nepal except in the new supermarkets in Kathmandu. Burn them out of sight of others and bury the ashes. A "potty" or chamber pot for toilet-trained children may be helpful. Otherwise, unfamiliar surroundings may make defecation difficult for them unless the parent "practices" with the child. Even older children may need to practice defecating in the squatting position.

Food for children can vary a great deal. The children of one trekking family soon became willing consumers of *daal bhaat,* the local rice-and-lentil dish. Those on treks organized by professional agencies have few problems if the cook prepares familiar foods. A great deal depends on the parents' attitude and their children's food fussiness. I strongly encourage you to try whatever is being served in the house, if you stay in local homes. This may not work with the very fussy child, so bring some very familiar foods in quantity to supplement the local fare if necessary.

Parents who have hiked with their children under various conditions should have no difficulties choosing clothing for them. Synthetic-pile garments, worn over a zippered pajama suit, may be the best choice for infants on cold days. Such clothes are warm, light in weight, and quick drying.

Discuss each day's plans with the children, what the trail might be like, the kind of people they'll meet, their fears, and how to interact with Nepalis. Rules for youngsters on the trail should include no running downhill, no getting out of sight, and no rock-throwing. Drink plenty of liquids, and put on extra clothing right away when stopping in the high, cold regions. Consider a sleep schedule that is close to

Your children may play at village work. (Robert Zimmerman)

the child's norm; this makes for happier kids. Usually they are pretty tired out so it is not a problem.

Uphill portions become a challenge varying with the age and temperament of the child. Telling stories, singing songs, playing games, and focusing on the nearby surroundings may make a 2000-foot climb go by painlessly. They all take effort, the amount varying with the character and fatigue level of the parent, as well as that of the child. Try placing a bell on the parent's pack and have the child herd the "yak" up the hill with a long light stick. Give points to your daughter or son for gentle prods with the stick. Play hide and seek along the trail—here are many places to hide. Or guess the number of steps to the next tree, house, or *chhautaara,* and then have the child count them. Try using baby steps, giant steps, or animal steps. Count anything else—flowers, birds, porters, children. Count by 2s, by 5s.

Telling stories to their children along the trail can be natural to many parents but daunting to some. Don't think you can't—try. Choose the child's favorite characters and draw out the story—one tale can get you up several hills if related in chapters. Stories are best used before a child is whiny or cranky, a kind of preventive.

The longer flat trails along the way invite singing. Good songs include the old favorites, especially those with endless repetitions and cacophonous sounds. Rounds would be great for getting several kids along the stretch. As a last resort for the exhausted parent, consider a portable tape player for stories and music.

It helps to choose daily destinations where there will be Nepali children to play with. So aim for villages, rather than lofty sites where there are only lodges for trekkers or lonely campsites. Make an effort to stay in a local home, rather than lodges or camping, for at least one night, and try this before the last day of the trek. This "night to remember" could be the highlight of the trek. You may want to continually put up in homes to share in the details of daily life: food preparation, family interaction, household tasks, use of water, and the open fire. In one such overnight stop, you may see many different kinds of food being prepared in ways unheard of back home, observe hauling water, using a dung fire, experience staying in a one-room upper-story with the stable below with novel sleeping arrangements, together with spinning of yarn from yak wool, planting food, and using the compost toilet! It is especially rewarding if the host family has children of similar ages, but even without this Nepalese are very family-oriented and will delight in the presence of children. There may be Nepali children in lodges with their innkeeper parents and this could dictate your choice of a lodge. To get the children playing together and over the language barrier, use a simple play item such as a doll, jump rope, or coloring book to facilitate the process. You the parent might play together with both sets of kids to get things going.

Most young kids will enjoy playing with Nepali children; you will be astonished to discover few language barriers among preteens. Your children may be surprised to see that Nepali children have few toys. It is wise to bring a few items to keep your children amused because they won't be as inspired by the beauty of the countryside or the spectacular mountains as you. Playing with toys with the Nepali children could be fascinating for your children, but avoid setting an unfortunate precedent by indiscriminately giving out toys to local children. Nepali children are quite happy with the limited toys they have, and they could become quite envious if they knew about the toys they don't have. Getting your children to play with the simple toys that Nepali children use could be an important formative experience.

Most children, like many adults, find it difficult to be stared at. This may happen when staying in a Nepali home that is not set up as a hotel, with separate rooms for trekkers. To avoid this problem, take a tent or choose one of the popular treks with lodges or hotels along the way. A tent gives your children a familiar place to go, away from the prying eyes of the crowds that always assemble to stare at the funny

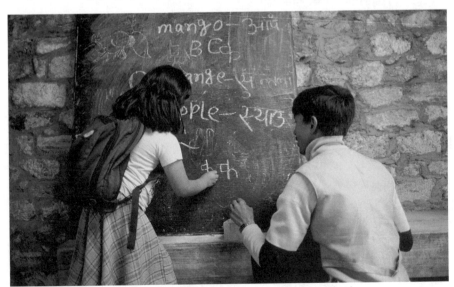

The author's daughter Maia learns the alphabet in a Nepali school.

little foreign kids. Some children may find it reassuring to sleep between their parents when staying in unfamiliar surroundings.

Consider getting your child to wear local dress. It is often easy to have clothes tailor made in rural areas or in Kathmandu before you leave. Hygiene can be a problem along the trail. Do the best you can, but you will not be able to attain the standards you left behind at home. Aim for a daily wet washcloth wash. Focus on cleaning the child's hands before eating, and keeping everything out of their mouths except food and water.

School work should probably be carried out for long trips, and the child's teacher may request this and provide lesson materials. Build in time each day for this, preferably earlier before there is much fatigue. Be sure to bring adequate supplies of pencils, paper, and erasers. Keep all the materials and lessons in one special bag. Plan the approximate amount of material to be covered with the child each day but be flexible with long days, illness, and so forth. Like the trail, go at it one step at a time. Make visits to local schools, and consider having your child sit in on the classes, which are usually quite informal anyway.

Be aware of the physical hazards in Nepal. There are plenty of places inside homes, along the trails, and in the fields where a slip or fall could be disastrous for a child. Dogs (particularly rabid ones) represent an occupational hazard for trekkers in Nepal, and even more so for children. Exercise extreme caution around all dogs and villages, as options after being bitten are few and unpleasant. Children should avoid petting stray dogs. Although they are not known to be carriers of rabies, water buffalo frequently have surly dispositions and delight in charging small children. I advise getting the preexposure rabies vaccine for your children.

Altitude may affect children more than adults. Also, it may be difficult to ascertain whether it is altitude or some other illness that is causing symptoms in infants and young children. (See altitude illness in chapter 4.) Like most aspects of trekking in Nepal, the experience of going as a family can be rewarding and enlightening if you prepare yourself adequately.

Cross-Cultural Clues for the Survival of Trekking in Nepal

Our hosts have more to teach us in regard to living in contentment, than we can possibly teach them. In the unfussed ways of villagers met on trek, we learn that patience, humility and tolerance for all are virtues worth striving for.

> Kev Reynolds, *Langtang, With Gosainkund and Helambu*

The fullest enjoyment of Nepal in all its myriad aspects comes to those who attempt to transcend the cultural and linguistic differences between themselves and their Nepali hosts. Such people are more easily accepted into the social framework of Nepal and there are many rewards.

At times some trekkers have offended their Nepali hosts. Others have taken great advantage of traditional hospitality without considering the consequences. Still others, realizing how much farther their money will go in this country, have made a big display of their wealth. They have handed out large (for Nepal) sums of money and given away many of their possessions. Trekkers have disgraced religious customs and shown great disrespect for their hosts' beliefs. The local people have adapted somewhat to this breach of courtesy and ethics by these foreign invaders, even coming to expect it along popular trails. Generally they both admire and envy foreigners and detest their behavior. Partly for this reason, traditional Nepali hospitality is less obvious along these trails. The Nepali people will not let you know of their displeasure—it isn't their way. But among themselves they will have less respect for you and less desire to treat you as an honored guest. But should you make the effort to stand apart from the other trekkers, to respect the Nepali people and their customs, they will relate to you in positive ways you couldn't have imagined. You will find yourself more respected in turn.

Nepal is a complex social mosaic, with Hindu and Buddhist traditions of the Indo-Tibetan frontier overlaying local animistic and shamanistic beliefs. Many of the customs stem from Hindu concepts of purity and ritual pollution with influences of Tibetan looser networks and monastic religious ideas. The hills of Nepal, as the interface, has been increasingly Indicized or Sanskritized, but American influences are ever more present today. With the advent of political change in the 1990s, some ethnic groups are subtly reasserting their own cultures. Still in the major population centers, Hindu religion has increasing influence.

INDICIZED POLITIES	TIBETICIZED POLITIES
center–periphery relations more direct	networks looser in more severe terrain
culture heart of North Indian plains, one of the most densely settled areas of world	culture heart of central Tibetan plateau, one of the most sparsely settled areas in the world
rice–cow subsistence system	cold crop, herding subsistence
dominated by Chhetri–Brahmin alliances	dominated by nobility–monastic alliances
high caste landlord elite	nobility and monastic landlord elite
expansive patrilineage dynamic	less expansive system
caste hierarchy as socio-religious ideas	endogamous social groupings and monastic religious ideal
Indic calendar	Chinese calendar

Todd T. Lewis and Theodore Riccardi, Jr., *The Himalayas: A Syllabus of the Region's History, Anthropology and Religion*

There are basic rules governing acceptable behavior in Nepal that have knit the social fabric together over centuries of change. An outsider may feel vulnerable, anxious about making a fool of him or herself by behaving inappropriately. With so many different cultural traditions in this country, no Nepali is facile in more than a few. Hence an outsider, if he or she is seriously trying to be culturally cognizant, will be noticed and respected. The rules are not difficult. You need only observe what Nepalis around you are doing and act accordingly. What follows classifies and expounds on this.

This section, the most important part of this book, is an attempt to provide you, the guest in Nepal, with the information to act in ways that constitute reasonably acceptable behavior to your hosts. Most of the material here has been subtly gleaned from Nepalis or from the experiences of sensitive visitors to Nepal. If your attitudes are right, and your practices are acceptable, then a few faux pas will be overlooked. All outsiders in Nepal have, at times, acted incorrectly. That is how I've obtained most of the information presented here. But once you have learned acceptable norms of behavior, the benefits should make all the effort worthwhile. Encourage others who have your confidence to do likewise. This is essential if trekking in Nepal is to continue to be one of the supreme experiences in social-cultural peregrination.

When talking to trekkers in Nepal, I compare the experience of those who are behaving in a fashion sensitive to Nepali customs with those who aren't so considerate. The thoughtful trekker has invariably had a more intimate relationship with the Nepali people, has encountered fewer problems, and is eager to come back.

Travellers and Tourists, Dave Cook

The term "traveller" much beloved by the backpackers I would sometimes meet, made my hackles rise. It is pure snobbery. To the local people we are all tourists— period. . . . They are not fooled by the traveller's attempts to create the illusion that they too are really part of the world's poor. They know that the scruffy denims contain a passport that will blast aside frontiers closed tight shut to them, and a piece of plastic able to release a cascade of banknotes from a hole in a wall. Best avoid the posing and pretence—as tourists we have responsibilities—and that applies to us all, not just to those on package holidays.

LANGUAGE

Along the popular trails, Nepalis who deal with trekkers have learned basic English, travelese, and other foreign languages to enable them to please their guests. Even off the trekker trails, some English is spoken; but in remote areas you are less likely to find translators to help communicate.

Everyone who attempts to learn some rudimentary Nepali will find his experience in the country much richer. You will be more welcome, people will be friendlier, and they will go out of their way to help if you try to speak some Nepali.

Nepali is an Indo-European language that is easy to learn. It is used as the second tongue by half of Nepal, so people commonly hear many variations in how it is spoken. Hence your efforts to speak the national language will immediately make you welcome and help you stand out from other visitors. It is the first step in transcending cultural differences to make for a more rewarding interaction.

To help you learn the language, order the pocket-size book *Nepali for Trekkers*, published by The Mountaineers Books, and practice with the accompanying language tape (see Appendix C for ordering information). From the questionnaire included with the first edition of the book and tape, I have learned how much a difference it makes for trekkers to practice with the tape at home before they leave and to make every attempt to speak Nepali. *Everyone*, linguist and nonlinguist alike, has found their attempts very well received and been uniformly positive about the experience. People report playing the tape repeatedly in their car or while doing other mindless chores and thus assimilating a sense of the sounds.

Whether or not you try to speak Nepali, be prepared for the questions you will be asked. They want to know: whether you're married? (and if not, who is the man or woman with you); how many children do you have? (if none, they will be extremely puzzled); how much money do you make? (perhaps you can answer in terms of what fraction of your rent it pays); what does your camera cost? (it helps to have forgotten); can you give me some medicine? You may be surprised at how much they know about you. Recently, a *Tamang* to whom I was speaking in Nepali told me I was from America because of the slang expressions I was using!

DRESS

The dress code for men is as important as that for women but is often neglected. Men wearing shorts have low status in Nepal. Don't wear them when visiting monasteries. Men should never bare their chests, except when bathing discreetly. Wear a shirt at all times.

Women should attempt to wear full, long skirts, midcalf at least, as often as possible. It is important that women do not expose their legs. Wearing long underwear is helpful if your skirt is shorter than midcalf. In fact, you can put long underwear, pile pants, and the like on when it gets cold and take them off quite discreetly when it warms up. Shorts are not acceptable for women. If women wear shorts, Nepali men and women make rude remarks about them among themselves. Attire appropriate for the beaches of Cannes is not appropriate for Nepal, just as attire for Papua New Guinea Highlands is inappropriate in Perth. Skirts can allow a woman to urinate with some privacy if there aren't enough bushes around, especially if she doesn't wear underpants.

For women, a *lungi* or tube of material can be purchased in any cloth shop in Nepal and custom-sewn in 10 minutes into a suitable garment. Have a pocket or two sewn in. An elastic waistband or drawstring is helpful for washing discreetly. Perhaps easier to wear is the *AAgi*, or *chubaa*, a long sleeveless *BhoTiya* dress that ties in back. In Kathmandu you can sometimes purchase a ready-made cotton one. Or it can be made from wool or polyester. Long skirts brought from home are also excellent. Some women have made them of denim, or with beautiful patterns. Skirts should be full (not tight) and in a lightweight fabric (cotton or synthetic) will be as cool as shorts, and definitely cooler than trousers. Wool is best for the cold. If you must wear baggy pants for the arduous part of the day's walk, change into your skirt in the evening when in a village or when dealing with Nepali people.

In Kathmandu and trekker tourist areas such as north of Pokhara and in Khumbu, you will find some young Nepali women wearing pants. This causes concern among many Nepalis there (not unlike the concern voiced by older people for the current younger fad in America of piercing many body parts). By wearing skirts you earn respect quickly, deserving of a sensitive guest.

Several women on one trek reported a phenomenal difference in acceptance by Nepalis depending on whether they wore skirts, pants, or shorts. One woman in another group of women decided to not wear a skirt while her companions did. She wrote me that her friends received all the attention from Nepalis and she was ignored. This all changed after a visit to the tailor along the way when in desperation she had one made and wore it ever since. One woman who started trekking in a skirt decided it wasn't necessary and changed into shorts. In an hour she was accosted by a Nepali man. Another changed from wearing shorts into a skirt and found that, rather than being stared at as a curiosity, she felt more accepted by Nepalis. A Nepali hillsman who married a trekker reported that he was attracted to her in distinction to other women because she wore a skirt.

Trekkers who have questioned Sherpas or other Nepalis about appropriate attire have countered my arguments by quoting their answers. The Nepalis always answer to please, even though their feelings are offended. Donald Messerschmidt, a savvy Nepal anthropologist from whom I first learned about trekking in 1969, was talking with a shopkeeper in Tirkhedhunga when a French couple walked by, dressed as if on the Riviera, the man in a tiny brief, the woman in a skimpy bikini. The shopkeeper asked Don what country they came from. Don, having heard them speak, replied France. The shopkeeper then asked, "What's the matter, don't they have cloth in their country?" Consider how you might feel if a Papua New Guinea highlander male, wearing only a penis shield, walked near your home and spoke to you. Would you treat him in a friendly manner and invite him inside? Nepalis feel equally put off by the dress of many foreigners. Along the well traveled routes, they have seen it all.

Jewelry: Nose and Ear Ornaments

Women pierce the nose on the left side (the female side) in the Hindu castes and insert a discreet stud. Many hill ethnic groups—*Tamang, Gurung, Magar, Rai, Limbu,* and Hindus—pierce the left nostril and septum. You may find a ring on the left side or a flat or dome-shaped plate of gold, with or without a colored stone. While the latter may be glass, or plastic because of its attractive color, the gold is usually real and quite pure. Brass or alloy is occasionally seen.

Ears are pierced early in life, as earrings are considered auspicious and gold helps the ears to hear *dharma* and the mind to understand it. There is great variety in the ornaments worn on earlobes, with no clear representational design. Some earrings will have *makar* (dragon) heads on either side, similar to the fish design of old water fountains. Large, up to 3 in. (8 cm) in diameter, lightweight gold earrings, held stiff by their rim (*chepTisun*, meaning "flat gold") are worn by *Tamang, Magar,* and *Gurung*, especially.

In the hills, many groups (except Sherpas and other *BhoTiya*) wear large *dhungri* through the stiff center cartilage of the ear. These may be so heavy that the ears flop over, a traditional sign of beauty among some peoples. The ear

A married Rai *woman wearing a* tilhari *and nose ring*

rims of some individuals may also have as many as eighteen to twenty tiny holes for carrying little rings. Some men, notably the *Jyapu*, pierce the right (male) side of the ear, high up. *BhoTiya* men and women wear coral and turquoise on strings through the earlobes.

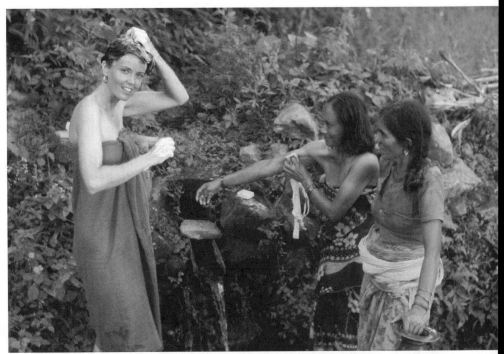

Participating in activities of daily living such as bathing Nepali style will help you have a more meaningful experience with the people. (Mary Anne Mercer)

BATHING

Trekkers often like to relax in hot springs or swim and wash in rivers or lakes. Nepalis are usually very shocked if this is done with genitals exposed. Women should not bare their breasts, especially those who have not borne children. Men may go bare-chested only while swimming or bathing. If you wish to swim in the nude, do so out of sight of Nepalis. Also be modest while washing yourself within view of others. Women wearing skirts can bathe discreetly when not alone by hitching the skirt up, using it as a tent. Clothes can be changed under it too, and an elastic waistband or drawstring makes it easy if your skirt is not too bulky. A tank suit underneath the skirt makes it easier to swim. Read the section on fuel under "Conservation" for energy efficient ways to keep clean.

BARGAINING AND BUYING

To understand the custom of bargaining, which is almost universal in Asia, one must realize that it is a game, not an impediment to friendship. Westerners, by contrast, often harbor bad feelings after the bargaining process. Yet once a price is agreed upon, it is "fixed." Language trouble can also create misunderstandings. I can well remember bargaining with a taxi driver to take me to the start of a trek out of the Kathmandu Valley. He named a price and I began to bargain with him, but named a higher price, as my command of Nepali numbers in 1970 was poor. He quickly agreed, and it was only as the ride began that I realized my mistake. Nevertheless, I paid the price I had agreed upon.

Try to find out the going price for an item before you begin bargaining. Failure to do so hurts everyone. As an example, if a Nepali will sell an egg to his neighbor for Rs. 5, but finds he can get Rs. 10 from a trekker, he will be less likely to sell that egg to his neighbor. The price of eggs goes up. The Nepali is hurt, but not the trekker, to whom the difference in price is negligible. Such inflation is common. It behooves the trekker to always pay the lowest going price in any transaction, especially for something Nepalis buy also. In some tourist areas, two prices are used, one for foreigners and one for Nepalis. Although it makes sense, given how much more money we have, it will increase prices for Nepalis.

In many places, people want Western gear, such as down jackets, windbreakers, and other items of apparel or equipment, more than they do your money. So you can either plan to bring extra to trade, or barter unneeded items toward the end of your trek.

Trekkers with their large sums of disposable currency have significant economic impact along the trail. By spending for locally produced goods and services, they can stimulate and support the local economy. This keeps people gainfully employed with respect and dignity, lessening the push to move to Kathmandu and work in sweat shops there. Eat local food, buy locally produced crafts, and limit purchases of imported products (foods, souvenirs brought from Kathmandu, bottled drinks, etc.).

Bargaining effectively takes time, so be leisurely and relaxed. Don't show too much interest in the item and certainly don't begin by offering the top price you are willing to pay. If you are hung up over the last stages of the bargaining process, remember the monetary exchange value of the amount in dispute. Sometimes it may just be a few cents and not worth the haggle for something a local wouldn't buy. Prices are fixed for certain items, usually food and commodities, especially along well-traveled routes. In the ACAP areas, lodge management committees have standardized menus and lodging with fixed prices for foreigners. In other national park areas, this is happening to different extents. Do not bargain here, or in other areas where prices have been fixed. Prices increase the further from the supply. In high altitude areas where Nepalis don't normally go outside of seasonal animal pasturing or on trading trips, they will be steep. Recognize that the local perception of cheap travelers is that they are fools. Moderate extravagance and generosity are appreciated by the Nepalis. Traveling cheaply, easy in Nepal, should not be the goal of your travel.

EATING

Hindus are concerned about ritual pollution of food when it is touched by anyone outside their caste or religion. As a foreigner, you are outside the caste system or considered an outcast or untouchable. Thus, do not touch any cooked foods on display, though it is usually all right to handle uncooked foods such as fruit and raw vegetables. When drinking from a container used by others, avoid touching your lips to it; pour the liquid into your mouth. Similarly, when drinking from a water bottle, do not touch your lips to it—at least not in sight of your hosts. Wait for food to be served to you rather than helping yourself. Do not give leftovers to your hosts, even though they may be rare delicacies brought from home. Do not offer a person anything from which you have taken a bite or sip. This is the *juTho* concept of food—if any food is touched by someone's mouth, the entire plate is contaminated and the utensils must be washed before anyone else uses them. By the same token, all leftover food or drink must either be thrown away or fed to animals. The only exception is that a wife may eat from her husband's plate. Hence, do not accept more food than you can eat. In a tea shop, put your empty glass where the Nepalis put theirs. Trekkers who visit Brahman houses or villages can expect to be served apart from others, usually outside their host's house. They will not be allowed to sleep in a Brahman house. In general, don't offer to share food in a group of Nepalis unless you have enough for everyone.

Don't touch food with your left hand. Nepalis use the left hand for cleaning after defecating. It is offensive for them to see food in it. Eat with your right hand and use your left for picking up a glass or holding something not edible. Before and after meals, you will be offered water and a place to wash your hands and rinse your mouth. Wash your hands separately, or your left one not at all. Your right hand may be used to wipe your mouth, never your left. Give and receive food items with your right hand. In eating *daal bhaat* and vegetables, where the meal is served in separate containers, keep them that way, except for small portions that you mix on your plate prior to eating. Spoons for eating are often available, but try eating with your right hand. It's fun! It's also the most popular way of consuming food in the world.

Nepalis never touch their lips to a container when drinking, but pour the liquid down without spilling a drop.

In hotels that cater to trekkers Western habits are more customary. All the same, the more a trekker is aware of the usual Nepali manners, and the more he or she uses them in everyday behavior, the more comfortable a Nepali host will be with that person.

GENEROSITY AND GIFT-GIVING

In rich countries, many of us feel we can buy whatever we want, whereas Nepalis tend to make things happen by creating social obligations. Many Nepali ethnic groups exchange goods and services by reciprocal relationships without involving money, while other traditional patron-client relationships are more hierarchical. Economic reciprocal exchanges based on social bonds of caste, kinship, and family are found in many Nepali ethnic groups with modern versions used to facilitate business transactions—the so-called "source-force" exchanges, for example. This practice involves utilizing access based on these bonds to gain power—be it jobs, contracts, or other advancement.

The trekker can unknowingly enter into these kinds of reciprocity relationships. Many foreigners feel the trekking experience to be a sacred journey, requiring physical and emotional stamina in an exotic environment. Special bonds develop over the course of a trek between the trekker and his or her employees because the work involves social interaction as well as physical labor. These bonds are more like the implicit trust of kinsmen than of unrelated people and are not found in most other types of tourism exchanges. Trekkers complete this journey with unfulfilled (?) gratitude and try to express this feeling through generosity to their staff. They may do so through giving tips, or even financially sponsoring some of their employees or children in their families for education and opportunities. The staff in turn reciprocate through special ceremonies and exchanges, hoping to establish long-term bonds between the hosts and guests.

These interactions may represent an attempt to replicate the egalitarian nature of pre-tourist relationships which have served humankind for countless millennia. Some foreigners have assumed long-term responsibilities in the relationship, even bringing some of the staff to the United States in return for assistance in their future sacred journeys. However, such associations tend to become hierarchical over time. The beneficence rarely involves the lowly porters and others who have little contact with the trekker, and this selectivity can increase the gulf between the rich and the poor, the haves and the have-nots. The lesson: try to maintain reciprocity and egalitarianism however you can, in spite of the hierarchical nature of touristic encounters. Any attempt to maintain these equitable traditions will benefit us all.

In dealings with people, pay the going rate. Never walk off without paying. In tipping people for their services, be reasonable. Routine tipping is not a Nepali custom. Some people tip much more than the salary or cost of the service they are paying for. This only reinforces the belief that the foreigner does not know the value of his money, and thus should be relieved of as much of it as possible.

Giving to monasteries is an extremely important tradition in Nepal and elsewhere. Buddhist cultural values are related to the number of monks and their devotion as well as the existence of teachers to carry on traditions. The decline of monasteries is more likely to affect faith and values than the pollution of sacred sites by unknowing tourists. You gain *dharma* and help conserve Buddhist culture. The main way the religion continues to survive the onslaught of western culture is through charitable largesse to the monasteries. Most have a donation box. Be generous. Villagers' sense of your respecting their culture also ensues. Hinduism is less dependent on the presence of *sadhu* (holy men), but giving to them is also appropriate.

Bringing small gifts for people who have helped you along the way is a good idea. People you wish to be generous to may appreciate a look through your camera or binoculars or at the pictures in this book or others you may have. Allowing people to look through picture books from home (those with farm scenes are most appreciated), post cards of temples and other sights of Nepal, or to see photographs of your family, is a most welcome gesture. Sing songs for them, dance with them, or play a musical instrument. Those artistically inclined should bring a sketchbook and share drawings with them. Let them draw for you. One trekker brings string and plays string games with children and adults, something that is imaginative, cheap, and portable. Flossing your teeth can provide entertainment. Displays of generosity should be limited to appreciation for something extraordinary that has been done for you. When you give or receive something to or from someone hold onto the object with both hands, a sign of respect.

Gifts should emphasize the transcendent values of friendship, knowledge, and health over material wealth. Beware of the long-term repercussions of anything you do. When Daniel Taylor-Ide who was working in family planning in Kathmandu in 1969 suggested that I distribute condoms during my treks, it seemed a great idea. Reluctant to demonstrate their proper use to adults, I blew them up as balloons for children. This was a highly successful public relations gesture, but people following my path were besieged with requests for condoms and balloons. Currently such litter abounds. Bring small useful items like strong sewing thread, needles, cloth, and rope. Whether or not you travel with small children, baby clothes will be appreciated. Consider bringing your older clothes that are out of style, or older camping or trekking equipment that is no longer used to give to porters and people as gifts, again within the grounds noted above.

BEGGING

Give me one pen, miThai, *bonbon. Give me one rupee.*
The sounds of Nepali children the
trekker hears today

Trekkers may sometimes encounter beggars to whom it is appropriate to give. There are few traditional beggars in the hills, but occasionally *sadhu* travel through, begging as part of their lifestyles. Monks and nuns occasionally beg. Food such as rice is an appropriate gift item for them. Sometimes destitute people are encountered and gifts of clothing, food, and occasionally money are appropriate. Note the actions of Nepalis around you when deciding whether to give.

It is instructive to watch patterns of begging develop along the trekking trails over the years. When I first came to Nepal in 1969 there was no begging in the hills. Yet children and others along the trekking trails are now constantly begging for candy, money, pens, and cigarettes. A few hours' walk off these trails, people do not beg at all.

Why do trekkers give money, pens, cigarettes, candy, and other items to children? Clearly they like the happy smiles they receive. And in Nepal, foreigners can feel generous without having to give very much. Others feel guilty about the great gulf in material wealth between themselves and Nepali people. If you are one of these, realize that you are making beggars out of children who once were spontaneously happy. To encourage and support begging is an example of cultural arrogance. Do you want Nepalis to lose their self-respect? If everyone stopped reinforcing inappropriate begging, it would cease in a generation or less. To sample the experience without begging, take a trek away from popular areas. You'll be convinced.

Nepalis have had good dental hygiene in the past, due mostly to their low consumption of sugar. Don't work against this by giving candy. The amount of tooth decay in the trekker areas from consumption of sugar in the form of candies has increased dramatically. This was the major reason to establish a dental clinic in Namche Bazaar. Don't encourage smoking by handing out cigarettes. Some Nepalis will not allow smoking inside their inns! Handing out money to everyone who asks or giving money for posing for pictures is not a good idea. Parents of Nepali children are usually quite ashamed to learn that their children have been begging, and they try to stop it, except in areas where begging has been so reinforced that parents have become a type of pimp.

When approached by a beggar, ignore the person and walk away disinterested. For begging children, consider using one of the phrases in *Nepali for Trekkers.* Talking to Nepali children about begging is not effective, it is like "Just say no" at home. Don't taunt or ridicule the beggar. Sarcasm is not understood in Nepal.

Adults are approaching trekkers asking for various opportunities such as help in getting a visa or for airfare to a foreign country (yours) or for support for their children to go to school in Kathmandu. Trekkers have been generous in these ways and word gets around. Some trekkers enjoy a chance to help people poorer than they who have been kind to them also. It would be better to seek out the truly marginalized groups in Nepal who can't interact with trekkers the way lodge owners, sirdars, and other tourism workers do. But this is much harder and less likely for the trekker.

Sometimes trekkers are approached to donate money for village construction projects such as schools, trails, and bridges. That is probably legitimate and if Nepalis also contribute, then the trekker might too. In some places Nepalis will approach you to plant a *Tikaa* (red mark) on your forehead or garland you with flowers for which they expect you to pay. Avoid such people if you don't want the product. Sometimes trekkers will spend several days with a family and then decide to be generous with that family in some special way. That is perfectly appropriate, it is a part of normal social human behavior. It certainly doesn't encourage the kind of begging that has sprung up on the shoulders of trekker tourism.

"Oh money come to me." This may become the mantra of the future in Nepal if we who are fortunate enough to travel here don't exercise care and sensitivity.

THEFT AND SECURITY

Trekkers are usually surprised to find that Nepali people are genuinely friendly and extremely honest. If you find yourself suddenly surrounded by a group of onlookers in Nepal, robbery is the farthest thing from their minds. They are curious and eager to help; they are not afraid to get involved. However, Nepal, once renowned as a place where travelers had absolutely no worries about theft and violence, is slowly entering the late twentieth century.

There is occasional theft and petty vandalism; packs and luggage left on tops of buses are easy targets, as are unattended tents (some of which have even been slit open and robbed while occupied). More people are reporting items missing from their packs and sometimes thieves are seen rustling through packs left outside lodges or unattended along the trail. Pickpockets now work some of the popular trails. Misunderstandings have resulted in a few reported attacks, robberies, and even a rare death. There have been attacks on trekkers camping alone in areas with few people, attacks by porters, and instances where trekkers on an exposed area have been pushed off a precipice. Is there is an increase in the incidence of such episodes, or are incidents more publicized as the number of trekkers increase?

Some trekkers have been insensitive to local customs, have mistreated their porters, and have behaved in a manner outside the norms of Nepali experience. Trekkers who could not afford it at home could have servants do many of the distasteful and laborious chores of camping and backpacking. Porters and assistants were sometimes thought of as less than human. This was evident in the lack of responsibility that many took toward their employees. There has been a change in cultural values among some Nepalis living in the areas most heavily influenced by trekking. Some Nepalis believe that trekkers don't value their money because they don't try to get the best prices. Since they are so willing to pay too much, others try to relieve them of their seemingly unvalued money and possessions. Remember, however, that the risk of attack and robbery in Nepal is much less than in your home country. Better to be an American in Nepal than a German in Florida.

Try to prevent petty thievery by keeping a watchful eye on your possessions. Carry around exposed to view only the equipment you expect to use a great deal. Try to have all your gear stowed inside your pack and duffel bag, and keep the pockets done up. Lock items whenever possible. Discreetly inventory your gear in the morning and afternoon; it will be less likely to disappear through porter mishap.

When traveling by bus with your belongings in the luggage rack on top, either have someone in the party ride with them or be watchful of people climbing on top when the bus stops. During a bus stop for lunch, it is safest to bring your carry-on items with you, out of the vehicle. It helps to keep all easily removed items buried deep inside the luggage. In populated areas, don't leave your tents unattended. Don't trek alone, especially if a woman. Treat your porters with respect. Make sure they have equipment and food sufficient for the undertaking. In lodges and hotels where the honor system is used, be honest, and never run off without paying. Where this has happened too many times, the lodge has the trekker pay for each item as it is ordered. Carry money in a money belt around the waist, or deep inside the pack, which you don't lose sight of. Don't be tempted by greed into a potential confrontation where by sleight of hand you lose your money. This happened to me in Connaught Circus in Delhi and taught me a valuable lesson.

Jewelry: Tikaa and Other Adornments

A *Tikaa* is a mark of religious and decorative significance on the forehead of Hindus. They are given and received, particularly at festival and religious occasions, to express good wishes, friendship, respect, and honor. When a Hindu visits a temple or shrine, he or she often takes *Tikaa* from the officiating priest. One day each year, during the religious observance of *DasAAI*, the King gives *Tikaa* to the general populace. Outside of Kathmandu, the headman of a village substitutes for the King on this day of honor. Plain *Tikaa* of red or yellow powder is an essential part of *pujaa* (worship) for men and women. Black ones guard against spirits. Fancy ones, commercially produced, are worn by women as decoration or makeup in urban areas today.

Colored powder, usually red and orange, is put on images of gods, thrown at *Holi*, and slapped on cheeks at festivals. This custom of Hindu origin is a sign of reverence that pleases the gods and delights people by expressing their connection with one another and with the gods.

We are far behind Nepalis such as this Tharu woman when it comes to body piercing.

Children, who need protection from the "evil eye" of witches and from ghosts and spirits, wear black *gaajal* at the eyes and black strings at the neck, wrists, ankles, and waist. Similarly, silver anklets are thought to help their legs grow straight. Amulets with mantra papers are worn at the neck. *Rudaaksha* (seeds of *Eleocarpus ganitrus*) are a sign of respect to Shiva, while *Narasimha* images of copper protect against lightning and fright.

Woman are reporting sexual harassment with greater frequency. This can occur in lodges as well as along the trails. Pornographic videos from the United States, shown in parlors to the men after the Hindi films are over, have projected salacious images of foreign women. Police may not be sensitive or be eager to investigate. Dressing appropriately helps. Either ignore relatively minor episodes and leave or be indignant. If this happens in a lodge, threaten adverse publicity.

In case of theft, report this to the police. Likely you will have to travel to a major police station in Pokhara, say, or Kathmandu and file a formal report. Make copies of the original for processing, have your passport or trekking permit replaced, get airline tickets reissued, and so forth. Usually other trekkers will be generous enough to take care of immediate needs and even loan money on goodwill terms.

Be sure to register with your country's embassy or consulate when you arrive in Nepal. This is advisable for all trekkers, even those on organized treks. Let the embassy officers know your dates and itinerary, and give them a contact person should they need to follow up.

Aphorism Once Seen on the Wall of the Police Check Post in Jomosom

A smile costs nothing but gives much. It enriches those who receive without making poorer those who give. It takes a moment, but the memory of it lasts forever. None is so rich or mighty that he can get along without it, and none is so poor but that he can be made rich by it. A smile creates happiness in the home, fosters good will in business, and is the countersign of friendship. It brings rest to the weary, cheer to the discouraged, sunshine to the sad, and it is nature's best antidote for trouble. Yet it cannot be bought, begged, borrowed, or stolen, for it is something that is of no value to anyone until it is given away. Some people are too tired to give you a smile—give them one of yours, as none needs a smile so much as he who has no more to give.

MEDICAL TREATMENT OF LOCAL PEOPLE

In the past, medical facilities were very scarce in Nepal, and foreigners were almost the only source of Western medicines. Each passing traveler was considered a doctor and indeed, many people, both medical and nonmedical, devoted a large part of their energies to treating the ills of the local people. Today this effort is not warranted and may do more harm than good. It helps destroy confidence in health care services developing in rural areas. Besides the facilities staffed by doctors along the trails, there are many health posts manned by auxiliary health workers. It is doubtful that ephemeral medical care such as a trekker could dispense would result in a cure or significant benefit to the sufferer. Furthermore, the idea that a little medicine might help a sick person and enable him or her to get to proper medical aid just does not hold up. Based on my personal experience as a doctor working in remote areas of Nepal and on discussions with other medical personnel, giving medicine to someone whom you wish to refer to another facility is almost certain to deter that person from acting on the referral. Finally, the idea that a little aspirin won't hurt anyone is untenable because, since it will not effect a cure, it may help destroy confidence in Western medicine. In a country with many different medical practices, it is best to introduce those aspects of medicine that definitely work. This policy is in Nepal's best interests, several important Nepali organizations have publicly concurred.

This advice does not apply to your porters and other employees. If a problem presents itself that you can confidently manage, you should treat them to the best of your abilities. Otherwise, if the condition is serious, you are responsible for obtaining proper medical care for that person. In other situations, exercising normal humanitarian instincts and helping your fellow man is also appropriate. That is, don't walk away from the scene of an accident without rendering assistance in any way that you can.

MISCELLANEOUS CUSTOMS

> *By living with villagers primarily on their own terms, more bumbling initiate than intrusive, elite stranger, I felt that my body developed a partial, experiential understanding of their world, from the ways in which they held their bodies, to how they felt, hurt and healed.*
>
> Robert R. Desjarlias, *Body and Emotion: The Aesthetics of Illness and Healing in the Nepal Himalayas*

The fire and hearth are considered sacred in Sherpa homes, in those of most other *BhoTiya,* and in high-caste Hindu homes. Thus do not throw any refuse, including cigarettes, into a hearth, at least not without asking. Sherpas and other *BhoTiya* believe that burning or charring meat offends the gods. Do not roast meat on an open fire.

Shoes are considered the most degrading part of your apparel, so keep them on the floor or ground. Remove them before putting your feet up on anything. Shoes, especially leather ones, should always be removed before entering any kind of temple, *gomba,* or monastery. Do not touch anyone with your shoes. The greatest insult you can give a Nepali is to kick him or her with your shoe. Follow the example of your host in deciding whether to remove shoes before entering a Nepali home. If in doubt, remove them. When removed, keep the soles on the ground, not overturned. When sleeping in a temple or *gomba* don't point your feet at the images.

Don't wash your feet in water that will flow into a water-driven prayer wheel. If you must wash your feet in such a stream, do it after the water has passed through the entire series of prayer wheels. The head of an adult Nepali is the most sacred or ritually clean part of the body. You should never touch it. Similarly, don't touch anyone with your left hand. Pointing your finger at someone is considered rude.

Before sitting down on the ground, you will almost always be offered a mat to sit on. When sitting, do not point the soles of your feet at anyone. Nepalis will not step over your legs and feet. Be sure to draw them up to make a path for anyone coming or going. If you and your porters, or Nepali hosts, have to sleep on the floor together, sometimes around a fire, the arrangement should be sure to avoid anyone's feet being pointed at a Nepali person's head. As you go farther north, these Sanskritized concepts of purity and pollution become more relaxed and Tibeticization influences predominate. Watch your hosts and adjust your habits accordingly.

Public displays of affection are not the custom in Nepal. Young men may hold hands walking, and women may, but not men and women. So confine your amorous feelings to private places.

Trekkers going around the chorten, *keeping it on their right*

While traveling, you may pass Buddhist *mani* walls containing tablets with prayers carved on them in handsome Tibetan script. Walk by them, keeping them on your right, as Buddhists would do as a sign of respect. Similar treatment is given to the *chorten* and *stupa,* commemorative mounds sometimes modeled after those at Swayambhu or Baudha. If in doubt as to whether a structure is one of these, keep it on the right as you walk by. When visiting a monastery or *gomba,* a donation of money for the upkeep is expected as a gift. In paying respects to the abbot of a monastery, offer him a ceremonial scarf, or *kata,* obtained from another monk. Many Hindu temples will be out-of-bounds for non-Hindus.

Many Western habits are offensive to traditional Nepalis. Some, such as shaking hands, using dry toilet paper, carrying around a used handkerchief, and eating without washing, seem unsanitary to them. Many of these have become more accepted in time but respect for the native customs pays rich dividends to the trekker.

OTHER CONCERNS FOR THE TREKKER

Respect people's desires not to be photographed. This is quite common along popular treks now. Think how you would feel if hordes of invaders would regularly descend into your life, not say a word to you, but plunge long lenses into the midst of your daily routine and occasionally into your most private affairs. Many, especially elderly villagers, believe that being photographed can shorten their lifespans. Flash photography inside monasteries is thought to hasten the disintegration of paint there. Sometimes if you talk with them a while, they will consent. After you show them pictures of your family, they may be more willing to be photographed. Or let a recalcitrant subject take a photograph with your camera. After she snaps the shutter, she may change her mind and let you photograph. If I want a photograph badly enough, these techniques, respecting human dignity, work. Don't promise to send copies of photographs to people unless there is a reasonable chance that you can do so. Sending photographs through the mail in Nepal is becoming more reliable. Write down their names and postal addresses in English, which is sufficient for the envelope. You could also send them with another traveler or through your trekking agency in Kathmandu. Do not take flash photographs inside *gomba* while ceremonies are going on.

Some people who come to Nepal are attracted by the freely available marijuana and hashish. The plant grows as a weed in much of the country. Traditionally, older shopkeepers consumed it now and then at the end of the day. Young Nepali people never used it when I first came to Nepal in 1969. Now in their desire to copy foreign habits they indulge. Nepal now has a considerable hard drug problem among its natives, both as consumers and drug runners! Some trekkers smoking marijuana on the trails will offer it to wide-eyed young children. Consumption of this drug is a personal adult decision. It is illegal to carry and sell it. It is wrong to try to entice youngsters to use it.

Many trekkers purchase art and craft objects in the hills. Sometimes they buy valuable old art objects, often at modest prices. This is expressly illegal; it is prohibited to remove any valuable old items from their origins. Even transporting idols and artifacts has resulted in imprisonment to trekkers. Steadfastly deny any interest in old art, for if you don't, you encourage Nepalis to steal objects from sanctuaries, trails, monasteries, or temples in order to sell them to foreigners.

OBJECTIVE AND OTHER HAZARDS

Nepal, a mountain environment, has its share of dangers from rock fall, avalanches, and other acts of gods. In November 1995, a huge aberrant snowfall created extremely hazardous conditions for trekkers in the high country. Avalanches and landslides resulted in loss of life and in people being stranded for days. Huge rescue operations were mounted. Both trekkers and guides misjudged the hazards and bad luck befell as well. In October 1996, snow storms dumped many feet of snow on encamped trekkers who didn't continue digging out and succumbed. The worst tragedies occur to trekkers on organized agency treks, partly because they give up responsibility to the guides.

Bad weather happens. Snowfalls bury tents and cause avalanche-prone slopes to release. Steep faces are exposed to rock fall. Rocks frozen in place on glaciers release when warmed, scree slopes slide. Trekkers misstep and fall. Weather forecasts in Nepal can't warn of increased risk even if they could predict the weather. Other hazards include getting lost and being stormed in. One man split from his companion near Gosainkund Pass in a storm and descended into a cul-de-sac where he survived without food for 43 days before being rescued. While this was a remarkable survival story, the lessons are clear.

These lessons are to stay away from potential avalanche slopes when snow is falling or when warming trends could cause depth hoar to release loaded inclines. Like having serious symptoms of altitude illness, evacuation from these areas cannot be delayed. If you are in an organized trek, be as vigilant as possible, recognizing that those who are looking after your welfare are only human, and may have a more fatalistic outlook than yours based on their sense of karma. You may have to take charge in such circumstances. Be prepared for difficult conditions up high, and keep the party together. There is strength in numbers.

Mountain travel requires judgment about dangers, something that can't be assumed, nor learned from books, nor necessarily expected of guides and certainly not of porters. Prepare yourself beforehand by gaining as much mountain experience as you can.

CONSERVATION

Take nothing but pictures, leave nothing but footprints.
Sierra Club motto

Fuel

In addition to the effect trekkers have on the people of Nepal, they may have a profound impact on the countryside. Nepal's limited supply of firewood is being consumed for tourism. Trekkers increase the demand for wood, especially in alpine areas where forests are being cut down near treeline to provide it. Use of wood for trekking, especially in the high-altitude areas, must stop if trekking is to be a resource-conserving activity. Some may argue that wood is a renewable resource, while the alternative, kerosene, is a nonrenewable fossil fuel. True, but in Nepal the deforestation problem is too severe to be further worsened by trekkers. For those on agency treks, choose an agency that uses only kerosene as a fuel for all members and staff including the porters.

Independent trekkers who are camping should use kerosene stoves. Trekker pressure can exert a significant effect on innkeepers: if they cook food on kerosene, patronize them. Suggest to other hoteliers who don't how important it would be to their business to do so. Porters will build fires to keep warm unless you provide them with enough warm clothes and shelter up high when they will burn less wood.

Try to eat the more simple Nepali *daal bhaat* rather than the less fuel-efficient foreign menus that hotels try to prepare to help conserve Nepal's fuel supply. Hotels offer hot showers for trekkers and where the water is heated in a wood fire consider showering less often to conserve fuel wood. Patronize hotels that use solar water heaters for showers or who have a heat exchange device (back boiler) to utilize the hot exhaust gases of a wood stove to heat water. Consider lowering your standards of personal hygiene to use less fuel in marginal areas. Hotels burn considerable quantities of wood in heaters to keep trekkers warm. Put on more clothing to keep warm and lessen the need for fuel.

Alpine Preservation

When camping, especially in the frail alpine meadows, be careful not to add to erosion problems. It takes many decades to produce the vegetation that can be carelessly torn away by a boot or killed by a tent. Similarly, when following trails, stay on the path and do not cut switchbacks. If the vegetation surrounding the trail erodes, it is much more likely that the trail will wash out during the torrential monsoon.

Threats to Nepal's Natural Resources: Habitat Loss

The major threats facing wildlife in Nepal are the loss and deterioration of the country's forests. The Nepalis depend on forests for fuel, animal fodder, medical herbs, bamboo for making baskets, and a host of other basic materials. As the population continues to increase, the forests can no longer meet the requirements of the people. In recent times this has been most pronounced in the Tarai, but loss has also occurred in the hills, as people clear land for agriculture to support the increasing population.

In some places, however, and mainly in Nepal's well-visited protected areas, such as Sagarmatha and Langtang National Parks and the Annapurna Conservation Area, trekkers and mountaineering expeditions are making the problems much worse. Dr. Hemanta Mishra of the King Mahendra Trust for Nature Conservation discovered that a tourist trekker uses nearly five times more fuel than a local Sherpa in Khumbu. The forests that are suffering are some of the best for wildlife in Nepal. An example is the forests along the trail between GhoRepani and Ghandruk in the Annapurna Conservation Area, a route once almost never used by local people. A huge, unbroken oak and rhododendron forest covered the surrounding ridges, supporting such rare species as the lesser panda and the orange-rumped honeyguide. In recent years, the trail has become a popular trekking route, and an increasing number of large forest clearings have been created by tourist lodges. Another important consideration is that much of the forest and shrubbery being depleted by tourists lie in the subalpine zone and are especially sensitive because they grow extremely slowly.

During your visit to Nepal's protected areas, there are many ways in which you can help to ensure that you do not damage the environment (see chapter 3).

Waste Disposal

The difference in waste along trekker-frequented and -unfrequented trails is phenomenal, especially today with consumer goods more widely available. Along the trekker trails, there are all types of detritus, including tampons, condoms, pink toilet paper, and that offering to the great Western god, feces. Trekkers often discard litter in Nepal in a way they would never do at home. Perhaps trekkers reason that this is their once-in-a-lifetime trip, they aren't coming back, so it doesn't matter if they litter.

For some popular trails, the route description might as well read, "Follow the line of sahib's garbage—film boxes, food wrappers, foreign cigarette boxes, tin cans, toilet paper, tampons—for a week to reach the superb alpine pastures and majestic viewpoint." Carry your wrappers and other items throughout the day, and burn them in the evening. Remember, however, not to throw any items into your host's hearth fire, at least not without asking first. Giving metal and glass containers to villagers is no longer as appreciated as it once was because of the abundance of containers and trekkers offering them. Consolidate and carry out noncombustible items (metal, glass, and plastic). Burial is not an option. Spent batteries should be taken home out of Nepal and disposed of appropriately there.

Along popular trekking trails you see litter containers. Sometimes, the paper contents of these are burned, and the metal discarded. Or the contents are just pitched off the back of the lodge or shop; these litter areas are all too easy to spot. Talk to the lodge owners and operators about this, and give your preference for incineration. You can influence them, because they want to be liked, and to do the "right thing" to get your business. Those with guides and porters should not leave them in charge of garbage disposal. There is no way for you to ensure that the garbage is not being incinerated and simply being discarded. If you suspect the latter and make a fuss, chances are it will just be done out of your sight.

The consumption of bottled mineral water that is now available along the popular trekker routes is not ecologically sound, unless you can carry all the empty bottles back home or at least to Kathmandu. Empty plastic bottles in various stages of destruction create a new category of despicable litter. Some bottles are being refilled with any water, recapped, and sealed perfectly. Samples of popular brands have been tested and found contaminated. Iodizing water makes sense and it is far less costly. Add vitamin C powder if the taste bothers you. You will save a lot of money on the water; prices increase the farther away you get. A liter costs more than a night in a lodge in many places. Try not to consume bottled beverages, beer, and the like. Seeing the millions of bottles scattered in trekker-traveled areas will convince

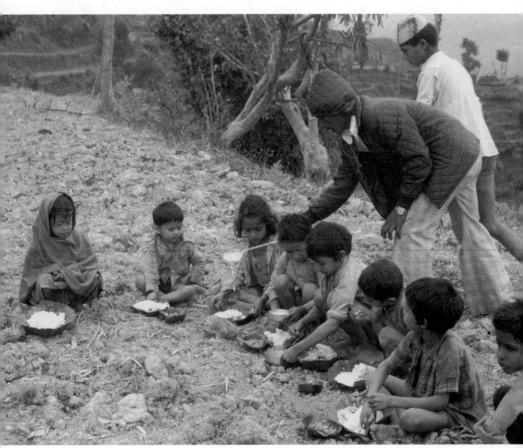

Disposable plates in Nepal are assembled from leaves held together with wooden picks. (Mary Anne Mercer)

you this is appropriate advice. The nonbeer popular brands of soft drinks are refillable, but they are being abandoned in remote areas as the deposit isn't enough to make it worthwhile to porter them out. Similarly, avoid packaged moistened towelettes for hygiene, carry a washcloth, and use your water bottle.

By not spending money for imported goods, you have money to spend on locally produced foods, services, and crafts, which benefits the local economy. Imported goods come from Kathmandu or abroad and do not help the local economy nearly as much.

Trekkers and mountaineers can contribute to "light pollution," especially in areas such as the Khumbu, through which pass expeditions bound for the heights. Often they carry along stickers with an expedition logo that they affix to walls, counters, and windows in hotels. Many, plastered on windows, results in less light getting inside dwellings with few windows. There is considerable wallpaper of unconventional sorts in these places, which seems a part of their decorative scheme. Help keep it off the glass windows.

Disposing of body wastes is another problem facing trekkers. Trekkers staying in lodges should ask where the latrine or toilet is and use that. Without American Standard, it is sometimes difficult to squat com-

Millions of empty bottles at the Shyang-boche airstrip await a ride to Kathmandu that will never come. Consider foregoing bottled beverages on your trek.

fortably, aim correctly, and avoid splattering. Those on large organized treks erect enclosed latrines at campsites. The feces and other material are then buried. This commendable practice avoids the unsightliness and potential for disease of piles of feces, each with a topping of toilet paper. In many areas, the pits are dug too shallowly, so the concentrated waste material easily contaminates the region. Ask for a deep hole to be dug. Travelers who are staying in someone's home should ask whether there are communal latrines (*chaarpi* or *toylat*) in the villages or if a family has one. One of the many positive changes over the past decade has been the establishment of latrines in certain heavily trekked areas. In addition, public health campaigns have resulted in the erection of latrine structures by many individuals near their homes. There are latrines in many of the villages of Langtang, Manang, Thak Khola, Solu–Khumbu, and other areas. Some have a container for used toilet paper so it won't clog the mechanism. Most homes in Khumbu and others in Helambu have traditionally had a convenient latrine arrangement on top of the hay pile situated in an alcove off the second floor, or more recently, a separate latrine near the house.

In much of Nepal, you will have to do as the Nepalis do. Usually, they perform their eliminations before dawn or after sunset in obvious places near the village. They carry a *loTaa,* or container of water, to wash themselves. Find a corner of a field or other sheltered spot away from running water and bury your feces, or at least cover them with stones. Carry a little plastic trowel for this. Keep a cigarette lighter or matches in a bag with your toilet paper and burn the paper or tampon first. Some people, those with old knees say, unable to defecate squatting, have taken small portable toilets for their personal use. (Rare trekkers have developed a dropped foot due to nerve compression from squatting.) Use a handkerchief rather than toilet tissue for nose blowing, or do it Nepali style.

Often you will find pariah dogs that eat feces—indeed, these are often summoned by villagers to clean up after young children. Disgusting as it may seem to non-Nepalis, it is certainly preferable to some alternatives. Whatever you do, be sure to exercise appropriate modesty and get out of sight of others. You never see an adult Nepali in an act of defecation. Nepali women and men often urinate discreetly by hunkering in their skirts. Some women trekkers find this quite appropriate if wearing long skirts with no underpants. If women separate their inner labia before urinating, it does away with the need for toilet paper and gives women more excretory freedom. If every woman did this, we would no longer see pink along the trail!

Threats to Nepal's Natural Resources: Hunting

Hunting poses a threat to some mammals and birds, although in most cases habitat loss is much more serious. One exception is the delightful Himalayan musk deer. Populations of this small deer are now much depleted as a result of over exploitation to obtain a strong-smelling secretion called musk, which is produced by the male. This is highly prized as perfume and is worth more than its weight in gold. The snow leopard, one of the world's rarest and most endangered mammals, is also threatened by hunting despite protection. This large cat has a beautiful, thick, spotted coat of soft gray and white fur, which is highly sought after to meet the demands of the fashion industry. Depletion in numbers of its prey (mainly bharal) are, however, thought to pose a much greater threat to its survival. Local hunting pressures on pheasants can be very high, such as in the Himalaya south of Annapurna. *Rhacophorus* frogs are hunted intensively near some villages because their dried extracts are thought to cure typhoid and high fever.

Endangered Species

Many wild animals and plants are being seriously threatened by illegal commercial trade. To combat this serious threat, many countries, including Nepal, have become signatories to CITES (Convention on International Trade in Endangered Species of Wild Fauna and Flora). Don't be tempted to buy the fur of a spotted cat, an orchid, a tortoise shell, or other animal or plant parts. To do so not only undermines Nepal's natural heritage, but breaks international laws. One person noted that 86% of the stores he visited carried coats made from protected species. In this survey, it was found that 700 protected cats had been killed to stock the fur coats in Kathmandu shops. Let store or hotel owners know your feelings if you see illegal items for sale.

Finally, in whatever you do, realize that you are not alone. If you carry off one *mani* stone from a prayer wall, saying that one less will make no difference, realize what would happen if everyone did so. Think of how you would like this country to be when you come to visit again, or when your children or grandchildren do. If we who travel in this exotic country respect its culture and customs, perhaps its spectacular countryside and the experience that we have found so worthwhile can be preserved for the benefit of Nepal and the enjoyment of future trekkers.

KEEP (Kathmandu Environmental Education Project)

This facility provides information to travelers in their offices in Tridevimarg, which are up the road from the Best Shopping Center, west of Kantipath and east of the main Thamel intersection. Open Sunday to Friday from 10:00 A.M. to 5:00 P.M., staff there can answer questions about trekking. There are informative notebooks in which trekkers record their experiences on the trails, a big help in finding out about local conditions and facilities. There is a convenient library and information programs. It is the best single source of information to extend this book. The phone number is 424698, fax 411533, and e-mail tour@keep.wlink.com.np.

Other Sources of Information on Trekking

Traditionally, trekkers read guidebooks, travel brochures, and stories of other's experiences and visit with returned travelers. A new phenomenon has invaded our time space, the World Wide Web. Below are some URLs, valid in early 1999, for various sites that may be of value. The web allows anyone with a home page to publish information. Much of this is of varying quality and accuracy, which sometimes may be difficult for the browser to assess. There are also mailing lists, such as the Nepal Digest, to which one can subscribe and post questions to be answered by others on the list. Treking agency contact information is available on the first page.

Home Page Title	Universal Record Locator (URL)
The Nepal Home Page	http://www.info-nepal.com/
Department of Tourism (Nepal)	http://south-asia.com/dotn/index.html
Himalayan Explorers Club	http://www.hec.org/
Nepal Information Directory	http://www.catmando.com/nepalihtm

There are many knowledgeable people in Kathmandu who are willing to help trekkers. Chris Beall presents slide shows on various treks at the Kathmandu Guest House, for an admission price, periodically during the popular seasons. These are informative, entertaining, and well-received.

Himalayan Explorers Club

This new U.S.- and Kathmandu-based organization provides services to members, and tries to give back to people of the Himalaya. The Kathmandu clubhouse is housed with KEEP, mentioned above. As a member, you can network with other travelers through their quarterly newsletter, find out about changes in Nepal through their web site (http://www.hec.org/), and use communication services, including e-mail, at the clubhouse. For information, contact them at P.O. Box 3665, Boulder, CO 80307, USA, (303) 998-0101, fax (303) 998-1007, e-mail info@hec.org.

Economic and Cultural Impact of Trekking

Tourism is thus not only the goose that lays golden eggs, but it also fouls its own nest.

Dr. Kamal Kumar Shrestha,
Nepali chemist

Tourism development proceeds through three (perhaps four) distinguishable stages. The first is "discovery," which for trekking in Nepal occurred in the 1960s and 1970s for the popular areas. Trekkers were addressed as sahib or memsahib, a colonial term of respect never heard today. There still are plenty of places in Nepal to discover today, even a few in this book. During the next stage, local resources are used for both traditional and touristic needs, under the control of local people. This is still happening in places visited by trekkers in small numbers. This contributes to the local economy significantly. In the third stage, tourism is institutionalized, with standardization for services and professionalization of tourist–host relationships. With increasing numbers of tourists in this stage, loss of local decision-making occurs, and profits from the growing competition for local resources flow outside the destination area. Goods and services for the tourist are imported, so much of the economic gain leaves the area. Most popular trekking areas in Nepal are either in this third stage or in a transition to it. A possible fourth stage would be when destruction or overuse of resources leads to a decline of tourism and consequent decrease in the local living standards. Some areas have noted a decline in trekkers presumably because of publicity regarding lack of hygiene. Marginalized groups have become poorer as a result of inequities in distribution of income from tourism.

Trekking tourism relies on a large trail network and inexpensive labor to porter. Most peasant farmers can no longer sustain their families on the available land, so they search out seasonal work. Trekking business produces social and spatial mobility and contributes to migration to the cities and adoption of market forces and urban values. Ancestral villages become abandoned, and languages are lost. Then helicopters put porters out of work. Some get rich, while many get poorer, losing their traditional means of support. Trekking tourism has thus radically altered conventional Nepalese society and culture; some have called it "wrecking in Nepal." It has contributed to the increasing disparity between rich and poor, the fundamental modern factor that is destroying the fabric of humankind everywhere. It doesn't have to; that is a key message of this book.

Essential Do's and Don'ts

Do

- plan enough time and limit your itinerary so you can enjoy your trek
- register at your embassy; let them know your itinerary, even if traveling through an agency
- verify the phone numbers for rescue on page 138-40
- wear a shirt if you are a man
- wear a long skirt if you are a woman
- take responsibility for your employees
- keep your valuables secure; locked up if possible
- keep prayer walls and *chorten* on the right when passing them
- pay the going price for food and other goods
- burn combustible garbage
- carry out unburnable garbage
- bury your feces and burn all toilet paper used
- draw up your legs while sitting on the floor so Nepalis can pass by you
- leave donations when visiting monasteries
- use kerosene stoves whenever you can
- patronize hotels and eating establishments that cook on kerosene; encourage others to do so
- patronize hotels that have solar-heated showers
- support local handicrafts that result from traditional cultural elements
- eat Nepali food for the most part
- limit consumption of bottled beer and other drinks to avoid bottle disposal problems
- compliment lodge and *bhaTTi* owners for the good aspects of their facilities
- smile—Nepalis tend to smile to relieve possible embarrassment; a return smile quickly eases tensions

Don't

- give to beggars unless Nepalis also do so, and give the amounts they do
- give money or items to people who have not done special favors for you
- give medicines to local people
- point the soles of your feet at anyone
- touch anyone with your shoes
- consume bottled water
- touch any Nepali's head
- give or receive food with your left hand
- eat off another's plate
- give food to Nepalis if you have touched it
- touch your lips to a drinking container that is to be used by others
- accept more food on your plate than you can eat
- walk out of a hotel or *bhaTTi* without paying your bill
- throw garbage in your host's fire
- photograph someone against their wishes
- defecate or urinate indiscreetly
- offer recreational drugs to Nepali children or adults
- travel alone, if a woman
- be sarcastic to a Nepali
- be openly affectionate

CULTURAL EROSION SONG

Open your ears and listen, brother, tradition is eroding
Both the drum and the breath of song are covered with a spider's web
Open your ears and listen, sister, tradition is eroding
Both the drum and the breath of song are covered with a spider's web

The older generation has not forgotten the traditional dress
You claim to be a son of Nepal, but don't wear a Nepali cap
Don't show off your long-haired hippiness
The Nepali cap is more appropriate

The women's skirt no longer has prestige
You claim to be a daughter of Nepal but are no longer recognizable
The roof on the house is torn apart and leaking, the skirt is eroding.

I recorded this song in the eastern hills in 1991; the adapation
of the lyrics from Lhakpa Norbu's translation is mine.

4   Health and Health Care

I suffered increasingly from mountaineer's foot—reluctance to put one in front of the other.

H. W. Tilman, *Nepal Himalaya*

Trekking in Nepal is beneficial to your health. Returning Nepal trekkers are commonly asked two questions. Did you have fun? And did you get sick? The answer is usually yes to both. (It is likely that you will have a bout of diarrhea and get a cold.) Field treatments and procedures are given for the medical problems you may commonly encounter in the hills. These are based on my own experiences as a physician who has worked and trekked in Nepal, as a specialist in travel medicine who has written a lay book on the subject and on altitude illness, and on discussions with other trekkers.

What follows may seem frightening to would-be trekkers who are used to the professional medical care available at a moment's notice in modern society. In Nepal you can be a week's walk or more from a doctor, though on popular treks you may find yourself surrounded by doctors! Hundreds of thousands of trekkers have followed precautions similar to those outlined here and have led a most enjoyable and healthy journey. For most people, trekking is not dangerous; it is the beginning of a new vitality.

Preparations and Posttrek Precautions

Many people come to Nepal with no hiking experience and, though in poor condition, take on their first trek, walk 100 mi (160 km) or more and thoroughly enjoy themselves. Some treks are more conducive to doing this successfully than are others. Still, I strongly recommend that those planning to trek undertake a conditioning program. Running several miles a day is about the best single conditioner. Taking hikes uphill with a heavy pack is a good activity to put variety into the regimen. Bicycling, cross-country skiing, swimming, and other aerobic activities are also excellent. But all of them must be started months ahead of time and carried on regularly with increases in the amount of exercise each week. Toughen your feet and break in your footwear through progressively longer hikes. Applying tincture of benzoin to your feet over pressure points where blisters may occur can toughen the skin.

Before you leave for Nepal, visit your physician and get necessary inoculations. The following immunizations are recommended: hepatitis A, hepatitis B, meningococcal meningitis, Sabin trivalent polio, typhoid, and tetanus–diphtheria. These vaccinations should be recorded on a World Health Organization–approved International Certificate of Vaccination, which can be obtained from the health department. Immunization against measles, mumps, and rubella is recommended for those not previously infected or vaccinated. Hepatitis A vaccine replaces gamma-globulin (immune globulin), long advised to protect against hepatitis. The only reason to use the less expensive but more difficult to obtain gamma-globulin is for a once-in-a-lifetime trekker who will never visit an area with poor hygiene or someone leaving less than two weeks before arrival in Nepal. Neither inoculation is needed if you have had hepatitis A before. There is some benefit to the old Whole

Cell Killed Typhoid vaccine over the newer oral and injectable vaccines in that it partially protects against paratyphoid fever, which infects travelers to Nepal. More people react to it than to the newer preparations.

Rabies exists in Nepal and you may wish to get the expensive human diploid cell vaccine. I have not heard of a trekker contracting rabies, but animal bites do occur and the risk is there. If you are bitten when you are far from anyplace where you could get the rabies shots, you face a dilemma. Should you abandon your trek and get to Kathmandu for the series of injections that take a month including the very expensive agent rabies immune globulin? A matter of time, inconvenience, and money. If you have had the preimmunization prophylaxis, then you need only get two doses of the human diploid cell vaccine, 3 days apart. It all depends on your level of risk assumption. Dr. David Shlim estimates that a foreigner in Nepal has a 1 in 6000 risk of acquiring a bite requiring rabies vaccine protection. If in doubt, I recommend the vaccine. If you have had it before, then you should either get your antibody blood levels tested or get a booster dose. The intradermal dosage scheme (0.1 ml on days 1, 7, and 21 or 28) is cheapest.

The old cholera inoculation was required in the past, but it was not particularly effective, and the World Health Organization has withdrawn it. Decline it and the new agent if offered; the risk of getting cholera for someone with the socioeconomic background to travel to Nepal is negligible. Other vaccinations that might be appropriate for specific groups include influenza (the yearly "flu" shot, available in the autumn in the United States) and pneumococcus (definitely recommended for those with chronic lung and heart disease, or over age sixty-five), as well as haemophilus B (routine now for young children). Several cases of meningococcal meningitis occurred in Westerners in Kathmandu during the mid-1980s. The single-injection meningococcal polysaccharide vaccine provides almost complete protection. Another risk is Japanese encephalitis, a potentially fatal viral infection spread by certain species of mosquitos. Many cases have recently been reported in Nepal, mostly occurring in the Tarai, during August and September. It is rare among world travelers from the United States; most cases occur in students, aid workers, or soldiers, not in casual tourists. There is an effective, low-risk vaccine available, which is recommended to those who will be long-term visitors in the Tarai during the monsoon. Others don't need it. All vaccines have some risk of adverse reactions and should not be used indiscriminately. Plague vaccine is not recommended in spite of the plague epidemic in South Asia in 1994.

A knowledgeable physician can time all of these inoculations properly. They should begin several months before departure. State and local public health departments usually have knowledgeable people whom you can consult. Visit a dentist to have potentially disabling dental problems cared for. There is no good dental service in Nepal outside of Kathmandu or Namche Bazaar. Women taking oral contraceptives should not stop them while trekking in Nepal.

Those with active chest and heart diseases that limit physical activity should avoid going to high altitudes. Individuals with the following conditions definitely should *not* go to high altitudes: primary pulmonary hypertension, cyanotic congenital heart disease, absence of the right pulmonary artery, chronic pulmonary disease with arterial unsaturation, coronary artery disease with severe angina or cardiac failure, congestive failure with arterial unsaturation, and disablingly symptomatic cardiac arrhythmias. These conditions are described in specific medical terms so the risks can be accurately assessed by your physician. Show this list to your doctor if you believe you have one of these conditions.

Some people with serious preexisting diseases have died while trekking. Those with sickle cell disease or sickle cell trait greatly increase their risk at high altitudes. People with recurrent deep vein thromboses and pulmonary emboli should also avoid high altitudes, but those with essential hypertension tolerate high altitudes well. Our knowledge of the effect of high altitudes on people with mild or moderate chronic disease, as well as on the elderly, is woefully inadequate. Information on drug effects at high altitudes is similarly lacking. Certainly many people in their sixties and seventies have trekked at high altitudes in Nepal with no problems. If you are in that age range or older and enjoy good health and physical conditioning, by all means consider trekking in Nepal, at least at moderate altitudes. You could later consider trying the high passes. Anyone with chronic diseases not discussed here should seek the advice of a knowledgeable physician and, if given the go-ahead, should first make supervised visits to high altitudes in his or her home country. My book *Altitude Illness: Prevention and Treatment* describes our understanding of people with various chronic diseases going to altitude. Similarly, those who wonder whether they have the physical stamina for trekking should first take backpack trips in hilly areas before planning a trek in Nepal.

Pregnant women have trekked and ascended to high altitude. There are no data on pregnant trekkers who venture to altitude for a short time. There is an increased risk (at the beginning of pregnancy and toward term) of problems, but it is probably small.

Those with stable chronic diseases who can undertake strenuous exercise can certainly trek. Such people may wish the security provided by an organized trek with a doctor along. Others may have enough self-confidence to trek in small groups without a physician. To my knowledge, people with diabetes, recurrent cancer, amputations, arthritis, after coronary bypass surgery, and even blindness have enjoyed trekking.

Diabetics who are insulin-dependent should be adept at regulating their own insulin dose based on blood glucose determinations. The exercise involved in trekking will usually result in lower insulin requirements, and this must be monitored en route. It is wise to carry snacks, as well as glucagon for insulin reactions. Companions should be well versed in dealing with these problems.

Ask your physician about taking malaria suppressants. Malaria was once endemic in the Tarai, but today it has been somewhat controlled in most areas. Nevertheless, incidents of malaria continue to occur. The usual form of protection is to take the suppressant chloroquine, 500 mg weekly. Except during the monsoon, the chances of contracting malaria while trekking in the hills and mountains is slight, especially above 4000 ft (1200 m). Malaria transmission is thought to occur sporadically in Nepal at altitudes above 4000 ft (1200 m), perhaps up to 6500 ft (2000 m), but I am not aware of trekkers who have contracted malaria at these heights. I do not take chloroquine prophylaxis while trekking. But you may wish to take the drug as an additional protection, especially if trekking in the monsoon. If so, start taking the pills one week before you reach the first area where there is a chance of getting malaria. Do not discontinue them until one month after you have left all infected areas. Rather than take it for prophylaxis, I would advise the trekker going outside of the monsoon season to carry some chloroquine for treatment of suspected attacks of malaria if his travels will involve a considerable stay below 4000 ft (1200 m). There is now chloroquine-resistant *falciparum* malaria in the southwest and southeast corners of Nepal. I do not consider this a threat to trekkers on the popular routes and so do not advise taking mefloquine for prophylaxis, but the situation could change in the future so get the latest advice before you depart. The U.S. State Department and the Centers for Disease Control (CDC), knowing there is some resistant malaria, make a general recommendation that all travelers take mefloquine. This is unnecessary.

Discuss the medical supplies mentioned here with your physician. Drugs and most supplies can be bought cheaply in Kathmandu.

In summary, every trekker should have current immunization status for polio, typhoid fever, tetanus, diphtheria, measles, mumps, rubella, and meningococcal meningitis, and especially hepatitis A. I recommend rabies vaccine but suggest that malaria prophylaxis not be taken, except possibly for lowland treks during the monsoon.

Consider obtaining travel and evacuation insurance in addition to standard medical insurance. This will not prevent you from having to arrange payment for a helicopter rescue should it be necessary, but it can help recover the substantial costs involved. Travel agents and insurance brokers can provide policies. Make sure the policy you obtain covers trekking travel in Nepal.

Finally, don't neglect health-promoting practices that are a part of your usual tradition back home. This can include meditation, yoga, and exercise. Similary, if you are accustomed to using various herbal, naturopathic, homeopathic, ayurvedic, or other preparations for illnesses, bring these with you. What follows is based on the allopathic or biomedical model for disease.

Health Care of Children

For those trekking with children, it is essential that a knowledgeable physician or other health professional be consulted before you leave home in order to get specific information appropriate to your children and their needs. See this person well in advance—several months may be necessary—to ensure that the required immunizations can be obtained in time.

The greatest health risk for children trekking in Nepal is the hazard of fecal–oral contamination. Children at oral stages tend to put everything into their mouths. Human and other animal feces are everywhere and tend to get into the hands and mouths of children. The problem is compounded because children with diarrhea and vomiting can get dehydrated quickly. Because there are essentially no medical care facilities in the hills, each family is on its own. Take solace in knowing that most trekking families have no problems.

Prevention is the key. Watch what your child puts in his or her mouth. Iodize or boil all water for drinking and feed your child only cooked food. Keep materials for making oral rehydration solution on hand in case diarrhea or vomiting develops. If the liquid losses in stool or vomitus are replaced gradually, no serious problems should result. Oral rehydration powder, Jeevan Jal in Nepal, can be purchased in drug shops and stores in (hopefully) most parts of the country. Mix one packet with 4 cups (1 liter) of boiled or iodized water, and feed it to the child a little at a time by spoon or cup. Try to get the child to drink at least as much liquid as he has lost. Check for signs of adequate hydration, such as normal frequency and amount of urination, moisture on the lips and mouth, and fairly normal behavior. If in doubt, get the child to take more fluids. Do not use opiates or other similar drugs to "plug up" diarrhea in children. Do not use tetracycline drugs in children under age eight. If you lack a commercial oral rehydration powder such as Jeevan Jal, a substitute can be made up almost anywhere. Add one three-finger pinch of salt and a three-finger scoop of sugar to one *maanaa* (2½ cups, or 570 ml) of boiled or iodized water. Add some orange or lime juice if available.

Colds and other upper respiratory infections are very common in Nepal, and your children may get their share. A bulb syringe can be handy for clearing a young child's snotty nose. Your child could get scabies while in Nepal so consider this if an itchy rash persists.

Children's doses for drugs are not given here. They vary, of course, with the age and weight of the child. They are listed in my book *The Pocket Doctor.* Be sure to discuss which drugs to take, and confirm their doses with your doctor. Liquid doses are best for young children.

The hazards of high altitudes are no less for children than for adults, and it may be even more difficult to determine whether a particular child's health problem is due to altitude or to some other cause. One family took their twenty-one-month-old child to 16,500 ft (5000 m) without difficulty, after appropriate acclimatization. An infant has been up Kala Pattar (18,450 ft, 5623 m). I have seen Sherpa mothers carry their one- or two-month-old babies over 19,000-ft (5800-m) passes. A woman who was six months pregnant ascended to 24,000 ft (7300 m). Such extremes are not recommended. Families should limit their treks to 13,000 ft (4000 m). With infants, 10,000 ft (3050 m) might be a safe limit. Unless born at high altitude, children tolerate ascent to heights less well than do adults. All people with children who venture to high altitudes should descend immediately if there is any difficulty with acclimatization. It may be difficult to determine whether a newly acquired unnatural behavior in a child represents altitude illness. My 3-month-old son became lethargic above 12,000 ft and improved dramatically with descent. Similarly, incontinence in a toilet-trained child at altitude could be a symptom of altitude illness. Descend in such circumstances to determine if it was the cause. The safety margin in waiting out the minor symptoms of altitude illness is significantly less in children than in adults.

The Medical Kit

A basic medical kit proposed here that can be purchased quite cheaply in Kathmandu will help trekkers be reasonably prepared for most problems and can be considered a kind of insurance. In most developed countries, prescriptions are required for some of the drugs. An understanding physician should give you these if you carefully explain why you need them. Do not use these medications when medical assistance is available nearby. When you are sick and there are appropriate treatments, it makes sense to use them. By following the suggestions in this chapter, the chances are excellent that you will recover, and the benefits of treatment far outweigh the risks. If you are not getting better in spite of self-treatment, then consider other alternatives, especially if the situation seems grave.

Names of drugs are always a dilemma. While the official or generic names are generally the same throughout the world, the advertising or brand names vary greatly from place to place. The generic names are used here whenever possible.

My recommended medical kit—enough for a party of two—includes the following:

Moleskin. Felt or foam (molefoam) padding (about 1 mm thick for felt, 2 or 3 mm for foam) with adhesive backing, used for the prevention of blisters. About half a square foot per person should be enough. It is not available in Kathmandu, but adhesive tape or zinc oxide strapping can be used as a substitute. See the "Foot Care" section for other alternatives.

Bandages. One roll of 2-in. adhesive tape, and five to ten adhesive bandages per person for small wounds.

Elastic Bandage. One 3-in. roll for relief of strains and sprains.

Thermometer. One that reads below normal temperatures (for diagnosis of hypothermia) as well as above (for fever).

Miscellaneous. Scissors, needle, or safety pin, and forceps or tweezers.

Plastic Dropper Bottles. One-ounce (30 ml) size for iodine. This is best brought from home. If your pharmacy no longer carries empty plastic dropper bottles for dispensing compounded ear, eye, or nose drops, buy a plastic dropper bottle of nose drops and dump the contents.

Water Purification Chemicals. Tetraglycine hydroperiodide or iodine in various forms (see next section). Vitamin C powder masks the taste.

Nose Spray or Drops (optional). Phenylephrine HCL (0.25%) for stuffed noses and sinuses. Put two drops in each nostril two or three times a day when symptomatic and when changing altitude. An alternative is oxymetazoline, used no more than twice a day.

Nasal Decongestant (optional). For those accustomed to taking these tablets for colds.

Antihistamine (optional). For treating symptoms of colds and hay fever. If you do not have a favorite, try chlorpheniramine maleate tablets (4 mg). Terfenadine and astemizole are expensive, nonsedating antihistamines you could try.

Aspirin or Similar Drug. Twenty-five tablets (5 grain, 325 mg) of aspirin for relief of minor pain, for lowering temperatures, and for symptomatic relief of colds and respiratory infections. Ibuprofen (200 mg) or acetaminophen (paracetamol) are appropriate substitutes for those who can't tolerate aspirin.

Codeine. Fifteen tablets (30 mg) for relief of pain, cough, and diarrhea. A good multipurpose drug. It is customarily compounded with acetaminophen tablets in the United States.

Anti-motility Agent. Codeine, as already mentioned, or loperamide (2 mg), or diphenoxylate compound tablets. Take twenty.

Antibiotic. The current trekkers' wonder drug is probably ciprofloxacin, in 500-mg tablets. Expensive, but adequate for most of the infectious bacterial causes of illnesses that might befall the trekker. Take twenty capsules at least; the dose is one capsule twice a day. An alternative is norfloxacin, 400-mg tablets, taken three times a day. A related cheaper drug, nalidixic acid, has been used successfully in Nepal and is the drug of choice for children for diarrhea. Other choices would best require that two different ones should be carried, a cephalosporin (cefaclor, cefuroxime, and cefadroxil are choices in the United States) and co-trimoxazole. Carry a 10-day supply of a 250-mg cephalosporin. The dose for the cephalosporin is either one or two every 8 hours (cefaclor) or 12 hours (cefuroxime or cefadroxil). If allergic to penicillin, you might also be allergic to a cephalosporin, but this is relatively rare. Erythromycin (250-mg capsule) would be the best choice for allergic individuals. Take forty. Bring co-trimoxazole (trimethoprim 160 mg and sulfamethoxazole 800 mg) in so-called double-strength tablets (abbreviated TMP/SMX later in this chapter) if not allergic to sulfa drugs. Bring twenty of these tablets. Be aware that there may be resistance to this drug in Nepal. For other choices, especially in diarrhea, read the section later in this chapter.

Antiprotozoan. Tinidazole is the best drug to self-treat presumed *Giardia* or *Amoeba* infections while trekking. It is not available in the United States but can be purchased in Nepal. Take twelve to twenty 500-mg tablets.

Antihelminth (worm medicine). Six 100-mg tablets of mebendazole. One tablet taken morning and evening for 3 days will take care of most worm infestations in porters. You won't be there long enough to require treatment in Nepal.

Oral Rehydration Solution (ORS, Jeevan Jal). A mixture of salts and glucose, this powder is added to a liter of water to provide the appropriate drink to rehydrate in almost any situation, but especially from diarrhea. Not easily available in the United States—buy it in Nepal.

Altitude Medicines. Acetazolamide (Diamox™), 250-mg tablets, take twenty, and also dexamethasone, 4-mg tablets, take five. The first is to treat symptoms of mild altitude illness, and the second is to take if someone has the serious, cerebral symptoms. The first drug is appropriate to use for prevention in suitable situations. Read the section on altitude illness, later, and consider carrying nifedipine in 10-mg capsules.

Gamow Bag™. A hyperbaric chamber for treatment of serious altitude illness. Enquire to Chinook Medical Gear, P.O. Box 1736, Edwards, CO 81632, phone 1-800-766-1365 or (970) 926-9277, fax (970) 926-9660. Recommended for parties in a group trek to significant altitudes (see trekking with an agency in the introduction).

Anti-inflammatory Agent. To be considered if you are prone to arthritic conditions or tendonitis. Aspirin or ibuprofen are good choices; acetaminophen is not as effective. If you've had such problems before, ask your doctor about indomethacin or meclofenamate. The latter is a good all-purpose pain medicine.

Sunscreen Preparation. One with a sun protection factor (or SPF) of at least 15 in order to get adequate protection from the sun on snow slopes at high altitudes. Sunscreens are best applied 1 or 2 hours before exposure and reapplied after heavy sweating. Be sure to apply them over all areas that can receive direct or reflected sunlight, especially under the nose, chin, and eyebrows. Lip balms containing effective sunscreens should also be used.

Topical Ophthalmic Antibiotic. Good choices of ophthalmic antibiotics are those that contain bacitracin, gentamicin, polymyxin, or tobramycin. Avoid any that contain steroids such as betamethasone, cortisone, dexamethasone, hydrocortisone, prednisolone, or others. If you wear contact lenses trekking, be sure to bring antibiotic eye drops.

Malaria Suppressant (optional). Chloroquine, for instance, if you and your doctor think it is necessary.

These items are considered a bare minimum by some, and too much by others; they are clearly adequate for most situations. Other items are mentioned in the next section and can be added if desired. I pack my kit in a zippered nylon bag. First I put the pills into small labeled plastic bags, such as the tiny bags that your airline cutlery is packed in cut short, and then assemble all these together inside a small plastic bottle. The whole kit never weighs more than a pound (½ kg). I would never go into the hills without an antidiarrheal, aspirin, iodine, a sunscreen, moleskin, and an antibiotic.

Pregnant women should consult a physician regarding medical problems they might encounter and the use of these or other drugs.

Nepalis have their own remedies for many illnesses. If you don't seem to be getting better, in spite of my recommendations, you might consider their suggestions. While working as a doctor in Nepal, I have sometimes been frustrated by my inability to help some unfortunate sick person only to discover later that the individual was cured by a folk remedy or by a shaman!

Health and Medical Problems

The vast majority of diseases that plague the trekker in Nepal are transmitted by food or water contaminated by infected human or animal feces. You should assume that all water and uncooked foods in Nepal are contaminated. This holds true in Kathmandu as well as along the trails.

WATER

Boiling. The safest procedure is to bring drinking water to the boil and let it cool before drinking. Boiling water on a trek, especially if wood is used, wastes scarce resources. Better to use a chemical disinfectant.

Filtering. Filters containing iodine exchange resins are effective for purposes claimed and produce potable water rapidly, but they are bulky, heavy, and expensive. Many trekkers like them. Other filters only remove parasites and bacteria but not viruses. If stuck without other options, filter water through several layers of cotton cloth.

Bottled Water. Bottled mineral water is available on the popular treks. It comes in sealed plastic bottles and is reputed to be safe although studies have found contaminated samples. Expensive, its use results in the profusion of empty plastic bottles scattered about. Empty used bottles are being refilled with any water and recapped to be sold in much of Asia. I advise that you use iodine instead.

Chemical Disinfection. Elemental iodine is the best agent, added by one of several means. The dose stated here is for clear water; double it for cloudy water. Once the chemical is added, the waiting time depends on the temperature of the water. Ten minutes is adequate for warm water; 20 to 30 minutes should suffice for cold water. For very questionable very cold water, double the dose and wait 30 minutes or more.

Iodine tablets (tetraglycine hydroperiodide, or Potable Aqua, Wisconsin Pharmacal). These tablets are most useful for water bottles. Use one tablet per quart (liter) of water.

Tincture of iodine (USP). This has several uses. Add five drops per quart (liter) or, conveniently, two drops per glass (250 ml). I carry this in an opaque plastic dropper bottle and use this technique exclusively. I tell them it is medicine for the water if people ask, and explain why. If water doesn't taste like iodine, it isn't water (unless I know it has been boiled). In the United States, or elsewhere, look for the USP designation (United States Pharmacopeia), which indicates that the product is compounded to the correct standard, with 2% free iodine. I find this material useful for removing leeches and with it I can disinfect the skin around a wound (do not put it directly into a wound). The iodine taste can be removed by adding ascorbic acid (vitamin C); 50 mg of powder (a minimal two-finger pinch) in a liter of water after contact time has elapsed.

Strong Iodine Solution (BP [British Pharmacopeia]) can be used in one-fifth the dose, that is, one drop per quart of clear water. It contains 10% free iodine. The Indian Pharmacopeia (IP) formulation is the same.

Weak Iodine Solution (BP) is used in the same dose as Tincture of Iodine (USP). The Indian Pharmacopeia (IP) formulation that is available in Kathmandu is used in the same dose as the BP.

Lugol's Solution if labeled Aqueous Iodine Solution BP (or IP) can be used, adding two drops to a quart (liter) of water.

Iodine solution. This solution is made by adding the supernatant of crystalline iodine carried in a glass bottle. This method is potentially lethal if crystals are ingested, and there are now commercial preparations (Polar Pure) available to make this unlikely.

Povidone iodine solution. This is used for surgical disinfection and usually comes as a 10% solution (do not get the scrub, which has a detergent added). It should probably be effective in a dose of eight to sixteen drops per quart (liter) of water, the higher amounts used in cold or cloudy water. The major advantage of this form of iodine is that it is less irritating than tincture of iodine when used around and in wounds.

Rare individuals may be allergic to iodine. These people would usually have a long-standing skin rash when taking iodine. They should not use this chemical for water purification. Pregnant women should have no problem with these chemical methods of water treatment though there is a theoretical hazard. Persons with thyroid disease might have problems with the iodine. Discuss this with your doctor. Experiment at home before you leave.

Powdered drink mixes to flavor the water can be added after the proper time has elapsed to render the water potable. The vitamin C method mentioned above works too.

I assume that water touted to have been boiled has not unless I have supervised it. All water should be purified, including that used for brushing your teeth and that used for making ice. If water is cloudy or murky, let it stand to clarify. Water used for cleaning open wounds is best boiled first and left to cool. However, if cleansing a wound concerns me, I will use any water available. With very cold water and iodine treatment, allow the water to stand twice as long, even up to an hour, before consumption. Bottled soft drinks and beer of well-known brands are considered safe.

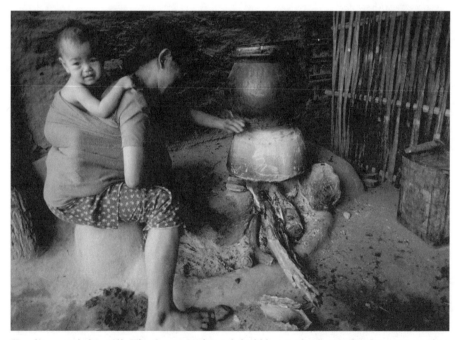

Tending a rakshi *still. The fermented mash bubbles on the fire, releasing vapors that pass through the column, condense on a copper cone cooled by water from above, and then drip into a cup.*

FOOD

Thoroughly cooked foods can be considered safe, but only if they are eaten soon after cooking. Fruits and vegetables that are eaten uncooked must first be washed and peeled under sanitary conditions. Leafy vegetables must be cooked, though it may be effective to wash them in a strong iodine solution and rinse with potable water. I don't trust anyone to do this carefully. Best to peel it, cook it, or forget it.

Food prepared by Nepalis can be assumed to be safe if it has just been cooked and not allowed to be contaminated by flies. Be wary of foods prepared in the morning in hotels and heated up later in the day. Contamination is also possible from the plates the food is served on, but this is very difficult to control.

Milk should always be heated just to the boiling point and allowed to cool before drinking, unless it is known to be already pasteurized. Curds are made from boiled milk and can be assumed to be safe unless recontaminated. Scraping off the top layer of curd should be sufficient. If milk has been diluted with water, it is necessary to bring the mixture to a boil. Buttermilk and cottage cheese, especially when prepared by herdsmen in their alpine huts, can be considered fairly safe.

It is difficult to follow rigorous advice concerning homemade alcoholic drinks. To be safe avoid them all. *Rakshi,* distilled from a fermented mash, is perhaps the safest because it has been boiled. The common fermented drink is called *chang* by the Sherpas and Tibetans and *jAAR* by other Nepalis. Unless the water from which it is made is known to be pure, it is possible to get sick from it (a hangover notwithstanding). Finally, in the east, there is *tOmba,* a fermented millet mash that is served in a bamboo canister with a straw. Hot, hopefully boiled, water is poured over it and the leach sucked up with the straw. Partly safe, except for the mash, container, and straw.

Recognize that if you follow these rules and those for water religiously, you may still get diarrhea. Most likely it results from contamination of the plates the food is served on.

DIARRHEA AND DYSENTERY

It's a brave man that farts in Asia.

Diarrhea and colds (upper respiratory infections) are the most common problems among trekkers. In fact, it is safe to say that almost every trekker will have a bout of diarrhea during his or her stay in Nepal. Diarrhea, frequent passage of loose stools, is not worth distinguishing from dysentery. You will know it when you have it. Back in the 1970s I wrote about self-treatment of diarrhea with antibiotics and now Dr. David Shlim has further perfected the regimen.

Note the number and nature of the stools and whether the diarrhea came on suddenly or gradually. Begin taking clear fluids such as water, weak tea with sugar, juice, clear soup, or soda pop that has been left to stand until the carbonation is gone. Avoid dairy products. Drinking a lot of fluids is necessary to avoid dehydration, but few trekkers get severely dehydrated in Nepal. Perhaps the best liquid to take is an oral rehydration solution. Jeevan Jal, a powder manufactured in Nepal, contains the needed salts. Mix one bag with a quart (liter) of water and drink it in small sips. For watery or loose diarrhea of *sudden* onset (you can recall when you first had the urge), take a tablet of ciprofloxacin, nalidixic acid, or norfloxacin and continue at the proper dosage regimen until the movements stop. Take this soon after the diarrhea begins. TMP/SMX used to be used, but there is increased resistance to this drug in Nepal. If the diarrhea is particularly bothersome, take an antidiarrheal, loperamide, codeine, or diphenoxylate. The one time I would be sure to use antimotility agents in diarrhea is before a long bus or plane ride. Norfloxacin and ciprofloxacin should be avoided by children and pregnant women. Nalidixic acid can be used in children. Return to solid foods gradually.

If your diarrhea comes on *gradually* over a few days, and perhaps you feel lethargic, then the protozoan parasite *Giardia lamblia* may well be the cause, especially if you have been in Nepal a month or more. It generally takes a longer time to acquire this infection than the bacterial ones, usually two weeks and sometimes longer, after ingesting the cysts. Stools will often contain mucus and smell like rotten eggs or sulfur, as will expelled gas (although this finding is not infallible). Trekkers presenting at clinics with diarrhea for two weeks or longer are more likely to have *Giardia* or *Amoeba* as the cause. If your symptoms persist for several days, it makes sense to treat yourself presumptively for giardiasis. Take 2 g of tinidazole (which is not available in North America but can be purchased in medical halls in Kathmandu) as a single dose and repeat in 24 hours. Some trekkers have developed *Giardia* neuroses, thinking that each loose stool has been caused by this comical-looking flagellate. There are other causes of loose stools and foul-smelling burps. For these people, taking tinidazole every few days could be risky.

If you are really sick, then rest, and if getting worse, seek attention. The diarrhea affecting tourists in Nepal is not the scourge that kills millions a year worldwide; only one tourist is known to have died from diarrhea in Nepal. Stool exams are not particularly helpful, as the labs in Kathmandu overdiagnose *Amoeba* and *Giardia*. If you had diarrhea before, treated yourself and were better for a few days, and now are sick again, it is likely you have been reinfected and should treat yourself again.

My personal regimen for treating my diarrhea is to (1) rehydrate if necessary, (2) decide if it might be *Giardia*, (3) if not, take a single dose of an antibiotic, currently ciprofloxacin, and (4) resume solid foods in a few hours. I do not recommend taking antibiotics to prevent getting diarrhea because the bacterial form is so easily treated, and antibiotics don't prevent the other types.

VOMITING

Nausea and vomiting, if unaccompanied by diarrhea at altitude, suggest moderate altitude illness. If there is no ataxia (see below), treat altitude illness as below. Don't ascend. Otherwise it is probably associated with a viral or food-borne infection and can be treated with liquids in small amounts as well as rest.

ALTITUDE ILLNESS

If you are not feeling well at altitude, it's altitude illness until proven otherwise.

Problems with altitude can strike anyone, even at relatively low altitudes such as 8000 ft (2450 m), where it has been fatal. But in general, trekkers going to higher altitudes quickly are more severely affected. People who fly to a high altitude and then proceed to an even higher area or cross a pass should be especially wary. Examples include flying to Lukla and Shyangboche and going to the Everest Base Camp, or flying to Jomosom or Ongre and crossing Thorung La. Some symptoms will be felt by most of those going to high altitudes. Those hiking up will have fewer problems than those flying up. Serious illness occurs in less than 2% of people who go to high altitudes. The fatality rate for trekkers in Nepal has fallen significantly from the early days of trekking as people have become more aware and acclimatized. Every altitude illness death in trekkers is preventable.

Altitude illness can be prevented by acclimatization; that is, by a gradual rate of ascent, allowing sufficient rest at various intermediate altitudes. The proper amount of rest and rate of ascent vary greatly from individual to individual and even over time in the same individual. For example, one person who previously had climbed Mount Everest later had difficulties at modest altitudes from ascending too rapidly. One protocol would be to spend the first night below 10,000 ft (3000 m), and not raise the sleeping altitude more than 1000 ft (300 m) a day and build in 1 day of acclimatization (rest) for every 3000 ft (900 m) gained between sleeping sites above 10,000 ft (3000 m). This is feasible only if everyone is on the lookout for the signs and symptoms of maladaptation to high altitudes. If the party acts appropriately should anyone develop altitude illness, serious problems can usually be avoided.

For example, in ascending to the Everest Base Camp, Kala Pattar, or anywhere above 15,000 ft (4500 m), allow at least 2 rest and acclimatization days. Three are preferable. One stop could be at 11,000 ft (3350 m) and the other at 14,000 ft (4250 m). On these days, people who feel good could take an excursion to a higher point, but return to sleep at the same altitude as the night before. In Khumbu, a rest day at Namche Bazaar and Khumjung or Pangboche, followed by another at Pheriche, would be the minimum requirement. Then spend a night at Lobuje, and ascend to Kala Pattar the next day, returning to Lobuje for the night. This may be too fast for many people, however.

If you are on a group trek going to high altitudes, ask how many rest days are built into the schedule and ask how flexible it is. Find out whether the leader has had significant problems with members getting serious altitude illness on previous treks. Individuals on group treks are at greater risk of bad outcomes from altitude illness compared to individual trekkers.

Trekking leaders should be aware that group members often withhold symptoms of altitude illness when asked. The leader must be a detective and look for clues. The most significant blunder likely to be made by a leader is to deny that a member's illness or symptoms represent altitude illness. Take this seriously; clients are in a more litigious mood these days (as if that should be the reason to be careful)!

There are other factors besides a slow rate of ascent that help in acclimatization. A large fluid intake to ensure good hydration is key. Four quarts (liters) or more a day of liquid are usually necessary. Urine volume should always exceed one pint (one-half liter) daily, preferably one quart (one liter). The urine color should be almost clear. A strong yellow color indicates that more fluids should be drunk. Some trekkers and Himalayan climbers find that measuring urine output daily with a small plastic bottle helps ensure adequate hydration. A simple way to measure urine output is to wait until you are absolutely bursting before urinating. The volume is then close to half a liter. Empty a full bladder at least twice a day. One sign of adaptation to altitude is a good natural diuresis (passage of lots of urine). If this is not found, be extra cautious. An easy way to judge the presence of dehydration is to compare heart rates standing and lying down, with a 30-second interval in between. If the rate is 20% greater in the standing position, the individual may be significantly dehydrated and should consume more fluids. This can be water, tea, soup, or broth. Alcoholic drinks should be avoided by dehydrated individuals and at high altitudes by everyone until well acclimatized. Besides being detrimental to acclimatization, the effects of alcohol at high altitude may be impossible to distinguish from symptoms of altitude illness.

Caloric intake should be maintained with a diet high in carbohydrates. The tasty potatoes found at high altitudes in Nepal are an excellent source of carbohydrates. A good appetite is a sign of acclimatization. Avoid excessive salt intake at high altitudes. Don't take salt tablets.

Rest is also important. Overexertion does not help acclimatization. Give up part of your load to Sherpas and other high-altitude dwellers who are already well acclimatized and can carry loads with ease. Avoid going so fast that you are always stopping short of breath with your heart pounding. Use the rest step and techniques for pacing yourself by checking your heart rate as described in the introduction to section II. Plan modest objectives for each day so that you will enjoy your altitude amble.

Many people who frequent the mountains and often make rapid changes in altitude find that forced deep breathing helps reduce the mild symptoms of altitude illness. However, if done to excess, it can produce the hyperventilation syndrome, in which shortness of breath, dizziness, and numbness are present. Breathing in and out of a large paper or plastic bag for a few minutes (sometimes 30 minutes) will relieve these symptoms.

Taking acetazolamide (Diamox™) has been shown to be beneficial in helping the acclimatization process especially if flying to altitudes. The dose is 125 mg by mouth two or three times a day, begun 2 days before the flight and continued for 3 days after ascent. Acetazolamide can also help when begun upon arrival at high altitude by plane and by those walking beginning it at, say, 9000 ft. Trekkers flying into a high-altitude area such as Lukla, Shyangboche, Jomosom, or Manang should consider taking it. Even one dose taken at supper may be beneficial. Common side effects are an increased urine output, some numbness and tingling in the extremities, and an unusual, perhaps unpalatable taste when drinking carbonated beverages, including beer. These are not reasons to stop taking the drug; they do not represent allergic reactions. Dexamethasone, a powerful cortisone-like drug, also prevents the symptoms of acute mountain sickness upon exposure to altitude. It has no effect on the acclimatization process, and I do *not* recommend trekkers taking it for prevention. However, it may have a place in treating severe symptoms of altitude illness. Other drugs for prevention of altitude illness that have been tried include furosemide, also called frusemide (Lasix™), and antacids. They are not helpful.

Personally, I do not use medicines to help me adapt to the altitude. On the other hand, I usually have few problems. If I had repeated, predictable difficulties in Nepal at altitude, I would try acetazolamide. If you have had HAPE before, discuss with your doctor using nifedipine as a preventive before ascent.

Most people trekking to high altitudes experience one or more *mild symptoms of altitude illness.* The symptoms include:

- headache
- nausea
- loss of appetite
- mild shortness of breath with minimal exertion
- sleep disturbance (difficulty sleeping)
- dizziness or light-headedness
- mild weakness
- slight swelling of hands and face

As long as the symptoms remain mild and are only a nuisance, rest at that altitude until better. As the HRA lecture states, "Do not take a headache higher!" Never ascent to sleep if you have mild symptoms. Symptomatic treatment with medicines may be helpful. If there is no improvement after a few hours, or after a night's rest, or there is worsening, descend on foot to below the altitude where symptoms first occurred. Then ascent at a more gradual rate can be considered after getting better.

Serious symptoms of altitude illness are a grave matter. They include:
- inability to recover from shortness of breath with rest
- delirium, confusion, and coma*
- loss of coordination, staggering*
- severe, persistent headache*
- rapid heart rate after resting—110 or more beats per minute
- wet, bubbly breathing
- severe coughing spasms that limit activity
- coughing up pinkish or rust-colored sputum
- blueness of face and lips
- low urine output—less than a pint (500 ml) daily
- persistent vomiting*
- gross fatigue or extreme lassitude*

If anyone in your party develops any of these symptoms, he or she should descend *immediately* on the back of a porter or animal to avoid undue exertion. Descend to below the altitude at which any symptoms of altitude illness first occurred. This treatment should not be delayed until morning when you may have a corpse to transport. The victim should be kept warm and given oxygen if available. Give acetazolamide, 250 mg every 8 hours. If dexamethasone is available, and the cerebral symptoms are present as noted above with an asterisk, give 4 mg every 6 hours. After a descent of only a few thousand feet, relief may be dramatic. At the point where relief occurs, or lower, rest a few days. Then consider ascending cautiously again only if none of the cerebral symptoms (*) were present and you have not taken dexamethasone.

Judgment is affected by altitude. Hence, possible altitude illness may be denied by the victim and his companions. To guide you, the clearest symptoms of significant altitude illness to watch for in *yourself* are:

- breathlessness at rest
- resting pulse over 110 per minute
- loss of appetite
- unusual fatigue while walking

The clearest ones to watch for in *others* are:
- skipping meals
- antisocial behavior
- the last person to arrive at the destination (i.e., people having difficulties with the walking)

It cannot be stressed too strongly that you *must* descend at the onset of serious symptoms. If in Khumbu, go to the hospital at Kunde, or to the Himalayan Rescue Association's clinic in Pheriche, if that is on your descent route. A hyperbaric pressure chamber (Gamow Bag™) to simulate the effects of descent is available there, as well as other resources. But don't stop descending in Pheriche unless the victim is considerably better. Trekkers have died in Pheriche from not heeding this guideline. Don't wait up high for a helicopter rescue. Many trekkers, including Olympic athletes, doctors, and experienced climbers, have died in Nepal from altitude illness because they failed to heed symptoms. A disproportionate number of physicians, who should know better, have died from altitude illness in Nepal. Finally, it appears that those trekking individually almost never die from altitude illness. It is peer pressure in groups that contributes to deaths among trekkers. Those alone descend early, while in groups there seems to be a tendency to not hold the party back.

The Gamow Bag™, a portable hyperbaric chamber, has had an impact in treating serious, potentially fatal, altitude illness. The victim is placed inside, and then the pressure inside is increased via an air pump to simulate descent of 3000 to 5000 ft. It can be useful for diagnosis, too. If you wonder if someone's symptoms might be due to altitude, put them into the bag and "descend" them 3000 ft or more and see if the symptoms improve. Treatment in the bag for an hour may produce temporary improvement in someone suffering from mild symptoms. For serious symptoms a minimum of 2 to 4 hours is required. The symptoms may recur once the victim leaves the bag, necessitating retreatment. Refer to the protocols provided with the bag. The bag requires continuous pumping to maintain air pressure, a tiring prospect. Use of the bag does not substitute for descent, so after initial treatment get the person down. Individuals successfully treated in the bag and then separated from it (another party took it on up), who didn't descend, have had symptoms recur and died.

The device is lightweight (less than 15 lb [7 kg] including pump) and expensive, but cheaper than the cost of a coffin. A large trekking group that will spend considerable time up high, where the way down is long and difficult, should carry one. It should be standard equipment for any group trek to altitude, but many group treks do not carry one to economize. If you are going on an expensive group trek, ask if they carry the bag, and if not, why not. Your money should be going to buy life-saving items such as this. The Gamow Bag™ should be standard insurance for all parties to altitude. There are two other products on the market now, the PAC (Portable Altitude Chamber) made by C.E. Bartlett in Ballarat, Australia, fax (03) 5338 1241, and the Certec, from Sourcieux le Mines, France, fax 33-74-70-3766. The original Gamow chamber is available from Chinook; the address is in the medical kit section.

The essential material on altitude illness has already been covered, and what follows is for trekkers who are suffering from altitude illness.

Altitude illnesses observed in Nepal include acute mountain sickness (AMS), high-altitude pulmonary edema (HAPE), peripheral edema (PE), high-altitude cerebral edema (HACE), and high-altitude retinal hemorrhage (HARH).

AMS commonly comes on after being at high altitudes for 1 to 2 days. A variety of symptoms are experienced, most often a persistent headache, usually present on awakening. The other mild symptoms listed above also occur. It is like an altitude hangover. Irregular or periodic breathing during sleep is common in most people at altitude. The rate and depth of respirations increase to a peak, then diminish, stopping altogether for a fraction of a minute, then increasing again. If none of the serious symptoms are present, there is no cause for concern. Physical fitness *per se* is of no benefit. This is true for most altitude illness. The treatment is to deal with each symptom with whatever means you have and to not ascend until better. Acetazolamide is useful in treating the symptoms of AMS. Try a 125-mg tablet at supper time and perhaps upon arising to see whether it helps the headache and malaise and sleeplessness. Do not take sleeping pills at high altitude; they may worsen symptoms and be dangerous. Don't leave such a person alone, for the mild condition may progress and the victim can become helpless.

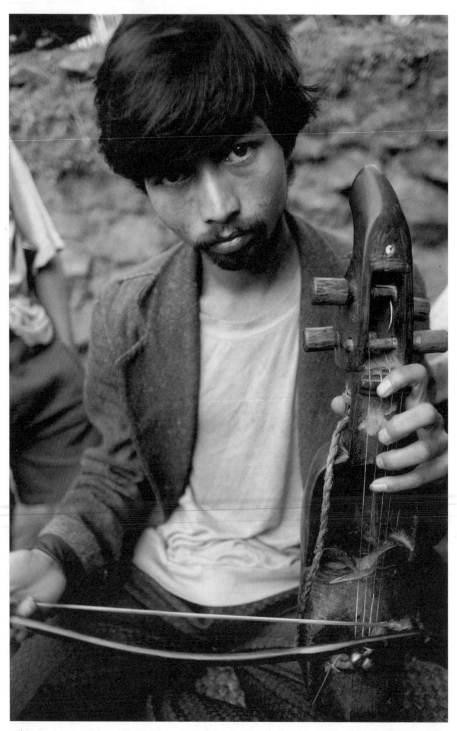

This gaaine *or minstrel wanders from town to town singing and playing the* saarangi.

Musics of Nepal

The hills of Nepal are alive with the sound of musics. Each of the many cultural groups have their own musical traditions, instruments, and means of aural expression. Like so many aspects of folkways, there are Tibetan influences in the north, and Indian in the south, with the hills the repository of indigenous musics. In the high regions of Himalayan culture, a chorus line of shuffling and singing at festivals is common, while men may strum a lute (*damyin* or *toongna*) while singing in falsetto. In the hills, at celebrations pairs of men and women alternate in rowdy repartees. During *tihaar* (*diwali*), the festival of lights or devotion to the goddess Laxmi, groups wander from village to village in the hills and sing. The barrel-drum, or *maadal,* is a common rhythmic accompaniment.

Music is a major part of religious expression. Tibetan Buddhist ceremonies with chanting, drumming, and cymbal playing use sound as a medium for meditation. What may seem to the outsider as cacophony is highly developed, articulate expression. Shamanic rituals use drumming as a means of invoking the spirits. *Newar* musics are incredibly varied and highly developed in the Kathmandu valley. Trekkers are attracted to devotional songs by ensembles at temples, while at festivals it is never silent. Many varieties of drums and nasal intonement, as well as horns, percussion, and shawms extend musical dimensions. The tailor caste, *damaai,* provides festive music (*pAchai baajaa*) at weddings and other Hindu rites. There is different regional emphasis on the performances, unending drumming being found in the far west, while large curved horns (*narsinga*) and shawms (sahanai) are prominent in central and eastern parts of the country. Circular breathing is used to play the shawm continuously.

There is considerable gender division in musical expression. Women sing while they work: transplanting rice, planting potatoes, or carrying along the trails. They sing at the female wedding party in Hindu celebrations at the groom's house, while the men are at the bride's. They sing on the fasting second day of the women's festival of *tij* in August–September to commemorate when Parvati, the daughter of the Himalaya, won the hand of Lord Shiva. They travel around in groups singing and dancing, replaying Parvati's dance before Shiva. Solo songs on themes of love, the pain of life, and contemporary issues are common among men and women in the hills and mountains. A minstrel caste, the *gaaine,* is found around Pokhara and to the north and occasionally in the Arun drainage. Individuals or groups who live near a Hindu village wander from place to place, gaining their livelihood by singing lyric, narrative, or religious songs for a donation, accompanied on a four-stringed bowed fiddle (*saarangi*). Many of their songs are full of outspoken political and social criticism, akin to that of blues and folk singers in the United States. Many simple homemade instruments, including bamboo flutes and Jew's harps, are found.

Many of these musics are being lost daily, reflecting cultural change as new genres, especially from Hindi cinema, replace them. Alas, much of current change reminds me of the ideas expounded by Warren Hern, who asked whether the human species was a cancer on the planet. Look at a definition for cancer and you will find four features: unrestrained growth, invasion of local tissues, distant spread, and dedifferentiation. Nepal provides a perfect example of this. Dedifferentiation is the process of "cells" becoming more primitive, or that human culture is becoming more American! But cultural death is a long way off in Nepal. You will discover this by listening to the sounds you hear while on the trail and in people's homes.

Tests for coordination (such as tandem walking) should be given. See if, after resting, the person can walk a straight line by putting the heel of the advancing foot directly in front of the toe of the back foot. Slight difficulty is tolerable if 12 ft (4 m) can be covered in a straight line. If in doubt, compare the individual with someone who is having no difficulty. Often the rugged terrain will make it harder for both to accomplish the maneuver. In exhaustion, hypothermia, or intoxication, mild degrees of loss of coordination (ataxia) can be seen, but there should be no staggering or falling. Ataxia is a sign of serious illness, probably HACE, and the person should descend while he is still able to do so under his own power, but always with someone else who is well. Even if this condition is diagnosed at night, descent should begin immediately. Give dexamethasone. If a Gamow Bag™ is available, place the person in it and descend him when better.

HAPE, the presence of fluid in the lungs, is a grave illness and is likely present if the respiratory problems on the above serious symptoms list are noted. The heart and breathing rates are useful clues. Do not delay in descending these individuals as death can be only a few hours away. Get them down while they can still walk on their own. There are usually some signs of AMS. Trained people using stethoscopes may hear sounds called rales in the lungs of trekkers with no symptoms. This is common and no cause for alarm. The presence of the above symptoms are grounds for descent. If the Gamow Bag™ or oxygen are available, use them.

Individuals with chest disease are more susceptible to HAPE, as are people who have previously suffered from it. Those with upper respiratory infections or common colds may be at an increased risk. Oxygen is beneficial and morphine may be, but other drugs used to treat pulmonary edema at sea level are probably not effective. Give acetazolamide. Medical personnel who are carrying nifedipine could administer a 10-mg capsule to the stricken individual, asking him to chew it. Trekkers ascending to significant altitudes can consider carrying it. Blood pressure may drop sufficiently making it difficult for the victim to climb down, and thus he becomes an evacuation problem. If this pulmonary artery vasodilator helps, it can be taken perhaps hourly for relief or the long acting preparation can be used in a dose of 30 mg three times a day. Descent for the seriously ill is best done without exertion, say on the back of a porter or a yak. Those with HAPE that has completely resolved with descent can consider re-ascending slowly.

PE—swelling around the eyes, face, hands, feet, or ankles—is present in some degree in many visitors to high altitudes. Women seem to be affected more than men. The hands are most often affected. Carrying a heavy pack with tight shoulder straps that affect venous return can be a cause. Remove or loosen rings on the fingers and constricting clothing or pack straps. Swelling of the feet and ankles should be treated by rest and elevation of the legs. Facial swelling, especially if severe enough to shut the eyes, requires descent. In general, check for other symptoms, and if any of the serious ones are present, descend. Otherwise, if the swelling is not especially uncomfortable or disabling and no other symptoms are present, continue cautious ascent. Such swelling can be an early indication of failure of the body to adapt to high altitudes. A diuretic to increase urination can be administered if swelling is an isolated problem; watch for serious symptoms. Others have used elastic compression bandages to the legs with good results.

HACE, or swelling of the brain, is a serious disorder that has killed many in Nepal. It usually occurs after a week or more at high altitudes and begins with mild symptoms that progress to the serious ones. Typically the heart and lung symptoms are not prominent. Characteristic features are a severe headache (usually but not always present), lack of coordination (tandem walking test already described is abnormal—this is the most reliable sign) progressing to severe lassitude, and total apathy, leading to coma and death. Do not leave such a person alone assuming that he is tired. A good night's sleep is not the answer. You may find a corpse in the morning. Descend. If you have a Gamow Bag™, use it. Give acetazolamide and dexamethasone, 4 mg every 6 hours for the latter as well as oxygen. Do not consider reascending after the symptoms of HACE have resolved.

HARH, or bleeding in the retina of the eye, is more common at extreme altitudes. But it does happen to trekkers occasionally and usually is symptomless unless the vision clouds somewhat or the bleeding is near the macula (center of visual acuity) in the eye. Double vision or noticeable blind spots are sufficient cause for descent. Vision clears and bleeding resolves at lower altitudes.

For more details, see my book, *Altitude Illness: Prevention and Treatment.* This information may seem frightening to the trekker bound for the heights, but it has to be put in perspective. If you have previous high-altitude experience, you have some idea of what to expect. If you have not been to high altitudes, don't be scared away from enjoying the mountains of Nepal. Ascend at a rate appropriate for the entire party—that is, at the rate appropriate for the individual having the greatest difficulty. Know the symptoms of altitude illness and what to do about them. If descent becomes necessary for some members of the party, make sure they are not sent down alone but are cared for by responsible, informed people. Don't always assume that your employees understand altitude illness. Give yourself permission to not be the high-altitude wanderer, summiter, and pass crosser, should you be one of the many who cannot tolerate high altitudes well. This does not reflect a lack of character or endurance.

FOOT CARE

Well-fitting boots or shoes and proper socks are a must (see chapter 2) to prevent foot problems. Tape, moleskin, or molefoam (foam with adhesive backing) tends to spread friction over a larger area and reduce local shear stress between layers of the skin. When you feel a tender or hot spot on the skin while walking, stop and investigate. Put a generous piece of moleskin, foam, or adhesive tape over the area. The best method is to place moleskin and cover that material with a piece of smooth (slippery) adhesive tape. Then the sock slides over this spot and less friction is generated. Don't remove it for several days; otherwise, you may pull some skin off with it. Begin your trek with padding applied to potential trouble areas. Other products used by trekkers to prevent blisters include Spenco Second Skin and plain open-cell foam that is used for packing and cushioning. The latter is cut in pieces about one-half inch to an inch thick and applied next to the skin, held in place over the friction point by the lightweight sock. This is especially useful for toes and irregular areas of the foot where blisters might form. If you are developing blisters, and have other footwear, change to it and see if this eliminates hot spots.

Keep the feet dry as moist feet are more prone to blisters. Change socks frequently in hot weather and do not wash or soak your feet too often. By keeping feet dry, you develop callouses over pressure points, and this protects your feet against blisters. Don't soak your feet in streams or hot springs if blister prone.

Once a blister has formed, there are two schools of thought on what to do. Some advocate leaving an intact blister alone, in fact protecting it by cutting a hole the same diameter as the blister in a piece of moleskin or foam and applying that around the blister. I prefer to drain the blister with a needle. Sterilize the needle in a flame until it turns red hot and allow it to cool. The needle should be inserted at the edge of the blister right next to the good skin. Then apply a sterile dressing or some moleskin or foam over it. Finally, if you have any of the biologic dressings that doctors use for wounds, they would be ideal for putting on broken blisters.

STRAINS, SPRAINS, AND SAHIB'S KNEE

As muscles flex, they shorten and move joints by means of tendons that attach to bones. Ligaments are fibrous tissue straps that cross joints and hold them together. Sprains are tears or stretching of ligaments; strains are tears in muscles. The tendons may get stretched, torn, or inflamed, too. For most trekkers, the prolonged, continual walking necessary to reach a distant point causes more wear on their musculoskeletal systems than they are used to. If you gradually increase the amount of activity, your body will toughen up and adjust. People who push themselves to walk long distances every day, especially with heavy packs, will find their poorly prepared body protesting. Strains, especially in the thigh and calf muscles, make climbing and descending painful. Knees will rebel, especially on the downhill portions, if the cartilage (the shock-absorbing pads in the joint) gets too much pounding. Those with weak cartilage lining the kneecap (chondromalacia patellae), women being more commonly afflicted, will especially have pain climbing and descending.

When tired, or not paying attention to the trail, anyone can twist and sprain a joint, most commonly the ankle. Ankle sprains are common when the foot turns inward momentarily with severe pain that can make walking difficult. Check for the points of maximum tenderness immediately after the injury. If they are just in front of the outside base of the ankle (lateral malleolus or distal fibula), and just below it, then you probably have the common variety of ankle sprain.

Treatment for strains and sprains is similar. Ice or cool the affected part, and elevate and compress the injured area. Compress with adhesive tape or an elastic bandage. Severe injuries will require rest for a few days. For strains in the bulky muscles of the thigh, there may be little you can do except to lighten the load and ease up on the amount of ground to be covered. This advice applies to sprains as well. Take pain medicine.

Individuals with preexisting knee or ankle problems should strengthen the muscles that pull across the joint by doing isometric exercises before they trek. Those with a tendency to ankle sprains should wear sturdy, over-the-ankle boots and do exercises to strengthen their peroneal muscles (those on the outside of the lower leg, done by pushing outward with the foot against an immovable object). Others prone to knee injuries should work on their quadriceps muscles (those on the front of the thigh, by keeping the knee straight and pushing up on a fixed object with the top of the foot—an isometric exercise). Those with knee problems will be better off wearing footwear with shock absorbency in the heel. Consider using ski poles to lessen the impact on knees and hips.

Everyone should pay attention to reducing the impact on the descent. Absorb the shock by bending the knee when the lower foot contacts the ground. Take short, choppy strides and don't keep the knees straight. Turn your feet sideways on steep descents. Watch how Nepali porters descend. Be sure to keep your shoes or boots laced tightly over the ankle during descents to avoid toe blisters.

HYPOTHERMIA

This condition, often termed exposure, occurs when loss of body heat exceeds gain and body core temperature drops. The body gains heat by digesting food, from an external source such as a fire, and through muscular activity, including shivering. Loss occurs through respiration, evaporation, conduction, radiation, and convection. The combination of physical exhaustion and wet or insufficient clothing, compounded by failure to eat, dehydration, and high altitude, can result in death in a very short time, even at temperatures above freezing. People venturing into cold, high regions must take adequate steps to prevent hypothermia and should be able to recognize its signs and symptoms. Be especially alert to its development in lowland porters, who may be inadequately clothed for cold. Obese people are better able to insulate their bodies against the cold than are slim individuals—a rare advantage to being overweight. Small adults and children are especially prone to hypothermia. Wear a well-insulated hat.

Initial symptoms of hypothermia are marked shivering and pale skin, followed by poor coordination, apathy, confusion, and fatigue. As temperature drops further, speech becomes slurred, and the victim has difficulty walking. Even at this stage, an external source of heat is needed to warm the victim. Further lowering of core temperature results in cessation of shivering, irrationality, memory lapses, and hallucinations. This is followed by increased muscular rigidity, stupor, and decreased pulse and respiration. Unconsciousness and death soon follow. Symptoms can appear in a few hours after the onset of bad weather, and the situation can quickly progress to the point where the victim cannot perform the functions necessary for survival. Hypothermia is easily diagnosed with a low-reading thermometer. Mild degrees of hypothermia are present when body temperature is below 94°F (34.4°C), most accurately measured rectally. But suspect it clinically whether you have a low reading thermometer or not.

Treat by stopping further heat loss, and for mild hypothermia, applying heat to the person's body core. Remove wet clothing and put the person in a sleeping bag together with a source of heat—a warm naked person, rocks warmed by a fire and wrapped in cloth, or hot water bottles. Place these under the armpits, and around the groin. Cover the person's head. Feed the victim warm drinks and sweets if he is conscious and able to swallow. Seek shelter. For body temperatures below 88°F (31.1°C), evacuate gently and quickly.

FROSTBITE

Frostbite, frozen body tissues, most commonly affecting fingers, toes, ears, noses, and chins, is rare in trekkers because the temperature extremes necessary are not usually encountered for long periods of time. But it happens, especially on high passes and trekking summits. Inadequate boots, skimpy gloves or mitts, and lack of experience are common causes. So-called easy passes can become frostbite traps after unseasonable snowfall. Beware of someone developing frostbite or hypothermia if your party is moving slowly over easy ground due to fatigue or is being delayed by route-finding difficulties or by having to help another member. Prevent with adequate clothing and equipment, eating enough food, and avoiding dehydration and exhaustion. Extreme altitudes increase the potential for the problem, as does a previous history of frostbite. Frostbite can occur at relatively warm temperatures if there is significant wind, if the victims are inadequately equipped, and if they suffer from dehydration and exhaustion. Affected tissues initially become cold, painful, and pale. Then they become numb. The trekker may then forget about the problem, with serious consequences.

An earlier reversible stage is frostnip. At this stage, the affected area becomes numb and white. Treatment consists of rapid rewarming by placing the part against a warm area of the body—an armpit, a hand, the stomach of the victim, or another trekker. Once normal color, feeling, and consistency are restored, the part can be used, providing it is not allowed to freeze again. A part of the body that has suffered frostnip before is more likely to get frostnip again. It may be difficult, especially when at altitude and dehydrated, to decide whether the injury is reversible or not. If you have a prostaglandin inhibitor pain medicine, preferably ibuprofen (aspirin and meclofenamate are others, but acetaminophen is not), take it.

Once an extremity has become frozen, it is best to keep it that way until help and safety can be reached. A frozen foot can be walked on to leave the cold area. Do not rub snow on the frozen area, nor rub it with your hands. Once feasible, the treatment is rapid rewarming in a water bath between 100°F (37.7°C) and 108°F (42.2°C). Thereafter, the victim requires expert care in a hospital and is not able to walk until treatment is completed. Trekkers are more apt to discover a dark toe or finger after an exhausting day crossing a high snowy pass. At this point, the part has already been rewarmed. Treatment consists of adequate hydration, elevation of the affected part, prevention of further injury, and evacuation.

HEAT INJURY

Not only does travel in Nepal pose problems in coping with extreme cold but also in dealing with extreme heat. Both can happen during the same trek, if it is from the hot lowlands to the cold, windy, snowy heights. Heat produced by the body is eliminated mostly by the skin through evaporation of perspiration. Acclimatization to heat takes around a week. When the body becomes able to sweat more without losing more salt, the ability to exercise in a hot environment improves. Maladaptation to heat can be prevented by an adequate intake of fluids and salt. Thirst mechanisms and salt hunger may not work adequately, so extra salt and water should be consumed in hot weather. In humid regions where evaporation is limited, it is a good idea to rest in the shade during the hottest part of the day. Cover the head and wear light-colored clothing to reflect sunlight. Soaking bandanas, hats, and shifts in water to cool the body in hot valleys is helpful too.

Suspect heat exhaustion when someone has a rapid heart rate, faintness, and perhaps nausea, vomiting, and headache. Blood supply to the brain and other organs is inadequate because of shunting of blood to the skin. The patient's temperature is normal. If the victim is treated with shaded rest, fluids, and salt, recovery is usually rapid.

Heat stroke is a failure of the swelling and heat regulation process, usually because of fatigue of the sweat glands themselves. The victim rapidly becomes aware of extreme heat and then becomes confused, uncoordinated (ataxic), delirious, or unconscious. Characteristically, the body temperature is very high, 105°F (40.6°C) or higher. The skin feels hot and dry and does not sweat. Treat immediately by undressing the victim and cooling him by any means available. Immersion in cool water, soaking with wet cloths, and fanning are all appropriate. Massage the limbs vigorously to promote circulation. Continue cooling the body until the temperature is below 102°F (38.9°C). Start cooling again if the temperature rises. The victim should be watched closely for the next few days and strenuous exercise should be avoided.

ACROPHOBIA, VERTIGO, BRIDGE, AND TRAIL PHOBIAS

These problems are common among those who trek in Nepal without previous mountain climbing and hiking experience. People with these fears usually choose environments and activities not requiring adjusting to exposure. Individuals living

Bamboo bridges are casually crossed by Nepalis, but challenge most trekkers.

in the flatlands may be unaware that they have this problem. Nevertheless, if you've come to Nepal and find yourself on a wobbly bamboo bridge, or on a ledge with a few hundred feet of drop-off, a few principles help. Obviously, don't look at the big drop-off, be it the river a hundred feet below your feet or the bottom of the cliff you are traversing. Instead, focus on a stationary object, say the end of the bridge. If feeling dizzy on a particularly exposed part of the trail, stopping and staring at a fixed object, even your thumb, can help. Don't hesitate for what seems an interminable time before you venture forth. As you walk the difficult portion, say a few verses of a familiar tune, or a prayer or mantra. This will give you an aural focus on the exposure, and you will not let your eyes wander. Breathe slowly, using your diaphragm—that is, pushing your stomach out as you inhale in. Don't stop in the middle and wonder what you are doing, or whether you will make it. For some, holding another's hand helps. A positive mental attitude is best. Just believing you can do it will result in it being so.

If you know that there will be a particularly difficult stretch coming up, plan to do it when you are not exhausted. Vertigo is worse when you are tired. Wear shoes that have good traction. This will give sufferers some added confidence. Find companions who are sympathetic. Nepali guides, once they understand the magnitude of the problem, will likely be more helpful than macho Westerners.

ANIMAL BITES

In case of an animal bite, treat by washing the site immediately with soap and water as well as a dilute solution of salt and water. Wash and irrigate the wound for 30 minutes or more. In animal experiments, inoculating of a wound with rabies virus has shown washing alone to be effective in preventing clinical rabies. Irrigation with a quaternary ammonium solution (cetrimide or benzalkonium chloride, also found in the antiseptic Savlon) within 12 hours is also effective. Those who have had rabies vaccine before coming to Nepal face less risk than others but should get postexposure inoculation as well, although they do not need rabies immune globulin.

If rabies is suspected, evacuate quickly so that the vaccine can be administered as soon as possible. The decision to seek help may be difficult if the animal bite is unprovoked and the animal appears healthy. If other animals in the area have been acting strangely recently, there may be an epidemic. Rabies is spread by saliva from infected animals penetrating the skin, usually through a bite or on a previous wound. Contact with rabid bats in caves has also caused the disease.

Leeches, abundant during the monsoon in the forests above 4000 ft (1200 m), are attracted to byproducts of respiration and drop onto you as you pass under them, or crawl up from the ground, or attach as you brush by leaves or rocks. Pick them off as soon as they latch on. When you feel a very localized cool sensation anywhere on your skin, stop immediately and investigate. It may be around your

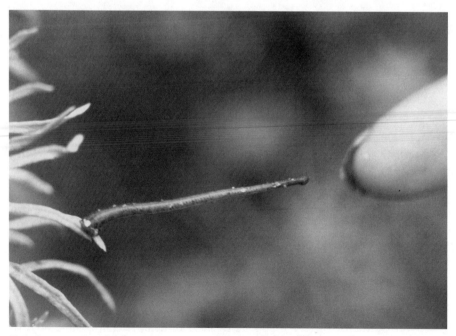

It is fun to tease a leech.

ears or neck, or just above your ankle. In leech-prone forests, stop periodically and search. You may find it amusing to tease the critters with your finger as they scan with their suckers while attached to a leaf or rock.

Once attached to your skin, they may often be pulled off. Holding a lighted match or cigarette to them also works well, as does some salt or iodine generously applied. The resulting wound may bleed considerably, a useful feature for improving circulation of reattached body parts. Control this with pressure and watch for signs of infection later. The usual insect repellents will work for leeches, as will dibutyl phthalate solutions applied to clothing around where leeches gain entry.

Ticks are best removed quickly, by grasping with a tweezer near the head, or with a gloved finger, and pulling out straight with increasing force. Lyme disease is not known to occur in Nepal.

FEVER

This section deals with fever when there is no apparent cause, such as a pneumonia or abscess. When associated with joint aches, perhaps nausea and vomiting as well as diarrhea, a fever is likely due to a flu illness. Aspirin and fluid replacement are appropriate. When the fever is severe, and the person very ill, sometimes delirious, enteric or typhoid fever may be the cause. Usually there is no diarrhea. Treat presumptively with ciprofloxacin, norfloxacin, or co-trimoxazole (TMP/SMX) if medical help is not available. If traveling in the Tarai, especially before and during the monsoon, and not taking malaria prophylaxis, periodic fevers might be due to malaria. In that case, try treating with chloroquine phosphate, 1 g (four 250-mg tablets) initially, then half that dose at 6 hours and repeated at 24 hours. If you get better quickly, assume that malaria was the cause and get treated with primaquine on return, for it is likely you had vivax malaria, which needs this additional drug to prevent relapses. Although there is no dengue fever in Nepal, travelers from other Asian countries, especially India and Thailand, might come down with it on the first few days of a trek if they set out soon after arriving in Nepal. The incubation period is around a week; the viral infection is transmitted by urban and jungle mosquitos that bite during the day. Abrupt onset with high fever accompanied by severe muscle aches, headaches, and blanching rashes are common in milder cases, which are the norm among travelers who have not been previously infected. The fever subsides quickly after 4 or 5 days. Treat with aspirin, acetaminophen, or ibuprofen. Fatigue and fevers after getting over the initial attack is seen as well.

SMALL WOUNDS AND INFECTIONS

Clean *any* wound that breaks the skin with soap and copious amounts of water, potable or not, to flush the wound and remove debris. Avoid using the common antiseptics, as they may damage healthy tissue. If you are using tincture of iodine or povidone iodine for water purification, you might cleanse the skin around (not in) the wound with this material. A large wound should be covered with a sterile dressing, which should be changed periodically until a good clot has formed and healing is well under way.

A wound infection is often the result of contamination and is evident by signs of inflammation (redness, swelling, tenderness, warmth) and pain several days after it occurs. They are more common at high altitudes, perhaps because the "resistance" of the body is less there. In this case, soak the wound in hot water for at least 15 minutes. Afterward, cover it with a sterile dressing. With severe spreading infections, antibiotics should be taken; the cephalosporin or erythromycin are preferable. For abscesses such as boils, the treatment is similar to that for wound infections, except that antibiotics probably do little to help unless the boils are a recurring problem. Drain the abscesses by soaking them in hot water for 15 minutes five or six times a day. They will usually spontaneously open, but you may have to assist the process with a sharp sterilized knife.

CONSTIPATION

This is not uncommon in the first few days of a trek, as you get used to the routine. A bulky Nepali diet usually prevents significant difficulties. If constipation does occur, drink plenty of fluids. Try a cup or two of hot water, tea, or coffee upon waking in the morning. In rare cases, mild laxatives may be needed. Better to just wait until the problem works itself out.

HEMORRHOIDS

These irritable dilated veins around the anus are usually a result of constipation. They may become larger while trekking, sometimes becoming hard with blood clots (thrombosed), not a threat to life, but a nuisance. There are various creams, ointments, and suppositories that may provide some symptomatic relief for uncomfortable hemorrhoids. When they become thrombosed, however, frequent warm "sitz" baths (sitting with the affected part in the water) are the answer.

BURNS, SUNBURNS, AND SNOW BLINDNESS

The severity of a burn depends on its area, its depth, and its location on the body. So-called first-degree burns are superficial—they do not kill any of the tissue but produce redness of the skin. Mild sunburn is a typical example. Second-degree burns kill only the upper portion of the skin and cause blisters. In third-degree burns, damage extends through the skin into the underlying tissues. First-degree burns require no treatment, but for the others wash the area gently with iced or cold water, and cover with a sterile dressing. Antibiotic ointments may relieve pain and make it easier to remove the dressing. Burns that cover more than 20% of the body surface are usually accompanied by shock, a serious threat to life. Attempt to get the injured person to drink plenty of fluids; the oral rehydration solution made from Jeevan Jal is best. Aspirin and codeine, two tablets of each every 6 hours, may help relieve pain. Evacuate the person to medical help.

Sunburn is common among trekkers visiting high altitudes, where there is less atmosphere to filter solar radiation, and where snow and ice can reflect additional radiation. Effective sun screening agents are listed as contents of the medical kit. Be sure to protect the lips and under the chin and nose when on snow. Treat sunburn as any other burn.

Eye protection in the form of dark glasses is needed on snow and generally at high altitudes. In an emergency, lenses made of cardboard with a thin slit to see through can be used, or a coarse cloth with small slits cut out can be tied over the eyes. Hair combed over the face, a method favored by Sherpas and Tibetans, is effective. Otherwise, snow blindness, a painful temporary condition, can result. The condition gets better in a day or two. Darkness and cold compresses over the eyes may help relieve pain. A poultice of tea leaves can provide some relief. Patch the eyes tightly so the lids don't move. Use your antibiotic eye drops. For severe pain, take aspirin and codeine, two tablets each, every 6 hours.

COMMON COLD

Upper respiratory infections, including the common cold, are very common in Nepal. Now that we have a good sense of how to treat diarrheas, respiratory infections are turning out to be very disabling to trekkers. Medical science does not offer any widely agreed upon remedies. Large doses of vitamin C may prevent a cold, cure it, or modify its symptoms in the early stages. The correct dose needs to be individualized, and you need to be aware of your body's reactions. When you sense a cold coming on, take additional ascorbic acid at that time, again sensing your body's needs. You might start by taking a gram of vitamin C a day and modifying this to suit the response.

Other ways of dealing with a common cold include rest, drinking plenty of fluids, and taking zinc. Do not smoke. Gargle with warm, salty water for a sore throat. Decongestants have been used for years by many people. You might want to try the antihistamine, chlorpheniramine maleate, suggested in the medical kit, at a dose of 4 mg four times a day. I would avoid decongestants containing many different drugs. People with high temperatures should not continue trekking. Investigate the cause for the fever. Normal temperature is 98.6°F (37°C), but there is little reason to be concerned if temperatures measured orally remain below 100°F (39°C) and the person feels pretty strong.

COUGHING

Coughing normally brings up sputum and is beneficial in ridding the body of it. Sometimes, however, an annoying cough occurs that does not produce sputum, even after a few days. Smoky interiors may be the cause or some respiratory virus. If this happens, take one or two tablets of codeine (30 mg) every 6 hours for a day or two. Read the section on altitude illness to make sure you are not dealing with HAPE. General measures in treating an annoying cough include drinking plenty of fluids and breathing moist air. The latter is difficult in dry mountain areas. Steam inhalation, that is, getting a kettle of boiling water and putting it inside a tent or under a blanket and breathing the water vapor, helps. Hard candy or throat lozenges provide some relief.

Serious coughing could be due to pneumonia. An affected individual would have high fevers, sputum thick with pus and possibly streaked with blood (but not frothy), and often localized chest pain that is most severe with a deep breath. The sick person is usually too ill to travel. Treatment consists of an antibiotic, aspirin for high fever and pain, and plenty of fluids.

Other commonly encountered causes of coughs are colds, asthma, and bronchitis. Bronchitis features inflammation of the airways in the lungs, the hallmark of which is the production of plenty of sputum through coughing. The sputum is usually yellow, or green, but in asthma it is usually clear. Sufferers are less sick than those with pneumonia, rarely have fevers, and if they have chest discomfort it is more likely to be central, resulting from the prolonged coughing. Try a week's course of antibiotics.

CONJUNCTIVITIS AND EYE PROBLEMS

Conjunctivitis is an inflammation of the delicate membrane that covers the surface of the eye and the undersurface of the eyelid. The eye appears red and the blood vessels on its surface are engorged. The flow of tears is increased, and material may be crusted in the margins of the eyelids and eyelashes. Irritation from the ubiquitous smoke in Nepali homes is a common cause, especially among the Nepalis. Apply ophthalmic antibiotic solution beneath the lower eyelid next to the eye every 4 hours until the symptoms disappear.

If you wear contact lenses, at the first sign of any eye irritation that is distinct from the irritation caused by dirty lenses, you should remove them and apply the antibiotic solution. In cases of problems persisting, especially if the eye is very sensitive to the light, patch it for 24 hours.

You may find your lenses need less frequent cleaning while trekking, because Nepal's hill and mountain air is quite clean. But don't neglect regular cleaning. If you do not want to bother with cleaning at all, disposable contact lenses may be the solution in Nepal. Once, while getting up in the night to answer the call up in the high dry air, my lens dried out, and I had to remove it. I used my iodized water to rehydrate it and replaced it in my eye. Some irritation persisted for an hour or so, presumably caused by the iodine residue. Better to carry some commercial normal saline for this purpose.

GYNECOLOGIC PROBLEMS

Women plagued with vaginal yeast infections when taking antibiotics might bring along appropriate vaginal suppositories. Those prone to urinary infections could consider carrying extra medicine for this problem. These individuals should make sure to urinate right after sexual intercourse, a preventive measure for recurrent infection.

Trekking is very strenuous and women who have been on the trail for a time may find that their menstrual periods stop. This is not serious; providing that a woman is not pregnant, periods should resume again with lessened activity. Vaginal bleeding may be profuse after one or two missed periods and will necessitate resting until the bleeding stops. Tampons or sanitary napkins are not available in the hills.

Heavy bleeding in a pregnant woman demands prompt medical attention, as does modest bleeding if accompanied by fever, light-headedness, pelvic cramps, or pain. If you are having profuse vaginal bleeding and there is not even the remotest chance that you could be pregnant, and you are far from any medical facility, you could try the following treatment. *Caution: If you are pregnant, this treatment could harm the fetus.* Take a birth control pill, if you have them, four times a day for five days. Bleeding should stop in a day or so. After stopping the pills, you should have a menstrual period within a week. If you don't, it is possible that you are pregnant and would need a termination because the hormone pills you have taken could harm the fetus. If bleeding doesn't stop, then prompt attention is warranted. An alternative to taking birth control pills for this is to take meclofenamate, the anti-inflammatory medicine suggested. The effect on a fetus is unknown.

Pelvic pain can have serious consequences if accompanied by fever (possibly due to an infection in the fallopian tubes) or associated with pregnancy (possibly a tubal gestation). This could be associated with vaginal bleeding. A leaking tubal pregnancy is a distinct possibility if defecation is also very painful. The treatment for a tubal pregnancy is surgical. Seek help immediately. If pain accompanied by fever is the predominant symptom, and you have had PID (pelvic inflammatory disease), or an infection in your tubes before, this could have recurred. If there are no medical facilities, you could take an antibiotic. Tetracycline, doxycycline, ciprofloxacin, or erythromycin would be the best choices from the drug list. If pelvic discomfort is accompanied by frequent and burning urination, sometimes with associated back pain, a urinary tract infection could be the cause. An antibiotic, especially co-trimoxazole, would be the treatment of choice. If you have co-trimoxazole, take a double-strength tablet twice a day for 3 days.

WORMS

You probably won't be bothered by a worm infection while in Nepal. But your porters may tell you they have passed worms. It is likely that there are more inside. A broad-spectrum worm medicine such as mebendazole (mentioned in the medical kit list) may be of some benefit. The porters will, however, get reinfected. Mebendazole is also a good drug to try if your porter complains of abdominal pain. Do not pass it out to villagers, for reasons explained in the previous chapter. And be sure to get your own stool examined when you return home if you have symptoms. Trekkers do pick up worm infections. Although the common roundworm will die of old age and you will be rid of him or her if you avoid reinfection, this is not necessarily true of other intestinal parasites.

APPENDICITIS

Trekkers out in the remote hills may worry about appendicitis. The chances of it occurring are very slight, so this in-

This man stands at the head of the 32-ft (9.75-m) tape worm he just passed. We used them for weight reduction a hundred years ago.

formation is for your peace of mind. The pain usually starts in the mid-abdomen, soon shifts to the right lower quadrant, and becomes accompanied by nausea. The victim rarely has an appetite, vomiting or diarrhea is rarely persistent. In a case where appendicitis is suspected, give fluids and an antibiotic, and evacuate the patient. Cases of acute appendicitis may respond to antibiotics and even improve without treatment.

HEARTBURN

This is fairly common among those prone to it, especially if they try to eat a Nepali diet in porter quantities. The burning is most likely to occur when on the trail soon after a meal. Better to eat smaller amounts. Don't fasten your pack waistband right after meals. Antacids may help, too. The liquid preparations are best in doses of two tablespoons every hour for symptomatic relief. Preparations are available in Kathmandu. The pain of heartburn could signify a heart attack. Such a person will usually look and act very sick, perhaps perspire profusely, and need gentle evacuation.

DENTAL PROBLEMS

Most dental problems are unlikely among trekkers if they see a dentist before going to Nepal. For simple toothache, a small wad of cotton, soaked in oil of cloves and inserted in the appropriate cavity, often relieves pain. Codeine and aspirin, two tablets each every 4 to 6 hours, help relieve severe pain. Abscesses, characterized by swelling of the gums and jaw near the site of the toothache, and often accompanied by fever and chills, as well as persistent hot and cold sensitivity, call for the care of a dentist. In the interim, take an antibiotic.

One possible hazard is breaking a tooth while eating because of the possible presence of small stones in the rice or *daal*. Take pain medicine and avoid foods of extreme temperature. Be aware of the excellent dental clinic in Namche Bazaar.

SINUSITIS

Sinusitis, an inflammation of the sinuses often following a cold, can be characterized by headaches of a dull nature, pain in the sinuses, fever, chills, weakness, swelling of the facial area and discomfort in the upper teeth if the maxillary sinus is involved. For severe symptoms, rest, drink plenty of fluids, take two aspirin every 4 hours for the fever, and use phenylephrine nose drops three times a day. Start an antibiotic if the temperature extremes are significant. This course should be continued for seven days no matter when the symptoms subside. The best antibiotic is cotrimoxazole, amoxicillin, a cephalosporin, or ciprofloxacin.

URINARY TRACT INFECTIONS

These are common in some women, especially after vigorous sexual activity. If you experience burning, frequent urination, passing small amounts of urine, without a fever or back pain, and are not pregnant, take co-trimoxazole, ciprofloxacin, a cephalosporin, or tetracycline for 3 days. If you have a fever, or back pain, or are pregnant, in addition to the preceding symptoms, take any antibiotic in its appropriate dose for a week.

PSYCHOLOGICAL AND EMOTIONAL PROBLEMS

> But at times I wondered if I had not come a long way only to find that what I really sought was something I left behind.
>
> Tom Hornbein,
> *Everest, The West Ridge*

Trekkers and travelers to exotic countries can have emotional problems adjusting. I can well remember squatting in the bush with diarrhea on the first few days of my first trek in Nepal on my first journey away from North America and pondering whether this was my reaction to being separated from my familiar environment and whether trekking was all it was cracked up to be.

While trekking, you may have to deal with more physical closeness than you are used to, being in a small tent with someone you only just met in Kathmandu 2 days ago or not having accustomed privacy in toilet or other personal matters. Some married couples at home have developed ways of living apart but, on a trek, are suddenly cast together with no easy escape, and this can lead to serious difficulties coping. You may be a very individualistic leader, who now has to cooperate in a group and agree to what the trip leader or guide decides. Giving up such control can be very difficult. You may be separated from friends and familiar places realizing that you are essentially alone a week or two from "civilization" and 15,000 mi (24,000 km) from home. Unexpected environmental stimuli including new sounds such as the incessant barking of dogs, the flap of the tent in a wind, or exotic smells including the everpresent stench of filth in some places, or the sights of abject poverty set in cultural wealth, all may overwhelm individuals. Prior expectations of one's performance in a new environment and a feeling of lack of control in unfamiliar surroundings must be dealt with. Accomplishing simple tasks such as finding a place to stay for the night or a place to eat can be very trying. The heroes of screen and stage are not flustered by unexpected obstacles. Most of us try to emulate this in our lives. Yet here on a trek, you get ill despite all your efforts at being careful, you are dirty and unkempt, unable to wash in the cold, you can't eat the food, you are too tired to enjoy the view, or bad weather has prevented you from seeing Mount Marvellous or has delayed your flight for 4 days! You want to cry, yet think you should appear in control. As trek leader, you may have to deal with your reactions to the client's moods. Other travel-related factors can compound the difficulties (disturbed sleep, jet lag, fatigue, altitude, alcohol or other recreational drugs, prescription medicines, and the stresses of the life left on hold back home).

Prevention is the key to not getting "burned out." Steps depend on the individual and the situation. Deciding on a reasonable goal for the trek before starting out can be helpful in limiting expectations. Make the journey a goal; it is the adventure itself, not standing on some patch of ground you have read about. If you have a secret spiritual agenda, it may be necessary to keep it in proportion to the realities of the trek. For some who never undertake new paths alone, it may be ensuring that you are with friends, with whom you can share the experience. For those who are fastidious in their personal habits, it may mean a daily bath, shaving every day, keeping hair combed, and putting on a clean change of clothes every few days. Use ear plugs or short-acting sleeping pills (when not at altitude) to deal with sleep disturbing noises at night. Sometimes the daily routine of constant walking, eating, and sleeping is too much. Take rest days every now and then and pamper yourself. For some it may mean acceptance of the reality that the schedule they have set for themselves is too ambitious or that difficulties in adjusting to altitude will prevent them from getting to that famous viewpoint or crossing that pass. Some people should not go trekking. Those with significant psychiatric diagnoses, such as bipolar disorder, might be better off on a private trek than a group trek.

Panic attacks are becoming more commonly recognized among travelers, perhaps because of increased awareness among clinicians or because less hardened adventurers are taking to the trails. Symptoms of these can be chest pains, palpitations, difficulty breathing, trembling, sensation of choking, nausea, tingling, weakness, dizziness, cramps, or a sense of impending doom. They peak in intensity in 10 minutes and typically subside spontaneously in half an hour. Those afflicted feel they are dying. Often there is no apparent cause, everything had been going well up to that point. Others may not have been aware of the stresses they were under. There may be a history of these attacks occurring back home. Steps to take are to make certain there is no physical disorder that is causing the symptoms, then to reassure the sufferer, and provide support. Various medicines can help prevent these attacks. Sometimes an evacuation may be necessary.

What if you are getting quite depressed or close to a "nervous breakdown"? First do some familiar, relaxing, comforting routines, such as bathing, shaving, washing your clothes, or putting on clean ones. If alone, find other trekkers to join. If carrying a heavy load, hire a porter. If sick and weak, rest and eat better foods frequently during the day. If consuming marijuana and other mood-altering drugs, stop them. If appalled by the conditions in Nepal and among the Nepalis, take comfort in the fact that you can leave if you choose. Ask yourself whether the people you see behave as if they are actually suffering or unhappy. If your mood does not improve, head back to Kathmandu or Pokhara by plane if possible. But be careful not to end up waiting a week for a plane when you could have walked in 3 days. If you have trouble adjusting to conditions in Nepal, don't go to India.

If you are a trip doctor, and may have to deal with sequelae of such problems, consider including an injectable anti-psychotic drug such as haloperidol in your kit. Stabilize a patient as quickly as possible and try to repatriate the individual accompanied by a reliable person. Many episodes occur in people without prior psychiatric history and may represent an acute situational psychosis or the first manifestations of further problems. Other victims may be those with a history of mental illness, some of whom have stopped their medicines or who are sliding into psychosis.

Few people end up having to curtail their treks in Nepal for these reasons. Rather, many will undergo a "culture shock" upon returning home as, based on their experience in Nepal, they question the values of the environment in which they have grown up. But trekking in Nepal is not for everyone. Don't despair. There are many other superb activities elsewhere waiting for you.

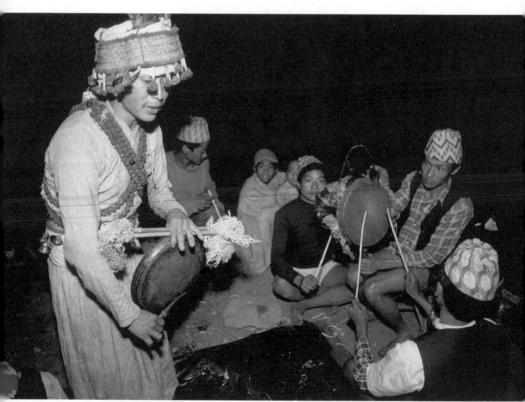

This jhankri, *while in a trance, becomes a spirit medium to facilitate healing.*

Oh mommy, take me home.
> The mantra of the burned-out trekker

Ritual Healing

Healing in Nepal is pluralistic; the afflicted try many remedies including seeking a spirit medium. Western attention has focused on a variety of shamanic traditions in Nepal that are widely dispersed and highly developed, especially among the hill ethnic groups. Some such as that of the *Kham-Magar* are related to the classic Inner-Siberan legacy. Shamans are vehicles by which normal individuals communicate with divinities. Causes of illness are thought to be naturalistic, in that spirits for various reasons have conspired to cause sickness. The shaman drums and shakes rattles, enters into a trance, and can make spirit flights or become possessed. In the seance, the spirit speaks through him (usually), describing the reason for the sickness and what needs to be done. This community-approved practice can allow for the resolution of inner conflicts in the face of cultural norms. Shamans are often low status individuals, who exemplify the ability to communicate with the spirit world early in life. Through training, they gain status and prestige, especially after an elaborate initiation ceremony where they demonstrate magical powers. Trekkers may encounter shamans in distinctive symbolic dress, drumming and performing healing rites, as well as those leading the dead to their proper dwelling places.

Emergency Care and Rescue Facilities

Nepal's health plan involves setting up hospitals to provide secondary health care, staffed by physicians in each of the seventy-five districts. Primary health care is provided by health posts staffed by paramedical personnel and female community health volunteers scattered throughout each district. None of these facilities, including the hospitals in major cities, can provide health care to a standard that even approximates that available at home.

If an emergency occurs, try to enlist the help of Nepalis. If in a district center, contact the CDO (Chief District Officer), who will usually speak English. Otherwise, seek out elected officials. Schoolteachers may be helpful. A seriously ill person can be carried by a porter, a horse, or a yak. You or your fellow trekkers can carry the person, too. Amazing resources can be mustered in the most desperate of circumstances.

If faced with a life-threatening emergency in the hills, you should try to get word to Kathmandu to effect a rescue. Telephones, now rather widely available, are the best means of communication. If an air rescue is necessary, send a message to Kathmandu for a helicopter. These days, there is widespread availability of helicopters, mostly Russian behemoths and others.

If the problem is not life-threatening, but requires evacuation, consider using porters, yaks, horses, or commercial air services.

Public telephone access, run by private business, is rapidly changing the communication pattern in Nepal. Previously, emergency communication links were limited

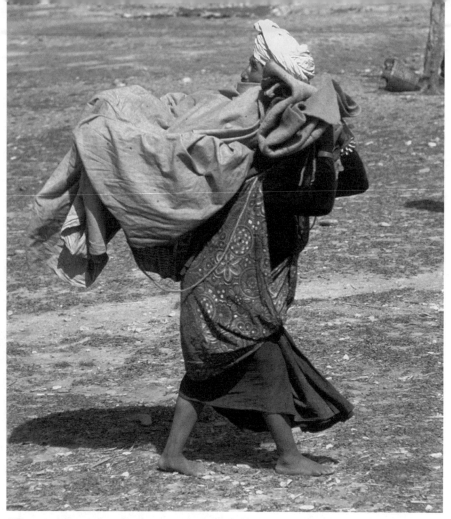

The usual form of medical evacuation available to Nepalis.

to various radio stations that were civilian-operated, part of the telecommunication systems at district centers, or army, police, HRA (Himalayan Rescue Association), or national park posts or others related to police check posts or army installations and telegraph links. Telephone communication centers, operated by VHF relay, and solar or electricity powered, are cropping up in towns all over the country. There is a desire to have them fit a grid, half a days' walk apart. Some have fax machines. You can call home from these places (expensive) and receive calls, and this is becoming the most appropriate way to send an emergency message. No comprehensive listing of them can be given as new ones are added frequently; you can ask and many people will be able to direct you to the closest one. Like anything in Nepal, they may be broken when you try to use them.

HOSPITALS, AID POSTS, AND SOURCES OF HELP
Kathmandu

There are several choices for trekkers seeking health care services. Check with your embassy for advice. Many travelers use the CIWEC international clinic (phone 228531, fax 224675) near the Yak and Yeti Hotel. The Nepal International Clinic, between Durbar Marg and Naxal (phone 412842, fax 419713), has Western-trained Nepali doctors. The Patan Hospital in Lagankhel (Patan) offers good care. There is the Tribhuvan University Teaching Hospital, in Maharajganj, which is affiliated with Nepal's first medical school. Private surgical palaces, known as nursing homes, abound.

North of Pokhara

Pokhara has a regional government hospital, and an airport. Radio stations are located in the Machhapuchhre Base Camp, Khuldighar, GhoRepani, Chame, Kusma, Baglung, Beni, Jomosom, Besisahar, and Manang. STOL strips are found in Jomosom, Hongde, and Balewa (south of Baglung, across the river from Kusma). There are district hospitals in Baglung, Besisahar, and Jomosom. An HRA Trekker's Aid Post at Manang is staffed by a doctor during much of the popular trekking season. A small aid project staffed by a French doctor in Tatopani could provide assistance.

Solu–Khumbu and Rolwaling

There are government health facilities in Jiri, Namche Bazaar, Phaphlu, and Charikot. A hospital staffed by foreign physicians is in Kunde. There is an HRA Trekker's Aid Post, staffed by a doctor during most of the trekking season at Pheriche but there is no radio or phone link there yet. Phone service is available in Namche Bazaar where there is also a modern dental clinic.

Langtang, Gosainkund, and Helambu

A government hospital is in Trisuli and Dhunche. Radio stations are in Langtang at the army office or in Dhunche. There are private phone offices in Malemchighyang, Tarke Ghyang, and Sermathang.

Eastern Nepal

There are radio stations at Chainpur, Khandbari, Taplejung, Phidem, Bhojpur, Terhathum, Dhankuta, Dharan, Ilam, and Chandragari and STOL strips at Tumlingtar, Lamidanda, Bhojpur, Chandragari, and Taplejung. There are government hospitals in Chainpur, Taplejung, Bhojpur, and Dhankuta.

Western Nepal

In addition to the facilities in Baglung and Beni already mentioned, there are radio stations in Dunai, Sumduwa (Shey Phoksumdo National Park headquarters), Jumla, and Tansen. There are radio stations at the Royal Dhorpatan Hunting Reserve post in Dhorpatan, ChAUmri Pharm, and Goatichaur. STOL strips are found at Dhorpatan, Jumla, Jufal, and Chhaaujhari. There is a government hospital in Jumla.

EMERGENCY MESSAGES AND RESCUES

In organizing a rescue requiring a helicopter, it is important to provide the proper information and make sure it reaches the proper place. It is wise to send several messages to different organizations to ensure that at least one is delivered. Write them up beforehand, and take extra time to make sure they are comprehensible by nonnative English speakers. Addresses should be as specific as possible to speed delivery. The phone numbers of the agencies and rescue facilities should be rechecked once you reach Kathmandu. Phone numbers change all the time; there is no

911system as in much of the United States. Rescue messages should be sent to one or more of these (redundancy helps ensure that one message will arrive) in order of preference:

- The embassy or consulate of the victim (for USA, phone 413836, fax 413936)
- The trekking agency that organized the trek; if applicable see Appendix A (get the home phone number of the managing director before you leave Kathmandu)
- Helicopter services
- Royal Nepal Army, 474953, 473297, 471653 (24 hours), fax 474607
- Asian Airlines, 423273-4, 416116, fax 423315, 411878
- Cosmic Air, 427150, 416881, 427358, fax 427084
- Dynasty Aviation, 414625-6, 414627
- Gorkha Airlines, 475855, 472989, fax 471136

The message should contain the following information:

- Degree of urgency. **Most Immediate** means death is likely within 24 hours. **As Soon As Possible** is used for all other cases in which helicopter rescue is justified.
- The location, including whether the victim will remain in one place or be moved down along a particular route. Give the altitude of the pickup place. Generally, 17,000 ft (5000 m) is the limit for helicopter pickups. Describe the route of evacuation, if you will be moving the victim. Describe the pickup point in relation to other nameable features, and if you can, give the town, ward number, village development committee (*gAU bikaas sammitti*), and district.
- Name, age, sex, and country of the victim, passport number, visa and trekking permit number, trekking agency if any, and information as to other destinations to which the same message will be sent (embassy, trekking agency, airline, etc.)
- Medical information, including the type of sickness or injury, and whether oxygen or stretcher immobilization (as for back injuries) is needed
- Whether a doctor is at the scene, and whether one might be required from Kathmandu. It may be difficult to send a physician along, and usually is not necessary, since the evacuation will bring the victim to medical attention.
- The name, nationality, age, and sex of all people to be evacuated
- The sender's name and organization, along with information on the method and source of payment for the rescue. Include any local phone numbers, especially where you are calling from. Generally, airlines will not fly rescues without written assurance of payment, so include this in the message. This can sometimes be provided by the embassy of the victim. A credit card number may sometimes be accepted for payment.

When sending a message, you will usually not be able to verify that it has been actually transmitted unless you can phone when there is a better chance to judge reception.

A rescue can take several days, especially if a runner has to be sent with the message, to a site for transmission, or if there is airplane trouble or bad weather. If notification to a helicopter company is received after 12 noon, there is little chance of a flight that day. It is wise to move the person along the route, waiting each day until 10:00 A.M. to start. In each sleeping place, a large, smoky fire should be built each morning, and a landing site cleared and marked with a large X, preferably using international orange garments or a colorful sleeping bag or tent. Improvising a secure, colorful wind sock would be helpful. If you have a mirror to signal with, use it. If you are directing a helicopter to land, stand at the end of the "pad" with your back to the wind, and wear brightly colored clothing so that you are easily seen.

Once the helicopter is preparing to land, remove the signal garment or sleeping bag and any other material that may be blown around by the rotor down draft while the helicopter is approaching or leaving. Do not signal a helicopter unless you can direct it to the victim. Locating the stricken party from the air can be quite difficult and pointless waving has resulted in dangerous landings, increased costs, and delay in evacuating severely ill patients. Approach and leave the helicopter in a crouched position, always in view of the pilot and never toward the rear of the helicopter, and only after the pilot has signaled you to move. You will rarely have a flat landing site, so on uneven ground, always approach and leave on the downhill side. When boarding, carry any material horizontally, below waist level, and never on your shoulder. Secure any loose articles of clothing before you approach.

The cost of a helicopter rescue is high—an hour of helicopter time costs over U.S.$800 for a small chopper. This has to be borne by the party involved, unless rescue insurance has been taken out previously, which alpine clubs in your home country can sometimes provide. Some trekkers might wish to obtain a comprehensive travel, accident, and rescue insurance policy before they leave home. Register at your country's embassy in Kathmandu, in case they receive a rescue message. Approximately 75 people are helicopter rescued for every 100,000 trekking permits issued.

In the tragic event that a porter or trekker dies, be aware that airlines will not transport corpses on their scheduled flights. You might be able to charter a helicopter or carry the body out, though you may find it very difficult to hire porters to do this.

It is best to cremate the body and have this witnessed, preferably by a local policeman, village headman, or person not associated with your trek. Record the victim's name and address, as well as those of any witnesses, remove all valuables, and keep the ashes for relatives. If Westerners die, realize that even in Kathmandu there are no public cemeteries, or mortuaries, or even a morgue. If you do get the body to Kathmandu, further difficulties in transporting it to your homeland ensue. The body must be embalmed. Enquire at the Department of Pathology, in the Teaching Hospital in Kathmandu.

The risk of death while trekking in Nepal is estimated to be 15 per 100,000 trekking permits issued. Common causes of death are injuries, usually from falling off the trail, altitude illness, and the afflictions of older age. Your risk if staying at home is certainly higher!

Overleaf: *Kambachen on the way to Kangchenjunga Base Camp*

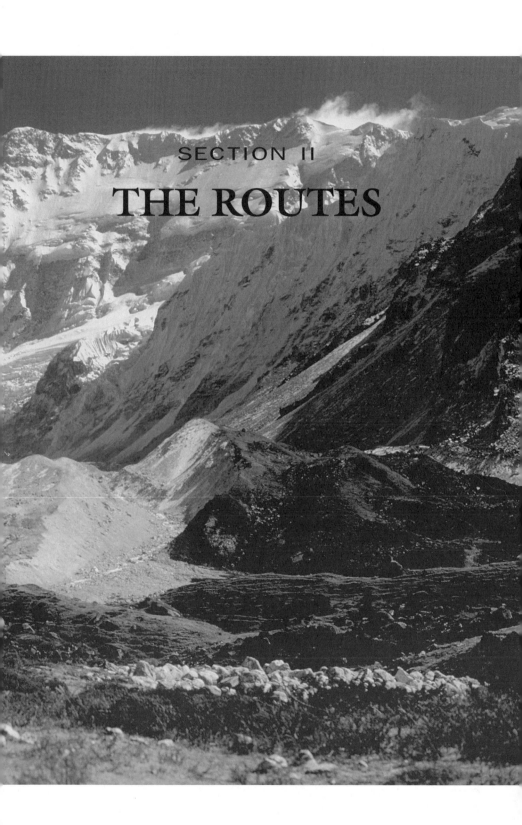

SECTION II

THE ROUTES

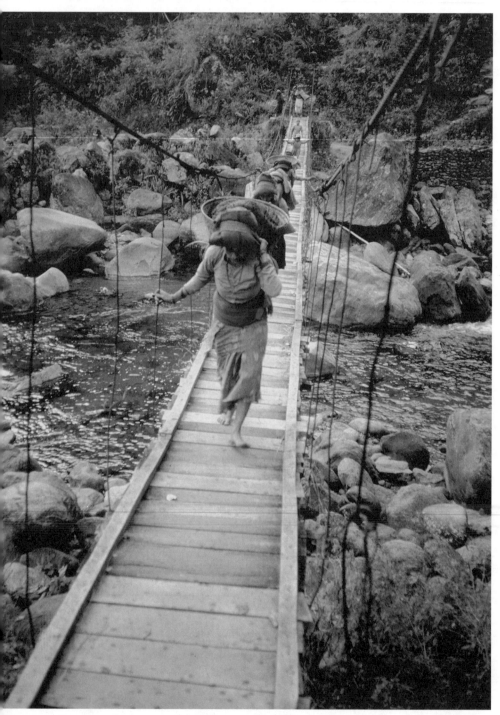

Heading for the Saturday market in Namche Bazaar.

Following the Route Descriptions

No one goes so far or so fast as the man who does not know where he is going.

H. W. Tilman, *Nepal Himalaya*

Walking Times and Trails

In the route descriptions that follow, the times listed between points are actual walking times, usually those I took myself. They *do not* include any rests. This has been strictly adhered to by using a chronograph. Over most of the trails I carried a moderately heavy pack. I almost never walked the segments in these times. Like everyone else, I rested, photographed, talked with the people, and so forth.

The times are fairly uniform in that, if a person takes 90 minutes to cover a stretch listed as taking an hour, then it will take that same person one and a half times as long as the time listed to cover any other stretch—providing the same pace is maintained. Some people have commented that they find the times too long, but most find them too short. The latter is usually because they do not add rest times to the estimates. The times are in boldface in descriptions to make them easier to total the time for a particular stretch. Times not in boldface are either noted for additional information or in reference to a side trip. These estimations help trekkers know what to expect and thus find the way more easily, and they make it easier to plan where to eat and to spend nights. These times are not meant as a challenge but, rather, as a guide.

At the end of each description of a major route, I have added a graph of cumulative walking times (excluding stops and rests) and altitudes from the start of the trek to significant points along the way. This does not include trail variations or side trips. Each graph tries to depict the high and low points along a trek, to give you an estimate of the effort required. Note that the abscissa (horizontal scale) is *not* horizontal distance (miles or kilometers) but, rather, hours of walking per the text. Until someone runs an odometer over the trails in Nepal (it won't be me), you'll have to judge for yourself how far the trails go. By reading off altitudes and times between points, you can estimate your night stopping points.

Treks are not set out on a day-to-day basis. Instead of adhering to a daily schedule, each party can adjust for long rests or interesting diversions. Those committed to straight traveling can count on covering about 5 to 7 hours of the given route times in a day, allowing a 2-hour food stop. In winter there is less daylight than at other times. If you have many porters, expect to cover shorter distances. For those wishing a day-to-day itinerary, start with about 5 hours of trekking times, and use the trail profiles and route descriptions to select destinations. If necessary, you can adjust your itinerary as you progress.

For many trekking routes, the distance has traditionally been measured in number of camps (or days) necessary for large parties of trekkers accompanied by numerous porters to complete the route. Camp days make sense for large groups who need space for tents and allowance made for the porters to carry the loads the required distance. I do not follow this convention here, to allow trekkers to plan the days as they wish.

Experienced trekkers find that often the first day on the trail seems fast. The next two or three days can be slow and painful. As the body strengthens and adjusts to the pace, the miles and hills seem to go by more effortlessly.

The altitudes listed in the descriptions are taken from several sources, including recent maps whose accuracy can be trusted and my own altimeter. I initially used a Thommen instrument, but most recently I have been using a Casio Alti-Depth™ or Citizen Altichron™ watch with altimeter for all but the highest readings, which are still taken on the Thommen. The readings have not been corrected for temperature changes, but they are adequate to indicate the order of climbing or descending.

Ascent rates of 2000 ft (600 m) per hour are difficult to maintain for any length of time. Most trekkers find 1000 ft (300 m) per hour a reasonable rate if the trail is good and the climb easy. Similarly, a descent rate of 1500 ft (450 m) per hour is reasonable. Altitudes are usually converted from feet into meters and are not rounded off; they are only approximations at best and can be in error by a few hundred feet. Altitudes of most towns in the hills are difficult to interpret accurately because several hundred feet of elevation may separate the highest and lowest parts of a town.

Routes are described in one direction only. They can easily be followed in the opposite direction. The time for the trip in the reverse direction can be figured approximately if altitude to be gained or lost and the rate of ascent or descent is taken into consideration.

Directions in the trail descriptions are given with reference to the compass. In addition, right- and left-hand sides of rivers are indicated to avoid confusion. **Right** and **left** refer to the (true) right and (true) left banks when *facing downstream*. Sometimes they are abbreviated TR and TL, respectively, to designate true right and true left.

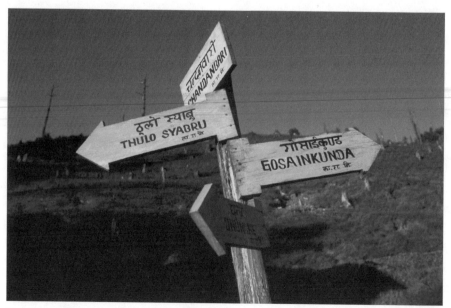

Signposts such as this one at Sing Gomba have become more common along trekker trails.

Questions to Ponder: Walking and Portering

What styles of walking and carrying loads do you see among the Nepali people? Slow, steady pace? Many stops? What do they do when they stop? Estimate the weight of the heaviest porter load you see and compare it with his or her body weight. Try lifting it with the tumpline. Compare a porter's foot, especially one walking barefoot, with your own—its shape, position of the toes, and so forth. Your little toe probably curls under. Why?

Observe the age ranges of Nepali people who undertake long journeys. Does this reflect the proportions present in the population? Do women undertake long trips?

Often there are branches off the main trails that lead to houses. You'll quickly discover if you've taken one of these. If you follow large trekking groups, you may find direction arrows scratched in the ground or on rocks to help indicate the way. Nepalis do not do this for themselves.

Trekkers, even experienced backpackers, are sometimes surprised to find the trails more difficult and rugged than the ones they are used to back home. Trails are maintained by local governments, who are improving trails because of the increasing popularity of trekking. However, they don't have the machinery and resources to produce the quality of trail found in national parks and forests back home. Nor is the wear of countless animals and monsoons anything like what it is in Nepal. Improved trails may take different routes from those described here, and routes can shift in popularity for a variety of reasons. I have walked most of the trails described in this book at least twice. Notable changes range from improvements in some trails to erosion and damage on others to finding more villages and settlements catering to trekkers along the popular routes. Landslides on steep valley-floor trails result in almost cyclical rerouting over a period of years to decades.

Travel along trails in the high country where there are no settlements is seasonal. Most Nepalis go there only during the monsoon when few trekkers are afoot. Animal trails may be confused with human trails. Forest, fog, or whiteout may make finding the route difficult or impossible. Trekkers have become lost in such circumstances, and it is easy to remain lost for several days, especially if trying to bushwhack to a trail you don't know. If lost, backtrack to a point you know, rather than trying to push onward. It is prudent to travel with a guide in such country. Often one can be hired locally for a few days.

Trails vary considerably with the seasons. During and soon after the monsoon, when the rivers are still swollen, travelers take ridge trails rather than those following the valley floors. But in the dry season, November through May, many trails on ridges are abandoned in favor of more indirect river routes. In addition, shortcuts across dry paddy fields are favored over the well-worn trails. These shortcuts can be numerous and at times misleading, but they are still preferable in most cases. Other times, you may precariously balance on walls of irrigated terraces or end up sloshing on muddy trails. Appropriate trail etiquette is to let the uphill traveler have the right-of-way.

Along the popular trekking trails, it is likely that you will find many more hotels, tea shops, lodges, and so forth in places where I haven't reported them. Local people are responding to the increased demands of tourism. It is hard to know what to call a hotel, or a tea shop, inn, or lodge. I have tried to use the term *bhaTTi* to refer to a traditional Nepali inn, one used by local people, but as an area becomes popular with trekkers, these are often the first to cater to outsiders. Consider all the terms to be used interchangeably. Trekking times change also, usually decreasing as the trails improve through use. Please note down any changes or new information and send it to me in care of the publisher.

Names of towns and villages are taken from two sources: maps and other documents, and my phonetic rendering of the names I heard. I spell the names according to the principles in my language book, so you may find my spellings differ from those found on signboards, though occasionally I will list some local English spellings.

In the route descriptions, the names of some towns are in boldface. They are usually large, well-known places whose names the trekker should use when asking the way. Food and accommodations are usually available in these towns. This should help you plan your journey. No recommendations for places to stay are given. These change constantly, and there is no way I can evaluate them or describe them in Travlish, that evanescent dialect found in traditional guidebooks. Ask other trekkers about the latest finds, which, depending on your point of view, might be places to avoid. Stay in people's homes where you can, and discover a different Nepal.

Place-names in Nepal are not unique. There are many Bhote Kosis (rivers from Tibet), Benis (junctions of two rivers), Phedis (foot of hill), and Deoralis (passes). In addition, some villages may be called by two different names, but this should not cause much confusion in actual practice. Finally, as facilities that cater to trekkers are built in remote mountain regions, they may take on English names, such as Bamboo, albeit pronounced in a confusing Nepali fashion.

The pronunciation and transliteration guide in Appendix C indicates the correct way to pronounce the place-names. It is important to place the stress on the first syllable of most words—for instance, Kathmandu, Pokhara, and Tengboche. The meaning of capital letters occurring within words is explained in Appendix C. Place-names and other proper nouns are capitalized in spite of the transliteration system. The only place-names that would be capitalized if the transliteration scheme were followed strictly are *RaRa, Dumre, AAbu Khaireni,* and *RiRi.* A correct spelling of Kathmandu in this transliteration system is *kaaThmaanDu,* but for the sake of convenience, the common spelling is used.

A *chautaaraa,* referred to in the trail descriptions, is a rectangular rock platform with a ledge for resting your load. Sometimes a pipal and a banyan tree are planted side by side in the center. In the east, you are as likely to find wooden benches. You can look forward to these welcome structures, found on many of the well-traveled routes. A *chorten* is a Buddhist religious structure, often cubical, with carved tablets. The term entrance *chorten* refers to a covered gateway or arch decorated with Buddhist motifs. A *stupa* is a very large *chorten. Mani* walls are rectangular and made of stone tablets carved with mantras and prayers.

Hints for Walking

Everyone should learn the rest step for ascents. As you advance your uphill foot, plant it and then, before transferring your weight to it, consciously rest briefly with your weight on your downhill foot. Do this continuously and the hills come easier. Try to coordinate your breathing with your steps. That is, breathe in on raising the left foot and out on raising the right. Or breathe in on raising each foot, if the ascent is very steep. This will also make the ascent less tiring. It is better to take several short steps up, rather than one long one, just as for going down.

Here's how the leader of the first ascent of Rum Doodle, at 40,000½ ft, did the rest step:

I tried to remember all I had read about climbing at such heights. I took one step, then waited for 10 minutes. This I understood was essential; our predecessors were unanimous about it: one step, then 10 minutes rest, or seven in an emergency. I found it more difficult than I had anticipated. To remain in one position for 10 minutes was not all easy. First, I tended to fall over sideways; then I got cramp in the calf; then my nose started to itch; then my foot started to vibrate and had to be held down by both hands. This was very tiring, and when I crouched to hold my foot I was lower than I had been before making the step, which caused me to wonder whether I was gaining height or losing it; and the mental strain was so great that I lost control of myself and fell off my step. . . .

W. E. Bowman, *The Ascent of Rum Doodle*

On descents, tighten your shoe- or bootlaces so that your toes are not crammed into the front of the shoe with each step. Take short steps, bending your knees and hips to absorb the energy of the descent. Be limber. Watch the porters to see how they walk. People can easily get knee problems by not descending with bent knees. Knee injuries take a long time to heal and can be quite disabling if they occur many days away from the road.

Arrange your clothing in easy-to-doff and -don layers so you can adjust to temperature changes due to the environment and your own heat production. It is pointless to sweat profusely, only to get freezing cold as a blast of icy wind hits your wet body. Anticipate your increased heat production going uphill, and doff clothing soon into the climb, yet put some on just before a rest stop, so you don't chill. I use garments with underarm zippers that allow me to remove my arms from the sleeves and adjust to different temperatures easily.

Morning along the Mayagdi Khola

During a walk of many weeks in such spectacular country, it is easy to let your mind wander from the task at hand, to daydream or gaze at people, mountains, or scenes. You must *always* pay attention to the trail in front of you and where you put your feet. This may sound obvious, but too many careless trekkers have had serious accidents or falls, and even lost their lives. As the late veteran trekker Hugh Swift stated, "Look when you look, walk when you walk." When passing animals on the trail, keep to the uphill side, where the fall is much shorter should you be nudged by a yak or buffalo. Drivers of yak trains want you to pass on the downhill side of yaks. They feel the yaks are spooked less by this. I wouldn't, unless the downhill side is perfectly safe!

In the mountainous regions you may be threatened by an ornery yak. If a yak makes an aggressive move, stand your ground, raise your hand, and shout! Loud, threatening dogs are sometimes met along the trail. They rarely attack but, just to be sure, carry a long stick and pass them assertively. Often you meet large Tibetan mastiffs, but they are usually chained, except possibly at night and near herders' camps. If you suspect that there might be an unchained mastiff about, call and get the attention of people at the camps and ask them to chain the dog. Do not approach chained dogs.

At rest stops, drink fluids and elevate your feet. Take off your shoes, remove the insoles, and let the sweat dry off your feet, socks, insoles, and shoes. Don't point your feet at any Nepali. Do not roll rocks off trails to see how far they go. This is especially important if traveling with children who may be eager to do this. People, animals, and villages are almost always downhill!

The Religion of the Hills in Nepal

People like simple classifications of other people's religions but dislike such efforts to their religion. The religion of the hills of Nepal is like that, with animistic and shamanistic practices, interwoven with Hindu and Buddhist influences. Animism and shamanism are concerned, respectively, with spirits that exist in nature and with the human condition, body and soul, alive or departed. Animistic beliefs and shamanic ritual permeate both of the "high" cultures of Buddhism and Hinduism. At virtually every wayside shrine, in almost every religious rite, in ceremonies performed by lay people as well as by Hindu temple priests (*pujaari*), Buddhist priests (*lama*), or village shaman (*jhAAkri*), you will see some form of worship (*pujaa*) focusing on both the animate and inanimate objects of nature. Funerals, rites of passage, and curing ceremonies are all richly ornamented with the animist's and shaman's concern for placating local spirits and natural forces. If you happen upon a religious ceremony, your presence may be offensive (your proximity to food preparation or to hallowed ground, for example, may be deemed ritually polluting). As you observe ritual events, be aware of the sensitivities of the officiants and participants. And open your senses to the fullness of their expression, especially to the sometimes awesome respect shown for nature—to the moon, earth, fire, water, and air; to cow dung and smoky incense; to cow's urine and curds; to the blood sacrifice of chickens, pigeons, goats, and buffalo. Therein you will begin to glimpse a very close association between villager and nature, a necessary relationship that many people, caught up in the frenetic pace of the modern world elsewhere, seem to have forgotten or have uncaringly abandoned.

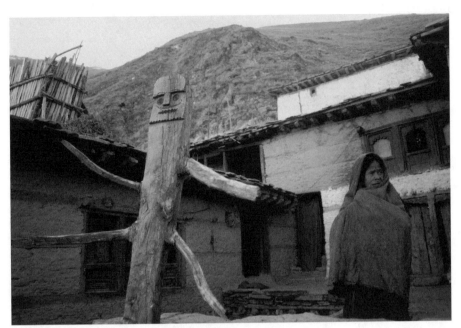

This komba *or protector deity wards off evil spirits in the west.*

Trails

During the day, especially along less trekker-frequented trails, you may pass many Nepalis who greet you and ask where you are coming from and where you are going. The accepted form of greeting or taking leave of a person is to place the palms of your hands together in front of your face as if to pray and say *namaste* or *namaskaar.* The latter is more respectful and formal. Both have the connotation of "I salute the god within you." Children will often badger you with endless such greetings. Always use the less formal greeting with children and don't overdo it. The best way to identify a neophyte trekker is to hear him or her greeting everyone on the trail. To set yourself apart from them, use *namaste* followed by an appropriate kinship term such as *didi* or *bahini, daaju,* or *bhaai,* as in the "Getting Someone's Attention" section of the language guide, *Nepali for Trekkers.*

During the day's walk, you may pass through several villages and farming areas, cross major rivers, climb to the crest of one or more ridges, and descend down into the valleys again. When trekking without a guide, it is necessary to constantly ask the name of the current village and the way to the next village. Except along the most popular trekker routes, there are few trail signs in Nepal, and finding the route is a matter of asking the way as the Nepalis do. Nepali people traveling in unknown areas are constantly asking the way and exchanging news. Often you may be confused by the answers Nepalis give to your questions about trails or times. If so, repeat the question or phrase it differently until you are satisfied with the response. The problem may be your pronunciation. Ask the next person on the trail, too. It's all part of the fun of trekking and finding your way in Nepal. Along the more popular routes local people make a commotion when they think you are on the wrong trail. This can create problems when you deliberately wish to take a side trip. When asking the

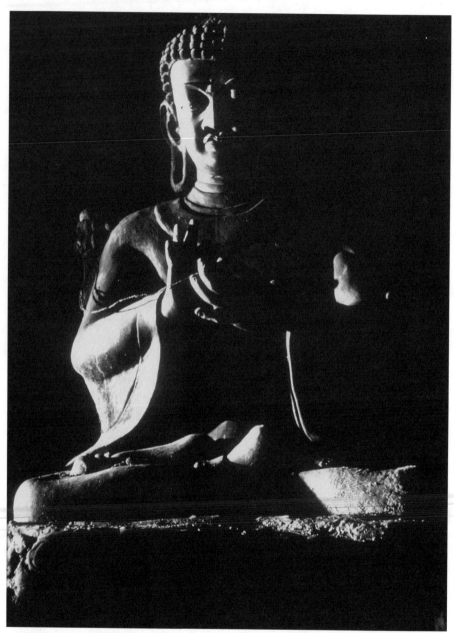

Buddha in the Braga Gomba

way, keep in mind both the next town's name as well as a larger, well-known town farther along. Often the names of small settlements may not be known, but nearly everyone knows the names of big centers, even though they may be a few days' walk away. Because of the lack of standardized spelling, names on many maps may lead to improper pronunciation.

Religion in Nepal: Hinduism and Buddhism

Spiritual mysteries—as opposed to spiritual answers—are one
foundation of Indian religious faith.
Daniel Taylor-Ide, *Something Hidden Behind the Ranges*

Nepali religion is based on two "great" or "high" traditions—Hinduism and Buddhism—each underlain by expressions of local "little" traditions of animism and shamanism. (Of course, practitioners of the latter do not necessarily see their religion in this way; the dichotomy is only for purposes of analysis.) Because only a very small percentage of Nepalis are Muslim, or *Musalmaan*, and as most of them live in the Tarai, they will not be considered here.

"Hinduism is not a religion, but a way of life," states ethnologist A. W. MacDonald. This seems evident from observing the devout in Nepal. Hinduism is rooted in the texts of the ancient Vedas dating to 2000 B.C. As it evolved, three main deities became focal: Brahma the creator, Vishnu the preserver, and Shiva the destroyer. In their varied manifestations they pervade daily ritual and symbolize the cycle of life. There are no basic dogmas, no qualities that define a Hindu, except perhaps whether that person employs a Brahman as a priest. It is left to each individual to decide the form of his or her worship. The caste system is a fundamental aspect of Hinduism. An individual who aspires to rebirth in a higher caste must live a proper life in his present caste. This precept has exerted a significant stabilizing effect on Indian and Nepali societies. Caste etiquette was codified as law in Nepal in the Muluki Ain of 1854. Although this law has now been repealed, it still governs behavior.

Buddhism, on the other hand, is more a philosophy than a religion. Founded by the disciples of Siddhartha Gautama, born at Lumbini in Nepal's Tarai around 623 B.C., Buddhism is based on the four noble truths: Existence is suffering, craving and attachment cause suffering, the attainment of nirvana is an end to this suffering, and there is a path to nirvana, the eightfold way. These are: right views, right resolve, right speech, right action, right livelihood, right effort, right mindfulness, and right concentration. Buddhism depends on the institution of a monastery and monks. The Buddhist community supports a monastery and derives strength from it. Meditation and observance of moral precepts are the foundations of Buddhist practice. To trekkers, the recitation of the esoteric mantra *Om mani padme hum* and the spinning of prayer wheels are examples of meditative practice observed by the common folk.

In Nepal, Hinduism is reflected both in the system of caste, which defines social status, and in a subsistence economy based on rice agriculture and a highly ritualized cattle culture (cow worship). Buddhism, principally the Mahayana ("Great Vehicle") Tibetan form, with strong tantric expression, is found among the *BhoTiya* people of the northern border area. Vajrayana Buddhism is practiced by Buddhist *Newar* of the Kathmandu Valley. Buddhism and Hinduism tend to blend in many settings, such as the Kathmandu Valley, where indigenous *Newar* practice both religions, side by side and intermixed. The various local expressions of these two religions, and of animism and shamanism, are so conceptually interwoven that it would take much more than this short account to untangle and explain them accurately and clearly.

Nepalis are eager to please Westerners and, in their enthusiasm to do so, often give incorrect answers to questions. For example, a Nepali might say that a particular destination you ask about is close when it is actually a long way off. Or he might say that the trail you are on goes to the place you are asking for, rather than upset you by telling you the truth. And people who don't understand your questions sometimes answer nevertheless. Learning to get around these problems is all part of the experience. It isn't insurmountable or fraught with hazard.

Even if you ask the way, there are times when you might get lost, especially along the less trekker-frequented trails. If this happens, it is preferable to backtrack to a place that you know rather than bushwhack ahead. If faced with an unknown trail junction, refer to the general route description, and apply it to the topography in your situation to arrive at a decision. Go off and see if the trail seems to be going where you expect it to.

Check in at police posts along the way, should you need to be traced in an emergency. Getting a small group processed at a police check post may take up to 30 minutes, but check posts along the popular trails have become much more efficient. The official will usually make a note in your trekking permit. Do not produce your passport unless absolutely necessary or there may be further delays. If you are carrying binoculars, keep them discreetly out of sight, or the officials may suspect you have motives other than bird-watching. The same discretion is advised for other belongings. Be patient and courteous in dealing with officials.

Don't always be in a hurry, eager to cover as much ground as possible. Sometimes, stop at noon and watch village life or explore the surroundings. Consider spending an entire day in some place that is *not* the highest, the most spectacular, the most beautiful, and just let things happen.

Many trekkers have found their greatest enjoyment from finding new trails little used by foreigners. After you get the hang of it, don't be afraid to venture forth on undescribed terrain, especially if you are trekking independently. Encouraging you to explore on your own, without route descriptions at hand, may be the best advice I can provide.

Questions to Ponder while Trekking

The real voyage of discovery consists not in seeing new landscapes, but in having new eyes.

Marcel Proust

Nepal provides marvelous food for thought. A manifold society with almost unfathomable ethnic diversity is layered over landscapes varying from tropical rain forest to snowy heights and desert. Paradoxically, the forces that shape Nepal are essentially very simple: its people endeavor to survive, while the land attempts to self-destruct through natural erosive forces.

There are too many facets to Nepal for an outsider to absorb in a single trip—or a lifetime. When I first came to Nepal, attracted by the incredible mountains, I was partially blinded to the people living among them. After spending more time in Nepal, however, I found the people—the culture, their ways of surviving in this harsh, upturned land—at least as interesting as the great peaks themselves. Once, some years ago while I was working in western Nepal, a trekking group of expatriate schoolchildren from Kathmandu and Barry Mateer, their teacher, visited my project. They peppered me with good questions about the work being done there.

Indeed, I later learned that each of them had been given a list of questions to report on after their trek. But the questions they were asking me were not from the list. The listed questions had merely heightened their curiosity.

I wish to share similar questions with you, to use as you see fit. These are inserted throughout the book. Please don't try to read all of them at once. But when the urge strikes, perhaps after a few days on the trail, you might read a few to see how they sit. They are not a test or catechism, but one way perhaps of organizing the myriad impressions and observations that are accumulated during an extended trek in Nepal. There are no real answers for many of the questions, but I have occasionally indicated directions in which you may find it helpful to proceed.

Enhancing Your Cultural and Environmental Experience

To a person uninstructed in natural history, his country or seaside
stroll is a walk through a gallery filled with wonderful works of art,
nine-tenths of which have their faces turned to the wall.
                                        Thomas Huxley

Geology

According to the theory of plate tectonics, the Himalayan arc has formed as a result of the "collision" between the Indian subcontinent and Asia. Prior to approximately 180 million years ago, all the present-day "southern" continents, including South America, Africa, Australia, Antarctica, the Arabian Peninsula, and the Indian subcontinent, formed one large, southern hemisphere "supercontinent," known as Gondwanaland. A vast ocean, the Tethys Sea, separated the northern margins of Africa and India from the southern margin of Laurasia, the northern hemisphere supercontinent composed of Asia, Europe, and North America. About 180 million years ago Gondwanaland began to break apart. Between 75 and 80 million years ago the Indian subcontinent, containing present-day India, Pakistan, Nepal, Bangladesh, and Sri Lanka, broke away from Antarctica and began its northward "drift" toward Asia. The Indian Ocean, which separates India and Antarctica, began opening up through the sea-floor spreading along the mid–Indian Ocean Ridge at this time. India and Antarctica traveled away from each other at an initial rate of about 16 cm per year, separating the two continents a distance of 3200 km over the next 20 million years. While to the south of India new oceanic crust was being produced at the mid-ocean ridge and the Indian Ocean was being created, to the north of the Indian continent the Tethys Sea was closing and the oceanic crust underlying the Tethys Sea was being subducted (consumed) beneath Tibet.

About 55 million years ago, the Indian subcontinent slammed into Tibetan and southern Asia. Seafloor-spreading has continued in the Indian Ocean since the collision, and India has continued to move northward relative to Tibet and Asia. With the Indian subcontinent plowing into Tibet and southern Asia, something has had to give. The result has been the crumpling-up, folding, faulting, and uplift of the northern margin of the Indian subcontinent to form the Himalaya, as well as the uplift of the Tibetan plateau by the Indian subcontinent being thrust under it.

Four Physiographic and Geologic Divisions of the Himalaya

The northern boundary of the Tibetan Himalaya is the Indus–Tsangpo Suture, along which the Indus and Tsangpo Rivers flow. The Indus–Tsangpo Suture is the actual collision zone and boundary between the Indian subcontinent and the Tibetan microcontinent. Along some sections of the Indus–Tsangpo Suture, oceanic crust and the subcrustal mantle have been squeezed up between the Indian and Tibetan continents and thrust over the oceanic sediments of the Tibetan Himalaya. This oceanic crust, along with the Tethyan sediments of the Tibetan Himalaya, is all that remains of the Tethys Sea today.

The *Tibetan* or *Tethys Himalaya* lie between the Indus and Tsangpo Rivers to the north and the high summits of the Higher Himalaya, which form the backbone of the Himalayan range (for example, Mount Everest, Annapurna, and Dhaulagiri), to the south. The Tibetan Himalaya include the Tibetan Marginal Range, a range of mountains that lies to the north of the High Himalayan peaks and includes the Dolpo, Mustang, and Manang regions of central Nepal as well as the Tingri region of southern Tibet. The Tibetan Himalaya are composed of Cambrian to Eocene sediments, which were deposited in the Tethys Sea between 500 and 55 million years ago on both the northern margin of the Indian continent (the continental platform underlain by Higher Himalayan rocks) and in the deep ocean basin between the Indian and Asian continents. These oceanic sediments include limestones, sandstones, and shales and contain abundant fossils, including brachiopods, oysters, occasional plant fossils, and the famous Upper Jurassic ammonites found in profusion around the sacred area of Muktinath. The Nilgiri Limestones (named after the peak of Nilgiri in the Annapurna region) were deposited in the Tethys Sea during the Ordovician period (500 to 435 million years ago); they presently form the summits of Nilgiri and the Annapurnas and are found on the northern flanks of Dhaulagiri. Similar early Paleozoic sediments cap the summits of Mount Everest, Lhotse, Kanjiroba, and Nanda Devi; thus, it is true that many of the highest summits of the world are capped by rocks that were once deposited in an ocean. Because these early Paleozoic Tethyan sediments in the Annapurna and Everest regions lie at the base of a 12-km-thick sequence of Tethyan sediments, and because the summits of these mountains are presently over 8 km high, these sediments have been uplifted some 20 km since the onset of the Himalayan orogeny (mountain-building event) 55 million years ago. During the Himalayan orogeny, the Tethyan sediments have been extensively faulted and folded; this can be seen between Marpha and Muktinath and north of Manang in the Annapurna region.

The physiographic *Higher Himalaya* includes the high mountains of the Himalaya proper (for instance, Kangchenjunga, Makalu, Everest, Cho Oyu, Shishapangma, Manaslu, Annapurna, Dhaulagiri, Kanjiroba, Api, and Saipal) and the valleys within the high mountains. The Higher Himalaya are generally considered to include those regions with altitudes over 4000 m that lie south of the Tibetan plateau and the Tibetan Marginal Range. Geologically, the Higher Himalaya consist of highly metamorphosed and extensively deformed schists and gneisses (crystalline rocks). These rocks were the original Precambrian continental crust of the northern margin of the Indian continent. (The Tethyan sediments of the Tibetan Himalaya were deposited upon these Higher Himalayan rocks.) About 25 million years ago, a deep, east-west–trending fracture formed within the Indian continental crust. The continental crust on the north side of the fracture (the Higher Himalayan rocks) was shoved over the continental crust and its sedimentary cover rocks south of the fracture (the Lesser Himalayan rocks). The Higher Himalayan crystalline rocks (to the north) were thrust over the Lesser Himalayan sedimentary rocks (to the south) along a fault known as the Main Central Thrust. The Main Central Thrust is the geological boundary between the Higher Himalaya and the Lesser Himalaya. Higher Himalayan rocks have been thrust over the Lesser Himalayan sediments a minimum of 100 km into eastern Nepal. Between 25 and 10 million years ago, at about the same time as thrusting was taking place along the Main Central Thrust, very high temperatures in the Higher Himalayan rocks melted the schists and gneisses, forming large granite bodies in many of the Higher Himalayan Peaks. These granites can be seen on Makalu, Everest, Lhotse, Shishapangma, and Manaslu.

The physiographic *Lesser* (or *Lower*) *Himalaya* is divided into two distinct regions in Nepal: the Middle Mountains and the Mahabharat Lekh. South of the Higher Himalaya lie the heavily inhabited Middle Mountains, from which almost all treks to the Higher Himalaya begin. Elevations in the Middle Mountains range from a few hundred meters in the valleys (for example, Tumlingtar at an elevation of 457 m) to 4000 m on the ridges. The Middle Mountains are dissected by major south-flowing rivers, such as the Karnali, Kali Gandaki, and Arun Rivers. The ridges that come off of the southern flanks of the Higher Himalaya also trend roughly north–south. The Mahabharat Lekh, an east-west–trending range of hills with summit elevations of 2000 to 2500 m, runs the whole length of Nepal south of the Middle Mountains and north of the Siwalik Hills. The Mahabharat Lekh can be seen south of Kathmandu and the Kathmandu–Pokhara road and is breached by the Trisuli-Narayani river, along which the road from Kathmandu to Narayangarh and India runs.

Much of the physiographic Lesser Himalaya are underlain by rocks belonging to the geologic Lesser Himalaya. The geologic Lesser Himalaya consist of variously metamorphosed and deformed sediments that were deposited in an inland basin from Precambrian times (more than 570 million years ago) up to about 50 or 60 million years ago. The original sediments of the Lesser Himalaya included shales, sandstones, conglomerates, limestone, and some acid-volcanic rocks. During the last 25 to 30 million years, these were metamorphosed to form the slates, phyllites, metaquartzites, marbles, and granitic augen-gneisses that make up the Lesser Himalaya today. Practically no fossils are seen in the Lesser Himalayan metasediments. It is interesting to note that the hills encircling Kathmandu, and the Mahabharat Lekh in eastern Nepal, which belong to the physiographic Lesser Himalaya, are actually composed of Higher Himalayan rocks—schists, gneisses, and granites—that have been thrust over the Lesser Himalayan sediments along the Main Central Thrust.

The *Sub-Himalaya* is the geologic name for the Siwalik Hills, the foothills of the Himalaya lying between the Mahabharat Lekh to the north and the Indo-Gangetic Plains of north India to the south. These hills rarely exceed 1200 m in elevation. The Siwalik Hills are composed entirely of shales, sandstones, and conglomerates less than 20 million years old, which are the product of the erosion of the rising Himalaya to the north. Thus, the Siwalik Series sediments record the uplift of the Himalaya. The Siwalik sediments contain scattered fossils of crocodiles, rhinoceroses, and elephants, all present-day inhabitants of the few wild regions left in the Himalayan foothills, such as Royal Chitwan National Park. Presently, the Lesser Himalaya, including the Mahabharat Lekh, are being uplifted and thrust southward over the Sub-Himalayan Siwalik Hills; the Siwalik Hills are being uplifted and thrust southward over the Ganges plain.

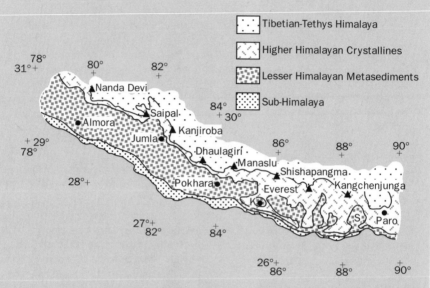

Figure 2. Map of the Himalaya showing the four tectonic zones. K = Kathmandu, S = Sikkum. (From Pecher and Le Fort, 1986.)

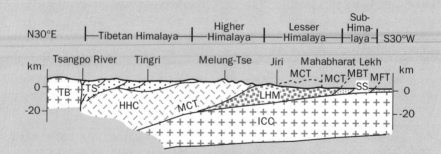

Figure 3. Crustal-scale cross-section of southern Tibet and eastern Nepal. TB = Tibetan Block north of the Indus–Tsangpo Suture, TS = Tethyan sediments of the Tibetan Himalayas, HHC = Higher Himalaya crystalline rocks, LHM = Lesser Himalayan metasedimentary rocks, SS = Siwalik Series sediments of the Sub-Himalaya, ICC = Indian Continental Crust, MCT = Main Central Thrust, MBT = Main Boundary Thrust, MFT = Main Frontal Thrust. (From Brunel, 1986, and Schelling, 1989.)

Major Habitat Types

Nepal's major natural habitat types are forests, grasslands, and wetlands. Nepal has rather few wetlands, but their ecological diversity is very great. For instance, a total of over 160 indigenous species of fish have been recorded. There are three major river systems, which are fed by the Himalayan snows and glaciers: the Kosi, Kali Gandaki, and Karnali. Other wetlands include a number of small lakes scattered throughout the country. The Kosi Barrage area, a large expanse of open water, marshes, grasslands, and scrub lying in the Kosi's floodplain in the far eastern lowlands, is by far the most valuable wetland in the country. It is internationally important as a staging point for migrant water birds. Over 50,000 ducks are estimated to be there in February.

Only small areas remain of the country's lowland grasslands, and almost all of these lie within protected forest areas. They are important for a number of threatened animals, including the swamp deer, Indian rhinoceros, and two of the world's most endangered bustards, the Bengal and lesser floricans. In spring and summer, a mass of colorful flowers bloom on alpine grasslands. A number of mammals, such as the bharal and common goral, depend on these grasslands for grazing and in turn they form the vital prey of the threatened snow leopard.

Forests form the major natural vegetation of Nepal. In his classic work *Forests of Nepal,* Adam Stainton identified thirty-five different forest types—an extraordinarily high number for such a small country. These include dry coniferous forests on the northern Himalayan slopes, rhododendron shrubberies in the subalpine zone, temperate oak forests draped in mosses, and lush, wet tropical jungles. The main reason Nepal is of great value for birds is because of its forests. There are as many as 124 species of breeding birds for which the country may hold significant world populations. Nearly all of these are dependent on forests. Nepal's forests also support a rich variety of mammals, although those in the Himalaya have been little studied so far. Relatively few species have adapted to habitats heavily modified or created by people, such as gardens, scrub, and cultivation. Most of them are widespread and common, such as the Asian magpie robin and jungle crow, while many animals dependent on natural habitats are declining.

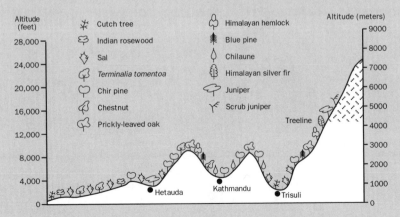

Figure 4. North–south profile through central Nepal showing altitudinal forest distributions.

Nepal's Species Richness

Nepal has a remarkably high diversity of flora and fauna considering its small size. There are over 830 species of birds, more than 600 of butterflies, and about 6500 of flowering plants.

Nepal's species richness can be partly attributed to the country's extremely varied climate and topography. The altitudinal range is greater than in any other country, ranging from almost sea level to the highest point on earth, Mount Everest. In the lowlands, such as in Royal Chitwan National Park, there are tropical forests, which support the greatest number of species. Here can be found some of the Indian subcontinent's large mammals, including the Indian rhinoceros and tiger.

Pleione humilis, *an orchid in the cloud forest above the Arun*

At the other extreme is the alpine zone of the high peaks, which holds the smallest number of species. Among these is the Tibetan snow cock, a large gamebird that normally summers above 4500 m.

The other major factor contributing to Nepal's species richness is its position of overlap between Asia's two great biogeographic realms—the Oriental and Palearctic, produced by the collision of the Indian subcontinent and Asia. Palearctic species originating in Europe and northern Asia are dominant in the Himalaya. For example, birds include accentors, redstarts, and rosefinches. Primulas, gentians, and edelweiss flower in the alpine grasslands, attracting Apollo butterflies. Oriental species are the most common in the tropical and subtropical zones of southern Nepal. Hornbills feed in large fruiting trees of the forest canopy while gaudy pittas search the leaf litter below, and large, colorful butterflies, such as the yellow and black birdwings, flutter past.

In the boxes that follow with information on plants and animals encountered by the trekker, common and scientific names are given with Nepali equivalents, in brackets, that are consistent with Regmi, Agriculture Projects Services Center (APROSC) Glossary, listed in Appendix B.

Observing Plants and Animals

Flowers [*phul*]

The main flowering season in the Himalaya is from mid-March to the end of May, while the period between November and late March is a good time to look for flowering plants in the lowlands.

Birds [*charo*]

The period between mid-March and the end of May is excellent for birds because many residents and summer visitors are at a peak of activity. Late May is the best time to bird-watch on the high-altitude treks, such as those to Langtang and Solu–Khumbu. Although it is very hot, late April is exciting for bird-watching at Chitwan, and probably other lowland forests, because large numbers of migrants are passing through the lowlands on their way to the hills and most summer visitors have arrived, while a few winter visitors still remain.

Between December and mid-March is a very interesting time due to Nepal's numerous winter visitors. Look for birds while you trek to the Thak Khola and around Annapurna. In October and November, small numbers of passage migrants can be seen flying south along the Himalayan valleys. In recent years, thousands of birds of prey have been reported northwest of Pokhara, moving west along the southern edge of the Himalaya.

When bird-watching, remember that most birds are active early in the morning and that their movements are affected by the sun. Slopes bathed in sunshine attract birds away from slopes in the shade, except during hot midday periods, when birds tend to be inactive. When walking in forest you may hardly see any birds for several hours. This is because most birds from one area of forest often join together to form a fast-moving party of different species.

Mammals [*janaawar, pashu* (domestic)]

In general, mammals can be seen throughout the year, although the best months are March to May in the lowland, protected forests of Chitwan, Sukla Phanta, and Bardia. During these months, the regrowth of grasses after the annual grass-burning attracts large numbers of herbivores and with them their predators.

Unlike birds, mammals are usually difficult to see in Nepal. Many of them are only active at night and are usually silent. The first 2- or 3-hour period after sunrise is a productive time to look for nocturnal mammals. They are often still active then and the trail is more likely to be undisturbed. Most mammals are shy and wary of people, so dress in clothes that blend in with your surroundings. Greens or browns are suitable in forest, and pale colors in the Himalaya when they are snow-covered. Remember to be silent and to walk lightly, with slow body movements. Large carnivores and some other mammals, notably the Indian rhinoceros and sloth bear, are potentially dangerous and should never be approached.

Insects [*kira*]

June to September is the best time for insects, but the monsoon weather will present difficulties in finding them. Many species can be seen in other months—for example, many butterflies [*putali*] emerge in March and April, becoming abundant by May and June.

Hill and Mountain Peoples of Nepal: Association and Diversity

Nepal is a land of great diversity. Its social, cultural, religious, geographical, floral, and faunal varieties fascinate and challenge the imagination. The diversity across the land is quickly seen and felt by trekkers. In a relatively short distance (although it may be days of arduous walking), a trekker can leave the low, subtropical Tarai forests and ascend northward into the high alpine meadows. The *Tarai-wala* (a person of the Tarai) is left behind for the *PahAARi* (hillsman), the *Lekhali* (person of the high country), the *goThaalo* (alpine herdsman), and the *BhoTiya* (Tibetan) of the hills and mountains.

Variations in social and cultural expression seem to parallel the physical, geographic, and biotic changes associated with altitude and latitude. The trekker sees an ever-changing variety of farmsteads, villages, and bazaars; passes the shrines of Hindu, Buddhist, and animist; encounters farmer, trader, storekeeper, pilgrim, innkeeper, and herder; and notes changes in the architecture of homes and religious edifices. The colorfully diverse expressions of human adaptation to the Himalaya are unexpectedly fascinating for a land to which most visitors come expecting only spectacular mountains, smiling guides, yak herds, and pagoda-like temples.

Nepal has dozens of ethnic and caste groups, each differentiated by unique aspects of language, dress, locale, lifestyle, house style, economy, and religion. At one level of analysis, however, certain elements of uniformity tend to knit all the diversity together. Take language. It divides Nepalis into two major camps: those who speak Nepali as their mother tongue—primarily the caste groups—and those who speak languages identified by linguists as part of the Bodic division of Sino-Tibetan (sometimes called Tibeto–Burman)—that is, the hill ethnic groups and those of close Tibetan affinities. At another level, however, language draws them together; most Nepalis, regardless of local dialect, speak Nepali in the public forums of trade, education, government, and daily encounters with outsiders. (In some places, English has become the second major language of the land.)

Another of the more visible attributes of uniformity in Nepal is a marked association between cultural groups and the altitude/latitude where they traditionally live. Each distinct group can be identified in great part by the ecological niche it occupies. Each niche is characterized by similarities in dress, house style, religious expression, patterns of trade, and subsistence. Caste groups, for example, tend to occupy the lower valleys in dispersed settlements, where they raise rice on irrigated paddy fields. Ethnic groups tend to cluster in nucleated villages on higher, more northerly ridges, where they raise upland crops such as millet, corn, barley, and wheat. Each depends on the other for exchange of produce and for other economic, social, and religious interaction. In addition, Nepal's rich cultural heritage has been heavily influenced and sometimes irrevocably changed by the recent influx of tourism, education, technology, mass communications, and other aspects of modernization.

Characteristics of the Physiographic Regions of Nepal: The Inhabited Areas

Features	Tarai	Siwaliks	Middle Mountains	High Mountains	High Himalaya
Elevation ft (m), approx.	300–1000 (100-300)	650–5000 (200–1500)	2000–8000 (600–2500)	3300–13000 (1000–4000)	6500–17000 (2000–5000)
Climate	Tropical	Subtropical	Cool temperate	Alpine	Alpine to arctic
Major natural vegetation	Sal and mixed hardwoods	Sal and mixed hardwoods, pine	Pine and mixed hardwoods, oak	Fir, pine, birch, rhododendron	Open meadow, tundra
Major crops	Rice, maize, wheat, mustard, sugarcane, tropical fruits	Rice, maize, wheat, millet, radish, mango	Rice, maize, wheat, millet, barley, pulses, potato	Oats, barley, wheat, potato, buckwheat, yam	Grazing (monsoon)
Livestock	Cattle, buffalo	Cattle	Cattle, sheep, buffalo, pigs	Cattle and crosses, sheep, goats	Yaks and crosses, sheep, goats
Textile materials	Jute, straw, grass	Bamboo	Nettle, hemp, bamboo, sheep's wool	Nettle, bamboo, sheep's wool, yak and goat hair	Sheep's wool, yak and goat hair
Ethnic groups	*Tharu*, Hindu castes, migrants, Musalman	*Tharu*, migrants from middle mountains	*Gurung, Magar, Tamang, Newar, Rai, Limbu*, Hindu castes	*Thakali*, Sherpa, *Tamang, Chhetri, BhoTiya, Gurung*	Sherpa, *BhoTiya*

(After Dunsmore, 1993.)

Nepal has always been a meeting ground for different people and cultures.

Dor Bahadur Bista,
Nepali anthropologist

5   North of Pokhara

If there be a Paradise on earth, it is now, it is now, it is now!
Wilfred Noyce, describing the area above
NagDAADa in *Climbing the Fish's Tail*

Scenic Pokhara is the starting point for at least four treks described in this book. The three described in this chapter are the traditional trek to Thak Khola, Jomosom, and Muktinath; the trek to Manang starting at Dumre east of Pokhara; and the trip to the Annapurna Sanctuary. A circuit of the Annapurna massif combines spectacular mountain scenery with incredible ethnic and cultural diversity and traverses through very different ecological life zones. This classic trek is among the world's best.

Many people take shorter journeys from Pokhara. Popular options for short trips include GhoRepani and Poon Hill, down to the Kali Gandaki, to Baglung, and then to Pokhara, or a circuit through Ghandruk, possibly including GhoRepani. The relevant trail portions can be picked out from the descriptions that follow. A short trek, almost all downhill, is to fly to Jomosom, perhaps paying a visit to Muktinath if you first acclimatize, then walking south to Baglung in 4 to 5 days, and then taking a vehicle to Pokhara. Those wishing to get a taste of a climb and views could cross GhoRepani and pick up the bus at Naya Pul.

The section from Jomosom to Tatopani is the most westernized rural area in Nepal. It is very popular with trekkers. Lodges and restaurants provide many tourist facilities unheard of elsewhere in Nepal. For this reason, some trekkers prefer to avoid this area, but it is very attractive to many others. You can assume that any place-name referring to a village in the route descriptions that follow have lodges for trekkers. I'll mention any that don't.

Many of these treks begin at low elevations and follow valley floors. It can get very warm in late spring so dress appropriately and don't push yourself, especially in the first few days. Relax during the midday, try to be in the shady side of the valley in the afternoon, or carry an umbrella.

In the route descriptions that follow, the times listed between points are actual walking times, generally those I took myself. They *do not* include any rests. This has been strictly adhered to by using a chronograph. Over most of the trails I carried a moderately heavy pack. I almost never walked the segments in these times. Like everyone else, I rested, photographed, talked with the people, and so forth.

To Thak Khola and Muktinath

The trek from Pokhara to Jomosom on the Kali Gandaki, or the Thak Khola, as the river is called in its northern portions, is one of the easiest and most comfortable treks, in addition to being the most popular, in Nepal. There is relatively little climbing, cooked food and lodging are easily available along the entire route, and the terrain is more varied than on any other trek of comparable length. Although the route passes among some of the highest mountains in the world, the scenery may not be as exciting as in, say, Khumbu. On this route you are likely to encounter colorful mule caravans made musical by the tinkling of neck bells. There are several side trips out of the Kali Gandaki valley less frequented by trekkers. Though strenuous, they reward tired hikers with spectacular views and give them a glimpse

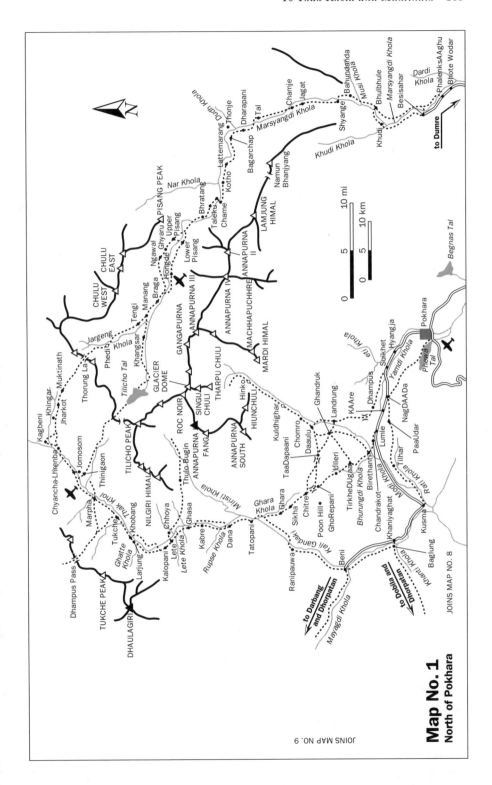

Map No. 1
North of Pokhara

JOINS MAP NO. 8

JOINS MAP NO. 9

to Dumre

of the immense scale of the valley. Muktinath, a Hindu and Buddhist pilgrimage site, is a day's walk north of Jomosom.

Unless you plan a side trip to one of the uninhabited areas, there is no need to take food or shelter. Lodges or hotels in most villages offer food and accommodations that are "Western" in style, with more variety, most likely, than back home. These places are run by the *Newar, Thakali, Gurung,* and *Magar* ethnic groups.

Transportation from Kathmandu to Pokhara is available daily via several airlines or by road, and from India by road. You could take a plane to or from Jomosom or Ongre in Manang to avoid backtracking. It may be difficult to get a seat on a scheduled flight to or from these places, as flights are often canceled due to bad weather and the high winds. Flying into these areas is not recommended because of the rapid altitude gain.

A road exists from Pokhara all the way to Beni. If you prefer to walk all the way, trek to Dhampus from Suikhet, and then go on to Landrung, cross to Ghandruk, and head over to GhoRepani. See page 193 for the route from GhoRepani to Ghandruk. My first trek in 1969 began from the airstrip in Pokhara because there was no road.

The Annapurna Conservation Area Project (ACAP) has sought to standardize facilities for trekkers and to facilitate travel north of Pokhara. Trekkers will find signboards at the entrance to many villages in this area. Developed by the ACAP, they indicate the route through the village as well as the registered establishments. There is an ACAP trekker's information center in Mahendra Pul in Pokhara, with a meeting board for getting together with other individuals.

POKHARA TO TATOPANI

(Map No.1, Page 165)

From the **Pokhara** airstrip (2713 ft, 827 m) you can board a bus or taxi to Mahendra Pul in the downtown area. The bus from Kathmandu also brings you here. If going by road to Beni, or Nayapul (for access to Birethanti), or near Lumle

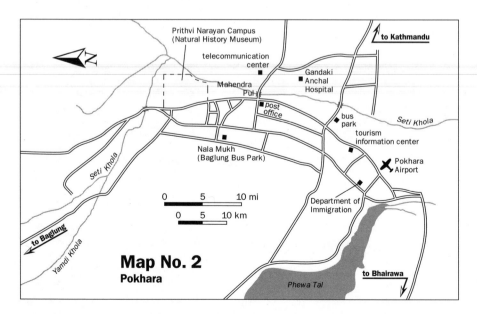

Map No. 2
Pokhara

Try winnowing soybeans with a manglo *to appreciate the skill involved.*

(to get to Chandrakot), get to the Baglung bus station (Nala Mukh or Besi Parak different from the Bas Parak, near Mahendra Pul), on the western side of the dense business section of Pokhara. Buses leave regularly. You can also take a bus directly to Beni from the Naya Bas Parak, near Baleju in Kathmandu. There is both day and night bus service, with tickets purchased a day in advance. The first place trekkers leave the road is south of Lumle, after passing through KAAre. Lumle is the site of a British agricultural development project where former Gurkha soldiers are trained in farming. It has one of the highest rainfalls in Nepal. Walk from **Lumle** (5300 ft, 1615 m) to **Chandrakot** (5250 ft, 1600 m) at the west end of the ridge in **30 minutes.**

The views from Chandrakot are unforgettable. You will cross the Modi Khola, which flows south from between the peaks Annapurna South and Machhapuchhre, which stand before you. The Annapurna Sanctuary, which lies upriver inside the gate formed by Machhapuchhre and Hiunchuli, the peak east of Annapurna South, is a worthwhile side trip described later.

The trail descends to the Modi Khola, follows its east (left) bank southward a short distance to a suspension bridge, and crosses to the prosperous town of **Birethanti** (3600 ft, 1097 m) **1¼ hours** from Chandrakot. Trekkers usually come to Birethanti by taking the bus going to Beni and getting off at **Naya Pul,** a short 15 to 30 minutes south of Birethanti and on the opposite (true left) side of the Modi Khola. If coming from Naya Pul cross the Lumle Khola from the bus drop-off point and walk up to the suspension bridge just east of Birethanti. There is a police check post in town where you register. From here, one trail heads up the Modi Khola on its west (right) bank toward the Annapurna Sanctuary. The trail to Thak Khola heads west. Just up from the town by a picturesque waterfall is a cool pool on the Bhurungdi Khola. If you swim here, be sure to wear clothing in order not to offend the Nepalis. Follow the Bhurungdi Khola westward, at first through forests. Stay on its northeast (left) bank, passing several suspension bridges. Cross several tributaries, and then pass through two settlements, Lamthali and Sudame. In times of low water, the trail may even cross the main river to avoid steep areas. Do what the locals are doing, but stay on the northeast (left) bank except for these short diversions. **Hille** (5000 ft, 1524 m) is reached in **2 hours,** and shortly beyond is **TirkheDUgaa** (5175 ft, 1577 m). Farther on, the branches of the Bhurungdi Khola are crossed on several bridges (5075 ft, 1547 m). The steepest climb so far, up to picturesque **Ulleri** (6800 ft, 2073 m), a *Magar* village, takes **2 hours** from Hille.

If you want to pace the climb, there are 3767 steps to ascend to Ulleri; trekker Lance Hart counted them! Note the handsome slate roofs on the village houses. Near the last house is the new stone commemorating the death of a Dutch trekker. Higher up, at a *chautaaraa* on the left, is a worn rock tablet faintly inscribed as follows: "Once, sweet, bright joy, like their lost children, an Ulleri child." It is a memorial to 18-month-old Ben, the son of anthropologist John Hitchcock. Ben died here in 1961 while his father was doing fieldwork.

Forests of the Temperate Zone

The temperate zone can be divided into the lower temperate zone (approximately 6500 to 9000 ft/2000 to 2700 m in the west and 5500 to 8000 ft/1700 to 2400 m in the east) and upper temperate zone (9000 to 10,200 ft/2700 to 3100 m in the west and center and 7800 to 9200 ft/2400 to 2800 m in the east). Oak, rhododendron, and fir forests dominate the zone. Upper temperate forests are much less disturbed than those lower down, especially those in the west, because they mainly lie below the limit of cultivation.

In wetter parts of the lower temperate region, there are mixed broad-leaves with abundant laurels (*Lauracea*) and oaks (broad-leaved evergreens with acorns): *Quercus lamellosa* [*bAshi, shaalsi, gogane*], a very large tree with a massive spreading crown, and alternate, toothed, oval leaves with dark green uppersides and bluish green undersides, in the east; and *Q. floribunda* [*bele kharmendo*], with small, leathery, spiny-margined leaves, in the west. Drier, lower temperate forests consist of *Q. lanata* [*bAAjh*], with leaves dark shiny green above and rust-colored below; *Q. leucotrichophora*, with undersides of leaves covered in dense, white, woolly hairs; and Himalayan blue pine (*Pinus wallichiana* [*gobre sallo*]), a conifer with clusters of long, cylindrical cones and drooping, gray-green needles in clusters of five.

Rhododendrons [*lali gurAAs*] are common in the upper temperate zone in the center and east, either as the dominant tree or scattered among other forest types. They grow as shrubs or trees and are broad-leaved evergreens with shiny, leathery leaves. The rhododendron is the national flower. The gorgeous flowers, colored red, pink, and white, are the most conspicuous Himalayan feature in this and the subalpine zones.

Forests of *Q. semecarpifolia* [*khasru*], with leathery, sometimes prickly leaves and globular fruits that have concave cups, occur throughout the upper temperate region, especially on south-facing slopes. Mixed broad-leaved forests grow in wetter places, while coniferous forests occur in the west.

Look for Himalayan blue pine; Himalayan hemlock (Tsuga dumosa [thinge salla]), a conifer with distinctive small, egg-shaped cones and flat needles that are dark green on the top and silvery white underneath, in two rows; and others, including Himalayan silver fir (Abies spectabilis [talis patra]), which has flat needles with two whitish lines on their undersides spread around the branchlets, and west Himalayan spruce (Picea smithiana [jhule sallo]), a floppy-looking tree with vaguely four-sided, pendulous branches, and needles arranged in a spiral, leaving scars where they have fallen off. In the drainage of the Thulo Bheri and Karnali, look for the Himalayan cedar, or deodar (Cedrus deodara [devdaar]), with its pyramidal crown and three-sided needles mostly scattered in tufts on the branches, and cones that have fan-shaped scales. Also limited to the west is Himalayan cypress (Cupressus torulosa [raaj sallo]), a large tree with pyramidal crown, horizontal to up-sloping branches, small, flat, triangular leaves that overlap each other closely, tiny cones, and gray-brown bark that peels off in strips. The larch (Larix griffithiana [lekh sallo]), a deciduous tree, golden in autumn, is found in dry inner valleys of the northeast corner as well as in north central Nepal.

Bamboo (*Bambusa* spp. and *Arundinaria* spp.) flourishes in very high rainfall areas. In a few places, such as in the Modi Khola valley on the Annapurna Sanctuary trek, it forms dense stands up to 7 m high. Elsewhere, bamboo occurs in the forest understory. The damper forests of the center and east are draped in mosses and lichens. In spring, beautiful epiphytic orchids, such as the white *Coelogyne,* bloom on the tree trunks. Ferns and numerous wildflowers, including fritillaries, primulas, and many orchids [*sunaakhari*], grow in damp ravines and along streams.

Note the following associations: Himalayan fir in rhododendron and oak forests on northern slopes, and with Q. semecarpifolia on southern aspects; west Himalayan spruce in the drier region around Jumla but as far east as Ganesh Himal; and Himalayan hemlock, found almost exclusively on northern aspects.

From Ulleri, the trail climbs steadily, enters lush oak forest, and crosses numerous small streams. It is a great place for bird-watching. An hour above Ulleri you come to Banthanti (7775 ft, 2307 m), meaning "a place in the forest," and 1½ hours later to Nayathanti (8550 ft, 2606 m), literally meaning "new place," both having recently expanded with lodges. Lone trekkers have been attacked by bandits in this forest. If by yourself, hire a porter or join up with others. This caution applies all the way to Chitre.

The trail emerges at **GhoRepani** (9250 ft, 2819 m), a cluster of hotels and an ACAP office below the pass some **3 hours** from Ulleri. GhoRepani, meaning "horse water," is now a far cry from the one building I saw on my first trek in Nepal in 1969. Then it truly was a watering hole for the horse caravans that traveled between Pokhara and Mustang. There is public telephone service here. There are more hotels at the pass, GhoRepani Deorali, which is 200 ft (61 m) higher. Trekkers should make certain they catch the views, either from the pass itself, which is now incredibly deforested, or from east or west of the pass. On my first trek, there were no views from the pass, as it was in a dense rhododendron forest.

Poon ("Pun," as it is pronounced, is the name of a *Magar* clan) Hill (10,478 ft, 3194 m) on the ridge to the west is a popular viewpoint. Reach the hill in less than 1 hour. Signs point the way to Poon Hill from GhoRepani and from the pass.

The best flour is ground by hand.
(Mary Anne Mercer)

Make sure you take all the water you can to Poon Hill, as sources there are very limited. There are no facilities there, though there once were. Enterprising Nepalis sometimes sell hot chocolate during peak-season frosty mornings. Hopefully reforestation will return this area to the serene place it once was. Views of Dhaulagiri and the Kali Gandaki gorge are best in the early morning, when it can get pretty crowded. Some people enjoy the view best an hour after sunrise, when most trekkers have left. The south face of Dhaulagiri, the most impressive feature seen, was climbed first by a Japanese party in 1978 via the left buttress and by a Yugoslav team in 1981 via the eastern. The most challenging central section awaits an ascent.

From the pass, a trail follows the ridge to the east to link with the trail from Ghandruk. The views to the east along the ridge are very impressive too. This route, which will be described later, offers a different return to Pokhara for those who have traveled north from Ulleri.

To continue to Thak Khola, descend through rhododendron forest, then prickly-leafed oak, to cultivated areas. Facilities begin 300 ft (91 m) below the pass. Reach the right fork to Ghandruk (8020 ft, 2444 m), with **Chitre** below, and cross landslides to **PhalaTe** (7400 ft, 2256 m), before reaching **Sikha** (6820 ft, 2079 m) in a notch that is **2 hours** from the pass. This unforgettable descent offers views of the immense south face of Dhaulagiri to the north. There are plenty of facilities all along here. Reach **Ghara** (6000 ft, 1828 m) less than **1 hour** from Sikha.

Questions to Ponder: Typical Days

What is a typical day like for an average person in the hills? How does this differ between men and women? How much do people rest? What are the sleeping arrangements in Nepali homes? What do people seem to talk about with one another?

Continue through a notch now called Durbin Danda ("binocular ridge"), and descend steeply to the south (left) bank of the Ghara Khola. Cross it on a wooden bridge (3850 ft, 1173 m) and reach the few houses called Ghara Khola above the junction of the Ghara Khola and the Kali Gandaki. As the junction of two rivers, this area is sacred and has a little temple below. The trail to Beni continues south on the east (left) bank of the Kali Gandaki, but you should head upstream, cross the Kali Gandaki on a suspension bridge, and go on to **Tatopani** (3900 ft, 1189 m),

1½ hours from Ghara. Nilgiri is the summit in the valley floor, and the photograph of it silhouetted by porters crossing the old suspension bridge here graced the covers of the first and only coffee-table book on Nepal for decades. If you head up to Kagbeni, you will go around Nilgiri to the north side.

In September 1998, a large landslide dammed the Kali Gandaki south of Tatopani for 7 hours. Water levels rose, flooding several homes before the Kali Gandaki cut a passage through the western end and waters receded. There is a 1000-kilowatt mini-hydrogenerator upstream, beyond the Miristi Khola, north of town. This facility drops water after diverting it through a hillside where the river takes a bend.

Tatopani, a prosperous *Thakali* town, takes its name (*taato paani*, literally "hot water") from the hot springs located along the banks of the river, near the middle of town, reached by a trail to the riverbank. There are currently two pools, one very hot and the other hot. Pay the usage fee to maintain the facility. Don't foul the water with soap even though some locals may. Wash in the effluent below the pools, or in the river, rinse, and then soak in the hot water. Be discreet and modest, as the Nepalis are.

The Kali Gandaki Valley—A Great Biogeographic Divide

When trekking up the Kali Gandaki valley to the Thak Khola, you experience changes in flora and fauna that are more dramatic than anywhere else in Nepal. For example, in 1 day you can climb down from the arid Tibetan steppe flora at Tukche through temperate coniferous forests to reach the humid subtropical zone around Tatopani. The Kali Gandaki has cut the world's deepest river gorge right through the Himalaya. The river runs from the Tibetan plateau to the north, through almost the center of Nepal and the middle of the Himalaya.

The valley is a biogeographic divide for Himalayan flora and fauna. Forests to the west of the valley are generally drier and have fewer plant species than eastern forests. In their field guide *Birds of Nepal*, the Flemings point out that the Kali Gandaki is a very distinctive break in bird distribution. Some species, such as the fire-tailed myzornis and the brown parrotbill, are restricted to the valley and farther east, while others, the cheer pheasant for instance, only breed in the valley and westward. Forests to the east of the valley are significantly richer in bird species than western forests, even taking into account that western forests are relatively poorly recorded.

TATOPANI TO MUKTINATH

Head north from Tatopani, passing the few houses of Nagdhunga and then Jalkale, near the junction of the Miristi Khola and the Kali Gandaki. Beyond is BhuiTe, where a suspension bridge leads to the powerhouse, which you see on the east side. Stay on the west (right) bank of the Kali Gandaki and pass through Sukebagar to **Dana** (4600 ft, 1402 m) by the Ghatte Khola. This wealthy, stretched-out former customs post is reached in about **1½ hours** from Tatopani. In the lower end of Dana you can see the spectacular west face of Annapurna. It took me five trips before the clouds cleared enought for me to see it. Continue on the west (right) bank to Titar, and then climb to the few houses of **Rupse Chhaharo** (5350 ft, 1631 m), named after the waterfall above the bridge. Rupse Chhaharo is reached in **1¼ hours** from Dana. Note the appropriate technology water mills here.

There are two route choices here: the east (left) or the west (right) bank. The east-side trail is currently the more used and is probably safer in the monsoon, but inquire locally about conditions. Trekkers have succumbed, slipping on this path. The more spectacular west-side route suffered a serious slide in 1988 and has been repaired.

EAST SIDE ROUTE

To follow the east-side trail between Rupse Chhaharo and Ghasa, fork right just after the bridge at the waterfall. Descend to cross the Kali Gandaki on a wooden bridge (5360 ft, 1634 m) at a narrow point in the gorge. Head upstream, keeping close to the powerful torrent, now chocolate brown carrying sand and soil south. Go through a big slide area to Kopche Pani, with several small clusters of tea houses (5500 ft, 1676 m), in **30 minutes.** A further **hour's** steep climb on a scree-boulder trail brings you to a similar spot, **Pahiro Tabla** (meaning "landslide place," 6400 ft, 1951 m). As you go along, look for the trail on the west side and the ancient pilgrim trails above it. Along the way, you may see monkeys in the forests. In another **45 minutes,** reach the suspension bridge and trail junction (6400 ft, 1951 m) a few minutes below Ghasa.

WEST SIDE ROUTE

On the west-side route, climb above the tea houses of Rupse Chhaharo to reach Kabre (5600 ft, 1707 m) in less than 30 minutes. Kabre is the northernmost village inhabited by hill castes in the Kali Gandaki valley. From Kabre, continue north along the steep cliff side to where the valley narrows spectacularly and the cascading river torrent resounds across the canyon walls. Probably the world's steepest and deepest large gorge, the gradient to the summit of Dhaulagiri is more than 1 mi (1.6 km) vertical to 1 mi (1.6 km) horizontal (1:1.05 to be exact). The steepest part, however, is south of the line between the two summits. Just beyond the main gorge you can see the old trail, cut like a three-sided tunnel into the wall. Above it are older pilgrimage routes. Pilgrims traveled this dangerous trail to Muktinath as long ago as 300 B.C. Beyond the most impressive narrow section, the trail crosses a boulder-strewn flat and reaches a *chautaaraa*, where the east-side trail rejoins it 2 hours from Kabre and a few minutes south of Ghasa.

It takes 30 minutes to get through **Ghasa** (6700 ft, 2040 m), a sprawling, flat-roofed *Thakali* village in the middle of which an army barrack sits.

Note how remarkably the land has changed over this short stretch, as the climate becomes colder and drier. To the south, you may see lizards throughout the year, but from here northward none are seen in the cold season. Similarly, as you head north, you will encounter more pine forests and fewer broad-leaved trees. The houses beyond here have flat roofs because there is less rainfall. The changes will be even more dramatic farther along. Be careful not to twist your ankle on the river-worn trail boulders.

To continue north from Ghasa, cross a tributary, and pass through Kaiku and the few houses of Gumaaune (literally "walking around"). There is a huge landslide scar on the east side. Reach a still active bridge over the Lete Khola (8000 ft, 2438 m), a tributary from the west, and cross it to a lodge. **Lete** (8100 ft, 2469 m), some 30 minutes beyond, is **2 hours** from Ghasa. There is a trail coming in from the southwest before you cross the Lete Khola. It offers a high route over the south shoulder of Dhaulagiri to Beni. Annapurna I, the first 8000-m peak ever climbed, can be seen to the east from Lete. Again, note the change in ecology; Lete gets 124 mm (49 in.) of rain a year, whereas a mere half day to the north Tukche gets only 20 mm (8 in.).

Heading north, pass the police check post in the spread-out village of Lete, which then blends into **Kalopani** (8300 ft, 2530 m). Sunsets from Kalopani and Lete are memorable. Cross a tributary north of town to reach your choice of two bridges over the Kali Gandaki in **30 minutes** from lower Lete. In the dry season, cross it if there is a good temporary bridge to cross back over the Kali Gandaki farther upstream, which is only possible in low water. Check what others are doing. If you cross to the east (left) bank here, the trail passes through Dhampu and KokheThAATi before crossing a series of bridges back to the west (right) bank just below **Larjung** (8400 ft, 2560 m), **2 hours** from Kalopani. Oftentimes cool wades and icy fords are necessary.

In the monsoon, or if you wish to reach the area below the southeast Dhaulagiri Icefall, stay on the west (right) bank and cross a river delta with its alluvial fan to reach the houses of Chatang in 30 minutes. Just beyond is a *chautaaraa* with a plaque commemorating the 1969 Dhaulagiri tragedy, in which seven members of a U.S. expedition were killed in an ice avalanche. The trail to the icefall cuts off left just to the north. If continuing on to Larjung, cross another tributary, enter a pine-and-juniper forest, and then cross the broad delta of the Ghatte Khola, wading where necessary, to rejoin the forest. Larjung is just beyond, perhaps 2¼ hours from Kalopani. To the west is the incredibly foreshortened summit of Dhaulagiri, almost 3.5 mi (5.5 km) higher. The temples above Larjung are where the local deities are kept for Thakali clans residing here. There is a festival honoring them every twelve years.

From Larjung, head north, cross a tributary, and in a few minutes enter the fascinating town of **Khobang** (8400 ft, 2560 m). The trail passes through a tunnel, and doors to the houses open off it. The village is thus protected from the strong winds that blow up the valley almost every afternoon. The northern, open segment of the series of settlements is called Kanti. The dry-season path keeps closer to the river. Cross another tributary, either on a temporary bridge or upstream on a more substantial one. **Tukche** (8500 ft, 2591 m), an historically important town, is **1 hour** beyond Khobang.

Pheasants of the Temperate Zone

Nepal is famous for its variety of Himalayan pheasants. There are six species, all of which can be seen in the Annapurna Conservation Area. Most are shy and difficult to see unless you flush them from the forest. They call frequently in spring. The Kalij pheasant (Lophura leucomelana [kaalij], length 60 to 68 cm) inhabits all types of forest with dense undergrowth, especially near water, and also occurs in subtropical and tropical zones. The male is mainly black with a long tail and red on the face; the female is reddish brown with a shorter tail. The Koklass pheasant (Pucrasia macrolopha [phokraas], length 52 to 61 cm) inhabits oak and conifer forests from the Modi Khola valley westward. The male is dark, with a long crest and tail, black head, and white ear patch. The female is brownish, with a shorter crest and tail. It crows loudly at dawn. The satyr tragopan, or crimson-horned pheasant (Tragopan satyra [munaal], length 59 to 68 cm), is found in damp oak and rhododendron forests with dense undergrowth. The male is bright red, spotted with white and with a blue wattle; the female is mottled brown. In spring, it makes a strange, mammallike "waaa" noise at dawn and dusk.

Tukche was once an important center for the trade of Nepali grain for Tibetan salt through the valley of the Thak Khola. *Thakali Subbha,* or customs contractors, controlled it and exacted taxes at Tukche in the summer and at Dana in the winter. The handsome architecture and great wood carving in Tukche attests to the importance of this town. By the middle of this century competition had reduced this trade, and the enterprising *Thakali* turned their attention south and became more involved in business ventures around Pokhara and in the Tarai. Their spread throughout many of the trade routes in Nepal resulted in the establishment of many *bhaTTi* even before trekking became popular. With the coming of foreigners, the *Thakali* developed hotel facilities for them, and many of their family homes have been developed into lodges. I urge you to try to find a traditional *bhaTTi* and sample a good Nepali meal of *daal bhaat tarkaari* (lentils, rice, and vegetables) or at least have such a meal in a tourist restaurant. The *Thakali* seem to prosper in whatever they turn to. In comparing my visits to this region twenty years apart, I find the improvements impressive—water systems, latrines, more schools (indeed, *functioning* schools), better trails, more varieties of crops, and cleaner homes. The *Thakali* have always exhibited a strong ethnic group consciousness, and Thak Khola is their homeland. Many of the towns have been electrified through the installation of a mini–hydroelectric generator across and up from Khobang on the Chhokopani Khola, which produces 260 kilowatts. Visit the active *gomba* at the northeast end of town and tour the distillery (the first of many to the north).

A strong wind blows from the south up the valley, beginning in the late morning and lasting most of the day. This is caused when the air mass over the plateau to the north warms, rises, and creates a pressure difference. The best time to head south is in the early morning when the wind may be from the north. As you go up the valley from Tukche, notice that there is relatively little vegetation on the valley floor itself, but there are trees and forests on the walls. The valley floor is in a rain shadow due to the strong winds. When the wind is blowing, you may notice that there are no clouds over the center of the valley, but clouds do hang on the sides.

A trail to Dhampus Pass (described later) goes up the hill to the west of the *gomba* at Tukche. For variety, you could cross the Thak Khola north of Tukche and visit Chhimgaon and Chaira and then recross below Marpha. Most people will stay on the west bank to reach **Marpha** (8750 ft, 2667 m) in **1½ hours**. About 15 minutes before Marpha, pass by the Marpha Agricultural Farm, which has introduced many of the new crops you see around.

Marpha, a charming town, has a fine sewer system—a series of canals flowing down the streets. There are plenty of choices for accommodation and food here especially given the variety of fruits and vegetables available. Some of the hotels here, and also in Jomosom, advertise pony rides as far as Muktinath. Visit the new large *gomba* in the center of town. Dhampus Pass can also be reached from Marpha.

To continue upstream, leave the town through the *chorten* and cross first a tributary and then the Pongkyu Khola, another alluvial fan, with a water mill, that flows from the west. Along the trail you will see willow plantations, part of a reforestation project. The town of Syang is beyond, and its monastery is up the hill a bit farther. On certain days during late October to early December, monks stage dance festivals in the *gomba* of Marpha, Syang, and Tukche. Somewhat similar to the *Mani-rimdu* festivals of Solu-Khumbu, they are definitely worth seeing. The Nepali name for such a festival is *dyokyapsi*. Consider a side trip east across the river to the *gomba* on the hillock with its commanding views of the valley.

Peoples of Central Nepal: Thakali and Other Peoples of the Thak Khola

Above the dramatic gorge of the Kali Gandaki, north from the town of Ghasa, is the region known as Thak Khola. *Thakali* villages line the route north along the high Kali Gandaki valley. Their language is very close to *Gurung* and *Tamang*, but their cultural history has been more influenced by Tibet. The *Thakali* are noted for their strong trading spirit, which they developed as middlemen in the formerly very active Nepal–Tibet rice and salt trade through their region. The largest town until recently was Tukche, the center of the *Thakali* ethnic culture and, for many decades earlier in this century, the regional center of the Tibetan salt trade. Since 1959, when the Tibetan border trade diminished, the Tibetan salt business has come to a virtual standstill in Thak Khola, and many *Thakali* have turned southward for other economic opportunities. Today, Jomosom, the district center north of Tukche, is much larger and at times Tukche appears almost abandoned. Some *Thakali* have dropped their Tibetan and Buddhist predilections and have adopted Nepali culture and Hinduism. Some have moved permanently out of Thak Khola to take advantage of business ventures in the larger bazaars and trade centers of Nepal.

Despite their uniform appearances, Thak Khola is actually the home of two similar ethnic groups and one quite distinct group. The *Thakali* proper live between Ghasa and Tukche. North of them, and virtually indistinguishable, are a people known as *PaunchgaaUle* (which literally means "people of the five villages"—Marpha, Syang, Chiwong, Cherok, and Jomosom-Thini). The *PaunchgaaUle* sometimes call themselves *Thakali* but intermarriage between them and their "true" *Thakali* neighbors is not condoned. The third group are a *BhoTiya* people who inhabit the valley of Muktinath, from Kagbeni east to the Muktinath shrine at the base of Thorung Pass. They are also sometimes called the *BaragaaUle,* or "people of the twelve villages." Muktinath is a special place to these *BhoTiya* people, as it is a Hindu–Buddhist shrine of great significance. There are many religious observances throughout the year that attract Hindu and Buddhist pilgrims. The most important event to local Buddhists is the celebration of the *Yartung* festival in the fall, when the animals have been brought down from the high pastures for the winter. *Yartung* is highlighted by horse racing and great revelry. For Hindus, one of the largest events of the year falls on the occasion of Janai Purnima, the "full moon day (*purnima*) of the sacred cord (*janai*)." The sacred cord is worn by men of the highest twice-born Hindu castes, as a sign of their privileged social status and religious sanctity. More about Muktinath as a sacred center is given later in this section.

Cross a tributary farther up the valley, and reach **Jomosom** (8900 ft, 2713 m), the capital for the Mustang District, **1½ hours** from Marpha. There is a STOL airstrip here with scheduled service to Kathmandu, but because of the winds service can be unreliable. Winter winds regularly reach 30 to 40 knots, with gusts to 70! Some of the airlines now use helicopters to service this area. If you fly in and head upvalley to rarefied air, beware of altitude illness. Other facilities include banks, a hospital, rather luxurious food and accommodations, some climbing cliffs with a sign welcoming you there, and, of course, a police check post. An ecomuseum has opened at the southern end of town and has informative displays. This town has prospered immensely over the years and has expanded to both sides of the river to provide space for the many government employees and offices. Many of the pony caravans bring food to Jomosom to feed the bureaucracy.

The countryside to the north is very arid, not unlike the Tibetan plateau farther north. To the south, Dhaulagiri impressively guards the Thak Khola valley. It is much less foreshortened than at Larjung. To the east, across the river on a shelf of land, is the traditional town of Thini (9500 ft, 2897 m), reached in 30 minutes from Jomosom. The inhabitants are technically not Buddhists (though they may say otherwise) but followers of Bon-po, the ancient religion that antedated Tibetan Buddhism.

Muktinath Pilgrimage

Muktinath, located in a poplar grove, is a sacred shrine and pilgrimage site for Hindus and Buddhists. The *Mahabharata,* the ancient Hindu epic written about 300 B.C., mentions Muktinath as Shaligrama because of its ammonite fossils called *shaligram.* Brahma, the creator, made an offering here by lighting a fire on water. You can see this miracle (burning natural gas) in a small Buddhist shrine (*gomba*) below the main Hindu temple (*mandir*). Many people from Mustang and other areas come to sell handicrafts to the pilgrims. Some sell the *shaligram,* the mollusk fossil dating from a period roughly 140 to 165 million years ago before the uplifting of the Himalaya. These objects, treasured for worship by Hindus, are said to represent several deities, principally those associated with Vishnu, the Lord of Salvation. You are apt to find them along the flats north of Jomosom and for sale in Baudha. You are not allowed to export them, however.

Hindus named the site Muktichhetra, meaning "place of salvation (*mukti*)," because they believed that bathing there gives salvation after death. Springs are piped into 108 water spouts in the shape of boars' heads near the temple dedicated to Vishnu, the focal point for Hindus. The boar was the third incarnation of Vishnu. Because Buddha was the eighth incarnation, the Hindus tolerate the Buddhists here. The Buddhists consider the image of Vishnu in this typically *Newar* style temple as the Bodhisatva Avalokiteshwara. Vishnu is in the shape of an icon as well as a large ammonite fossil. The same fossil image is worshiped by Buddhists as Gawa Jogpa, the "serpent deity."

The miraculous fire revered by Buddhists and Hindus burns on water, stones, and earth, and is inside the Jwala Mai Temple, south of the police check post. Natural gas jets burn in small recesses curtained under the altar to Avalokiteshwara. On the left the earth burns, in the middle water burns, and on the right the stone burns. One flame has died out; only two remain lighted. Sherpas and Buddhist porters with you may ask you for a bottle to take some of the "water that burns" with them. Be sure to leave an offering of money for temple upkeep.

Padmasambhava, who brought Buddhism to Tibet in the eighth century, is believed to have meditated here. His "footprints" are on a rock in the northwest corner of this sacred place. On their way to Tibet, the eighty-four *siddha* ("great magicians") left their pilgrim staffs, which grew into the poplars at the site. You will find many old *chorten* and temples cared for by Nyingmapa nuns or old women from the nearby villages. A full moon is an especially auspicious time to visit Muktinath. In the full moon of August–September, thousands of pilgrims arrive.

Up the valley east of Thini is Tilicho Pass and Tilicho Tal. The latter, at 16,140 ft (4919 m), is one of the highest, most spectacular lakes in the world. Once open to trekking, this area has often been closed to access from the west because of a Nepali army camp on this side of the pass, used for mountain warfare training. You might have noticed their "R&R" facilities in Jomosom.

To continue on to Kagbeni and Muktinath, you can travel on either side, depending on the condition of a temporary bridge over the Kali Gandaki. If you stay on the east (left) side, you will either have to climb to avoid wading the separate rivulets of the river or stay on the valley floor close to the river and get your feet wet. If you take the west (right) bank trail, there may be a temporary bridge crossing upstream. Either way, in 1½ **hours** reach the trail junction of Chyancha-Lhrenba (9050 ft, 2758 m). This place is known locally as **Eklai BhaTTi,** meaning "lonely inn," which bespeaks a former time.

The left fork continues up the river to Kagbeni (9200 ft, 2804 m) in 30 minutes, while the right ascends out of the valley and heads more directly to Muktinath. The right fork reaches the junction (10,350 ft, 3155 m) of the trail from Kagbeni to Muktinath in 1½ hours.

The name Kagbeni aptly reflects the town's character—*kak* means "blockade" in the local dialect and *beni* means "junction of two rivers"—and this citadel does effectively block the valley. River junctions are especially sacred to the local people. Since the town is at the confluence of trails from the north, south, east, and west, the ancient king who sat here could control and tax the exchange of grain from the south and wool and salt from the north. The ruins of his palace, which can still be seen, are a reminder of the ancient kingdoms that predated the unification of Nepal. Some scholars believe the family that ruled here was related to the ancient kings of Jumla. The Sakyapa monastery here is run down but worth a visit. You may see two large terra-cotta images of the protector deities of the town—a male at the north end and the remains of a female at the south. This mingling of old animistic beliefs with those of the more developed religions is common in Nepal. People here call themselves *Gurung* but are clearly not the same as the *Gurung* to the south. People from Tibet who have settled in Nepal often call themselves *Gurung* to facilitate assimilation. This practice has continued with the recent immigration of Tibetan refugees in the 1980s.

The impressive folding of the cliffs west of town illustrates the powerful forces of orogeny. You can just make out the crest of Thorung La up the valley to the east of town. Try to make out Kagbeni from the pass. The trail to Mustang and the kingdom of Lo crosses the Kali Gandaki here and heads up the west (right) bank. There is a police check post in Kagbeni, at the northern limit for trekkers who have not made special arrangements to go to Lomanthang.

To go to Muktinath from Kagbeni, cross the Dzong Khola, the tributary from the east, and head east through terraces to the trail's junction (10,350 ft, 3155 m) with the trail from Chyancha-Lhrenba in 1½ hours.

Whether you go to Kagbeni or not, it will take **3 to 3½ hours** to reach the junction from Jomosom. Continue east, noting the caves on the north side of the valley. So ancient are these caves that no one remembers if they were used by hermits or troglodytes. On a clear day, the walk can be ethereal, as the dry valley sparkles and the north wall seems suspended close to you. Climb to **Khingar;** the old part of town is north of the trail. Continue to **Jharkot** (11,850 ft, 3612 m), a crumbling but still impressive fortress perched on a ridge 1½ **hours** from the trail junction above Kagbeni. Jharkot, called Dzar by Tibetans, is believed to have been the home of the ruling house of this valley. Note how some houses around the ruins of the fort are made of blocks of earth.

Continue climbing and contouring, often staying near an irrigation trough. Along the trail there are little piles of stones made by pilgrims returning from Muktinath in hopes of obtaining a better reincarnation. Go on to **Ranipauwa** (12,200 ft, 3718 m), a village of sorts, with a large rest house for pilgrims, many hotels, and a police check post you should visit. It is **40 minutes** from Jharkot. Across the valley you can see the extensive ruins of Dzong ("castle" in Tibetan) and the town built around it, the original seat of the king of this valley. Consider a side trip to there from Jharkot or here. **Muktinath** (12,475 ft, 3802 m) is less than **15 minutes** farther. Dhaulagiri (26,795 ft, 8167 m) looms impressively to the south. It was first climbed from the north, the view you see here, by a German expedition in 1960. Trekkers are not allowed to stay inside the fenced compound. The considerable cement poured here has decidedly changed the character of this previously locally cared-for sacred spot.

To the east is Thorung La (17,700 ft, 5416 m), which leads to Manang. Crossing the pass from Muktinath to Manang is more difficult than crossing in the other direction, for in the dry season there are few if any suitable campsites with water on this side of the pass. It is a very long day to ascend from Muktinath to the pass and then to descend to the first campsite on the other side. In season, there may be a hotel for trekkers partway up. Altitude illness may jeopardize those who are unacclimatized. Crossing from Manang, on the other hand, is easier because of the comparatively long time spent at high altitudes before approaching the pass and because of the higher campsites below the east side of the pass. The pass is often crossed from Muktinath, but it certainly is more difficult and hazardous. Under no condition should you ascend from either direction unless the entire party, including porters, is well equipped to camp in snow should a storm arise. The trail descriptions for the Manang to Muktinath crossing are given with the Manang section later in this chapter.

RETURN JOURNEY VARIATIONS

On the return journey, consider some variations, such as returning to Marpha via Thinigaon, which is approached from Jomosom on the east (left) bank of the river; returning to Pokhara by following the Kali Gandaki south from Tatopani past Beni, to Baglung, where you meet the road; and returning from Chitre to Ghandruk and Dhampus. These last three variations are described in greater detail later, but first some side trips out of the Thak Khola valley are described. All are strenuous trips to substantial altitudes where food, fuel, and shelter must be carried. At certain times of the year, snow can make the trips almost impossible. Parties should be prepared for cold at any time of the year. It is always best to have someone along who is familiar with the route.

DHAMPUS PASS

Dhampus Pass (17,000 ft, 5184 m) connects the valley of the Thak Khola with Hidden Valley. It lies beyond the treeline and is often snowed in. Huts used for pasturing yaks can be used for shelter and cooking en route to the pass. There are no facilities at the pass. Carry food, fuel, and shelter. Temperatures below freezing can always be expected and in the winter months the temperature drops below 0°F (-18°C). A trip to the pass is ideal for those who want a more intense experience of the mountains. Reach it from Tukche or Marpha by going to some yak

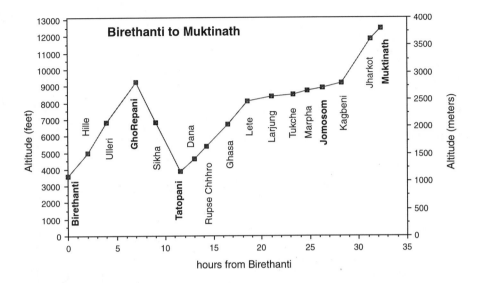

huts (13,000 ft, 3962 m) the first day and to the pass the second. This may be too rapid an ascent for many people. If you are unprepared to spend a night at the pass, you could go up and return to the yak huts in a day.

To trek from Tukche to Dhampus Pass, go to the large open field at the north end of the village. Just behind the village, to the east, is a steep earth cliff. Follow a plainly defined switchback trail to the top and continue along the ridge behind the cliff. You pass through scattered apricot trees and horse pasturage for 1 mi (1.6 km) to arrive at the base of a high rock cliff. Keeping well to the east, the trail ascends this steep but not technically difficult cliff and comes out just above where the ridge plunges down to the Kali Gandaki far below. You are now on the end of the ridge defining the north side of the Dhampus Khola. There are fantastic views up the Kali Gandaki toward Mustang and a panorama from Tilicho Peak in the east round through the Nilgiris, the Annapurnas, and Dhaulagiri to Tukche Peak in the southwest.

Up to this point, the trail is fairly well defined. But on the ridge it degenerates into myriad cow and yak trails, and you are pretty much on your own. Continue up the north side of the ridge for about 2 hours until you come to a low point (relatively speaking), then cross the south (Dhampus Khola) side of the ridge. Looking up the Dhampus Khola valley, you can see a large rock ridge going off your ridge and dropping steeply into the Khola. It is perpendicular to your line of travel. Traverse upward slightly toward this ridge to a wide trail, which takes you around and behind the ridge. This is the main trail to the upper portion of the Dhampus Khola valley and is used by local herders taking their yaks up to graze during the summer. Yak yogurt is delicious—during the warm season you should try to buy some at the herders' huts along the way.

After crossing the rock ridge, climb obliquely upward by obvious routes to Dhampus Pass, which is not visible at this point. If there is any possibility of cloudy weather, hire a local man from Tukche as a guide. Once clouds settle in, it is very easy to get lost. If fog becomes a problem, don't descend to the Dhampus Khola to escape, because the Khola is impassable due to rock cliffs in its lower portions. If you become confused in a fog, stay up high and traverse eastward back toward

Marpha or Tukche. Again, be sure to descend if severe symptoms of altitude sickness come on.

Beyond the pass, you can descend into the upper (southern) end of Hidden Valley for excellent views of Dhaulagiri's north face and the glaciated pass called French Pass, which lies between Dhaulagiri and its sister peak to the west, Dhaula Himal. You may see the remains of a plane near the pass, the Swiss Pilatus Porter that crashed in 1961 while ferrying people and loads from Pokhara for the Dhaulagiri Expedition. You may encounter semiwild yak herds, snow leopards, and blue sheep in Hidden Valley.

DHAULAGIRI ICEFALL

The area below the east Dhaulagiri Icefall abounds with yak pastures and was the location of the 1969 American Base Camp. At a lower altitude than Dhampus Pass, it has correspondingly less severe conditions. The views of the mountains are excellent, possibly better than at Dhampus Pass.

To reach this area, proceed from the trail junction north of the few houses of Chatang between Kalopani and Larjung. The trail leaves the valley near a *chautaaraa* with a plaque commemorating the seven members of the 1969 American Expedition to Dhaulagiri who died in an ice avalanche. Again, it is best to hire a local guide. The area below the icefall (12,400 ft, 3780 m) can be visited in a very long day from the Kali Gandaki, but it's better to camp and enjoy the sunrise and sunset. Beware of avalanches in the vicinity of the icefall.

NORTH ANNAPURNA BASE CAMP

The route to the original Annapurna Base Camp was discovered by the 1950 French Expedition to Annapurna led by Maurice Herzog. The French first tried to climb Dhaulagiri but found it beyond their capabilities and instead tried to find a way to the base of Annapurna. They had difficulty getting there from the Kali Gandaki, and the route still has a bad reputation. It is seldom used except by shepherds and mountaineering expeditions. However, in the relatively snow-free early fall and late spring, the route is neither very difficult nor dangerous. The trail is often indistinct and traverses steep grassy slopes. Porters do not like this trail, but it is certainly no worse than little-used trails in many other areas of mountain wilderness.

The views along the way are spectacular. As the trail climbs steeply out of the Kali Gandaki valley, the incredible gorge becomes more and more impressive. The views of Dhaulagiri and Annapurna from the crest of the ridge separating the Kali Gandaki from the Miristi Khola are breathtaking. Only from this perch (14,000 ft, 4267 m), some 7000 ft (2134 m) above the valley floor, can you appreciate just how high these mountains are. From the foreshortened view from Kalopani, it is hard to believe that Dhaulagiri is the sixth highest mountain in the world. If you venture beyond the base camp toward Camp One, on the north side of Annapurna, you can appreciate the impressive features of that side of the mountain.

There are neither villages nor shelter from Chhoya onward, so you must be self-sufficient for at least 5 days. It is best to hire someone from Chhoya to show the way. In times of high water, it may be impossible to cross the Miristi Khola and reach the base camp without building a bridge, an undertaking most trekkers prefer to avoid. But with the increasing number of expeditions to Annapurna, the chance of finding a usable bridge is good. Check beforehand to find out if there has been a recent expedition. In low water, the river can be forded with some difficulty downstream. If there is no bridge, consider at least climbing to the height of land for the spectacular views.

Yartung Festival

At about the same time as the major pilgrimage to Muktinath in the full moon of August–September, local Tibetan villagers of the valley hold a great horse festival called Yartung—a time of horse racing, gambling, and general merriment. With its themes of "food, sex, and violence," it bears a striking resemblance to the European Carnival, according to anthropologist Charles Ramble. This is held on the race grounds of Ranipauwa, adjacent to the Muktinath pilgrimage site in the Mustang District. BhoTiya people from all over Bargee (the Muktinath or Dzong river valley), and Lo-Manthang (upper Mustang), and some from Manang (east of Mustang) and Dolpo (west) attend. The men of BaragaaU region compete in a day of horse racing, a raucous occasion spiced by drinking and gambling in tents set up on the hills around the small community below Muktinath. The day begins with processions of laymen and monks in colorful attire, some riding equally decorated horses, from each of the surrounding villages. The monks lead the processions to circle the Muktinath shrine, before the secular fun starts. Yartung signals the return from the highlands of the animals, which are pastured in the lower valleys during the coming winter. Yartung annually attracts the majority of *BhoTiya* people from throughout upper Thak Khola, northern Mustang, and neighboring Manang District (over Thorung Pass). The participants wear their traditional ethnic dress.

If you are coming from the south, turn off the regular trail just after crossing the Lete Khola on a new suspension bridge. Keep close to the Kali Gandaki for some 10 minutes before crossing the tumultuous river on a wooden bridge to reach Chhoya (8000 ft, 2400 m). If you are coming from the north, take a left fork a few minutes before reaching Lete and after passing through Upala Lete (8150 ft, 2484 m). This left fork takes you through a beautiful pine forest before you descend slightly in 10 minutes to the same wooden bridge to Chhoya. You can get provisions in Chhoya or in Lete. From Chhoya, cross the delta of the Polje Khola and ascend to the few houses of Poljedanda (8175 ft, 2492 m). Then turn right and head southeast to the few more houses of Deorali (8275 ft, 2522 m) 30 minutes from Chhoya. This is the last village on the route. Here the trail forks left and you contour above fields to enter the valley of the Tangdung or Bhutra Khola, a little more than 30 minutes later. Contour below a small waterfall of a tributary to the main river (8075 ft, 2461 m) after a short, steep descent through forest. The river is 1¼ hours from Deorali. There should be a wooden bridge here unless it has been washed out during the monsoon. Fill up all your water containers, as you may not get another chance during the next day.

The next section of the trail ascends 6000 ft (1829 m) and is unrelentingly steep. There are few suitable campsites until near the end of the climb. After crossing to the southeast (left) bank, ascend a cliff and enter a mixed broad-leaved forest. The trail is easy to follow and the forest is pleasant. There are occasional vistas to inspire the weary. In the upper reaches you find areas of bamboo, then rhododendron, fir, and birch forests. In 2½ hours, reach a saddle called Kal Ghiu (11,000 ft, 3383 m). Some trekking groups call this place Jungle Camp. Camping is possible here if you can find water down the other side of the saddle. Keep close to the crest of the ridge as you pass several notches. Enjoy the rhododendrons in bloom in the spring. After keeping to the southeast side of the ridge and leaving the forest, the trail becomes fainter, reaches a minor ridge crest (12,600 ft, 3840 m), and crosses over to the northwest side. Keep climbing to a prominent notch with a *chorten* (13,350 ft, 4069 m), some 2 hours from Kal Ghiu. The views of Dhaulagiri are unforgettable.

The slope eases off now and continues over more moderate grazing slopes to a place near a ridge crest called Sano Bugin (13,950 ft, 4252 m), where herders stay during the monsoon. There are rock walls here that the herders convert to shelters with the use of bamboo mats. If there is no snow to melt, water may be difficult to obtain. The gigantic west face of Annapurna, first climbed by Reinhold Messner in 1985, is before you. Head north along the ridge crest, or on the west side. The trail is marked with slabs of rock standing on end. In 1 hour, reach another

Birds of the Subtropical Zone (3300 to 6500 ft/1000 to 2000 m in the West, to 5500 ft/1700 m in the East)

Birds of prey either kill other animals or feed on their bodies. Nepal has over seventy species, including twenty-one owls. Egyptian vulture (*Neophron percnopterus,* length 60 cm) is a familiar small vulture around villages. It has a wedge-shaped tail. The adult is white with black flight feathers and yellow head (immature is brownish). It also occurs in tropical and temperate zones. The steppe eagle (*Aquila nipalensis,* length 74 to 81 cm) is a large eagle with long, broad wings and medium-long tail. From below, while in flight, it looks dark brown with one or two white wing bars across the undersides of its wings. It is a common winter visitor between September and April and occurs from tropical to alpine zones.

Its call monotonously repeated all day in spring and summer, the barbet usually remains hidden in tree tops. The blue-throated barbet (*Megalaima asiatica,* length 22 cm), green with a blue throat and face and red forehead, makes a loud "chuperup." It also occurs in tropical and temperate zones. The coppersmith (or crimson-breasted) barbet (*Megalaima haemacephala,* length 14 cm), greenish with yellow throat and reddish breast, makes a metallic note said to resemble a coppersmith beating on metal. It also occurs in the tropical zone. The Indian cuckoo (*Cuculus micropterus* [*kaphal pakyo*], length 33 cm), like several other cuckoo species, is grayish above and on the throat, with the rest of the underparts barred black and white. It occurs in tropical and temperate zones. Its bubbling call sounds like "one more bottle." It calls all night, as does the common hawk cuckoo or brainfever bird (*Hierococcyx varius,* length 34 cm), which is gray above and mottled or barred brown below. It occurs in the tropical zone. Calls start slowly and accelerate to a high pitch.

Nepal has six species of minivets, these long-tailed, brightly colored arboreal birds. Long-tailed minivet (*Pericrocotus ethologus* [*Ranichara*], length 18 cm) males are red and black, females yellow and black. Flocks often perch on treetops and twitter to each other as they fly from tree to tree. They occur in the temperate zone.

The Asian magpie robin (*Copsychus saularis,* length 19 cm) is a long-tailed, black-and-white robin. The male is black above, on throat and breast, and rest of underparts; the wing bar and outer tail coverts are white. In the female, black is replaced by gray. Common in gardens, it has a sweet song of short, repeated phrases.

The spiny babbler (*Turdoides nipalensis,* length 24 cm) is Nepal's only endemic bird. It is very secretive and rarely seen but fairly common in thick scrub. Grayish brown and streaked, with a long tail, it also occurs in the temperate zone.

ridge crest (14,375 ft, 4382 m) and cross to the southeast side of the ridge. This may be the "*passage du avril 27*" that Herzog's expedition discovered in order to get to the base of Annapurna. You are now in the drainage area of the Miristi Khola, the river that enters the Kali Gandaki above Tatopani.

Continue contouring for a few minutes to Thulo Bugin (14,300 ft, 4359 m), where herders stay. There is a small shrine here. Contour, crossing several tributaries of the Hum Khola, a tributary of the Miristi. The last stream (13,375 ft, 4077 m), reached in 30 minutes, is a little tricky to cross. Climb on, at first gradually, then more steeply, to reach a flat area sometimes called Bal Khola (14,650 ft, 4465 m) in 1¾ hours. Camp here, for there are few other suitable places until the river is reached. The west face of Annapurna looms before you. Local people do not venture much beyond here in their tending of sheep and goats.

Descend and round a ridge crest to the canyon of the Miristi Khola proper. The river is almost a mile below you, yet its roar can be heard. Continue on steep grassy slopes and pass an overhanging rock (14,075 ft, 4290 m) suitable for camping, 45 minutes from the high point. Descend more steeply on grass, cross a stream, and go down into shrubbery until it appears that a 1000-ft (300-m) cliff will block the way to the valley floor. The trail heads west to a break in the rock wall and descends through the break to the river (11,500 ft, 3505 m) 1½ hours from the overhanging rock. The impressive gorge at the bottom gives a feeling of isolation. Head upstream on the northwest (right) bank. The dense shrubs may make travel difficult. There are campsites by some sand near a widening in the river (11,575 ft, 3528 m), where it may be possible to ford in low water. Otherwise, head upstream for 10 minutes to a narrowing where there may be a bridge. Cross the river, if possible, and camp on the other side if it is late.

Once on the southeast (left) bank of the Miristi Khola, follow the trail upstream. The vegetation soon disappears as altitude and erosion increase. The trail becomes indistinct in the moraine. As the valley opens up, bear right to the east and leave the river bottom to climb the moraine to a vague shelf. Continue beyond to a small glacial lake in the terminal moraine of the North Annapurna Glacier. Cross its outflow to the right and climb the lateral moraine to the left. There are views of the Nilgiris to the west. The base camp for the various attempts to climb Annapurna from the north is on a flat shelf of land (14,300 ft, 4359 m) to the north of the

Traditional Papermaking

The centuries-old technique of making paper in Nepal has been revived by outsider interest in "rice" paper. In addition to the manufacturing along the Kali Gandaki, you will find it along tributaries of the Arun and parts in between. The *Daphne bholua* shrub grows at elevations of 7000 to 11,000 feet (2100 to 3300 m), and the barks used for making paper are called *lokta* or *baruwa* locally. The out barks are stripped off, cleaned, then soaked in water and dried and carried down to the processing area. The alkali leachate of wood ashes is used for digesting the barks by boiling the mixture in copper vessels, cutting them, and continuing the process until they are soft and breakable. The bark material is then pounded into a pulpy mass and mixed into a dense emulsion with water. The casting of the pulp into paper is done by a stream or pond by mixing the concentrate in a tank of water, and swirling just the right amount on a mesh frame. The frames are left to dry in the sun, when the paper is removed.

An immense wall of ice rises above Tilicho Tal

glacier. There is a steep drop-off to the glacier valley to the south and east. The base camp is reached in 3 to 4 hours from the crossing of the Miristi Khola. Annapurna (26,545 ft, 8091 m) was the first 8000-m peak to be climbed, in 1950, by the French from this side.

The view of Annapurna I from the base camp is minimal. Better views can be obtained by contouring and climbing to the east to a grassy knoll from which much of the north face can be seen. You could also proceed toward Camp I by dropping from the shelf and climbing along the lateral moraine of the glacier to 16,000 ft (4877 m). Exploratory and climbing journeys will suggest themselves to those with experience. The Great Barrier, an impressive wall of mountains to the north, separates you from Tilicho Tal. Be sure to take enough food to stay awhile and enjoy this unforgettable area.

TILICHO TAL

Currently, approach to the lake is restricted from the west because the area is used as a mountain warfare training ground for the Royal Nepal Army. The restriction is relaxed for trekking groups going through an agency, so the route is described here.

To reach Tilicho Tal from Thak Khola proceed up the trail from Thini (9500 ft, 2897 m). The trail winds up the north side of the valley, leading to the pass to the east. There is little or no water along the lower part of the route. Pass through rhododendron, fir, and birch forests to reach alpine vegetation. Soon after crossing two tributaries, the trail leads to a *goTh* (14,000 ft, 2468 m), some 6 hours from Thinigaon. Another day takes you over Tilicho Pass (16,730 ft, 5100 m) to the majestic ice walls beyond. The pass itself is not clearly seen from the *goTh*. It is glaciated, so those who are not equipped for ice climbing may prefer to head up one of the gullies north of the pass. The climb is higher, up to 17,500 ft (5334 m) or so, but the route is preferable for most parties. A trip to the lake and climbs of nearby summits are rewarding. The lake is often frozen. Trekkers attempting to climb up to the lake from the valley in 2 days must be especially watchful for signs and symptoms of altitude sickness. They should descend at the first signs of severe symptoms. You can also reach the lake from the east, heading up from Khangsar in Manang (described later).

TATOPANI TO POKHARA VIA BENI AND BAGLUNG

The return to Pokhara from Tatopani via Beni mentioned earlier involves much less climbing. You may not want to go this way in late spring, as it is much hotter than the higher route. To proceed from Tatopani, cross the suspension bridge to the east (left) bank of the Kali Gandaki and cross the bridge over the Ghara Khola to its south (left) bank to rejoin the Kali Gandaki instead of taking the trail climbing to GhoRepani. Proceed south on its east (left) bank. There are undeveloped hot springs below the lodges near a suspension bridge over the Kali Gandaki.

After 2½ hours on the trail, which in places is carved into the rock cliff and passes through subtropical valley forests, cross to the west (right) bank at Tiplyang (3400 ft, 1037 m) and climb high up the west (right) bank passing through Baisari. Eventually descend to Ranipauwa (3900 ft, 1189 m), also called Galeshwor, and cross the tributary RahughaT Khola. Ranipauwa, some 4 hours from Tatopani, is the site of the annual *mela* (fair), which is usually in mid-November or early December.

An hour after crossing the tributary, come to a suspension bridge over the Kali

Gandaki, just before Beni (2700 ft, 823 m), the administrative center for the Mayagdi District. Board a bus at the road head on the true left side of the Kali Gandaki, across the downstream bridge in Beni. You can get an early morning bus to Kathmandu. When I stay in Beni, I try to find the breeziest place to avoid being eaten by the mosquitos. You can walk to Baglung (3150 ft, 960 m), and along the way, especially on the east bank, you may see traditional Nepali papermaking, using the bark of the Daphne bholua shrub, collected up high and then cooked into a pulp. The slurry settles on a screen that is set out to dry. UNICEF has a depot here to collect the product to send to Bhaktapur, where cards are printed. Don't forget to look behind you for immense views of the south face of Dhaulagiri from Baglung if you climb up there.

The Annapurna Sanctuary

Walking the uphill staircases in Gurung country is a mantra.
Trekker Anne Outwater

The term Annapurna Sanctuary, coined by outsiders, denotes the high basin southwest of Annapurna and the headwaters of the Modi Khola. This vast amphi-theater, surrounded by Himalayan giants, was explored by Jimmy Roberts in 1956 and brought to the attention of the Western world by the British Expedition to Machhapuchhre in 1957. The gigantic mountains named for the goddesses Anna–purna and Gangapurna, important figures in Hindu myth and folklore, justify calling it a sanctuary. Its gate, the deep gorge between the peaks Hiunchuli and Machhapuchhre, marks a natural division between the dense rain forest and bamboo jungle of the narrow Modi Khola valley and the scattered summits and immense walls of the mountain fortress inside. This area is also referred to as the Annapurna Base Camp and the Machhapuchhre Base Camp.

Trekking possibilities are varied. Those without time to head up to Thak Khola can make a circuit from Pokhara into the sanctuary, in less than 10 days, with little backtracking. However, to enjoy the route and the sanctuary itself without feeling rushed, plan a few more days. This area can be easily combined with the entire Annapurna circuit or with a trek to Jomosom that offers various link-up possibilities.

The route up the Modi Khola has always had a reputation among porters for being slippery and difficult. While lodges and inns that cater to the trekker now exist outside the inhabited areas, the trail hasn't changed much. It is often wet, and in the steep and slippery places a fall could be disastrous. But the trail never lived up to its old reputation; the route to the North Annapurna Base Camp is a much more serious undertaking.

You can find cooked food and lodging along the entire route in season (ask at Chomro before venturing forth at other times). During winter months, snowfall may make the trip difficult or impossible, and avalanche hazard can increase the risk.

This is the homeland of the *Gurung* people, an ethnic group renowned for brav-ery in the Gurkhas. They speak their own unwritten language, a member of the Sino-Tibetan family, and names of villages don't transliterate accurately into Nepali. Hence the variations in spelling that you will see on signboards here. Is it Ghandrung or Ghandruk? Landrung or Landruk? Chomro or Chomrong? Kyumunu, Kimrong, Kymnu, Kyumnu, or Kimnu? I try to use the ACAP spellings.

For those traveling from Pokhara, one access route to the sanctuary leaves the

Left: *Scooping the pulp slurry out onto the screen to make so-called rice paper.*
Right: *Peeling off dried rice paper which will be transported to Kathmandu for sale.*

trail at Chandrakot. This is not a popular approach, as more people head there from GhoRepani, or Dhampus. A route from Phedi could be followed in the opposite direction as part of the circuit from Pokhara. If coming from the Thak Khola region, you could leave the standard trail at GhoRepani or Chitre. These options will be described in the Chomro to Suikhet section, along with a route from the Sanctuary to Pokhara through Dhampus.

BIRETHANTI TO ANNAPURNA SANCTUARY

Accommodations are available in almost all towns en route with opportunities to stay in traditional *bhaTTi* lower down. For those who are camping, they must be self-sufficient in fuel; there is a kerosene depot in Naya Pul, on the road from Pokhara. From **Birethanti** (3600 ft, 1097 m), reached from Naya Pul on the road, a half hour south, head east past the school, keeping close to the river, and passing fields and forests, to Chimrong in **40 minutes.** Here you could cross the river and climb up to Chandrakot. However, keep to the valley to Syauli Bazaar, cross a tributary, and begin a long climb along a remarkable staircase to reach **Thamle** (5600 ft, 1707 m) at the entrance to *Gurung* country in **70 minutes** from the Modi Khola.

Peoples of Central Nepal: Gurung

The *Gurung* are most prominent on high ridges and upper valleys below the Annapurna and Himal Chuli massifs north and east of Pokhara, eastward beyond Gorkha. They are an enterprising upland farming and herding people; their sheep herds are often seen along the Manang trail on the Marsyangdi river route. They are subdivided into many clans, but except for the *Ghale* (pronounced like "golly"), who prefer to use the clan name, most call themselves, simply, *Gurung*. They, like their *Magar* counterparts, occupy some of the most inaccessible villages, high on the mountainsides above the trekking routes. Young *Gurung* men are often encountered as porters; older *Gurung* of distinction may have served in the Gurkha regiments, and many have interesting tales of exploits from World War II. If you happen to stop at a *Gurung* village for the night, you might see their colorful dances, or other ritual or festival activities, some of which display very ancient characteristics. Especially interesting are *Gurung* funerary rituals (called *arghun*), which are described later.

Another **15 minutes** beyond are the houses of Kimche (5775 ft, 1760 m). A trail forks left here to TirkheDUgaa in the headwaters of the Bhurungdi Khola, on the way to GhoRepani. Along the way, you would pass through the villages of Moriya, Dhansing, and Sabet, taking some 4 hours to reach TirkheDUgaa. You could travel from Thak Khola by this route instead of one of the other trails from GhoRepani or Chitre.

From Kimche, cross a tributary a few minutes later and continue through or above a recent landslide. You can expect the people to rebuild the land here and further stabilize the hillside. Those coming from Landrung will join this trail just beyond a *chautaaraa* and by a *goTh* on the right side (6300 ft, 1920 m) 30 minutes beyond Kimche. Ahead is the large, affluent *Gurung* village of Ghandruk. Their wealth comes from handsome pensions provided to *Gurungs* who have served as Gurkhas in the British Army. This income was one of several factors that changed their primary livelihood from herding and hunting to sedentary farming. Tourism has further increased their wealth. Shrines along the trail receive offerings for the god Meshram Baraha, to ensure a safe journey.

Reach **Ghandruk** (6600 ft, 2012 m) in **40 minutes** from Kimche. At the upper end of Ghandruk, the trail leads to Banthanti and GhoRepani, at least a day's walk. You can also join this trail by heading upstream by Kimrong Khola in the next major tributary valley to the north. These will be described later. It takes **15 minutes** to pass through Ghandruk. Do pay a visit to the Annapurna Conservation Area Project (ACAP) headquarters on a spur near the lower end of town to see the energy conservation technology they espouse. There is also a locally run Traditional Gurung Museum. Sometimes, Gurung dancing and singing can be staged for trekkers willing to pay. A Local Youth Eco-Trekking Centre has been set up where local guides can be hired and tours arranged. In the heart of town is an Eco-Camping Place, a model camping ground. There is public phone service too. In the future you may be able to book a room at a lodge or arrange a guide by phone from your own country, if that is your desire!

Leave the town to the northwest, cross a tributary, and mostly contour through fields and oak forest in a side draw to reach Kimrong Danda (7400 ft, 2255 m), a prominent notch with houses and lodges, **1 hour** beyond Ghandruk. Descend into the valley of the Kyumnu Khola (also called Kimrong, Kymnu, Kyumnu, and Kimnu) on a trail much improved over the one I got lost on in 1969. Just below the crest of the ridge take the right fork and descend steeply to reach the river in **45 minutes** (5940 ft, 1810 m). A trail, described later, heads upstream in this tributary valley to reach GhoRepani and Chitre. Cross to the left bank and ascend to the few lodges of Kimrong Khola just beyond. Now climb steeply up the hillside and traverse east higher up to enter the Modi Khola valley at **Daaulu** (7160 ft, 2182 m), **70 minutes** from the Kyumnu Khola crossing.

At this junction of the two valleys, there are several lodges for trekkers as well as signs pointing out the routes. On the return you can take the right fork here and descend the spur below, cross the river beyond, and reach Landrung directly. This pleasant, direct route from Pokhara is now possible, thanks to a bridge over the Modi Khola.

But to head to Chomro, contour and climb to enter the tributary valley draining the south side of Annapurna South (left) and Hiunchuli (right), the major peaks before you. Descend to **Chomro** (also called Chomrong), a prosperous *Gurung* village (6725 ft, 2050 m), reached in **30 minutes** from Daaulu. Pass the school 400 ft (122 m) above the center of town. There are many large hotels for trekkers here where you can rent climbing equipment and down jackets as well.

Questions to Ponder: Interactions with Innkeepers and Nepalis

Discuss with innkeepers and villagers your concerns about conservation of Nepal's resources. Ask them about plans for the future in their area. Would they want to install a portable electric generator as some, where electricity is not planned, have stated? How would you feel about modern conveniences that might change the experience of trekking?

What do the Nepali people you meet have that you don't? Materially? Otherwise? What do you think they would most like to have of yours? What about your encounter do you think they talk about among themselves after you have left?

From Chomro descend northward to cross the main tributary on a suspension bridge (6200 ft, 1890 m) **20 minutes** beyond. Climb through terraces and the few houses of Kilche (6700 ft, 2042 m) to contour and enter the main Modi Khola valley, which you will follow for the next 2 days. The trail was previously used only by shepherds, who drove their flocks of sheep and goats up during the monsoon to browse in the forests and the shrubbery above tree line.

You reach Bhanuwa entering the main valley and then **Sinuwa** (7625 ft, 2324 m) **1½ hours** beyond the suspension bridge. This last permanent settlement resulted from the trekker traffic. Contour along a reasonable trail in an rhododendron-and-oak forest, reaching growths of bamboo as you go farther up the valley. Reach **Kuldhighar** (8200 ft, 2499 m) in **70 minutes** as you go through increasingly dense forest. There is an ACAP center here, with informative programs and interesting activities. The ACAP has a check post here as well. The trail drops slightly from here and then appears transformed into the stone staircases of the *Gurung* villages to the south, but with the addition of drainage ditches.

The main mountain visible at the head of the valley is Annapurna III; Machhapuchhre, the "fish-tail" mountain whose name has been obvious for several days now, is off to the right. After you leave this improved trail, descend over a series of slabs, which require care to negotiate. Enter a dense bamboo rain forest. The area around Pokhara and south of the main Himalaya receives considerably more rainfall than almost any place in Nepal. South of Pokhara the Mahabharat Lekh, the range of hills above the Tarai, is lower than in other parts and doesn't block the northerly flow of moisture. The trail is always wet in this jungle.

Uses of Bamboo

Bamboos are prolific, especially in the high-rainfall areas around Pokhara and the eastern hills. They can be found at altitudes up to 13,000 ft (4000 m) in the east. It is a multipurpose raw material with an incredible variety of uses. Some species are very hard and can withstand great compressive forces as pillars. Bamboos don't last long, so need to be replaced regularly. The softer ones are flexible and thin strips can be woven into baskets and trays. They provide good protection against erosion because of their dense surface roots. This rhizome root system can hold up terraces and road banks. Villagers cultivate many species and harvest them in controlled fashion by thinning older poles, preserving the clump to protect the soil. Because they grow so rapidly new shoots are soon out of the reach of grazing animals. Species take long periods to flower, sometimes up to 150 years. Some can be a foot (30 cm) in diameter and used as pillars or storage containers but are too large for most purposes. Smaller culmed species are used as fodder, while shoots are eaten by people. There are well over twenty species found, usually with specific Nepali names. Broad categories include *bAAs,* the large-stature species, at moderate altitudes; *nigaalo,* the smaller species; and *maalingo,* at higher altitudes, which produce the best weaving materials. Human torpedoes may be met catapulting down steep trails headed for home as they clutch their bamboo charges under their arms. You will often see people in villages weaving articles of bamboo. Bamboos are used as building materials for bridges, roofs, floors, ceilings, and walls. Sitting mats (*gundri*), winnowing trays (*naanglo*), twine, sieves, pipes, water carriers, containers, straws, and a large variety of baskets are other uses of this versatile grass.

Reach a clearing and some lodges, **Bamboo** (7700 ft, 2347 m), in **35 minutes.** Cross several substantial tributaries. The third has an overhanging rock upstream that could serve as a shelter in a pinch. Eventually, you reach **Dovan** (8550 ft, 2606 m), with several inns, in **1 hour 20 minutes.** The rhododendrons festooned with moss in the forest beyond are gigantic; sometimes orchids can be spotted. This region has over 100 varieties of orchids. There are hemlocks too but, because of excess rainfall, not as many as elsewhere at this elevation.

The Modi Khola seems much closer as you wend your way through the jungle. Across the valley, some 30 to 40 minutes later, you'll see streams of water plunging thousands of feet into the river. At a very slight rise at the neck of the gorge, called Deorali (8950 ft, 2728 m), 35 minutes after Dovan, you'll find a small rock shrine (Panchenin Baraha or Barahathan) and strips of colored cloth. Local custom dictates prohibiting buffalo, chicken, eggs, or pork north of here, or else risking the anger

This human bamboo torpedo careens down trails from the harvesting area above to the weaving area by the village.

of the mountain gods, whose revenge will be sickness and death in your party. Nepalis explain the misfortune that has befallen some trekking groups and mountaineering expeditions in the sanctuary by breach of this custom. Just beyond is a spot where you can stand closer to the center of the valley to see the torrent rushing below you and the weeping wall across from you coming down from Machhapuchhre, a gift from the god Baraha. Shortly beyond, the forest opens slightly and again, by venturing closer to the river from the main trail, you'll see a 100-ft waterfall thundering down this canyon.

Continue to a clearing, called **Himalaya** (after the first lodge there, 9425 ft, 2873 m), **1 hour** beyond Dovan. After another stretch of dense forest, the valley begins to open up. In **45 minutes** reach **Hinko** (10,300 ft, 3139 m), a large over-hanging rock.

The next hour or more of trail is subject to avalanches. You may find the re-mains of some near the trail. After heavy snowfall above, which may be rain along the trail, the safest course may be to wait a few days for the slopes to clear. Because none of the avalanche slopes can be easily seen from the valley floor, it is difficult to be sure when it is safe to proceed. If up in the sanctuary, wait a few days if food supplies allow. Be aware that trekkers have been buried by avalanches along here. If you need to cross this portion, you could cross to the east bank of the Modi Khola.

Cross several streams and reach another **Deorali** (10,600 ft, 3231 m) **35 minutes** from Hinko, where there are several lodges. Notice the beautiful birch forests across the valley. Most of the trees have been cut on this side. Pass some old huts. As you proceed along, you can admire before you the triangular snow-and-rock face of Gangapurna, which has actually been climbed. There is a cave of snow from avalanches off Hiunchuli above that persists through the monsoon and has never been known to disappear. It seems to be getting smaller, perhaps an effect of global warming.

Suddenly, you cross the imaginary gates and are inside the sanctuary! A stream flows in from the west and a large grass-covered moraine is ahead of you, with more grassy slopes beyond. Reach a shelf with several inns, the so-called Machhapuchhre Base Camp (12,150 ft, 3703 m), in 1¼ hours. There has not been a legally sanctioned expedition to sacred Machhapuchhre since 1957, and that one stopped short of the summit. The west face of Machhapuchhre looms above you, but the other views are limited to Annapurna South to the west.

Be cognizant of the rapid gain in altitude but, if conditions permit, try to stay higher to gain better views. The trail heads west in a trough between the moraine and the north slopes of Hiunchuli. In 1 hour, the halfway point to the Annapurna Base Camp is reached (12,925 ft, 3939 m). The views are much better from here but are even more spectacular farther on, at the Annapurna Base Camp, where food and shelter are available during peak season. This flat area (13,550 ft, 4130 m) was first used by the British in their successful first ascent of the South Face of Annapurna in 1970. It is the coldest and windiest of all places to stay but is well worth it if you are acclimatized and suitably equipped. Venture beyond to the crest of the moraine to gaze upon the awesome mountain walls. From left to right they are Hiunchuli, Annapurna South, Fang, Annapurna, Annapurna III, and Machhapuchhre. Tent Peak and Fluted Peak, rising above the hills to the north, complete the unforgettable panorama. Look for ghoral. Wander around and feel at peace with the earth.

People with time and equipment (which might be rented from lodges up here) may want to venture across the rubble-covered glacier to the north and explore further.

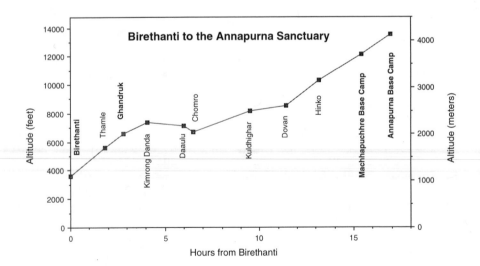

GHOREPANI TO GHANDRUK AND CHOMRO

The route keeps high, traversing the ridge system to reach Ghandruk. A policy requiring the use of kerosene and gas only in the lodges along here has been in effect. This limits firewood consumption for trekkers. Do not travel this route alone, as bandits sometimes work the forest. Begin at **GhoRepani Deorali** (9450 ft, 2880 m), and head east through the forest, keeping close to the ridge. Reach a clearing (10,360 ft, 3158 m), in **40 minutes,** with an immense panoramic view from Machhapuchhre to beyond Gurja Himal that rivals that from Poon Hill. Climb a little more, and before descending to the next notch you can see east to Annapurna II and Himalchuli. Reach this pass, **Deorali** (10,160 ft, 3097 m), in another **40 minutes.** Here the trail mentioned earlier in the descent from GhoRepani to Tatopani, which heads south from Chitre, joins and offers another route to Ghandruk. There are several inns here. Head south to descend a steep gully that is treacherous when wet or icy. Pass another lodge, and switchback by a tiny waterfall in a moss-festooned rhododendron forest until you reach **Banthanti** ("place in the forest" with inns now) (8740 ft, 2664 m) beneath a steep cliff in **1 hour.** Himalayan Black Bear has been recorded here, but your chances of spotting one are slight for it is nocturnal.

Continue traversing east and descending, passing another lodge in 15 minutes and then a campsite by a stream, before climbing up to **TaaDapaani** (meaning "far water," 8800 ft, 2682 m), beautifully situated in a notch, in **1 hour.** All of the facilities at these places where there is no farmland have been set up for trekkers. There was no sign of habitation here twenty years ago. Just below the pass, to the southeast, there is a trail fork, with the right branch going to Ghandruk, the left to Chomro. Both options will be described.

To go to Ghandruk, take the right fork through rhododendron forest to BhAIsi Kharka ("buffalo pasture," again with lodges these days, 8260 ft, 2518 m) in **35 minutes,** and then continue a descending traverse in a narrow valley to Sitke (7120 ft, 2170 m) in **1 hour.** Reach the upper portion of Ghandruk in another **30 minutes,** and descend to lodges.

If taking the left fork at TaaDapaani to go to Chomro, descend and head northeast. Reach MelAAje (7260 ft, 2213 m) in **50 minutes** and fork right at the school, climb the fence, and descend very steeply among terraces to the Kyumnu Khola. Head downstream to a suspension bridge to meet the trail coming from Ghandruk (5940 ft, 1810 m) in **30 minutes.** The way to Daaulu and Chomro has already been described.

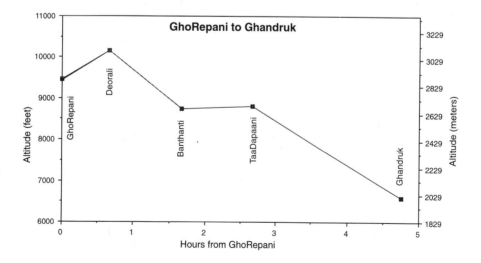

CHOMRO TO SUIKHET

This route avoids some backtracking and could be followed in reverse as a direct route to the sanctuary.

From Chomro return to **Daaulu** (7160 ft, 2182 m), above the spur of mostly terraced land that appears to jut out into the Modi Khola valley. Take the left fork that descends steeply, going around and through terraced fields of millet. Take the steepest choice at trail forks. Near the spur of land, which is just a shoulder of the Kyumnu Khola valley, cross a fence to keep to the crest of the spur. Reach the few houses of **Chinu** (5660 ft, 1725 m), **40 minutes** from the junction. This is a settlement of *Jaishi* Brahmans. There is a hot spring near the river about 15 minutes' walk north, and a sign points the way.

Beyond, the main trail drops on the south side of the spur, heading toward the Kyumnu Khola. Just before reaching it, fork left to a log bridge (5180 ft, 1579 m), some **15 minutes** from Chinu. Cross the tributary and climb up the south bank pass, called Samrung, and then return to the Modi Khola valley at around 5425 ft (1653 m). Reach forest and go almost all the way around a small side valley before dropping down to the lodges at **Himalkyo** (5050 ft, 1539 m), some **35 minutes** from the previous bridge. Popularly called New Bridge, or Naya Pul for the now old structure 100 ft (30 m) below, the *Gurung* name meaning "water from the snows" is much more appropriate. Hopefully with the newer Naya Pul south of Birethanti this name will be forgotten.

Cross the Modi Khola to the left bank and head downstream, past ChiURe, then climb and contour, reaching terraces. An **hour** from Himalkyo, cross a suspension bridge over a tributary (5175 ft, 1577 m). Some **5 minutes** beyond, reach the main trail from Landruk to Ghandruk (5325 ft, 1623 m), by a lodge. A short climb brings you to **Landruk,** a large *Gurung* settlement. At a fork in the middle of town (5340 ft, 1628 m) take the right branch to contour southward.

The trail heads down the valley to climb out of it into the Pokhara drainage. Leave Landruk, and contour south through several tributary valleys to reach **Tolka** (5660 ft, 1725 m) in **45 minutes.** Continue through more lodges of Tolka in the Bhichok or Ghirsung Khola valley. Cross this tributary to the left bank and climb out of the valley to **Bhichok Deorali** (6880 ft, 2097 m) in **1 hour.** There are now plenty of facilities for trekkers along here, and it is difficult to get lost. Continue in the same direction you have been walking and cross to the opposite (east) side of the ridge to contour above the Indi Khola valley. Descend slightly to the lodges and tea shops at **Potana** (6460 ft, 1969 m) in **30 minutes.** Shortly beyond, the trail forks. The right fork, which goes through forest to KAAre, comes out at the pass just to the west. This route may be a useful link, depending on your plans.

To return to Pokhara via Dhampus, don't take the right fork, but continue and descend, reaching fields on the north side of a ridge in the Indi Khola valley in 30 minutes. The village of **Dhampus** is spread out farther along the north side of this ridge. Reach the far end of town (5560 ft, 1695 m) in 1 hour from Potana. There is a police check post here. The views of the giants to the north are worth waiting for if the weather has been bad. You can continue along the ridge to Dhital, Henjakot, and Astam before descending to Suikhet at a narrowing in the Yamdi Khola valley. Those wishing longer views along the ridge will enjoy taking this route.

Most trekkers will want to descend, following the stairs, joining trails coming in from the right. Keep close to the crest of the hill, along terraces. Reach a *chautaaraa* 35 minutes below (4575 ft, 1394 m) and descend into forests of *chilaune* trees. *Chilaune* means "itch" in Nepali, and if you rub sap of this tree on your skin, you will learn how it got its name. As you drop down to the Yamdi Khola valley floor, you'll be impressed with this uncut forest so close to Pokhara. The people of Dhampus have traditionally protected this forest, and governmental programs are only now realizing that this traditional, social forestry should be encouraged. Reach the valley floor (3750 ft, 1143 m) and the road to Baglung in **45 minutes** from Dhampus.

If taking this trail in reverse, look for the small (50 ft, 15 m) waterfall on the north side of the valley, near the start of the climb. The trail begins a few minutes beyond.

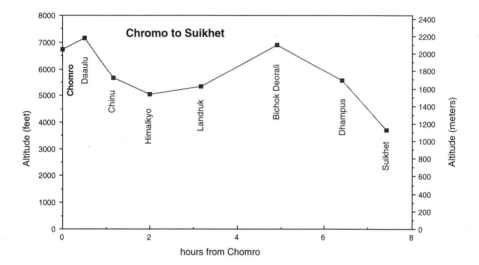

To Manang and over Thorung La

DUMRE TO MANANG

The Manang area offers many of the same attractions of a trek to Jomosom via Thak Khola. The *Manangba,* the people of Manang, are a most worldly ethnic group and some of the men may have traveled farther on the globe than you. The mountain scenery is perhaps more breathtaking than on the other side, if only because the peaks in the open Manang Valley are closer. It takes over a week to reach the town of Manang if you walk the entire way from Dumre or Pokhara, though most trekkers now take a vehicle to Besisahar, shortening the walk by 2 days. There are no *Thakali* here running the kind of hotels and lodges for tourists that you find on the trail to Jomosom, but the local people have set up comparable inns and hotels that cater to Western tastes.

Enjoy it all. Cross Thorung La and circle the Annapurna massif. It is a walk of over 150 mi (240 km), but the rewards certainly compensate for the effort. The circuit takes at least two and a half weeks, perhaps a week more than just walking to Manang and then retracing your steps, but this includes time for some diversions. There are now inns temporarily set up on both sides of the pass so it is possible to cross without being self-sufficient, though storms that catch you up high may make it difficult to reach one. A number of trekkers have died because they pushed on in deteriorating conditions when not adequately prepared with food, clothing, and shelter. Bad weather can threaten the party at any time, and it is prudent to wait it out or turn back rather than risk lives. Serious frostbite is not uncommon among trekkers who are inadequately prepared. Crossings can be difficult or impossible if there is deep, soft snow on the pass. Such conditions can be expected from January to March, and often longer. The police check posts on either side of the pass will advise you when conditions prevent safer crossings; however, this is not a substitute for good mountain sense.

The route is described from Dumre on the Kathmandu–Pokhara road. You could begin by walking directly from Pokhara to intersect the trail described here at either Khudi or near Tarkughat. The Khudi-to-Pokhara route is described briefly below (p. 199). The reasons for not going counterclockwise have already been discussed.

The basic route description is very simple. The entire trek is spent going up the Marsyangdi Khola to its headwaters and then crossing a pass to reach the Kali Gandaki drainage. The lower portions of the valley are broad, and then the modern trail passes through the bottom of the gorge where the river cuts through the main Himalayan system, until it finally opens into a broader alpine glacial valley. Like the next major valley to the west, the Kali Gandaki, the Marsyangdi Khola was once a major salt-for-rice trade route. I have borrowed shamelessly from Liesl Messerschmidt K.C.'s booklet on the local lore.

Dumre (1500 ft, 457 m) is reached in some 5 hours by bus from Kathmandu, or 2½ hours from Pokhara (more or less, depending on road conditions). Board the bus in Pokhara at Mahendra Pul or at the main bus terminal at Chhaina Chowk, just east of the town–airport road junction, on the south side of the Kathmandu–Pokhara road. The bus terminals are often called *bas parak* ("bus park"). There are direct buses to Dumre or Besisahar from the *Naya bas parka* near Baleju in Kathmandu with tickets purchased a day in advance.

Dumre is one of the many towns that have sprung up along the road to serve the needs of travelers, traders, and villagers. It is a principal staging area for people arriving and departing for the hinterland of the Marsyangdi Khola. This is a place to purchase a range of provisions at reasonable prices, although more and more goods can be bought at main towns along the dry-weather feeder road that parallels the Marsyangdi Khola on the west bank and goes to Besisahar. Porters can be hired at Dumre or at the terminus of the feeder road, and sometimes a guide may also be engaged.

The feeder road is passable for four-wheel-drive vehicles from October to May or June, depending on weather conditions, and now trucks and buses make the journey. Jeeps may be hired on a "reserve" basis (expensive) or you can pay by the seat (crowded but inexpensive). There is usually a nominal charge for baggage in addition to the seat charge. Taking a vehicle along the road saves 2 or more days of walking, but the rugged trucks and wagons take their toll as they pitch and heave. Larger and taller people are advised to keep their centers of gravity as low and as far forward as possible on the trucks.

Those wishing to trek the entire way (and avoid the road) should get off the bus from Pokhara at Bimalnagar, east of Dumre. Cross the suspension bridge and walk up the east side of the Marsyangdi Khola. You can rejoin the trail described here at either Tarkughat, PhalenksAAghu, or Besisahar, or you can stay on the east side all the way to Syange. Bimalnagar to PhalenksAAghu takes about 8 hours. Traditional inns or *bhaTTi* are the fare along here. A fine alternative to walking from Dumre is

Consider asking the woman of the house if you may stay in her home for the evening to experience a different Nepal, away from the lodges.

to walk from Pokhara to Khudi. The basics of the route are described from Khudi to Pokhara below.

DUMRE TO BESISAHAR

This description is included in case you can't get a vehicle out of Dumre, or the bridges are out, necessitating a walk. To walk from Dumre (1500 ft, 457 m), head north to reach Bhansar (1650 ft, 503 m) in 40 minutes, then Barabise (1650 ft, 504 m) in 40 minutes and Chambas (1759 ft, 533 m) in 45 minutes, and then Turture (1725 ft, 526 m) in another 45 minutes. Turture sits above a suspension bridge over the Marsyangdi Khola. Just north of the Paundi Khola, on the banks of the Marsyangdi Khola, is a large sandy beach, good for tent camping (watch for thieves) and swimming. North of Turture the trail passes through many small hamlets, including Tharpani (1875 ft, 556 m), in 1 hour. Beyond there are fewer settlements and more farmland until 1 hour later you come to the new town of Kalimati. This area was the intersection of the major trail between Kathmandu and Pokhara that mail runners used. I recommend this trail to veteran trekkers looking for new routes. (From Pokhara, the towns en route to Tarkughat would be Deorali, Sisaghat, and Kunchha. East of Tarkughat, you would climb to Luitel Bhanjyang, on to Khoplang, then to Gorkha [also at a roadhead], and then to Khanchok Bhanjyang. Drop to cross the Buri Gandaki at Arughat, then to Sallentar, Hanse Bazaar, Katunge to Samri Bhanjyang. Descend to Kagune Bazaar, and meet the road again at Trisuli Bazaar. It takes 2 to 3 days from Pokhara to Tarkughat and another 3 to 4 days to Trisuli Bazaar, at a leisurely pace in the cool winter months.) Below and across from you, on the east (left) bank of the Marsyangdi Khola, you can see the town of Tarkughat.

Questions to Ponder: Villages

Why are some villages composed of clustered houses, reminiscent of downtown Kathmandu, while others have dwellings either widely scattered over the hillside or within shouting distance? What factors influence this diversity? (Ethnic group? Terrain?) Why are some villages close to the main trail, while others avoid it? Why do some villages near the trail have shops, while others don't? Why do homes and villages face the directions they do? How have people adapted their town plan to the environment?

Some villages have decorative adornment, such as painting on walls or carved windows, yet this is absent in others nearby. Why? What materials are used to build homes? Roofs, walls, doors, floors? If there is electricity, how is it wired and used? Consider the relationship of bamboo stands to villages. How many different types of this grass do you see, and what uses is it put to?

Have you noticed lines of communication in villages that follow an organized pattern? Is there a town crier? What influence does the transistor radio have? What happens if a printed note or letter arrives? What evidence do you see of modern improvements to people's houses? How well maintained are they? What nonlocally produced materials are required for building? Who builds and maintains bridges, trails, water systems, and other community projects? Why do so many of them seem in disrepair?

Have you taken trails in high-mountain areas without signs of much tourism and found the trails and bridges much better than lower down, where there may be more people traffic? Why?

To go to Manang, follow the road north, and in 30 minutes cross a suspension bridge over a tributary, the Paundi Khola (same name as the river near Turture). Climb up to reach Paundi Dhik (1900 ft, 579 m) a few minutes later. There is a good swimming place under the bridge (*paundi* means "swim"). The road goes out across the fields. Stay on the trail through this small town. Don't take the left fork at the top end of the few shops, but continue north along the west edge of the fields. The trail soon rejoins the road, sometimes staying with it, sometimes avoiding it on shortcuts. Reach opposite the large tributary, the Dardi Khola, that you see joining the Marsyangdi Khola on the east (left) bank, in 50 minutes. An hour farther, cross another tributary to Udipur (2450 ft, 747 m) 5 minutes beyond. The forests that remain are tropical sal but have been cut extensively. Continue on to the rapidly growing village of Bhote Wodar (also called Suidibar).

In 30 minutes the trail reaches PhalenksAAghu. Follow the road through the high part of this town, unless you want to cross the Marsyangdi Khola here, in which case you should descend into the old town by the bridge. The name PhalenksAAghu comes from the English word "plank" and the Nepali word for a rather primitive bridge, *sAAghu*. There was once a plank bridge here, and the name stuck. Such combinations of Nepali and English words can often cause difficulty when they are pronounced with a Nepali accent or spelled in the local script. Another name for this town is Dalal, meaning "black market," a reference to activities of an earlier time.

An alternative trail here crosses the bridge and ascends the east (left) bank of the river to rejoin the other trail above Bhulbhule. This east (left) bank route is slightly shorter than the west (right) bank route and has more spectacular views. In the winter, many *Manangba* camp and trade on this side of the river. Ask the way or take a guide. Another variation, or even a side trip, is to cross the Marsyangdi Khola here and climb to the lakes on the Baahra Pokhari Lekh for fine views of Manaslu, Peak 29, and Himalchuli. You could even head north from the lakes to rejoin the main riverside route a day beyond. The route from PhalenksAAghu to Baahra Pokhara takes about 2 days of steady climbing.

If you don't cross the suspension bridge at PhalenksAAghu, continue on up the west (right) bank through stands of wet subtropical forest (good birding, and even a squirrel or two may be seen, especially on early mornings). The trail on to Besisahar generally follows the road. Reach a small town, Nadiwal (2650 ft, 808 m), in 45 minutes. Take the shortcut right, down, and across a small stream, then continue along the wide roadbed to Bakunde (2675 ft, 815 m) in another 30 minutes. You will see the large buildings and roofs of Besisahar in the distance. Descend to cross a tributary stream in 45 minutes, then ascend to Besisahar (2700 ft, 823 m) 15 minutes beyond. The old Lamjung Darbar, a palace fortress, once the center of a princely state, is high on the ridge southwest of the town. Besisahar has two sections; the main part of town is 5 minutes beyond, across a small stream.

The bridge across the Marsyangdi Khola to the east (left) bank is reached by a trail that turns off near the south end of the main old bazaar, near the hospital. It can be used by those taking the east (left) bank trail from PhalenksAAghu or by going to Bhulbhule on the east (left) side of the valley

Besisahar (2700 ft, 823 m), a major town situated on a shelf of land above the Marsyangdi Khola, is the Lamjung District headquarters and the site of a police check post. The town also has a district hospital, a prison, a high school, government offices, shops, a cinema, lodges, and electricity. It is a real "boomtown" in every sense, with new construction visible on all sides of the old bazaar. The road ends here but there are plans to push it farther. Above Besisahar on the ridge to the west is Lamjung Durbar, which was the summer palace of the sixteenth century Ghale Gurung Rajas, who wintered down below. Climb up there for a view and a sense of the history of this region.

To proceed from Besisahar on the west (right) bank, continue north through town to the end of the wide roadbed. The peak up the valley is Gyahi Kang. Descend from the shelf and cross the tributary PoDjo Khola some **15 minutes** later. Climb up steeply and then contour in wet subtropical forest and rice fields to Tanaute (2800 ft, 853 m) in **15 minutes.** Just beyond, fork right, to contour, rather than climb. Continue north above the Marsyangdi Khola to the Khudi Khola, a main tributary stream that drains the east end of the Lamjung Himal. Reach the old suspension bridge in **70 minutes.** The mountains up to the northeast are Ngadi Chuli and Baudha Himal. Either cross the old bridge (2600 ft, 792 m) or ascend 10 minutes upstream to cross a new suspension bridge and return from "new Khudi" (Naya Khudi) at the new bridge site. On the east (left) bank of the Khudi Khola, pass through **Khudi** to rejoin the Marsyangdi River trail. The Marsyangdi valley turns, narrows, and changes character now.

KHUDI TO POKHARA

If returning from Manang, you might consider walking directly to Pokhara from Khudi and avoiding Dumre. This route takes 2 to 3 days and there are traditional accommodations, nothing like the usual trekker lodges. Most of the villages passed are inhabited by *Gurung,* who farm the high hills and raise sheep. Trekkers wishing to meet few other foreigners should consider this route. The trail climbs from Khudi through Lamagaon, to Baglung Pani (5220 ft, 1591 m), across the Badam Khola to Nalma (3900 ft, 1189 m), and across the Midam Khola, passing Kala Pattar to Begnas Tal, the lake in the eastern part of the Pokhara Valley where there is a road and bus service to Pokhara.

To reach Manang from Khudi, continue up the Marsyangdi north (right) bank northeastward, and pass above the Khudi school stone pillar and tree nursery. Continue along the Marsyangdi Khola another **20 minutes** to a long suspension bridge (2720 ft, 829 m). Bagartol refers to the hotels and houses on this side. Cross to the south (left) bank to **Bhulbhule.** There is an ACAP checkpoint here. The village gets its name from the sound of a natural spring that bubbles up from cracks in the rocks nearby.

The route continues eastward out of Bhulbhule along the south (left) bank of the Marsyangdi Khola; later it turns northward again. Continue upstream from Bhulbhule and pass the first beautiful, thin waterfall on your right. You discover the rest! Below it is a fine pool for bathing—much better than the main river but this is the town water supply! Beyond, fork left, rather than climbing up the stairs, except in the monsoon. Pass Tarante, and just beyond fork left, rather than climbing.

An **hour** from Bhulbhule, reach **Ngadi** (3000 ft, 914 m), on the banks of a small tributary stream. There is more town beyond, and you reach a suspension bridge (3060 ft, 933 m) over the Ngadi Khola in **10 minutes.** Cross it to the right bank of the Ngadi Khola, and take the left of the two trails, which heads over to the Marsyangdi Khola on a wide trail. Cross a landslide via a detour. If the landslide is no longer visible, then the Nepalis have rebuilt the area, something that foreign experts have realized is the common way the peasant farmers deal with these land movements. Beyond, climb through Lampata, to reach **Bahundanda** (literally meaning "Brahman hill"), on the right of a prominent brow at a saddle (4300 ft, 1311 m) **1 hour** from the crossing of the Ngadi Khola. There is a police check post here and good views to the north if the weather is clear. On the high hills all around are Gurung settlements, and this used to be the northernmost settlement of Brahmins in this river system. There is an undeveloped hot springs (taato paani) at the edge of the Marsyangdi Khola, below the knob of Bahundanda hill, but it is a steep descent (and return ascent) and takes some time and effort to find. Ask locally for the way.

Descend into another tributary valley and in **45 minutes** cross its river on a cantilever bridge (3700 ft, 1128 m). Ascend to the main river valley and follow the trail beautifully carved out of the rock wall of the valley. Pass the houses and lodges of Khanegaon (3900 ft, 1189 m) in **30 minutes,** and contour to the first houses of **Shyange** (3725 ft, 1136 m) in **30 minutes.** This village was named after the sound the waterfall makes in a nearby side stream. The village used to be higher up during the heydays of the salt trade but was relocated as the valley floor became the main route through here. Arrive at the large suspension bridge over the Marsyangdi (3700 ft, 1128 m) and cross it to the west (right) bank to pass through more of **Shyange.**

You are now in the gorge of the Marsyangdi Khola. The trail is much improved from the salt trade trail that snaked up and down the cliffs on bamboo ladders high up the walls. Then there were no settlements in the floor of the gorge, but as the trail was improved the ups and downs diminished; traffic and facilities followed. There are overhanging rocks that can provide campsites. The trail continues 1¼ **hours** to the village of **Jagat** (4400 ft, 1341 m), meaning "toll station"—also called Gadi Jagat or Chote—situated in a saddle in the forest. This used to be an old customs post for the salt trade with Tibet until 1950 and is inhabited now mostly by *BhoTiya. Thakali* not from here were given the power to collect taxes and were resented by the *Gurung* residents.

The trail continues up and down and has detours to avoid slide areas. An **hour** beyond Jagat, reach the small settlement of **Chamje** (4560 ft, 1390 m), which has a large overhanging rock between two groups of houses, both with lodges. The overhang was a convenient sleeping spot for the porters carrying rice to trade for salt. There are many changes in the people, architecture, and vegetation as you head upstream. Houses are now built of rocks, the vegetation is less tropical, and the culture is more Tibetan-like.

Forests of the Subtropical Zone (3300 to 6500 ft/1000 to 2000 m in the West, to 5500 ft/1700 m in the East)

Extensive forests of chir pine (*Pinus roxburghii* [*khoTe sallo*]) occur throughout the subtropical zone in western Nepal and on drier slopes in the east. The forests are typically open, with no understory, because of frequent fires. Chir pine is a conifer with needles arranged in clusters of three. Broad-leaved, evergreen forests of *Schima wallichii* [*chilaaune*] and chestnut (*Castanopsis indica* [*dhalne katus*]) once covered much of subtropical central and eastern Nepal. Almost all of them have either been converted to agriculture or are much depleted, as they lie in regions of highest population density. Both species have oblong-elliptical, leathery leaves, alternately arranged on the twigs. The chestnut has silvery-gray fissured bark, while that of *Schima* is dark gray and rugged. The chestnut has a prickly-covered fruit. Riverine forest with *Toona* spp. (compound leaves divided into eight to thirty pairs of leaflets) and *Albizia* spp., or Nepali alder (*Alnus nipalensis* [*utis*]), often grow along streams. The alder has elliptical leaves alternately arranged on the twigs, and the fruits resemble miniature fir cones. Alder also frequently colonizes abandoned cultivation and landslides. There are small areas of evergreen forest in the far east. The showy, large, red flowers of the silk cotton tree (*Bombax malabaricum,* syn. *B. ceiba* [*simal*]) are a characteristic feature of the subtropical zone in spring. The flowers are clustered toward the ends of bare horizontal branches and are alive with mynahs, sunbirds, drongos, bulbuls, and other birds that feed on nectar. This tall, deciduous tree has branches that grow out from the trunk in regular whorls.

Just beyond the town, the gorge is very impressive. Descend for less than **10 minutes** and cross to the east (left) bank of the Marsyangdi Khola on a suspension bridge (4420 ft, 1347 m). The forests are temperate broad-leaved with bamboo. Continue upstream, usually high above the river, for almost **1½ hours** until you emerge from the gorge with its torrent below. An ancient landslide from the mountain to the east filled the gorge here, creating a lake that has become silted in above. The river itself flows buried beneath the rubble and is muffled but not seen.

Enter a broad, pleasant, flat valley with a somewhat quieter river; there are a few houses (Tale) and then a suspension bridge across the river that isn't taken. You have entered the Manang District. Continue ahead to the houses of **Tal** in the center of the flat valley (5460 ft, 1664 m) in **1½ hours** from Chamje. There is a police check post here. Try to spend a night here, for there is nowhere else along the trek quite like it. The area of Manang to the north is called Gyasumdo, meaning "meeting place of the three highways," referring to the proximity of three rivers, Marsyangdi, Didh, and Nar Kholas, to the north of here. It is inhabited partly by *BhoTiya,* who are primarily agropastoralists. These people were the real trans-Himalayan traders of the region until 1959 or 1960, when the trade closed after the Chinese takeover of Tibet.

Legend of the Formation of Tal

Tal, meaning "lake" in Nepali, refers to the feature created when a gigantic landslide, whose scar can be seen at the southeast end of the valley, blocked the outflow of the Marsyangdi. Eventually the lake became silted in and became this flat area.

Liesl Messerschmidt K.C. describes a *Gurung* legend about this lake. The mountains on either side of the valley are sacred deities. The east one is *Akhe Kai Du,* meaning "old grandfather rock," which looks to local people like a *torma,* the Buddhist ritual *tsampa* offering. The western one is *Pakre,* which is the entire eastern end of Lamjung Himal. These two deities, angry with one another, started to fight and threw boulders across the gorge, until *Pakre* won. The fight caused the slide on *Akhe's* side. Afterward, they made up and became blood relatives or *mit.* In front of the falls, you may see a *chorten* built by the local Lamas to appease the gods to not send more landslides.

The current route is to cross a cantilever bridge (5540 ft, 1689 m) **30 minutes** north of Tal. Pass a few houses, then proceed on a section that has been blasted out of the rock along the right (west) bank. In **45 minutes** come to a long suspension bridge (5960 ft, 1817 m) and cross to the left (east) bank of the Marsyangdi and Khotro, also called **Karte.** In **20 minutes** cross back to the west bank (6100 ft, 1859 m). **Five minutes** beyond is **Dharapani** (6180 ft, 1884 m). The lower portion is where traders used to graze their pack mules in the fields overnight.

Continue on upstream and note the valley coming in from the northeast some **10 minutes** beyond. It comes down from the Larkya Pass and leads north of Manaslu to the Buri Gandaki. The village of **Thonje,** which in *Gurung* means "pine trees growing on a flat place," lies at the confluence of the Dudh Khola and the Marsyangdi Khola. Such river junctions are always powerful places in Nepal; there is a small shrine located there. Don't fork right to cross the wooden cantilever bridge over the Marsyangdi Khola upstream of the river junction. There is more village and a police check post here. Some **10 minutes** beyond the confluence, take the lower fork—the upper leads to some higher villages. The general direction from here is northwest, rather than north. In the winter, you may see some highlanders, sun birds, camped along here. The *Gurung* along here practice shamanism with blood sacrifice, which is distinct from the Tantric Buddhism of the *Lama* who migrated here from Kyirong to the north which proscribes such practices. Such tolerance of different traditions is the norm in Nepal.

A pleasant **30-minute** walk brings you around the corner to the town of **Bagarchap** (6900 ft, 2103 m), meaning "butcher's place." This town has flat-roofed houses, indicating that rainfall is less here because the monsoon clouds first unload some of their water to the south. The waterworks flowing through the town are unusual—you will see nothing remotely similar until you reach Marpha in the Thak Khola across the Annapurna range to the west. The Diki Gomba of the Nyingmapa sect is worth a visit. There are views of the Annapurnas and part of Lamjung Himal. Note that this town was hit by a landslide in the winter of 1995, so parts of it have been destroyed.

Just beyond the town, take the left fork and do not go down to the cantilever bridge crossing the Marsyangdi Khola. Then fork right on a wider trail **17 minutes** from town and come to **Danakyu** (7140 ft, 2176 m) **15 minutes** beyond. There are attempts to cultivate fruit trees along here. Continue in the picturesquely narrow valley of temperate mixed broad-leaved forest.

You may see four light-colored diamond shapes on the rock to the left, near the middle part of the waterfall above the only concrete cantilever bridge I can recall in these parts. Local legend holds that a lama painted these auspicious symbols centuries ago. Unlike similar valleys in eastern Nepal, there are not many rhododendron trees along the trail.

Come up to **Chaumrikharka** (7380 ft, 2249 m), with its few houses and a lodge, in **45 minutes.** Timung and the trail to the Namun Bhanjyang is 1 hour above here. This high pass crosses the Himalayan barrier east of Lamjung Himal. Once heavily traveled, it is now only occasionally used by *Gurung* shepherds who pasture their sheep and goats on the high slopes. The newly constructed trail along the Marsyangdi Khola has replaced the dangerous old river bottom route that people avoided by taking the strenuous high route.

Birds of Prey of the Temperate Zone

The Himalayan griffon vulture (*Gyps himalayensis*, length 122 cm), like most vulture species, has long, broad wings and a short, broad tail. It sails majestically on motionless wings over mountains and valleys searching for food. From below, adults show white underparts and forewing and a dark trailing edge to the wing; immatures are dark brown. Occurs from subtropical to alpine zones.

Continue to **Lattemarang** (7720 ft, 2353 m) in **30 minutes.** This place's name evolved from *lato maanche*, meaning "a deaf mute," the first settler. Across the river, reached by a bridge that heads off between the two groups of lodges, are several hot springs. Fork left after you cross the bridge and reach the two pools.

Twenty minutes later is Tanshe Beshi. Keep on the left bank and fork right on a bigger trail in 25 minutes, and reach **Kotho** (meaning "walnut" in *Gurung*, 8300 ft, 2530 m) in **1¼ hour** from Lattemarang. The prominent tributary valley heading north is the Nar Khola, which drains the region called Nar Phu, whose inhabitants are traditionally pastoralists. Don't take the right fork heading there, just beyond the police check post in the upper part of Kotho (also called Qupar). The valley walls here might remind you of Yosemite.

To continue to Manang, enter **Chame** (8580 ft, 2615 m) in less than **30 minutes.** The name means "fields in the warm sunny corner under the cliffs," a brief daily occurrence. Note the unusual entrance *chorten* containing Hindu elements, the result of being a government town, the district center for Manang. It has a bank, a health center, electricity, and many shops. The nongovernmental people live at the west end of town, where there is a *gomba*. At the far end of town, first cross a tributary from the south and then the main Marsyangdi Khola, on either a cantilever or suspension bridge (8620 ft, 2627 m) to the north (left) bank. There are more houses here as well as some hot springs right at the river's edge about 200 yd (200 m) south of the bridge over the Marsyangdi Khola on the north (left) bank, beyond a lodge about as far as you can go downstream.

Go up the valley past more of Chame, to **Taleku** (8960 ft, 2731 m) in **30 minutes.** Continue in the unrelentingly narrow valley of pine, hemlock, and cypress forest, almost 1 hour to **Bhratang** (9340 ft, 2847 m). The apples you may enjoy in the northwest come from the orchards around here.

There used to be a *Khampa* village situated across the valley from here. These Tibetan refugee warriors settled here after the Chinese occupation of Tibet in 1959 and made raids to the north. They built several bridges; when I first journeyed up here, the bridge here was still in use and had remnants of a gate used to maintain control over all traffic in the valley. You still might see its remnants in the riverbed some 15 minutes upstream. The former village had a huge meeting hall for strategy sessions. The *Khampa* were all resettled in 1975 and the town was eventually destroyed, only to be rebuilt on the other side of the river to serve trekkers.

Head upstream on a new trail carved out of the narrow canyon walls, through hemlock and pine forest. Cross again to the south (right) bank in **35 minutes** on your choice of a suspension or cantilever bridge (9740 ft, 2969 m), and then climb into a serene pine, hemlock, and fir forest. After the days in the gorge, you can appreciate the beauty and silence of these **45 minutes.** Pass a rest house, a rock cairn memorial, and a clearing. There are facilities at Dhukur Pokhari Danda (10,200 ft, 3109 m).

As you look west, behind you, the Great Wall of Pisang rises almost 5000 ft (1500 m) up from the valley floor. The names for it include *Oble* in *Gurung*, *Yunga Drag Thang* in Tibetan, and *Paungda Danda* in Nepali, all roughly equivalent to the "Mountain of Heaven." This arc of slate portrays the intense folding of lakebed sediments that were upturned in the creation of the Himalaya. At the top are two stone formations, locally known as a temple with a dog-hitching post next to it, or the house of the wise old grandfather, with he himself standing beside it. Legends regarding it involve the Manang salt trade and *Gurung* death rituals. For the *Gurung* traveling to this wall was an important life milestone. As they passed it, they would ask the grandfather up above the price of salt up higher and dance and drum before continuing on. For the *Gurung* of Gyasumdo below, this dome is the entranace to the land of the dead. The spirits of the dead must be led by a shaman's ritual, and the huge boulders at the top represent the temple of the dead. For details, see Mumford's book listed in Appendix B. Relatives of the dead travel to the wall to pay their respects; they build *chorten* and make offerings and shout their ancestor's names, which echo back to them.

Just beyond the *mani* wall, if you fork right, the trail goes directly to a bridge over the Marsyangdi Khola to the north (left) bank (10,220 ft, 3115 m). Then you climb directly to Upper Pisang. The left fork keeps to the valley floor and Lower Pisang. Take this trail, and reach Lower **Pisang** (10,280 ft, 3133 m) in **45 minutes.** This town is now mostly a collection of lodges. Its name is derived from a word in the *Managi* dialect meaning "to work together at something." You can cross the river at the western part, fork right, and climb up to Upper Pisang (10,600 ft, 3231 m), where there is a *gomba* and amazing views of Annapurna II. An essential side trip.

MANANG TO THORUNG LA AND MUKTINATH

You are now in the wide, dry, arid region of Manang called Nyesyang, an abrupt change from the gorge. Because it is in the rain shadow of the Himalaya, which acts as a barrier to the wet monsoon clouds from the south, the area gets little rain in the summer. Snow falls here in the winter and remains on the ground much of the time. Unlike the people in the gorge to the south, the inhabitants here have been here for centuries. The men are traders and part-time farmers, and the women are full-time farmers. There is comparatively little animal husbandry. In the winter many leave for warmer places. You may meet many young men with considerable facility in English who have traveled far and wide in Asia. They may try to sell or trade almost anything. The people of Nyesyang were granted special trading privileges by the king in 1790. This included passports and import and export facilities. These privileges have been extended to all the people of the Manang District. Initially they traded local items, mostly medicinal herbs, animal products, and semiprecious stones for manufactured goods, usually in India and Burma, but more recently they have begun using hard currency from the export of expensive items to import machines and other manufactured goods from most South Asian countries. The resultant seasonal migration means less development of agriculture and animal husbandry, so you won't see many herds of yak, sheep, or goats at the higher elevations. These people are thus quite dependent on food imports.

From lower Pisang there are basically two routes, which join up in the valley below the village of Braga. The direct route keeps to the valley floor, staying mostly on the south (right) side. The other trail ascends on the north side of the valley to reach several villages on the north (left) side of the valley. The views of the mountains from this route are more impressive than from the floor, and the villages are quite interesting, but it takes perhaps 2 hours more to reach Braga. You will find fewer facilities here and, as well, fewer trekkers. I strongly advise you to take this way, and stay in local people's homes.

PISANG TO BRAGA VIA THE LOW ROUTE

For the lower route, start from lower Pisang, cross a tributary from the south, just beyond, regain the main Marsyangdi by a row of *mani* walls, and continue on its south (right) bank. Climb to a ridge crest, Ngoro Danda (11,060 ft, 3371 m), in **45 minutes.** Villagers may sell refreshments and souvenirs to trekkers here. Beyond, look up the hill to the north for the "red fort on the hill" mentioned below, the Manang Raja's fortress. **Hongde** (or Ongre, Omdhe, HumDe, or Hongre, 11,060 ft, 3371 m), a sprawling new settlement with an airstrip at its upper end, is reached in another **45 minutes.** The name degenerated from the Tibetan word meaning milk, referring to what was available when many yaks were pastured here. The RNAC office is here along with a police check post. If you are waiting for a flight here, recall what the letters stand for: Royal Nepal Always Cancels! Continue along, on a two-lane highway, to cross another tributary from the south in **20 minutes.** Here is a hydroelectric project to provide electricity for upper Manang Valley, but it can't provide enough, so there is load shedding as in Kathmandu. Some **20 minutes** later, cross the Marsyangdi Khola (11,160 ft, 3401 m). Ascend along the north (left) bank for 10 minutes to Munchi (11,240 ft, 3426 m), a dilapidated series of houses where the high, north-side route joins the main valley route. Stay on the north (left) bank of the Marsyangdi, and in **30 minutes** come to the base of **Braga** (11,320 ft, 3450 m). There is a cooperative hotel below the village but few facilities in the town perched above.

PISANG TO BRAGA VIA THE HIGH ROUTE

The high, north-side route begins in lower Pisang. Like many villages here, the town is constructed using flat roofs. The roof of one house serves as the yard or open area of the house above it. There is a long, handsome wall of prayer wheels in an open space below a little-used *gomba*. To head up the valley on the north side, cross the Marsyangdi Khola (10,260 ft, 3127 m) and immediately fork left to head upstream. Cross a tributary (10,800 ft, 3292 m) and contour northwest in a pleasant pine and juniper forest. Pass by a small green lake. If you are coming from upper Pisang, and contour, you will reach this lake. Continue contouring to a long *mani* wall. Then descend to cross a tributary (10,775 ft, 3284 m) a little over **30 minutes** from Pisang. Take the upper fork and begin a steep climb for 1 hour to **Ghyaru**, meaning "goat pasture," at 12,050 ft (3673 m). Lore has it that when Tibetans came here to see if this was a good place to farm, they planted some wheat seed inside a yak horn. If the seeds germinated, as they did, it would be a good place to settle. The surrounding fields of wheat and buckwheat attest to that prophesy. Spectacular views of Annapurnas II and III and Gangapurna are the main attractions, along with the dark, tunnellike streets of the town.

Contour out of the town to the west, cross a tributary (12,075 ft, 3680 m), and reach a ridge crest (12,375 ft, 3772 m) some 100 ft (30 m) above some ruins of an old fort, the Tiwol Danda ("red fort on the hill") in **45 minutes.** The fortress perched on this strategic site was the palace of the Manang Raja before the Gurkha conquest in the late eighteenth century. Rest here and enjoy the views of Gangapurna, Glacier Dome, and Tilicho Peak to the west. North of Tilicho Peak lies the "great frozen lake," named by Herzog, although it is out of view from here. If you cross Thorung La, you will eventually return to Pokhara by heading well north and then west of this peak.

Continue contouring, cross a tributary, and pass three trails joining yours on the left. Cross another tributary to **Ngawal** (11,975 ft, 3650 m) **45 minutes** from the ruins. Descend to cross a tributary in a few minutes, and then continue descending, avoiding a left fork (11,625 ft, 3543 m) 10 minutes beyond town. Descend to the valley floor (11,325 ft, 3452 m) and, in **1¼ hours** from Ngawal, reach the few houses of Munchi (11,425 ft, 3482 m). Here the trail meets the main lower trail from Pisang. **Braga** is 30 minutes away.

Braga (the name refers to the white cliffs above), a large and interesting village, is the seat of the oldest monastery in the area. The *gomba* is perhaps 900 years old, and belongs to the Kargyupa sect of Tibetan Buddhism. Like most of the *gomba* in this region, it is not very active but is well worth a visit, for it contains some unique works of art and is spectacularly situated. The *Konyer* ("custodian") will show you around, sometimes with varying amounts of patience. The main temple holds 108 terra-cotta statues, each about 2 ft (60 cm) high, arranged in rows along three of the four walls. They represent the Kargyupa lineage and much more. There is another three-story temple above this main building. The temple is described in detail in David Snellgrove's *Himalayan Pilgrimage.*

The village of **Manang** (11,480 ft, 3499 m) is **30 minutes** beyond Braga. Between two tributaries along the way, on a ridge to the north, lies the Bod-zo *gomba*. Reach this *gomba* by climbing upstream before crossing the second of the series of tributaries. Head up the valley for 30 minutes to the ridge crest (11,750 ft, 3581 m). Directly to the north of it, across a tributary, is the new Kargyupa *gomba*. Before going to either of these, try to determine whether the key bearer is around.

You can restock your provisions in Manang, but prices are high. Attend one of the Himalayan Rescue Association post's daily lectures on altitude illness. If you are planning to cross Thorung La and reach the Kali Gandaki to the west, it is important to spend a day or two acclimatizing here before proceeding. Don't go on to sleep higher if you have a headache. If you have flown to Manang, you should spend at least 3 or 4 days in this region before attempting to cross the pass. In addition, it is advisable to spend an additional night at Leder, before going on to Phedi. Acclimatization days are best spent being active and climbing to high elevations for views but returning to lower altitudes to sleep. There are many suitable hikes on both sides of the valley. These extra acclimatization days may be unnecessary for some or not long enough for others. They are guidelines on how to proceed with less risk.

For people traveling without food or tents, it is now possible to cross the pass relying on local facilities, except during the winter, when crossing the pass is a mountaineering endeavor. However, it is best to bring some extra food from Manang. Ask here if Phedi is set up to provide services outside of the usual trekking season. This has recently been the case, even in the monsoon!

Peoples of Central Nepal: *BhoTiya*

Tibetan *BhoTiya* groups of northern central Nepal come from Nupri (northern Gorkha District, upper Buri Gandaki river), Manang (upper Marsyangdi river), Lo–Manthang (upper Kali Gandaki river), and from Dolpo and Tarap (north of the Dhaulagiri massif). During the winter months, large numbers of these high-mountain peoples trek south to the lower hills and are often encountered in and around bazaar towns, where they engage in trade and sometimes run inns and small shops. Many of the pony and donkey trains encountered along the Thak Khola trek route are operated by *BhoTiya* men from the Lo–Manthang region, northern Thak Khola, and the valley of Muktinath, all in the northern Mustang District.

Finally, north of the Muktinath Valley, there are the *Lopa*, the *BhoTiya* people of the upper Mustang District, in what was once the petty kingdom of Mustang. Their lives center around high, dry-land agriculture on oasislike farmland wherever nearby streams can be diverted for irrigation water, and they follow pastoral pursuits with sheep, goats, and yak. In winter, many of them migrate south as traders and pony drivers. These people are Tibetan Buddhists, and some practice the pre-Buddhist religion called Bon. There are a number of small monasteries of both religions throughout the Thak Khola and upper Mustang. In their northernmost walled town of Manthang lives the king of the *Lopa*, the Raja of Mustang, whose allegiance is firmly with the government in Kathmandu.

REST DAY ACTIVITIES NEAR MANANG

There are several "rest day" activities possible. Perhaps you may see an archery contest or a horse race! An hour above the town, there is a lama who likes to receive visitors and give blessings. Manang itself is spectacularly perched across from a glacial lake formed by water from Gangapurna and Annapurna III. Cross the Marsyangdi below town by the school and fork right to go up to the lake. Go around it and visit the caves at the foot of the icefall. Or climb up the lateral moraine on its southeast side for good views of the Chulu peaks and Manang.

A good half-day hike is a circuit to Khangsar, the last town before Tilicho Tal. A visit here may give a glimpse of what the region was like before Westerners invaded. To get there, go through Manang, and then 3 minutes beyond, where you pass a *mani* wall with prayer wheels, fork left and descend to the bridge by the river. Cross it and head upstream to climb to a shelf. Contour into the valley of the Khangsar Khola and cross a small slide area. Continue through a serene forest, eventually descending to cross the Khangsar Khola. Ascend to Khangsar (12,180 ft, 3712 m), 1½ hours from Manang. To return, keep high on the north side of the valley until you reach a plateau with some ruins, and then descend its north side to cross the Marsyangdi and head downstream to the bridge you crossed before.

TILICHO TAL

Beyond Khangsar is the impressive north face of Tilicho Peak. An approach to the lake at its foot has been described from the Kali Gandaki side. It can also be reached from Khangsar in 2 days and camping is necessary. Parties must be acclimatized. Check in Khangsar to see whether the lodge that has been constructed halfway up the valley is in operation. From there you could make a long day trip to see the lake and return, without having to camp and allowing a 2-day side trip in good conditions.

To proceed there from Khangsar, take a trail that follows the river; it takes about 4 hours to reach a meadow (14,100 ft, 4298 m) to camp, where there is water and the lodge. A further 3 hours' climb along a series of ridges, followed by an unpleasant traverse, will bring you to the crest of the moraine. The lake can be seen from beyond there. In bad weather it can be difficult to find the lake from the east. It is frozen in winter, and periods of thaw vary from year to year. You can pick a route down through the moraine to reach the lake in another 2 hours. Be aware that storms can blow up unexpectedly from the south in this region. On one trip, it went from not a cloud in the sky to pelting-down snow in an hour—and an accumulation of several feet by the morning!

To proceed from Manang over Thorung La, cross a tributary below a falls northwest of Manang and climb up to Tengi (11,950 ft, 3642 m) in **30 minutes.** This last permanent settlement below the pass has few tourist facilities. Climb gradually to reach some *goTh* and hotels at Ghunsang (12,725 ft, 3879 m) in **1 hour. Ten minutes** farther is a higher settlement of *goTh* and another hotel, called Thora. The trail has now turned northwest up the valley of the Jargeng Khola. Pass some *goTh,* cross small tributaries, on variable bridges, and contour along pleasant meadows with occasional birch groves. If you are here early in the morning or late in the afternoon, look for herds of blue sheep, which may descend for water. Reach Yak Kharka (13,020 ft, 3968 m) in **1½ hours,** with hotels there, and one 10 minutes before. Letdar (13,700 ft, 4176 m) is **1¼ hours** from Yak Kharka. The original two-story shelter is beyond the hotels. It is possible to hire a horse from here to the summit of the pass. People have been put on a horse only to arrive higher up unconscious and moribund from altitude illness. Acclimatizing and walking is safer.

Do not attempt to cross the pass unless all of the party, including the porters, are equipped for cold and bad weather. If the weather is threatening, do not proceed. Lives of trekkers and porters have been needlessly lost on this pass because parties proceeded in bad weather. Recently, many people have been crossing the pass wearing running shoes and other light footwear. If you do not carry proper boots, at least recognize that there is risk of frostbite should a storm occur. I have seen trekkers get serious frostbite on this pass. Losing fingers and toes is a big price to pay! If stuck with poor footwear, in bad conditions, and unwilling to turn back, wrap your feet in plastic socks as a vapor barrier. This may help, but there are no guarantees. There is safety in numbers, so travel in groups.

From Leder, climb, pass above a tarn, contour, and then descend to the river by a bridge (14,000 ft, 4267 m) in **45 minutes.** Cross to the west (right) bank of the Jargeng Khola, and climb and contour upstream to reach the riverbed and campsite (14,450 ft, 4404 m), called **Phedi**, meaning "foot of hill," in **45 minutes** from the bridge. Landslides along here may change the route. There are lodges and a police check post another **15 minutes** up the hill (14,660 ft, 4468 m) during the trekking season. The police may advise you as to the feasibility of crossing the pass in current conditions. A lucky trekker has spotted a snow leopard near here at dusk!

Mammals of the Alpine Zone

The snow leopard (*Panthera uncia* [*hIU chituwaa*], length 100 to 110 cm) is one of the Himalaya's most elusive animals. It occurs above the treeline, mainly in the trans-Himalayan region near the Tibetan border. Well adapted for life at high altitudes, it has a long, thick coat. There have been recent sightings by trekkers near Thorung Phedi, north of Manang, south of Ganja La, and in the Kangchenjunga region.

The Himalayan marmot (*Marmota bobak* [*himali marmot*], length 60 cm) has a distinctive squat build, medium tail, and very small ears. Large colonies live in deep burrows in the open country of the trans-Himalayan region.

The blue sheep, or bharal (*Pseudois nayaur* [*nyaaur*], shoulder height 90 cm), is intermediate in appearance between sheep and goats. It has long backward-curving horns. Herds of ten to fifty graze on grass slopes between treeline and snowline, usually within cover of rock cliffs, rarely descending below 12,000 ft (3660 m) in winter. It can be seen in the Manang District east of Thorung La on the Annapurna circuit, near Kangchenjunga, or north of Dhorpatan.

Leave at daybreak. It takes a long day to cross the pass, but doing the first quarter in the dark is unnecessarily tiring, and stumbles and falls can result in injury, fatigue, and getting wet, which can lead to hypothermia and frostbite higher up. As well, the wind is too variable to predict.

The trail now leaves the river valley, which continues northwest and then ascends west. In dry weather, water can be scarce the next day, so fill up. There are no good campsites with water beyond the pass unless you camp on snow in the appropriate season. In early-season snow (November through December) or early-spring conditions (March through April), don't underestimate the difficulties of proceeding, especially if you don't have mountaineering experience. In deep snow, an ice ax, ski pole, or walking stick is helpful. Some parties bring a stove to melt snow and rehydrate along the way.

From Phedi, ascend to a notch (15,725 ft, 4793 m) in 1¼ **hours** and head left (west), traversing to the base of a prominent lateral moraine (15,900 ft, 4846 m) in **30 minutes.** Reach its crest (16,050 ft, 4892 m) a few minutes later, and continue west along less steep terrain. After many false crests, reach Thorung La (17,769 ft, 5416 m) in **2 hours** if you are adequately acclimatized. A large cairn marks the pass, but it may be almost entirely covered with snow. The pass is exhilarating in that it is an abrupt transition from one major Himalayan valley to another, but views from the pass are probably less impressive than those on either side. Far below you to the west is the Kali Gandaki. Those with sharp eyes and binoculars can pick out the green oasis of Kagbeni.

The descent from the pass is gradual at first and follows the middle of the valley for the first hour. It becomes considerably steeper and keeps to the south side of the valley on scree. The first campsites, with some *goTh*, called Thante (14,450 ft, 4404 m), are some 2 hours down from the pass just after crossing a tributary to the right. Locals are only here during the monsoon. In the dry season, after and just before the monsoon, when all the snow has melted, there is no water available, necessitating a further descent. There are more *goTh* frames around 13,720 ft (4182 m), but the nearest lodge or inn is Chatar Puk, or Chambar (13,500 ft, 4115 m), perhaps **3 hours** from the pass. Just as at Phedi, there will be no one here in the middle of the winter—if you are coming up from Muktinath at that time, ask there first. Because fewer people cross the pass from this side, there is not a great deal of sleeping space, compared to the Phedi side. Cross a tributary (which may be dry) to the left (it flows from the south), and descend to a major tributary in the valley floor (12,650 ft, 3856 m). Cross it to the south (left) bank and ascend a bit to continue down the main valley. Reach **Muktinath** (12,460 ft, 3798 m) after rounding a corner **1 hour** from Chatar Puk. There is a police check post here, and they may advise you against proceeding to Thorung La in marginal conditions.

To continue, reverse the trail descriptions given earlier for the trek from Pokhara to Muktinath.

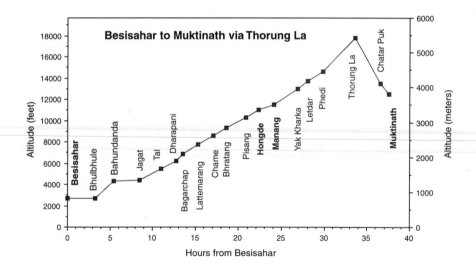

Questions to Ponder: Cultural Conservation

Why do Nepali people seem to cling to old ways that may, on reflection, seem to be foolish or counterproductive? If your return home from Nepal was suddenly made impossible, which of your cultural trappings would you cling to most tenaciously? Which would you insist on passing on to your children and grandchildren? If you had to live in the Nepali village you are in, what changes would you want to make? Would you be successful? What would be the hardest part of adapting? What would be the joys of staying here?

Fifty or a hundred years from now, imagine going through a Nepali museum showing artifacts of particular villages you have been through. Compare this imagined trip to one through a North American Indian Tribal museum you may have taken recently or (as I did) a Ukrainian outdoor museum.

6   Solu-Khumbu (The Everest Region)

Because it's there.

> Replied George Mallory, one of the first climbers to attempt Everest, when asked why he wanted to climb it. He disappeared into a cloud near the summit in 1924, where his body was found in 1999.

There are several possible ways of reaching the Solu-Khumbu District of Nepal. The classic way to Khumbu, the northernmost part of the district, was to walk from Kathmandu. But because roads continue to be built ever closer to Khumbu, the route now begins at Jiri, reached in less than a day by bus from Kathmandu.

Scheduled inexpensive plane service to Lukla and some service to Shyangboche has markedly changed access and egress to the Khumbu region. Gone are the days of acrimonious bottlenecks at Lukla, as stranded trekkers desperately tried to get back to their hectic home schedules. This change in tourist access has significantly impacted the local economy, as lodges on the Jiri to Lukla route stand empty, and trekker porter wages can no longer supplement the food deficit that most peasant households in the area have to endure. The lodges between Lukla and Namche Bazaar have also suffered a decline in business as a result. Projected increase in Khumbu trekker traffic has resulted in much lodge building there, and the benefits from tourism continue to contribute to regional economic inequality. Trekkers who walk from Jiri to Khumbu, continuing the tradition of the past, often find that part of the journey the most enjoyable. If trekker traffic from Jiri continues to decline, the lodge situation described here (lodges all the way) may decline, and trekkers may be more inclined to sleep in traditional inns or people's homes—and experience hill Nepal!

Rapid ascent to high altitudes can be dangerous, even fatal, so it is safest to walk to Khumbu and fly out, if you want to fly a segment. If you must fly in, choose Lukla as the destination, rather than Shyangboche, because it is sufficiently lower to make it somewhat safer. At the time of writing (early 1999), Russian Mi-17 helicopters are taking passengers to or from Shyangboche, but other charter services are also available. If you are walking one or both ways, the journey from Kathmandu to Khumbu can be combined with the trek from Khumbu to the Arun Valley in eastern Nepal, using air transportation from Tumlingtar to Kathmandu or getting to the roadhead at Hille. This is described in chapter 8. You can also reach and leave the Khumbu region via Rolwaling to the east by crossing the Trashi Labsta, a high, glaciated pass to the west (18,885 ft, 5775 m), and going through Rolwaling to the Kathmandu–Kodari road. This long crossing is hazardous and requires some mountaineering skills and equipment and considerable stamina. The pass is currently restricted to those with a trekking peak permit for Pharchamo, which can be obtained by interested parties wishing to take this route. Sir Edmund Hillary once said it was one of the hardest passes he had ever crossed. This trek, best attempted in the early autumn or late spring, takes a minimum of 10 days.

In the route descriptions that follow, the times listed between points are actual walking times, generally those I took myself. They *do not* include any rests. This has been strictly adhered to by using a chronograph. Over most of the trails I carried a moderately heavy pack. I almost never walked the segments in these times. Like everyone else, I rested, photographed, talked with the people, and so forth.

Jiri to Solu-Khumbu
(Map No. 3, Page 214)

JIRI TO CHOPLUNG/LUKLA

The walk from Jiri to Khumbu is recommended as an introduction to the hills of Nepal. A few pleasant diversions along the way are described. Average walking time to Namche Bazaar is 7 to 9 days from Jiri, though athletes can do it in 4 or 5. You more than climb Everest along the way if you total all the ascents, but it is well worth it. The main rivers run south and are separated by high ridges, so the route is a succession of ups and downs. Compared to the trek between Pokhara and Kathmandu, which also goes against the grain of the land, the ridges and valleys are much higher and the climbs and descents are more strenuous. There are lodges all the way, and there is much less trekker traffic because the helicopter access to Khumbu has improved. The route is strongly recommended.

Take the bus heading to Jiri, which leaves from the staging area north of the Kathmandu city hall, east of Tundikhel. The ride takes a day. Buses leave at 5:00, 6:00, and 7:00 A.M. Buy a ticket on the morning you leave, as you can't in advance. More buses go to Charikot and Tama Kosi, which can give trekkers a different starting point and a walk to get to Jiri. Be aware that there have been incidents of theft on the public buses that take trekkers to Jiri. Luggage is broken into and pickpocketing occurs. Try and carry your pack inside the bus, perhaps buying a seat for it. Be watchful, and consider getting on the rooftop if others are up there. Or hire a private vehicle (and still be watchful!). It can be difficult to arrange a private vehicle back from Jiri. Jiri was the site of a Swiss hill development project that built a hospital and technical school and focused on agricultural inputs. A police check post is located near the market site, before the trail descends to the valley floor. There are tourist lodges in Jiri in the valley floor where you can arrange porters and buy last minute items.

From **Jiri** (6250 ft, 1905 m) there are two choices. One route passes through Those, a *Newar* bazaar with an old iron manufacturing center. The other route ascends higher and offers distant views of mountains.

To take the more popular high route from Jiri, climb the east side of the Jiri Valley in a rhododendron forest, past the tea shops at Chitre, to reach a pass with more tea shops (7875 ft, 2400 m) after 1½ **hours**. Then descend to a bridge over the Yelung Khola. Along the way are more simple tea shops and lodges. As you drop down, notice the cliffs on the north side, and look for beehives. In late spring, villagers will dangle on rope ladders to harvest honey from them. Cross the bridge to the northeast (left) bank and go on to a suspension bridge over the Khimti Khola. **Shivalaya** (5900 ft, 1800 m), the village on the other side, is 1½ **hours** from the pass.

The route from Jiri through Those follows the east (left) bank of the Jiri Khola south past the hospital to about 6125 ft (1867 m) and ascends, passing near the village of Kune (6775 ft, 2064 m), where it meets the preroad route. The trail continues to a notch marked with *chorten* (8800 ft, 2070 m) in a chir pine and oak forest and then descends, passing the settlement of Kattike to the south, to the

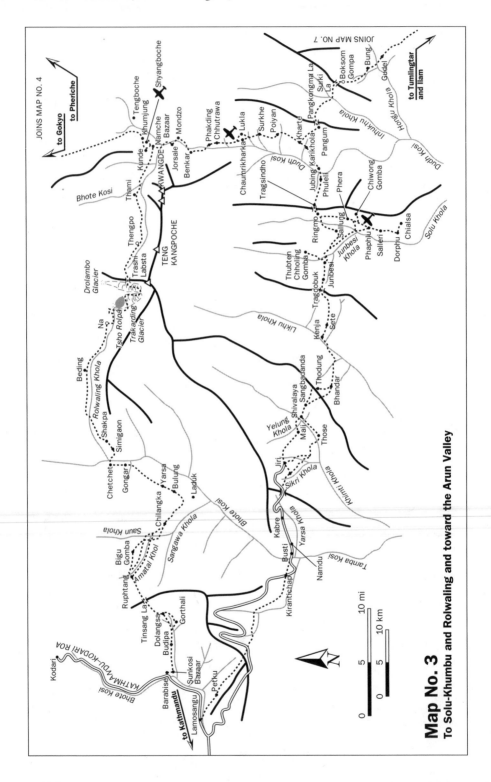

Map No. 3
To Solu-Khumbu and Rolwaling and toward the Arun Valley

Khimti Khola (5750 ft, 1753 m), which is followed on its west (right) bank to a suspension bridge. Cross it and follow the river north to **Those** (5775 ft, 1760 m). From Jiri to Those takes **2½ to 3 hours**. From Those, follow the river on its east (left) bank, walking upstream for **1½ hours** to **Shivalaya** (5900 ft, 1800 m).

All the route choices end up at Shivalaya, the home of Shiva, where there are lodges and a police check post. From here the trail climbs steeply up the ridge to the scattered village of **Sangbadanda** with its schoolhouse (7350 ft, 2240 m) in **1¾ hours**. Just up from the schoolhouse, the trail branches. If you take the right fork, shortly beyond is Kasourbas, another Sherpa settlement. The left branch heads up past the village of **Buldanda** (8200 ft, 2500 m) to the Swiss-designed cheese factory and lodge at **Thodung** (10,140 ft, 3091 m), about **2¾ hours** from Sangbadanda. Besides buying cheese here, you can get a good view of Gaurishankar to the north. This peak (23,459 ft, 7150 m) was once thought to be the highest in the world because it was visible from so far away. Thodung is definitely a worthwhile detour. There is a monastery 30 minutes south of the cheese factory. To rejoin the regular route, head south along the ridge to the pass (8900 ft, 2713 m), reaching it in 1 hour.

Questions to Ponder: Ethnic Groups and Gender Roles

Do people wear makeup? Which sexes or ethnic groups? What materials do they apply? Do you see mirrors? Are people concerned about their appearance as much as you expected? How physically close can people be to one another without feeling uncomfortable? What about eye contact, body language, posturing, and physical contact? Is there much physical display of affection?

What distinctions do you see between gender roles and identity? What kind of work do men do? Women? Who does what work and how does this vary with ethnic groups? What do children do most of the day? What do they play with? Do they cry as often as you might expect? Do you see them sucking their thumbs? At what age are children weaned? How many children go to school? Mostly boys or girls? Are they in school during harvest times or other periods of intense farm work? Where are the village schools built? How many of them function? Are the classes held inside the building? What supplies does the school have? What means of learning are used? How much teaching is done by chanting? What jobs are available to the educated?

What is the role of young unmarried women? Do you ever see them alone, or are they always in groups? Do you ever see them talking to single men? How do teenagers entertain themselves? What are the status and role of old people?

The direct trail to the pass, the right fork, continues along the north side of the valley of the Mohabir Khola, crossing numerous tributaries and entering a rhododendron and broad-leaved forest until the pass (8900 ft, 2713 m) is reached. It takes **1¾ hours** to reach the pass from Sangbadanda. The pass originally had no name (being insignificant in the Nepali perspective, so as settlement occurred and trekkers asked the name, Deorali, or "pass," was the obvious choice. There are now tea shops and lodges run by Sherpas at the pass and also one of the largest collections of mani walls in Nepal. From the pass, take the left fork. The trail descends into the beautiful, lush valley to the east and heads toward the large *stupas* by a small gomba at the town of **Bhandar**, called Chyangma by Sherpas (7200 ft, 2194 m), where there are plenty of comfortable lodges. This walk takes **1 hour**.

From the scattered village of Bhandar, descend the fertile plateau toward a notch to cross a river (6600 ft, 2012 m) on a covered bridge. Just beyond, take the fork to the far left. Then go on through forests and terraces, asking villagers the way to Kenja, as there are numerous trail junctions, to cross the Surma Khola (5100 ft, 1555 m) to its north (left) bank. Continue to the Likhu Khola and cross it on the second suspension bridge (5060 ft, 1543 m) to its east (left) bank. It takes **2 hours** to reach the river from Bhandar and then less than 1 hour of walking upstream along its east (left) bank through broad-leaved forest to reach the Kenja Khola, which is crossed to **Kenja** (5360 ft, 1634 m) with its numerous lodges.

The biggest climb of the journey so far, up to Lamjura Pass (11,580 ft, 3530 m), begins behind the town and follows a ridge more or less on its south side through oak forest to the settlement of **Sete** (8450 ft, 2575 m), which has lodges and a small *gomba* above it. Be sure to obtain water from the streams crossing the trail below Sete, as there is little until you have descended the other side of the pass. It takes **2¼ to 3 hours** to reach Sete from Kenja. Beyond, the trail continues along the ridge in a prickly-leaved oak forest. Reach the few houses and lodge of Dakchu (9350 ft, 2850 m) 1 hour beyond. A water-supply system may be functioning here. Goyun (10,350 ft, 3155 m) is a small cluster of tea shops and lodges 1 hour beyond. The trail passes through impressive stands of fir. The ridge you have been following meets the main ridge striking north–south, and you fork left at a *mani* wall (11,300 ft, 3444 m). Contour in a once splendid rhododendron grove to reach the pass and beyond. There are now tea shops and lodges along the way to the pass. During the monsoon, people use makeshift shelters along the way to churn milk into butter or *ghiu*. The pass (11,582 ft, 3530 m) is **3 to 4 hours** from Sete. There were lodges here in 1996. Despite the height of the pass, there is no view of the mountains, but those with time and energy can climb several hours to the peak north of the pass (13,159 ft, 4010 m) for views in good weather.

From Lamjura Pass, the trail descends through a fir and rhododendron forest past a lodge and emerges at **Tragdobuk**, also called Taktor with several lodges (9380 ft, 2860 m), in **1½ hours**. Continue on the north side of the valley, avoiding right forks, round a notch, and drop down to the town of **Junbesi** (8775 ft, 2675 m) in 1 hour. The Serlo Monastery above the village is quite active. The monks print ancient Buddhist texts from woodblocks. Junbesi with its many lodges has prospered from trekkers, Hillary's Himalayan Trust development efforts, and the dedication of western Buddhist seekers. *Rhythms of a Himalayan Village* is an informative book about this area's past. Now there is television and phone service.

THUBTEN CHHOLING GOMBA

About 1½ hours off the main trail to the north of Junbesi lies Thubten Chholing Gomba, an active monastery with 150 monks. The abbot there, Trulshik Rimpoche, was formerly at the Rongbuk Monastery on the northern slopes of Mount Everest in Tibet. The small *gomba* is exquisitely painted and definitely worth seeing. To reach it, head north from Junbesi past some *chorten* and *mani* walls to a bridge (9000 ft, 2743 m) over the main Junbesi Khola, 30 minutes from town. Continue up the east (left) bank until you spot the monastery on a shelf above you to the east. Follow the main trail past fine Sherpa homes until you are just about under the *gomba* and head directly up to it. The town of Mobung is nearby. The *gomba* is 1 to 1½ hours from Junbesi. Rimpoche was the subject of a 1986 British documentary film entitled *Lord of the Dance, Destroyer of Illusion*. There is a high-level route linking this area with Ringmo. From Junbesi you can also head south to the major Solu towns of Salleri and Phaphlu. The *Shorong/Hinku* map of the Research Scheme Nepal Himalaya covers the trek from here to Namche Bazaar.

Questions to Ponder: Pets and Other Animals

What role do pets play in Nepali people's lives? Do you see many cats? What do Nepalis feed their pets and how do they treat them? Are they affectionate toward them in ways you would expect?

What domestic animals are given status in the community? How big are they compared to similar breeds in your home country? Who cares for them? What evidence of disease do you see? In what parts of the country do they keep pigs regularly? Why aren't there more horses? What parts of the animals do they use? At what age can a child begin tending an animal? Are wild animals hunted? With what? Which animals are feared? What parts of wild animals are used?

To continue to Namche Bazaar from Junbesi, cross the Junbesi Khola on a bridge below the *stupa* (8700 ft, 2552 m) and above the hydrogenerating station, seen once you cross. Take the extreme left or upper trail up the valley to the south (the right heads to Phaphlu and Salleri). The trail passes through blue pine forest to rhododendron and prickly-leaved oak forest typical of western midland forest. Such forests are often found on south-facing slopes in this region. Reach open country, round the crest (10,000 ft, 3048 m) of the Sallung ridge, and look for Mount Everest on a clear morning. There is a view lodge here. You can climb up the ridge to the north for better views. Head north up the valley of the Ringmo Khola to the town of Sallung (9700 ft, 2953 m), with more lodges, about **2 hours** from Junbesi.

From here, the trail descends through oak forests to cross two tributaries, below the peaks (Numbur and Khatang) where the local gods reside, and then the main river of the Ringmo Khola (8525 ft, 2599 m). The trail then ascends to the houses of **Ringmo** (9200 ft, 2805 m), **1½ hours** from Sallung. En route, the trail branches after crossing the river. The right branch heads south to Phaphlu. You could also head north to yak pastures and reach the Dudh Kosi, but this is a challenging route. From Ringmo, the wide trail ascends east through juniper woods past some rectangular *mani* walls to Tragsindho La (10,075 ft, 3071 m) with *chorten, mani* walls, prayer flags, and hotels. To the south, 450 ft (137 m) below, there is a cheese factory on the west side of the river. You probably will have seen signs pointing the way there. To the east is the valley of the Dudh Kosi, and the region called Pharak (meaning "different" from Solu, and Khumbu). You will follow the valley north to Khumbu. Meanwhile, 460 ft (140 m) below you is **Tragsindho Monastery** with lodges nearby. To reach it, take the left branch of the trail at the junction 100 ft (30 m) below the pass on the east side. The other trail passes above the monastery and rejoins the monastery trail 100 ft (30 m) below the *gomba*. It takes **45 minutes** to reach the pass from Ringmo and another **15 minutes** to reach the Gelugpa monastery.

From Tragsindho, the trail forks right, descends to the southeast, passes through forests, and emerges at the prosperous Sherpa village and lodges of **Manidingma** (Nuntale) (7200 ft, 2194 m) in **1½ hours**. A mini-hydel plant powers the village.

Beyond, descend past terraces into oak forests to emerge at a bridge over the Dudh Kosi (4900 ft, 1493 m) 1½ **hours** from Manidingma.

The trail crosses the river to the east (left) bank and heads north to reach Namche Bazaar in 3 days. Sometimes the trail is over a mile above the river, which falls through a steep gorge. There have been many improvements in agriculture in Pharak over the years. You may notice fruit trees and many varieties of vegetables. The main trail north of here is being continuously improved. Ask locally for the latest routes.

Follow the river through forests, and then climb through terraces to reach the *Rai* village and lodges of **Jubing** (5500 ft, 1676 m) in **40 minutes.** This is your only opportunity along this trek to see a settlement of these people who populate so much of eastern Nepal. The British found the *Rai* to be excellent soldiers and actively recruited them as Gurkhas. *Rai* are ethnically and linguistically diverse, speaking many different languages, with attendant different customs. Climb through the village, round a ridge, and aim for the prominent notch in front of you where there is a check post. From the notch (6900 ft, 2103 m), contour to the village of **Karikhola** (6575 ft, 2004 m) inhabited by Sherpas, *Rai,* and *Magar.* Karikhola is 1½ **hours** from Jubing. The *Magar* hail from western Nepal, settling here generations ago. They no longer speak their native language. The town has prospered with many lodges and shops.

Mammals of the Temperate Zone

The gray langur (*Presbytis entellus* [*bAAdar*], head and body length 60 to 75 cm) is long-tailed and long-limbed, with silver-gray fur and a distinctive black face. Troops inhabit forests and feed on leaves, flowers, and fruits. Easily seen on the Thak Khola trek near Ghasa and GhoRepani, it occurs from tropical to alpine zones.

The lesser (or red) panda (*Ailurus fulgens* [*haabre*], head and body length 60 cm) is rich chestnut above with a white face, dark legs, and a long, ringed tail. A forest dweller, it is nocturnal, remaining in treetops during the day. It has been seen in Langtang National Park and between GhoRepani and Ghandruk in the Annapurna Conservation Area.

The yellow-throated marten (*Martes flavigula* [*malsAApro*], length 45 to 60 cm), a lithe, arboreal predator, has a yellow throat and a long tail that makes up over a third of its length. It also occurs in the subtropical zone.

The leopard (*Panthera pardus* [*chituwaa*], length 185 to 215 cm) is rarely seen but not uncommon; you may find tracks on the trail. Found in open country, scrub, dense forest, and near villages, it also occurs in tropical and subtropical zones.

The Himalayan musk deer (*Moschus chrysogaster* [*kasturi mriga*], shoulder height 50 cm) is a small deer with large, rounded ears. The male has long upper teeth that form tusks. Now rare because of persecution, it inhabits upper temperate and subalpine forests and shrubbery.

The Indian muntjac (*Muntiacus muntjak* [*ratuwaa*], male shoulder height 50 to 75 cm) is also known as the barking deer after its distinctive barking alarm call, which sounds remarkably like a dog. It inhabits forests and forest edges, especially rocky ravines, and also occurs in tropical and subtropical zones.

The mainland serow (*Capricornis sumatraensis* [*thar*], male shoulder height 100 to 110 cm) is a thickset, goatlike mammal. Chestnut or blackish, usually solitary, it occurs in thickly forested ravines and steep slopes.

Cross the bridge over the Kari Khola, and ascend its north (right) bank below the scattered settlement of Kharte. Reach **Bupsa,** with lodges (7700 ft, 2347 m), in an **hour** on a redirected trail that avoids over 2 hours of climbing. Visit the *gomba* here. Contour into the next valley, pass some lodges, and climb below the old trail. If coming from Pangkongma La, and the Arun Valley, the trail meets above Bupsa at upper Kharte.

The next tributary valley to the north has to be traversed. Descend 1000 ft (305 m) and cross the tributary. Round a crest below Khari La where you can see Cho Oyu and Gyachung Kang. Continue on the north side of the valley to reach **Poiyan** and its lodges (9175 ft, 2796 m) in **3 hours.** Continue to below Chutok La (9100 ft, 2773 m) on the crest of a ridge. Enter the valley of another tributary, the Poiyan Khola. Almost due north is the sacred mountain Khumbiyula at the head of the valley. The village and lodges of **Surkhe** (7525 ft, 2293 m) on both sides of the tributary are **2 hours** from Poiyan.

The trail now leaves this tributary valley and heads more directly north toward the town of Chaumrikharka, another scattered village. Along the way, pass the fork to Lukla (7850 ft, 2393 m), 30 minutes beyond Surkhe. This junction is reached just before the main trail crosses a stream on a small cantilever bridge. The STOL field (9350 ft, 2850 m) is 1 hour from here. Before ascending to **Chaumrikharka** (8500 ft, 2591 m, to 8900 ft, 2713 m) the main trail crosses a spectacular deep gorge with a high waterfall (7900 ft, 2408 m). Upper Chaumrikharka (8700 ft, 2652 m), with several large slopes, stupas of varying designs, and a *gomba*, is 1¾ **hours** from Surkhe. From here on, the going is easier; the major climbs are over. The trail from Chaumrikharka (which means "pastures for yak-cow cross-breeds," referring to days long past) traverses through pleasant fields and ascends to a small ridge (8775 ft, 2674 m), where the trail from the south at Lukla joins the main trail up the Dudh Kosi valley at **Choplung.** This is **30 minutes** from Chaumrikharka. There is also a direct trail to Lukla from Chaumrikharka, reaching the village just north of the school.

LUKLA/CHOPLUNG TO NAMCHE BAZAAR

Lukla (9350 ft, 2860 m) has become a major trekking center over the years. The name Lukla means "place with many goats and sheep," but clearly things have changed. In addition to the airstrip nestled among spectacular mountains, there are now many hotels featuring food and accommodations of varying standards. Lukla is now a major staging area for treks to Khumbu. There are many regular helicopter and still some fixed-wing flights here from Kathmandu, so it is no longer the bottleneck it used to be. If you plan to fly out, reconfirm your ticket with the airline as soon as you reach the town.

To proceed from Lukla to Khumbu, head north, past a *chorten* with prayer wheels sporting the usual mantra written out in English letters, and join the main trail at **Choplung** (8840 ft, 2696 m) in less than an **hour** where there are lodges. (All trekkers heading to Khumbu, whether on foot from Jiri or by plane to Lukla, will end up at Choplung.) To proceed from there, head north, crossing the Thado Khola (8380 ft, 2554 m) with the awesome trekking peak Kusum Kanguru at its head and lodges at the bridge. Soon, come to a bridge over the Dudh Kosi, with the village of Ghat (8350 ft, 2545 m) on both banks. There are lodges here. Proceed on the east (left) bank through to **Phakding** (8700 ft, 2652 m), now expanded to both sides of the river. Phakding is 1½ **hours** from Choplung and 2½ hours from Lukla. It is a common overnighting spot for trekkers flying to Lukla and is thus often crowded. Consider other choices. Cross to the west (right) bank (8600 ft, 2621 m) of the Dudh Kosi. Continue through blue pine and rhododendron forests, past a settlement of metal-workers (called Tok Tok, for their hammering out vessels), to the village of **Benkar** (8875 ft, 2905 m) with lodges, which is reached in 1 hour from Phakding. Watch for large, hanging, tonguelike beehives just beyond a waterfall on the east (left) bank cliffs opposite you in this steep-walled canyon. In a short while, cross to the east (left) bank and climb up through Chumowa, with extensive vegetable farms. Cross another tributary, the Kyangshar Khola (9100 ft, 2773 m), before climbing up a cleft in the canyon wall to **Mondzo** (9300 ft, 2835 m) about **45 minutes** from Benkar. Enter Sagarmatha (Everest) National Park here and pay the entrance fee if you did not when you obtained your trekking permit. Your porters may be questioned. The park regulations are covered in chapter 3. The trail then descends in a cleft to the left of a huge rock and crosses to the west (right) bank of the Dudh Kosi on a suspension bridge (a part of the old wood one is below) to reach **Jorsale** (Thumbug) (9100 ft, 2774 m) in **45 minutes.** This is the last village before Namche Bazaar. You can see the route on the *Khumbu Himal* map of the Research Scheme Nepal Himalaya.

 ## Peoples of Eastern Nepal: The Sherpas

Next to the Gurkha soldiers of Nepal, it is perhaps the Sherpas, famous as mountain guides and porters, who have attracted the most worldwide attention. Some Sherpas dwell in the remote Rolwaling valley, and as far west as Helambu region north of Kathmandu, but the most renowned come from the villages of Shar–Khumbu (Solu–Khumbu), along the upper valley of the Dudh Kosi and its tributaries, in the Mount Everest region. Sherpas are relatively recent immigrants to Nepal. Pangboche, their oldest village and one of the highest in the world, is thought to have been built a little over 300 years ago. The Sherpas speak a Tibetan dialect, dress like their Tibetan neighbors—or often like Western trekkers—and live as traders and agropastoralists, farming their high fields (mostly potatoes, wheat, barley, and buckwheat) and herding yak and sheep in alpine pastures up to 17,000 ft (5000 m). Their region is divided into three subregions: Solu, Pharak, and Khumbu. Solu, at the south, includes such villages as Junbesi and Phaphlu, and the monastery at Chiwong, in picturesque valleys at approximately 9000 ft (2700 m). Pharak is situated between Solu and Khumbu along the steep banks of the Dudh Kosi. Most Sherpa mountaineers hail from Khumbu, the highest and most northerly of the three regions, at elevations of 11,000 ft (3300 m) and up. Their villages include Namche Bazaar, Thami, Khumjung, Kunde, and Pangboche, as well as the famous and beautiful Buddhist monastery of Tengboche. Among the Sherpas, the practice of Tibetan Lamaism remains strong.

People from other areas have adopted the name Sherpa, including the upper Arun and upper Tamur. These include migrants from Solu–Khumbu, but also other Tibetan origin peoples who live in the northern regions, or more Hindu-acculturated peoples on the interface between the mountain and hill cultures. This may be for status, but often because when such people were given citizenship papers, or asked about their ethnicity for a census, their responses were constrained into a few available categories. Recent census figures show the number of Sherpas increasing faster than birth rates and migration could allow. Some have avoided this dilemma by adopting the surname Lama. It is mostly our problem trying to classify things.

Their religion gives Sherpas a concern for all living things and for their Western clients on treks and expeditions. Their warmth of character, shared by many Himalayan peoples, is perhaps best displayed in their sense of hospitality. Visitors to a Sherpa house are considered guests of honor, for whom nothing is spared (sometimes to the point of embarrassment for Westerners). The best response to an outpouring of generosity by a Sherpa, or any Nepali host, is reciprocity—your own generosity and care in their regard.

Sherpa names of men often reflect the day of the week on which the boy was born. Nima on Sunday, Dawa on Monday, Mingma on Tuesday, Lhakpa on Wednesday, Phurbu on Thursday, Pasang on Friday, and Pemba on Saturday. Like any tradition, this one is not strictly adhered to.

The Sherpas have received considerable attention from anthropologists, mountaineer-writers, and traveling journalists, so we need not go into detail here (see Appendix B). One facet of Sherpa culture not often described in the literature is the Namche Bazaar Saturday market, which is interesting from a traveler's perspective because of the chance to see several ethnic groups and a wide variety of local handicrafts and trade goods on display. If traveling toward Namche Bazaar immediately before a Saturday, trekkers may see many groups of lowlanders, mostly *Rai* and a few Brahman and *Chhetri*, carrying baskets of produce such as rice, corn, and fruits to sell or trade for highland produce such as wheat, wool, potatoes, *ghiu* (clarified butter, or *ghee*), and other animal byproducts. This is part of the natural economic exchange that keeps each community supplied with the produce of the other. The lowlanders are easily singled out by their style of dress (light, tie-across Nepali shirts and baggy trousers that fit snugly at the calves) from the Sherpas and Tibetans. Sherpa and Tibetan men, by comparison, prefer heavy woolen cloaks and trousers, with leather or woolen boots. And these days, some dress in down jackets as well. At the market itself, Tibetan boots and handicrafts of silver, wool, and leather are displayed. A market day is a lively occasion, a time when Tibetans, Sherpas, *Rai,* and others (including Western visitors) intermingle to trade, gossip, eat, drink, and even dance and sing in a spirited, sharing atmosphere.

The *BhoTiya* people east of Makalu, out to Kangchenjunga, sometimes call themselves Sherpa, sometimes not. Generally their language is Tibetan, which is distinct from the Sherpa dialect of Solu–Khumbu.With the increasing numbers of trekkers flying to Lukla and quickly climbing to Namche, they miss the opportunities to appreciate the valley below the Bazaar and to get a sense of hill Nepal. Consider spending two nights in this region and making side trips up tributary valleys to the east or west. Visit small conventional villages and handsome *gomba* nestled in temperate forest with snow-clad peaks at the valley heads. Stay in Sherpa homes there rather than in lodges. Observe traditional lumber making. Benefits include a warmer climate, less risk of altitude illness later, and sylvan surroundings.

Continue briefly up the west bank from Jorsale through blue pine forests to a bridge that crosses again to the east (left) bank. This area has had the bridges rebuilt several times because of large floods. I expect there will be more changes in the future and that you will have no difficulty finding the way. The latest trail proceeds above the confluence of the Bhote Kosi from the west and the Dudh Kosi

Stay in a Sherpa home and have riltok sen.

from the east, to cross high above the east fork to its west (right) bank at a narrowing (9400 ft, 2865 m). The climb to Namche Bazaar proceeds in pine forest. Some 800 ft (244 m) higher up the crest of the prow, you have your first view of Everest behind the Lhotse–Nuptse ridge! A water source is shortly beyond. **Namche Bazaar** (11,300 ft, 3446 m), the gateway to Khumbu, is **2 or 2½ hours** from Jorsale. The village is expanding down the hill and everywhere else. NAUje is the preferred Sherpa pronunciation, referring to a big forest, which may again be realistic with the fenced-in reforestation projects above town.

Namche Bazaar is a remarkable entrepreneurial town. The electricity here and in surrounding villages comes from a generating plant up the Thami valley that came on line in 1995. As the administrative center for Khumbu, Namche Bazaar has many officials and offices, including a police check post and a bank. Namche Bazaar used to be a trading center, where grain from the south was exchanged for salt from Tibet, and it remains a trading center even though the salt trade has ended. Sherpas run the stores, hotels, and restaurants. Prices are high, but most staples are available. Old expedition food and equipment are available in the shops. You can even sleep in the bed that Jimmy Carter used on his trek here. There is a dental clinic to the east, staffed by Canadian-trained Sherpas designed to stem the decay wrought on Sherpa children by well-meaning trekker candy dispensers. Trekkers can use the excellent facilities (closed on Sunday) with reasonable prices. Visit the Khumbu Environmental Conservation Committee center in town (formerly the Sagarmatha Pollution Control Committee, whose acronym is preferred to the new one, which connotes feces) and the national park museum above town (now called Choi Gang), where the headquarters of Sagarmatha National Park are located. The weekly market, held on Saturday, is colorful and well worth seeing. If you find Namche too commercial, stay in Kunde or Khumjung. But spend at least the first night in Namche to help acclimation before sleeping higher. An excellent day hike for acclimatization is to explore the crest of the ridge above Shyangboche before descending to Khumjung and Kunde. Another would be to head up the Thami Valley as far as Thamo.

Khumbu

(Map No. 4, Page 224)
To arrive by foot in Sherpa country is to gain some insight into what it was like for the Israelites to reach the promised land.
Mike Thompson,
anthropologist and climber

There are enough things to do in Khumbu to occupy two or three weeks. Four main river valleys can be explored, each with spectacular mountain scenery. You can visit two monasteries and at least three village *gomba*. And perhaps most appealing are the Sherpa people and their culture. If you have employed a Sherpa whose home is in Khumbu, you may likely be given the hospitality of his or her home. Those fortunate enough to be in Khumbu during the full moon in May or November to December may see *Mani-rimdu,* the Sherpa drama festival depicting the victory of Buddhism over Bon. The May production is usually at the Thami Monastery and the November to December one at the Tengboche Monastery. Most trekkers want to head to the foot of Everest, and there is no circuit route so bottlenecks exist. If you can be satisfied by breathtaking mountain scenery that doesn't include Everest up close, follow some of the alternative routes described here.

A reasonable itinerary for a grand tour of Khumbu for those with at least three weeks available would be to proceed to Namche, then to Dingboche, Chhukhung, and beyond, and then to Kala Pattar and the Everest Base Camp. If conditions permit, cross Cho La; otherwise, backtrack to Pheriche, then go on to Pangboche, and take the high-level traverse to Phortse. Continue up the Gokyo Valley to Gokyo, where both the Cho La and Phortse routes converge. Explore here and then descend the west side of the valley to Khumjung and Kunde. End by going up the Thami Valley. Those with less time must decide how important the base of Everest is to them and whether they want to spend more time in permanently settled areas or head for high-altitude areas. One itinerary for the latter is to head from Namche to Gokyo and then over to the Everest Base Camp area via Cho La or the high traverse from Phortse to Pangboche. Then return via Tengboche.

In a survey conducted in October 1978, trekkers rated the following trails according to number of trekkers (in order from highest to lowest): Namche Bazaar to Pheriche; Pheriche to Lobuche; Namche Bazaar to Khumjung–Kunde; Namche Bazaar to Thami; Lobuche to Kala Pattar; and Namche Bazaar to Gokyo, to Phortse, to Chhukhung, to Gokyo's Kala Pattar, to Everest Base Camp, to Island Peak, to Trashi Labsta, to Cho La.

TO EVEREST BASE CAMP
Namche to Pheriche

The times given for the journey beyond Namche Bazaar are quite variable. They depend on the weather conditions as well as the fitness and acclimatization of the party. Allow at least 5 days to reach Kala Pattar from Tengboche, the absolute minimum time. Hire porters to carry your loads, because they can handle the altitude much better than you. If you are going to high altitudes, be prepared for cold winds and snow. It is critical to heed the warning signs of altitude sickness described in chapter 4. Many trekkers have died in this region because they did not do so.

From Namche Bazaar the trail rises to the saddle to the east, Choi Gang, where the Sagarmatha National Park museum (11,550 ft, 3520 m) sits. You could head

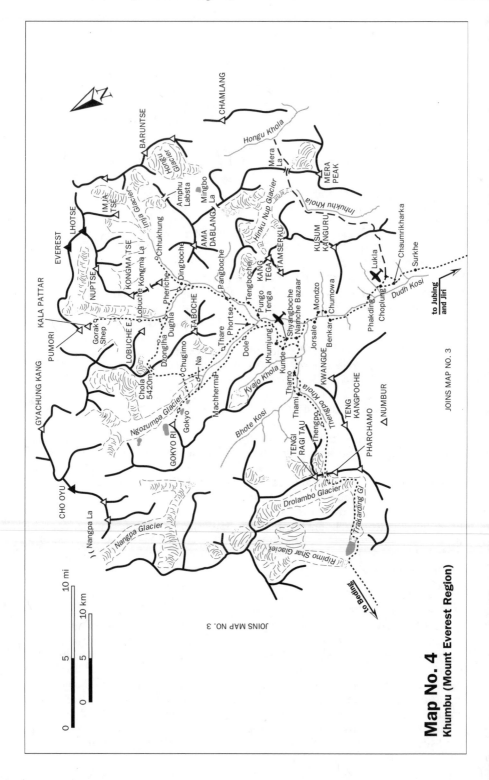

Map No. 4
Khumbu (Mount Everest Region)

northwest to Shyangboche from here. Instead, contour high above the Dudh Kosi, past a lodge (Kyangsuma), until, by some large boulders, a few minutes later with lodges nearby **Sangnasa** (11,800 ft, 3597 m), this trail joins the one from Khumjung. As well, a trail leaves this major juncture to ascend to Mong and the entrance to the Gokyo Valley. To go on to Tengboche, continue through forests of blue pine and rhododendron, passing below the village of Trashinga and through the tea shops of Labisyasa and more lodges below near the forest nursery to reach the Dudh Kosi (10,650 ft, 3247 m), where there is a small settlement called **Pungo Tenga,** with several mills, a series of water-driven prayer wheels, and some hotels, on both banks. It is **2 hours** from Namche Bazaar. Consider spending a night at this lower altitude, especially if you flew to Lukla and spent only one night in Namche or if you made the mistake of leaving Namche with a headache. The trail crosses to the true left at a narrowing and climbs past the prayer wheels through very pleasant forest, with occasional impressive views of Kangtega, to **Tengboche** (12,887 ft, 3867 m), about **2 hours** from the river. The portion from Namche to Tengboche is approximately 12 mi (19 km).

There are few choices for food and lodging at Tengboche, and the limited space does not begin to accommodate everyone during popular times. The latrines and hygiene facilities here handle fewer trekkers than other sites en route. Camping parties dig minimal latrines, so the waste is easily unearthed. When helicopters land, the shit flies. The water supply is below the ridge, and waste effluent flows into it, resulting in many trekkers getting sick here. Better to spend the evening at Pungo Tenga, or closer to Khumjung, visit Tengboche, and continue on to spend the night east at Deboche or beyond. The trekker traffic also disrupts the functions of the monastery. There are plans for separating the touristic activities from those of the monastery in some way, possibly a wall or rerouting the main trail to bypass this place. Moral dilemmas here.

The forest of pine, fir, black juniper, and rhododendron en route is remarkable. Early in the morning or late in the afternoon, if you are quiet, you may be able to spot a musk deer along here. Across the valley to the south, there are silver birch forests, which grow well on the colder north slopes. Look for blood and Impeyan pheasants feeding near Tengboche in the morning. There are many places to explore around the monastery; those feeling strong can climb the ridge to the south.

Tengboche Monastery

The Tengboche Monastery was founded in 1916 by Lama Gulu, and the building was completed three years later, but the main temple was destroyed in the 1934 earthquake and rebuilt. The monastery was electrified in 1988, and on January 19, 1989, the *gomba* burned to the ground. It has been again rebuilt, this time with foreign and local funding. The monks follow the Nyingmapa sect of Buddhism. Currently there are some forty monks and thirty students, all of them Sherpas. Sometimes respects can be paid to the venerable abbot, an incarnation of Lama Gulu. Tours of the monastery are often available. Donations for the monastery are appropriate. When visiting the abbot, be sure to offer him a ceremonial scarf or *kata* obtained from another monk. Be aware that the heavy use of this area for tourist purposes is disrupting the religious life here. There is talk of building a wall to seclude the monastery! Be sensitive to these issues.

Musk deer can sometimes be spotted in potato fields.

From Tengboche the trail heads east and descends slightly, past several lodges some 15 minutes beyond and 400 feet (121 m) lower. Head past the nunnery (Ani Gompa) at Deboche (12,325 ft, 3757 m), which is worth a visit. In the formal Buddhist tradition, monks and nuns are considered equal, but there are fewer nunneries than monasteries, for families find it more difficult to support daughters in religious pursuit. Presently there are only a few older nuns living here. Shortly beyond are more lodges at Milingo, all the while traveling in a fine forest of rhododendrons and birch. Where you have a choice, take the lower trail. These trees are festooned with moss lower down. Continue to the river, the Imja Khola, and cross it at a narrowing on a suspension bridge (12,400 ft, 3780 m), from which you get a spectacular view of Ama Dablang. This is 45 minutes from Tengboche. Note that map names for rivers in this area vary greatly. Some 5 or 10 minutes beyond, just past a small notch, the trail forks. The left (higher) fork ascends to the Pangboche Gomba (13,075 ft, 3985 m) and upper Pangboche, while the right goes directly to the village of lower **Pangboche** (12,800 ft, 3901 m), some **1½ hours** and 3 mi (4.8 km) from Tengboche. The *gomba*, the oldest in Khumbu, was built some 300 years ago at the time that Buddhism is said to have been introduced into Khumbu. According to legend, Lama Sangwa Dorje tore out his hair and cast it around the *gomba*. The large black juniper trees surrounding it sprouted from those hairs. They are so large because it is forbidden to cut them. For side trips, explore the slopes to the north. Residents here are especially sensitive to intrusions by camera-wielding trekkers. Upper Pangboche appears to maintain more traditions than the lower villages. For the trekker willing to seek out staying in a family's home as a guest, here is a chance to glimpse typical Sherpa life. The National Geographic's *Mount Everest* map shows the area beyond Pangboche in great detail.

Continue northeast from either the village itself or from the *gomba*, with the last views of Everest for some time, to reach the junction west of a *chorten* above a cantilever bridge over the Imja Khola. Beyond is Shomare with new lodge construction and then another at Orsho. Continue to reach a trail fork above a small summer yak herding pasture (Warsa, 13,725 ft, 4183 m) 1½ **hours** beyond Pangboche. The right fork goes toward Dingboche, while the left fork climbs past one hut to the crest of a small ridge (14,050 ft, 4282 m), from which Pheriche can be seen. From this crest, one can climb up to the north on the ridge to get great views including the west face of Makalu. Altitudes above 5000 m can be attained by the acclimatized before technical difficulties intervene. To proceed on, descend a short distance to the bridge over the Khumbu (or Lobuche) Khola (13,875 ft, 4229 m) and cross it to the west (left) bank to reach **Pheriche** (13,950 ft, 4252 m) in some **2 or 3 hours** and 3 mi (4.8 km) from Pangboche, depending on acclimatization.

Questions to Ponder: Tourism and Encounters with Trekkers

Reflect on the friendliness of trekkers in different areas and circumstances—remote areas where few trekkers go, the well-trodden lodge routes, and so on. What differences in ecological behavior do you see among trekkers from various countries? Any generalizations?

Does tourism in Nepal replay the history of the white man coming to North America and changing the lives of the natives by economic and cultural exploitation, not to speak of genocide?

Pheriche to Everest Base Camp

Pheriche, once a *yersa* or temporary yak herding area, is now settled throughout the winter—entirely because of the trekking traffic. It is a very different place from the one I encountered on my first visit in 1969. There are hotels built from blocks of sod, exhumed from the top soil en route, a garbage dump, and some latrines. Pheriche is usually crowded with people, although slight solitude can be found in nearby Dingboche. There is a Trekker's Aid Post, which was set up by the Himalayan Rescue Association in 1973. The post provides medical care to trekkers and porters. Attend the daily altitude educational session held each afternoon. Every party should spend two nights, or at least a complete day and night, at Pheriche or Dingboche. During the day spent here, an ascent or hike is an especially good idea. You could spend this day going to Dingboche and farther east up the Imja Khola, as described later, or you could climb the ridge to the northeast to as high as 17,000 ft (5030 m) for views of Makalu to the east and of nearby summits. There is a hermitage on the way. You could also recross the Khumbu Khola and climb up on the shoulders of Taboche to the west as already described, or simply do the next day's walk, but return to Pheriche for the night. If you are already bothered by the altitude, it may be best to walk along the valley floor or just rest. Check the section on altitude illness in chapter 4. If going beyond out of the popular season and dependent on facilities, enquire if they are open.

To go on to the foot of Everest, continue north from Pheriche along the flats past the *yersa* of Phuling Karpo, and then turn northeast up a grassy lateral moraine of the Khumbu Glacier. The route from Pheriche crosses the moraine's crest, descends to cross a glacial stream emerging from the snout of the glacier, which is covered by the moraine (15,025 ft, 4579 m), and ascends to the lodges at **Dughla** (also called Tuglha, 15,075 ft, 4593 m). If coming from Dingboche, there is a high route that doesn't descend to Pheriche but traverses more directly along the lateral moraine to Dughla. It takes 1½ **hours** to reach Dughla from Pheriche, a distance of 3 mi (4.8 km). If you have a headache, stop here for the night rather than push on. Accommodations may be limited in peak season for trekkers who want to stay in lodges in Dughla or beyond, so early starts are advised. Those prepared to camp should have an easier time. Climb to pass to the right of stone memorials on a ridge crest. These are built for climbers killed on expeditions to nearby summits, mostly Everest—there were none here when I first walked up this valley in 1969. The trail then contours on the west side of the glacier. After crossing another stream of meltwater, the trail heads northeast to the more primitive lodges of **Lobuche** (16,175 ft, 4930 m), situated below the terminal moraine of a tributary glacier. Lobuche is about **1½ hours** and a little over 2 mi (3.2 km) from Dughla. Sanitation facilities are limited at Lobuche and higher up. A climb to the ridge crest to the west provides fine views, especially at sunset. The Italians have constructed a pyramid research station north of Lobuche to study altitude phenomena.

Birds of the Alpine Zone

Snow cocks (*Tetraogallus* spp.) are represented by two Nepali species. Large, mainly gray gamebirds, they frequent steep grassy slopes and stony ridges up to 18,000 to 19,700 ft (5500 to 6000 m) in summer, then descend to the sub alpine zone in winter. They escape from people by running uphill. These birds can be seen on the Muktinath side of the Thorung La pass on the Annapurna Circuit and in Sagarmatha National Park.

The snow pigeon (*Columba leuconota*, length 34 cm), a pale gray and white pigeon with a black head, occurs in flocks on rocky cliffs. It may descend to 5000 ft (1500 m) in severe winter conditions.

Most of the nine Nepali species of pipits (*Anthus* spp., length 14 to 23 cm) inhabit grasslands. Slim, brown, and streaked, they run or walk quickly and have both an undulating flight and song flight.

Accentors (*Prunellidae,* length 15 to 16 cm), of which Nepal has seven species, resemble sparrows but have sharp, pointed bills. Most are drab gray or brown and heavily streaked above. They feed quietly on the ground, often in small groups in winter. Look for them on grassy and rocky slopes or, in winter, in open forest.

The grandala (*Grandala coelicolor*, length 23 cm) belongs to the thrush family. The male is deep, brilliant purple-blue; the female is brown with a white wing patch. It forms flocks of several hundred birds in winter and inhabits rocky slopes and stony alpine meadows. It can be seen on Laurebina Pass on the Gosainkund trek and between Dole and Gokyo in Sagarmatha National Park.

Choughs in Nepal include the red-billed chough (*Pyrrhocorax pyrrhocorax*, length 46 cm) and the alpine, or yellow-billed, chough (*Pyrrhocorax graculus,* length 40 cm). Both are all black, except that the former has a red bill and legs, and the latter yellow. Behavior and appearance are crowlike: sociable and noisy. They engage in fantastic aerial acrobatics.

It is possible to use Lobuche or Dughla as a base to climb to Kala Pattar for views and to return the same day. This is advisable to avoid altitude problems.

To the southeast of Lobuche lies a pass, Kongma La (18,135 ft, 5527 m). A good side trip is to cross the Khumbu Glacier, ascend the pass, and head south to Bibre as described later. This trip takes a very long, strenuous day and requires confidence on rock. Pokalde Peak, south of the pass, could also be climbed.

Beyond Lobuche the trail follows a trough beside the Khumbu Glacier and then climbs through the terminal moraine of another tributary glacier. From a high point here the rubble-covered hill of Kala Pattar (black rock), in front of Pumori, can be seen, with an often frozen lake at its base. Those planning to go to Gorak Shep, at the northeast end of the lake, should drop to the sands and contour the lake on its northeast shore to the rock monuments to persons who have died nearby. **Gorak Shep** (17,000 ft, 5184 m) is reached in **2½ to 3 hours** and 3 mi (4.8 km) from Lobuche. Again there are simple lodges here. You may see Tibetan snow cocks here and approach them quite closely. Gorak Shep is the starting point for the world's highest marathon race, the Everest Marathon to Namche Bazaar, which began in 1987 and is run on alternate years. Data from it has allowed me to quote trail mileage figures.

The cairn of upper **Kala Pattar** (18,450 ft, 5623 m), to the north of the rounded hill that is the surveyed point of Kala Pattar, can be reached in **1½ hours** from Gorak Shep by ascending directly and keeping slightly to the northeast. You can see the South Col of Everest from here, as well as the immense west and south faces. This is certainly one of the most majestic mountain viewpoints in the world. Alternatively, by proceeding from the terminal moraine, you can head directly up to Kala Pattar without going to Gorak Shep. It may be difficult to find the "trail" through the moraine, especially if there has been a recent snowfall. Trail sense is an asset, though small cairns mark the way. Consider an early start to get here at sunrise, or wait here until the sun sets for a light show when it becomes apparent, as Tom Hornbein remarked, that "Everest is a jewel and the earth is a garland around it"!

The world's highest mountain was named after Sir George Everest, the head of the Survey of India from 1823 to 1843. Sherpas use its Tibetan name, Chomolongma, which means "Goddess of the Wind." Sagarmatha, its Nepali name, means "the Forehead of the Sky" or "Churning Stick of the Ocean of Existence," from a Sanskrit interpretation. Current estimates of its height above sea level are 8846.1 m, plus 2.55 m of snow, making it 8848.65 m (29,031 ft) high!

The mountain was first explored by outsiders from the Tibetan side beginning in 1920, with the last early expedition there in 1933. A joint British–U.S. group visited the south side in 1950, and climbing attention shifted to Nepal. It was first climbed in 1953 by Sir Edmund Hillary and Tenzing Norgay. The Swiss reached the summit the following year, and the mountain rested until 1963, when the Americans climbed it by the West Ridge and came down the original route, the first and only traverse of the mountain. Activities resumed in earnest in the 1970s, mostly nationalistic endeavors. By 1990 it was being exploited by commercial expeditions who tantalized climbing wannabees with fat wallets. Recent carnage there reminds us of the powerful forces residing on the big summits. A fatality rate of almost 3% accompanies those who try to climb and those who are paid to climb it, especially guides and high-altitude porters.

The sites of the various base camps used for climbing Everest are close to the foot of the Khumbu Icefall (17,575 ft, 5357 m) and can be reached from Gorak Shep in a few hours by venturing over the rubble-covered surface of the Khumbu Glacier. Many trekkers find the serac formations along the glacier a fascinating change from the majestic mountain walls, and this is the prime attraction for the journey toward base camp. There are no good views from the base camps. As you approach the first evidence of base camp garbage, note that recent base camps are 1 hour or so beyond, right at the foot of the Khumbu Icefall. If you are here when no expedition is climbing Everest, it may be tedious and time-consuming to find the exact location. Even if there is an expedition there and you are not following a supply team, it is easy to get lost and wander about. It is possible to visit the base camps from Lobuche and return the same long day if you are well acclimatized. There is no accommodation or food for trekkers at base camp.

Questions to Ponder: Mountaineering as Metaphor

Consider mountaineering as done in Nepal. Does this have metaphorical vestiges of imperialism as climbers conquer summits in other countries, helped by high-altitude porters who function as an organized militia? Why did one of the first two climbers of Everest say upon first meeting his teammates, "We knocked the bastard off"? The rate of mortality on high Himalayan climbs is similar to that of the U.S. casualties in Vietnam (almost 3%). One is a totally voluntary activity. Why do climbers accept such a risk?

Better views of the Khumbu Icefall and the north side of the Lhotse–Nuptse Wall can be obtained by climbing up the southeast ridge of Pumori. This ridge is reached by going partway to the base camps and turning northwest. Do not go out on the Khumbu Glacier to reach the ridge; stay on the lateral moraine. You will be able to see the North Col of Everest before encountering technical difficulties. Lhotse can also be seen. The view of the massive hulk of Everest is not as good from here as from Kala Pattar. Gorak Shep is the best base for this trip.

You can vary your return trip in several ways. Crossing Chugima Pass (Cho La) offers one route. You can also take a trail on the left side of the Imja Khola, crossing it below where the Khumbu (or Pheriche) Khola enters. Cross back before

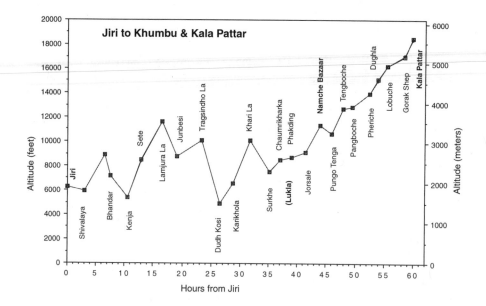

Pangboche, or continue on the south side to meet the trail to Tengboche.

An excellent route back from Upper Pangboche, where the *gomba* sits is to traverse over to Phortse on a new trail then either head up to Gokyo, or cross the river and climb up to Khumjung or Namche. The high-level traverse from Pangboche to Phortse is exhilarating for mountain panoramas. It takes 2 to 3 hours to reach Phortse and *tahr* may be seen en route.

Up the Imja Khola: Dingboche and Beyond

There are several ways to reach Dingboche, depending on where you happen to be. If coming from Pangboche, and heading directly to Dingboche, it is best to avoid going to Pheriche, which is generally cold and windy. Dingboche can be used as the stopover en route to Kala Pattar; it is less windy and sunnier. More village activities can be observed.

At the trail junction by the confluence of the Khumbu and Imja Kholas, about 1½ hours from Pangboche, take the right-hand branch (the left goes to Pheriche, as already described). Descend and cross the Khumbu Khola, and then climb above the Imja Khola to reach old moraine terraces. Continue heading east into the Imja valley, climbing gently to reach the outer fields of Dingboche. Follow the stone-walled path through the fields to reach lodges on the far side of the village in about 2 to 3 hours from Pangboche.

Reach **Dingboche** as already described or climb up and over the ridge (14,250 ft, 4343 m) behind the Trekker's Aid Post at Pheriche and descend to it in 30 to 45 minutes. You can also take a shortcut from Lobuche by crossing the stream that emanates from the snout of the Khumbu Glacier and climbing up the lateral moraine. Then follow a trail that contours to the south, passing the small temporary village of Dusa before dropping down to Dingboche. This third possibility is the quickest route from Lobuche.

Dingboche is temporarily settled by Sherpas and, because fields can be irrigated, the site for growing revered barley for *tsampa*. Many new lodges abound.

From a little west of Dingboche, you can climb up to Nangkartshang Gomba (15,430 ft, 4703 m) in 1½ hours for fine views of Makalu to the east. This is a detour if you are going to Chhukhung, but you could then head east to join the trail coming from Dingboche at Bibre (15,000 ft, 4571 m). Bibre with its tea shop, is reached in 1¼ hours from Dingboche by the direct valley route. The trail continues east, crossing numerous streams that flow from the Nuptse and Lhotse Glaciers, to the new luxurious lodges at Chhukhung (15,535 ft, 4734 m), perhaps a half hour after Bibre. This area is less crowded and perhaps more spectacular than the way to Kala Pattar; consider it for an acclimatization stage.

You can now see Ama Dablang's east face. It is worthwhile to spend a day or two traveling around to the east and to the northeast for close views of the incredible Lhotse–Nuptse Wall. Lhotse (27,923 ft, 8511 m), the stupendous summit above the 2-mi-high rock wall, was scaled from this side in 1990 by Tomo Cesen, a Yugoslav. It was first climbed by the Swiss in 1956 from the Western Cwm, beyond the Khumbu Icefall. The *Khumbu Himal* map is very useful here and suggests many hikes. Imja Tse (Island Peak), a trekking summit, is northeast of Chhukhung and the base camp south of the peak is a popular trip. Chhukhung Ri (18,238 ft, 5559 m), to the north, as well as a lesser plateau are shorter destinations that provide views of the incredible amphitheater you are in as well as of the west face of Makalu. To reach these viewpoints, there are two choices of trails. They both cross the stream behind Chhukhung on a small bridge. To reach the nearer lower plateau, follow the trail that climbs the left-hand ridge of the moraine north of Chhukhung. If you lose the trail in the sand, veer left. A flat crest viewpoint is reached (16,666 ft, 5080 m). This site is suitable for camping if you melt snow or carry water. You could continue and climb the higher summit involving a rock scramble, from here or a slightly lesser crest below. Or from the bridge, you could head east and pick up a more direct trail in the next draw to reach either viewpoint. The National Geographic *Mount Everest* map is helpful for other hikes.

Khumjung and Kunde

The airstrip of Shyangboche (12,205 ft, 3720 m), with lodges, is reached in less than 1 hour from Namche Bazaar, by taking the trail that climbs up from the *gomba*. This is the helicopter landing site, as well, and a repository for hundreds of thousands of beer bottles. Consider restraining your consumption to limit this desecration. If you flew here from Kathmandu, descend to Namche Bazaar for the next two nights to acclimatize. You can fork left above at a *chautaaraa*, proceed past the yak farm preserve to the northwest, and climb to a crest (12,700 ft, 3871 m) in peaceful juniper forests and descend to Kunde (12,600 ft, 3841 m) 30 minutes from Shyangboche. The north end of this town is the site of Kunde Hospital, built by the Himalayan Trust established by Sir Edmund Hillary. There are some lodges here. Consider a side trip to the crest of the ridge north of Kunde to gaze on the steep cliffs to the north.

To reach Khumjung, the "sister city" of Kunde, you can either traverse east from Kunde, or go directly from Shyangboche by climbing northeast from the airstrip

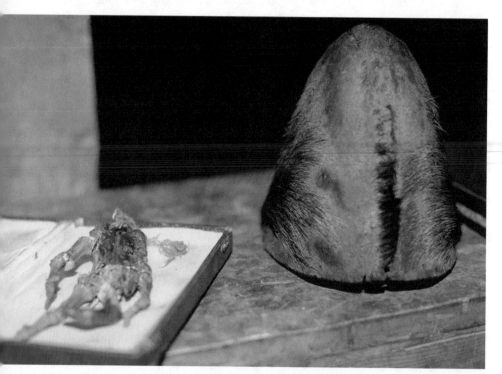

This yeti scalp and hand have now been stolen from the Pangboche Gomba.

past a large *chorten* in a blue pine forest. Descend past the Himalayan Trust school buildings to the recently constructed lodges and the few remaining potato fields below Khumjung (12,400 ft, 3780 m). A village *gomba* in a juniper grove to the north contains yeti relics that can be seen for a donation.

Of interest is the Everest View Hotel, beautifully situated on a shelf (12,700 ft, 3870 m). To visit this place, there is a trail from the lower end of the airstrip, but the main trail is the one leading southeast from the large *chorten* above the top end of the airstrip. It climbs gently across the hillside above the side of the airstrip to reach the ridge crest and then turns sharply north above the Dudh Kosi and traverses under the ridge crest to reach the hotel. The trail from the lower end of the airstrip joins this main trail at the ridge crest. Or you can reach it from the eastern end of the potato fields and lodges below Khumjung. This luxury hotel was built in 1974 and continues to be plagued by guests who ascended too rapidly from Kathmandu and are sick from altitude illness.

Changes in Khumbu over 27 Years

Much has changed in this area since my first visit in 1969. Immediately noticeable are the new houses with Western-style windows, painting of trim on houses, electric lights and hot plates, corrugated tin roofs, and more efficient mudded stoves. People are much more cautious with their use of firewood since it is so time-consuming to search for it. Families have a greater variety of Western goods. With the availability of electricity in lower Khumbu since 1995, satellite TV and video is making an impact. Modern clothes are usually worn rather than traditional apparel. Some Sherpani women dress in pants. Wealth is more often measured in terms of equipment and money rather than traditionally in the size of yak and sheep herds. The general level of education has improved greatly, but few Sherpas have gone on to finish high school or beyond, preferring to work in the tourist industry, which provides great monetary rewards. Sweet tea is replacing the salt-butter variety (solja). Many Sherpa families now prefer to live in Kathmandu and can afford to send their children to private schools there. Many such Sherpa do not speak their mother tongue. A major change in Sherpa society is the breakdown in the extended family, with elders alone in their senescence as young sons based in Kathmandu make their fortunes. It was traditional for a family to send the youngest child to the monastery, but now such practices are less common. It is not uncommon to find widows caring for children and looking after homes. Mountaineering expeditions take their toll and the Sherpas as an ethnic group were never large in number. The recent increase in the helicopter access has severely disrupted the local porter economy. The overall net gain in the economy is negative as funds leave the country to pay for improved machinery, fuel and technicians. Some of the changes are for the good, and some are questionable. No matter how we perceive it, the Sherpas feel their lot is better now.

To Gokyo

This valley has become a justifiably popular destination as the trail takes you to summer yak-grazing country, to beautiful small lakes, and to the foot of Cho Oyu and Gyachung Kang peaks. Lodges now abound everywhere. There are three choices to reach this valley. One heads north from below Khumjung on the west side of the valley, and the trail can be accessed from Namche. Another reaches Phortse on the east side of the valley from Pangboche, or below Tengboche. Finally, you could cross Cho La to the east, as you leave the foot of Everest. Some trekking parties avoid the foot of Everest and visit this region instead. There is disproportionately more serious altitude illness among trekkers who venture up here from the low-lands, because elevation gains can be great, given the short horizontal distances. Spend several nights at Namche, and then take at least 3 more days to get to Gokyo. This may not be slow enough for some.

The west-side trail goes northeast from the major junction, **Sangnasa** (11,800 ft, 3597 m), below the east end of Khumjung. It can be accessed from Namche as well. The trail climbs along the side of Khumbiyula, crossing a prominence below the rock. There is another higher trail below Khumjung that ascends the rocky promi-nence on steps in a cleft to join the lower trail above. Both reach **Mong La,** a crest of a ridge (13,000 ft, 3962 m), where there is a *stupa,* some lodges, and a pan-oramic view. This takes **2 hours** from Khumjung. Above you, on the slopes of Khumbiyula, watch for a herd of Himalayan tahr (called *ghoral* by locals). Phortse is across the river. A side trip would be to ascend to the north. The trail descends steeply to **Phortse Tenga** (11,950 ft, 3643 m) with lodges near the river in an **hour.** The right fork descends to cross the river and climb to Phortse. The left fork here heads north and, after an hour or so, Cho Oyu is visible. You cross many spec-tacular waterfalls that are frozen in winter and pass a national park office that may check your permit and an army post, apparently built to check smuggling. After emerg-ing from the birch and rhododendron woods, the trail passes several summer yak herding huts, or *yersa,* including Tongba (13,175 ft, 4015 m), Gyele, and **Dole** (13,400 ft, 4084 m), where there are lodges. It takes **2¾ hours** from Mong La to Gyele.

From Gyele, Lhabarma, with a lodge (14,200 ft, 4328 m), is reached in less than **1 hour,** and **Luza,** in a small tributary valley, with lodges (14,400 ft, 4390 m), is another **hour.** In the next tributary valley is **Machherma** (14,650 ft, 4465 m), another **45 minutes** away, with several lodges. Explore the valley to the west. Go on for **1 hour** to **Pangka** (14,925 ft, 4548 m), with a few lodges, and where a huge snowstorm in November 1995 dumped over 2 m of snow and caused an avalanche that killed some twenty-five trekkers and porters nestled against the hillside in a lodge. There was a huge rescue mission to recover those who were stranded. From Pangka, descend slightly, following one of the melted glacial rivers that flow down the west side of the Ngozumpa Glacier, which is to the east now. The trail crosses this river at a narrowing and soon emerges at the first of several small lakes (15,450 ft, 4709 m), **1½ hours** beyond Pangka. Look for Brahminy ducks resting at these lakes. Another **45 minutes** brings you to the next lake, or *tsho,* with the *yersa* Longpanga at its northern end. Continue for another **30 minutes** to the third lake (sometimes called Dudh Pokhari) and the tourist development of **Gokyo** (15,720 ft, 4791 m) on its northeast shore. There is a trading library here and garbage left over from a 1991 balloon voyage over Everest! This place is also called Goyo by Sherpas.

From Gokyo, Cho Oyu (26,749 ft, 8153 m) looms to the north. It was first climbed in 1954 by an Austrian expedition from the northwest. The face you see has also been climbed. There are many places to go for views and excursions, which make this an attractive place to spend a few days. Currently the most popular is to ascend the ridge to the northwest to a summit Gokyo Ri (17,990 ft, 5483 m). This climb takes 2 to 3 hours for those well acclimatized and provides an excellent pan-orama from Cho Oyu, to Everest, to Lhotse, and all the way to Makalu. Consider being here at sunset or sunrise. Renjo La, the pass to the west, provides an alpine

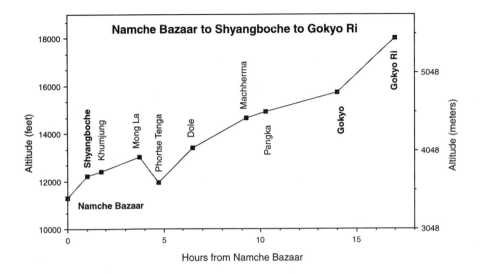

experience and takes 3 hours of climbing. Reach the western end of the lake, and follow a path or cairns. Routefinding ability is an asset. You can follow the trail north between the lateral moraine of the glacier and the hills to the west until you reach the next lake (16,150 ft, 4923 m) about 1½ hours from Gokyo or follow the moraine crest for better views. A climb of a few hundred feet up the hill to the north of the lake provides fine vistas, but climbers can get much higher with the rewards of spectacular views. You could also continue another 1½ hours to the last large lake, which offers a fine panorama from the moraine to the east. Beyond are smaller lakes and even more spectacular views. The *Khumbu Himal* map may suggest many other hikes.

You can return from Gokyo by following the east side of the valley, reaching it from below the snout of the glacier at Pangka, as described at the end of the next section. Alternatively, you could follow the route described below in reverse to reach the Khumbu Glacier and the foot of Everest.

Cho La (Chugima)

For people who want to combine visits to the Everest Base Camp region with one to the upper reaches of the valley beneath Cho Oyu without extensive backtracking, Cho La is a scenic and enjoyable route. It does involve a short glacier crossing, for which a rope and ice ax are advisable; however, there are no serious dangers or technical difficulties. In the process, you circumnavigate Jobo Lhaptshan (21,128 ft, 6440 m) and Taboche (20,869 ft, 6367 m) for excellent views of Cho Oyu to the north.

Be aware that fresh snowfall on the pass seriously increases the difficulty and the risk of frostbite. If you do not have enough experience to be sure that the new snow will not cause problems, consider skipping the pass. In the autumn of 1982, snowfall resulted in at least five trip-ending cases of frostbite, and some trekkers suffered permanent damage. At that time, renowned mountaineer Reinhold Messner assessed the conditions and elected to avoid the pass and go around via Phortse. Deaths from rockfall and other hazards have also occurred. If depending on the lodges for accommodation, verify in Dughla that they are open.

To descend from the Everest Base Camp area, follow the trail down below Lobuche some **15 to 30 minutes** as far as the stream crossing on the lateral moraine (16,000 ft, 4877 m) but, instead of crossing it, contour along a trail on the side of the valley, eventually turning northwest into the valley of the pass. You can thus stay at a high elevation instead of descending to the shores of the lake below you (Tshola Tsho). Cross the main stream that feeds into the lake higher up. Pick the trail up again near the stream crossing if it has been lost. The trail ascends to the *yersa* of Dzonglha with its lodges (15,869 ft, 4843 m), beautifully situated on a shelf of land with fine views in every direction. It is about **2½ hours** or more from Lobuche. This is a very good spot to stay, either in tents or in the lodges. The feeling of sitting under the north face of Jobo Lhaptshan is unforgettable.

Alternatively, if approaching this area from the south, go to Dughla and follow the trail slightly below it before bearing west to the small trail that skirts the end of the Tshola Glacier moraine, which has almost blocked the valley and formed Tshola Tsho (lake) above it. Reach the end of the lake (14,804 ft, 4512 m)—it is ice-covered in November—in **30 minutes.** The best camping spot for spectacular views is near here, but the only huts are some distance farther on. The trail follows the north shore of the lake and rises gradually until it reaches Tsholo Og (15,306 ft, 4665 m), a *yersa* of several huts, in **45 minutes.** Water must be carried from a stream **10 minutes** farther on. **Dzonglha** (15,889 ft, 4843 m) is another **hour** up the faint trail and lodges function here when trekkers cross the pass. Above this *yersa* the trail is less distinct.

Cross a small crest just above Dzonglha and descend slightly into the gentle valley coming down from the glacier in the pass to the northwest. The pass, sometimes called Chugima or Cho La by locals, is the 17,783-ft (5420-m) crossing marked on the Schneider *Khumbu Himal* map. There is a small trail aiming for the glacier-smoothed rock to the east of the glacier itself. Look for cairns to mark the route. The moraine at the head of the valley is reached in 1 hour from Dzonglha. Ascend to the right of the glacier, sometimes on loose rock, sometimes on large slabs with handsome grain, until you reach a small valley or moat between the rock and the glacier. Eventually, gain the glacier around 17,350 ft (5285 m). Keep to its south side and ascend steeply at first (30°) on the snow-covered surface. Watch for crevasses covered by snow and the bergschrund where the glacier pulls away from the rock. The surface may be bare ice and require crampons. Porters sometimes make do with rope tied to their footwear. You may be able to avoid the ice by keeping to the south. The glacier levels out and the pass (17,783 ft, 5420 m) is reached in at least **2½ hours** from Dzonglha. A new valley and new vistas open up before you. From the pass there are no views of the giants but an opportunity to appreciate the lesser, often more beautiful, mountains. Those with experience and equipment may want to scramble up the snow to the minor summit to the south.

The descent on the west side of the pass heads south, initially down steep, hard snow and then onto variegated talus. Beware of ice avalanches and loose rock from the hanging glacier on the peak marked "5686 m" on the Schneider map. Reach the valley floor, with its boulders and hummocks.

If heading to Gokyo, you then bear west to a saddle, without losing much altitude, and then descend steeply to reach Dragnag (15,387 ft, 4690 m), which has lodges functioning when people are crossing the pass. It takes 2 hours from the pass to here in good conditions. Proceed up the lateral moraine to a cairned notch, and then cross the dry (that is, the crevasses are not hidden under snow) Ngozumpa

Glacier. Ascend the moraine and come out near the lake below Gokyo and join that trail. This takes about 2 hours. You can now head north to Gokyo.

If heading south to Na to descend the east side of the Gokyo Valley or to cross the Ngozumpa Glacier at its snout, continue along the trail through the boulders and hummocks near the main stream in the rather flat main valley. Near the end of the shelf there are caves by the stone fences of Chugimo (16,175 ft, 4930 m). They are suitable for shelter or camping. Reach them in **2 to 3 hours** from the pass. As you leave the flats, follow the trail on the north (left) side of the stream and reach Charchang, a beautiful *yersa* (15,100 ft, 4602 m) within sight of the terminal moraine of the Ngozumpa Glacier in **45 minutes.** Cross the river on a rock bridge to the south (left) bank. The river may be concealed beneath it. Don't descend, but contour **15 minutes** to a *yersa* of Tsom (15,000 ft, 4572 m). Alternatively, you could descend from Charchang to **Na** (14,435 ft, 4400 m), which is below the tongue of the glacier. From here, you can join the route described earlier, on the west (right) bank of the Dudh Kosi, by crossing the stream west of Na and contouring gently up to the south to reach the shelf above the river in **30 minutes.** Before you proceed, note the view of the impressive south face of Cho Oyu to the north.

To head south to Phortse from Na on the east side of the valley, go south, and cross a tributary to reach the valley floor and Kanasa with some huts (no lodges), potato fields, and yak pastures. Reach **Thare** with lodges (14,250 ft, 4343 m) on the hillside in **45 minutes.** Another **30 minutes** of traversing brings you to Thore with a lodge (14,435 ft, 4400 m). After a couple of tributaries, and the tea shop at Genkewa (or Genjha), the *yersa* of **Konar** with lodges (13,425 ft, 4092 m), in an idyllic tributary valley, is reached in **1½ hours.** Consider staying here and exploring the valley below the south face of Taboche. The ambrosia along here in the spring is intoxicating.

Planting potatoes at Phortse

Continue into a handsome juniper and birch forest to a tributary that is the source of the Phortse water supply. Continue through rhododendrons to upper **Phortse** (12,140 ft, 3700 m), some **45 minutes** from Konar. Phortse (also pronounced "Furtze") is perched on the flats you have probably seen from the west and south. It dominates the entrance to the valley you have descended. Phortse itself appears to be least affected by trekker tourism. Silver birch and rhododendron forests surround it, and more wildlife may be seen nearby than near any other village in Khumbu. Homes tend to have fire pits for cooking, rather than the more efficient mudded *chulo,* because pressures on nearby forests are less. Spend a night here in one of the lodges or in someone's home and explore the surroundings.

To leave Phortse, toward Namche, descend for **30 minutes** through the fine forest to the west to the Dudh Kosi (11,200 ft, 3414 m) and then ascend to meet the trail from Khumjung to Gokyo at Phortse Tenga, which has already been described, in another **30 minutes.** Another option is to continue east on the high traverse to Upper Pangboche, a recommended 3-hour walk already described.

Pheasants of the Subalpine Zone
(10,000 to 13,800 ft/3000 to 4200 m in the West, to 12,500 ft/3800 m in the East)

Himalayan monal, or Impeyan pheasant (*Lophophorus impejanus* [*DAAphe*], length 72 cm), is Nepal's national bird. The male has nine iridescent colors but at a distance looks black; the female is dull, brown-mottled buff. Both sexes have white rumps and brown tails. It summers on grassy slopes above the treeline and winters in oak and rhododendron forests. It is easily seen on the Gosainkund trek and in Sagarmatha National Park.

The blood pheasant (*Ithaginis cruentus* [*chilime*], length 46 cm), a small short-tailed pheasant, is often tame and curious. The male is pale gray, green, and red; the female is reddish brown. Both sexes have red legs. It is found in rhododendron, juniper, or bamboo, and is most easily seen in Sagarmatha National Park.

To Thami

The trail to Thami begins at Namche Bazaar and heads west going below the *gomba.* You can also take the trail heading west from Shyangboche before the descent to Namche Bazaar. The trail contours the Nangpo Tsangpo Valley through fir forest and emerging at Phurte (11,400 ft, 3475 m), with its tea shop and nursery. Cross the main tributary from the north, the Kyajo Khola (11,200 ft, 3414 m), at the small town of Kyajo. Continue on to **Thamo,** with lodges (11,300 ft, 3444 m), 1½ **hours** from Namche Bazaar or less from Shyangboche. To the north above the trail is a monastery (Laudo Gomba) where Westerners affiliated with Kopan at Baudha sometimes study. Thamo is the headquarters for the 630-kilowatt power project built with Austrian assistance. It came on line in 1995 and electrifies the western end of Khumbu. In towns, the distribution wires are buried. The predecessor of this project was flooded when a glacial lake burst, and the remnants can be seen across the valley to the south. There are two route choices to Thami from here, and I recommend you make a circuit.

Proceed to **Samde** (11,980 ft, 3652 m), with some tea shops. The trail continues to follow the river and comes to a thundering narrow crossing (12,060 ft, 3676 m) some **45 minutes** beyond Thamo. Ascend on its south (right) bank and reach the Thengpo Khola, flowing east from Trashi Labsta Pass. Cross it to the north (left) bank (12,075 ft, 3880 m) and ascend a small hill to the north to the valley flats and the town of **Thami** (12,400 ft, 3780 m) half an hour from the river crossing. There is a lower part, Thami Og, and an upper part, Thami Teng, where the monastery (12,925 ft, 3940 m) sits in a cliff, which is worth a visit. Near the lower part is the intake for the hydroelectricity project and a small holding pond. To the north up the main riverbed lies Nangpa La (18,753 ft, 5716 m), an important pass into Tibet that was once the popular trading route. Farther to the east at the head of the valley is Trashi Labsta, a high pass (18,882 ft, 5755 m) leading west to the Rolwaling Valley. It is described later. To complete the circuit back to Thamo, find the reconstructed trail east of the holding pond, and follow it down to the powerhouse in a draw to the south (11,760 ft, 3584 m). Cross the main river just to the north, and head downstream through the village of Hungo (Thamo on maps), to reach Thamo in less than two hours from Thami.

Other Side Trips

Many places in Khumbu are worth a detour. Almost any ridge can be hiked up for views, and some are mentioned in the route descriptions. Climbing to base camps such as Ama Dablang, reached from Pangboche in a long day, provides a different Khumbu perspective. Hikes west of Lobuche provide different views than from Kala Pattar. The Gokyo Valley is full of numerous wonderful smaller valleys and ridges to explore.

Mammals of the Subalpine Zone
(10,000 to 13,800 ft/3000 to 4200 m in the West, to 12,500 ft/3800 m in the East)

The Asiatic black bear (*Selenarctos thibetanus* [*himali kaalo bhaalu*], length 140 to 170 cm) is all black with a creamy V on the chest. A powerful and potentially dangerous animal, it is seldom seen. Active between dusk and dawn, it inhabits subalpine forests in summer and descends to temperate or subtropical forests in winter.

The common ghoral (*Nemorhaedus goral* [*ghoral*], shoulder height 65 to 70 cm) is one of the goat-antelopes. Found singly or in small groups on steep grass- and rock-covered slopes, it can be seen on the Gosainkund and Helambu treks.

The Himalayan tahr (*Hemitragus jemlahicus* [*jhaaral*], male shoulder height 90 to 100 cm) is a large goat with a black face. The male has a shaggy shoulder ruff. It grazes in herds at 12,000 ft (3660 m) and below, on precipitous slopes and in dense forests and scrub, and can be seen above Langtang village and around Phortse and Pungo Tenga in Sagarmatha National Park.

Royle's pika, also known as the mouse hare (*Ochotona roylei* [*musa kharayo, pikaa*], length 15 to 20 cm), is a delightful small mammal. It has a short muzzle, small ears, and no visible tail. It lives above the treeline in open country among rocks and can be seen on the Gosainkund trail, at Lobuche, and along the trail above Pheriche in Sagarmatha National Park.

Outsider interest in the dance drama festival of Mani-rimdu *has fostered excellent presentations. (Robert Zimmerman)*

THAMI TO ROLWALING AND BARABISE VIA THE TRASHI LABSTA

This spectacular high route leaves Khumbu via a glaciated pass (Trashi Labsta) and reaches the Rolwaling Valley to the east and its major settlement, Beding, in a minimum of 4 days. There are no villages or shelters along the way, and the route is dangerous even in the best of conditions. Only experienced mountaineers should attempt it, and then only with a party that includes some Sherpas who have been over it before. The entire party, including all the porters, must be equipped for severe conditions of cold and high altitude. Because it is necessary to camp on ice, parties should carry tents and fuel for everyone as well as ice-climbing equipment (ice ax, rope, crampons, and ice screws). Under ideal conditions, the crossing need not require technical climbing, but such conditions cannot be counted on. Storms should be expected, and food for at least 5 days should be carried in order to be able to wait out bad weather. Temperatures below freezing are always encountered. Crossings have been made at all times of the year, but the best time is probably April to early December. Falling rock is the danger most often encountered. Ice avalanches are also possible. Many people have died attempting this crossing, but competent, well-equipped parties should have little trouble. Sherpas even take yaks over it! You must be very aware of the hazards of rapid ascent to altitude and of hypothermia. There are no quick escape routes, especially on the Rolwaling side of the pass, should altitude illness become serious.

The route is described from Thami to Rolwaling, thus offering a challenging route out of Khumbu. This direction is also preferable because parties attempting the crossing have usually acclimatized first in Khumbu. Furthermore, if altitude problems strike on the ascent, it is easier to retreat to lower altitudes from this side than from the other side, where technically difficult terrain and long glaciers must be negotiated. The times listed here, of course, depend on the acclimatization of the party.

Thami to Trashi Labsta

From **Thami** (12,400 ft, 3780 m), described earlier, head west, passing below the monastery to reach a *yersa*, Kure (13,875 ft, 4229 m), in **70 minutes**. The next *yersa* (14,050 ft, 4282 m) is **10 minutes** beyond. Proceed as the valley of the Thami or Thengpo Khola opens up and admire the peaks on its south side, especially the north face of Teng Kangpoche. The extensive *yersa* of Thengpo (14,175 ft, 4321 m) is reached in **25 minutes.** Climb through the various fenced-in fields of this *yersa* and continue up the north side of the valley. Traverse a rock slide from the north to the end of the slide (15,465 ft, 4714 m), **1 hour 20 minutes** from lower Thengpo. The best views east, including the west face of Makalu behind Ama Dablang, are along here. Continue on a grassy slope, then begin climbing a loose moraine to reach a flat area suitable for camping (15,910 ft, 4849 m) in **30 minutes.** Climb the moraine for **1 hour** to Ngole (16,745 ft, 5104 m), located below an icefall to the north. Ngole, which has tent sites and overhanging rocks for shelter, is protected from the icefall and is a good place to camp below the pass. To avoid rockfall off the southern slopes of Tengi Ragi Tau, the peak to the north, it is wisest to ascend beyond here in the early morning. There is another possible campsite (17,150 ft, 5227 m) **30 minutes** beyond. Below and to the south a lake lies in the moraine.

Creatures of the Aeolian Zone

This is the region where snow lies permanently, although much terrain is not covered because snow accumulates unevenly. A. F. R. Wollaston, writing in *Mount Everest, The Reconnaissance, 1921*, records the highest flowering plant species as a small, white-flowering sandwort (*Arenaria bryophylla*) at 20,277 ft (6180 m). Some invertebrates make their homes at even higher altitudes. Large populations of fairy shrimp have been reported in glacial pools at 19,000 ft (5790 m), for example. Insects, such as snow fleas (*Proistoma*) and some carabid beetles, feed on pollen grains, spores, seeds, dead spiders, and insects uplifted on air currents from the distant plains of India. Permanent life even exists at the highest point on earth: samples of soil and snow collected on the summit of Everest were found to contain microorganisms. Birds and mammals are brief visitors to the high peaks and passes. Flocks of bar-headed geese (*Anser indicus*) have been seen flying over the summit of Everest at over 30,500 ft (9300 m). Mountaineering expeditions have reported alpine choughs scavenging from tents above 26,900 ft (8200 m).Continue climbing beyond this last site on snow or rock, as the season dictates, to another level area (17,700 ft, 5395 m) in 30 minutes. Some 15 minutes more of climbing, closer to the face of Tengi Ragi Tau, brings you to yet another small campsite (17,850 ft, 5441 m). These last two campsites are not entirely protected from rockfall, a hazard that varies with the time of year. Be on the lookout for serious symptoms of altitude illness, and descend if they occur.

The icefall before you, which has been visible for some time, is from Trashi Labsta. Ascend a scree slope to the northeast of the icefall and traverse to a sheltered spot (18,250 ft, 5563 m) under the rock face of Tengi Ragi Tau in another **30 minutes.** If coming from Rolwaling, this sheltered spot could be an appropriate place to pitch a tent and camp. It is safer to camp lower, but you should not descend late in the day if much rock is falling. To proceed over the pass, climb on snow east of the icefall to a long, more gradual slope. There are sheltered spots under overhanging rocks under the face of Tengi Ragi Tau, but it is not a good idea to camp this high, because the risk of altitude illness is greater. Better to sleep low and climb high. Proceed west to the height of land and Trashi Labsta (18,882 ft, 5755 m)—the name means "luck-bringing prayer flags"—in another **45 minutes.** There is a cairn with prayer flags at the pass. The times listed here are actual traveling times, and most parties take at least half a day from Ngole to here when rests are included. New vistas open up to the west, but the views to the east are limited to Teng Kangpoche. Directly south is the peak Pharchamo (20,582 ft, 6273 m), a trekking summit.

The Yeti

It was north of this area in the autumn of 1951 near Menlung La that the famous yeti (abominable snowman) footprint photographs were taken. The footprints were found in the afternoon at around 16,000 ft (5000 m) on a snow-covered glacier among crevasses. They were about a foot long (0.3 m) and half as wide. Could it have been a person traveling several hours from the nearest habitation without shoes and with deformed feet? I have seen mountain people carry heavy loads barefoot in the snow. Others have documented individuals with seemingly superhuman abilities to adapt to extreme temperatures unclothed.

Sherpas and other mountain groups speak of a hairy apelike creature, and scalp and hand bone relics have been on display at Khumjung and Pangboche (the former can still be seen by the trekker, the latter has been stolen). Sir Edmund Hillary's 1960–61 expedition took the Khumjung relics on an around-the-world trek to authenticate them without success. Other expeditions have tried to find this animal. Many years ago, when outsiders expressed disbelief in the creature, a Sherpa said, "You tell us of buildings as tall as our hills, with magic carpets in them that carry you to the top, and we can't believe this, so how can we expect you to believe in the yeti?"

Trashi Labsta to Beding

The descent is over a snow-covered, moderately steep glacier with crevasses and requires roped travel and the ability to do crevasse rescues. The route may take you near the cliffs to the north—where there may be a potential rockfall hazard. Reach the Drolambo Glacier (17,850 ft, 5440 m) in perhaps **45 minutes.** Parties wishing to explore further can get plenty of ideas from the Schneider map. Note that the route marked on Schneider's *Rolwaling Himal* map is not the one described here, as the marked route (which is perhaps more hazardous) is no longer in use. The route in use when you cross could be different. Thus, it is advisable to have along a Sherpa familiar with the current way.

Head south along the Drolambo, proceeding near a medial moraine. It is safest to camp above the icefall that lies at the snout of the Drolambo, which in turn lies above the Trakarding Glacier. Camping here will enable you to get an early start and minimize the danger of rockfall from the medial moraines. A campsite (17,750 ft, 5410 m) can be found in about **30 minutes** after reaching the valley glacier. Unlike the narrow upper part of the eastern side of Trashi Labsta, the country here is open.

Continue descending the Drolambo, staying east of the first medial moraine and of an icefall that you pass in **30 minutes.** Most likely you can travel in a trough that is easy and quite safe, providing you have made an early start and the sun hasn't hit the walls. Late in the day the ice-bound rocks loosen and you may feel like a target in a shooting gallery in the middle of a waterfall! In the usual trough, there is one steep ice step, perhaps 40 to 50 ft (15 m) high, where it is best to belay the party down. Crampons, ice axes, rope, and ice screws are usually necessary. Descend carefully on snow and ice-covered rock, keeping close to the rock face to the right to avoid falling rocks and ice. In **2½ to 3 hours** from the camp above, reach a spectacular rocky spur (16,950 ft, 5166 m) below the icefall on the Drolambo, but still considerably above the Trakarding Glacier below. There are plenty of campsites here that are safe from falling rock and ice. If ascending to the pass from Rolwaling, it would be prudent to camp here if you arrive late in the day, unless it is very cold and the rocks are frozen in place. If there is no sound of falling rock when you stop here on the way to the pass, it is probably fairly safe to continue. Along the way, there are several points where your porters might appreciate a rope to use as a hand line.

The yeti lives!

The Trakarding Glacier is the long, rubble-covered ice river flowing northwest below you. It is reached in **30 minutes** from the spur (16,125 ft, 4915 m). Rock overhangs that provide shelter should be apparent. Traverse northwest under the icefall of the Drolambo Glacier to a campsite called Thakar (16,075 ft, 4900 m) in **15 minutes.** There are few if any good campsites on the extensive moraine of the glacier until the lake is passed. Finding water is also a problem. Keeping close to the northwest side of the glacier, follow an indistinct trail marked with cairns. There is sometimes falling rock from the northwest, so be cautious. The going is slow along this moraine. Occasional rock overhangs are passed that would make possible campsites.

About halfway toward the big lake—Tsho Rolpa or Chu Pokhari—the current route crosses the dry Trakarding Glacier to the southwest side and ascends the moraine to a shelf or pasture, Kyidug Kangma (15,682 ft, 4780 m), where you could camp, providing water is available. This is **2 to 3 hours** from the rock overhangs. The route used to follow the northeast side of the glacier and cross the lake on that side, but the moraine along the lake has become virtually impassable. From Kyidug Kangma follow the trail up steeply to the 4886-m (16,830-ft) high point marked on the Schneider *Rolwaling Himal* map. Descend into a trough with pleasant pastures and streams once you reach Kabug (14,875 ft, 4534 m), where there are overhanging shelters you can camp under. Reach it in **1½ hours** from Kyidug Kangma. Proceed along more friendly terrain to reach the terminal moraine of the Ripimo Shar Glacier.

Outbursts of Glacier-Formed Lakes

Tsho Rolpa is a pristine example of a lake created by a glacier behind a fragile dam of rock and ice. Another is a lake on the Imja Glacier beneath Island Peak that appears to be less than 35 years old and is growing rapidly. Such structures are going to burst unexpectedly at some future time, as the pressure of the water backed up exceeds the breaking point of the dam. Sometimes an avalanche that commonly lets loose can trigger the calamity and catastrophically flood the valley below. The trail on the north side of the lake has become too dangerous to take, and glacial movement has changed the strength of the dam below. Such outbursts have occurred at least six times in the last 40 years on the Khumbu side, destroying hydroelectric projects under construction, as well as myriad bridges over the rivers. Although the local people can quickly rebuild the bridges and reroute the trails, the bigger outsider-driven projects can take decades to complete after such incidents. When motorable roads and other modern amenities get built and the population becomes dependent on them, those calamities can have much more far-reaching effects on the population than the simple technologies that they replaced but were under local control. Such potential disasters on the Arun to the east were factors stressed by groups concerned about the impact of the hydroelectric project that was to be financed there.

Descend just beyond to pass through a small *yersa* of unroofed frames, Sangma (14,175 ft, 4321 m), reached in **45 minutes.** Descend to cross the outflow (13,900 ft, 4237 m) of the lake to the left a few minutes later. Descend the broad valley and enjoy the fragrant shrubs. In **30 minutes** cross to the north (right) bank of the Rolwaling Khola (13,725 ft, 4163 m). There is a route to the south over the ridge via Yalung La, a pass to the Khare Khola. But continue on the usual route and reach the west end of the settlement of Na and the limit of the glaciated valley. Downstream, the Rolwaling Valley is a sharp, river-worn V. Na is a large *yersa* at the base of an impressive peak to the north. It is occupied by inhabitants of Beding part of the year, depending on the potato harvest. The Sherpas of Rolwaling believe that their valley was formed by the sweep of a giant horse and plow guided by Padmasamblava, who brought Buddhism to Tibet from India. According to one source, *rolwa* means "a furrow," while *ling* is "a country." Another meaning for *Rolwaling* is "the place where the *dakini* play." They also feel it is one of the eight *beyul*, or "hidden valleys," in the Himalaya. Because of this, they do not allow anyone to kill animals in the valley.

Descend 125 ft (38 m) to the lower part of Na and in 1 hour reach rhododendron and juniper forests, a pleasant contrast to the barren landscape above the lake. Pass through another *yersa*, Dokare (12,575 ft, 3833 m), 15 minutes later and continue to **Beding** (12,120 ft, 3694 m), **1½ hours** from Na. This is the main settlement for the Sherpa inhabitants of the Rolwaling Valley. It is located in a narrow gorge and gets little direct sunlight. There is no farmland nor mountain view, save that of Gaurishankar before you reach the village. The *gomba* here is impressively located and worth visiting to see the fine paintings. There is a school built by Sir Edmund Hillary and some interesting flour mills. People wishing to take a side trip with a view of spectacular Menlungtse (Jobo Garu on the Schneider map) can ascend to Manlung La in a day and a half from Beding if they are already acclimatized. There is some trade to Palbugthang and Thumphug over this pass during the summer—mostly rice exchanged for Tibetan salt.

BEDING TO BARABISE

Leave Beding and pass through a *yersa* (11,975 ft, 3650 m) in **10 minutes.** Then cross a tributary (11,875 ft, 3584 m) in another **10 minutes.** This river, the Gaurishankar Khola, has eroded a gap in the wall, allowing a pretty waterfall to cascade through. Just beyond is a *yersa*, Chumlgalgya, and there are two more in **5 and 10 minutes,** respectively (the last at 11,700 ft, 3566 m). The trail continues into a pleasant fir, rhododendron, and birch forest and descends in **20 minutes** to a small sanctuary (11,275 ft, 3437 m) dedicated to the Nepali deities Sita Mahadev and Kanchi Mahadev. A cantilever bridge here to the south (left) bank of the Rolwaling Khola is the beginning of a trail that leads to Daldung La. It offers a higher route out of the Rolwaling Valley to use in the monsoon, when the main route may be too wet. Don't take it unless so advised by the locals. Continue in forest for **35 minutes** until you cross a tributary from the north. Here there is a good, though very foreshortened, view of Gaurishankar to the north. Some **10 minutes** beyond, come to a covered bridge crossing the Rolwaling Khola (10,200 ft, 3108 m). Cross to the south (left) bank and keep to the south side of the narrow valley. Notice how everything is much greener and lusher here, perhaps because this north-facing slope receives less direct sun. In addition to the deciduous vegetation, there are impressive fir trees.

Continue on the south side above the valley floor and enter a burned area (9350 ft, 2850 m) in **35 minutes.** Some **20 minutes** beyond reach some steep slabs (9150 ft, 2789 m). Leave the riverbed and ascend the slabs along an impressive, locally made ramp. Reach a clearing in **30 minutes**—you are still in the burn, which has more growth the farther west you go. **Ten minutes** beyond is a campsite under an overhanging rock, and nearby is a fault cave. Continue high on the side of the valley to stands of oak. Pass under a swirling waterfall (9175 ft, 2797 m) **1 hour** beyond the slabs. Continue contouring for almost **1 hour** before descending to reach the few *goTh* of Shakpa (8700 ft, 2652 m). Descend in less than **1 hour** to the village of **Simigaon** (6550 ft, 1996 m). Sherpas and hill Nepalis inhabit this lush oasis, which has interesting fruits and vegetables in addition to the predominant millet fields.

Descend steeply to the river, the Bhote Kosi, passing under some large rock overhangs. Cross to the east (right) bank on a suspension bridge (5000 ft, 1524 m) **45 minutes** from Simigaon. The trail rises above difficult stretches of an impressive gorge to the south. Traverse the few fields of Chetchet 15 minutes beyond and admire the falls that tumble at least 300 ft (100 m) down the east (right) bank. Some **35 minutes** beyond Chetchet, the trail forks. The lower fork keeps close to the river and is suitable during low water. The upper fork is for use during the monsoon. In **30 minutes** the valley widens and in its floor ahead is the village of **Gongar** (4525 ft, 1410 m). Cross the Gongar Khola, a tributary from the west, to the trail fork beyond. The left fork keeps close to the river and goes to Charikot. You can take it to join the usual Everest Base Camp route from Lamosangu. The right fork, described here, ascends and heads to Barabise. Climb on a spur through terraces to a *chautaaraa* (5150 ft, 1570 m) **30 minutes** from Gongar. Contour and cross two tributaries in **30 minutes.** Climb another **25 minutes** to a Shiva sanctuary (5825 ft, 1775 m) to the left of the trail. Surrounded by a rock wall, this sanctuary contains a few bells and innumerable tridents of iron in various shapes and sizes. Climb another **30 minutes** to **Thare** (6475 ft, 1974 m), a scattered *Tamang* village. It is not marked on Schneider's *Lapchi Kang* map.

Continue contouring to **Dulang** (6225 ft, 1897 m), the next scattered village. Another **50 minutes** brings you to the ridge where the Warang school (6600 ft, 2012 m) is located. Enjoy the views of Gaurishankar to the northeast. Pass through the settlement of **Yarsa** (6225 ft, 1897 m) **25 minutes** beyond, and then contour and descend for **20 minutes** to cross the Warang Khola (5775 ft, 1760 m). Contour another **25 minutes** to the scattered village of Bulung (5850 ft, 1783 m). Continue to a high clearing, the site of the local middle school (6335 ft, 1931 m), some **25 minutes** beyond. You are now leaving the valley of the Bhote Kosi for the tributary valley of the Sangawa Khola. Contour for **45 minutes** to a *stupa* and then to a *chautaaraa* with Tibetan-style religious paintings. Pass above the scattered village of Laduk and reach the school situated above it (6810 ft, 2075 m) in **20 minutes.** Don't climb beyond, but take the lower fork and descend slightly. Cross a recent slide, then the Thuran Khola (6260 ft, 1908 m), in another **1¼ hours.** Above you is the town of Charsaba, but the main trail ascends and contours below it. Beyond a main ridge, the town of Chilangka (6310 ft, 1923 m) is reached in **65 minutes.** Descend past another small slide and cross the Jorang Khola (5585 ft, 1702 m) in **25 minutes.** Contour through chir pine forest to reach **Lading** (5835 ft, 1778 m) in **50 minutes.**

Beyond there is a choice of routes. The left fork descends to the river (the Saun Khola), crosses it to the east (right) bank on a log bridge, ascends near a tributary (the Amatal Khola), and passes the village of Amatal to the few houses of Ruphtang (7670 ft, 2335 m) in approximately 4 hours. This route is more direct than the other, but it avoids the climb up to Bigu Gomba, one of the most fascinating Buddhist nunneries in Nepal.

To head to Bigu Gomba, also known locally as Tashi Gomba, don't descend the Saun or Sangawa Khola, but contour around a ridge and descend to the Samling Khola, a tributary from the north. Cross it on a cantilever bridge (5710 ft, 1710 m) to the west (right) bank in **45 minutes.** Begin climbing up to **Bigu Gomba.** The entire terraced hillside has numerous houses and is called Bigu. It takes **2 hours** or more to reach the actual nunnery (8235 ft, 2310 m), a long, white building in front of the temple itself, which is set among juniper trees. This nunnery of the Kargyupa sect was built around 1933 and houses some thirty-six nuns, most of them Sherpas. It is unusual because its east and west walls are lined with interlacing statues of Avalokiteshwara, each with eleven heads and a thousand arms, hands, and eyes. You are not allowed to photograph the inside of the *gomba.*

To leave Bigu, traverse north on a high trail, and then contour and drop to join a main trail west of the *gomba* near three *stupa* (7895 ft, 2406 m) in less than **30 minutes.** Continue until you spot Ruphtang, one house on top of a small hill; take a left fork to descend and cross a tributary from the north on a covered bridge by some mills (7460 ft, 2275 m). Climb the hill to **Ruphtang** (7680 ft, 2335 m) **30 minutes** from the *stupa*. This may be the last habitation below the pass, Tinsang La. Climb beyond, steeply at first, then more gradually in a forest of prickly-leaved oak. There is a tea shop (8740 ft, 2664 m) some 55 minutes above Ruphtang. Continue climbing in impressive fir forest with numerous campsites. There is a *goTh* (10,240 ft, 3121 m) **2 hours** from Ruphtang and a pleasant stream some 500 ft (150 m) higher. The pass itself (10,890 ft, 3319 m), with several *goTh* nearby, is **30 minutes** beyond. The view of the Himalaya, although somewhat distant, is breathtaking. The tower of Chobo Bamare is quite close.

Buddhist Festivals: Mani-rimdu

Mani-rimdu is a Sherpa dance drama performed in the Khumbu region. It is held annually at Tengboche and Chiwong monasteries during November or early December and at Thami each May. Although usually held during the full moon, this is sometimes scheduled at a more auspicious time, so inquire in Kathmandu and along the way to learn when it will take place. This colorful, uniquely Sherpa festival has its origins in ancient Tibetan theatrical genres. The performers are monks, but the occasion is highlighted by much gaiety and feasting by monks and lay spectators alike.

From the pass, descend into rhododendron and fir forest that becomes almost pure rhododendron forest lower down and then blends again into prickly-leaved oak forest. A small *gomba* above **Dolangsa** (8165 ft, 2489 m) is reached in **65 minutes** from the pass. There are many variations in the route down the Sun Kosi to its junction with the Bhote Kosi below Barabise. You can head south through Nangarpa and cross the main river west of Gorthali before proceeding along its north (right) bank. Or you can keep to the north side of the valley, crossing tributaries and going below a pretty waterfall (7390 ft, 2252 m) **65 minutes** beyond the *gomba*. Beyond, you can continue contouring, or you can descend closer to the river. If descending, reach **Kabre** (5265 ft, 1605 m) in **70 minutes** from the waterfall. Continue west, crossing a tributary from the north on an old suspension bridge (3890 ft, 1185 m) in **35 minutes.** Contour another **10 minutes** to the first stores of **Budipa** (3790 ft, 1155 m). The main trail continues contouring about 500 ft (150 m) above the main river and passes through the scattered houses of **Simle** (3550 ft, 1080 m) in **55 minutes.** The solace and freedom from the noises of the twentieth century are almost over. Horns can soon be heard. The trail rounds a ridge to descend to **Barabise** (2690 ft, 820 m) on the west (left) bank of the Bhote Kosi in 45 minutes. Buses leave this staging center for Kathmandu periodically during the day.

There is another high pass leading out of the upper Rolwaling Valley, Yalung La (17,422 ft, 5310 m). The descent is made to the southwest to Suri Dhoban. Inquire at Beding for a guide.

An alternative route from Rolwaling branches from Simigaon and, instead of crossing to the west (right) bank of the Bhote Kosi, heads south on its east (left) bank, passing through Tashinam to Manthali (3450 ft, 1080 m), approximately 1 day from Simigaon. The Sieri Khola, a tributary from the east, is crossed en route. Continue on the east (left) bank of the main valley and cross the Suri (or Khare) Khola at Suri Dhoban (3215 ft, 990 m). Continue to Tyanku in a day. Cross the main river, the Tamba or Bhote Kosi, at Biguti (3150 ft, 960 m) and climb up to Dolakha (5580 ft, 1700 m), which has several interesting temples. Shortly beyond, reach Charikot (6560 ft, 2000 m), less than a day from Tyanku. The main trail to Solu-Khumbu is soon intersected; Lamosangu is a day and a half farther. This trail is somewhat shorter than the higher Tinsang La trail, but less scenic.

7 Langtang, Gosainkund, and Helambu

If you walk the trails of Nepal, you will know what Buddhist dharma is all about.

Tengboche Rimpoche

Most of Langtang and Gosainkund has been included in Langtang National Park, and there is an attempt to create uniform restaurant and lodging services as in the ACAP region north of Pokhara. Gosainkund is the site of several sacred lakes that lie south of a major ridge between Helambu and the Trisuli River to the west. The area is uninhabited for the most part, but every August as many as 50,000 pilgrims crowd into the area for a festival by a lake that figures prominently in Hindu mythology. Trekkers can visit this area from Dhunche or Syabrubensi, which is reached by road from Kathmandu and, if conditions permit, cross a pass to link up with Helambu. It is spectacular in the spring when rhododendrons are in bloom. Trekkers heading into this area may find accommodations for all of the journey in the popular season.

Langtang, a Himalayan valley north of Helambu and Gosainkund, is inhabited by *Tamang* and Tibetan (Bhote) peoples and provides a glimpse of mountain life. Trails are straightforward, yet you can head east in the Langtang Valley beyond the last habitation to spectacular remote mountain areas, taking various side trips. Food and lodging are available except for the highest areas. Linkups with Gosainkund are reasonably simple, but to link with Helambu requires crossing a substantial pass, for which you must be self-sufficient.

Helambu, the region closest to Kathmandu, can be approached from the northeast rim of the Kathmandu Valley. The name refers to a region at the north end of the Malemchi Khola. It is inhabited by *Yolmo*, who also are called Sherpas. This region south of the main Himalayan chain provides an example of typical hill life in Nepal. A circuit can be made through the area from Kathmandu. The route begins in areas of Hindu influence and goes through Buddhist villages. There are distant views of the Himalaya. Rather than backtrack to Kathmandu, a circuit is described to reach the road, either at Malemchi Pul if you head south from Shermathang or at Chautaaraa if you take the Panch Pokhari side trip, which is a challenging trek to some high-altitude lakes not visited by many trekkers.

In the route descriptions that follow, the times listed between points are actual walking times, generally those I took myself. They *do not* include any rests. This has been strictly adhered to by using a chronograph. Over most of the trails I carried a moderately heavy pack. I almost never walked the segments in these times. Like everyone else, I rested, photographed, talked with the people, and so forth.

Langtang

Langtang is a spectacular valley nestled in the Himalaya. Lodges and food are available for most of the way, but it is best to arrange food and shelter to be able to explore the upper part of the valley; this can be organized at Kyangjin Gomba, the last area with lodges. First the trip from Dhunche (or Syabrubensi, a quicker

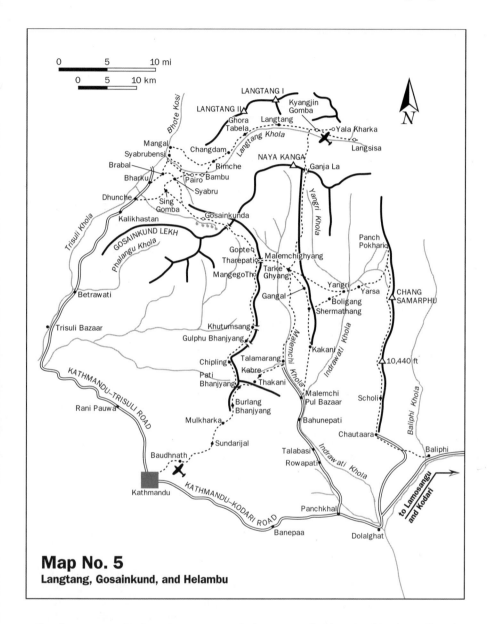

Map No. 5
Langtang, Gosainkund, and Helambu

valley-bottom option) to Langtang and then several side trips up the valley are described. There is a high pass, the Ganja La, which links Langtang with Helambu. A brief description of this route is given; going with a guide is advised. Return routes to avoid backtracking from Langtang and linkups with Gosainkund complete the description.

Dhunche was the traditional starting point for the trek. With the construction of a new trail from Syabrubensi, to Pairo, it is possible to cut about a day off the usual trekking time, but the price paid is not passing through Syabru, missing views of the Ganesh Himal and peaks to the north in Tibet, and opting for an entire valley-bottom route. If you are going on to Gosainkund, you will pass through Syabru anyway, so this option makes sense. You could also vary your return by traversing high on the north side of the Langtang Valley and reaching Syabrubensi from the north. The start from Syabrubensi is described first, followed by that from Dhunche.

The first part, often the most difficult, consists of road travel. If you have the resources, consider hiring a taxi. Trekkers have occasionally chartered a helicopter to Kyangjin Gomba and descended from there. Altitude illness is more likely to strike such groups. Better to board a bus from Kathmandu to Dhunche or Syabrubensi. Some buses go directly to Syabrubensi; others go only as far as Dhunche. Departure points for these tourist buses are from the Naya Bas Parak ("new bus park") near Baleju on the Kathmandu Ring Road. Purchase the tickets the day before, and specify which destination you want. The road first reaches Trisuli, the district center for the Nuwakot District, and then goes north up a rough road to Dhunche and beyond to Syabrubensi. Travel beyond into the Ganesh Himal area to lead and zinc mines at Somdang is by private vehicle. The road to Trisuli rises out of the northeast end of the Kathmandu Valley on a decaying track. There are views of Ganesh Himal and west to Himal Chuli and the Annapurna Range. North of Trisuli the rough feeder road climbs up from the valley bottom. Views of Langtang and Paldor as well as the incredible gorge below you give a sense of the scale of the terrain. Beyond Trisuli, pass through Kalikhastan and the entrance to Langtang National Park. Trekking permits are inspected along the road and rarely after you leave it. Check posts like being on the road.

SYABRUBENSI TO KYANGJIN GOMBA

Instead of starting at Dhunche, if you stay on the bus until **Syabrubensi** (4650 ft, 1417 m), at the junction of the Langtang Khola with the Bhote Kosi, the route is shorter. You can stay on either side of the river. This large town contains a settlement of Tibetan refugees, as well as *BhoTiya,* who call themselves *Tamang.* The newer part of town is on the south. A VHF public phone system operates here. Near here on the TR bank of the Bhote Kosi below the bridge across it, there are some hot springs that used to be clean enough for bathing but more recently have become too polluted. There are attempts to clean them up so enquire locally if they are usable. Begin on the south side of the Langtang Khola and pick up the trail that follows the Langtang Khola upstream on the TL bank. Don't take the right-hand fork that leaves the valley to climb up to Syabru. In 1½ **hours** cross the Ghopche Khola to reach the few tea houses of Domin (Dhoban, 5380 ft, 1640 m). Along the way, after about an hour, you will pass a temporary bridge over the Langtang Khola that is the way across for the slightly shorter dry-season route that begins on the north (TR) bank of the river in Syabrubensi. This route could also be taken if it is known that the bridge is there. Ascend to join the trail from Syabru just west of a major landslide (5800 ft, 1768 m) in **30 minutes.** Turn left and head up the valley, crossing the landslide of 1987 near its terminus, to reach **Pairo** (5500 ft, 1676 m), meaning landslide, in **20 minutes**. The first lodge has piped hot water from a hot spring, across the river, that is not accessible currently, as there is no bridge. A short climb up brings you to more lodges of the same settlement. Most of these are operated by *Tamang* until you get well into Langtang.

Continue upstream from Pairo in a lush oak forest to reach **Bambu** (6480 ft, 1975 m), a collection of lodges in a cleared bamboo jungle with spaces for tents in another **hour.** Water cascades off the north side of the impressive canyon here.

Climbing beyond, cross a tributary and in **30 minutes** come to the bridge across the Langtang Khola (6920 ft, 2109 m). There are simple lodges on both sides and little sunshine as the water tumbles down from above because of recent landslides. Cross to the true left, and climb upstream, being careful of the nettles that guard the sides of the trail in this wild jungle. Reach the first lodges of **Rimche** (7840 ft, 2390 m) in **less than an hour**. A further **30-minute** climb brings you to another lodge, misnamed for a view not possible from there (8200 ft, 2500 m), where the high north-side trail to Syabrubensi leaves to traverse above treeline for the most part. This is described below. Five minutes behind is another lodge, and all these are referred to as Rimche. Only the upper ones enjoy mountain views to the west.

The forest here abounds with wildlife, martin, bear, langur monkey, and red panda, which one lucky trekker watched and photographed on his first trek in Nepal in the winter months!

BAMBOO IN THE MOONLIGHT

Moonlight,
Filtering silvery through a grove of whispering bamboo,
Moonlight,
Caressing fondly the branches that sway as nature dances,
Moonlight,
Smiling down in this bamboo
That bids farewell and welcomes you,
That closes in the farmer's fields,
That rocks the child and soothes his dreams,
A door that every family needs

Then one day in our final year
This same bamboo becomes the bier
That carries us to burn
And lastly, when it is our turn,
The blazing pyre will heavenward go
Towards the moonlight's lasting glow
High still above, the thick bamboo
From birth to death remains for you
The moonlight,
The never-ending moonlight.

Megh Raj Manjul

Compare the forests on both sides of the valley; they go much higher on the north-facing aspect, even though it receives less sunlight, because there is more rainfall there. Descend slightly to reach **Changdam** (8140 ft, 2481 m) in **20 minutes,** a group of lodges in a clearing, that is more usually referred to as Lama Hotel, after the first structure built in 1973. That building is gone, but the builder of the original hotel continues in a new hotel; there are many more fancier ones as well. You may prefer to stay back to enjoy the views if the weather is suitable.

Relax your vigilance for nettles now, and climb into more lush forest with hanging moss, and be glad the huge landslide on the other side didn't catch you in this orogenically active area. Nevertheless small parts of the trail slide away, so it is being constantly rerouted and rebuilt. Reach several lodges 10 minutes apart, known collectively as **Gumnachowk**, meaning "trekker's corner" (9100 ft, 2774 m), in **1¼ hours**. Look for troops of well-fed monkeys. Climb on through more hobbit forest to reach **Ghora Tabela** (9860 ft, 3005 m) in **1¼ hours** as the valley opens out. This was once a settlement of Tibetans, then a Khampa staging center, and now the army has taken over. As well, there are a few lodges that operate here. Your national park permit will be checked just beyond here, and you will be asked to sign a register when you leave. Beyond here the steep climbs are over, but the altitude gain should make you cautious to look out for signs of mountain sickness.

Climb on, being wary of slippery sections of the trail when cold temperatures freeze the water in tributaries coming off the walls to the north. You will pass several pasturing settlements where lodges operate, including Thang Shyap (10,400 ft, 3170 m), in **less than an hour** where you leave the forest behind and Tchamki a further **15 minutes**. In another **45 minutes** reach some lodges below Kangtangsa, the gomba near Langtang. This gomba and the one at Kyangjin operate with villagers performing the rites, and monks visiting occasionally to officiate, in the Nyingmapa tradition. Pay a visit and leave a donation, asking at the lodge for the whereabouts of the key custodian. Continue climbing in the widening valley, and approach Langtang village. Lodges are concentrated on the newer lower part of town. There, off to the north, is a small hydroelectric power supply that powers a community-run bakery where you can get fresh cookies! **Langtang** (11,220 ft, 3420 m) is **30 minutes** up from Kangtangsa. This place is the first opportunity you have in this valley bottom to stay in a village. Choose one of the simple home lodges in the traditional upper part of town to get a better sense of life in this valley. Every other place up to here, if you came from Syabrubensi, has been built for tourists. The people, although they call themselves *Tamang,* have a much different culture than the relative lowlanders, much more Tibetan, as is their language. If you later go to Helambu, compare the peoples there with those here.

 Buddhist Festivals

Losar, the Tibetan New Year, is in mid-February. There are festive activities at Baudhnath and Swayambhunath temples in the Kathmandu Valley and at the Tibetan refugee center near PaaTan. Festivals are also held in outlying Tibetan refugee communities, such as in the Pokhara Valley, in the Langtang Valley, and at Chialsa. Buddhist pilgrims visit the big temples and monasteries at this time, and family reunions—with feasting, drinking, and dancing—highlight home life.

Buddha's Birthday in May is a solemn occasion. Foreign dignitaries are usually invited to observances during the day at Swayambhunath, where Tibetan and *Newar* Buddhist monks perform elaborate rituals in their brightly colored robes. Observances are also held in other Buddhist temples and monasteries. Prayer flags fly overhead, and at night the Swayambhunath hilltop is brightly lit. The celebration of Buddha's Birthday is less elaborate in outlying Buddhist communities, where observances at the local *gomba* or monastery are common.

Dalai Lama's Birthday, on July 6, is a time for prayer, invocation of blessings, and feasting, especially by Tibetan refugees. For some refugees it is a time of patriotic expressions in remembrance of former times, when the Dalai Lama was the supreme ruler of Tibet. Prayer flags fly overhead, and within the monasteries, butter lamps are lit in the name of the Dalai Lama. Prayers are said for his long life and good health.

Climb on, passing many *mani* walls, and notice how there are no new carvings, reflecting the decline in this practice. The beautiful peak at the head of the valley is Gangchenpo. As you go below Mundu in 30 minutes, a village off the trail, there are tea shops, and a school and 15 minutes beyond is Simdum. Look ahead at the U-shaped glacier-scoured valley, and contrast it with the V-shaped river eroded valley behind you. A bleaker hour's walk brings you to a couple of hotels (12,160 ft, 3706 m). Ahead is the terminal moraine of the Ledrup Lirung Glacier, and you cross its outflow in a few minutes and then climb over the boulders of the moraine to drop down into Kyangjin Gomba, just below the Gomba (12,795 ft, 3900 m) in 30 minutes. There are many lodges here—a destination resort (a far cry from the yak pastures I found almost 25 years ago).

Cuckoos and Barbets of the Temperate Zone

Cuckoos and barbets call repeatedly in spring and summer while concealing themselves in treetops. The great barbet (*Megalaima virens*, length 32 cm) has a large yellow bill, dark head, and red vent. It sings a duet with its mate: he repeats "pir-ao," while she replies with a trilled "pur." It occurs in oak forests; it is also found in the subtropical zone. The common (or Eurasian) cuckoo (*Cuculus canorus*, length 33 cm) is a familiar bird in Europe. It sings its English name. Found in open wooded country, it also occurs in tropical, subtropical, and subalpine zones. The oriental (or Himalayan) cuckoo (*Cuculus saturatus*, length 33 cm) makes a monotonous "oop-oop" call. The appearance of both species is similar to Indian cuckoo (see "Birds of the Subtropical Zone"). The large hawk cuckoo (*Cuculus sparverioides*, length 38 cm) has a call and appearance similar to the common hawk cuckoo but is larger and occurs at higher altitudes. The latter two species are found in oak and rhododendron forests. The orange-rumped (or Himalayan) honeyguide (*Indicator xanthonotus* [*mauricharo*], length 15 cm) is a drab, sparrowlike bird, which is remarkable for its ability to digest beeswax. It will defend the nest of the giant honeybee from other honeyguides and can be seen on cliffs north of Ghasa (on the Thak Khola trek) and near Syabru and Changdam (on the Langtang trek).

STARTING FROM DHUNCHE

If you get off in **Dhunche** (6450 ft, 1966 m), the center for the Rasuwa District, located at the junction of the Trisuli Khola and the Bhote Kosi, you will find shops, comfortable lodges, and an army check post. Pay the park entrance fee at the Langtang National Park headquarters just before reaching the town if you didn't in Kathmandu. Keep the receipt with your trekking permit. There is international phone service available. A useful area map is available at the Hotel Langtang View. Most of the newer part of town is run by *Newar* and serves district government functions as well as tourists. The older charming *Tamang* town is below and worth a wander. The trail will be described to Pairo, near the junction with the trail from Syabrubensi.

From **Dhunche** walk or ride the road 6 km to **Thulo Bharku** (*Thulo* means "big"; there is a smaller settlement above the road) (6050 ft, 1844 m), reached in **1½ hours** or less. There are shortcuts to avoid long switchbacks up to the Trisuli Khola crossing (5908 ft, 1823 m). Head through town and, just after the first hairpin turn (where a road heads off to the Gosainkund trail), a small trail descends a few steep steps to reach the road where the powerline crosses by a hotel. Continue further on the road and bypass another hairpin turn by a branch trail on the left. Just before and just after Bharku, there are camping sites. The trail now leads off up the hill on your right. Pick it up either behind the school or above the road crossing of the tributary near the mill.

Peoples of Eastern Nepal: *Tamang*

The *Tamang*, a very large and widespread hill group, are among the most recent groups to have settled along the northern border regions and higher hills, having come, it appears, from farther north and east. *Tamang* have retained much of their Tibetan and Buddhist heritage. They have many villages all around the Kathmandu Valley, especially north, toward Helambu, and east, on the Mount Everest trek. They also populate the upper Trisuli Valley, on the Langtang trek. *Tamang* are well known to Himalayan climbers, who hire them for the long haul into base camps. At the higher elevations, however, the Sherpas tend to dominate the portering.

Continue contouring and rising beyond Bharku through pleasant chir pine and rhododendron forests. Pass a lodge in 20 minutes and rise above some beautifully terraced fields (Mungra) to the west and then another simple lodge. Cross several tributaries to reach the few houses of **Brabal** (7560 ft, 2304 m), in **1½ hours** from Bharku. There is a monastery, Shedup Cheling Gomba, sitting majestically on a spur splitting the two parts of this town. Consider donating for its completion and support of the Lama, as it is needy. You have great views of Ganesh Himal and peaks to the north in Tibet. You also see the road winding west out of the Bhote

A Tamang *lady and a young* Bahun *woman converse about village events.*

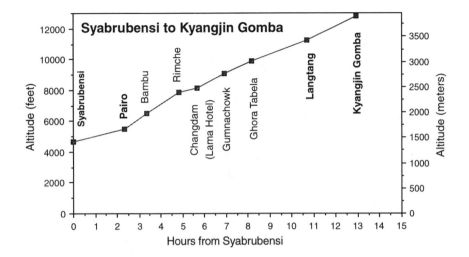

Kosi valley to cross high ridges. Round a bend to a rest spot with the first views up the Langtang Valley in **20 minutes**. You will follow the valley floor ahead of you for several days. Contour and descend another **45 minutes** to **Syabru** (7350 ft, 2240 m), a village commandingly strung out along a ridge. Notice the fine carved windows on the older houses below the new construction for trekkers. Consider staying in one to get a sense of nontouristic life here. The fertile fields to the east and south support this region.

Descend toward the bottom of the houses on the ridge and pick up a trail that traverses the fields to the east, past a few lodges, to cross the Gopche Khola, a tributary of the Langtang Khola draining from the Gosainkund Lekh (6500 ft, 1981 m), in **40 minutes**. Climb up beyond to pass two simple hotels, and then descend into a lush bamboo jungle to reach a trail junction (5800 ft, 1768 m), near the Langtang Khola in less than an **hour** from the Gopche Khola crossing. Here the left fork descends to Domin and the quick route to Syabrubensi. Continue crossing the landslide near its terminus, to reach **Pairo** (5500 ft, 1676 m), meaning "landslide," in **20 minutes**. The trail up the Langtang Valley beyond this point has already been described.

UPPER LANGTANG VALLEY

Kyangjin Gomba (12,795 ft, 3900 m) is an excellent base for exploring the idyllic upper reaches of this valley. The *Langthang Himal West* sheet of the Alpenvereinskarte 1:50,000 map, published by the Austrian Alpine Club, is most helpful. The cheese factory near the Gomba here was started as a Swiss project in 1955, with rounds of cheese carried to Kathmandu over the Ganja La. The original simple technology can be observed from May to October, when they produce 5000 to 7000 kg of *nak* (female yak) and *chAUmri* (yak crossbreed) cheese. Visit the *gomba*. As you acclimatize, consider hiking north to reach the glacier and icefall in less than 3 hours. Climb the lateral moraine to the east of the glacier. If you climb up the trough on the west side of the glacier, you will come to an often frozen lake. All of the suggested hikes here are nontechnical unless otherwise stated. Musk deer may be spotted in the forest to the south or even closer to the settlement in winter. Tibetan horses can be hired here for more leisurely sightseeing, but don't take a horse higher if you couldn't walk it yourself—or if you have a headache. You could also use one to return to Syabrubensi. You can hire tents and climbing gear and arrange guides for exploration farther up the valley or to cross the Ganja La.

Stream Birds in Nepal

Several conspicuous bird species can be found along fast-flowing streams throughout Nepal.

The ibisbill (*Ibidorhyncha struthersi,* length 39 cm) is a gray wader with black forehead and face and a long decurved red bill. Shy, it breeds in gravelly river beds, such as those near Kyangjin in the upper Langtang Valley. It winters on stony riverbeds in foothills.

The brown dipper (*Cinclus pallasii* [*dubulke charo*], length 20 cm), a plump, all-brown, short-tailed bird that bobs up and down while standing on boulders, can feed by walking underwater on the streambed.

The plumbeous redstart (*Rhyacornis fuliginosus,* length 14 cm) is robinlike. It constantly pumps its tail up and down and makes short flights after insects flying over the water. The male is slate blue with a reddish tail; the female is pale gray with a white rump.

The white-capped redstart, or river chat (*Chaimarrornis leucocephalus* [*taukecharo*], length 19 cm), is a handsome maroon and black bird with a contrasting white cap. Both sexes are alike in appearance. It fans and pumps its tail as it flies from one rock to another.

The blue whistling thrush (*Myiophoneus caeruleus* [*kalchande*], length 33 cm) is a blue-black thrush with a bright yellow bill. It has a beautiful whistling song and harsh alarm call, both of which penetrate the sound of rushing water.

Nepal has four species of forktails (*Enicurus* spp. [*kholedobi*], length 13 to 27 cm). Black and white birds with long, forked tails, they are shy and fly off quickly, making a harsh alarm call, when disturbed. Three species can be readily seen along the Bhurungdi Khola near Birethanti on the Thak Khola trek.

Begin with a **1-hour** climb to the north up a small hill behind Kyangjin Gomba. Find the trail just behind the volleyball field at the cheese factory. It climbs through some boulders and then traverses east across the face before switchbacking up the eastern side to come below the rocky crest Brana Chumso (14,300 ft, 4359 m), festooned with prayer flags. You can always see the prayer flags as you ascend. A slightly more gradual ascent would be to head up the valley to the east of the hill and then gain the ridge to the west north of the first prayer flag summit. You can follow this ridge to **Menchamsu** (15,260 ft, 4651 m), where there are more prayer flags in **another hour**. To the east is Dag Batse Ri (15,660 ft, 4773 m), an even more spectacular viewpoint.

Consider taking a tent and camping at Yala Kharka, where other ascents can be made. To go to Yala, head east from Kyangjin Gomba and, after about 10 minutes, contour the hillside to the north, reaching a few *goTh* in 1 hour. Another hour's contouring and climbing brings you to another series of *goTh* (13,650 ft, 4160 m). Round the ridge crest and contour another slope for 30 minutes to another ridge (14,400 ft, 4389 m). Climb north beside a small stream (Chubi Chu) to reach the buildings at Yala Kharka (15,200 ft, 4633 m) in less than 1 hour. There is a small cheese factory here, too. To reach Tsergo Ri (some call this Yala Peak), an excellent viewpoint, head west from Yala Kharka, or continue circling the hill, reaching the prayer flag–festooned summit (16,353 ft, 4984 m) in 2 hours. To the south, you can see the Ganja La, the pass leading into Helambu and Naya Kanga, the trekking peak summit to its west. The surrounding peaks are quite spectacular. There is Tsergo Ri North (5440 m) due north of Yala Kharka. Yala Peak is the 17,849-ft (5520-m) glaciated peak to the northeast; other summits beyond to the north, including Tsergo Peak (18,862 ft, 5749 m), require familiarity with glacier climbing. To the east of Yala Kharka are several summits of Tsergo Ri East (16,513 ft, 5033 m). Many other climbs may suggest themselves to the experienced, and ice axes and crampons can be rented in Kyangjin Gomba.

Butterflies of the Subalpine and Alpine Zones

In spring and summer, butterflies are common in the subalpine and alpine zones, feeding on the nectar of the numerous blooming flowers. Common blue Apollo, Queen of Spain fritillary, and common yellow swallowtail are frequently seen; the latter two species are also found in subtropical and temperate zones.

From Kyangjin Gomba, you can also head up the valley to **Langsisa**, the next to last summer pasturing settlement. Cross an alluvial fan (12,250 ft, 3734 m) 20 minutes beyond and reach the abandoned STOL airstrip (12,425 ft, 3786 m), crossing its western end. In less than **30 minutes**, reach the north (right) bank of the Langtang Khola and continue upstream. Another **45 minutes** brings you to Chadung, a summer settlement (12,500 ft, 3810 m), and **another hour** brings you to a second, Numthang. Big lateral and terminal moraines of the West Langtang Glacier loom ahead. Contour around its south terminus, crossing a recent slide on the moraine and reach the lone hut of Langsisa (13,650 ft, 4160 m) in **another hour**. Consider camping here away from the crowds at Kyangjin Gomba. Ahead lies the main Langtang Glacier and the Tibetan border, a hard day's climb away (some trekking maps are grossly in error regarding the border). To the south lies beautiful Buddha Peak and the terminus of the East Langtang Glacier. Up this valley lies a difficult pass leading to the region east of Helambu. The first recorded crossing was probably by H. W. Tilman in 1949. There are many places to explore.

There is a big reddish rock at Langsisa that, according to legend, is that color because a holy man living outside the valley lost his yak and tracked it to this place. The yak died here (Langsisa means "place where the yak [*lang*] died"), and the lama, wanting its hide, skinned it and spread the skin on a rock to dry. But the skin stuck and remains there on the rock to this day! This is the legend of the discovery of the Langtang Valley. *Tang* means "to follow," hence the name Langtang. Before, this place was considered a *beyul*, or hidden valley. A few miles up the valley to the southeast, two big rock gendarmes stand a hundred feet above the glacier. They are said to represent two Buddhist saints, Shakya Muni and Guru Rimpoche.

There are several possible linkup routes to avoid backtracking. You can descend to Syabrubensi from Pairo, if you came from Dhunche, or vice versa. From Syabru you can ascend to Gosainkunda and on to Helambu. For experienced parties, the Ganja La leads to Helambu. This pass is normally possible from May to November, sometimes longer in dry years. Food, fuel, and shelter for 4 to 5 days must be carried. It is necessary to have someone along who is familiar with the route, as it is quite easy to get lost in poor weather. Hire a guide in Kyangjin Gomba.

THE GANJA LA

To cross the Ganja La from the Langtang Valley, follow the main route from Kyangjin to Langtang for a few hundred yards (meters) down the old moraine to where the main trail swings west down the valley. Another trail leads off near here and continues straight on down to the Langtang Khola, which can be crossed by a log bridge between massive boulders. This is reached in 15 minutes from Kyangjin Gomba. Then upstream on the south (right) bank are a few huts and meadows (Tshoma Kharka). Pick up a trail at the edge of the forest behind the meadows and climb in an easterly (upriver) direction through birch and rhododendron forest, and then rhododendron scrub, to come out at the stone huts and pastures of Ngegang (14,450 ft, 4404 m) in **2 hours**. Stay here (where water flows underground), or proceed to a site an hour farther (Yajukesa, named as the place where a sour plant can be found), where there may be water.

Climbing **4 or more hours** brings you to the pass, which may be difficult to spot from below. Basically, you continue easterly, climbing steeply for the first 1½ to 2 hours and contouring until you reach the slopes of the moraine and a glacier, below the pass. Nasumkang is the campsite here. Keep to the west side of the valley coming down from the pass. The last 100 ft (30 m) to the pass (16,805 ft, 5122 m) is a scramble, either on rock or on mixed rock and snow, depending on the conditions. Mountaineering experience, with the ability to use a rope and ice ax, is necessary here. To the northeast is Shisha Pangma—the fourteenth 8000-m peak, across the border in Tibet—that was first climbed in 1964.

At the pass, descend steeply over scree for several hundred feet to reach more gradual broken rock. Keep to the eastern side of the basin, at times on the crest of a moraine, avoiding the glacier. In **2 to 3 hours**, reach a cairn. Then descend steeply over easier ground, on a trail, to a small meadow where there may be a stream. This takes less than **30 minutes**, and the site, Kanjapukpa, may be a suitable campsite. Keep to the east side of a mossy rock, and enter the left (northeast) side of the Yangri Khola valley. Reach meadows with old *goTh* in **1 to 1½ hours** from the previous campsite. Cross a tributary of the Yangri Khola here to the right side where there is another *goTh* frame. Do not descend farther into the Yangri Khola valley. Ascend on a faint trail to some more meadows and keep high up on the east side of the ridge, passing several broken-down *goTh*. There is little water along this route most of the time, but several possible campsites. Hopefully snow to melt can be found. Avoid trail forks descending into the valley to the east.

Reach Kelchung, or Kildangphu, a series of *goTh* in poor repair, in **2 to 3 hours**. Continue south, crossing several shoulders, for the most part tending to the east side of the main ridge. Staying high on the main ridge, reach Dukpu (13,200 ft, 4023 m), a group of *goTh* in better shape, located near scrub, in another **3 to 4 hours**. In between is Chachar, another group of roofless *goTh*. Contour and then ascend to a notch (Tongla) to the northeast of a prominent hill, where there are prayer flags and cairns, **in 1 hour**. Enter fine rhododendron forests, crossing and recrossing the ridge crest. Pass through a clearing (Balucho) with a hut (10,900 ft, 3322 m) **in 1 hour**. An hour beyond is a trail fork, the right heading to Malemchighyang. Take the left branch toward Tarke Ghyang, reaching it after **2 to 3 hours**, the last part a steep descent. Routes linking Tarke Ghyang with Kathmandu have been described in the Helambu section of this chapter.

LANGTANG TO SYABRUBENSI VIA THE HIGH ROUTE

If you came to Langtang without visiting Syabrubensi, consider varying your exit by following the Langtang Valley downstream, high on the north side, to Syabrubensi. This route has become less popular with trekkers, who take the quicker valley-bottom trail to Syabrubensi, described earlier. It is recommended for those preferring to take a high trail away from the bulk of trekkers. Descend on the usual trail from Ghora Tabela, and reach the trail junction at **Rimche,** by the lodge misnamed Ganesh View (8200 ft, 2500 m). The left fork descends to the bridge over the Langtang Khola and out via the quickest route to Syabrubensi. It has already been described above. The right fork ascends through open, steep country where you might spot some interesting animals, such as goral or serow. The trail passes a lodge and descends to the houses of Syarpa or **Syarpagaon** (8225 ft, 2507 m) in another **hour.** There are lodges here. Continue contouring and climbing on the steep valley wall for **2 hours** until you round a ridge to an oak and blue pine forest and the valley of the main Bhote Kosi. Rarely, red panda have been spotted in this forest. A **30- to 45-minute** descent brings you to **Khangjung** (7250 ft, 2210 m), a scattered village with cultivated fields where there are lodges. This is an old Tibetan refugee settlement and still comprises Tibetans as well as *Tamang.* At the lower end, the trail forks near a water source and *mani.* The right fork heads north to Rasuwa Garhi, while the left descends through terraces into chir pine forest to Mangal (4900 ft, 1494 m), near the bottom of the Bhote Kosi valley, in a little over **1 hour.** There are tea shops here. Head downstream (south) from here, following the main trail on the east (left) bank of the Bhote Kosi for **30 minutes** to **Syabrubensi** (4650 ft, 1417 m). A bus can be taken back to Kathmandu.

Questions to Ponder: Seasonality

I was struck by the seasonal and diurnal pulsations of human activities, the great mobility of people in pursuing these activities, and the interaction of various ethnic groups within, between, and among the environmental zones of Nepal.

Thus wrote the late mountaineer and geographer, Barry Bishop, after several journeys in Nepal in the 1960s. How does economic development change these pulsations which are in some sense natural? If you stay in places with electricity, what happens to your sleep pattern? If you have central heating, how does this affect your activity levels? How have these changes occurring in such a brief period of time worldwide affected human evolution?

Gosainkund

Here is the description of a trek from Dhunche, up the Trisuli Valley to the sacred lakes of Gosainkund, and beyond to Helambu. Another starting point is Syabru, reached on return from a Langtang visit, and this linkup will be described. Such a circuit is an excellent short trek from Kathmandu that has no backtracking. It is not feasible in the winter, when snowfall makes the passage a mountaineering expedition.

Reach **Dhunche** (6450 ft, 1966 m) from Kathmandu as already described in the preceding Langtang section. It is a climb of 8700 ft (2652 m) to the pass. The first

4300 ft (1311 m) is rather steep and there is little water. From Dhunche, the current trail begins at the first hairpin turn on the motor road out of town. There is a mineral water bottling plant under construction where the trail begins, and it may be rerouted slightly at this point. A road continues straight instead of turning, and this becomes a trail that traverses to cross the Trisuli Khola (6000 ft, 1829 m) to the TR. It is now just a small tributary of the Bhote Kosi, the major river in this valley from Tibet. Continue up the bank of the stream by the first bridge. Climb up the gully to reach the crest and the trail junction. Reach Deurali (Thangjin locally, 6560 ft, 2000 m), where there is a tea shop, in **2 hours** from Dhunche. Take the right-hand fork, climbing steeply to the east, and follow it for another **2 hours** to reach Thomje, or Dimsa (9840 ft, 3000 m), with a few more tea shops. Climb on to **Sing Gomba** (10,840 ft, 3304 m) in another **hour.** Pass through oak forests to reach an impressive fir and rhododendron forest before arriving at the lodges.

Forests of the Subalpine Zone (10,000 to 13,800 ft/3000 to 4200 m in the West, to 12,500 ft/3800 m in the East)

Forests of Himalayan silver fir (*Abies spectabilis*) are widespread and are often superseded above 11,500 ft (3500 m) by birch (*Betula utilis* [*bhoj patra*]), which grows up to the treeline. Birch is deciduous, with oval leaves that are woolly-haired below, and white to gray-brown bark. Rhododendron forests or shrubberies often replace other forests in wetter places, while junipers (*Juniperus* spp.), coniferous shrubs with berrylike, fleshy fruit, occur in drier areas. Bamboo (*Arundinaria* spp. and *Bambusa* spp.) is common in the understory of high rainfall areas and sometimes forms pure stands. Some of the least disturbed forests occur in this zone, although trekkers and mountaineers are posing severe threats.

If you come from **Syabru** (7350 ft, 2240 m), begin at the signpost at the upper end of town and climb past the school, going up the east side of the ridge close to the crest and by the army post. Fork right where there may be a signpost, and keep close to the ridge crest. The trail then leaves the town and switchbacks up in the forest passing a metal-roofed government building in 20 minutes. Continue on switchbacks, taking the upper fork at junctions and the bigger trail where you have a choice. Pass through an open area with prayer flags and a *chorten* and then by a couple of seasonal tea shops to reach a simple year-round lodge at **Dursakang** (8940 ft, 2725 m) in **1¼ hours** from Syabru. Continue climbing in forest with no water, taking a left fork 20 minutes beyond to reach the simple lodge of **Probang Danda** (10,500 ft, 3260 m), spectacularly perched on the ridge in another **1½ hours**. There are impressive views of Ganesh Himal and the Langtang peaks from this site. If you fork right here, you will descend to Brabal. Instead, turn left (east) and, on a wide trail, enter a magical forest of large fir trees, impressive juniper, and rhododendrons covered with moss. Just before **Sing Gomba**, pass through a fenced compound, and reach the collection of year-round lodges, a little-used gomba, a cheese factory, and a private phone system (10,840 ft, 3304 m) in an **hour.** The other name for this site in a burned area is Chandan Bari. There are no mountain views from here. A radio-collaring project to study the red panda took place north of here.

There is an alternative trail from Syabru to Cholang Pati that avoids Sing Gomba. You begin on the regular trail and then fork left an hour above town and climb for

4 hours. It is hard to wind through the maze of farm trails and houses, so a guide is essential, because you cannot see the objective until just below it. If returning from Gosainkunda, it might be easier to independently take the trail from Cholang Pati to Syabru, because you can see your destination.

From Sing Gomba, head east along the south side of the ridge, following a wide trail. At first, where there was once a big burn, the slope is covered with *Piptanthus nepalensis* shrubs with yellow flowers. Then the trail enters a rhododendron and fir forest and, in **1¼ hours,** reach **Cholang Pati** (12,040 ft, 3669 m), where the trail is joined by one coming up from Syabru. There are lodges here open during the trekking season and the view of Ganesh and Langtang Himals is worth a rest if not an overnight. Farther to the west, Himal Chuli and Manaslu dominate the sky, and beyond you can make out the Annapurnas, including the top of Annapurna between Machhapuchhre and Annapurna IV.

Continue for **45 minutes** on the north side to the seasonal lodges, perched on a windy ridge, called **Laurebina** (12,800 ft, 3901 m) or Laurebina Yak. The name means "without walking stick," referring to the practice of pilgrims leaving their sticks behind here, for they are in the hands of the gods as they proceed to the lakes. You can look back and see your starting point, Dhunche or Syabru. Natural water is scarce along here, but a piped water system has been constructed. Climb on, reaching a notch in the ridge (13,750 ft, 4191 m) with an unusual Buddha shrine and prayer flags in an **hour.** Beyond, cross the ridge to the south side and notice the steeper character of the valley. To the south, you see yak and sheep pastures and other trails converging. Traverse and be careful of the steep drop-off to the south from the wide trail. Beyond, you begin to see the lakes. The first is Saraswatikunda with an impressive waterfall below you, followed by Bhairavkund, and then Gosainkunda. This third lake (14,374 ft, 4381 m) is reached by descending from a small crest in an **hour.** There are several lodges on the north shore, operated most of the year. There is a protected Shiva shrine, bells to announce your presence to the gods, and rest houses for pilgrims. On my first visit here in 1970 there was only a simple stone hut, a freestanding Shiva *lingam* ("phallic symbol"), and *nandi* ("bull") made more powerful with the eerie howls of a jackal spooking me in the late afternoon. *Gosain* means "priest," and *kund* is "lake."

Every year during the full moon between mid-July and mid-August, thousands of pilgrims and devotees come to bathe in this lake and to pay homage to Shiva. There are several legends, all similar, concerning the formation of this lake and its significance. One story is that the gods were churning the ocean, hoping to obtain from it *amrit*, the water of immortality. They extracted burning poison from the seas and turned to Shiva, who had come to the foothills to meditate. Realizing that the poison might harm the gods, Shiva drank it. The poison caused him a great deal of pain and thirst, as well as a blue discoloration of his neck. To relieve the fever and suffering, Shiva traveled to the snows of Gosainkund. He thrust his trident, or *trisul*, into the mountainside and three streams of water sprang forth and collected in the hollow beneath, producing Gosainkund Lake. Shiva stretched along the lake's edge and drank its waters, quenching his thirst. There is an oval-shaped rock beneath the surface near the center of the lake. Worshipers say they can see Shiva reclining on a bed of serpents there. The lake is said to be connected via subterranean channels to the Kumbheswar Mahadev Temple in Kathmandu. Pilgrims coming here from the lowlands during the monsoon suffer from altitude illness just like the trekkers.

In good weather, consider climbing the hill to the north for a view, as no peaks are seen from the lake. Or circumambulate the lake on the new trail or bathe in it if you are brave, all to gain *karma*. To continue to Helambu, contour the north side of the lake and as you ascend look back to see Shiva reclining. Regain views and pass four more lakes (Bhairunkunda, Saraswatikunda, Dudhkunda, and Surjekunda— often they may be covered with ice) on the often snowy trail marked with cairns, to Laurebina Pass (15,121 ft, 4609 m) in **1 hour.** There are cairns, *goTh* frames, and a *chorten* up the hill to the south. You could climb the hill to the north for views. Look east into the valley that you will follow on the north side to reach Helambu. Off to the east, there is a spur coming down the main ridge that you will crest and head off to Tharepati, which is visible on the major north–south ridge beyond.

Pilgrimage

The Himalaya are a great attraction to Nepali, Tibetan, and Indian pilgrims. Pilgrimage sites are common—a high "milk lake" (*dudh pokhari* or *kunda*), the confluence (*beni*) of sacred rivers, or an especially prominent shrine or temple. Some of the most famous pilgrimage sites for Hindus are at Gosainkunda, Dudh Pokhari, Panch Pokhari, and Baahra Pokhari. Muktinath and several other high-mountain shrines are sacred pilgrimage attractions to Hindus and Buddhists alike. Likewise, there are many shrines and temples within the Kathmandu Valley— Swayambhunath, for one—that are sacred to both religious groups. Baudhnath and Pashupatinath, on the outskirts of Kathmandu city, are especially sacred to Buddhists and Hindus, respectively.

Pilgrims come to Nepal from all over southern Asia, and as travel conditions allow, from Tibet. Hindu holy men stand out clearly by their attire (or relative lack of attire, as the case may be). The occasion of *Shiva Raatri* is especially significant both to holy men and Indian lay pilgrims, who flock to the Kathmandu Valley. Sometimes holy men may be encountered who are observing vows of silence; they sometimes go for as long as twelve years without speaking.

Lay pilgrims are commonly seen throughout the year on popular routes to the high-mountain shrines or lakes. For example, there are many seasonal events that attract pilgrims to and from Muktinath shrine above Thak Khola. Many of them have planned for years to come to a certain Himalayan Shaivite or Vaishnavite shrine (devoted to Shiva and Vishnu, respectively). Others seem to come on the spur of the moment: some to cleanse themselves from sin or bad luck; others, just for the pleasure of doing something different and unusual, or to see the country. For Hindus, water is an essential element at pilgrim shrines, and bathing is a central feature of the ritual observances. Sometimes Hindu and Buddhist shrines offer other attractions as well, such as natural gas fires, the presence of sacred fossils, hot springs, an ice cave, a sacred footprint or other holy mark or memory of the gods, or a rich mythology of sacred events that adds to the attractiveness of a place. Legendary accounts of sacred pilgrimage sites and events in the Himalaya are recorded in the ancient literature of Hinduism, some works dating back over 2000 years.

From the pass, descend to the valley below heading southeast on the north side of the valley, skirting ice in the cold season and following a trail marked with cairns. The numerous *goTh* frames attest to the heavy use pasturing sheep and yaks during

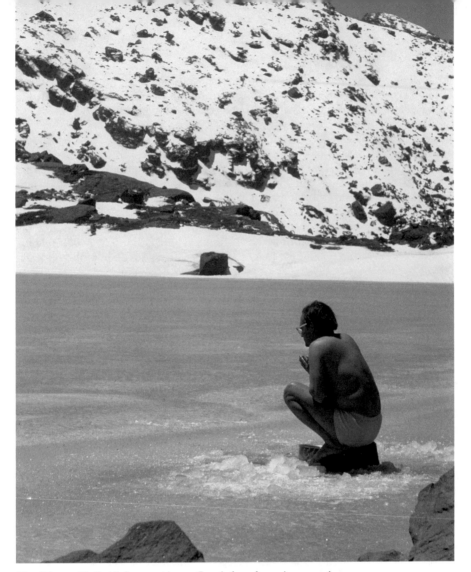

Dr. Durga D. Joshi does a puja *at Gosainkund one icy morning.*

the monsoon when the vegetation is intense. Reach Bhera goTh, a seasonal tea shop (13,850 ft, 4221 m) above a trail junction in **1 hour.** The left-hand trail, a supposed shortcut to Tharepati, contours high around the northeast side of the valley, eventually coming out on the ridge above Tharepati. This killer trail traverses steep country, where slides and ice make it treacherous, so no Nepalis use it, and you shouldn't either unless you chance a rapid descent into the valley below.

Take the popular trail, by forking right below Bhera goTh and descending. Eventually reach scrub vegetation and a spur with a waterfall on your left. Descend to **Phedi** (12,400 ft, 3780 m) with a couple of simple seasonal lodges on the hillside near the bottom of the waterfall in an **hour.** James Scott, the Australian who was ascending here in the winter of 1991–92, split from his companion and descended to the south in bad weather for about 2 hours, where he stayed in a cave for 43 days awaiting rescue. If the weather is bad, don't split from your party, and don't descend into unknown terrain.

Descend a steep draw and cross a stream below the waterfall to the TL (a source of the TaDi Khola). Then cross another picturesque waterfall that may be dry in the winter. The trail contours with ups and downs on the south-facing hillside, all the way to Tharepati. Reach Dubichaur (11,760 ft, 3584 m), some seasonal tea shops, and *goTh* in **45 minutes.** If you look carefully to the south of the waterfall south from Phedi, you may see a few shiny reflections that are about all that remains of pieces of the Thai jet that crashed here in the monsoon of 1992. Other fragments may be seen as building materials. It is more comforting to look south and pick out Shivapuri, the summit of the north end of the Kathmandu Valley. To the east of it are hillocks resembling Swayambhunath.

Continue on a tiring trail to reach the **crest** of the spur you saw from near the pass (12,000 ft, 3758 m) in another **hour.** Reach **Gopte** (11,180 ft, 3408 m), a flat spot on a spur with a few simple lodges, in **45 minutes.** Take the trail that passes just below the overhanging rocks to your left (don't descend the steep trail here). Reach more suitable shelter just beyond. The variety of primulas blooming in the spring between Phedi and Gopte is unparalleled. The trail continues through beautiful moss-draped rhododendron and fir forests and then comes up in the open to ascend through juniper woods to reach the lodges at **Tharepati** (11,920 ft, 3633 m), just below the ridge west of the Malemchi Khola in another **2 hours.** There are good views to the northeast from the easternmost crests of the ridge and from the lodges at the north end. The nonrecommended trail mentioned above proceeds north near the crest and leads to Bhera goTh. You could walk up it an hour and then head north to the crest to gain views. There are no views from the trail unless you climb up from it.

You have two choices at this point. Either you can traverse south along the main ridge to Pati Bhanjyang and reach Kathmandu via the high route, or you can descend east to the Helambu village of Malemchighyang. I will describe this latter route, heading east farther to Tarke Ghyang and descending to Malemchi Pul Bazaar, where a bus can be taken back to Kathmandu in the following section. The other route is given as a route of ascent into Helambu and can be followed in reverse to leave.

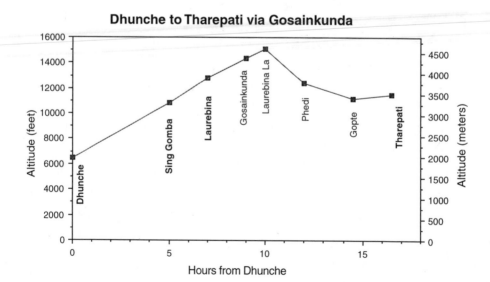

Dhunche to Tharepati via Gosainkunda

Helambu

SUNDARIJAL TO THAREPATI

Helambu or Helmu is the name of a region at the northern end of the Malemchi Khola valley. At one time it was a "hidden valley," or *beyul*. Helambu is derived from the local words for potato (*he*) and radish (*labu*), the two principle upland crops in that area. The trek starts from **Sundarijal** (4560 ft, 1390 m), a small dam and hydroelectric station in the northeast corner of the Kathmandu Valley where the Himalayan Rescue Dog Squad is headquartered. The trail begins west of Sundarijal at the end of the auto road, where the large water pipe comes out of the hill.

There is now bus service to Sundarijal from Baudhnath. A taxi can also be hired or you could walk. There is now daily jeep service from Sundarijal to Pati Bhanjyang. To walk, begin at the bus park in Sundarijal and reach the large water pipe. Cross under the pipe and proceed along its west side. Much of the way is up stairs. Continue, eventually turning left to cross over the dam of a water reservoir (5200 ft, 1585 m) in **40 minutes.** Across the dam continue uphill, crossing the watershed management road, which winds around the hillside. There is a lodge near here.

Climb through wet, subtropical forest to an oak forest and on to **Mulkharka** (6220 ft, 1896 m), in an **hour.** This is a scattered *Tamang* village with lodges and views of the Kathmandu Valley behind you. Don't walk the next area alone, as there have been rare instances of attacks north of Mulkharka, and take care of your belongings—but you know that anyway. The trail continues up, first in open country and then in oak forest, often in a small gully, and enters the Shivapuri Watershed and Wildlife Research area, after passing an army station. The trail ascends to a pass, **Burlang Bhanjyang** (8000 ft, 2438 m), with houses and lodges below it on the north side, in **2 hours.** This pass marks the Shivapuri ridge, Kathmandu Valley's rim. The trail descends through a pleasant oak forest, past some houses and lodges on the left, **Chisapani** (7200 ft, 2194 m), meaning "cold water," to a flat portion where another trail joins from the right and a road crosses. In clear weather there are good views of the Himalaya to the north and in the spring rhododendrons bloom. The trail continues to descend through open farmland to reach **Pati Bhanjyang** (5800 ft, 1768 m), sitting in a saddle 1¾ **hours** from the Burlang Bhanjyang. There are lodges and a police check post here.

From here, there is a choice of two routes. One continues along the general ridge system heading north and eventually descends east to the Sherpa village of Malemchighyang. The other heads east, descends to the Malemchi Khola, and proceeds up its east (left) bank toward Tarke Ghyang, situated opposite Malemchighyang on the east side of the river. The ridge route goes much higher (almost to 12,000 ft, 3658 m) than the other route, and there may be snow on its upper portions in the late winter or early spring. There are no permanent villages between Khutumsang and Malemchighyang on this route, but if you leave Khutumsang in the morning, you should reach Tharepati, where there are lodges, that afternoon. This part of the route offers excellent views of the mountains. If it clouds over, as often happens late in the day, consider spending a night up high in a seasonal lodge or hoping for views in Tharepati. Then hope for good views the next morning.

The circuit to the north along the ridge and the return via the east side of the Malemchi Khola valley is described. But if the weather is bad, it is wise to head up the east (left) side of the Malemchi Khola and then, if conditions have improved, to return via the high route. In this case, follow the directions in reverse.

Peoples of the Kathmandu Valley

The early inhabitants of the Kathmandu Valley were farmers and herders. The indigenous *Newar* are a mixture of those peoples and other migrants who found their way, over the centuries, to this fertile basin. Each conqueror of the valley, some from the eastern hills of Nepal (of *Kiranti* stock) and some from north India, added to the cultural heritage to make the ethnologically rich *Newar* culture and society of today. *Newar* make up the bulk of the merchants and shopkeepers (alongside more recently arrived Indian merchants) in the three cities of Kathmandu, PaaTan, and BhatgAAU (Bhaktapur). *Newar* are also the predominant shopkeepers in outlying rural bazaars and, throughout the country, make up a considerable percentage of the Nepali civil service.

The Kathmandu Valley is also populated by large numbers of Brahmans and *Chhetri*. They too are farmers and many have become professional and civil servants in the capital city.

Other peoples often seen on the streets of the capital are Hindu peddlers from the Tarai, *Tamang* hill people who work as coolies and day laborers, *BhoTiya* (including many Sherpas) from the north, *Gurung* and *Magar* from central and west Nepal, and *Kiranti* (*Rai* and *Limbu*) from east Nepal. Since 1959, many Tibetan refugees have also settled in the valley. Monks and other Tibetan men and women are found in the Buddhist temples and monasteries of Baudhnath and Swayambhunath, on the outskirts of Kathmandu, and at the refugee and handicraft center at Jawalakhel, near PaaTan. Tibetan handicrafts—especially articles of woolen clothing and colorful carpets—are well known to tourists in Nepal and in the export marts of Europe and America.

In medieval times, *Newar* craftsmen developed the distinct architectural and decorative motifs and religious arts of the valley and, not insignificantly, of Tibetan Buddhism as well. They became active traders when, for centuries, a main trade route between India and Tibet passed through Kathmandu and BhatgAAU. In time, *Newar* extended their craftsmanship and business enterprises to Lhasa and other Tibetan trade centers. After the defeat of their valley kingdoms by the Shah rulers from Gorkha in 1769, the *Newar* proceeded to take economic advantage of the Gorkha conquest. As Gorkha military and administrative outposts were established to tie the new Himalayan kingdom together, *Newar* merchants went along to set up shops. They created many of the hill bazaars that trekkers encounter throughout Nepal, and they continue to serve as suppliers for many of the still remote government outposts.

Not all *Newar* are businessmen or civil servants. Members of one subgroup known as *Jyapu* are seen tilling the vast fields of rice, wheat, and vegetables in the valley. Others are stone and wood carvers, carpenters, potters, goldsmiths, blacksmiths, butchers, and Hindu or Buddhist temple priests. *Newar* peasant communities are even occasionally found in the outlying districts. Most *Newar*, no matter how far dispersed, try to keep kinship and ritual ties with the Kathmandu Valley because it is their homeland.

To head north from Pati Bhanjyang, climb up the north side of the hill forming the saddle heading to the left. Shortly (100 ft, 30 m), the trail forks. The right fork heads to Thakani, a *Tamang* village, and beyond to the Talamarang Khola and Malemchi Khola. This is where it meets one return path.

Take the left fork instead, climb a little, and contour for **30 minutes** to reach another saddle, Thana Bhanjyang (5800 ft, 1768 m), with tea shops. Continue climbing steeply north for **1¼ hours** to the town of **Chipling** (7100 ft, 2165 m), scattered along the hillside with simple lodges at the beginning. Climb on, taking the uppermost fork at major junctions, up to the crest of Joghin Danda (8050 ft, 2453 m), and begin descending through the oak forest and the scattered village of **Thodhang Betini** (6860 ft, 2091 m), with a variety of accommodations. Continue to **Gulphu Bhanjyang** (7020 ft, 2141 m), a *Tamang* village where there are lodges, **1¾ hours** from Chipling. The trail is not very direct over this portion. A few minutes north of the town, reach a clearing and a trail junction where the left fork contours while the right climbs near the ridge. Take the right fork. Almost **1 hour** beyond Gulphu Bhanjyang, at 7975 ft (2430 m), there is another fork. Take the left fork up to 8350 ft (2545 m) just west of the summit of the hill and descend to the houses and trekker lodges at **Khutumsang** (8100 ft, 2469 m), situated in a pass. Reach it in **1¾ hours.** Khutumsang was a place with no settlement when I first came here in 1970. Now it is full of lodges, and the national park office requires that you show a receipt in lieu of paying a fee there. There are no permanent villages between this town and Malemchighyang, a day away, but trekker accommodation is available in Tharepati and likely MangegoTh during the popular seasons.

Porters climb out of a mist-filled valley north of Kathmandu.

From Khutumsang the trail ascends the hill to the north. Climb through a prickly-leaved oak forest that becomes a rhododendron and fir forest in its upper reaches. Reach a notch containing several *chorten* (10,600 ft, 3230 m) after climbing for **2½ hours,** mostly on the east side of the main ridge. Just beyond the notch is a clearing. Continue, keeping more level, on the west side of the ridge. Another clearing containing some *goTh* (10,450 ft, 3185 m) is reached in **30 minutes.** There are tea shops along here. At the north end of the clearing, a little to the west, there is a freshwater spring. Water can be difficult to find along this ridge during dry weather. From here on, there are two route choices. One keeps close to the ridge crest, the Turin Danda, while the other contours over portions on the west side.

Weaving Traditions: Wool

Trekkers commonly come across wool weavers during their travels in the high country. Nepal has been famous for millennia as a source for woolen blankets (*raDi*) that are rainproof as a result of the felting process used. They were mentioned in the emperor Ashoka's time, the third century b.c. The local sheep's wool is very suitable for felting, and you may observe this process in your travels. The carpet industry that has become one of Nepal's biggest exports uses different wool, preferably from Tibet, but sometimes from New Zealand. Felting is done with most woolen garments, either on a large flat stone, or on bamboo mats. Hot water is poured over the folded *raDi* on the stone and it is walked on using the toes to fold the edges under, while holding on to support poles. This rhythmical dance is not unlike using the treadmill or stair machine in exercise centers back home, except that it usually goes on for many hours, sometimes a day! The *raDi* maker is given nutritious food, or it is believed he or she will get tuberculosis. Once completed the *raDi* has shrunk considerably and the garment's texture makes it hard to believe it was woven. Such wool clothing is durable, and warm, even when wet.

The wool is prepared for weaving by washing and spinning it, then using a backstrap loom, much as described for the nettle fiber in the next chapter. Yaks are also a source of wool. Its outer hair is cut before the monsoon, using a sharp two-edge knife, leaving behind the soft, downlike inner layer which is plucked when the yak loses its winter coat. The yak hair is sorted and fluffed up as is sheep's wool and spun using a spike spindle, the twisted strands of hair feeding off rings on the arm. The outer hair makes strong, durable rope used to tie loads on animals. I urge you to try spinning, to appreciate the skill involved. Natural dyes used to be used exclusively, but these days powdered dyes from India are often mixed with natural dyes and mordants to fix them. Natural colors are obtained from madder, collected in the forests in winter when leaves have fallen and it is easier to spot, walnuts, sorrel, and rhubarb.

From the clearing, contour on the west side to reach **MangegoTh** (10,775 ft, 3285 m) in **30 minutes.** This is the largest group of *goTh* before Tharepati and also the site of an army guard post. There are trekker hotels here. Continue north on the east side through pleasant rhododendron forests. Cross over to the west side in **15 minutes,** and then contour to reach some *goTh* (11,125 ft, 3390 m) in less than **30 minutes.** Continue on the west side to the ridge crest in another **45 minutes** to **Tharepati**

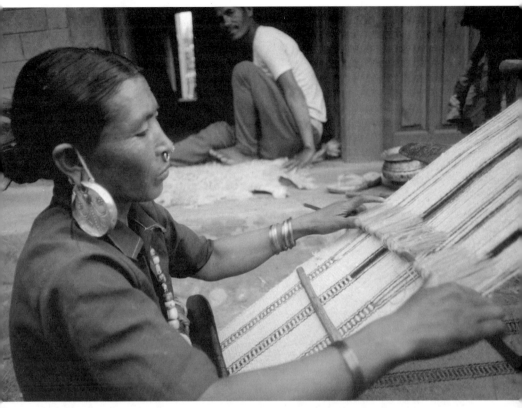

This woman with cheptisun *earrings is weaving on a backstrap loom.*

(11,920 ft, 3633 m), with a series of lodges clustered along the ridge crest. If you descend to the west, you pick up the trail to Gosainkund, which has already been described in the other direction. There are good views of the mountains from the next lodged notch north (12,000 ft, 3658 m) from where the trail leads down to Malemchighyang. This notch is north of a *chorten* with prayer flags.

Flora of the Alpine Zone

The alpine zone lies between the treeline (12,500 ft/3800 m in the east and 13,800 ft/4200 m in the west) and the region of perpetual snow. Shrubs grow above the treeline up to 16,000 ft (4870 m), with rhododendrons abundant in the east and junipers in the west. In the northwest and north of the Dhaulagiri–Annapurna massif, there is extensive steppe country dominated by *Caragana,* a low, spiny shrub typical of the Tibetan plateau. Flowers in both the subalpine and alpine grasslands produce spectacular colorful displays in late spring and summer. There is an amazing diversity of plants: gentians, anemones, saxifrages, geraniums, primulas, cinquefoils, and many others. Isolated plants are common up to 18,000 ft (5500 m).

Spinning wool while walking along the trails is commonplace in Nepal.
(Mary Anne Mercer)

THAREPATI TO SHERMATHANG AND MALEMCHI PUL BAZAAR

To continue to Malemchighyang and the villages of upper Helambu, descend east from the northernmost notch mentioned above along a steep trail in a juniper, rhododendron, and birch forest with impressive fir trunks. It descends the crest of a spur and blazes on the trees reassure you. In a little over an **hour** reach a cairn, as the trail reaches a streambed/broad trail (9780 ft, 2981 m). Finding this spot is important if you are coming up from Malemchigoan, for there you would bear right. Such cairns in the forest are most unusual in Nepal, so you should have no difficulty locating it. On the descent, turn left, cross a difficult icy stretch in the winter where there is a streambed, and cross another streambed, to contour on the TL bank and soon reach a small *chautaaraa* and a *chorten* above some *goTh* (9600 ft, 2926 m) in a clearing. Traverse left across the top of the meadow and, beyond, join a trail coming in from the lower end of the *goTh* meadow. In less than an hour from the cairn come to a clearing and a *chautaaraa* with a view of Malemchighyang across the tributary valley before you. Descend to cross a tributary (8400 ft, 2560 m) after **70 minutes** from the cairn. Traverse to Malemchighyang (8400 ft, 2560 m). The town's name is commonly written Malemchigaon, meaning the town of Malemchi, but *ghyang* means temple in the local dialect.

The people here began calling themselves Sherpas within the last century, perhaps because of outsiders' needs to classify things. Their relationship with the Sherpas of Solu-Khumbu is distant. The languages spoken are different, though both are derived from Tibetan, and the two groups don't intermarry. A more appropriate name might be *yolmo wa*, the peoples of Yolmo, "the place screened by snow mountains," or the Lama People of Helambu. There is a *gomba* on the east end of the town, and the interesting rock home of a hermit on the west end, currently unused. You can call home from here. Stay in a home rather than a lodge, and admire the extraordinarily clean interiors here. Every home has a smokeless *chulo* kept spotless. The Helambu *Yolmo* are incredibly fastidious now, something I can't recall from visits several decades ago. Electricity lines come up here from below and power light bulbs, but in low water flow times they will barely flicker.

There are no more towns farther up this valley. To Tarke Ghyang, proceed down below the *gomba* to descend steeply on a small spur. Reach a crest, Tarke Dau, with a tea shop, prayer flags, and *chorten* in 35 minutes (7100 ft, 2164 m). If coming up to this point, take the trail beyond that climbs. You can see the bridge below, north of where the powerline crosses, so take whatever trail junction you need to reach it (6200 ft, 1890 m) and a lodge on this side in **2 hours** from Malemchighyang. Legends say that a fierce dragon once guarded the river crossing between Malemchighyang and Tarke Ghyang requiring human sacrifice to get across. Guru Rimpoche, who brought Buddhism to these parts, transformed the monster into a boulder, which now guards above the bridge. Up above Malemchighyang, he made a shelter by placing a large boulder above smaller ones, creating the hermitage there.

Cross to the east (TL) bank, go downstream a bit, and then take the uphill forks to ascend to terraces. Just before you reach a *chorten,* fork left, and cross terraces, a small tributary to the TL, go downstream slightly, then climb again. Asking the way is usually necessary, and the powerlines indicate where the village sits. Reach a *gomba* (Palma Chholing Monastery) in 20 minutes from the crossing. Traverse up south of the *gomba,* contour around a small spur ahead with a *chorten* on top. Cross another tributary with a couple of mills one above and another below the bridge. Beyond, reach the tiniest of *chorten* and bear left steeply up a spur. Climb the spur and don't head into the next tributary valley but reach a big *chorten* (8020 ft, 2445 m) in 1 hour 20 minutes. Pass south of a *gomba,* and descend into a draw and climb out of it to the tight cluster of houses called **Tarke Ghyang,** a *Yolmo* village (8400 ft, 2560 m), **3 hours** from the river crossing.

Birds of Prey of the Subalpine Zone (10,000 to 13,800 ft/ 3000 to 4200 m in the West, to 12,500 ft/3800 m in the East)

The lammergeier, or bearded vulture (*Gypaetus barbatus* [*giddha*], length 122 cm), a magnificent vulture, has a characteristic wedge-shaped tail. Rusty-white on the head and below, dark brown above, it drops bones from a height to splinter them on rocks below and then feeds on the bone marrow. It soars along mountain slopes on motionless wings with hardly a wing beat; it occurs from the subtropical to alpine zone.

The town's name means "temple of the 100 horses" and was taken from the name of a temple established in 1727 by a lama who was called by the king of Kantipur to stop an epidemic in Kathmandu. As his reward, the lama asked for 100 horses, which he brought here. The local temple, rebuilt in 1969, follows the Bhutanese style. But another characteristic of this area is the presence of many *gomba,* each with its own lay *lama* or officiator. These *lama* are married village priests, the lineage passed from father to eldest son. They are all Nyingmapa and religion is a family affair. The village with its tight cluster of houses, narrow lanes, and court-yards reminds one of what a medieval village that has just been electrified and punctured with TV antennas might look like. Apples became a successful cash crop around here, but recently the orchards have been decimated by disease. For a day hike, climb up east past the schoolhouse to the ridge and climb north to the prayer flag viewpoint, Yangri Danda (12,372 ft, 3771 m), as if setting out for the Ganja La.

From Tarke Ghyang you can head north for 3 days to reach the Ganja La, a high pass (16,805 ft, 5123 m) leading to the Langtang Valley. Food, shelter, and fuel have to be carried, and the party should be equipped for snow climbing. This route has been described in the reverse direction earlier in this chapter. A second option is to continue south along the ridge, the Palchowk Danda, from Tarke Ghyang to reach the road at Malemchi Pul Bazaar, the junction of the Malemchi Khola with the Indrawati Khola, a very very long day's journey, better done in 2 easy days so you don't have to sleep in the hot lowlands. The third option from Tarke Ghyang follows the river southward and offers another route to return directly to Kathmandu without using the road. It is outlined below.

Questions to Ponder: Spiritual Activity

How much evidence is there of religious activity in the hills? Are there daily practices? How does this vary among ethnic groups in the same area? Do you see statues, symbols, or idols that don't seem to belong to one of the two major religions in Nepal? The Swastika is an ancient oriental symbol of welfare, the name is Sanskrit meaning "aiming at doing good for all." Among the Buddhists, the four stretching hands represent the four merits: friendship, compassion, happiness, and indifference (the opposite of discrimination). The six-pointed star, or *katcorn* or *satakaaon,* is a Hindu symbol of divine knowledge. The two sets of overlapping triangles symbolize Shiva, the eternal being, and Shakti, the most active female force, and their union, the ultimate source of the entire cosmic energy. It is also the symbol of Saraswati, the goddess of creative arts and wisdom, and is found on schools.

To take the second option to the road at Malemchi Pul Bazaar, head south from the lower end of Tarke Ghyang by the *gomba* past a large *chorten,* just above the large Hotel Tarke Ghyang. At the stream crossing here you take the left fork, rather than the right, which descends and will be outlined later. The powerlines that contour along the hillside for the first hour are your guide. Pass below Shettigang (8580 ft, 2615 m), a few houses with a *gomba* under construction, in 20 minutes. The trail contours in a prickly-leaved oak forest, crossing several tributaries and *chorten* to reach **Gangal** (8320 ft, 2615 m), with a *gomba* and lodges on the crest of the ridge in **1½ hours** from Tarke Ghyang. Continue contouring, taking the uphill fork at any junctions for another **1½ hours** to reach **Shermathang** (8540 ft, 2603 m), situated in another notch in the ridge. Here there are several *gomba* including one on the east side of the pass that was recently rebuilt from one built 800 years ago! There are lodges here as well.

Looking back to the northwest, if you try to make out your route from Gosainkund, if you came that way, neither of the two high passes that descend into the Malemchi Khola are the ones you traveled. The Laurebina La is less prominent behind the ridge on the west side of the valley, where you can see your route if you came up from Kathmandu. From Shermathang, there are views of the summits to the east, including Dorje Lhakpa and an array beyond. You can head east from here to Panch Pokhari, a series of small lakes (about 13,000 ft, 3968 m) that are pilgrimage sites. There is a fine view from the ridge nearby. You can then head to the Kathmandu–Kodari road. This option is not a well-traveled route, and there are few houses or lodges along the way unlike the second or last choice. This route description follows that for the stretch from Talamarang to the Kathmandu–Kodari road.

Sundarijal to Tharepati to Malemchi Pul Bazaar via Shermathang

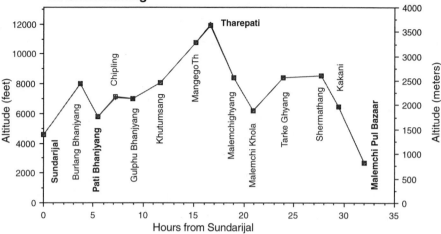

Head south, enjoying being near the ridge crest and passing an occasional house and many *chorten*. In less than an hour, you reach the end of the flat part of the ridge and have a last chance to enjoy the mountain panorama. Descend, bypassing Raitanyang (7300 ft, 2225 m), in 1¼ **hours** from Shermathang, with the trail in a gully. Reach a pine forest, and continue on the ridge to **Kakani** (6460 ft, 1969 m) in a notch in the ridge south of the school where there are simple lodges, in another **30 minutes.** This is not the town of the same name on the direct descent route from Tarke Ghyang. Here, if you take the large trail that descends to the west, you will reach Talamarang and the route back to Pati Bhanjyang, described later, in 2 hours.

Your goal is to reach the prow at the bottom of the ridge, but the next section is a little tricky. Head east from the pass, contouring south on a narrower trail, and regain the prow south of a small hill to continue descending on a wider trail. Descend steeply now on a reddish trail that will be treacherous in the monsoon (*raato maato chhiplo baaTo,* "red mud slippery trail") and notice the altitude when rice paddies appear (5280 ft, 1609 m), the usual limit in the east. Rice grows several thousand feet higher in far western Nepal. Reach **Dubhachaur** or **Pokhari Bhanjyang** (5260 ft, 1603 m), a *Tamang* village with handsome thatched roofs strung out on the ridge, in another **hour.** Continue descending the ridge, with **Malemchi Pul Bazaar** at the confluence of the Malemchi and Indrawati Kholas below. The steep trail comes out at a long suspension bridge over the Malemchi Khola (2716 ft, 828 m) in 1½ **hours** from Dubhachaur. Cross it to the TR, pass above the road-sized track that continues to Talamarang, and climb over a small height of land to reach the road and vehicles beyond. Here you can catch a bus to Kathmandu (last bus leaves around 3:00 P.M.) or to Banepa, where another vehicle can take you back to the city.

TARKE GHYANG TO SUNDARIJAL VIA PATI BHANJYANG

To take the third route above from Tarke Ghyang, head south at the low end of the village past the large new *gomba* and rows of *mani* walls to cross a stream. Take the lower fork just beyond, pass fields and forest. After 1 **hour,** cross a tributary (7000 ft, 2134 m) to a different **Kakani** than above, a small scattered Sherpa village (6750 ft, 2058 m) **30 minutes** after the tributary. Upon rounding the next

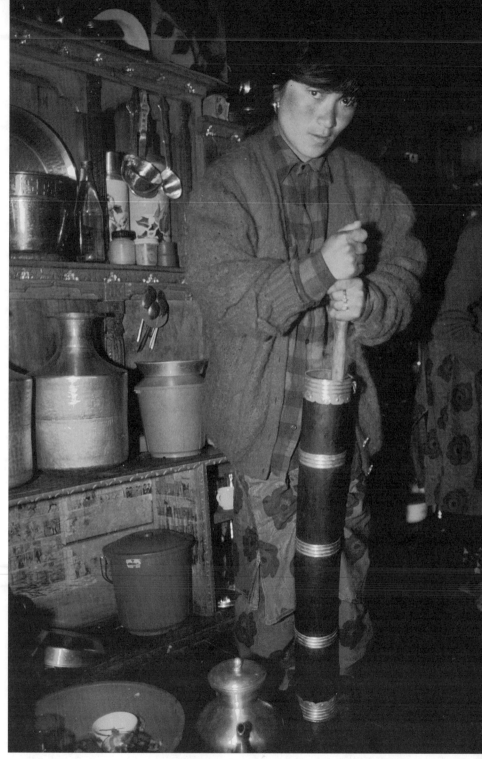

Freshly churned solja *or salt-butter tea will warm your spirits in a Yolmo home in Tarke Ghyang.*

ridge crest, you reach a clearing in the oak forest with *chorten, mani* walls, and an entrance *chorten.* Descend from here into the valley of the next tributary. Rather than head east to cross the tributary upstream from the main river, the trail descends near the ridge past a large *chorten.* In 1½ hours from Kakani, you reach **Thimbu,** another scattered Sherpa and *Tamang* village (5000 ft, 1524 m). Below it, the trail descends for **15 minutes** to cross the next tributary (4550 ft, 1486 m). It contours then drops steeply to the Malemchi Khola.

The trail now follows the east (left) bank of the Malemchi Khola, close to the water for the most part, but rising occasionally to clear difficult stretches. The forest is again subtropical. In less than **1 hour,** descend to a suspension bridge across the river (4050 ft, 1234 m). Do not cross it, but continue on the east (left) bank, crossing several tributaries along the way. A road is being built up from Talmarang on the west bank. At some future point, you may wish to cross sooner on one of the first two bridges. About 1½ **hours** beyond the first suspension bridge, you come to the third bridge (3500 ft, 1067 m). Cross this to the west (right) bank and continue south on a wide trail. There is an interesting-looking Brahman village (Sarha) on the right, and 1¼ **hours** beyond the suspension bridge you pass high above another. Then shortly, you descend to **Talamarang** (3150 ft, 960 m), a town with shops and tea houses.

The next section of trail is currently little used by trekkers because incidents have occurred to those alone. Keep company if you go and, if you decide not to, follow the main river down to Malemchi Pul Bazaar and catch a bus. To return from Talamarang via Pati Bhanjyang, cross the suspension bridge over the tributary, the Talamarang Khola, and head west up its south (right) bank. There is a direct trail, which is difficult to find, up the ridge to Thakani. Instead, stay close to the river most of the time. Try to follow a small trail that meanders about the river and crisscrosses it irregularly. The forest is chir pine and *chilaauni* again. Almost **3 hours** later (4700 ft, 1433 m), cross a large landslide through which a prominent tributary from the south flows. **Half an hour** beyond, on the south (right) bank of the Talamarang Khola near the hill to the south, you come to a small water-operated mill (4750 ft, 1448 m). A trail rises near the mill and essentially climbs the ridge north of the tributary valley mentioned before. Follow the trail to the *Tamang* village of **Kabre** (5500 ft, 1676 m), which is **45 minutes** from the riverbed.

Continue along the ridge through oak forest past another *Tamang* village. Take the right fork beyond to head west and rise to a *chautaaraa* (6050 ft, 1844 m) **30 minutes** from **Kabre**. The trail continues to ascend and reaches a ridge crest (6200 ft, 1890 m) in **20 minutes** near the *Tamang* village of **Thakani**. There are good distant views from here in clear weather. The trail now crosses to the south side of the ridge and contours, heading west, for 1¼ **hours** to the trail you took on the way out, just north of Pati Bhanjyang. Descend to **Pati Bhanjyang** in a **few minutes** and retrace the route described earlier to Sundarijal.

Panch Pokhari

For people who approach Helambu from the west or south, this route is an alternative means of return to the highway through an area south and east of Helambu. While slightly longer, it does offer some fine scenery and a ridge route that is cooler during the hot months. From Panch Pokhari ("five lakes") itself, there is no view of the snow-covered mountains because the cirque the lakes are set in faces southeast. But a half-hour climb to the crest of the cirque yields a spectacular vantage point. Five or six days should be allowed for the trip.

Reach Shermathang as already described. Descend, while going diagonally north, to **Boligang** in **1½ hours,** passing **Samil** about halfway. The trail is rather obscure and the town, inhabited by Sherpas and *Tamang,* is notably poorer than the Sherpa villages of Helambu. Continue heading north along a better trail, which reaches the town of **Yangri** near the intersection of the Ripar Khola and the Indrawati Khola in **1 hour.** This town may be reached more directly from Tarke Ghyang by climbing up (2000 ft, 609 m), crossing the ridge directly, and descending via the Ripar Khola to Yangri.

Cross the river at each of the branches over somewhat treacherous bridges and take a short, steep climb along a cliff between them. Instead of taking the path diverging right toward Bhotung, climb straight up through millet fields to **Yarsa** in **1 hour.** From Yarsa, take the main path on the left, going gently up, but avoiding steeper alternative paths, past *chorten* and clusters of houses until you come to a rushing stream in **1 hour.** Cross the stream on a bridge and then go steeply up on your left along a well-built trail. Halfway up, take the steeper path (the other trail flattens out) and reach the crest in **1 hour.**

The trail continues gently up for **15 minutes** to **Dukang,** a settlement with two permanent houses and many *goTh.* This is the last human habitation for the next several days. Panch Pokhari can be reached from here in 1 long day.

Go rather steeply up to reach another ridge crest in **1¼ hours,** and then contour left for **1 hour** to a stream. Here the trail is easy to lose due to floods, but proceed up the stony bed for a few hundred feet, cross a temporary bridge, and go diagonally left very steeply up the hillside. Soon the grade eases, and in **45 minutes** you enter pleasant terrain. Cross two streams (the last water before Panch Pokhari) and go left up across the hill. This section may be seen from the level section of the trail before the stream. In another **45 minutes,** gain the crest near some abandoned *goTh* and continue gently up to the left on fine rock slabs to reach the saddle (12,000 ft, 3658 m) in the Panch Pokhari ridge in **1½ hours.** There are numerous *chorten* and a trail shelter here, but water may be difficult to find.

The trail to Panch Pokhari runs along the left side of the ridge and is generally well built, but it has numerous ups and downs that are tiresome at that altitude. Reach one slightly dilapidated, but usable, shelter to the north of the ponds in **3 hours** from the point of gaining the ridge. There is room for only three or four people to sleep on the boards, but many more could be accommodated on the dirt, and there are plenty of fine camping places. Because the area is just above the tree line, firewood is scarce. A Hindu shrine and numerous Buddhist prayer flags are nearby, making it a very peaceful place. From the cirque crest (about 13,000 ft, 3962 m), there is a splendid view of the Himalaya all the way east from Langtang to beyond Everest.

The return to the Kathmandu–Kodari road is almost entirely along a ridge route with only a couple of short climbs to break the 11,000-ft (3354-m) descent. Follow the ascent route back for **2 hours** to the shelter (12,966 ft, 3958 m) in the saddle north of Chang Samarphu. The old trail went up almost to the summit, but the new route skirts the west side of the peak on a nearly level trail consisting of easy slabs. Rejoin the former trail in **1½ hours** at the col on the south side where there are remains of some *goTh.* The next hill is also skirted on its west side in **30 minutes.** Midway on this section are a couple of caves suitable for housing four or five people, but the nearby watercourses are sometimes dry outside of the monsoon. About **10 minutes** short of the next col there are some meadows that provide excellent camping and some shelter in abandoned *goTh*. Water is available at a good stream at the col, but there is no campsite any closer.

From the col, take the main trail, which branches east (left). At first it is fairly level, then goes upward, crosses several streams, and reaches the crest in 1¼ **hours.** From the open, flower-filled meadows, there are fine views of the mountains. Now descend rather steeply for 500 ft (152 m), and then go down more gradually over a series of bumps to reach the lowest col (10,440 ft, 3182 m) before the peak in 1½ **hours.** The remains of many fires indicate where water is found some 200 ft (61 m) east in small semiclear pools. Campsites, as well as some small grass and leaf lean-tos, are available. In the monsoon, the meadows and *goTh* are quite damp, basically a quagmire. This is the last water for about 5 hours.

From here there are two route choices, keeping close to the ridge or heading off to the west. The latter route avoids the ridge crest by taking a lower, level trail on the west side that passes through three groups of *goTh*. This trail crosses numerous streambeds, which may have some water in the dry seasons. This lower trail is preferable in bad weather and it is not as exposed as the upper trail. To take the ridge crest trail, proceed diagonally, going gently up, around, and down the west side of the peak (10,440 ft, 3187 m) until, in 1½ **hours,** four chimneylike cairns are reached just beyond a shallow, sandy depression in the ridge. There is a good view from here of the ridge below as it goes south before doglegging southwest. The fine trail continues 1 **hour** down to the dogleg and then stays fairly level for another 1½ **hours.** An obvious level trail cuts off to the left (southeast) here and goes out to the end of a subsidiary ridge. Then it heads down steeply to a series of plateaus, where the first houses are found and where water is probably available, though not along the trail. As you descend, the town of Scholi can be seen. Farther away, Chautaaraa, which has a particularly large, white building, is nestled in a saddle in the ridge.

Continuing, skirt gently down across the southwest face of a large hill where two small streams join. Cross the saddle to the east of the next hill and drop steeply down to **Scholi.** It has a small bazaar with a rest house about **45 minutes** from the stream crossing and perhaps 2½ **hours** from the beginning of the steep descent. From Scholi, proceed for 1½ **hours** along a very wide, flat trail, which meanders along the ridge top and around hillocks before going more steeply down to **Chautaaraa.** This large bazaar is the headquarters for the Sindhu Palchowk District. There is a road to the Kathmandu–Kodari road, and bus service is available from here to Banepa and Kathmandu. As well, the foot trail follows the motor road east for 1½ **hours** until you come to several tea shops. From here, descend steeply to **Baliphi** on the main road, where a bus to Kathmandu is available.

8   Eastern Nepal

Eastern Nepal is characterized by additional hill ethnic groups different from those in the central and western regions, more development efforts in the hills, and perhaps a higher standard of living. Much of the difference is attributable to several factors. The east receives more rainfall generally, and this increases agricultural productivity; proximity to Darjeeling has always resulted in a greater awareness of the outside world; and the Gurkhas, the soldiers recruited for service in the British army, traditionally came from four ethnic groups, two of which, the *Rai* and *Limbu,* are concentrated in this region. (*Magar* and *Gurung,* the other two, are from near Pokhara, another comparatively well-off area). As a consequence, the eastern Tarai was the first segment to be developed, large towns and cities first appeared and continue to grow here, and construction on the East-West Highway was begun in the east. Air links were also concentrated here. By contrast, the inhabitants of the mountains have tended to maintain their links with Tibet and have shared in economic development to a lesser extent. Ethnically, these mountain people are somewhat apart from the Sherpas around Khumbu.

This area is attractive because it is less visited by tourists, the rhododendron forests are spectacular, and the mountain scenery offers new vistas. There are fewer of the trekker lodges and inns that characterize the region north of Pokhara, north of Kathmandu, and on the way to Everest. Travelers here must be more self-sufficient or able to live in a modified Nepali style. The high mountain regions are pretty well uninhabited, so those venturing there must be entirely self-sufficient. There are no organized help or rescue facilities like those in Manang or in Khumbu run by the Himalaya Rescue Association.

Three trekking regions are described here. One focuses on Kangchenjunga, and the second includes different routes to or from Khumbu, traversing from the eastern hills. Finally, treks in the Arun Valley, including a visit to the Makalu Base Camp, are described. Many of these treks begin at low elevations and follow valley floors. It can get very warm in late spring, so dress appropriately and don't push yourself, especially in the first few days. Relax during midday, try to be in the shady side of the valley in the afternoon, or carry an umbrella.

In the route descriptions that follow, the times listed between points are actual walking times, generally those I took myself. They *do not* include any rests. This has been strictly adhered to by using a chronograph. Over most of the trails I carried a moderately heavy pack. I almost never walked the segments in these times. Like everyone else, I rested, photographed, talked with the people, and so forth.

Kangchenjunga Base Camp

A circuit is described, starting in Kathmandu, traveling by air to Tumlingtar, crossing the Milke Danda (ridge) to the valley of the Tamur Khola to reach the Ghunsa Khola, the major river draining the northwest side of the Kangchenjunga Himal. This torrent is followed upstream to near its source, where the base camp is located on the north side of Kangchenjunga. Then after retracing your steps partway, back as far as Ghunsa, the route will take you to the south side of the massif, crossing a

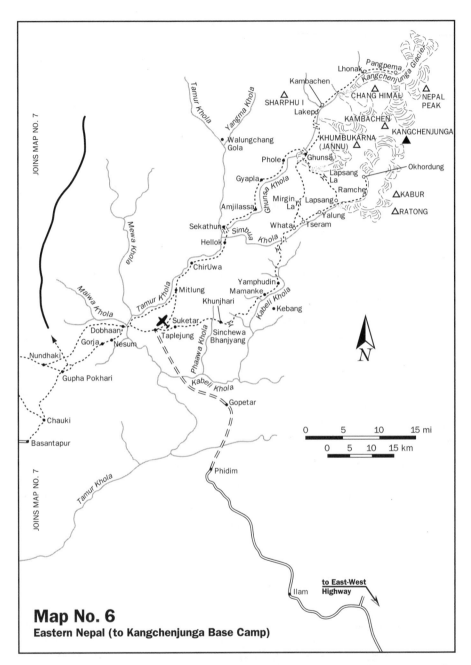

Map No. 6
Eastern Nepal (to Kangchenjunga Base Camp)

high pass. From there, you head south to reach Taplejung, the district center for the northeast corner of Nepal. In contrast to the outbound route, this one is primarily a high traverse that only occasionally follows roaring river bottoms. The described return rejoins the major ridge, the Milke Danda, and follows it south to reach the road at Basantapur, where vehicles can take you to the Tarai. Options then include returning to Kathmandu by road or flying from Biratnagar.

Such a trip will take at least three and a half weeks, though four to five weeks is preferable. It can be shortened by trying to fly in and out through Taplejung, but this may be difficult to arrange, and schedules and arrivals can be erratic. Such a course misses out on traveling through some fascinating middle hill country and on the unforgettable long-distance views from the Milke Danda. Those wishing a more denture-rattling journey can take vehicles from Kathmandu to Basantapur on the road north of Dharan, or to somewhere north of Phidim on the road north of Ilam. Currently the former road is preferred, but the road north of Ilam reaches Taplejung during the dry season. Bus service is available to Kabeli Khola and, beyond that, only occasional trucks and jeeps from various offices use the road.

For those with less time, consider an itinerary that starts with a flight from Kathmandu to Biratnagar to Taplejung, proceeds to the south side of Kangchenjunga, crosses the Mirgin La to visit the north side, and then descends to meet the road at Basantapur. More trekkers head to the north side of Kangchenjunga, the south side is less visited. There are many possibilities for travel in this region.

Trekker lodges and tourist facilities are being increasingly developed. Trekkers can get a permit for the Kangchenjunga Base Camp (the area beyond Taplejung) only by going through an approved trekking agency. You may be able to have such an agency get the permit for you and allow you to travel without many porters. You could live with Nepali people for the most part, but to get to the base camps you must be self-sufficient. Of course, below this high mountain area, a special permit is not necessary and you can travel in any style you wish. The Indian (Sikkimese) side of the mountain has been designated a national park. There are plans to create a conservation area on the Nepal side, somewhat akin to that in the Annapurna region.

TUMLINGTAR TO GUPHA POKHARI

To begin, fly to **Tumlingtar** (1500 ft, 457 m) (see Map No. 7), a broad, flat plateau on the left (east) bank of the Arun Khola. The grass landing strip is located on a convenient shelf dividing the valley of the Arun and the Sabhaaya Kholas. There are hotels on the eastern side of the airstrip and, surprisingly, you see modern electric wires and sturdy metal poles. There is a hydroelectric project on the HEwA Khola to the east of Tumlingtar, and the juice is routed north to the district center of the Sankhuwa Sabha District at KhAADbari as well as to the former district center and brass-making center of Chainpur, east from here. If stuck here waiting for a plane back to Kathmandu, you can wander over to the main river and perhaps take a ferry boat across it. It can even be swum, as can the Sabhaaya Khola off the plateau to the east. If impatiently stuck here, you might consider walking south to Hille, on the road to Basantapur. It takes a long day, and then a half-day vehicle trip to Dharan, hopefully to catch an overnight bus to Kathmandu. (Before heading east, stock up on oranges at the airstrip during the November–December season, as they become scarcer for a few days.)

From the airstrip, head south along the main trail, and pass many laden porters as they head north to the district center from Hille. Reach a few houses in **15 to 20 minutes.** Shortly beyond, take a left fork (the right goes to Hille and is described below), to descend a rocky gully from the plateau to the major valley of the Sabhaaya Khola. Arrive at its junction (1100 ft, 335 m) with the HEwA Khola, a lesser river from the northeast. You arrive on the right bank after **10 minutes.** There is no bridge, so you have to either ford at an appropriate spot, or take a brief, exhilarating ferry ride across during the high-water season, eventually ending up on the left bank of the Sabhaaya Khola. Then cross the smaller HEwA Khola to its left bank. There is really only one main trail to find; it climbs up the hillside to the east.

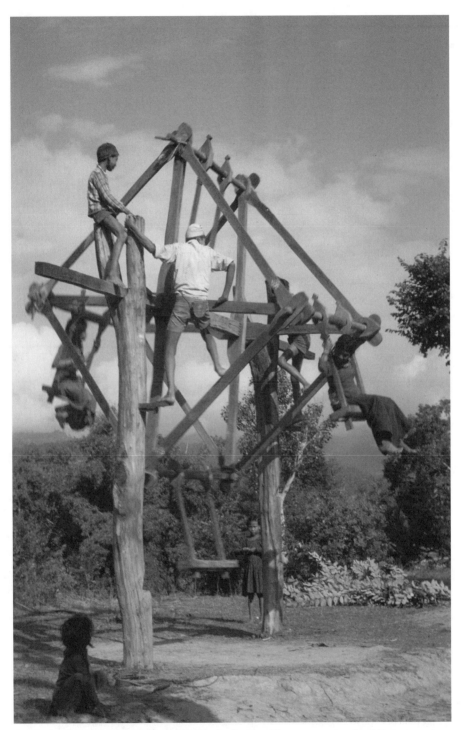

In the lowlands during the dassAAI *festival, you will see many people riding on a* ping, *the Nepali Ferris wheel. (Mary Anne Mercer)*

Hindu Festivals: DasAAI

DasAAI (*Dusserah* in India) lasts for ten days at the time of the new moon in mid-October. This is Nepal's most important festival. It commemorates the legendary victory of the goddess Durga (Kali) over the evil demon-buffalo, Mahisashur. One highlight is the ceremonial decapitating of buffaloes at the *koT* (fort) near Hanuman Dhoka on the ninth day of the festival. The tenth day, called *Vijaya Dasami* (literally, "Victorious Tenth Day") is the day of the *Tikaa* ceremony and symbolizes victory by extermination of the demon-buffalo by Durga. On this day, the King and Queen receive citizens at the royal palace, where they give *Tikaa,* and village leaders dispense *Tikaa* to their constituents in the hinterlands. Schools and government offices are closed during *DasAAI,* and the holiday is considered a time for family reunions all over the country. On rural trails, one will see women and children returning to their *maiti ghar* (or mother's home) during the time of *DasAAI* and/or during *Tihaar,* which follows. At this time of year, the Kathmandu Tundikhel is alive with goats and sheep brought into the valley from northern districts and with buffalo from the Tarai. These animals are for sale and are ultimately used in the necessary sacrifices and feasting of the occasion. The whole *DasAAI* season is one of feasting and merrymaking.

Climb up through light forest and then farmland, reaching a house, which is part of a scattered village, Gahate (2100 ft, 640 m), and soon obtain some views of Makalu and Chamlang to the northwest. Reach the ridge crest and a *bhaTTi* at Luwakot (3125 ft, 952 m) in 1¼ hours from the river ford below. Continue on up, sometimes along another ridge crest, sometimes contouring, to the pleasant town of **Kharaang** (4335 ft, 1321 m), reached in 2¼ **hours** from the ford. Climb west along the ridge, reaching a fork in 30 minutes, and take either the left fork trail that climbs more or the right fork that passes above some houses, enters a bamboo thicket, and soon gives you views of Chainpur in a pass ahead. About a half hour beyond Kharaang, above the right-hand fork, there is a charming old temple to Mahadev, with a *dharmsala* for pilgrims and a sacred pond. As you descend a ridge crest toward this major town, you enter a new suburb, **KatarigAAU** (4375 ft, 1333 m), a little over **1 hour** from Kharaang. Cardamom (*alAIchi*) is the successful cash crop in this region.

Another **20-minute** descent brings you to the field at the western end of **Chainpur** (4300 ft, 1311 m), a beautiful, ridge-crest *Newar* bazaar. Plan to have enough time to explore and savor this wonderful offspring of Kathmandu, where traditional craftsmen continue their brass work.

Continue on by taking a right fork up stone steps at a clearing in the center of town, before you encounter the brass workers, and follow the stone-paved bazaar path to pass south of a Buddhist temple at the high eastern end of the town ridge (4525 ft, 1379 m). The trail climbs the ridge, passes south of the houses of Okharbhote (or DAgigaon), **15 minutes** from town, and then enters broad-leaved forest, meeting a trail coming in from the left by a water faucet **35 minutes** from Okharbhote (5075 ft, 1546 m). Enquire here about a trail leading off to the right a short way down from the main trail to the Siddhakali temple, a beautiful example of Nepalese pagoda temple architecture and home to a very powerful goddess.

Brasswork

Artisans from the Shakya clan of Kathmandu (their ancestors moved here eons ago) continue the centuries-old process of making the attractive small brass vessels Nepalis drink from and take to the fields. The process begins with a clay or metal mold that is covered by a thin layer of soft wax. This model is fitted by a lump of wax onto a hand-driven lathe, and the artist carves. The model is then encased in a clay-dung coating with outlets for the wax and inlets for the brass. It is heated in a charcoal oven, and then the outlets are opened to extract the wax. The mold is then fully baked. When ready, molten brass is poured into the mold. After cooling, the molds are broken open to remove the vessel, which is finished on the hand-driven lathe which is rotated much faster. Complicated designs are made in separate parts, which are later joined together. The decorated patterns are made by a similar process, adding wax elements with the designs embossed into the wax mold. Later the artwork is completed with fine tools. Separate sections are then joined together. To obtain the intricate floral designs often seen, wax layers containing the carved designs are pasted on the plain wax forms created as above. The same clay coating is then carried out and final finishing done by hand.

The other major center for this craft in the east is in Bhojpur west of the Arun River. The brasscraft is sold by weight. The brass comes from Singapore or from recycled old objects (*khu*). Interestingly, the biggest consumers of this dying art are in the Kathmandu Valley, where the urban people have a taste for this fine craftsmanship. Elsewhere in Nepal, cheaply produced stainless steel, aluminum, and plastic ware, as well as discarded tin cans, have become commonplace. If you don't wish to buy examples of their work here and carry it with you, it is available in Kathmandu, at of course much higher prices, or in Dharan at the foot of the hills before you return to Kathmandu.

The Shakya artisans in Chainpur make brass vessels, following a centuries-old tradition.

Fifteen minutes beyond is the town of **Pokhari** (4950 ft, 1508 m), a few houses in a saddle on the ridge. Here you see the first chorten, indicating your arrival at the edge of Buddhist *Tamang* and Sherpa lands. Follow the main trail around to the right, contouring more or less level along the ridge slope from Pokhari. Tanglewa (5150 ft 1570 m), a *bhaTTi* and a few houses, is 1 hour beyond Pokhari. The scattered houses beyond belong to the village of **Chitlang**, and the trail wanders in and out of tributary valleys until you reach a suspension bridge over the Pilua Khola (4450 ft, 1356 m), **2½** hours from Pokhari. Cross it to the left bank and pass by some stalls used for a market every Tuesday. A steep climb follows, to the scattered town of **Nundhaki** (5350 ft, 1631 m), home to *Limbu*, *Gurung*, and Sherpa tribes people, a little over 30 minutes from the bridge. In Nundhaki, climb up in the valley above the *YAUra Khola* (you are on its right bank) and on the south side of the ridge. Reach the crest of this spur, and follow it to a school with a prominent field (6350 ft, 1935 m), some **45 minutes** above where you first come to the town. Along the way, you have probably noticed what appear to be coffins set on prominent parts of the hillsides. These are *Limbu* and *Rai* graves, with the dead interred in the stone-and-concrete structures. Various sizes suggest the ages of the deceased. Traditionally, there are four tiers of stones for a male, three for a female. The cement is inscribed with the name and age of the person.

There are two trails beyond to choose from. The more direct one climbs steeply to the northeast. It crosses the major ridge separating the Arun Khola valley from that of the Tamur Khola (to the east) at a place called the Milke Danda. (In fact, that is the name for the ridge crest along this portion, but it is used locally to indicate the pass crossing.) The trail then descends to Dobhaan, on the Tamur below Taplejung. The other trail, less used by locals, ascends more easterly to reach the ridge crest at an idyllic lake setting called Gupha Pokhari. Both have views; the latter takes longer but offers a convenient place to break the journey at the ridge crest, with the recent settlement with hotels at the lake. The views, however, are better the farther south you are, because Jannu appears more separated from the Kangchenjunga massif and Everest peers out from behind Lhotse Shar. Indeed, this subsidiary summit hides the earth's high point when you are up this close but still at a relatively low altitude in comparison to the Himalaya. The main trail north from the current road head at Basantapur follows the ridge crest to Gupha Pokhari and then descends to Dobhaan. From Gupha, you could walk the ridge crest north as well, to join the other trail from Nundhaki and avoid the major trade trail from the road. No matter which trail you choose, the distant views from the ridge of Everest, Makalu, Kangchenjunga, and the lesser peaks are outstanding.

The route from Nundhaki to Gupha Pokhari and beyond to Dobhaan will be described here. At the school field in Nundhaki, the left major fork climbs steeply up to the Milke Danda. Take the right fork, which ascends more gradually at this point, to Gupha Pokhari. The trail climbs but mostly contours through forest, crossing a tributary below a waterfall (6340 ft, 1932 m) in **50 minutes** from Nundhaki School. Just beyond is another tributary and the few Sherpa houses of Bhittri. These Sherpas are referred to as *Samyukpa,* a clan that does not intermarry with other Sherpas. Women wear striped posterior aprons, full pleated skirts, and heavy necklaces. Continue on fairly level trail to cross two branches of the YAUra Khola, **15 minutes** beyond, on cantilever bridges below a recent slide (6675 ft, 2034 m). Climb up through terraces to reach the houses of DAADa Kharka (7050 ft, 2149 m), in **15 minutes.** This is the last settlement before Gupha Pokhari. If you climb up into the forest in the morning or evening, you might spot a leopard or maybe see some tracks or fresh spoor. Cross a tributary (8850 ft, 2697 m) in **1 hour,** but this may be dry in late spring.

The trail is not very prominent, but there is little to do but climb to reach the ridge crest and the serene lake of **Gupha Pokhari** (9525 ft, 2903 m) in another **30 minutes.** The recent settlement, with hotels, is on the other side of the rock-fenced lake. The water all comes from the dammed, stagnant pond. Even locals take to boiling it, because they experience illness coming from drinking it straight! Excellent Tongba is available in several of the hotels here, especially those run by *Wallungchung* people. Yak herders from the Jaljale Himal may be seen with their animals grazing in the winter months. Views of the Kangchenjunga (to the east) and Khumbu Himals (to the west) are distant but outstanding, especially at sunrise and sunset. It is hard to see Everest itself, because it is hidden by Lhotse Shar, the subsidiary summit of Lhotse. From the southeast, the face of Everest is all snow-covered and very different from the conventional views. It becomes easier to make out as you head south, toward Basantapur.

Funerals

Funerals can be observed in the city and countryside at any time. Most Nepalis burn the dead, preferably at the riverside (*ghaaT*), within a few hours of death. Hill villagers, far from the river, prefer prominent hillsides on which to burn or bury the dead. *Rai* and *Limbu* tend to bury. The other ethnic groups prefer cremation. Funeral parties are obvious from the presence of a white-shrouded corpse carried on a bier either prone or bound tightly into a sitting position. Male relatives at the funeral typically shave their heads; women frequently loosen their hair, letting it hang unadorned down the back. Drumming is uncommon, except on the occasion of postfunerary ceremonies held sometimes months after death to celebrate the passage of the deceased's spirit into the afterlife. Such post-funerary rituals are common, for example, among the hill ethnic groups such as the *Gurung, Tamang,* and *Thakali.* These are occasions for great feasting, dancing, drinking, and serious and ancient religious rituals conducted by shamans and Bon or Buddhist monks. Such postfunerary events are sometimes known in Nepali as *arghun* in the hills of west and west-central Nepal.

GUPHA POKHARI TO GHUNSA

From Gupha, you can head south to the current road head at Basantapur; this will be described later. You can also head north to join the other trail crossing the Milke Danda, which forks from Nundhaki. However, the direct trail to Dobhaan, which the heavily laden porters ferrying supplies to Taplejung used to use, will be described here. There are always choices, and here you have one. The old trail dropped to the east a few hundred feet, and then contoured and climbed to a ridge crest, Bhuje, of gneiss and schist (9725 ft, 2964 m) 1 hour from Gupha. Some 15 minutes before reaching this small pass, and 300 ft (91 m) below, you meet a newly cut trail entering from the left. If you want to take this more direct route with more ups and downs, instead of dropping to the east from Gupha, head north along the pleasant ridge crest for about 10 minutes to a right-hand fork, which heads off to the northeast. The other trail heads north along the Milke Danda to join the previously mentioned trail from Nundhaki. It also continues north, following the wild ridge crest for many days, into the Jaljale Himal. This would be a great monsoon walk when the highlands would be full of yaks pasturing but well guarded by leeches lurking in the vegetation along the way.

Either way from Gupha, you end up at the small pass **1 hour** beyond and then drop 50 ft (15 m) to reach the temporary tea houses of Akar Deorali, the name of the pass above you. The next **2 hours** are spent on a spur in mixed rhododendron forest, with occasional clearings and temporary tea houses; one comes up in 45 minutes at Buje Deorali (9325 ft, 2842 m). About 30 minutes beyond is Fokde (8525 ft, 2598 m), and you reach the few houses at Mulpakuri (8460 ft, 2578 m) in another 30 minutes. In less than **1 hour,** you come out of the forest to reach terraces and substantial houses, and the spread-out settlement of **Gorja** (6825 ft, 2080 m) or Gorja Taar. Consider spending a night here for the sunsets on the Kangchenjunga massif. Jannu (25,295 ft, 7710 m), also called Khumbhakarna Himal, is the spectacular face before you. It was first climbed by the French in 1962. You can look across the Tamur Khola valley at Taplejung, the airstrip above it, and the all too common road scars.

Hindu Festivals: *Tihaar (Diwali)*

Tihaar or *Diwali* is a 5-day festival in mid-November. The last 3 days are the most interesting. The third day is *Lakshmi Pujaa,* dedicated to Lakshmi, goddess of wealth and associated with light. Houses are trimmed with hundreds of tiny oil lamps, which transform Kathmandu into a beautifully lit city at night. Lakshmi's blessings are invoked, and a new business year is officially begun. In Newar communities, the streets are overhung with paper lanterns that are lit each evening. During *Tihaar* various creatures, including humans, are singled out for attention—on the first day, the crow; on the second day, the dog; on the third day, the cow; and on the fourth day, the bull. On the final day, *Bhaai Tikaa,* sisters ceremonially give their brothers *Tikaa* on the foreheads and wish them prosperity and long life. This is the only time of the year when public gambling is condoned, and you will see many crowds around groups of *juwaa* (cowrie shell) players, or card players. During this season, girls and boys also carol in the streets and alleyways of towns and villages. Girls carol on the night of *Lakshmi Pujaa,* and boys carol on the next night. A popular treat during *Tihaar* is the rice-flour doughnut, called *sel roti.* Finally, among the *Newar* merchant community, *Tihaar* marks the beginning of their New Year, and *Newar* bazaars, in particular, are festooned with decorations and crowded with well-wishers and merrymakers. At this time, the sweet shops are overflowing with pastries and candy treats.

Both *DasAAI* and *Tihaar* mark the end of the farming season, the bringing in of the harvest, and new beginnings. This time of year is especially joyous for individuals and families alike, and most people prefer to be at home with relatives and friends.

Continuing on the main trail below Gorja, reach the few tea houses of Chedarpati and then the scattered village of **Nesum** (5125 ft, 1562 m), **1 hour** from Gorja. Keep descending to Bhajogara (3125 ft, 952 m), with some houses, 1 hour beyond.

You approach Dobhaan (2150 ft, 655 m), a large town at the confluence of the Maiwa Khola valley, which enters from the west, and Tamur Khola, the major river draining the snows to the north. Meet power lines from a hydroelectric project on a tributary of the Tamur south of here. **Dobhaan** is reached in **70 minutes** from Nesum. If you crossed the Milke Danda north of Gupha Pokhari, you will enter Dobhaan by descending in the Maiwa Khola valley via SAAghu and Dhunge SAAghu. Dobhaan is the last major town en route, with banks, a number of stores, and the chance to stock up on supplies, unless you climb up to Taplejung on the other side of the valley. There is a police check post here. For those wishing to camp, the area near the confluence of the two rivers is a pleasant site.

As you pass through Dobhaan, you reach the right bank of the Maiwa Khola and then cross it on a suspension bridge to another collection of houses and hotels on the north (left) bank. Head east to the large suspension bridge over the roaring Tamur, and cross it to the left bank. Immediately after crossing the bridge, you meet a staircase heading up. This leads to Taplejung and would be the route to take if you wanted to head to the south side of the Kangchenjunga massif first. However, the route described here leads to the north side of the range, and the trail to it diverges left immediately after crossing the bridge, before climbing any stairs. It is indistinct, and you cross through some bushes to descend to the Tamur Khola. Sometimes a trek guide has inscribed an arrow pointing left just at the end of the bridge to help his clients find it. Arrows like this were common in 1988, when the area first opened. Because Nepalis do not do this for themselves, the arrows can probably be followed with some confidence if you are heading up to Kangchenjunga.

Head north on the left bank of the Tamur, following the small trail through rice paddies close to the main torrent. Soon you see another major confluence ahead, that of the Mewa Khola from the north and the Tamur Khola from the northeast. There is a suspension bridge over the Mewa Khola above the confluence, which, luckily, you don't have to make your way to! There may be a bamboo bridge over the Tamur here at Handrung, which is rebuilt yearly after the monsoon. There are no large villages along the route for the next several days. You'll understand why as you encounter the difficult terrain and sense the tension in this roaring river-valley bottom.

Reach the confluence in **30 minutes** from the last bridge crossing, and then head up the left bank of the Tamur. Boulder-hop and cross tributaries as the trail gets a little more prominent. Sometimes it wanders along sandy flats and other times climbs into subtropical forest to avoid steep sections the river has carved or to bypass slides in this eroding valley. But you stay close to the bottom of this wild, roaring river for the next several days. Where you have choices in the trail, and no arrow or person to indicate the way, take the choice that keeps you closest to the river bottom. Reach Tumma (2700 ft, 823 m) in **1½ hours** from the confluence, then pass above a suspension bridge (it is not crossed on this route), and go by a few more tea houses. An hour later, you cross a tributary (2800 ft, 853 m) in a slide area and then climb steeply up the debris on the right bank to rejoin the main valley to enter **Mitlung** (3025 ft, 922 m), a town with a few shops and at least one lodge, **30 minutes** later. The trail from Taplejung joins here.

Continue along the southeast side of the river valley, on the narrow trail. In **45 minutes**, cross a tributary (the Sisne Khola) either by the suspension bridge upstream, or in low water by hopping rocks (3075 ft, 937 m). Pass above a suspension bridge **40 minutes** beyond, just before reaching the town of **SInwa** (3225 ft, 983 m), with some shops, a telephone, and a health post. An **hour** beyond, come to a bamboo suspension bridge over the Tamur (3525 ft, 1074 m), which (thank the gods) you don't have to cross unless you want a frightful feeling of adventure. In less than **30 minutes,** you pass by a tall cascading waterfall on the other side of the gorge, and in **1 hour 35 minutes** from SInwa, you reach a powerful narrowing in the river where a big boulder splits the flow into two halves. The trail traverses a slide (3825 ft, 1166 m), and there are tall cliffs on the opposite side of the valley. Notice that on these overhanging portions there are large beehives. Nepal's so-called honey hunters dangle from bamboo ladders and cut down portions of the hives for honey. (See Eric Valli and Diane Summers's outstanding photo essay *Honey Hunters of Nepal* for the details.)

Insects of the Temperate Zone

The temperate zone is rich in insects, although there is less variety than in the subtropical zone. Temperate-zone species include praying mantes, fireflies, cicadas, beetles, bugs, bees, ants, moths, and butterflies.

Butterflies are most common in open forests, forest clearings, and grassland. Common species include the common windmill (also found in the tropical zone), Indian fritillary (also occurs down to the tropical zone), painted lady, Indian red admiral, and Indian tortoiseshell (the last three species common from the tropical to subalpine zones). The giant honeybee (*Apis dorsata* [*maahuri*]) is a large bee that forms highly sophisticated colonies. Common in the Himalaya, it makes a distinctively shaped hive—a single exposed sheet of wax hanging down from beneath a rock overhang or ledge.

Proceed almost another **hour** to ChirUwa (4175 ft, 1272 m); the village has several lodges and is by a suspension bridge, which is not crossed. Beyond you pass some overhanging cliffs and enticing fault caves. An hour from ChirUwa, cross another tributary to the right bank on a suspension bridge (4550 ft, 1387 m)—notice that the main valley is heading east now. Some 15 minutes beyond, the valley opens up, and you come to a new suspension bridge across the Tamur, which is not crossed. Up the hillside to the south is a checkpost and teahouses at Thapethok. The trail over the next section has been considerably improved due to the efforts of the local village development council. **Two hours** from ChirUwa cross a tributary, the ThAkyak Khola (4900 ft, 1493 m), on a suspension bridge and again notice the scattered houses of ThAkyak on the hillside above you. Climb up a spur to the lone bamboo hut of Chilaauni (5225 ft, 1593 m), **20 minutes** beyond. *Chilaauni* means "itch" and also is the name of a tree found near here that produces the same irritation.

Continue high above the valley in a forest. A little over 20 minutes beyond the hut is a left fork that goes to a suspension bridge over the Tamur—don't cross this bridge, but in 5 more minutes do take the lesser left fork. The bigger trail at the second fork here climbs to the town of Hellok, which you can skip unless you want to spend the night there or get food. The lesser left fork descends to near the river again and crosses a fresh landslide to enter the valley of the Simbua Khola, which drains the southwest side of Kangchenjunga. You reach the recently constructed Hellok suspension bridge (5200 ft, 1585 m), **45 minutes** from Chilaauni, and cross it to the right bank. The town of Hellok is above the bridge on the south side.

Immediately after crossing the river, turn left, and contour north into the main Tamur valley. Almost immediately meet another side valley from the northeast, that of the Ghunsa Khola. Cross a suspension bridge to the right bank of the Ghunsa

Khola, your companion for the next week or so. The bridge (5225 ft, 1593 m) is **30 minutes** from the Hellok one. Again, if you want to reach Sekathun, a *BhoTiya* village, turn left and climb up. The more direct way heads right after crossing the bridge to continue upstream on the right bank. (If you go to Sekathun, you join this trail a little higher up.)

The next day or two is spent in this wild, steep valley, usually high up on its side, on a surprisingly narrow and exposed trail. There are few habitations. You encounter numerous delightful waterfalls. If you return via the southern route I suggest, you'll look down upon this valley from a high ridge—quite a contrast.

Climb up, and in a little over 1 hour, pass under a waterfall that seems surprisingly warm—there must be a hot spring above that partly feeds it. There is another waterfall shortly beyond and high above. Climb up a fault between a large cliff (on the right) and the main valley to reach Ghaiya Bari, a few houses scattered 800 ft (243 m) between each other on the steep hillside. Continue on to the upper few structures (6725 ft, 2050 m), some **1¾ hours** from the bridge. Watch for monkeys. The trail then climbs up 1000 ft (305 m) and traverses one of the steepest valleys in which you'll find an open trail in Nepal. Don't let your mind wander from your feet and sense of balance. The exposure is fierce, and the slides you traverse remind you that active erosion is taking place. Because of its steepness and northerly aspect, I doubt it was ever forested—unlike the opposite side, which receives more rainfall. Pass by yet another impressive waterfall, to reach **Amjilassa** (8250 ft, 2514 m), a few houses and simple tea shops, **2½ hours** from Ghaiya Bari. You are leaving the hill Nepal culture behind and entering the *BhoTiya* domain of the mountain region.

Continue traversing the valley, which is now less nerve-racking, and head north. There is more vegetation, bamboo, oak forest, and, higher up, some rhododendron—and always, wonderful waterfalls. There are many tributaries to cross. At times the trail is close to the river, but it often climbs and descends to circumvent obstacles. There are no campsites along this difficult portion, and again, like the trail before Amjilassa, this section is best done when well rested. Pass Thanyan in 2 hours to reach **Gyapla** (8875 ft, 2705 m), **3¼ hours** from Amjilassa. Just up the trail a bit there is a thin waterfall on the Ghunsa Khola. You notice burned stumps on the hillside above, from a 1981 fire—an important reminder of the precarious balance of which you are a part.

Just beyond Gyapla, cross a tributary, head east again, enter an impressive forest, and take a right fork 30 minutes beyond the village. Continue crossing tributaries, at times near the main river, and notice that the valley has opened up a little, easing the tension of walking in the narrow river bottom. The bridges and trails have become more substantial, because *chAUmri* are taken along here. Notice the fir forests, especially on the east side of the valley. Climb up to the sprawling *BhoTiya* settlement of **Phole** (10,475 ft, 3193 m), **2½ hours** from Gyapla. Here there is a settlement of Tibetan refugees, and many people of Ghunsa move down here during the winter. There is a *gomba* at the upper end of town. Descend to cross the Yangma Khola (11,000 ft, 3353 m) 30 minutes beyond the *gomba*.

Here you first meet larch forests, along with juniper and rhododendron. The larches are golden in the autumn, a delightful sight that is rare in most of Nepal. They are common in Bhutan and Sikkim but only sporadically reported in a few other places in Nepal. Enjoy them all the way up to Kambachen.

To continue to Ghunsa, come to a pair of restful benches across the trail at about the halfway point (11,025 ft, 3360 m), and then continue close to the right bank of the Ghunsa Khola. Beyond, you come to a left fork, which heads to the *gomba*, but you should continue to the wooden cantilever bridge over the main river (11,225 ft, 3421 m), **1 hour** from Phale. Cross it to the left bank and climb up to the village of **Ghunsa** (11,300 ft, 3444 m), some **10 minutes** beyond. The police check post is just on your right as you reach the bench the town sits on.

Ghunsa is a traditional *BhoTiya* settlement of sturdy wooden houses, surrounded by potato fields and magnificent forests. There are lodges and camping facilities here. The people's values center around their yak herds, which will be found pastured up as far as Pangpema beneath the north face of Kangchenjunga during the summer months, or down as far as Phole during the winter. Indeed, in the middle of winter, the village may seem deserted. People have moved "south" to Phole, leaving only the police to shiver here, although you may find Tibetans tending yak herds farther up the valley. But there is no permanent settlement beyond. No major trade routes traverse this area. The lack of substantial numbers of trekkers and climbers presents an outwardly different culture than is found in, say, Khumbu. There are now enough tea houses for the journey to just before Pangpema on the north side.

The altitude is probably having an effect on you here. It is a good place to take a rest day. Explore the *gomba* or the wonderful forests. The best side trip to the latter is an excursion toward the Lapsang La, the high pass leading to the south side of the Kangchenjunga massif. This will be described with the other pass leading to the south side.

GHUNSA TO PANGPEMA AND THE NORTH KANGCHENJUNGA BASE CAMP

The route to Pangpema, a summer yak pasture and the site of the North Kangchenjunga Base Camp, takes at least 3 days from Ghunsa and involves an additional elevation gain of over 5500 ft (1676 m), so trekkers must watch for signs of altitude illness and be ready to descend should serious ones occur. There is food available beyond Ghunsa in the trekking season. There are sturdy huts in Kambachen and Lakep. The only other structures are rock walls for erecting the yak-hair Tibetan-style tents used by yak herders. So tents for trekkers are necessary, before this route gets too popular and before locals construct lodges.

Head northeast, up the valley from Ghunsa. Avoid the right fork that climbs into a forest, but cross a small tributary above a tiny bluff festooned with prayer flags, and then go by a fenced-in pasture. Admire the rhododendrons, larch, and huge fir trees in this impressive forest. Cross a tributary to its right bank 1¼ hours after leaving Ghunsa on a wide log bridge made for yak herds. Kabur, not Jannu, is the mountain up at the headwaters of this tributary. Eventually descend to the main river, reach a wide cantilever bridge with a tea shop, and cross the Ghunsa Khola to its right bank **2 hours** from Ghunsa (12,450 ft, 3795 m). Proceed along to Lapuk Kharka, another pasture, 10 minutes beyond. There are rock overhangs here that would make good shelter. Enter an idyllic rhododendron- and juniper-forested valley, which ends all too soon as you cross a tributary with a spectacular waterfall at its head 15 minutes from Lapuk Kharka (12,900 ft, 3932 m). Just beyond is Lapu Kong, a flat pasture area. Along the way, the birch trees festooned with hanging lichens are memorable. Take the lower fork beyond, as the upper goes to higher yak pastures. The impressive summit to the east–northeast is Kambachen. But as you ascend farther, it disappears and you see Jannu, or Khumbukarna Himal.

Questions to Ponder: Hazards and Catastrophes

Do you see any evidence of natural catastrophes? What factors contribute to erosion besides deforestation? Are most landslides the results of human factors (deforestation), or are they the norm, so-called mass-wasting due to mountain-building forests. What kinds of wood-cutting practices do you see in different areas? Do you see evidence of reforestation? What attempts do you see by the Nepalis to control erosion?

What physical hazards are hill people exposed to as they go about their daily lives? What tools are used, and how did they evolve to their present designs? Which items are made locally and which are imported? Do you suspect that local production has increased or decreased?

The next part of the trail crosses a slide area, another indication of the active orogeny still going on. Sometimes the slopes are active, and boulders can roll down, usually in the early morning when the sun melts the ice "glue." If you hear activity, it is best to cross one at a time, with someone spotting for missiles. It is not a place to gawk at Jannu—you'll have plenty of opportunity for this later. Across the slide, descend a little to the lone house of Lakep (13,450 ft, 4099 m), 1¼ **hours** from the crossing of the Ghunsa Khola. There is an alternative trail that avoids this slide section, so enquire locally.

Lakep is the place to be awestruck by Jannu's northwest face. Sunsets are particularly grand. This rock stock, reminiscent of Ama Dablang in the Khumbu area, pokes into the sky only a little short of the magical 8000-m mark. Its altitude is 25,294 ft (7710 m). Jannu was first climbed by the French in 1962 from the south and now has been ascended several times by the difficult side you see here, climbers reaching the rock at the top by its left (north) ridge. Parties of trekkers might wish to head up to the base camp used for these climbs on the north side. The route actually branches off beyond Ghunsa, before crossing the river and proceeding up the Jannu or Khumbukarna glaciers. The mountain is called Khumbukarna (its official name) by locals, especially in the south, and Jannu by others. The only problem with camping at Lakep is that water is far away at the river below. Twenty minutes away is Kambachen, a large summer settlement of sturdy stone huts, with easy water, but alas, less impressive views, as all but the rock stock of Jannu is hidden.

From Lakep on, look for blue sheep in the mornings and afternoons. In the middle of winter they will come down here, usually browsing on grass within reach of cliffs and rocks that offer protection. The herds migrate up the valley to stay near Pangpema during the summer.

Reach Kambachen by heading around the next bend to the northeast and descending to cross two tributary streams (of the Nupchu Khola) from the north 15 minutes beyond (13,450 ft, 4099 m). No matter where you spend the night, take time to explore. A rest day to acclimatize might be in order. Wander up the Nupchu Khola valley. In the dead of winter, you might find Tibetan snow cocks here (in warmer seasons, they head up the main valley).

Climb up the hill behind Kambachen and continue along the northeast side of the main valley, reaching the potato fields of Lungba Chemu, then another pasture, before traversing scree and boulders near the river. Pass below a spectacular waterfall and follow the trail up through the boulder field along the river. A cairn, located where the trail levels off above, may be visible to the keen eye. After climbing up from the river, continue along a fairly flat trail. Avoid the animal trails and herder trails used to get to yak pastures. Reach Ramdang Kharka (15,025 ft, 4579 m), another pasture with a small *chorten* situated across from another impressive mountain face, that of Kambachen. This is 2¼ **hours** from the huts at Kambachen. This impressive mountain, like Jannu, is a mere 25,925 ft (7902 m), and therefore short of the 8000-m dividing line that compels climbers. It was first ascended in 1974 from the side you see from here, first by Polish and then Yugoslavian expeditions. The route proceeded to the ridge west of the summit via the valley between Jannu and Kambachen, up the Ramdang Glacier in front of you.

Up the main valley, you may have seen a lone pillar (gendarme) on the south side of the valley, set off from Chang Himal. Lhonak is across the Kangchenjunga Glacier from it. To reach it, the trail descends an old lateral moraine, crosses a river from the north (possibly difficult, depending on the conditions), then crests another old lateral moraine before coming to the sandy valley from the north. Descend to the yak-herding area of Lhonak (15,700 ft, 4785 m), some 1½ **hours** from Ramdang Kharka. You may find some yak herders in their tents here even during winter. The yaks seem content to scratch at the sparse grass found at that time. Notice that the surrounding rock is primarily gneiss; as you proceed, you will encounter granitic elements.

The foot of the north side of Kangchenjunga, which remains hidden still, is finally seen at Pangpema, a summer yak pasture and the base camp for ascents from the north. You can either pack your supplies up there and camp, or make a day trip from Lhonak. For those who are well acclimatized, it is a glorious place to spend the night. Make your decision on how well the slowest members of the party are acclimatizing and on how well clothed the porters are.

To proceed, continue on up the flats from Lhonak, cross some wet areas, descend an old moraine slide, and walk in a trough, sometimes strolling on pleasant grassy slopes, other times dealing with the occasional boulder. There is a new lower route that drops down 120 ft (40 m) toward the glacier and follows it along a lateral moraine, eventually meeting the other trail. A cairn on the right, a half hour beyond Lhonak, marks the drop-off point to the glacier. An **hour and a half** from Lhonak, reach a big plateau with an impressive boulder in the center. This is Jorju (16,475 ft, 5021 m). As you continue up-valley, Kangchenjunga begins to come into view; it has been well hidden by its neighbors up to now. Reach the shelf of Pangpema (16,875 ft, 5143 m), where there are some rock walls for herders' tents, in 1 hour from Jorju. Kangchenjunga's north face is immense, just like the rest of the mountain. This massif is probably the second largest mountain mass in the world. (Mount Logan in the Yukon Territory of Canada is reputed to be the bulkiest.) The face you see has been climbed on the left (east) side, first by an Indian expedition in 1977. "Kangchenjunga" is a Sikkimese name, roughly translating to "the five treasures of the great snow." It is considered a god and a protector by the people of Sikkim to the east.

There are many options for side trips. At least climb up the hillside to the north. If you ascend the boulder ridge crest that bounds the Ginsang Glacier from the north some 700 ft (213 m), you'll come to a plateau with even more impressive views of Kangchenjunga's face. You can continue higher for a more panoramic

Opposite: *The immense North Face of Kangchenjunga from above Pangpema*

sense of the area, or head northwest, where you may find a small lake at about the same altitude. There are plenty of choices for following the glacier valleys to the north and east. It would be grand to make a circuit of the entire Kangchenjunga massif, but political considerations and international boundaries make this impossible at present. In retracing your steps, you'll probably admire the lesser summits, such as the rock spires of Sharpu III below Kambachen, and have more time and patience to stalk blue sheep. If you are well acclimatized, you can do the trip to Ghunsa in 2 very long days, but spend 3 and enjoy it.

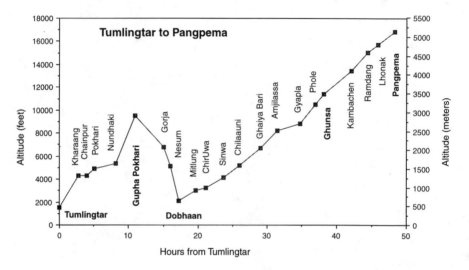

GHUNSA TO THE SOUTH SIDE OF KANGCHENJUNGA

Besides returning from Ghunsa down the Ghunsa Khola valley, the way you came, there are two other feasible exits that head over to the south side of Kangchenjunga. These allow you the option of visiting the base camps there and give you a return to Taplejung, where there is an airstrip and a seasonal road. The two exits both cross high passes from Ghunsa and arrive in the Yalung Glacier–Simbua Khola valley.

The higher route crosses the Lapsang La, a 17,250-ft (5258 m) pass, to reach the herding area of Lapsang near the snout of the Yalung Glacier. En route, it heads up to the Yamatari Glacier, crosses its moraine, and ascends the valley of the Lasampa Glacier to the pass. The way is loose and rocky and requires 2 days' travel, with an intermediate camp at the Lumba Sumba Kharka, across from the Yamatari Glacier lateral moraine. This route is not recommended because of the additional altitude gain, the lack of views, the length, and the increased difficulties on the trail, especially for the porters. If you plan to do it, hiring extra porters to carry loads makes sense. Snowfall can make the way hazardous.

The lower route, essentially a high-ridge, upper-valley traverse, is exhilarating and can be done in a long day. If you wish to break it up into two, which would be more enjoyable, there are suitable camping sites and parties must be self-sufficient in fuel. There are several names for points reached, including Sinion La, Tama La, and Mirgin La. The maximum altitude reached is 15,250 ft (4648 m). This is the route locals use for getting back and forth. It also has a bonus: a more complete view of Jannu from the southwest than the former route. If you climb above the trail near the high point, you can also see the Khumbu Himal peaks and Makalu. On the descent toward Tseram, there are panoramic views of the south face of Kangchenjunga and surrounding peaks. Finally, there are two exit options (to Ilam and to Basantapur) that allow a more direct route for parties not wanting to return to Tumlingtar.

To proceed on this lower route, climb up behind the schoolhouse at the south end of Ghunsa into a forest to reach a fork **10 minutes** beyond (11,500 ft, 3505 m). The left fork goes to Lapsang La; going partway up can make a pleasant day hike for people adjusting to the altitude at Ghunsa and provides some closer views of the west side of Jannu.

To continue south, take the right fork at the junction shortly beyond Ghunsa, and reach the Yamatari Khola, which you cross to its left bank. Just beyond is the pasture called Yamatari. Make sure you get water here. Find the trail into the forest at the end of the corral area and follow it to the forested crest of another old lateral moraine. The route then climbs steeply on the impressive rhododendron-forested side of the valley to reach a prayer flag–festooned spot on the open ridge crest (12,950 ft, 3947 m) in 1¼ **hours** from the fork. Called the Tama Lasi, it is not really a pass. Proceed up near the ridge crest and then on its right (west) side. Look down on your route up the Ghunsa Khola valley—Phole and Gyapla are easily spotted. To the north is the Yangma Khola valley, which leads to the Nango La, the pass connecting Ghunsa with Wallungchung Gola.

The ascending traverse is serene. Reach a spring (13,400 ft, 4084 m) in 45 minutes, just below a ridge crest called Tynuma, which you cross into another draw to the south. I well recall the exotic ambrosia along here. Continue along to Mani Bhuk (13,975 ft, 4259 m), a fine campsite with a pleasant stream, 1½ **hours** from the Tama Lasi. Eventually, Jannu's west face pops up above a ridge behind you. An hour beyond Mani Bhuk, you reach a level area (14,325 ft, 4366 m), after which you leave the views of Jannu. In some seasons, if water is available, this would be an idyllic spot to camp. If not, continue up to another notch, the Margin La (15,250 ft, 4648 m). In 1 hour, this leads into a very different series of valleys.

After more pleasant traverses, you reach a small draw with a prominent spire (gendarme) and attendant sphinx-like consort, called Menda Puja (15,250 ft, 4648 m), up the valley. Notice the many rock cairns along here. Local people feel the gendarme is a deity and make cairn offerings to it. Finally, reach the last ridge crest (15,250 ft, 4648 m) Sinion La, in **2 hours 10 minutes** from Mani Bhuk. At this point, you can look down into the Simbua Khola valley to see a fork in the trail. The left fork traverses and then descends to the yak pastures at Tseram. This is the choice for those planning to see the south side of Kangchenjunga close up. The right fork descends more directly into the valley, and would suit those wanting a more direct exit.

The right-fork trail will be described. Descend, and reach some scree, pretty much the first such rubble along this trail. Below you are two lakes. The trail drops to pass to the south of the lower lake, which is called Tsojung Tanga (14,300 ft, 4358 m) and marked Chhudung Pokhari on the recent Survey of India maps. Reach it in **40 minutes** from the pass. There are a few rock monuments out in the lake, a sign of its sanctity to the locals. To continue, descend steeply, first a small spur, and then a side valley, to reach the forest. At a fork in the forest (12,400 ft, 3779 m), turn right to traverse rather than heading down more steeply, to eventually reach the main trail up the right bank of the Simbua Khola by a small stream (11,800 ft, 3596 m), 1¼ **hours** from the lake. If you turn left here, you will reach Tseram in 2½ hours. But turn right, and head downstream to cross a tributary just beyond on a log bridge (11,715 ft, 3571 m) to reach the tea house of Whata Phedi **10 minutes** beyond.

TAPLEJUNG TO MITLUNG

Those arriving by air to Suketar, or by road to Taplejung, can join the trail to the north side of Kangchenjunga by descending to Mitlung on the Tamur. The trail is a continuation of main street in Taplejung, leaving from the northeast corner of town.

In 20 minutes cross an extensive low-angled landslide. Soon after, a faint trail leads down—keep right to maintain height. In 50 minutes from Taplejung, reach the first of several house clusters, each called Hangdewa. A huge Pipal tree stands beside a tea shop and school. The trail drops steeply along the crest of the ridge to a suspension bridge over the Hangdewa Khola in 80 minutes (3215 ft. 980 m.) One minute past the bridge take the left fork in the trail and contour across steep a landslide to pass a house with a nice view back down the Tamur Valley. In 30 minutes reach Mitlung. Continue upstream on the trail already described earlier.

THE SOUTH SIDE OF KANGCHENJUNGA

The south side of Kangchenjunga presents a rugged, somewhat more open valley that sees less local presence than the north side because of its distance from permanent habitation. But it is similarly used as yak-pasturing grounds and, because of the southerly exposure and increased rainfall, it gets better grass growth. It was the focus of attempts to explore and first climb the mountain in the early 1950s. The route of the first successful ascent of the mountain by the British in 1955 went up the Simbua Khola valley. If this area is your goal and you are crossing Mirgin La, described earlier, then instead of dropping right from Sinion La traverse northeast and descend to Tseram. If you are coming up from Taplejung, following the directions in reverse, then head up to Tseram from Whata, which is described next. Be aware that there is no food or shelter available beyond Yamphudin, so all parties must be self-sufficient. This includes carrying fuel, because these magnificent forests *must* be preserved.

From Whata, proceed up the valley floor in larch forests with some rhododendron, like those near Ghunsa, eventually reaching the two large terraces of Tseram (12,700 ft, 3870 m) with a tea house in **3 hours.** You may find some caves here to stay in. The other fork of the Sinion La trail comes in just above the upper terrace, where there may be water for camping. The small shrine of Devi Than is downstream. It is said that if you pray there once a year, your prayers will be answered. The major mountain massif up the valley is Kabur. Across the Simbua Khola to the southeast is the valley of the Yamagaachha Khola, which heads up to Kang La, a 16,580-ft (5053-m) pass into Sikkim. It was used by outsiders as an early approach to this side of the mountain.

To continue on, head upstream on the same right bank in a broader valley, climbing rapidly at first, reaching Yalung (13,550 ft, 4130 m) after **1 hour,** just after crossing a stream. The forests below Yalung are the last woods and porters may want to carry wood from there, but I advise that the party be self-sufficient in fuel.

Yalung, with a stone hut and potato fields, is below the terminus of the large valley glacier of the same name. There are striking views of Kabur, Kabur Dome, and Ratong. Climb on to Lapsang (14,540 ft, 4432 m), in **2 hours.** The trail keeps to the plateau between the lateral moraine of the glacier and the steep valley wall, near where the Simbua Khola also flows. The trail from Lapsang La, mentioned before, comes in here from the north, and there is a small pond. However, neither the trail nor the pass is visible from the main trail. The path continues climbing over the plateau, coming to a small pond and then continuing another **hour** to Ramche (14,700 ft, 4480 m). There is a large meadow here as well as a stone hut, and beyond there is a *chorten*. Views of Koktang, Ratong, and the Kabur Dome, the massif to the east, are most impressive. You may see blue sheep along here, the only place besides Dhorpatan where they may exist south of the main Himalayan chain. Tibetan snow cocks can be seen in this valley, too.

From Ramche, the trail gently ascends along the ridge above the moraine of the Yalung Glacier. About an **hour** above Ramche, the trail rounds a corner to the left and you can see the main mass of Kangchenjunga. If you then climb up to the crest of the ridge above the moraine, you will find a good trail that continues along the edge of the moraine. After about **1 hour** on that trail, there is a spectacular panorama of the Kangchenjunga massif and the edge of the Jannu ridge.

The trail heads more northerly, to Okhordung (15,520 ft, 4730 m), labeled Oktang on some maps, reached in another **1½ hours.** From the *chorten* there, on the lateral moraine, there is a grand panoramic view of the Kangchenjunga massif, including Jannu, which looks quite different up close from this angle than it does from the north and southwest. Climbers can head up a ridge on a small peak to the west, reaching 17,700 ft (5395 m) in some 3 hours, for even better views. To reach this peak, turn left before the *chorten* and skirt the first group of rocks on the right. Then head left, behind the rocks, and follow the ridge to the top, being careful on the loose rocks higher up. To head on toward the actual base camps of Kangchenjunga climbing expeditions, you have to cross the Yalung Glacier and head onto the slopes of Ratong. The way is difficult, especially for those unfamiliar with unstable, rubble-covered ice, and the views are not better, except perhaps of Jannu. Kangchenjunga (28,209 ft, 8598 m) was first climbed by a British Expedition from this side in 1955.

All the times along here, of course, depend on the state of acclimatization of the party. Those who have already visited the north side and been acclimatized there will be much quicker than those coming up from the south. Be prepared to take your time.

SOUTH KANGCHENJUNGA TO TAPLEJUNG

The return to Taplejung from Whata will be described here. This becomes the exit from the south side of Kangchenjunga for trekkers. To identify Whata Phedi, look directly across the main valley, up a tributary valley to a forked peak. To proceed, go southwest, keeping close to the eroded bank of the raging torrent of the Simbua Khola. In **1¼ hours** from the junction at Whata, the trail crosses a small tributary and heads inland to a rhododendron forest for a respite. In another **½ hour,** at a slight clearing called Toronten, don't continue along the forested trail, but fork left to descend to a wooden cantilever bridge over the Simbua Khola (9,950 ft, 3033 m) and cross it to the left bank.

Head downstream on the much wetter side of the valley, as you notice more bamboo growth. In 15 minutes, you begin to climb out of the main valley, traversing an impressive fir forest. A half hour later, cross a stream, the last running water for some time, and continue traversing and climbing in a small side valley to reach a clearing at Thangsetang (10,350 ft, 3155 m), used as a midway point in dried cheese (*churpi*) trade. This is 1¼ **hours** from the Simbua Khola crossing. Climb up through a rhododendron and birch forest to reach more open slopes and a kind of pass, Lassi Than (11,425 ft, 3482 m). The actual pass is a little lower down, but the trail avoids the low point, 125 feet below, which is more hazardous. Continue on to the southwest, to a clearing and the pasture of Lassi (11,375 ft, 3467 m), **1 hour** from Thangsetang. With the now-distant views of Jannu behind you, this is a spectacular spot to camp, but water may be hard to find. It is available about a half-hour's descent directly to the southeast, below the pass.

There is also a fine viewpoint of the south side of Kangchenjunga, which is reached by taking the ridge-crest trail that heads northeast from where you meet the ridge at Lassi Than. After a 35-minute walk through rhododendron forest, you come to a rock outcropping (12,150 ft, 3703 m). A brief scramble to the small summit gives great views of Jannu and Kangchenjunga. The peak to the west of Jannu is Sharpu I. You can look back at Makalu, the white pyramid, before reaching this point.

To head on from Lassi, continue for **30 minutes** along the trail in a rhododendron forest to a clearing called Lamite (10,750 ft, 3276 m). Another **30 minutes** down in a bamboo forest and you come to Chitre (9725 ft, 2964 m), another clearing, with little chance of finding water in the dry season. Continue into an oak forest, and just before coming out of it, **20 minutes** beyond Chitre, fork right (9150 ft, 2789 m) to stay in the woods. After a clearing, the trail switchbacks along a new, slippery, pebble trail. Finally reach water, as you cross a tributary on stepping stones (7475 ft, 2278 m), to its right bank. Traverse along to Tzenday Portok, a *chautaaraa* **30 minutes** beyond.

This area has farm fields without terraces, which you also notice across the valley, to the southeast. It is an example of slash-and-burn agriculture, where every five years or so the area is burned and one crop of corn is grown. The land lies dormant for another five years. Population and food pressures have resulted in the use of more marginal lands in this manner. To do otherwise would require these slopes to be terraced. Further pressures on the land might result in terracing at some future date.

Here, I took the right, lesser fork, which descended to a pool below a waterfall in 10 minutes. To reach it, however, you have to descend some 30 ft (10 m) on a cliff. It has good foot- and handholds, as well as a vine rope to hold on to, but it is a scramble. The payoff is that the pool could provide a cool, refreshing bath. Cross the tributary to the right (6900 ft, 2103 m) and climb up a faint trail, which then traverses and ascends. A high trail joins this one **30 minutes** beyond; take the lower left fork just before the main trail coming up from the bridge is reached on the right.

If you take the left fork from Tzenday Portok, the trail descends a spur to cross the Tzenday Khola to the right bank on a cantilever bridge and then ascends.

Either way, the settlement of **Yamphudin**, the first since Ghunsa, is just beyond (6825 ft, 2080 m), less than **1 hour** from the *chautaaraa* called Tzenday Portok. The people here are mostly *BhoTiya*, like those in Ghunsa with *Gurung* and *Rai* as well, but as you head along toward Taplejung, *Limbu* predominate and the town names reflect their different linguistic origins. There are several small hotels here.

These villages are usually quite scattered; denser collections of houses usually reflect the presence of other ethnic groups.

From Yamphudin there is a trail to Hellok at the junction of the Tamur and Ghunsa Kholas. This takes 1 long day and climbs to 12,850 ft (3916 m). It could be used to give you access to a different arrival or departure route. It is not described here.

The trail now for the most part travels through farmland. To continue from Yamphudin, descend through town to a spur and meet trails coming from the right and then from the left. Descend to the Kabeli Khola valley floor, and cross a tributary en route. Reach it in some 35 minutes from town. You are on the right bank, and should follow the river downstream. The main trail then climbs over a steep part of the valley, and there, at **45 minutes** from Yamphudin, just beyond a *chautaaraa* (5500 ft, 1676 m), there is a left fork that descends to a suspension bridge over the main river. This would be the fork to take if you were heading to Gopetaar.

This route would take 2 days and follow the Kabeli Khola for the most part. The towns along the way are Kebang, Barundin, Dandagaon, Panchami, Tharpu, and then Gopetaar.

To continue to Taplejung, however, take the right fork and climb up a bit to traverse in and out of side valleys of the Kabeli Khola. This is done for almost 2 days, before descending to Taplejung. At forks, always choose the more prominent or bigger trail. After traversing along the main trail for **1½ hours** from the *chautaaraa,* you cross a tributary from the north. The first houses of **Mamanke** (6075 ft, 1852 m) are **15 minutes** beyond, but the school is on a spur almost **30 minutes** farther. Notice how schools are almost always sited on the land most unsuited for agriculture. There is a tea shop/lodge/camping site here.

The trail then descends and traverses to cross a major tributary, the Takshewa Khola, to the right on a suspension bridge. Climb up to the few houses and shops of Pumpe (6150 ft, 1874 m), **1 hour** from the school. Continue traversing, mostly in mixed broad-leaved forest with some rhododendron. A half hour beyond is an arboreal surprise for this region: some pine trees! These are the three-needle chir pine, *Pinus rhoxburghi,* called *khoTe Sallo* by Nepalis. Almost an hour beyond Pumpe are two small but idyllic waterfalls you pass below.

Pass above the scattered *Limbu* houses of Yampung, then round a spur and reach the town of Pum Pung (6050 ft, 1844 m), **1½ hours** from Pumpe. This town is referred to as Funfun on some trekker maps, a decidedly difficult *Limbu* name to exactly pin down. Here you finally leave the Kabeli Khola valley and enter the tributary valley of the Nangden Khola. The traverse continues, crossing below a waterfall in a fault with pleasant, shallow pools below. Shortly beyond is a weeping wall, then another tributary to cross on a log bridge, before the steep climb up to Kheshewa (6450 ft, 1966 m). It is reached in **1¼ hour** from Pum Pung.

Ascend to a small pass, **Sinchewa Bhanjyang** (7050 ft, 2149 m), where there are some tea shops. This is **45 minutes** from Kheshewa. The Kangchenjunga massif is seen behind you. The trail to Taplejung turns right here to descend into the Phaawa Khola valley. At a *chautaaraa* on the notch of a spur, some 25 minutes beyond, head down the other side, and 15 minutes later reach the first houses of **Khunjhari** (6325 ft, 1928 m).

Upon reaching some shops, turn left and continue down a spur, reaching a few covered stalls in **1 hour** from Sinchewu Bhanjyang (5700 ft, 1737 m). There is a market here on the first day of the Nepali month (*sAAgrAti*). The school is just below. Descend to the suspension bridge over the Phaawa Khola in another **30 minutes.** Cross it to the right (4700 ft, 1432 m), then climb up the other side. **Half an hour** later, take the left fork and reach **Simbu** (5600 ft, 1707 m), **10 minutes** beyond. Continue climbing and traversing and, in a half hour, fork right to climb rather than traverse (6175 ft, 1882 m). Round a spur crest, head into another tributary valley, and proceed to the scattered village of Tembewa (6325 ft, 1928 m), **10 minutes** beyond. Just before coming to a school, fork right to climb rather than heading lower to reach the school. Here begins a long, ascending traverse in this valley.

Pass several streams in a draw to reach a house in **1 hour 10 minutes** (7475 ft, 2278 m). Climb into an oak forest to reach a spur crest **10 minutes** beyond (8675 ft, 2644 m), but there is another **1¼ hours** of climbing, until you reach an open, lofty area (8700 ft, 2652 m). Here you see Makalu to the west, as well as the Jaljale Himal. Traverse a little farther to a crossroads, where five trails converge. You head southwest on a forested ridge, taking some stairs up from the junction. Cross to the northwest side of the ridge, on a very wide, almost jeepable road, and enter an open area. As you walk down this hillside, you can look back at the Kangchenjunga range you were so intimately connected with not so long ago.

The walk down is a restful contrast from the endless forest to the crest. Soon you reach a modern fence, and beyond is the airstrip of **Suketar, 30 minutes** from the crossroads. The top of the runway is 8000 ft (2438 m). There are several hotels here, and a sense that much expansion will take place here. The district center and large bazaar of **Taplejung** is another **30 to 60 minutes** beyond. Some hotels are below the hospital (5850 ft, 1783 m). The dense collection of shops is a little farther below. There is a weekly market on Saturdays, held near the district army headquarters, south of the main bazaar. There is a police check post here where you should register. The road from Ilam to Taplejung is passable during the dry season, but buses only go to Kabeli Khola, and beyond only occasional trucks and jeeps currently ply the route. It may be possible to catch a ride on a truck.

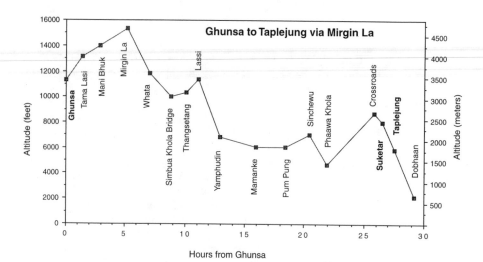

Ghunsa to Taplejung via Mirgin La

CHILDREN GOING TO SCHOOL

Do not ask these little children
coming toward you all in a line,
do not ask them where they are going.
They have their own roads to travel,
their own tools for creating themselves.

They have feet you cannot see,
do not ask about when and where,
these children are their own open sky,
their wings they make themselves.

Their language is different, meanings diverge,
if they are noisy, it does not matter.

Do not try to understand what they say:
these are the books of tomorrow's Nepal

Hem Hamal, circa 1982

This geometry lesson for 6th graders living a week's walk from the nearest road is of questionable practical value.

TAPLEJUNG TO BASANTAPUR
Taplejung to Dobhaan

The trail to Dobhaan and the segment from Gupha Pokhari will be described here, to allow you to link up with the road to Dharan. Even when regular bus service is established to Taplejung, I would advise walking the trail south from Gupha Pokhari. It is a most pleasant day, spent along a ridge crest for the most part, with views of the Khumbu Himal and Everest massif, as well as the Kang-chenjunga region.

From Taplejung, descend past the primary school (5800 ft, 1768 m). Follow a big trail to **Deolinge,** some houses with a school (3675 ft, 1120 m), an hour from Taplejung. Twenty minutes below are the tea houses of Nangesuri (2975 ft, 907 m), and as you approach the suspension bridge over the Tamur, across from Dobhaan, there are a few more tea shops. The bridge is **1 hour 40 minutes** from Taplejung (2125 ft, 648 m).

The trail from Gupha Pokhari to Dobhaan has already been described, so those descriptions can be followed in reverse.

Questions to Ponder: Consumer Goods and Economic Development

. . . our Western consumption of resources, no matter how greedily we gorge our lifestyles, leaves us still fundamentally hungry inside. And it is also true, and apparent as you live with these people in these hills, that millions of people here in the Himalaya, regardless of specific religious insight—Hindus in Nepal, Buddhists in Tibet, animists in the back hills—do not hunger inside as we do.

Daniel Taylor-Ide, *Something Hidden Behind the Ranges*

They have everything that money can buy, and they still want something. That you can't buy with money.

Chundak Tenzing

Both these remarks, one by a Nepali about his impressions of life in North America, and the other by a Westerner who has spent much time in the Himalayan region, reflect on materialism and other lifestyles.

What kinds of goods are available in local stores? On the main trekking trails, what goods are purchased by the local inhabitants? Which are staples and which are luxuries? What is produced locally and what is imported? How dependent are the hill and mountain people on imported goods? What crafts are produced locally? Compare the use of the wheel in your society and in a remote area of Nepal.

What modern consumer goods do you see in use? What did they replace, and how dependent are the people on them? How has this affected local craftsmen? How important is cash in trading and commerce? What are the major influences on the economy of the region you are passing through? How important are Gurkha pensions in supporting the hill economy? Can this have a deleterious effect? What are the specific and general benefits as well as the negative influences that road building has brought? What will be the changes in this area in ten years? Twenty years? How can you influence those changes positively?

What changes can you see that have resulted from modern development? What would be the major development effects you could make if you were the party in power? What problems would you foresee?

Gupha Pokhari to Basantapur

The trail segment from Gupha Pokhari to Basantapur will now be documented. From Gupha Pokhari (9950 ft, 3033 m), head south to reach Korunga, a few tea houses on the ridge crest (10,075 ft, 3071 m), **30 minutes** beyond. Like almost all the settlements along this portion to Basantapur, they are temporary, set up to serve the porter traffic to Taplejung. How they will change once regular road service is established to Taplejung is unclear.

Cross a ridge crest to reach Lam Pokhari, **15 minutes** beyond. There is a long lake almost pinched off in the middle here to contemplate. The next collection of tea houses is Bhaalukhop (9650 ft, 2941 m), 20 minutes farther, and then Sirmani, before reaching **Manglabari** (9100 ft, 2774 m), **1 hour** from Lam Pokhari. Climb up a bit, and contour on the west side of the ridge crest, before reaching **Chauki** (9250 ft, 2819 m), **35 minutes** farther.

The views of the Khumbu Himal are impressive, but it is hard for the uninitiated to pick out Mount Everest. Certainly the locals all along here tend to point to Makalu when asked where Everest is. Farther north, around Gupha Pokhari, it is especially hard to make it out, since it is blocked by Lhotse Shar.

Continue on to Madan Sing, then Phedi, and begin a climb to Tinjuri Deorali, a few tea houses just below a notch where the trail crosses to the south side of the ridge. This spot (10,100 ft, 3078 m) is **1 hour 10 minutes** from Chauki. Alas, the mountain views are over for now. Below, you can see the substantial town of Basantapur and the road. Traverse along the southeast side of a ridge, to reach Durpani, then Dur, and finally Deorali in a notch, all collections of tea houses. At Deorali (8850 ft, 2697 m), **1 hour** from Tinjuri Deorali, you end the traverse, and turn left to head south. Reach **Basantapur** (7950 ft, 2423 m) in another **45 minutes.** The odyssey is over.

Links between the Dudh Kosi and Arun Valleys
(Maps No. 3, Page 214, and No. 7, Page 310)

The following route descriptions provide alternatives to getting to Khumbu and the Everest region from the Arun Khola, one of Nepal's three major river systems. The first route, over the Salpa Bhanjyang, is close to the original one to the Everest region taken by outsiders in 1949. It does not have quite as many ups and downs as the way from Jiri, and is much less popular with trekkers. More lodges and other facilities for trekkers are being built. Enquire locally to see whether they are open up high. The trek also offers an excellent way of varying your route of exit from Khumbu, when followed in reverse. Some trekkers have been doing a "grand traverse," starting in Kathmandu, going to Everest, then leaving heading east, going to the Makalu Base Camp, and finishing up with the Kangchenjunga circuit. This is at least a two-month odyssey, but what a glorious gambol! Another route is described afterward, involving a much less used pass, Kemba La, through *Rai* country to reach the Arun Khola.

TUMLINGTAR TO KHARTE (IN THE DUDH KOSI VALLEY) VIA SALPA BHANJYANG

Fly to **Tumlingtar** (1500 ft, 457 m), a broad, flat plateau on the east (left) bank of the Arun Khola. Once there, spend the night in hope of getting the spectacular early morning views of Makalu and Chamlang to the north. To head to Khumbu, head north for **45 minutes** and fork left at a *chautaaraa* (ask the way here) to drop steeply northwest down to the Arun Khola (1000 ft, 305 m). Head upriver on its left bank.

There are two trails: a monsoon track that proceeds up higher and the more usual valley-bottom trail. It is usually quite hot here, and if you care to swim or bathe in the river beware of powerful currents. Reach the suspension bridge in **3½ to 4 hours.** Cross (1200 ft, 366 m) to **Kartikeghat** on the southwest (right) bank of the Arun. Continue upstream on a rice paddy trail to the Chikhuwa Khola, in **30 minutes.** Cross it to the north (left) bank and ascend a major ridge system to the northwest, climbing out of the valley of the Arun Khola.

Ask the way at junctions for the trail to Phedi. Gain the ridge crest (3000 ft, 914 m) in 3 hours and traverse north to descend into the south side of the Irkhuwa Khola valley. Cross it on a wooden cantilever bridge at 2200 ft (671 m) in an hour. Trails exist on both sides of the Irkhuwa Khola; ask which is the best this year. It depends on which bamboo bridges remain from the last monsoon. Continue up the Irkhuwa Khola, reaching the village of **Dobhane** in **4 hours** from the crossing of the Chikhuwa Khola.

TUMLINGTAR TO DHOBHANE VIA DINGLA

Those wishing to take the higher, less trekker visited, trail from Tumlingtar should descend from the north end of the plateau to the Arun and cross to the west (TR) bank by ferry. Climb to Dingla (3900 ft, 1189 m), where there is a Saturday market, in 3 hours. Ask the way to Mulpani, then drop to cross the Chikhuwa Khola below Kaule in 2½ hours. Ascend steeply to the ridge crest between the Irkhuwa and Chikhuwa Khola at the Kaule school, then head west to Taabu in 2 hours. Contour around to Dangmaya before descending to Dobhane in another 2½ hours.

Carefully cross several tributaries to reach **Phedi** (4900 ft, 1493 m), in **3 hours** from Dobhane. This is a large *Rai* village with lodges on the prow between the Irkhuwa Khola to the west and the Sabu Khola to the north. There is a signficant *lokta* paper-making industry up from here.

Climb up steeply through Phedi to the ridge crest to the northwest toward Salpa Bhanjyang. An hour beyond Phedi at Jaubari there are some lodges, as well as at Suranse below the pass. A spectacular causeway brings you to a group of *goTh*, Tamdse Dingma, in a meadow with a pond (9300 ft, 2835 m). It is **5 to 6 hours** from Phedi. There are campsites here, but the pond may be dry in the spring. The many *goTh* along here are used by shepherds during the monsoon.

A **half hour** above the pond there are also good campsites with water near more *goTh* at Gauracha where there may be a *bhaTTi*. Carry water beyond. A further hour will bring you to **Salpa Bhanjyang** (11,018 ft, 3349 m), with its large *chorten* and good views of Numbur and Katang to the north as well as more distant views to the east and west.

Descend steeply through dense coniferous forest to cross the Lidung Khola to the north (right) side and traverse to the Sherpa village of **Sanam** (8530 ft, 2600 m) in **2 hours** from the pass. There are several developed lodges here. Enjoy delicious curds during milking times.

Stay high, traversing above the river to round a ridge promontory, and see the large *Rai* village of **Gudel** (6560 ft, 2000 m) directly below you. This village is **3 hours** from Sanam and in between is the Sherpa village of Nimchola (Limsolar) (8100 ft, 2469 m) with some lodges. Camp at the school, or stay in a *bhaTTi* or recently built lodges. Then descend very steeply to cross the Hongu Khola to the northwest (right) bank on a suspension bridge (4318 ft, 1316 m). Ascend through the large hillside village of **Bung** (5250 ft, 1600 m). Reach it in **1½ hours** from Gudel. There are several lodges here as well as a Makalu Barun National Park office where you show your park permit. Continue up through the village and head north to Lenji Kharka and on to **Boksom Gompa** (8399 ft, 2560 m) in **3½ hours** from lower Bung. Once a beautiful Buddhist monastery, it is now in disrepair. The distinctive ring of juniper trees surrounding it were introduced from Darjeeling.

Weaving Traditions: Cotton

Cotton originated in South Asia, and it has been grown in Nepal for at least several hundred years. Cheap imported cloth has stifled much local production. Imported yarn is spun into lively attractive patterns for producing *dhaka* cloth made into the traditional men's hat or *Topi*. The *Rai* and *Limbu* of the eastern hills are the source of this tradition and Terhathum south of Basantapur is a major production center. Weaving takes place in groups near home, with children playing about. Men make the loom, and the women weave. Inlay and tapestry patterns are continually being created, and the interplay of colors produce desirable textiles, as well as caps. Much of this material has made its way to Kathmandu and is being used by fashion designers there and exported as well.

Reach a promontory with *chorten* in **30 minutes.** Climb through rhododendron forests to Surki (Sipki) La (10,120 ft, 3085 m), some **2 hours** from Boksom Gompa. A steep, slick, rocky descent follows. Reach **Najingdingma** (8531 ft, 2600 m), where there are lodges in **45 minutes.** Traverse and descend through the pastoral village of **Gai Kharka.** Continue descending to cross the suspension bridge (6200 ft, 1890 m) of the Inhukhu (Inkhu) Khola to the west (right) bank. The trail on both sides is extremely steep and exposed. It is **1½ hours** from Najingdingma.

Climb very steeply to the ridge crest at the Sherpa village of **Shibuche** (9000 ft, 2743 m), where there are lodges. This takes **2 hours.** Head west up the ridge crest and traverse over to Pangkongma La (10,410 ft, 3173 m) in **1½ hours.** Mera Peak is at the head of the Inhukhu Valley to the northeast. Descend past the *gomba* to Pangkongma, or **Pangum** (9338 ft, 2846 m), in **45 minutes,** where there are several lodges. If heading toward Everest, take the right-hand fork and traverse to Kharte in **3 hours.** You can now follow the trek descriptions in chapter 6 to Khumbu or perhaps continue west toward Kathmandu.

KHARTE TO BUMLINGTAR VIA KEMBA LA

This unknown trail follows the preceding one for about a day (described below in the opposite direction) and then branches off to cross a local-use pass through wild country. You must be self-sufficient for a day, and otherwise stay in Nepali homes, or camp, as there are no lodges. The descriptions are brief, appropriate for those with previous experience in Nepal, who are able to ask the way.

Leave the main Dudh Kosi trail at Bupsa, climb up to Kharte, and from there ascend to the village (with some lodges) of Pangkongma (9338 ft, 2846 m), 3 hours from upper Kharte. You could also reach this village up the valley to the east of Karikhola. Continue up Pangkongma La (10,410 ft, 3173 m) 40 minutes beyond, a pass in a rhododendron forest. Descend to the east, through Bosmeh Satu, to Shibuche (also called Basme and Chatuk) (9000 ft, 2743 m), where there are a few lodges, in an hour. Descend, forking right steeply to cross Hinku Khola to the TL in 1 hour 30 minutes (6201 ft, 1890 m) below the junction of a tributary from the east. Climb through Gai Kharka (no lodges) and on to Najing (8860 ft, 2700 m) on a shelf with some temporary shelters set up as lodges (2 hours from the river). Ascend to Surki La (10,120 ft, 3085 m), in another hour.

Myths of *Rai* Origin

The *Rai* are aboriginal *Kiranti* people and of the four original Kiranti brothers, the oldest was Khambulang, the second eldest Mewahang, the third eldest Limbhuhang, and the youngest was Med Koce, who stayed in the Tarai, and gave rise to the Tharu people there. The other three came up to Barahachhetra. Mewahang asked the eldest brother how he crossed the river there, and was told he gave the blood of his sister. Mewahang sacrificed another sister who was traveling with him, and crossed, then found the older brother had tricked him, as he left his sister hidden in a Doko. Mewahang cursed his older brother, saying he should only acquire bad land and have illnesses. Khambulang moved up the Dudh Kosi and Mewahang the Arun. Limbhuhang moved up the Tamur, and the *Limbu* are descended from him. You may often find the Mewahang with better land than the Kulung, descended from Khambulang, and this explains why.

Descend from Surki pass, and don't take the left fork just east of the pass (which goes up to a series of lakes called Panch Pokhari [five lakes] and is the way to Mera Peak and the Hongu Basin), but pass through scattered houses, fields, and forests heading east (instead of southeast to Boksom Gompa and the Salpa Bhanjyang) to reach a river at 6420 ft (1956 m) in 4 hours. Cross it to the TL, and then climb to the spread-out houses of Papelung (6620 ft, 2018 m). Climb through more houses to round a ridge, and reach Chheskam, also spread out (6560 ft, 2000 m), an hour from the river crossing. Head up to the northeast, through Chheskam and Chhemsing, two large *Rai* villages, with a market center (*Tundikhel*) separating them, on the TR bank of the Hunku Khola.

Head up the valley to a narrowing and a bamboo bridge 1½ hours from Chheskam (5370 ft, 1637 m). Cross the Hunku Khola to the TL and then climb to the Sherpa village of Boksuwar (7550 ft, 2301 m) in 1 hour 40 minutes. This is the last habitation before Kemba La; hire a trail guide here. Climb steeply up the crest of a ridge, passing several *goTh* and pasture ensembles (Bokulu Kharka and Kemba Kharka), heading to the northeast, into the head of a valley striking to the south. Contour and climb to reach Kemba La (12,839 ft, 3913 m), approximately 7 hours from Boksuwar. You can see Kangchenjunga to the east and Makalu to the north.

Traverse east, and descend, with the Arun Valley in the distance. Descend very steeply, in a lush forest, eventually reaching more *goTh* and bamboo forests, before arriving at Chitre, a Sherpa village (7550 ft, 2300 m) some 7 hours from the pass. In the forests above here, people gather nettle to weave into cloth as well as daphne shrub bark to make so-called rice paper. You may also see human torpedoes carrying down *nigalo* bamboo to their villages. Descend through Teyung, a scattered area of *Rai* houses, to reach Sisuwatar (2280 ft, 695 m) in the valley bottom, at the junction of the Sisuwa and Sankhuwa Kholas in another 5 hours. Here there is a colorful weekly Wednesday market and a nettle cloth weaving factory.

To head onto the Arun, cross the bridge to the TR of the Sisuwa Khola, above the junction with the Sankhuwa Khola, and head downstream, east to Bumlingtar (1320 ft, 402 m) in 2½ hours. Just downstream on the TR bank below Sisuwatar is a large paper factory, using *lokta* bark from up the valley, to produce so-called rice paper, which is made on contract to sell in Kathmandu. Typical of many such enterprises, the investors are outsiders, and the workers (who hail from outside as well) do piecework. Upon reaching Bumlingtar, consider swimming below the suspension bridge over the Sankhuwa Khola, a wonderful respite on a hot day. Bumlingtar is comprised of a few houses, even a lodge, on the shelf to the south.

Peoples of Eastern Nepal: *Kiranti* (*Rai* and *Limbu*)

The *Kiranti* live in the easternmost districts and are found even around Darjeeling in West Bengal. Like the *Gurung* and *Magar* farther west, the *Kiranti* are renowned for their exploits in the British and Indian Gurkha armies. *Rai* was originally an honorific term bestowed by the Gorkha conqueror, designating village headmen who acted as intermediaries between local people and the government. Today it stands for a number of ethnic groups who speak a variety of interrelated dialects that are often unintelligible from one watershed village to the next. *Limbu* inhabit lands east of the Tamur, and *Rai* west. Among the subgroups of the *Rai* are *Bantawa, Chamling, Dumi, Khaling, Kulung, Mewahang, Thulung, Yakka,* and *Yamphu.* Most members of one of these groups live in relatively close proximity and speak languages different from the others. There are many more groups, and there is a saying among the *Rai* that there are as many different languages as there are *Rai.*

Kiranti economy is fairly self-sufficient. (The description that follows fits the Nepali hill peoples in general.) Rice is raised in lower, well-watered fields. Upland crops, such as corn, millet, barley, wheat, and potatoes, are raised on higher, drier, and steeper or terraced hillsides. No mechanized farm equipment is found in the hills (except an occasional threshing machine or rice mill). Tilling is done either by hand with a short-handled hoe (seen most often in the Kathmandu Valley) or with bullocks pulling iron-tipped wooden plows. All hills people eat what they raise, and market what little surplus they may have. Some supplement their incomes by selling oranges or fish. The wealthier may engage in money lending. Others work seasonally in neighboring India as porters, Gurkha soldiers, policemen, or watchmen. In the far eastern hills bordering the Darjeeling District of West Bengal, there are tea plantations—Nepal's own brand of Ilam tea is exceptionally tasty. Many *Limbu* work the tea plantations on both sides of the border. Some hills people make and sell bamboo baskets and mats, and where sheep are raised on the higher slopes the people weave and sell the woolen blankets, rugs, and feltlike capes and jackets that are often seen in Kathmandu's street bazaar. Trekkers are most likely to encounter *Kiranti-Rai* along the lower trail through the Solu District on the trek to Mount Everest and around Makalu and Kangchenjunga.

Weaving Traditions: Nettle

Trekkers commonly come across weavers during their travels. A variety of fibers are used, including the giant Himalayan nettle (*allo*) in the east for making clothing, casting fish nets, and tumplines; *raDi,* a rough, felted woolen cloth used as a hooded blanket; or cotton used for the *dhaka* cloth to make traditional Nepali hats for men (*topi*).

With nettle as an example, the fiber is harvested after the monsoon before the plant flowers. Hands are protected by a bundle of cloth used to strip off thorns and leaves. The stems are cut, then the outer bark of a bundle of five is stripped off by incising the stem with the harvester's teeth and pulling with the hands supporting the end by the feet. The outer barks are stored in twisted bundles and then boiled in a water ash mixture. The subsequent washed fibers are rubbed with clay to separate them and then dried. The fibers are teased apart by stretching between the upper arm and toes and then spun using a hand spindle. The tip fibers are kept for fine yarn, the coarser middle ones for making mats. Trekkers often see people spinning while walking along the trail or attending to other chores. Borrow the "works" and see if you can do it!

Nettle is woven on backstrap looms in the winter when there is little fieldwork to be done. First the warp yarns have to be prepared for the loom and assembled, often stretching them around stakes in the ground. The loom's warp beam is attached to the roof rafter or on a support beam and weaving begins. Items made from *allo* include sacks (*bhangra*) done in about 5 days, smaller bags (*jhola*), tumplines (*naamlo*), jackets (*phenga*), often with cotton embroidery along the seams, and casting fish nets (*jal*) woven exclusively by men.

Women have been organized into weaving cooperatives, and nettle cloth and finished products are exported to Kathmandu from this area. Marketing of these items remains the biggest problem today. I have had a handsome sports jacket made from the strong, fascinating material.

Makalu Base Camp
(Map No. 7, Page 310)

Trekkers wishing an opportunity to visit wild cloud-forest jungle festooned with orchids, pass through *Rai* villages with their incredibly varied use of bamboo, see whether their spiritual preparation allows them to enter hidden valleys, or leave hill Nepal along the spine of a ridge to enter wild and sacred mountain terrain will be well rewarded in trekking to and in Makalu–Barun National Park. The park also has a surrounding conservation area where there are villages. The current park headquarters are in KhAADbari, with offices scattered throughout the region.

A route is described to the Makalu Base Camp from the Tumlingtar airstrip used for the Kangchenjunga treks, as well as an alternative route up the Arun Valley. In a separate section, routes to Khembalung and Saisima, and beyond toward Tashigaon are briefly described. Next, an exit from Tumlingtar to the road at Hille is described. Finally, an exit from Tumlingtar, following the Arun all the way south to leave hill

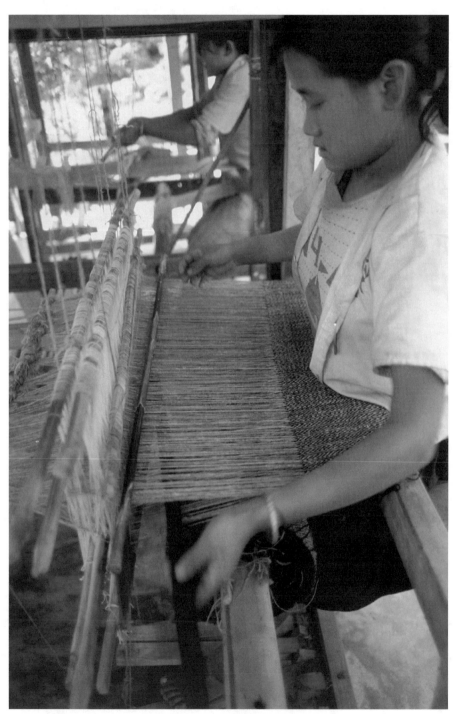

This woman weaves nettle cloth at the Sisuwatar weaving center.

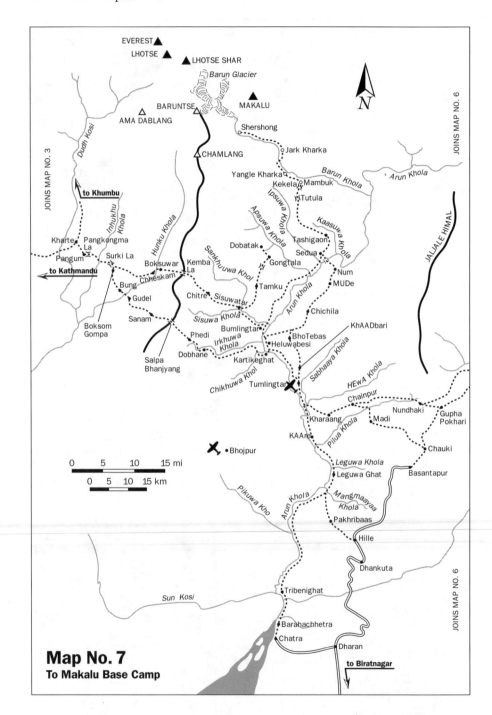

EVEREST ▲
LHOTSE ▲
▲ LHOTSE SHAR

Barun Glacier

MAKALU ▲

BARUNTSE △
AMA DABLANG △

Shershong

JOINS MAP NO. 3

Dudh Kosi

to Khumbu

△ CHAMLANG

Jark Kharka

Yangle Kharka

Barun Khola

Arun Khola

Kekela Mambuk

Tutula

Ipsuwa Khola

Apsuwa Khola

Kaasuwa Khola

JALJALE HIMAL

JOINS MAP NO. 6

Inhukhu Khola

Kharte Pangkongma La
Pangum

Surki La

Hunku Khola

Dobatak

Tashigaon
Sedua
Gongtala

Num
MUDe

Sankhuuwa Khol

Kemba La

to Kathmandu

Boksuwar

Chheskam

Bung

Gudel

Chitre Sisuwatar

Tamku

Sanam

Sisuwa Khola

Arun Khola

Chichila

Boksom
Gompa

Bumlingtar

Phedi

KhAADbari

Dobhane

Irkhuwa Khola

Heluwabesi

BhoTebas

Salpa
Bhanjyang

Kartikeghat

Sabhaaya Khola

Chikhuwa Khol

Tumlingtar

HEwA Khola

Chainpur

Nundhaki

Gupha
Pokhari

Kharaang

Madi

✈ Bhojpur

KAAre

Pilua Khola

Chauki

0   5   10   15 mi

0   5   10   15 km

Leguwa Khola

Leguwa Ghat

Basantapur

Pikuwa Kho

Arun Khola

*Mangmaayaa
Khola*

Pakhribaas

Hille

Dhankuta

JOINS MAP NO. 6

Sun Kosi

Tribenighat

Barahachhetra

Chatra

Dharan

Map No. 7
To Makalu Base Camp

to Biratnagar

Nepal behind and enter the Tarai is noted. This is an excellent way out during the cool winter that passes the physically and spiritually powerful junction of the Tamur, Arun, and Sun Kosi rivers that drain all of eastern Nepal's Himalaya.

TUMLINGTAR TO SEDUA VIA KHAADBARI

Tumlingtar (1500 ft, 457 m) is a long plateau with a grass airstrip, hotels nearby to the east, and the main town just north. To head to KhAADbari, head east, up a hill, on a major trail a minute north of the airstrip, just south of some ponds. Reach **KhAADbari** (3500 ft, 1067 m), a *Newar* bazaar and the district center, spread out along the ridge in about **2¾ hours.** The Makalu–Barun National Park office head-quarters are here as well as a police check post, many shops, hotels, a hospital, and both a Wednesday and Saturday market.

Head up to the small *Newar* Bazaar of **Manebhanjyang** (3700 ft, 1128 m), along the major ridge north–south. There are some hotels and tea shops for trekkers along the ridge, with more expected in the future. If you head west from Manebhanjyang, by

Insects of the Subtropical Zone (3300 to 6500 ft/1000 to 2000 m in the West, to 5500 ft/1700 m in the East)

Insects are particularly abundant in the subtropical zone. Common butterflies in-clude the plain and common tigers and blue and peacock pansies (all four also in tropical and temperate zones) and common Indian crow (also tropical zone). Large and especially colorful species occur, such as the golden birdwing (also tropical and temperate zones), Paris peacock, and glassy bluebottle (also temperate zone). The orange oakleaf, as its name implies, closely resembles an oak leaf when its wings are closed; it is also found in tropical and temperate zones. There is a be-wildering variety of other butterfly groups with evocative names such as sailors, sergeants, windmills, and jezebels.

Cicadas are large insects that resemble the color and pattern of the tree bark on which they live. Countless numbers make a prolonged, monotonous trilling in the forest. The noise is so loud that it has a deafening effect. Males sing by vi-brating a membrane on each side of the abdomen to attract females, which are incapable of making sounds. There are at least four distinct sounds. One is a low-frequency rattle made in the night by the *shechshelli*, another the continuous pitch made during the day by the *jyaaUkiri*, one sounding almost electronic, and a fourth that is wavering and intermittent. A local saying is that "cicada has a pleasant life for it has a silent wife." Cicadas also occur in tropical and temperate zones.

Fireflies (*Lampyridae* [*junkiri*]) are tiny beetles. Wingless females resemble lar-vae and are also called glow worms. At night, winged males flash lights on and off in flight during their courtship display. Lighting is produced by special glands in the abdomen. Each species has a distinctive glow. They also occur in tropical and temperate zones.

Stick insects (*Phasmida*) have slender bodies up to 20 cm long, usually green or brown. They resemble twigs or branches amazingly well and stay motionless at the first sign of danger.

Praying mantids (*Dictyoptera*) are so called because, when waiting for prey, they hold their forelegs folded in front as if in prayer. Any insect, lizard, or small bird that comes by is snapped up with lightning speed by the viselike grip of the forelegs. They also occur in the tropical and temperate zones.

the school, you can reach the Arun southeast of Bumlingtar, and then follow the route to Saisima, which is described below. On to Sedua, pass through BhoTebas (5900 ft, 1798 m) below the ridge crest in 3½ hours from KhAADbari. There are simple lodges here. The trail continues close to the crest of a ridge (Chyankuti Bhanjyang), passing through Chichila (where there are simple lodges) in 2¼ hours. Look for the park signboard describing the mountain panorama seen. Continue in a glorious mixed broadleaf verdant hobbit forest, with moss everywhere. Don't travel alone in this forest as incidents have occurred to solo travelers. Reach MUDe (6500 ft, 1981 m) with lodges in another 3½ hours. Here you can see the route toward the Makalu Base Camp, while closer to hand, Nepalis may be carrying a shrub, bound together on their backs. This is chiraito, a medicinal plant sold at the road head. Head north, along the west side of the ridge mostly, sometimes on a red mud (rato mato) trail that is even more treacherous in the monsoon. Continue on to reach Num TUDikhel (4920 ft, 1500 m), on the ridge with a few shops in 3 hours. Here you leave the main north–south trail and descend steeply east through incredibly wet jungle on the east side of the valley where the sun rarely shines to reach the suspension bridge over the Arun at 2260 ft (689 m) in 1½ hours. Downstream are some of the more difficult kayak and rafting ventures in Nepal. Cross the torrent to the TL and climb up to Sedua (5000 ft, 1524 m), a few shops, and school in a flat area in 3 hours.

Arun III Dam

Along the way, you may spot some unlikely modern buildings on the east side of the Arun, just before the river doglegs east. These were built at the proposed outlet site of the run of river electricity–generating Arun III project, developed by the World Bank. Costing a billion (1994) dollars, it was to be the largest project ever undertaken in Nepal. Appropriate opposition to this foreign-dominated development project was mounted by Nepali environmentalists, who pointed out that Nepal could build smaller facilities themselves, and the installed cost of the electricity would be much higher than what they could afford. In 1995, it was cancelled, representing a major victory for Nepal. Politicians in Kathmandu wept, most likely because of the loss of leakage of project funds, commonly estimated at 10%. There is talk of transnational corporations taking on an even bigger project to generate 400 megawatts here.

BUMLINGTAR TO SEDUA VIA WEST SIDE OF ARUN KHOLA

Reach Bumlingtar as above by crossing Kemba La or from upstream of Kartike reached from the Salpa Bhanjyang. There are simple lodges here. To head on to Sedua from **Bumlingtar,** cross the Sankhuwa Khola, the tributary from the west, to the TL, and head north up the Arun Valley's west side (TR) on a well-used old trail, crossing tributaries, and scattered houses, taking **5 to 6 hours** to reach the bridge over the Apsuwa Khola (2000 ft, 609 m), crossing to the TL. In the valley bottom are *Rai* but also Hindu castes, including *Bahun* and *Chhetri*. There is a fascinating variety of ways that bamboo is used along here. There are higher trails up the hillside to the west, but the valley floor, hot though it may be, is direct and easy. There are no trekker lodges along here—I recommend you stay in people's homes and ask them to cook for you.

Continue from the Apsuwa back up the Arun, which heads east and north, to reach the Ipsuwa (Isuwa) Khola crossed to the TL (2540 ft, 774 m), in another **2 hours**. Climb up toward **Sedua** (5000 ft, 1524 m), in another **2 to 3 hours**, meeting the trail from Num at the school.

SEDUA TO MAKALU BASE CAMP

All routes to the Makalu Base Camp begin at **Sedua** (Murmidanda). Here there is space for camping, as well as a police check post and national park offices where your permit will be checked. Take the KhAADbari route in, and walk out down the Arun for variety. It is good sense to hire porters who are familiar with the way to base camp; these could be hired here or in Tashigaon. Make sure everyone is adequately clothed and equipped.

From Sedua, basically climb up a ridge between the Ipsuwa (also called the Isuwa) Khola to the west and the Kasuwa Khola to the east, passing a ridge crest with a school at Cheksedanda (6100 ft, 1959 m). Then traverse less steeply, the hillside striking northeast, entering Sherpa country, passing through Geng, above Hindrungma, and Ropessa to reach **Tashigaon** (6860 ft, 2090 m) in 3½ **hours** from Sedua. This is a cluster of Sherpa homes. There is a variety of trails that can lead here from Sedua, all converging at the water mill below the village. Beyond there are no settlements, but lots of seasonal use in the monsoon. Many trekkers going on report bad weather prevents them from seeing the mountains. Good luck! There are several lodges here that cater to trekkers; you should enquire about whether there are any facilities farther on toward the Makalu Base Camp when you are here. A private kerosene depot has been established and you must use this fuel beyond. You can rent stoves and blankets here as well. Because there are no villages beyond, you must be self-sufficient for the rest of the journey. There are seven signed campsites ahead designated by the park for use by trekkers. There are minimal or no toilet facilities developed there at present. While some lodges may be in operation beyond, they are only temporary, pending new park regulations.

From Tashigaon (literally, "luck village"), head north, crossing a few streams, on a wide trail in a lush cloud forest, pass trees festooned with orchids, to reach a notch at 10,140 ft (3090 m). Enter the national park and descend in more open country on the west side of the ridge to Ongshisa (10,240 ft, 3121 m), with *goTh* frames. Water is a problem along here if there is no snow to melt. Continue out of the forest along a ridge crest, and look back to get a sense of climbing the backbone of hill Nepal to leave it behind. Reach **Kongma Danda,** a flat area for camping (11,420 ft, 3480 m), with water sometimes available in sink holes. There are overhangs that can be used as shelters to the east. It takes **4 hours** from Tashigaon. Be on the lookout for altitude illness, and return should there be anything other than mild symptoms when you could wait one night at Kongma Danda. Otherwise, if it strikes down in the Barun, you have to ascend to get out.

Continue along the ridge, past Gongru La, festooned with prayer flags, with views of Makalu, Chamlang, and Baruntse, as well as Kangchenjunga and Jannu to the east, to Sano Pokhari (12,720 ft, 3383 m) (little lake) in 1½ **hours.** Peaks 6 and 7 reflect in the waters. Climb to the first of two passes, the **Tutula,** at 13,875 ft (4429 m), in 2¼ **hours**, and descend 575 ft (175 m) to Thulo Pokhari, the magical lake between the two passes. Climb again to the **Kekela** (13,725 ft, 4183 m), in **45 minutes** from the other pass. Westerners call the first one Shipton Pass after the first westerner to cross them. It is so signed but I prefer the Sherpa name. Make a mental map of the route you have taken, for if returning in a whiteout, locating the snow-covered route could be a nightmare. Don't go on unless everyone is well equipped and not suffering from altitude illness.

Gaze off north into Tibet. Descend to the north, entering the fir, rhododendron, and birch forest of the Barun Khola valley to reach **Mambuk** by an overhang with spaces for camping (11,690 ft, 3563 m) in **2 hours** from the pass. The descent can be treacherous if frozen. Reach the Barun Khola at 10,380 ft (3162 m), and head upstream on the TR, south bank to reach Jate (or lower Mambuk) with space for camping, as well as an overhang in another **hour.**

Plunge down to head up the valley in the Barun canyon, reaching Zhante before taking an hour to cross an active slide area. There is talk of rebuilding the trail to avoid this dangerous section. As the upper part of Makalu comes into view, pass Pematang, another flat area, to more open meadows among forests of silver fir and birch (**Yangle Kharka**) (11,800 ft, 3597 m) in **3 hours** from Mambuk. This is another designated camping site with a small *gomba*. There are small caves nearby. Look south at the northeast side of Peak 6 and its ice-covered neighbors. A simple bridge often spans the river here, but the usual route stays on the south side. Contour along turning into an avalanche fan through scrub alders, to **Neghe Kharka** (12,160 ft, 3706 m), a serene, powerful pasture of frames, and another designated campsite, a further **30 minutes** along. Guru Rimpoche stayed in a cave up high to the south and made a fist with his upturned thumb that is sculptured in one of the rocks. During the full moon of August in the monsoon, there is a festival held here, and people go up to the cave, where it is said that if you are infertile or barren and do a *puja*, you will bear children. Of the sheer cliffs to the south, the one on the right is the mother, on the left the father.

Shortly beyond, cross the Barun Khola to the TL on bridges between the huge boulders in the river (12,240 ft, 3730 m), then wind up behind in a quiet, peaceful valley, to come up to a clearing, where to the south you can see two revered pregnant rock formations, Aama Phisum, that may account for the local fertility legends. Many waterfall slivers cascade off the canyon walls if not frozen, one even emerges from a cave 100 m up—ice climbs and Yosemite walls for the next century. Reach the opening of Ripu Maidaan (13,040 ft, 3975 m), and then cross many tributaries to Tadosa (meaning "horse tie," where Shiva tied his steed). Continue to **Jark Kharka** (13,850 ft, 4221 m) with its roofed hut, near the upper limit of forest **2 hours** from Neghe Kharka. Be wary of altitude illness and quick to descend. Note how the valley above changes from a water worn V below to a glacier scoured U above.

Continue past Langmale Kharka where a lodge may be in operation and kerosene supplies may be replenished. Then crest a ridge from where you can see the lateral moraine of the Barun Glacier, pass **Merek,** a string of stone enclosures and a designated campsite where there are currently no lodges, to **Shershong** (15,450 ft, 4710 m), in **2½ hours**, also a campsite. This broad plane puts you on the Schneider Khumbu Himal map. The valley turns north. Thrushes may flock around nearby. Supplicate beneath the immense south face of Makalu in the throne room of the gods. To appreciate the 2-mi-high face, camp near a flat sandy shelf an hour up on the protected west side of a lateral moraine at 15,825 ft (4824 m), or make hikes from Shershong, which is less exposed. This area was the original site of the base camp for the 1955 French first ascent of Makalu (27,825 ft, 8481 m), an expedition where all members reached the summit! They headed northwest of here to cross a col to reach the north side of the mountain. Its name is taken from Maha-kala, meaning "the great black one," clearly appropriate for this rocky massif.

Currently, expeditions head northwest up the Barun Glacier rubble to the so-called Hillary Base Camp, a tiring day's hike up, where the views are minimal. Instead, climb up to the east, take a tent after you have acclimatized, and consider camping on the crest of the ridge (17,800 ft, 5525 m) to get the sunrise and sunset views if you can melt snow. The broad white Kangshung (east) face of Everest can be seen, as well as Lhotse, unfamiliar views to most trekkers. You can see the flanks of their ridges reaching down into Tibet. Some call the rocky black ridge crest above Kala Pattar (black rock). Spectacular Chamlang looks very different from the peak you have been seeing. Many other hikes will suggest themselves to the energetic explorers.

The descent can be made remarkably quickly, but if you have good weather take time to enjoy this special place.

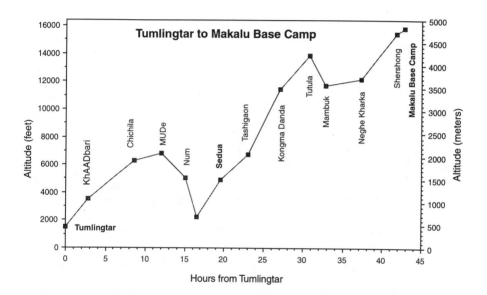

Additional Routes in the Makalu Barun Area

There are many satisfying route options in the Arun Valley area, especially in the cooler months when most trekkers are afoot. First, a route linking the airstrip at Tumlingtar with the road provides an option in case you don't want to fly. Then a route is described following the Arun south to where it exits abruptly from the hills to the Tarai. Finally, links of Tumlingtar with Bumlingtar are given, allowing visits to the southern portion of Makalu Barun National Park and the nunnery at Saisima. All descriptions are brief and presume trekking experience in Nepal. There are essentially no facilities for foreign trekkers. You have to be comfortable traveling Nepali style or camp.

BASANTAPUR TO KHAADBARI

An alternative way to reach this area would be to motor up to Basantapur from Kathmandu or from Dharan at the base of the hills to the south. Then head over to the Arun to KhAADbari directly, rather than take off from Hille and follow a different route described near the end of this chapter. This could allow different links of the Kangchenjunga side with the Arun side. This route, briefly outlined here, traverses pleasant *Rai* hill country. To do so, get to Chauki above, then fork left, just north of it, and traverse, descending on the west side, passing fields of cardamom, a successful cash crop here, to Madi (5540 ft, 1689 m), a large town in some 7 hours from Chauki. Descend crossing tributaries to reach Chainpur (4300 ft, 1311 m) in another 6 hours. It is described above in the trek from Tumlingtar to Kangchenjunga. Reach KhAADbari passing through several small villages and crossing tributaries (including the HEwA and Sabhaaya Kholas), in another 6 to 7 hours. Below, the trails to the Makalu Base Camp from the Tumlingtar airstrip are described.

Weddings

Hindu weddings can be observed almost any time, but most are held during the months of January and February. Wedding parties can be observed traveling to and from the bride's house, sometimes over a long distance and for several days. In rural villages, weddings are loud, colorful affairs accompanied by hornpipers, drummers, and dancers. Wealthy city weddings often include professional bands, and the house where the wedding feast is held is decorated with strings of lights at night. Hindu marriages are traditionally arranged by the parents of the couple; horoscopes are compared by a priest, and an auspicious date is set. Dowries are often demanded, and can be quite expensive. Child marriage, now prohibited, was traditionally the norm among orthodox Hindus.

Buddhist weddings in the hills and mountains are less elaborate, more relaxed affairs, with great attention paid to ostentatious display and reciprocity in gift giving. Among Sherpas, for example, a wedding is preceded, sometimes years earlier, by betrothal rites and often by the birth of a child. There is much beer drinking and dancing. Monks from a nearby monastery attend to the actual ceremonial activities.

Today, throughout Nepal, the customs surrounding the securing of a marriage partner are greatly relaxed compared with the past. Love marriage and marriage between castes and ethnic groups are not uncommon. Nonetheless, arranged marriages of alliance between families in proper caste or ethnic categories are still contracted, especially among the more traditional and orthodox people.

TUMLINGTAR TO HILLE

From the Tumlingtar (1500 ft, 457 m) airstrip (sometimes delightfully fog-bound in the cool early morning), head south on the plateau, pass many houses, and dodge bicycles, for **45 minutes** to reach a few shops at Kaflebhanjyang, before the end of the plateau. Drop off to the east, and cross the Sabhaaya Khola (1060 ft, 323 m) to the TL bank. If heading to Gupha Pokhari, you don't go this far but head east some 15 minutes after leaving the airstrip.

Reach Kakuwa, a few tea shops beyond the Sabhaaya Khola bridge, then along the TL side of the Arun Valley, pass Gandepani, Saptari, to KAAre, all tea shop stops for the trade route up the valley. Cross tributaries, sometimes wading, other times by an upstream bridge used in the monsoon. The river bottom passes through terraces, houses, and sandy beaches reddish tinted from small garnets deposited there. Swim in the Arun to cool off. The river outside of the monsoon is not too swift, and those with good swimming ability can get across. In some places, there are dug-out canoe ferry rides to the other side.

Present-Day Landforms and Rivers

While the Himalayan orogeny has been active for the last 55 million years, the present-day landforms of the Himalaya are the result of tectonic and erosional activity that has taken place during the last 1.6 million years (the Pleistocene and Holocene epochs). This includes the glacial activity that has carved out the mountain slopes and the U-shaped valleys of the Higher Himalaya and the Tibetan Marginal Range above approximately 3800 m; the erosional activity of water that has produced the deep, V-shaped valleys of the Higher and Lesser Himalaya, including the Arun and Kali Gandaki valleys, which vie for the honor of "deepest valley in the world"; the recent uplift of the Mahabharat Lekh, which has forced all the rivers of Nepal, except the Arun River, to turn abruptly from their north–south orientations to east–west orientations as they flow out of the Higher Himalaya or Tibetan Marginal Range; and the formation of, and subsequent drying up of, a number of lakes lying on the north side of the Mahabharat Lekh, including the Quaternary Kathmandu Lake, which has been uplifted and drained during the last 10,000 years to form the Kathmandu Valley.

Of particular interest are the numerous major rivers that originate on the Tibetan plateau and within the Tibetan Marginal Range that cut through the High Himalaya. Why doesn't the highest mountain range in the world, the Himalaya, form a hydrologic divide? These Himalayan rivers were flowing southward off of the Tibetan plateau onto the plains of north India prior to the uplift of the Higher Himalaya. The erosive power of these rivers has kept pace with the uplift of the Himalaya, cutting spectacular gorges through the Higher Himalaya as fast as the tectonic forces of the region could lift up the summits of the great Himalayan peaks. The Kali Gandaki, Arun, Bhahmaputra, and Indus are all examples of rivers that have maintained their original positions, and cut impressive valleys, during the uplift of the Himalaya.

Reach the Pilua Khola in 3½ hours, then the Kenwa Khola, then Leguwa Khola (1100 ft, 335 m) in another 2½ hours, and beyond is the settlement of Leguwa Ghat, where there is a suspension bridge spanning the Arun, as well as a cable car suspended in the middle, upstream of it. Round into the valley of the Mangmaayaa Khola and the village of same name on the TR (1100 ft, 335 m), in a long 7 hours from the Tumlingtar airstrip.

From Mangmaayaa, the main trail climbs up and out of the Mangmaayaa Khola valley to reach the road on the ridge at Hille (6450 ft, 1966 m) in 5 hours, passing through small settlements for the porter traffic, as well as Pakhribaas (5400 ft, 1646 m), a large village. Nearby is the Pakhribaas Agricultural Center, which acts as a research and demonstration center for improved agriculture and animal husbandry, as well as appropriate technology approaches to local problems. There are plans to build a road from Hille through Pakhribaas to the Arun and north to Num. It will facilitate access to this area. Hille is a major road head stop, with many provisions for people living in the hills, who make a yearly visit to resupply especially with salt. There are people resettled from Walangchung Gola in the northern Taplejung district here as well as many other ethnic groups. Here you can catch a bus to Dharan in the Tarai and make connections elsewhere. There is a night bus from Kathmandu to Hille leaving from the Naya Bas Park; buy the ticket the day before.

Secular Festivals

Several national holidays are celebrated throughout the country. The most colorful, from the standpoint of national culture and the prospect of photography, is *Prajaatantra Divas,* or Nepali National Day, February 19. It is highlighted by parades on the Tundikhel (parade ground) in the center of Kathmandu. National ethnic groups, dancing troupes, the military, and various peasant, class, and cooperative organizations participate, all dressed in their traditional finery. There is much pomp and splendor.

At least three different New Year celebrations are held in Nepal annually. The Lunar New Year begins in the Nepali month of Baisakh (mid-April). The Tibetan New Year, called *Losar,* usually falls in February. It is heralded by feasting and celebration among the Tibetan community. The traditional *Newar* New Year falls in October and is celebrated by the preparation and sale of great amounts of sweet cakes and candies, with colorful decorations throughout the streets of Kathmandu, PaaTan, and BhatgAAU.

Rural fairs or *mela* are countrywide and occur throughout the year at various locations. Many are held in the spring and in the fall after the harvest. Fairs are traditionally associated with local rural shrines, quite often for Hindus at the confluence (*beni*) of two sacred rivers or simply on the bank (*ghaaT*) of a sacred river. They usually coincide with a religious occasion and include worship at a local shrine. Some *mela* are quite large and last several days, attracting people from surrounding districts. Others are quite brief and limited to a small region.

ARUN (MANGMAAYAA KHOLA) TO CHATRA

This 2½-day trip, described from the settlement of Mangmaayaa Khola, in the river valley of the same name, a long day's walk south of Tumlingtar, is a wonderful continuation of the valley-bottom journey that brings you out into the Tarai. There is no other such abrupt exit to the flatlands that takes you through as many spiritually powerful areas as in this fantastic gorge.

Begin above the confluence of the Mangmaayaa Khola with the Arun, at the village there, and cross to the TL (1100 ft, 335 m), and then head northwest to rejoin the Arun. The trail on the upper portions here is less used, but navigable, so it is good to take someone along who knows the way here. Cross tributaries of the Chamlang Khola and the Andheri Khola (appropriately named for the steep dark [*Adhyaaro*] valley that strikes east of here) in about 3 to 4 hours from the Mangmaayaa Khola. Beyond there is a large suspension bridge crossing the Arun, and the trail over it leads to Bhojpur, the district center to the northwest in a day. You could cross here and continue on the west side, but those with trail sense can continue on the east.

Keep close to the river, on the east (TL) side, near the cliffs south of here, skirting difficult points. Continue passing across from the Pikuwa Khola that drains the valley where Bhojpur sits and where there is a major trail heading south along the Arun. Pass the major bridge over the Arun at Lamibagar (960 ft, 293 m), where the west-side trail crosses to become the major route south in 3 to 4 hours from the Andheri Khola.

Beyond, the Arun Khola meanders begin; the trail cuts around many of these, to reach another large bridge across the Arun in a narrow canyon with folded vertical strata in the walls in another 3 hours. Just beyond, the Sun Kosi enters from the west, then the Tamur Khola enters from the east, at Tribenighat—wonderful sandy beaches here. Upstream on the Tamur is a bridge, which is crossed to the TL, then rejoin the major valley, which some call the Sapt Kosi, or "seven rivers."

Kosi Tappu Wildlife Reserve

Kosi Tappu (175 sq km) lies in the Kosi River plain in the southeastern lowlands. The reserve consists of extensive marshes, grasslands, degraded scrub, and riverine forest. It supports some of the few remaining herds of the wild water buffalo, although they have interbred with the domestic buffalo. The reserve is a valuable wintering area and staging point for migrating birds, especially wildfowl, waders, gulls, and terns.

Hills start to fall away. Cross the alluvial fan of the Koka Khola to the TL bank and reach Barahachhetra (450 ft, 137 m), a sacred Vishnu Hindu site in an hour. It is one of four holy *chhetra* for Hindu pilgrims; one other, Muktinath, is in Nepal. Once upon a time, there was a strong demon that challenged the god Indra and started causing trouble on the earth and in the oceans. Other gods went to Vishnu and prayed for help. Vishnu said he would go into the ocean as a boar (*baraha*, the third of the ten incarnations of Vishnu), and fight with the demon. He killed him and held the earth up with his tusks, in the form of Bara, from this place. His head is a pig, and below it is the male form. A local custom here is for people to try and lift a large, heavy copper stone, by a temple, and if successful the individual will have good luck. Many come to perform obsequies and place the ashes in the Koka Khola. There is a bazaar here on Wednesday and a large pilgrimage during the full moon of October–November. If you are lucky, you may see some of the gharial crocodiles reintroduced here into the Sun Kosi after being raised to a decent size in the government gharial propagation center in Chitwan.

Continue south, see the flat lands of the Tarai below, and continue on a motor road to reach Chatra (375 ft, 114m), just nestled in the flats by the hills as they abruptly fall away, in another hour. There is a spur road from Dharan to here. You can find transportation back to Dharan, where a bus can be taken to Kathmandu, or you can continue on to Biratnagar and fly to Kathmandu.

TUMLINGTAR TO BUMLINGTAR

As you head north from the Tumlingtar (1500 ft, 457 m) airstrip, continuing on the plateau and not climbing to Khandbari, you pass a large walled compound on both sides of the trail, which are go-downs built for the now-canceled Arun III

World Bank electric-generating project. Whether or not the road that was planned will actually be built up the valley from Hille is unclear.

Descend from the plateau and continue on the TL bank to reach Chyawabesi (1200 ft, 366 m) in 3½ hours. Here a suspension bridge crosses the Arun to Kartike, and a trail heads up to the Salpa Bhanjyang, described earlier. But continue some 3 hours on the east bank to Heluwabesi, a few houses and a school above the next suspension bridge over the Arun. Drop off the plateau, cross it (1200 ft, 366 m), and head upstream on the TR bank of the Arun, staying near the water, before ascending to Bumlingtar by the confluence with the Sankhuwa Khola in another hour. There is a hotel in the town south of the tributary.

Earthquakes

The Himalaya remains a tectonically active region today. The magnitude of the present-day tectonic forces in the Himalayan region is demonstrated by the numerous earthquakes felt in the Himalaya, including the devastating "Great Earthquake" of 1934, which destroyed much of Kathmandu, and the more recent earthquake of August 22, 1988, which caused landslides, destroyed homes, and killed hundreds of people throughout eastern Nepal. As India keeps plowing northward into Tibet and southern Asia, the Himalayan orogeny continues, and the Higher, Lesser, and Sub-Himalaya continue to be uplifted and pushed southward (relative to north India) at rates of several millimeters per year.

BUMLINGTAR TO SAISIMA

Two choices are described. The first can be used if you might be coming from Khemba La, ending up at Sisuwatar, or if heading west up the Sankhuwa Khola from Bumlingtar. The other choice avoids Tamku and heads more directly.

Bumlingtar to Chamkharka

Reach Bumlingtar (1320 ft, 402 m) as above. Then head upstream on the TR bank of the Sankhuwa Khola, to Sisuwatar in 3 hours. This is just above the confluence with the Sisuwa Khola. Cross the Sisuwa Khola, pass through Sisuwatar (2280 ft, 695m), and soon cross the Sankhuwa Khola to the TL bank. Climb the hill to Tamku (4800 ft, 1463 m) in 2½ hours. From Tamku, climb up through forests to the flat area Nagitar, where there is a Makalu–Barun National Park office, just below the houses of Kannegaon. Then climb through those houses up to a ridge crest, and head north to Chamkharka (6900 ft, 2103 m), the last few houses on this side, below the ridge to the west, about 4 hours from Tamku.

The alternative route from Bumlingtar crosses to the TL of the Sankhuwa Khola, then heads up the Arun TR bank briefly to Dhoban (1540 ft, 469 m), and leaves the valley to climb north to Dopbewa (5200 ft, 1585 m) in 4 hours. Continue climbing to the ridge, and reach the houses of Chamkharka (6900 ft, 2103 m) in another 2 hours.

Chamkharka to Saisima

From Chamkharka, a few houses on the north side of the ridge, regain the Gopadanda Ridge and follow it in an orchid-festooned cloud forest, passing posts marking the boundaries of the Mangtewa VDC to the east and the Tamku VDC to the west. These define user groups' areas for forest conservation. In parts there are ladders to climb, as well as bypasses for animals. There are a few *goTh* (herders' shelters), too.

Questions to Ponder: Distribution of Wealth and Income

What evidence do you see of the distribution of income and wealth in the different parts you walk through? Are some areas more egalitarian than others? Near the road or roadhead? In bazaars and training centers? In remote villages? How does this affect the functioning of society, locally and nationally?

Compare the situation in your country of the differences between the poor and the well-off with that in Nepal. How much wealthier are the well-off in your country compared to the poor there? In Nepal? Look at aspects like diet, clothing, leisure time, luxury goods, or ability to get around.

Reach a summit of sorts, Deurali (10,020 ft, 3054 m), with prayer flags, in 4 hours, then descend into the Apsuwa Khola Valley to a clearing, Dhapkharka, and continue descending into the upper fields of the Sherpa village, Gongtala (7500 ft, 2286 m), in another 3 hours. For a side trip, head 1½ hours south, past an idyllic waterfall and weeping wall, to Yangdin (5400 ft, 1646 m), a Kulung Rai village that is quite a contrast from the wealthier Sherpa enclaves to the north. There is a trail from here to Wallung that would be another easier choice to get to Sedua, described below.

DOBATAK TO SEDUA CROSS-COUNTRY TRAIL

From Dobatak, there is a trail to Sedua (which takes at least 2 days) and the way to the Makalu Base Camp. If taking this option, descend to cross the Apsuwa below the waterfall seen to the north on a makeshift bridge, then ascend to cross a ridge, and descend to Wallung (Norbugaon), a Sherpa village, reached in 1 long day from Dobatak; there are camping sites in between but no settlements. From Wallung (5500 ft, 1676 m), descend and cross the Ipsuwa Khola to reach Dingjen, another Sherpa village in 2 to 3 hours. Continue another hour to Norbuchaur, then a further 3 hours to Sedua, and join the trail to Tashigaon.

To head onto Khembalung and Saisima, contour the rugged valley with Chamlang at its head, to reach Dobatak (6900 ft, 2103 m) on a shelf of land, in 2 hours. Dobatak, with its few houses and lodge, is the site closest to the sacred Khembalung cave, where many Nepalis come, especially *Rai* and Sherpas, but also *Tamang* and *Gurung*. To visit the caves, enlist a guide here, follow the cultural precepts, and do all you can to maintain the purity of the area. Such *beyul*, or hidden valleys, figure significantly in Buddhist mythology. If the seeker has the right spiritual preparation, she or he will have an experience that transcends that of the ordinary person.

KHEMBALUNG CAVES

The way includes circumambulating the large boulder outside clockwise, taking off your footwear at the entrance, washing your feet, and going barefoot along the stream that flows through them. The *kata*-adorned rock under the overhanging boulder is a fertility goddess. Also bring some oil or *ghiu*, a wick and matches to light lamps, and ceremonial scarfs, or *kata*. Be sure to leave a donation for the upkeep of this place. It takes a half hour or so. Walk up to the caves, passing the Seven Devi (goddesses) on the muddy trail. It is a cold, dark, claustrophobic experience, with some tight passages, so the wary, the very tall, and the rotund should sit at the entrance and contemplate this peaceful site. At the anteroom, there is an altar to the right with butter lamps. Prepare and light one. Here there are tubes to the right and left where a lama doing a blessing blows sounds, and a tube above that represents the teat of a cow's udder. At the narrowing beyond is a trident to the right and a bell on the left. Pass to the left of a serpent's nose; then to the right is the optional Dharma Dhoka, a room split by a central pillar, where one goes around clockwise, a tight fit for a tall body. Then stem a descent, traverse in a narrow passage, drink some of the sacred water that flows below you (as long as people are clean, there shouldn't be a problem with this stream), and pass through more narrowing and tight fits to a larger area where there is some sacred white crystalline material. Emerge into the daylight, leave the heavenly confines behind, circumambulate back to the entrance, and sit serene. Passing through the caves once or three times in a lifetime is holy.

To continue to Saisima, head up the valley crossing streams, and enter the national park, to reach the lower fields of Saisima (7500 ft, 2286 m), in 2 hours. The nunnery Detchencholling, related to the monastery Thubten Chholing near Junbesi, is above the fields to the north. There are no trekker facilities here.

9   Western Nepal

The fact that I could find almost no other information about the north-west of the country convinced me that that was where I should go.

John Pilkington, *Into Thin Air*

Western Nepal, the region west of the Kali Gandaki river, offers a chance to visit fascinating country and people and is a good choice for the trekker who has done the popular treks. It is more difficult to travel here than in the trekker-frequented east. Except for the Pokhara to Dhorpatan route, food and accommodations are difficult to obtain. Going with an agency or organizing porters yourself makes sense in most places here. Few people in the area speak English, trails tend to be more difficult, and the country is more rugged. The Nepali spoken is different, making it a further challenge to be understood. Different words are used than in the east. Except for the region around Dhaulagiri, the Himalayan scenery in this part of Nepal is less impressive than in the east. It is more difficult to get the feeling of being in the mountains that Khumbu, Kangchenjunga, Makalu, the Thorung La region, and Langtang provide. But for the seeker of impressive forests, rugged, sometimes stark terrain, and fascinating people with unusual customs, the west may be the best.

Two trekking areas will be described. Many, many others are possible. First, a route from Pokhara to Dhorpatan and then on to Dolpo, Nepal's "Hidden Land," is described, then continuing to Jumla, the district center for the roadless Karnali Zone. Then, a trek out of Jumla to RaRa Lake National Park completes our brief look at Nepal's Wild West! Look at *Nepal: The Far Western Region*, for more ideas.

Access to this region is from Pokhara by road or air and from airstrips at Jumla, and Jufal, near Dunai, in Dolpo. There are flights to Jumla from Nepalgunj, as well as from Pokhara, and Kathmandu. It is extremely difficult to get seats from Kathmandu on the infrequent flights. Dolpo flights originate from Nepalganj, except for a weekly flight from Pokhara. Nepalgunj, reached by road or air from Kathmandu, is your best staging point. Some of these treks begin at low elevations and follow valley floors. It can get very warm in late spring, so dress appropriately and don't push yourself, especially in the first few days. Relax during the midday, try to be in the shady side of the valley in the afternoon, or carry an umbrella.

In the route descriptions that follow, the times listed between points are actual walking times, generally those I took myself. They *do not* include any rests. This has been strictly adhered to by using a chronograph. Over most of the trails I carried a moderately heavy pack. I almost never walked the segments in these times. Like everyone else, I rested, photographed, talked with the people, and so forth.

Pokhara to Dhorpatan

The route from Pokhara to Dhorpatan offers a pleasant trek through mixed country and views of impressive mountains. The spacious Dhorpatan Valley is refreshing in this tangled country, and there are many intriguing side trips. In the winter, snow can make the crossing of the Jaljala, a moderate pass into Dhorpatan, difficult if not impossible for a few days. In that case, an alternative route heading west from Baglung and crossing a lower pass is briefly described. With the road to Baglung,

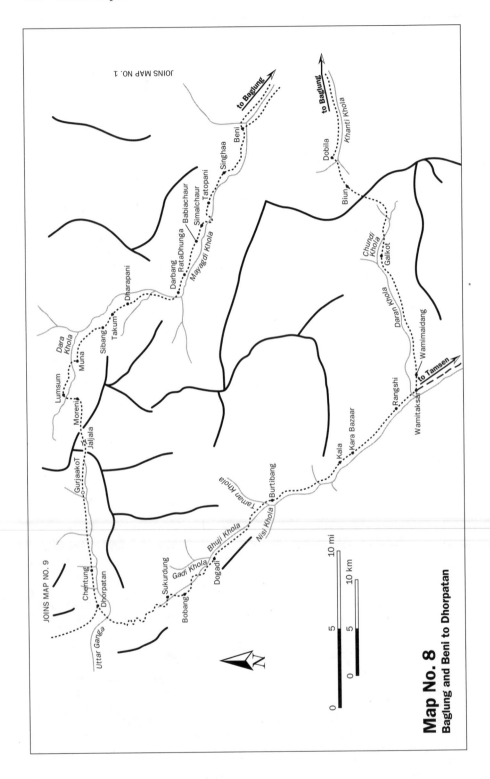

Map No. 8
Baglung and Beni to Dhorpatan

the trek is shorter than it used to be by 2 to 3 days. Food and lodging are available along most of the way. There might be a problem only on the last day, near the Jaljala, so food should be carried for that.

Most people doing this trek will drive to Baglung beyond where people on the popular route to Thak Khola get off and proceed from there. This is described.

BAGLUNG TO DHORPATAN VIA JALJALA

Most travelers take a bus for the half-day trip from Pokhara to **Baglung** (3110 ft, 948 m). Baglung, on a shelf above the river, is the administrative center for the Baglung District. Views of the south face of Dhaulagiri are particularly impressive from here. A sacred sal forest stands at the south end of the shelf.

To go on to Beni, you could cross the river at Khaniyaghaat (2740 ft, 835 m) below you and head up on the east side, a little easier but busier route. Along here, you may see villagers making "rice paper" from the bark of the *Daphne bholua* shrub (*baruwa* or *kagat pate* in Nepali), which is collected in the high hills here. The bark is pounded into a pulp, and the paper made from the slurry that settles on a screen and dries in the sun. It is used in Kathmandu, and you can buy cards and stationery made from it there. If you see a family making some, ask to buy a few sheets locally.

Continue north up the east bank, through Jimire, to **Pharse**, in 1 hour. Here there is a suspension bridge (2720 ft, 829 m) over the Kali Gandaki. Decide whether to cross it, depending on the weather and time of day and whether you want to be in the sun. Assuming you want to avoid the afternoon sun, your route will head north on the TR west bank and pass through the towns of Taremaregaon, Ratnaachaur, Lamogara, TAAgnebagar, and Jaremare, before coming to the Mayagdi Khola in 1½ **hours.** Here you cross the suspension bridge (2700 ft, 823 m) and reach **Beni,** the large town and administrative center for the Mayagdi District. The way west now heads up the Mayagdi Khola valley for several days before crossing the Jaljala to leave this major drainage system and enter that of the Bheri Khola. You could also continue north up the Kali Gandaki and reach Tatopani, with its hordes of trekkers, and go on to Thak Khola, between Annapurna and Dhaulagiri. This is described in chapter 6.

Proceed west from Beni up the left bank of the Mayagdi Khola, past a cable car over the river. The government buildings here were designed by the winner of an architectural competition held in Kathmandu. Pass many small villages, including Chutreni, Ghorsang, and Baguwa, to **Singhaa** (2800 ft, 914 m), reached in 1¼ **hours** from Beni. In **30 minutes,** reach the first houses of **Tatopani,** and after crossing a tributary, pass above a hot springs pool, where men bathe up to 4:00 P.M. and women after. Like similar places in other parts of the world, people with arthritis and other complaints have moved here to soak and soothe. The main part of town (2920 ft, 890 m) is **10 minutes** beyond. Below this part of town, by the river, are more hot springs emanating from the rocks, where you can wash. At the upper end of town there is a suspension bridge that you cross to the right and in **15 minutes** regain the northeast bank on another bridge to reach Simalchaur (3100 ft, 945 m).

Continue heading upvalley, staying on the left bank and not crossing any bridges over the main river, to reach **Babiachaur** (3220 ft, 981 m) in 1 hour. Upstream, pass through Ranamang, Shastradara, and Baloti to reach RataDhunga (meaning "red rock") in another **hour.** Continue on the same left bank, through Poteni, and reach the lone hut of Dharkharka in another **35 minutes,** where the trail now forks right to climb up above the huge landslide you have been seeing on the south bank. This slide rumbled for 5 minutes in September 1988, claiming the lives of over

100 people. The rock and debris washed across the river, taking out the trail on the north bank. Such major events are now considered more likely due to tectonic (mountain-building) forces than to deforestation. When I used to journey up this valley in the mid-1970s, there was a major slide before RataDhunga that I couldn't find in 1989. Nepalis are quick to rebuild the slides and reclaim farmland, so I expect that eventually even this scar will be invisible and the trail will not detour.

Nepali Cultural Groups: Hindu Castes

The Hindu castes are called by the general term *PahAARi* (people of the hills). They inhabit the middle hills and lower valleys, generally below 6000 ft (1800 m). Each caste has an ascribed profession, but many people no longer follow the rules.

High Castes
Today this group includes peasant farmers, civil servants, money lenders, and school teachers, as well as people following the traditional caste occupations.

Bahun (Brahman)—the traditional priest caste. In former times, the Brahmans did not handle plows or eat certain prohibited foods (e.g., onions, tomatoes, certain kinds of meat) or drink alcohol. These days, however, many of these prohibitions are ignored, even the rule against drinking. Some of these rules are still followed in the more remote and traditional rural areas. Brahmans can be grouped into those from the east (*Purbiya*) and those from the west (*Kumaon*). Offspring of irregular unions among Brahmans are termed *Jaishi Bahun.*

Chhetri—the traditional warrior caste. It includes much the same occupations as the Brahmans, as well as soldiers in the Gurkha armies. The King's family is *Thakuri,* a subcaste of *Chhetri.* The term *Matwali Chhetri* ("those who drink liquor") refers to western peoples who are not given the sacred thread characteristic of the "twice born" castes of Brahman and *Chhetri.*

Menial Castes
Many men and women of the three lower menial castes no longer pursue blacksmithing, shoemaking, or tailoring but work as day laborers on the land of others or as porters for large trekking parties or merchant-traders.

Damai or *Darji*—tailors and musicians for Hindu weddings and festivals

Kaami—ironworkers, toolmakers, and sometimes silversmiths and goldsmiths (*Sunar*)

Saarki—cobblers and leatherworkers

(These are the main castes found in the Nepali hills. Many other caste groups are found among the *Newar,* below, and in the Tarai regions.)

The detour climbs 300 ft (91 m) through terraces, crosses and follows an irrigation canal, contours, and then descends to the large town of **Darbang** (3520 ft, 1073 m) in **40 minutes.** You cross the Mayagdi Khola to the west (right) bank, and local villagers may collect a tax for porters crossing here. Go past the few more hotels in the village and head north to reach Phedi, the few houses at the foot of the climb to Dharapani, in **30 minutes.** Cross the tributary Daanga Khola on a suspension bridge upstream, or on rocks at low water, and pick up the trail that climbs the ridge. As you ascend, join a trail coming in from the right and reach the crest of the ridge. As you climb, on the right is subtropical forest and, on the drier left, chir pine. This results from the marked climatological changes on either side of the ridge. Reach the spectacularly situated town of **Dharapani** (5125 ft, 1562 m) in **1 hour.** Dhaulagiri is the massive mountain to the north, and off to the west is Gurja Himal. Between lie Dhaulagiri IV and V. Hope to get views (unfettered by clouds) here in the morning or evening. Don't despair, I had been by here several times in the mid-1970s, and it wasn't until recently that I saw the mountains not shackled by cloud.

The trail now contours high above the river, as it heads northwest toward the watershed. The views along this stretch are some of the finest in Nepal. Reach **Takum** (5500 ft, 1676 m), another idyllic setting, in **1 hour.** The predominant ethnic groups in this region are *Magar, Chhetri, Kaami, Damai,* and *Bahun.* Continue contouring through Sibang, and then climb up to Maachhim. As you round a bend by a *chautaaraa* (6600 ft, 2112 m) and begin to head northwest up the tributary Dara Khola, you can look north up the Mayagdi Khola valley, which drains the west side of Dhaulagiri. A strenuous high trek encircles the sixth highest mountain in the world by crossing French Pass at the headwaters of this valley.

Continue on to sprawling **Phaleagaon** (6200 ft, 1890 m) in **1½ hours,** where, at the outskirts, there is a recently constructed water mill run by an efficient turbine. During the trade embargo with India in 1989, the noisy diesel mills were laid to rest, and traditional mills flourished. As you head up, notice that you are at the altitude limit of rice cultivation. However, nearer to Jumla, it will be growing almost 2000 ft (610 m) higher! **Muna** (6460 ft, 1969 m), is **45 minutes** beyond. You have to take the uphill fork after you leave Phaleagaon, or you will pass below the village and head directly to the bridge over the Dara Khola. Across the valley is the spectacularly perched village of Dara.

Amphibians and Reptiles of the Subtropical Zone
(3300 to 6500 ft / 1000 to 2000 m in the West, to 5500 ft / 1700 m in the East)

Nepali amphibians and reptiles are primarily found in the warmer tropical and subtropical zones. A total of thirty-six species of amphibians, including frogs [*bhyaguto*], toads, newts, and a caecilian, have been recorded so far. One of the commonest is the aptly named skittering frog (*Rana cyanophlyctis*), which can float and skip over the water surface. The six-fingered frog (*Rana hexadactyla*) is the largest Nepali amphibian. Not aquatic, it is reported to feed on mice, shrews, birds, and lizards. In the breeding season it calls deep "oong-awang" throughout the night. Reptile species total eighty and include crocodiles, turtles, lizards, skinks, and geckos. Snakes [*sAAp, sarpa*] are elusive; most are nonpoisonous. One of the commonest is the buff-striped keelback (*Amphiesma stolata*), which occurs in grassy areas near cultivation. It is olive-green or brown above with black spots or bars intersected with buff stripes. Lizards [*chhepaaro*] are more obvious and can often be seen basking in the sun on stone walls or rocks. A familiar lizard is the Himalayan rock lizard (*Agama tuberculata*). It is coarsely scaled, has a long tail, and is generally colored brown with black spots; breeding males have blue throats.

Peoples of Central Nepal: *Magar*

The *Magar* are farmers and herdsmen who live along the tributaries of the Kali Gandaki River in the Myagdi District both north, west, and southwest of Beni. *Magar* villages situated under the Dhaulagiri Himal seem to cling like postage stamps to the high cliffs. In some regions, indigenous *Magar* call themselves by clan names, such as *Pun, Chantel, Kaiki,* and *Tarali. Pun Magar* are renowned for rock-cutting skills, which are visible along the Kali Gandaki river trail. Some of the more northerly trails were cut out of the cliffs in the 1950s by Tibetan refugee *Khamba. Chantel Magar,* who also dwell below the south face of the Dhaulagiri massif, are herdsmen and farmers who are noted also for their skills in local copper mining. The culture of the northernmost *Magar,* the *Tarali* of the Dolpo District, blends into that of the *BhoTiya.*

Reach the suspension bridge (6200 ft, 1990 m) over the Dara Khola in **15 minutes** and cross it to the left bank. Climb up to enter a side valley and reach the single house of Narja Khola (7060 ft, 2152 m) in **35 minutes.** Cross the tributary and reach a trail junction (7220 ft, 2201 m) **10 minutes** later. The right fork heads to Lulang, Gurjaakhaani, and the Gurja Himal region, but to head on to Dhorpatan, take the left fork. Pass above the houses of Lumsum to reach a hotel in **25 minutes** (7180 ft, 2188 m). Ask to find out whether the next village is occupied and whether food is available, if you need to. Cross the Dara Khola again in **20 minutes,** to the right bank, and head upstream to cross another tributary. Immediately turn left and begin to climb to **Moreni** (lowest at 7820 ft, 2383 m). The few houses, scattered 700 ft (213 m) up the hillside, are reached in some **40 minutes,** and they may be unoccupied in the middle of winter as the people descend to Lumsum. There may be little water along the way, so fill up at the valley bottom. Moreni is the last place to get food before Dhorpatan.

The trail heads southwest, reaching prickly-leaved oak forests, then rhododendron and birch higher up. After **2½ hours,** you reach a cluster of prayer flags and a *chorten* (11,200 ft, 3414 m). Continue to the west (don't take the left fork), pass a small spring, and reach the broad, flat plateau of Jaljala a few minutes later at a *chautaaraa.* The panorama from here takes in Machhapuchhre all the way to Churen Himal. Sunsets are supreme. There are some *goTh,* used in the monsoon by people from Muna as they pasture their animals on the lush grass.

From Jaljala, follow the trail on the left (south) side of the plateau, and don't descend into the river valley to the north. Descend some 15 minutes to reach a small saddle point (11,000 ft, 3353 m) that is the actual watershed between the Kali Gandaki and the Bheri–Karnali. Head for the valley V shape, through the pastures, and pass below a group of *goTh* to reach a lone stone one in **30 minutes** from the *chautaaraa.* Beyond, cross to the right bank of the Uttar Ganga ("north river"), which you will follow to Dhorpatan, and continue downvalley. Don't cross the cantilever bridge over the river 30 minutes beyond, but enjoy the rhododendron and juniper forests on the north side of the valley. Reach an open area with *goTh* in **1½ hours** from the lone stone *goTh.* GurjaakoT (9900 ft, 3017 m), the next cluster of *goTh* on this side of the valley, is **20 minutes** beyond. From here, cross several tributaries of the Simudar Khola on wooden bridges. As a variant side trip, you could head up this tributary valley, cross a

Gurja Himal from Jaljala

pass and get to Gurjaakhaani, and then head back to Lulang and Muna.

In **30 minutes** from the Simudar Khola, head upstream in another tributary valley to cross the Gur Gad to its right bank on a suspension bridge. Rejoin the main valley, and reach the beginning of the broad Dhorpatan Valley. The way keeps to the drier north side and reaches **Chentung** (9660 ft, 2944 m) and a few hotels in another **hour.** The main Tibetan village is across the tributary. The Bon-po *gompa* of this village, behind you on the hillside, follows the tradition that predated the introduction of Buddhism to Tibet. It has been much changed, so it is difficult to tell adherents apart. The best way is to see which direction they spin their prayer wheels and circumambulate *mani* walls.

Continue west and reach Nauthar, also called Chisopani, in **35 minutes.** Here Nepalis come up from the south in the summer to grow potatoes and pasture animals. This agropastoral style of life is followed by many Nepalis in these parts as they farm the lowlands in the winter, grow rice in the summer, and move up with their animals to the high country in the monsoon. Cross the next tributary and go on through another Tibetan settlement before descending to the flat area called Giraaund (9325 ft, 2842 m), meaning "ground," the local term for an airstrip. Reach it in another **30 minutes.** The airstrip is overgrown with vegetation; planes haven't landed here for several years. Before you reach the flats, pass below the Wildlife Conservation and Hunting Office, where they will ask to see your permits. They monitor the trophy hunting for blue sheep that goes on north of here.

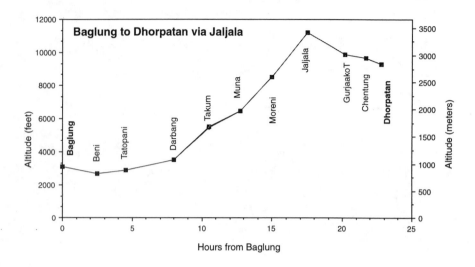

Baglung to Dhorpatan via Jaljala

Hours from Baglung

AROUND DHORPATAN

Dhorpatan is the name of the area, an unusually broad, flat valley (*paaTan*) in this rugged hill country. It was once a lake that was filled in. Many Nepalis from villages to the east, south, and west live here during the summer months, when they grow potatoes and pasture animals. Their settlements are seen along the perimeter of the valley, especially on its southern aspect, and at Nauthar. When Tibetan refugees were streaming over the hills during the Chinese takeover of 1959–60, many were directed to settle in this valley by leaflet maps dropped out of airplanes. Thus began one of the four original Tibetan refugee camps set up by the Swiss in the early 1960s. While many Tibetans moved to business centers and prospered, a few remained here, content in this remoter realm of Nepal. The two years I lived here were one of the best times of my life.

Although there are few views from the valley floor (Annapurna can be seen some 35 mi or 56 km to the east), easy climbs of the surrounding hills provide unparalleled views. You can travel a few days to the north into blue sheep country or up into the snows of the western Dhaulagiri range. The base camps of the various expeditions at the head of the Ghustung Khola are worth visiting. Also, the route northwest to Dolpo will be described. Food and shelter must be carried for all these trips to the north.

To the west and northwest live the *Kham Magar,* an ethnic group with strong animistic and shamanistic traditions. Food and shelter are difficult to obtain in this area and are best carried. A 4- to 5-day circuit through this region can be most interesting. After a long day down the Uttar Ganga, you reach the villages of Taka and Shera, where the flat-roofed houses are reminiscent of Thak Khola or of areas farther west. Cross the ridge up the tributary valley to the north and descend to Hukum (Hugaon), and go beyond to Maikot, on the north side of the Pelma Khola, in another very long day. The third day takes you through Puchhargaon and Yamakhar, where you meet the trail described below to Dolpo, which you can backtrack to Dhorpatan.

Those with less time should at least walk up one of the hills surrounding the valley for a view. The ridge crest directly south of the airstrip is the easiest viewpoint and takes less than 2 hours via one of its north-facing spurs. The view from here in clear weather extends beyond Langtang in the east! The hill to the north of the valley (13,600 ft, 4145 m) can be reached in 3 to 4 hours from the airstrip. Surtibang, the "writing desk" hill to the southwest, is an excellent viewpoint. Reach it by heading west for 30 minutes as the valley narrows to a bridge over the Uttar Ganga. Cross and ascend to the top (13,300 ft, 4054 m), in 4 hours from the airstrip. Hiunchuli Patan is visible to the west. Finally, the highest of the peaks surrounding the valley, Phagune Dhuri (15,500 ft, 4724 m), lying to the northwest, can be reached from the Phagune Danda pass, which is described in the route to Dolpo.

BAGLUNG TO DHORPATAN, AVOIDING JALJALA

An alternative, less scenic route from Baglung to Dhorpatan is suitable when snow blocks the route over Jaljala. It will be described very briefly, as few trekkers take it. From **Baglung**, walk west on the main street. Leave the town and contour close to the Khanti Khola. Reach Khare (3450 ft, 1052 m) in **1 hour**. Pass through **Dobila**, Biun, Tarakasi, and Dokapani to a notch (7100 ft, 2164 m) in **3¼ hours**. Take the left fork, which drops a bit, to Ragini, and then the left fork to Gasgas (5575 ft, 1700 m) in **1 hour**. Cross the Chundi Khola (4650 ft, 1417 m) to the north (right) bank in **30 minutes** and go downstream to Narethanti. Cross the next suspension bridge beyond the town to the south (left) bank and follow the river to **Galkot HaTiya** (4075 ft, 1242 m) in **1¼ hours**.

Shortly beyond the bazaar, cross a bridge to the north (right) bank to reach Banyan in **30 minutes**. Then cross a small tributary from the north to reach the Bas Khola (3850 ft, 1173 m) in another **30 minutes**. Cross again to the south (left) bank and reach Potsua. Do not cross either of the next two suspension bridges over the river, now called the Daran Khola, but reach Kanebas in **45 minutes**. Ascend to Wamiukaalo (3775 ft, 1151 m) in **1½ hours**. Climb for **30 minutes** to a notch in the ridge at Wamimaidang (4550 ft, 1387 m). Descend the south side of the ridge and, in **45 minutes,** take the right fork north to **Wamitaksar** (2900 ft, 884 m), some **15 minutes** beyond. Descend for **30 minutes** to the junction of the Daran Khola with the Bari Gad. Head northwest up the TL of the Bari Gaad (*Gaad* means river in parts of the west) to **Rangshi** (2575 ft, 785 m) in **30 minutes**. Cross the Labdi Khola, pass through Balua (2700 ft, 823 m), and reach **Kara Bazaar** (2850 ft, 869 m) in **2 hours**. Continue up the east bank of the river through Kala, cross the Bing Khola, pass through **Bingetti** (3400 ft, 1036 m), and cross a tributary to the east, the Taman Khola, to reach **Burtibang** (3600 ft, 1097 m) in **3½ hours**. Continue upstream on the Bhuji Khola, as it is called in the continuation of the valley northeast, cross to the west (TR) bank, and reach **Dogadi** (4775 ft, 1455 m) in **1¼ hours**. Continue upstream, cross to the east bank (5200 ft, 1585 m) at **half an hour**, and reach **Bobang** (5800 ft, 1768 m) in an **hour**. Ascend past the school house and recross to the west bank to reach **Sukurdung** (6700 ft, 2042 m) in an **hour**. Climb through prickly-leaved oak forest, cross and recross the river, and reach **Dowal** (7600 ft, 2316 m) in **1½ hours**. This is the last permanent settlement on this side of the pass. Ascend crossing a series of six or so bridges over the stream, and reach a pass (9625 ft, 2934 m) at the Dhorpatan Valley to the north in **2 to 3 hours**. Head downstream (west) for **half an hour**, reach a bridge at Nabe, and cross the Uttar Ganga to the TR north bank. You can proceed north toward the Jaljala or east toward hotels and the settlements of Dhorpatan.

Those wishing to make a brief circuit from Dhorpatan and not head north could follow the preceding descriptions in reverse and return to Baglung or head south to Ourli Khola, crossing the Bari Gad Khola and climbing up to RiRi Bazaar and the road. This would take 4 days, a pleasant journey through western hills. It could be made more interesting by heading out of the river bottom to spend some days in *Magar* country.

Dhorpatan to Jumla through Dolpo
(Map No. 9, Page 333)

This section describes the long route to Jumla through the recently opened southern part of the Dolpo District. A side trip to the pristine lake at Phoksumdo, coupled with the crossing of Kaagmaara La (a high pass) to avoid backtracking, is described. Trekking parties are required to be self-sufficient in food and fuel and to go through a trekking agency. In the monsoon, you might be able to hire horses at Dhorpatan to carry loads to Tarakot.

DHORPATAN TO DUNAI

The first part of the trip crosses a major ridge to reach the Pelma Khola and then crosses another ridge to reach the same river system higher up. Then the crest of this part of the Himalaya is crossed to reach Dolpo and the upper reaches of the Thulo Bheri river system. There are only two small, poor villages along this 4- to 5-day walk.

The description starts at **Giraaund,** just down from the Wildlife Conservation and Hunting Office. Cross a small stream and climb up a short hill to Shelpaki, the houses spread out on a shelf above the valley floor, and continue west. You see a low-lying notch to the northwest and fork right about 15 minutes beyond Giraaund. If you miss it, there is a more direct trail up to the notch, and you can go cross-country up to the trail that climbs more gradually to it. Reach the notch (10,120 ft, 3084 m), **1 hour** from Giraaund. Descend slightly to a plateau, and head toward the main Phagune Khola valley heading north up to the Phagune Danda pass. You proceed up the east (left) side of this valley lower down, reaching the main river in another **1½ hours,** crossing to the west (right) bank at 12,020 ft (3664 m) in another **30 minutes.** You then leave the river and climb up the valley wall to reach the pass (13,300 ft, 4054 m) in another **45 minutes.** Hopefully, weather will permit you to enjoy the panorama from Putha Hiunchuli to the north to Dhaulagiri in the east.

Look for blue sheep in the early morning and late afternoon to the north of the pass as you contour and descend in open country. In 1 hour, round the bend to the west and you can see the isolated peak of Hiunchuli Patan; then descend into rhododendron and birch forest. Reach a *goTh* and then descend a spur into the Ghustung Valley, ending the steep portion at Thankur, a broad, flat valley (10,800 ft, 3292 m) with several *goTh*, in almost **2 hours** from the pass. There are few suitable campsites for another 3 hours and, even there, water may be lacking.

Cross the small stream at Thankur to the left bank and head downstream on the left bank of the main Ghustung Khola valley. Descend through a magnificent forest to reach the river in **70 minutes,** and cross it on a cantilever bridge (9100 ft, 2774 m). Climb steeply on the much drier north side to the ridge crest, passing a few streams,

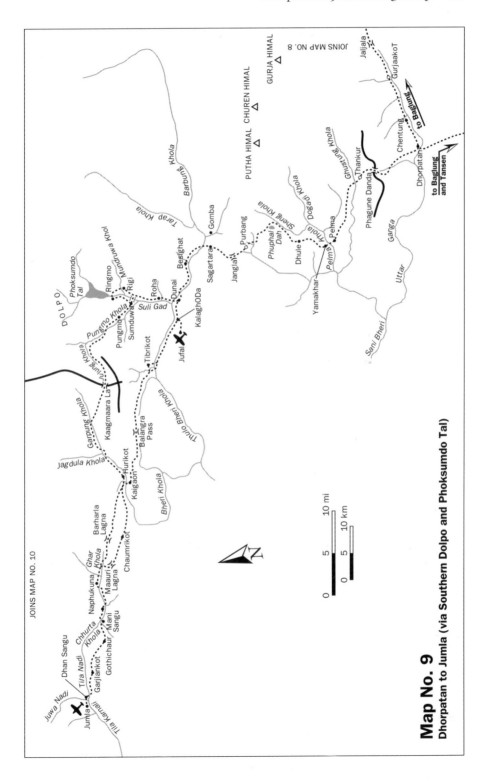

Map No. 9
Dhorpatan to Jumla (via Southern Dolpo and Phoksumdo Tal)

which may be dry in the spring. The trail heads west and keeps high to reach an open area and *goTh* frames (Kami Danda, 10,280 ft, 3134 m) in **1¾ hours** from the river. In another **45 minutes,** after a descent, reach a *chorten* (9800 ft, 2987 m) and look down upon the only villages for a few days, and gaze north toward the pass you will cross. Continue down to reach **Pelma** (8300 ft, 2530 m) in **45 minutes.** This flat-roofed village and the one across the valley are populated by *Kham Magar,* a fascinating ethnic group that continues shamanistic traditions closest to the classic Northern Siberian custom.

Questions to Ponder: Illness

Do you see a great deal of illness as you travel? Is this what you expected? Among which age group is the greatest sickness and mortality? Whom do you think are the greatest consumers of health care? What are the greatest obstacles to better health among the Nepalis? What practices do the people undertake that promote good health? Are there differences in this regard among ethnic groups? What are the most constructive steps that can be taken to improve the health of the Nepalis?

Descend to the gorge of the Pelma Khola and cross to the right bank (7620 ft, 2322 m) in another **15 minutes.** Ascend slightly and head downstream to pick up a trail after crossing a tributary that climbs steeply to Yamakhar (8200 ft, 2499 m) in **30 minutes.** Near the top of the village, the trail to Jangla forks right, while that to Puchhargaon and Maikot heads left and downstream. Take the right fork and switchback some forty-six times; the trail then levels out somewhat and ascends to the north to reach Askyur (9660 ft, 2944 m) in **1 hour.** Here there are fields and *goTh* tended by *Kham* villagers from Maikot. Climb for 15 minutes (10,240 ft, 3121 m) to traverse over to a ridge, rather than climbing up farther. Descend and wind around the hillside to the left and traverse across it; then join a more prominent trail that descends steeply at first, then more gradually to cross a tributary stream 20 minutes later. Ascend gradually to reach the crest of a spur above Shengam, where there are some fields and *goTh* (10,180 ft, 3103 m) tended by Pelma people.

Contour, then descend through a deciduous forest into a flat draw with a stream that you follow up on its right bank. Cross and recross it several times in a cold, mysterious, narrow canyon with caves that could be used as shelter in a pinch. End up ascending on the right bank to reach **Dhule** (10,920 ft, 3328 m), **2 hours** from Askyur. This semipermanent settlement serves the Nepali traffic over the Jangla, and *Kham* people from Maikot and Pelma stay here, except in the dead of winter. There are possible sites for camping. There is no water for a long stretch beyond.

Climb up another 400 ft (122 m) to a notch, then traverse left, and reach a ridge crest, which you follow north out of the woods to reach a *chautaaraa* (12,420 ft, 3785 m) in **1 hour.** Traverse northwest across a hillside, and then climb to a pass (12,900 ft, 3932 m) in **1 hour.** Descend into the wild Sheng Khola valley, passing rock overhangs that could be used for camping, and reach a tributary (12,140 ft, 3700 m) in **45 minutes.** Look for blue sheep near the cliffs. Along the west bank (right), pass above a flat area that is suitable for camping (12,800 ft, 3901 m) in **1 hour.** About **15 minutes** beyond, take the left fork (12,940 ft, 3950 m). The way up the valley floor would cross the river beyond and head east over the crest to Gurjaakhaani. Ascend to the north for **45 minutes** to reach a crest

(14,160 ft, 4316 m) with Phuphal Dah, a small pond, just below.

Head northwest in open country over a small pass and then on the left bank of a stream to reach a saddle (14,760 ft, 4499 m) in **45 minutes.** Descend into the drainage system of the Saunre Khola, reaching the major tributary at 13,000 ft (3962 m) in 1¼ **hours.** Cross it to the right and begin the final climb to the Jangla. A **10-minute** climb brings you to Purbang (13,160 ft, 4011 m), where there is a steel rigging system for a *goTh* that was installed around 1975 by the Nepali government as a shelter for Nepalis crossing the pass. The metal roof blew off ten years later. This entire area is monsoon pasturage.

Climb up to another crest (Majala, 14,200 ft, 4328 m), descend slightly to the last tributary, and be sure to fill every container with water here. Ascend to the Jangla (14,840 ft, 4523 m), reached in **2 hours** from Purbang if everyone is well acclimatized. Add a stone to the cairn as you enter the Dolpo District. Descend to the north, keeping to the east side of the valley, heading over to a notch (13,300 ft, 4054 m) in **1 hour.** There is another, less-used trail forking left, up high, that heads off northwest to reach Dunai.

Descend steeply northeast from the notch and enter an oak, then pine, forest, reaching Samtiling (9960 ft, 3036 m) in 1½ **hours,** where there is a *gomba.* This region, called Tichurong, is populated by people calling themselves *Magar,* with those in three villages speaking Kaike. (Read Jim Fisher's *Trans Himalayan Traders* for more information on their life.) Descend to **Sagartara** (9120 ft, 2780 m) in **20 minutes.** Below to the east is strategically situated Tarakot, once the fort town controlling access through here, and across the tributary valley to the east is Gomba, with its monastery. Both are worth visiting. Notice that the terraces are constructed differently from those you left. Rice, needing irrigation, can't be grown here.

Questions to Ponder: Government Influences

What evidence is there of governmental influence in remote areas? Any signs of political parties? Slogans painted on stones and walls, or symbols of the parties? Nepal is experiencing a growth of Non-Governmental Organizations (NGOs). What evidence do you see of these?

Can you envisage any recording of vital events (births, deaths)? Do you see many calendars in use? How many of the Nepali people you pass know the day, date, and year? How do people keep track of time?

There is a high route from here that goes north up the Tarap Khola to Tarap (in 2 to 3 days) and then west over two high passes to Phoksumdo Tal. Permission for this is occasionally granted to trekkers.

To continue on to Dunai, you descend to the main river and follow it west. From Sagartara, begin at the walnut trees below town and fork left to traverse west and drop down, passing above Ruma and reaching the valley floor (7800 ft, 2377 m), where there is a police check post, in **30 minutes.** Head downstream on the left bank of the Thulo Bheri Khola for a few minutes to reach a massive concrete suspension bridge (7680 ft, 2341 m), which you cross to the right bank, and then head downstream. Keep to the valley floor and descend close to the torrent. There are several possible campsites along here. Reach the Rishi Khola from the north in 1½ **hours.** Cross it either here or upstream, and reach the few houses of **Besighat**

(7500 ft, 2286 m). Head west in a pleasant pine forest and reach a cantilever bridge (7140 ft, 2176 m) in **1¼ hours,** which you cross to the left bank of the Thulo Bheri. Head downstream, passing Menosara in another **30 minutes,** to reach **Dunai** (6920 ft, 2109 m), the administrative headquarters for the Dolpo District. You will note that there is quite a different atmosphere in government towns from that in peasant villages.

From Dunai there are two route choices, both of which are described. To go to Phoksumdo Tal and beyond, over Kaagmaara La toward Jumla, you cross the river and climb up the valley to reach the Suli Gad valley, which you follow to the lake. To head directly to Jumla, continue downvalley on the left bank of the Thulo Bheri. This will also take you to the Jufal airstrip (called Dolpa on RNAC schedules). Snow can make the crossing of Kaagmaara La impossible and can force you to backtrack to Dunai to take the lower route. This description follows below.

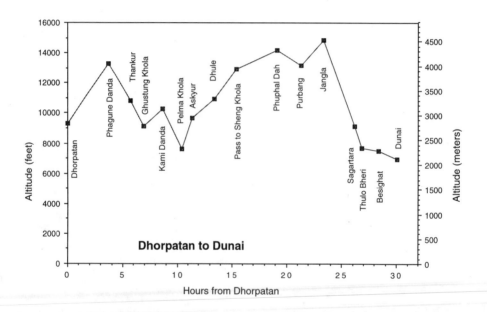

DUNAI TO PHOKSUMDO TAL AND OVER KAAGMAARA LA TO JUMLA

> *These villagers dwell in one of the most glorious places on earth without being remotely aware of it. But how should they be? It is we who have somehow grown weary of the benefits of modern life, who can tarry in such a place with keen enjoyment. We imagine that we should be content with the simplicity of their life, scheming how we would improve this within proper limits.*
>
> David Snellgrove, *Himalayan Pilgrimage,* speaking of Phoksumdo Tal

Cross one of the bridges at Dunai to the right bank of the Thulo Bheri and head downstream, forking right after 10 minutes to climb up to a spur (8180 ft, 2493 m) in **1 hour** from Dunai. Enter the Suli Gad valley and traverse through sage, bypassing a few Himalaya deodar trees as you contour into a tributary valley and see the small village of Parla across on the north side. Cross the stream (8220 ft, 2505 m) in this valley in **30 minutes** and get water here. Climb, rather than contour, to the village. Enter the next steep tributary valley upstream, that of the Phokso Khola, and reach the few houses of Pun Alduwa, and Eklai Tigho just beyond. Finding water is a problem for camping here. Cross the Phokso Khola in **1½ hours** from the previous tributary (9400 ft, 2865 m). Reach the outskirts of **Roha** (9660 ft, 2944 m) in **15 minutes.** This village is populated by *Matwali Chhetri*, who have more animistic traditions than the lower-elevation Hindu peoples. Notice the protector deities, called *komba*, on the houses. There is a Devi temple up above the village. Water is difficult here, too.

Pick up the trail at the lower west side of town and contour north, passing the stream, which is the town's water supply! Fork left (9520 ft, 2902 m) in **30 minutes** in an open area, and continue, rounding a bend into a glade with spruce and cypress trees in a steep tributary valley. Descend to a sturdy cantilever bridge, which is crossed to the right bank (8660 ft, 2639 m). Just beyond is **Anke,** the few buildings at the entrance to Shey Phoksumdo National Park (8720 ft, 2658 m). Pay the fee here.

Climb up and traverse into the main valley and reach the few Tibetan houses of Chepka (8600 ft, 2621 m) in **45 minutes.** The trail leaves the valley floor in less

You may be the center of attention in Rohagaon or other less visited places.

than 30 minutes, climbs up, then enters a tributary valley, and descends under a large, dripping overhang to cross the stream (9360 ft, 2853 m) in **1½ hours** from Chepka. Just beyond is an overhang suitable for shelter but too small for camping. Regain the main valley and ascend to 10,540 ft (3212 m) in an open, wider valley, where there are a few houses below, after **2 hours.** Enter a birch glade and descend steeply to reach the river and a rock causeway. Continue upstream to a bridge (9800 ft, 2987 m), across the Suli Gad, in another **hour.** If you cross it and head downstream a bit, you reach the few houses of RiAAjic.

Questions to Ponder: Families and Households

Who makes up the household? What happens to old people, the mentally retarded, the physically handicapped? How much evidence of alcoholism do you see? How much leisure time do people have and how do they spend it? Is there much obesity? How are bodies disposed of? Can you identify a person's caste or ethnic group without asking? What factors go into your hunch? (Facial and body hair? Facial shape? Eye folds? Jewelry? Dress? The way people interact with others? Where they locate their village? The kind of work they do?)

How big are families? Where is everyone? Why are family sizes large in remote hill areas? What value to a family does having more children bring? How much migration outside the village for wage labor is there? Has this changed recently? What will higher education do to this process?

To continue to Phoksumdo Tal, head upstream on the east (left) bank, passing a field on the left in **45 minutes** that is used for camping by trekkers (9940 ft, 3030 m). A minute north of this, find a little wooden bench with a big, flat rock as a backrest, and enjoy this seat!

Five minutes farther, come to a major junction, where the Pungmo Khola, which drains Kaagmaara La to the west, joins the Suli Gad, which drains Phoksumdo. You can head up either the east or west bank of the Suli Gad valley. The west is more direct, whereas the east gives a different perspective on Nepal's biggest waterfall, which drains the lake. The west bank route also passes through an interesting village. Go up one side and come down the other! Sumduwa, the headquarters of the national park and an army encampment, is a short climb up after crossing the river here. The way up the east and down the west is described.

Fork right at the sign by the bridge over the Suli Gad above the confluence. Head up its east (left) bank, passing another bridge over the river 10 minutes beyond. This is the place to cross if you want to ascend the west side of the valley. Shortly beyond is perhaps a better campsite than the one below the wooden bench because of views to the north. Traverse above some fields and climb up to a notch with a *chorten.* Here the trail heads east into the Mundruwa Khola valley, and soon you can look back and see the source of the roar, the magnificent waterfall. Continue along to **Rigi** (10,800 ft, 3292 m), **1¼ hours** from the confluence. It is also called Morwa, and Mondro, and provides a winter retreat for some people from Ringmo at the lake. The trail to Tarap heads east up the south side of the valley, reaching it after crossing two high passes, Baga La (16,569 ft, 5050 m) and Numa La (16,897 ft, 5150 m), in 2 days.

Hemp in the Himalaya

Hemp grows as a weed in a wide range of territory in Nepal. Although known as a source of intoxicants, and occasionally used this way by some people in Nepal society, it serves other purposes as well. Seeds from the female plant are collected and pressed into oil in large hollowed out wooden trays. The oil is used for cooking commonly out west and it can also be used for making soap and as a liniment. Male plants growing in hot humid regions of the hills provide the best fiber. They are harvested toward the end of the monsoon; the stems are left to dry, then soaked, and the fibers pulled out with the teeth. They are then dried in the sun, beaten to soften them, and spun. Hemp is then woven into ropes and twine or made into a type of toga.

Descend **15 minutes** to reach the Mundruwa Khola and cross it to the north (right) bank (10,700 ft, 3261 m). Just beyond, climb, head downvalley slightly, and less than 10 minutes from the crossing fork right to climb. The left fork takes a lower route to the lake. Climb steeply and, in 30 minutes, reach a trail joining from the east. Gain a crest at 12,320 ft (3755 m) in **1 hour.** Here a high trail (mentioned earlier) from the east joins. Traverse north on the west side of a small valley of pine and juniper. Reach the height of land (12,460 ft, 3798 m), and see the falls again and, just beyond, the lake. Cross the river draining the lake (11,900 ft, 3627 m) in another **30 minutes,** and climb up through the entrance *chorten* to **Ringmo** (11,940 ft, 3639 m) at its southern end. The local name for it is Tso-wa, or "lakeside."

The unearthly, azure blue waters of the Phoksumdo Tal change color constantly with the sun and clouds. Majestic small summits ring the water, and the entire area affords a peacefulness found in few other places. There is a Bon-po monastery by the water to the southeast of the lake that must be visited.

How the Yak Got His Long Hair and Why the Buffalo Has So Little and Is Always Looking Back

Kami Temba told me why the water buffalo has so little hair and is always looking over his shoulder searching. Once, the water buffalo was hairy, was a good friend of the yak, and they both lived in the lower regions. They both loved salt, but there wasn't much around. The yak said he would go to Tibet to get some if the water buffalo would loan him his hair so he could survive in the cold. The water buffalo agreed. The yak went off and never returned. To this day, the water buffalo holds his head up, searching around, awaiting the return of the yak with his hair and salt.

The trail to Shey is fixed to struts on the west side of the lake, but local officials will not permit you to venture forth on it. So, alas, you currently have to retrace your steps. To head down the west side of the valley, leave Ringmo by going past the school and its entrance *chorten* up on the right bank of the river. Follow the river, and look for musk deer in the forest before reaching an open crest (12,380 ft, 3773 m) with views of the falls after **35 minutes.** Descend to the winter houses of Palam (10,000 ft, 3048 m) in another **35 minutes.** Reach the park headquarters at Sumduwa (10,260 ft, 3127 m) in another **hour.** If you are not ascending Kaagmaara La there is little reason to go to the headquarters, and you could cross back over to the east (left) bank of the Suli Gad.

From Sumduwa, head up the north (left) bank of the Pungmo Khola for **1¼ hours** to reach **Pungmo** (10,840 ft, 3304 m). This is the last inhabited place before the pass, though in the warmer months people will be found up quite high. Don't head up in bad weather unless the entire party is experienced and well equipped. A further **30 minutes** beyond is KAAru (11,200 ft, 3414 m), with substantial houses. In another **45 minutes** is a lone house in a flat area that makes a good campsite. Cross to the west (right) bank of the Pungmo Khola (12,020 ft, 3664 m) **15 minutes** beyond, and continue upvalley, keeping to the same side. Head west beyond the confluence of the Pungmo Khola from the north, keeping to what is now called the Julung Khola. Reach Phedi, the bottom of the hill, and summer pastures (13,950 ft, 4252 m), in **2 hours.** There may be blue sheep along here. The route now heads south and climbs to Kaagmaara La (16,780 ft, 5114 m), in another **3 hours.** *Kaag* means "crow" in Nepali, while *maara,* "death"; Khumbu's Gorak Shep is Sherpa for the same thing.

From the pass, the descent angles down along a rocky slope into the valley of the Garpung Khola, keeping to its south (left) bank. There is a campsite (another "Phedi") at 13,120 ft (3999 m) in **2½ hours.** Continue to the bridge (12,150 ft, 3703 m) near the treeline, crossing the river to its right, in **1 hour.** Recross it again (10,400 ft, 3170 m) in another **hour.** Head downstream, below the junction with the Jagdula Khola, and recross it (9450 ft, 2880 m), to the north (right) bank in **45 minutes.** At the national park boundary, along the Jagdula Khola, there is an army camp with a radio. Another **2 hours** along the Jagdula Khola valley will bring you **Hurikot** (8500 ft, 2591 m).

There is a choice of routes at this point, depending on whether you want to take a direct, uninhabited, ridge route to cross the *lekh* at the Barharla Lagna, also called the Barbaria Lekh (14,050 ft, 4282 m), or a lower, longer, more populated route to cross at the Maauri Lagna (12,850 ft, 3916 m). Certainly in the middle of winter, the lower crossing is preferred, while the higher would be better in the monsoon. The lower is described.

From Hurikot, follow the river valley to the bridge across from **Kaigaon** (8740 ft, 2664 m) in **45 minutes.** There is a school, up the way. Keep to the right bank of the Jagdula Khola and pass by Topgaon, then on to Majgaon (9560 ft, 2914 m), at the school, in **1 hour** from the bridge. These villages are all in the **Rimi** village development council. Reach Jharkot, and continue on in a tributary valley to reach a notch (10,280 ft, 3133 m) in **1¼ hours** from the school. Descend northwest in another tributary valley, cross the stream, and reach **Chaumrikot** (10,200 ft, 3109 m) in **45 minutes.** Keep traversing west, crossing tributaries, then head northwest and climb up toward the pass. Leave behind the views of the Dhaulagiri peaks, and reach the Maauri Lagna ("bee pass") (12,850 ft, 3916 m), in **3 hours** from Chaumrikot. Here you leave behind the Bheri drainage and enter that of the Karnali. These rivers join down in the Surkhet District. Way off to the northwest is the massive peak of Saipal. To the northeast are the lower summits of Kang Chunne and Wedge Peak.

Descend steeply to the north on switchbacks and reach the Ghar Khola (11,540 ft, 3517 m) in **30 minutes.** Cross it to the right bank. The trail over the Barharla

Lagna comes in here. Head downvalley, contouring then angling out of the bottom of the valley to the north, crossing a tributary, the Gumaiya Khola, to the right bank, and come up to a fairly flat area suitable for camping (11,060 ft, 3371 m) in **30 minutes.** Continue downvalley, soon passing another campsite, and reach **Chhurta** (also called **Naphukuna,** 10,200 ft, 3109 m), a Tibetan *drokpa* (nomad) village, in another **hour.** The *gomba* above here is worth a visit. Just beyond, pass through more of the town, which looks distinctively Nepali in contrast, to reach a bridge over the Chhurta Khola in **30 minutes** (9700 ft, 2956 m). There are spots for camping here.

Cross the river to the left bank and continue downstream, not taking any uphill forks or crossing the river again until you reach a log bridge (9240 ft, 2816 m), **1 hour** later. Cross to the right bank and reach Mani Sangu (9100 ft, 2774 m) in **20 minutes.** Don't cross the bridge here, but continue on the right bank of the main valley, which heads northwest and opens up delightfully. Cross to the left bank on a large cantilever bridge (9020 ft, 2749 m) in **40 minutes.** Continue downstream, and soon head west up the right bank of the Gothichaur Khola a short way. Cross to the left bank via a little island (9000 ft, 2743 m), where there are a series of mills, in **15 minutes.**

Questions to Ponder: Farming

Some terraces are buttressed by rocks and others are not. Why? What crops are planted there? What crop patterns produce maximum productivity for the land? Do you see evidence of periodic slash-and-burn agriculture? What are the altitude limits for certain crops and animals? For what purposes are irrigation systems used, besides watering crops? How are they controlled? Do most of the farmers own the land they are working, or are they sharecroppers? Does having many children contribute to the family labor force? You often see fodder being carried to feed animals. Is its harvesting haphazard or on a planned basis? Do households have private or community forests they use? What is the situation regarding firewood? Does the food they produce last year-round, or do they have to supplement by migrating out to find work? What kind of outside work do they engage in?

Head up the valley and emerge from the narrow canyon into a broad valley. Head northwest to pass above the Gothichaur Sheep Breeding Farm, which has been active since the early 1970s trying to introduce Australian breeds of sheep and improved grass. Years ago, planes landed here. Before you leave this area, sit and gaze at the solitude around. Just before the fence for the farm, below you, is a pillar that is hundreds of years old. Some say it dates from the Hindu epic the *Mahabharata* and was built by Panchpanta, perhaps 2000 years ago. Gothichaur used to be a grazing area and is remarkable in being so verdant yet unsettled.

Ascend to a pass (9723 ft, 2963 m) in **1 hour** from the river crossing. Head northwest in another idyllic pastoral valley and in **1 hour** join a major trail from the right that comes from Gothigaon. In a few minutes, reach the first few houses of **Garjlankot** (8600 ft, 2621 m), and cross to the left bank there. The main valley of the Babila Khola enters to the north. Traverse on the south side of this valley. Note that they grow rice at this altitude—quite a contrast with the regions south of the

Himalaya! Continue through more houses of Garjlankot, especially a cluster situated strategically in a notch near the center of the valley, reached in **30 minutes**. The main river is called the Tila Nadi here; you follow it to Jumla. Meet electric poles and wires, and pass through Dipalgaon (7840 ft, 2390 m) after **45 minutes**.

Cross the Tila Nadi to the right in **30 minutes** and come up to the small town of Dhan Sangu, situated at the junction with the Juwa Nadi. Here there are several Hindu temples, common at river junctions, which are considered sacred. They are to the deities Shiva, Ganesh, and Mahadev. You are not likely to see the *komba*, or protector deity, on houses anymore. Continue through the suburbs to **Jumla** (7640 ft, 2329 m) in another **30 minutes**. Just before, at the few houses of Kali Khola, if you fork right, you will climb up to the airstrip (7660 ft, 2335 m). Here there are hotels, shops, and a hospital, as well as a strong government and development presence.

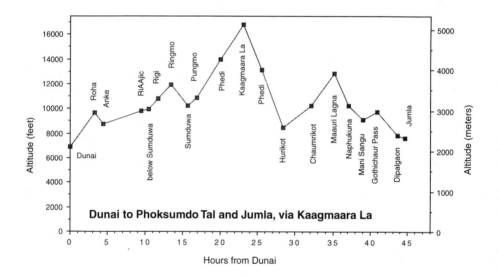

Dunai to Phoksumdo Tal and Jumla, via Kaagmaara La

DUNAI TO KAIGAON VIA TIBRIKOT

To take the low route to Kaigaon, and then on to Jumla, do not cross the bridge at Dunai. If you are backtracking from Phoksumdo Tal, do not try to cross the Suri Gad above its confluence with the Bheri (there is a bridge there), but retrace your steps to Dunai. The trail to Tibrikot on the south side of the valley is much easier. The route heads up the Bheri to a tributary and follows that valley up across a pass and down into the next drainage system.

From Dunai, head northwest along the sandy left bank of the Bheri Khola, and reach the few houses of Dhupichaur, named after the cypress trees near the river, in **30 minutes**. Pass through Rupcheghat at the crossing of the Rup Gad, and then come to the few houses of **KalaghODa** (6740 ft, 2054 m) in less than **1 hour**. Here the trail to the airstrip at Jufal forks left and climbs to reach it in 1½ hours. But keep to the barren valley floor, pass Bhertigaon on an alluvial flat, and eventually reach the few houses of Supani (6660 ft, 2030 m) after **2½ hours**.

There is a choice of trails beyond here. One goes to Likhu and avoids Tibrikot, whereas the other goes to this historically strategic site. The Tibrikot trail is described. Reach a new suspension bridge (6600 ft, 2012 m), and cross it to the

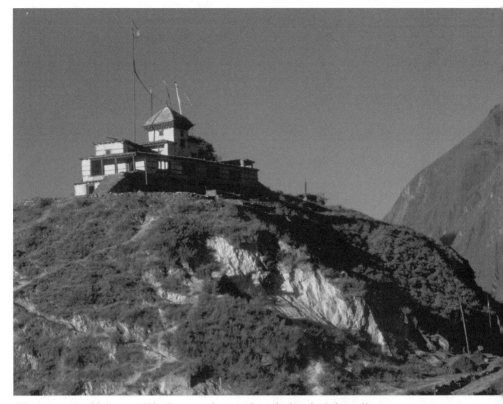

The strategic old fort at Tibrikot stands guard at the head of the valley.

right bank of the Thulo Bheri. Fork right a few minutes beyond (the left fork is the Likhu trail), cross the Galli Gad tributary, and climb. Reach **KoT** or **Tibrikot** (7020 ft, 2140 m) in **25 minutes** from Supani. To the south of the notch is presumably the old fort of a former king who could watch everything and everyone from there. It is now a temple to Tripureshsundari Devi. The town is now scattered in three nondescript clusters. Descend to the Chhal Gad, the tributary from the north, in **10 minutes** and cross it to the right bank (6860 ft, 2091 m). Be sure to get water here.

Head downstream a bit, and begin the climb up to the northwest. Pass a number of little shrines that bespeak the animistic feel of this area. Reach the crest of the spur in 1 hour, and then keep to it. Eventually, keep to the north side of the Khorain Khola valley and pass above the villages of Koragaon and Kamigaon. Halfway between them, just above the trail, noticed if you look back, is a segmented stone pillar that dates back to the old kingdom here. Pass through the bottom of Dagine (9760 ft, 2975 m) in **2½ hours** from the Chhal Gad crossing and then climb, eventually going into the forested tributary of the Kali Charo ("black bird") river. Cross the river and reenter the main valley to pass below the town of Kaliban ("black forest," 10,140 ft, 3091 m) and cross the tributary in **45 minutes.** When I asked trail directions from the people in Kaliban, they pointed down the hill and said the trail was over by those "forest people" there. I expected to see some wild hunter-gatherers there, and in a sense I did—langur monkeys!

Jewelry: Necklaces and Bangles

Necklace designs are shared among many groups. There may be large gold beads, lac-filled for strength and lightness, strung with coral, glass, or layers of velvet circles between them. While the necklaces were once silver, the trend is away from it to gold.

A *tilhari,* a long, cylindrical, repoussé gold bead that hangs in the center of a few to a hundred strands of fine colored glass beads (seed beads), is worn by married Hindu women. Red, followed by green, are the most popular color beads.

The most commonly worn necklaces are composed of multiple strands of small glass beads (*pote*). With the availability of Czechoslovakian and Japanese beads, color choices number in the hundreds. Necklaces may be choker length with just a few strands, or may hang to the hips and have numerous strands.

The most significant color is red, the color of marriage and fertility. Among the Hindu castes, the bridegroom placing a necklace of red *pote* in combination with the application of red powder (*sindur*) in the part of the hair constitutes the most important act in the wedding ceremony. The red beads are the sign of a woman whose husband is alive. When a woman becomes widowed, the beads are discarded.

BhoTiya wear big pieces of coral (often imitation) and turquoise (almost always real) as well as large black and white *dzi* beads. *Dzi* protect the wearer from stroke and lightning. They are believed to have a supernatural origin as creatures (worms) which were petrified

Bangles and a variety of necklaces, including one of musk deer teeth, adorn this woman.

by the contamination of human touch, but retain some of their supernatural power. *BhoTiya* will also wear prayer boxes of gold and silver, often with bits of turquoise and fine filigree work. Colored, knotted strings, blessings from lamas, are also worn.

Many women wear bangles of gold, silver, and Indian glass on the wrists. Red is the most auspicious color, and the clinking is considered mildly erotic. Ankles are less commonly decorated than in the past. The *Tharu* in the Tarai may wear hollow or solid heavy anklets. Hill ethnic groups used to wear dragon-like (*makar* or *singha mukh*) designs. Anklets display high relief when new, but wear down over the years to become almost smooth. Some may wear similar pieces on the wrist. Gold, a divine metal, sacred to Vishnu, is rarely worn below the waist (the more impure part of the body), so these are usually silver. Anklets are currently out of fashion.

An old carved Malla Vir Khamba *stands alone in a field, awaiting archeological investigation.*

Continue up the valley another **1¼ hours** to reach the **Chhaumri Pharam** (11,480 ft, 3499 m). Officials at this yak-breeding project may let you stay in their guest house. To head on to Balangra Pass (12,590 ft, 3837 m), either contour up high, or go through the forest, for **1 hour.** Descend to the west, keeping to the north side of the valley on a wide trail, passing by a tiny spring. Unlike the major Thulo Bheri cutting the landscape to the east, the western side of the pass is a jumble of ridges. In **1½ hours** take the right fork (10,850 ft, 3307 m) by a tiny stream, rather than the left fork, which passes below the lone house of Chiplaaina. In less than **20 minutes** reach a small notch (10,820 ft, 3298 m) and fork right to descend steeply into the Garpunk Khola valley (the left fork contours).

The descent to **Kaigaon** (8740 ft, 2664 m at the bridge) takes **1 hour.** You can fork either way halfway down, depending on whether you want to arrive at the bridge or pass through the upper part of town. On the left fork, you pass a few sheds with colored bits of cloth: temples to Masta, the local protector deity. To proceed on to Jumla, pick up the trail description at Kaigaon above.

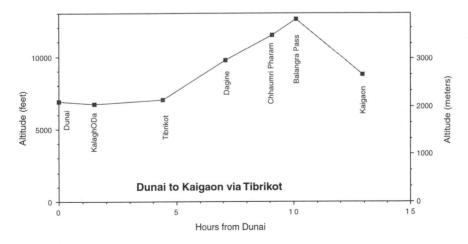

Peoples of Western and Far Western Nepal

This is the land of the ancient Malla Kingdom of the Karnali river basin. This region is literally littered with many of the cultural and historic artifacts of the Malla era, the twelfth to fourteenth centuries A.D. At one time, the Malla Kingdom included portions of western Tibet as well. After its decline, the *baaisi raja* (twenty-two kingdoms) of west Nepal emerged and were not ceded to the expanding Gorkha kingdom until the nineteenth century. (Historians have postulated a relationship between the Malla kings of west Nepal and those of the Kathmandu Valley just prior to the eighteenth-century Gorkha conquest, but there is no consensus.)

Along the former "royal highway" of the Malla Kingdom of west Nepal, a walking route stretching north from the inner Tarai through Jumla and into Tibet, there are various inscribed stones that scholars have used to determine the nature and extent of the Malla domain. And there are ancient shrines to be seen throughout western Nepal dedicated to the prominent local deity called "*Masta.*" On some trails in the west, one may see carved wooden spirit effigies, festooned with bells, flowers, and strips of colored cloth, set out to appease the spirits that haunt each locale. Trekkers are admonished—*please*—to respect local customs here and throughout Nepal and to refrain from handling or taking souvenirs beyond what can be captured on film. Much of what is seen and admired here is sacred, and local feeling toward holy objects is not unlike the reverence and respect Westerners feel in the sanctuaries of the great cathedrals of Europe or in their hometown churches and synagogues.

One fascinating cultural feature of some of the more northerly dwelling Hindus of this region is their apparent "Tibetanization." Unlike elsewhere in Nepal, some *Chhetri* and *Thakuri* of the west and far west are indistinguishable at first glance from their Buddhist *BhoTiya* neighbors. They wear the same style of clothing, construct similar flat-roofed houses, and pursue the same patterns of trade and subsistence economy. Their way of living is unlike that of their more "pure" Hindu caste neighbors to the south and east, who look down upon them in some respects. The *BhoTiya* cultural attributes noted here, and wherever they occur among non-*BhoTiya* people in Nepal, are reflections of the northern mountain environment.

Jumla–RaRa Lake Circuit
(Map No. 10, Page 347)

At the southern edge of the Mugu District, at an altitude of almost 10,000 ft (3050 m), lies RaRa, the largest lake in Nepal. It has a circumference of almost 8 mi (13 km) and is nestled between heavily forested, steep-sided ridges that thrust up from the fault lines that riddle this section of the foot of the Himalaya.

Scheduled flights to Jumla (7660 ft, 2335 m), the headquarters of the Karnali Zone, are operated by several carriers now. They originate in Kathmandu, Nepalgunj, and Pokhara. Jumla is situated in a broad valley 3 days' walk south of RaRa. Most flights originate from Nepalganj to the south, but there are less frequent direct flights from Kathmandu. It is possible to trek to Jumla from Pokhara (described earlier), but most people fly there. One can also trek to Jumla from Surkhet to the south, to

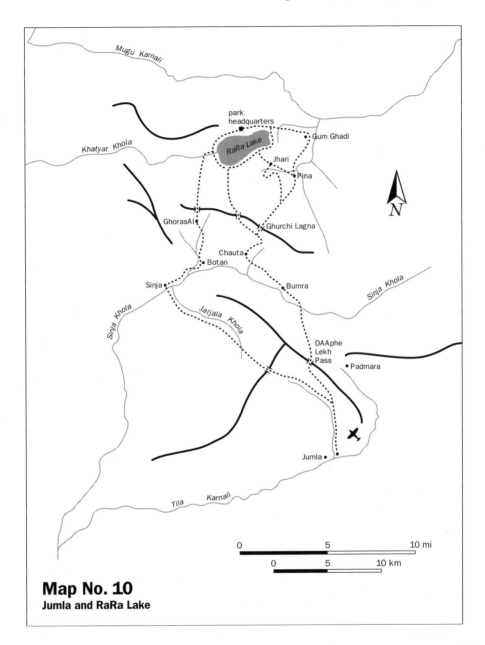

Map No. 10
Jumla and RaRa Lake

where there is a road. This takes about a week. Either of these might be viable alternatives for getting out of Jumla at the end of the trek. Finally, you could walk there from Khaptad National Park, another week's journey.

First, the usual route from Jumla to RaRa is described. There are two variations. Most people do well to take the longer route—at least if traveling without a guide thoroughly familiar with the shorter *lekh* route. Then the return route described follows a little-used trail to Sinja, an interesting, historic town. From here, a former trade and communication route leads to Jumla. Some food must be carried no matter which route you take. A local guide is advised.

Rice, wheat, potatoes, or beans may sometimes be available in the bazaar in Jumla, but food shortages are a recurring problem in this whole area. As far as possible, all supplies required for trekking should be brought from Kathmandu. Porters can be hired locally, but English-speaking ones are rare. Prices are high. It is essential to carry a tent when trekking in this area. Many of the people along this trek are *Thakuri,* the King's caste. They are loathe to allow anyone below their caste to enter or stay in their homes.

It is difficult to arrange return flights, either in Kathmandu or in Jumla. Once you arrive in Jumla, see the airline representative immediately to confirm your return flight. If you are stuck in Jumla, and unable to make direct connections to Kathmandu because of frequent "rice" charters into Jumla, it is easier to get a seat out on one going back to Nepalganj. There are daily flights to Kathmandu from Nepalganj. It is also possible to walk 7 days south to Surkhet and drive to Nepalganj.

JUMLA TO RARA LAKE

Looking north from the Jumla Bazaar, you can see most of the trail to the top of DAAphe Lekh. The trail goes just to the left of the highest point of this *lekh.*

Head out of the main bazaar from Jumla (7660 ft, 2335 m) on a wide trail along the east (left) bank of the stream heading north. Stay on this side more or less all the time until the climbing begins. The trail up this valley passes next to the buildings of a large technical school on the way to the pass. Run by the United Mission to Nepal, this school offers appropriate educational opportunities to people in this remote region. After **1 hour** begin the ascent from the valley floor, climbing toward the right. The trail rises through a series of cultivated fields, passes close to a few scattered houses, and ascends steadily for over **1 hour.** While still well below the main treeline, the trail rises steeply for about **15 minutes,** crosses a small stream, and enters one of the few clusters of blue pine trees on the open stretch of hillside. Near this spot—above the trail and slightly off to the right—is a campsite with a freshwater spring (9000 ft, 2743 m), a good place to rest and cook your morning meal. This is the last water before the pass. Don't go on in bad weather.

Ascending out of the trees, the trail opens out onto wide meadows rising gently to the north. **Fifteen minutes** beyond the trees, the trail forks near some stone huts. Take the less obvious right fork and, shortly after, reenter the forest. (The left fork is a more level main route to Sinja.) The trail emerges into high meadows, visible earlier from below, in **1½ hours** from the fork. Another **hour** on increasingly difficult rocky terrain brings you to the pass, the DAAphe Lekh (12,100 ft, 3688 m). The summit is marked with a small *chorten.* There is a small peak to your left (13,715 ft, 4180 m) and another to your right (13,807 ft, 4224 m). From this point you should have a fine view back down over the Jumla Valley to the 15,000-ft (4500-m) ridges to the south. There is no northern view until you cross the top of the pass.

From the *chorten,* follow the trail across the top of the ridge, winding through patchy forest to the north before dropping again into open meadows. Note carefully the spot where you emerge from the trees. If you come back this way, it is very easy to miss the opening. If you climb straight on over these meadows, you reach a different pass that leads to the village of Padmara to the southeast and a longer walk back to Jumla.

Leave the meadows, cross a small stream, follow the trail into the trees, and descend rapidly through dense, mixed forest for **2 hours.** Notice the magnificent birch trees, the bark of which is collected for use as paper. And keep your eyes open for a *DAAphe*—the multicolored national bird of Nepal. There may be *bhaTTi* for Nepali travelers along here.

Near the end of the descent, the trail drops very steeply to the Sinja Khola, which is immediately crossed by a substantial log bridge (8900 ft, 2713 m). Turning west, proceed along the north (right) bank of the river. Within the next hour choose any suitable campsite along the valley floor by the river.

Approximately **1 hour** from the bridge, the trail rises from the riverbed to pass near the village of **Bumra** (9350 ft, 2850 m). An alternative campsite could be in the vicinity of the village. Supplies such as eggs or firewood can sometimes be procured.

From Bumra, continue along the side of the hill, proceeding about 500 ft (150 m) above the river. Pass just above another small village within **15 minutes.** After another **15 minutes,** descend steeply to cross a small stream entering the main river from the north. On the valley floor, cross the main stream (9250 ft, 2819 m), and immediately climb steeply again for **30 minutes** to regain your former altitude. Within another **hour,** descend again to cross another stream entering from the north. At the foot of this descent, huddled beneath the steep rock walls on the far side of the stream, stand the few houses of **Chauta** (9000 ft, 2743 m). Splendid clay *chilim* (pipes) are made in this area and are sometimes sold at one of the hotels here. If you head downstream on the Sinja Khola, you will reach Sinja in less than a day. There is a route that returns to Chauta from RaRa Lake via Chabragaon. Hire a local guide if you wish to return this way and not do the long circuit via Sinja.

From Chauta, head north, following the trail gently uphill and crisscrossing the stream, the Chauta Khola, in a steep, narrow valley. Pass the RaRa Lake National Park Entrance station, where you will have to pay an entrance fee if you didn't in Kathmandu or don't have a receipt. A pleasant walk through groves of large walnut trees takes you to a small *dharmsala* ("resting place") with a good, clear-flowing spring. Reach some isolated cultivated fields in 1 hour. In another 15 minutes, the trail passes out of the trees and, leaving the course of the stream, swings left onto the high, open pastures. You are now climbing again to the pass of Ghurchi Lagna.

The wide trail proceeds almost directly westward, rising across a broad, grassy valley that runs almost at right angles to the final ridge. After you pass groups of large boulders for 30 minutes, the valley you are following splits into two distinct valleys. One heads northwest, and the other, containing the main trail, goes slightly northeast. The main trail heads up the right valley, climbing more or less north to the pass of the Ghurchi Lagna (11,300 ft, 3444 m), which is marked by a small stone *chorten*. The pass is some **3 hours** from Chauta.

Descend 30 minutes, and take an obvious newer trail branching to the left, and traversing without losing much height, through young pine forest. Cross a couple of meadows, and then descend steeply to a clear stream. Cross this stream and continue northwest above another valley and stream, which is eventually crossed before making a final climb to **Jhari** (8350 ft, 2545 m) some **5 or 6 hours** from the pass.

On the older trail from the Ghurchi Lagna pass, descend north again into forest. Some 5 minutes below the top is a *dharmsala* near a small stream. From here the trail is difficult, dropping very steeply away from the stream over a series of rocky outcrops. It descends in and out of belts of trees and emerges almost 2 hours later.

Traverse for another 30 minutes to the village of Pina (8000 ft, 2438 m). Pass a water source and suitable campsites on the way to the village. About 5 minutes before the village, come to a hotel, an isolated house directly on the main trail. If you are lucky, it may be open for business.

The village of Pina is grouped into upper and lower clusters, which are connected by an intricate maze of paths through the fields. The main trail from lower Pina proceeds in the direction of the river below, reaching Gum Ghadi (6500 ft, 1981 m) in about 3 hours. This is the government headquarters and police check post for the Mugu District. One trail from Gum Ghadi cuts back, ascending steeply to the northern ridge of RaRa. The other trail from the village continues dropping steeply to the Mugu Karnali River, the gateway to the trails into Humla and Mugu.

To proceed most directly to RaRa from Pina, take the new trail that splits from the main trail about 10 minutes above the hotel. It passes through upper Pina after beginning on the side of a valley at the edge of the village. To find the trail when descending from the Ghurchi Lagna pass, take the left fork at the first stream you come to after leaving the pass, a few minutes outside of Pina. Bearing to the left, the trail traverses the side of this westward-heading valley, passes through cultivated fields for 30 minutes, and gradually meets the valley floor and a stream at the end of the traverse. Cross this small stream by a mill (7500 ft, 2286 m) and climb again for 15 minutes before dropping almost immediately to the main valley stream. Follow the stream for another 30 minutes through more fields in an ever-narrowing valley. Cross the stream on a substantial wooden bridge and climb steeply to the north for 30 minutes to the village of Jhari (8350 ft, 2545 m).

Continue up through the village of Jhari to the north, pass some huge cedars, climb again through the forest, and emerge after about **2 hours** onto high, open pasture. Cross the easily gained summit (10,050 ft, 3063 m) and emerge at the "airstrip" on the south side of RaRa Lake (9800 ft, 2987 m). The airstrip, the only flat area around the shores of the lake, is no longer used. Directly across, toward the northwestern side of the lake, is the newer building of the national park headquarters and staff and army houses. There are several lodges here, one by the barracks and another alongside the stream that drains the lake.

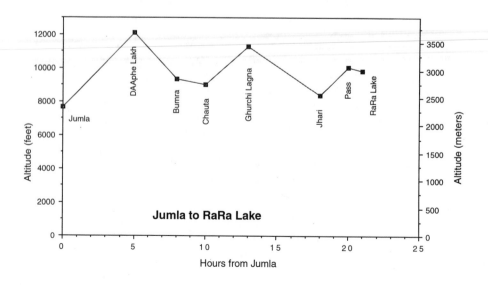

WHAT'S IN THE BASTARD HILLS?

Springing quickly from its source,
it hurries here, and loiters there,
but never glances back;
instead, the river is kicking hard
against the sickly mountains
which stand like statues on its banks,
as it runs away, and leaves this land.

Young sons are walking out,
leaving the places they were born,
taking loved ones with them,
carrying bags, neatly tied
with red kerchiefs on their shoulders.
Khukuri knives hang from their waists,
dull and unpolished for years;
they tell their sick old parents
to look after homes, homes which are lifeless.

Soft petals of gentle flowers, tender leaves of green,
flying in every direction,
plucked up by unseasonal winds
blowing from unknown lands.
Trees stand bare and disfigured,
like soldiers on parade along mountain ranges.

Flocks of doves like destitutes
are driven from their homes
by incessant storms, the deluge
which ends the longest drought;
their bodies are soaked by rain:
no hope of food to eat,
no place for them to rest.

Thus there is nothing in the hills
on which to pen a poem,
you could even say there is nothing there
for anyone to write;
it's like the soldiers always say
home for a few months' leave
"What's in the bastard hills?"

Sure there is something here:
dying mothers, newborn babies,
springs shedding sorrowful tears,
pools frozen like heaps of stone,
absolutely still,
where the rivers have left some dirty water
and a few frogs hop
as they give up hope and leave,
a few old people tending their homes, awaiting their time,
some mountains with finished faces,
some trees felled in their youth.

And there are the cooing destitutes,
piercing the heart, shedding tears of blood:
flocks of doves.

Minbahadur Bishta, circa 1982

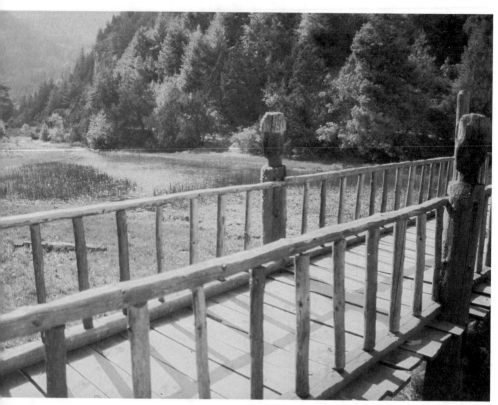

Protector deities on the bridge at RaRa Lake (Robin Biellik)

RARA

The area surrounding the lake, which was designated a national park in 1975, offers spectacular scenery, although views of snow-capped peaks are limited. Magnificent examples of fir, pine, spruce, juniper, cedar, birch, and rhododendron are found in the forest. Wildlife, including bears, cats, wolves, and deer, has been observed in the area. Around the shores of the lake are some fine "Malla Stones"— pillars of rock bearing Devanagari inscriptions and figures of the sun and moon. The inscriptions probably date from the Malla kings, who reigned over much of the western Himalayan region in the twelfth century.

The best camping areas are on the lake's south side, which has much more diverse topography and vegetation than the north side. Meadowlands blanketed with wildflowers, virgin spruce forest full of birds, and some streams on the southwest corner of the lake make for idyllic camping. Be aware that this area has a fragile ecosystem and cannot stand the excesses of contemporary trekking development.

Legend and folklore provide the bulk of knowledge about RaRa Lake. The villagers believe it is at least 1800 ft (550 m) deep. They feel it is fed from underground springs flowing from the Mugu Karnali River, which is located about 1800 ft (550 m) downhill from the lake on the other side of the north *lekh*. Given its size and location near one of the main trade routes to Tibet, it is surprising that the lake does not have greater historical or religious significance. Unlike many Himalayan lakes, it is not a pilgrimage site. An annual festival in July and August commemorates the intervention of the great god Thakur, who changed the direction of the outlet of the lake. Firing an arrow to the west, he opened the western hill to form the present outlet and, taking huge quantities of earth, he filled in the eastern outlet and stamped it firmly with his great feet. His footprints, embedded in a rock, are visible to this day at the eastern end of the lake. They are the festival's main objects of interest—other than the attractive dancers and the local brew.

The lake's inaccessible location has kept many of its secrets undiscovered. The potential for discovery may be one of the most exciting aspects of this trek.

RARA TO JUMLA VIA SINJA

You can return by taking a less-traveled, longer route through Sinja, the historical summer capital of the Malla Kingdom (twelfth to fourteenth centuries). Food, shelter, and a good map or a local guide familiar with the route are necessary.

From the park headquarters (9900 ft, 3018 m), take the shore trail southwest to the lake outlet, the Khatyar Khola (9780 ft, 2981 m), also called the Nisha Khola, in **45 minutes.** Do not cross the bridge here, but continue down the north (right) bank for **30 minutes** and then cross the stream on a log bridge. One trail continues west on the south (left) bank of the *khola* after ascending a 100-ft (30-m) knoll. Instead, take the left fork (heading south) up a small valley. Climb through the woods on a sometimes indefinite trail that keeps to the western side of the valley. Reach a meadow with a *goTh* (10,740 ft, 3274 m) on a crest in **1 hour.**

Continue south, climbing steeply through oak, then birch, then rhododendron forests, to reach an alpine ridge (12,500 ft, 3810 m) in **2½ hours.** Above to the left is Chuchuemara Danda. Traverse on its west shoulder for **15 minutes** and come out on a saddle above the Ghatta Khola. Descend 500 ft (150 m) to the headwaters of the river and continue down through the valley for 1 hour to GhorasAI, site of the army guard post (10,500 ft, 3200 m), in **1½ hours** from the saddle. Here the stream turns southwest. This is an appropriate and beautiful place to camp.

From GhorasAI, the trail at first heads down the right side of the valley and then soon crosses to the left, where it is very flat, to the top of the moraine wall. It recrosses the stream here and descends very steeply on the right-hand side. Botan can be seen ahead on the left-hand slopes of the valley. Regardless of trails heading off to the right in the general direction of Sinja, stay in this valley, taking the fork that keeps you closest to the Sinja Khola, until you reach it.

There is an excellent campsite at the confluence of the Jaljala and Sinja Kholas. Just below here, the Sinja Khola goes through a narrow gorge. The top end of the Sinja village is at the lower end of this gorge, an additional 15 minutes walk. Reach **Sinja** (8000 ft, 2438 m) in **4 hours** from GhorasAI. A bridge across the Sinja Khola at this point (top end of the village and lower end of the gorge) is crossed to pick up the trail heading up the Jaljala Khola. Food and lodging are difficult to find in Sinja, even for porters.

Sinja lies in a highly cultivated valley. To the south, on a prominent knoll, are the remains of the former capitol of this area. It is presently the site of a temple, Kankasundri. This area is well worth visiting by climbing the 400 ft (120 m) to the top of the knoll.

To return to Jumla, follow the historical route between Sinja and Kalanga, the old name for Jumla. The 2-day route through beautiful forests ascends a river valley to a *lekh* and descends to Jumla. A camp roughly halfway on the crest of the *lekh* (11,500 ft, 3505 m) is ideal.

From Sinja, ascend the Jaljala Khola to the southeast, keeping to the south (left) bank on a very good, clear trail for **6 hours** to reach the high point. On the far watershed, the trail descends through forests and pastures south to Jumla (7640 ft, 2329 m) in less than **4 hours.**

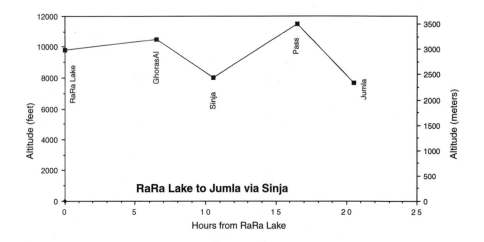

APPENDICES

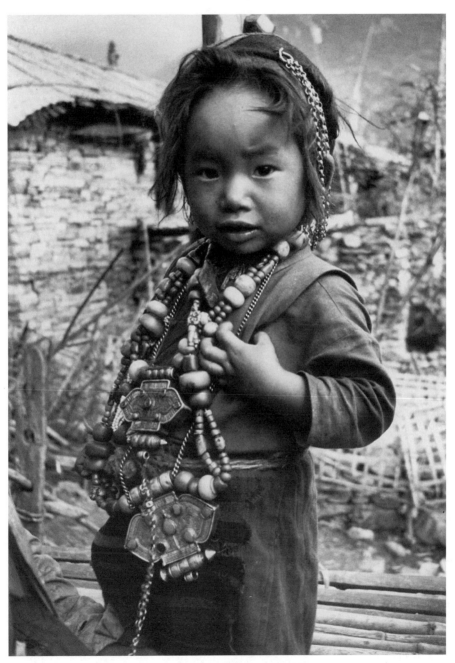

How do I look with my mother's jewelry? (Jeff Greenwald)

A Addresses

The following addresses could be helpful for organizing a trek in Nepal. Naturally, businesses come and go, and addresses change, but those listed here will provide a place to start if you want to organize a trek with a Nepali agency. *Inclusion in this list does not imply endorsement by the author or publisher.* There is little regulation of trekking agencies in Nepal, so standards of performance vary widely. Some are shoestring operations, yet trekkers report satisfaction from even the smallest mom-and-pop agency. The list of trekking agents is taken from the list of the Trekking Agents Association of Nepal as of 1994, determined to be active in 1996. This is not the latest list, as many new agencies appear and disappear. Use the Web sites on page 101 for the latest information. Those agencies active in 1990 are noted by an asterisk (*). They are establishments with a longer history. The first address shown is an example of a complete postal address in Kathmandu. Nepal's country code is 977, and the city code for Kathmandu is 1 while that for Pokhara is 61.

Trekking Agencies

Above the Clouds Trekking*
Thamel, Box 2230, Kathmandu
Nepal
phone 416909; fax 416923

Adventure Nepal Trekking*
Tridevimarg, Kesar Mahal, Box 915
phone 412508; fax 411245

Alpine Trekking & Expedition Services
Jyatha, Box 2796
phone 226980

Ama Dablam Trekking*
Lazimpat, Box 3035
phone 415372; fax 416029

Annapurna Trekking and
  Mountaineering*
Durbar Marg, Box 7145
phone 222339; fax 222966

Asian Trekking*
Bhagwan Bahal, Box 3022
phone 415506; fax 411878

Back Track Adventures
Siphal, Box 2212
phone 471504

Bhrikuti Himalayan Treks
Naxal, Box 2267
phone 413612; fax 413612

Boudha Himal Treks & Expeditions
Thamel, Box 5597
phone 211091

Cho-Oyu Trekking*
Lazimpat, Box 4515
phone 418890; fax 418890

Chomolhari Trekking*
Durbar Marg, Box 5619
phone 222422; fax 226820

Cosmo Treks*
Lazimpat, Box 2541
phone 416226; fax 415275

Crystal Mountain Treks
Naxal, Box 5437
phone 416813; fax 412647

Culture Trekking
Kantipath, Box 3263
phone 226603; fax 227583

Dhaulagiri Trek House
Chuchepati, Chabahil, Box 2583
phone 473308; fax 473234

Eco Trekking and Expeditions
Thamel, Box 6438
phone 417420; fax 413118

Everest Adventures
Ganeswor, Box 6964
phone 412516; fax 415126

Everest Express Trekking*
Durbar Marg, Box 482
phone 220759; fax 226795

Everest Trekking*
Kamaladi, Box 1676
phone 220558

Foothills Trekking
Lazimpat, Box 3966
Phone 417347; fax 417347

Four Season Trekking*
Jyatha, Box 1656
phone 214237; fax 221387

Ganga Jamuna Trekking
Thamel, Box 5054
phone 418518; fax 411933

GATES (Guiding and Trekking
    Expedition Services)
Kopan, Box 2081
phone 478963; fax 478962

Glacier Safari Treks*
Thamel, Box 2238
phone 412116; fax 418578

Gorkha Treks
Lainchour, Box 4509
phone 413806

Great Escapes Trekking
Baluwattar, Box 6550
phone 411533

Great Himalayan Adventure*
Kantipath, Box 1033
phone 216144; fax 228066

Green Lotus Trekking
Dhumbarah, Box 1019
phone 419138; fax 414267

Guides for All Season Trekking*
Gairidhara, Box 3776
phone 415841; fax 416047

High Adventure Service
Lazimpat, Box 6008
phone 416580; fax 220143

Highland Sherpa Trekking*
Jyatha, Box 3597
phone 226487; fax 226389

Him Treks
Lazimpat, Box 2383
phone 419233

Himalaya Expeditions*
Thamel, Box 105
phone 226622; fax 228890

Himalayan Adventures*
Lazimpat, Box 1946
phone 414344; fax 412083

Himalayan Encounter
Thamel
phone 417426; fax 417133

Himalayan Excursions
Thamel, Box 1221
phone 418497; fax 222026

Himalayan Explorers*
Sano Gaucher, Box 1737
phone 419853; fax 411069

Himalayan Horizons*
Pokhara, Box 35
phone 20253; fax 418382, in
   Kathmandu

Himalayan Journeys*
Kantipath, Box 989
phone 226138; fax 227068

Himalayan Paradise
Chabahil, Box 5343
phone 471103

Hiunchuli Treks*
Lazimpat, Box 3725
phone 411813; fax 229459

Inner Nepal Trekking
Kamaladi, Box 936
phone 226130; fax 225237

In Wilderness Trekking*
Baudhnath, Box 3043
phone 410760

Inter Treks Nepal
Pratap Bhawan, Box 2896
phone 225619; fax 225324

International Trekkers*
Chabahil, Box 1273
phone 413397; fax 221151

Jai Himal Trekking*
Durbar Marg
Box 3017
phone 221707; fax 226430

Journeys Mountaineering & Trekking*
Maarajgunj, Box 2034
phone 411989; fax 414243

Kailash Himalaya Trek
Gaidhara, Box 4781
phone 412049; fax 223171

Kanchenjunga Trek Travel
Thamel, Box 105
phone 229039

Kanjiroba Trekking
Jyatha, Box 2981
phone 229303; fax 227919

Khumbi-ila Mountaineering &
   Trekking*
Kamal Pokhari, Box 731
phone 413166; fax 416559

Khumbu HimalayanTrekking
Jyatha, Box 3956
phone 228597; fax 224621

Lama Excursions*
Durbar Marg, Box 2485
phone 220186; fax 227292

Lamjung Trekking*
Kupondole, Box 1436
phone 521607; fax 226820

Langtang Ri Trekking
Thamel, Box 2107
phone 412728; fax 417133

Last Frontiers Trekking*
Lainchaur, Box 881
phone 416146; fax 414512

Lotus Treks & Expeditions
Kamaladi, Box 2281
phone 230570; fax 245552

Lukla Treks & Expeditions
Lazimpat, Box 2025
phone 417190; fax 415346

Malla Treks*
Lainchour, Box 787
phone 418389; fax 418382

Mandala Trekking*
Kantipath, Box 4573
phone 228600; fax 227600

Mansarobar Trekking
Durbar Marg, Box 4685
phone 224516; fax 226912

Maya Trekking
Boudha, Box 1178
phone 470266

Monal Trekking
Kamaladi, Box 5002
phone 418950

More than mountain treks
Lazimpat, Box 4114
phone 418793; fax 226912

Mount Makalu Trekking
Nag Pokhari, Box 3039
phone 417166; fax 414024

Mountain Adventure Trekking*
Jyatha, Box 3440
phone 227040; fax 525126

Mountain Travel*
Lazimpat, Box 170
phone 414508; fax 414075

Mountain Way Trekking & Expeditions
Rastra Bank Chowk, Box 59, **Pokhara**
phone 20316; fax 21240

Mustang Trekking & Expeditions
Kamaladi, Box 1147
phone 212831

Natraj Trekking*
Kantipath, Box 495
phone 226644; fax 227372

Nepal Hanuman Trekking
Thamel, Box 2926M
phone 213625; fax 227919

Nepal Himal Treks*
Naxal, Box 4528
phone 419796; fax 411933

Nepal Insight Trekking
Purano Baneswor, Box 3851
phone 470299; fax 226820

Nepal Panorama Treks
Jyatha, Box 4529
phone 228033

Nepal Trek House*
Surepa, Lalitpur, Box 1357
phone 526990; fax 521291

Nepal Treks & Natural History
   Expeditions*
Ganga Path, Box 459
phone 222511

Nilgiri Treks & Mountaineering
Thamel, Box 4562
phone 414050; fax 222026

Numbur Himal Trekking
Jyatha, Box 5439
phone 215246; fax 220143

Overseas Adventure Trekking*
Thamel, Box 1017
phone 229145

Pabil Treks
Kamalpokhari, Box 2607
phone 418532; fax 414184

Parivar Trekking
Jyatha, Box 2414
phone 222835; fax 222835

Pleasure Trekking
Tridevi Marg
phone 226499

Poon Hill Trekking
Thamel, Box 2994
phone 229122; fax 226912

President Treks & Expeditions
Durbar Marg, Box 1307
phone 228873; fax 221180

Quest Horizon Treks
Kantipath, Box 1930
phone 215568; fax 227919

Rai International Trekking
Durbar Marg, Box 4627
phone 222726; fax 226820

Regal Excursions
Lazimpat, Box 4325
phone 415942; fax 412546

Rover Treks & Expeditions*
Naxal, Box 1081
phone 416817; fax 226820

Sagarmatha Trekking*
Naxal, Box 2236
phone 226639; fax 415284

Sherpa Alpine Trekking
Jyatha, Box 2390
phone 227239; fax 220143

Sherpa Cooperative Trekking*
Durbar Marg, Box 1338
phone 224068; fax 227983

Sherpa Society*
Chabahil, Box 1566
phone 470631

Sherpa Trekking Service*
Kamaladi, Box 500
Cable: Sherpatrek
phone 220423

Snow Leopard Trekking*
Naxal, Box 1811
phone 414719; fax 414719

Sports & Nature
Hattisar, Box 3048
phone 414890; fax 226588

Stupa View Trekking
Boudha, Box 5616
phone 417368; fax 472529

Summit Nepal Trekking*
Kupondole, Lalitpur, Box 1406
phone 521810; fax 523737

Swagatam Trekking & Expeditions
Jyatha, Box 3018
phone 215500; fax 419419

Thamserku Trekking*
Kamalpokhari, Box 3124
phone 414644; fax 227042

Tip & Top Trekking*
Keshar Mahal, Box 1760
phone 419973; fax 220143

Trans Himalayan Trekking*
Durbar Marg, Box 283
phone 224854

Trekking International*
Bansbari, Box 4431
phone 419946; fax 220331

Tukchey Treks & Expeditions
Nagpokhari, Box 5200
phone 419506

Venture Treks & Expeditions*
Kantipath, Box 3968
phone 221585; fax 220178

White Magic Trekking*
Jyatha, Box 3356
phone 226885

Wilderness Experience*
Tangal, Box 4065
phone 410518; fax 222096

Wonderland Trekking
Jyatha, Box 7309
phone 225293; fax 228194

Yak Trekking & Expeditions
Chhetrapati, Box 3506
fax 220143

Yalung Treks & Expeditions
Kantipath, Box 4652
phone 227423

Yeti Mountaineering & Trekking*
Ramshah Path, Box 1034
phone 410899; fax 410899

Yeti Trekking*
Kantipath, Box 2488
phone 225982; fax 227567

Nepal Book Dealers (Kathmandu)

Himalayan Book Center
Bagh Bazaar, Box 1339
phone 242085

Mandala Book Point
Kanti Path, Box 528
phone 227711; fax 227600
mandala@ccsl.com.np

Tiwari's Pilgrims Book House
Thamel, Box 3872
phone 424942; fax 424943; email
ifo@pilgrims.wlink.com.np

B   Further Reading

Many people come, looking, looking . . .
some people come, see.

Dawa Tenzing

I love Nepal. Ever since I first saw her in 1969, I have wanted to know all about her. The first experience led to questions, and answers to those lead to still more questions. By now I have come to know a little about much of her, but the spell has not waned. I want to share her with you. Maximum enjoyment will come through familiarity with her history, her culture, her geography, and her people. And as time passes, you see the changes. While this book is primarily concerned with the practical matters related to trekking, a kind of Kama Sutra, you will want to know more about her personality, in its diverse aspects. Reading helps.

Most of the books in the following annotated list focus on areas outside of the Kathmandu Valley and should help the trekker learn more about the various regions of this country. I have listed recent, in-print books, in the interest of saving space, and refer the interested peripatetic reader to the previous edition for more. There has been a proliferation of published material recently on diverse aspects of the Himalayan region, including fiction, which provides a glimpse of how Nepalis see things. Those wishing to pursue specific interests will be well rewarded browsing in Kathmandu, in both bookstores and agency offices. Books published in Nepal can normally only be purchased there. Some sources for ordering books by mail are listed in the "Addresses" section of Appendix A. I strongly urge you to order language materials published in Nepal from them. A U.S. source for many Nepali materials is Yak and Yeti Books, P.O. Box 5736, Rockville, MD 20855, fax (202) 347-3811.

General

Choegyal, Lisa. *Nepal.* Singapore: Apa Productions, 1994. One of the Insight Guides series, with contributions by experts.

Lewis, Todd T., and Theodore Riccardi, Jr. *The Himalayas: A Syllabus of the Region's History, Anthropology, and Religion.* Ann Arbor, Mich.: Association for Asian Studies, 1995. The comprehensive springboard for further study.

Moran, Kerry. *Nepal Handbook.* Chico, Calif.: Moon, 1992. Much thoughtful discussion.

Reed, David. *The Rough Guide: Nepal.* London: Rough Guides, 1996. An excellent guide to the rest of the country with much helpful information.

Anthropology

Bista, Dor Bahadur. *People of Nepal.* Kathmandu: Ratna Pustak Bhandar, 1996. Presents an excellent, though dated, synopsis of most of the ethnic groups found in Nepal.

Brower, Barbara. *Sherpa of Khumbu: People, Livestock and Landscape.* Delhi: Oxford University Press, 1991. A look at the yak and Sherpa society and changes brought by tourism.

Desjarlais, Robert R. *Body and Emotion: The Aesthetics of Illness and Healing in the Nepal Himalayas.* Philadelphia: University of Pennsylvania Press, 1992. Focused on Helambu.

Fisher, James F. *Sherpas: Reflection on Change in Himalayan Nepal.* Berkeley: University of California Press, 1990. A look at this legendary ethnic group seen through their eyes, interpreted by an anthropologist who first worked among them in 1964.

Gautam, Rajesh, and Asoke K. Thapa-Magar. *Tribal Ethnography of Nepal,* vols. 1 and 2. Delhi: Book Faith India, 1994. A huge treatise, at times sounding very colonial, but with helpful information.

Kipp, Eva. *Bending Bamboo, Changing Winds: Nepali Women Tell Their Life Stories.* Delhi: Book Faith India, 1995. A compilation of interviews with 14 women representing diverse situations in Nepal.

Macfarlane, Alan, and Indrabahadur Gurung. *Gurungs of Nepal (A Guide to the Gurungs).* Kathmandu: Ratna Pustak Bhandar, 1990. A concise synopsis.

Mumford, Stan Royal. *Himalayan Dialogue: Tibetan Lamas and Gurung Shamans in Nepal.* Madison: University of Wisconsin Press, 1989.

Salter, Jan, and Harka Gurung. *Faces of Nepal.* Kathmandu: Himal Books, 1996. Excellent sketches and details on the ethnic groups.

Stevens, Stanley F. *Claiming the High Ground: Sherpas, Subsistence and Environmental Change in the Highest Himalaya.* Berkeley: University of California Press, 1993. A cultural geography book suggesting that society was changing long before we came to speed it up.

Art

Singer, Jane Casey. *Gold Jewelry from Tibet and Nepal.* London: Thames and Hudson, 1996. This book looks at jewelry worn by Tibetans and highlanders in Nepal. Published materials on the jewelry of Nepal are limited.

Tingey, C. *Auspicious Music in a Changing Society.* New Delhi: Heritage Publishers, 1994. A look at the *damai* and their bands that play at hill weddings.

Crafts, Development, Economics, Environment, and Geography

Dunsmore, Susi. *Nepalese Textiles.* London: British Museum Press, 1993. Pays homage to the skills of weavers in Nepal.

Gajurel, C. L., and K. K. Vaidya. *Traditional Arts and Crafts of Nepal.* New Delhi: S. Chand, 1984. Invaluable for understanding many of the folk processes going on around you.

Hagen, Toni. *Building Bridges to the Third World: Memories of Nepal 1950–1992.* Delhi: Book Faith India, 1994. Insight on the "development process" by one of the first long-term visitors to Nepal who played a key role in the early stages.

Hutt, Michael. *Nepal in the Nineties.* Delhi: Oxford University Press, 1994. A compendium of essays on recent developments.

Ives, Jack D., and Bruno Messerli. *The Himalayan Dilemma: Reconciling Development and Conservation.* London: Routledge, 1989. A look at the myth of environmental degradation in the Himalaya. Is there a crisis or not? Important reading for Nepal cognoscenti.

Shrestha, Nanda R. *Landlessness and Migration in Nepal.* Boulder: Westview Press, 1990. "Help me, I am a development victim" sets the perspective of this book.

Toffin, Gérard, ed. *Man and His House in the Himalayas: Ecology of Nepal.* New Delhi: Sterling Publishers, 1991. Architecture and human ecology.

Tüting, Ludmilla, and Kunda Dixit. *BIKAS-BINAS/Development–Destruction? The Change in Life and Environment of the Himalaya.* Munich: Geobuch, 1986. A collection of reprints dealing with changes in Nepal wrought through development.

Valli, Eric, and Diane Summers. *Honey Hunters of Nepal.* London: Thames and Hudson, 1988. Ode to a dying art. Youth work in tourism rather than learn this skill and the beehives are declining. Locals cite the use of fertilizer as well as foreign experts removing queen bees for study as reasons.

History

Regmi, Mahesh Chandra. *Kings and Political Leaders of the Gorkhali Empire 1768–1814.* Himayatnagar, Hyderabad: Orient Longman, 1995. There are many more books by this prolific scholar, all helpful for understanding how Nepal got to be where it is today.

Language

Adhikary, Kamal R. *A Concise English–Nepali Dictionary (with transliteration and Devanagari).* Kathmandu: author, 1988. Very useful for the trekker who has mastered the basics.

Aryal, S. *El Amigo Nepal (Nepali–Español).* Kathmandu: author, 1996.

Bezruchka, Stephen. *Nepali for Trekkers.* Seattle: The Mountaineers Books, 1991. A book and accompanying language tape that sets trekkers apart from those with no Nepali skills.

Bloomfield, Andrew, and Yanki Tshering. *Tibetan Phrasebook* and *Tibetan Phrasebook Tapes.* Ithaca, N.Y.: Snow Lion, 1987. A useful beginning.

Chazot, Evelyne, and Soma Pant. *Dictionnaire Français–Nepali.* Kathmandu: Tiwori's Pilgrims Book House, 1981.

Friedrich, Georgia. *Wörterbuch Deutsch–Nepali in Devanagary und lateinischer Umschrift.* Kathmandu: Pilgrims Book House, 1996.

Goldstein, Melvyn C. *Tibetan for Beginners and Travellers.* Kathmandu: Ratna Pustak Bhandar, 1982. It is a place to start, but you need a teacher.

———. *Tibet Phrasebook.* South Yarra, Australia: Lonely Planet, 1987. Another resource.

Karki, Tika B., and Chij K. Shrestha. *Basic Course in Spoken Nepali.* Kathmandu: authors, 1996. Written for Peace Corps volunteers; stresses the situational approach, for the serious trekker. Trekkers wanting something to extend my phrase book should get this.

Manandhar, R. *Parler Nepalais.* Kathmandu: author, 1996.

Matthews, David J. *A Course in Nepali.* London: School of Oriental and African Studies, 1984. A useful formal text for those seeking an in-depth study.

Meerendonk, M. *Basic Gurkhali Dictionary.* Singapore: author, 1960. An excellent, dated, pocket dictionary. Some grammar is needed to use it.

O'Rourke, Mary-Jo, and Bimal Shrestha. *Nepali Phrasebook.* Hawthorn, Australia: Lonely Planet, 1996. A useful resource.

Schmidt, Ruth Laila, ed. *A Practical Dictionary of Modern Nepali.* Delhi: Ratna Sagar, 1993. For the serious student.

Sherchan, Bijaya et al. *An Exercise Book on Spoken Nepali Language*. Kathmandu: School for International Training, 1994. A helpful next step.

Sherpa, Phinjo. *Sherpa Nepali English*. Kathmandu: author, n.d. The first resource on the Sherpa language.

Terrell, Grace M., and Krishna B. Pradhan. *A Small World of Words*. Kathmandu, 1990. A pocket-sized Nepali–English and English–Nepali dictionary.

Literature

Dixit, Mani. *Over the Mountains*. Kathmandu: Ekta Books, 1995. An historical ethnic novel about contemporary Nepal by a prolific writer.

Dixit Kanak Mani. *Bhaktaprasad Bhyaguto: Adventures of a Nepali Frog*. Lalitpur: Rato Bangala Kitab, 1996. A delightful book for adults and children alike.

Hutt, Michael James, ed. *Himalayan Voices: An Introduction to Modern Nepali Literature*. Berkeley: University of California Press, 1991. A collection of poems and short stories that give a glimpse of Nepali writing.

Koirala, Shankar. *Khairini Ghat: Return to a Nepali Village*. Kathmandu: Pilgrims Book House, 1996. A contemporary look at village life.

Rana, Diamond Shumshere. *Wake of the White Tiger*. Kathmandu: Mrs. Balika Rana, 1984. An English translation of this popular historical novel.

Rubin, David. *Nepali Visions, Nepali Dreams*. New York: Columbia University Press, 1980. Translations of and commentary on the poems of the late Laxmiprasad Devkota, perhaps Nepal's finest poet.

Natural History

Fleming, Robert L., Sr., Robert L. Fleming, Jr., and Lain Bangdel. *Birds of Nepal*. Springfield, Oreg.: Nature Himalayas, (expected 1997). There are plans for a long awaited fourth edition of this comprehensive field guide. Inquire to Robert Fleming Jr., 88152 Keola Lane, Springfield, OR 97478-8535 for sources.

Inskipp, Carol, and Tim Inskipp. *A Guide to the Birds of Nepal*. Beckenham, England: Christopher Helm, 1991. This monograph contains range and distribution maps of species, aids for identifying difficult birds, and information on bird-watching areas. A complement to the Fleming guide for the keen birder.

Mierow, Dorothy, and Tirtha Bahadur Shrestha. *Himalayan Flowers and Trees*. Kathmandu: Sahayogi Prakashan, 1978. Pictorial material to aid in identifying plants with helpful notes.

Polunin, Oleg, and Adam Stainton. *Concise Flowers of the Himalaya*. Delhi: Oxford University Press, 1987. A portable wealth of photographs and descriptions of the most common species, listed in the 1984 work.

———. *Flowers of the Himalaya*. Delhi: Oxford University Press, 1984. Together with Stainton's supplement, the best photographic record of flowering plants.

Prater, S. H. *The Book of Indian Animals*. Bombay: Bombay Natural History Society, 1980. Useful descriptions.

Regmi, Puskal Prasad. *An Introduction to Nepalese Food Plants*. Kathmandu: Royal Nepal Academy, 1982. Very helpful to those trying to identify exotic foods.

Regmi, Puskal Prasad, and Deshav Chandra Sharma. *Glossary of Some Important Plants and Animals Names in Nepal*. Kathmandu: Agricultural Projects Services Centre (APROSC), 1991. The guide used for Nepali names in this book.

Smith, Colin. *Butterflies of Nepal (Central Himalaya)*. Bangkok: Tecpress, 1989. The long-awaited guide, with color photos, to all the species in Nepal!

Stainton, Adam. *Flowers of the Himalaya: A Supplement*. Delhi: Oxford University Press, 1988. More photographs and species to extend the seminal work of Polunin and Stainton.

Stapleton, Chris. *Bamboos of Nepal*. Kew: The Royal Botanical Gardens, 1994. A handy reference to the prodigious varieties in Nepal.

Storrs, Adrian, and Jimmie Storrs. *Discovering Trees in Nepal and the Himalayas*. Kathmandu: Sahayogi Press, 1984. A description of many of the species a trekker could see, together with black and white photographs.

Political Science

Bista, Dor Bahadur. *Fatalism and Development: Nepal's Struggle for Modernization*. Calcutta: Orient Longman, 1991. Sparked much controversy with its publication; this volume and Brown's help the outsider understand current Nepal.

Brown, T. Louise. *The Challenge to Democracy in Nepal: A Political History*. Politics in Asia Series, ed. M. Leifer. London: Roultedge, 1996. Essential beginning for understanding the reasons behind the lack of progress after the 1990 democracy movement.

Gellner, David, Pfaff-Czarnecka, J, Whelpton, J, editors. *Nationalism and Ethnicity in a Hindu Kingdom: The Politics of Culture in Contemporary Nepal*. Amsterdam: Harwood Academic Publishers, 1997. An insightful series of papers helping to understand the violent conflicts in the world from issues of ethnic nationalism that so far have had peaceful expression in Nepal. It presents discussions by experts on changes within various ethnic groups in diverse parts of Nepal. The overview alone places many contemporary world events in perspective.

Mihaly, Eugene Bramer. *Foreign Aid and Politics in Nepal*. London: Oxford University Press, 1965. An early study. His conclusions make sense today.

Regional

Bishop, Barry C. *Karnali under Stress: Livelihood Strategies and Seasonal Rhythms in a Changing Nepal Himalaya*. Chicago: University of Chicago Geography Research Paper, nos. 228 and 229, 1990. A look at village dynamics and mountain society around Jumla, showing that mountains have not been a barrier to movement.

Coburn, Broughton. *Nepali Aama: Portrait of a Nepalese Hill Woman*. Chico, Calif: Moon, 1991. A sensitive look at life in a *Gurung* village, told by an old woman.

Downs, Hugh R. *Rhythms of a Himalayan Village*. New York: Harper & Row, 1980. A photodocumentary of a Sherpa village in Solu—a most helpful book for understanding *Mani-rimdu* and how Sherpas may view their land.

Jefferies, Margaret, and Margaret Clarbrough. *Sagarmatha, Mother of the Universe: The Story of Mount Everest National Park*. Auckland: Cobb/Horwood, 1986. The best single source of information on the Khumbu.

Messerschmidt, Don. *Muktinath: Himalayan Pilgrimage, a Cultural & Historical Guide*. Kathmandu: Sayahogi Press, 1992. A glimpse of the importance of these trekker destinations to people of South Asia.

Messerschmidt, Liesl. *Kings, Myths & Apple Pie: Interesting Aspects of the Trek up the Marsiangdi Khola to Manang*. Kathmandu, 1992. A delightful book to enhance your visit to Manang. The source of much local lore in this book.

Rai, Ratan Kumar. *Along the Kali Gandaki: The Ancient Salt Route in Western Nepal, the Thakalis, Bon dKar and Lamaist Monasteries.* Delhi: Book Faith India, 1994. A look at the history and art by an artist.

Sherpa, Donna M. *Living in the Middle: Sherpas of the Mid-range Himalayas.* Prospect Heights, Ill.: Waveland Press, 1994. The insight of an American school teacher who meets and marries a Sherpa.

Thapa, Manjushri. *Mustang Bhot in Fragments.* Lalitpur: Himal Books, 1992. What does a Nepali woman who was raised and educated abroad see when she returns to Nepal and works there? This book opens a window on Nepal as seen by an unusual Nepali writer from whom we can expect more insight in future writing.

Taylor-Ide, Daniel. *Something Hidden behind the Ranges: A Himalayan Quest.* San Francisco: Mercury House, 1995. Well-written story of a yeti search and the Himalayan tree bear.

Zangbu, Ngawang Tenzin, and Frances Klatzel. *Stories and Customs of the Sherpas.* 3rd ed. Kathmandu: Mandala Book Point, 1995. A concise, helpful booklet recommended for all Khumbu trekkers.

Religion

Snellgrove, David. *Buddhist Himalaya.* Kathmandu: Himalayan Booksellers, 1995. A reprint of the 1957 edition that deals with the Solu–Khumbu region and the Buddhism of Sherpas and of Kathmandu.

Travelogues

Coburn, Broughton. *Aama in America: A Pilgrimage of the Heart.* New York: Anchor, 1995. Ever wonder what impressions of America an old *Gurung* lady of the hills would have?

Pye-Smith, Charlie. *Travels in Nepal: The Sequestered Kingdom.* London: Aurum Press, 1988. A visitor's view of diverse aspects.

Scott, J., and J. Robertson. *Lost in the Himalayas.* Delhi: Book Faith India, 1993. What it might be like if you wander off the trail alone in the winter near Gosainkund and wait 43 days for rescue!

Snellgrove, David. *Himalayan Pilgrimage.* Boulder, Colo.: Prajna Press, 1981. A chronicle of travel through northcentral and northwestern Nepal in the 1950s. Though scholars question his observations about hill regions, his wide range of interests and acute powers of observation make for fascinating reading.

Tucci, Giuseppe. *Journey to Mustang, 1952.* Kathmandu: Ratna Pustak Bhandar, 1977. Much of this early journey describes the popular trek to Jomosom. Read it to sense the changes.

Trekking and Related Activities

Armington, Stan. *Trekking in the Nepal Himalaya.* Hawthorn, Australia: Lonely Planet, 1994. Treks with general route descriptions on a day-by-day basis.

Burbank, Jon. *Culture Shock: Nepal: A guide to Customs and Etiquitte.* Portland, Oreg.: Graphic Arts, 1992. I wish I'd had this book when I first worked here.

Gibbons, Bob, and Sian Pritchard-Jones. *Mustang: A Trekking Guide.* Kathmandu: Pilgrims, 1993.

Gurung, Hum Bahadur, and Barry Arthur. *Eco-Trekking in the Southern Annapurna Himal.* Kathmandu: ACAP, 1995.

Kaplan, Amy R., and Michael Keller. *Nepal: An Essential Handbook for Trekkers.* Kathmandu: Mandala, 1995. General information about trekking.

Knowles, Peter. *Rafting Nepal: A Consumer's Guide.* Surbiton, UK: Rivers Publishing, 1994.

Knowles, Peter, and Dave Allardice. *White Water Nepal: A Rivers Guidebook for Rafting and Kayaking.* Surbiton, UK: Rivers Publishing, 1992.

Lama, Wendy Brewer. *Trekking Gently in the Himalaya: Essential Tips for Trekkers.* Kathmandu: Sagarmatha Pollution Control Project, 1992.

Lindenfelser, M. *Nepal: The Far Western Region.* Kathmandu: Tiwari Pilgrim's, 1993. A brief guide to places not covered in this book.

McGuinness, Jamie. *Trekking in the Everest Region.* 2d ed. Surrey, UK: Trailblazer Publications, 1996. A travelish guide to the area with detailed route maps depicting lodge locations.

O'Connor, Bill. *The Trekking Peaks of Nepal.* Seattle: Cloudcap Press, 1989. Also published in Great Britain by Crowood Press. A climbing guide to the eighteen summits.

Reynolds, Kev. *Annapurna: A Trekker's Guide.* Milnthorpe, Cumbria, UK: Cicerone Press, 1993.

———. *Langtang, With Gosainkund & Helambu: A Trekker's Guide.* Milnthorpe, Cumbria, UK: Cicerone Press, 1996.

Thomas, Bryn. *Trekking in the Annapurna Region.* Surrey, UK: Trailblazer Publications, 1996. An information guide to the area and lodges with detailed route maps.

Trekking Medicine

Bezruchka, Stephen. *Altitude Illness: Prevention and Treatment.* Seattle: The Mountaineers, 1994. Another slim volume to carry with details on understanding and coping with problems at altitude.

———. *The Pocket Doctor: Your Ticket to Good Health while Traveling.* Seattle: The Mountaineers, 1999. Another inexpensive, small, carry-along book to help you prepare for and deal with health problems while traveling.

C   Nepali Language Introduction

> *Refusal to accept anybody else's language as worth knowing reflects the same*
> *narrow-gauge kind of head, the same stubborn ignorance as that of the*
> *fundamentalist I heard about who denounced people speaking in other*
> *tongues, saying "If English was good enough for Jesus Christ, it's good*
> *enough for them." The story is apocryphal in both senses.*
>
> Flora Lewis

Nepali is an Indo-European language that is easy to learn. Get one of the language resources in the "Language" section in Appendix B. The *Nepali for Trekkers* booklet and tape is helpful. In what follows, the transliteration system used for Nepali words in this book is described, with a pronunciation guide to enable the reader to pronounce place-names and other words correctly. A few important phrases are given.

Pronunciation

Nepali is written in Devanagari script, but a system of transliteration to the Roman script is used here. Many of the letters denote their usual sounds and only the special sounds are described.

Stress

The stress usually falls on the first syllable (**chaá mal**) unless the first syllable has a short vowel and is followed in the second syllable by a long one. Then the stress falls on the second syllable (**pa kaaú nos**). **The single most common pronunciation error made by the beginning student is NOT putting the emphasis on the first syllable.**

Vowels

a	like the *a* in *balloon*. Never like the *a* in *hat*.
aa	long like the *a* in *father* or *car*.
i	like *ee* in *beer*, the short and long forms pronounced similarly.
u	like *oo* in *mood* or *root*, again with the long and short forms similar. Never like the *u* in *mute*.
e	like *a* in *skate* or like the French *e* in *café*.
ai	a diphthong with the first element like the *a* in *arise* and the second like the *y* in *city*. Together, somewhat like the *ay* in *laying*, but not like the sound of the word *eye*.
au	a diphthong in which the first element is like the *a* in *arise* and the second like the *u* in *put*.
o	like *o* in *bowl* or *go*.
aau, aai, and eu	not diphthongs, but vowels pronounced separately one after the other.

Capitalized Vowels

Capitalized vowels (**A, E, I, O, U**) indicate nasalization of that sound. Squeeze your nostrils together and force the sound to be made high up in the mouth.

Dental and Retroflex Consonants

With retroflexed consonants, make the sound farther back in the mouth, compared to the dental, which are made much more forward.

t   pronounced unaspirated, with the tip of the tongue on the teeth as in the French *petite.*

T   like the *t* in *little,* with the tongue slightly bent back when it meets the roof of the mouth.

d   dental like the French *d,* in which the blade of the tongue is pressed behind the upper teeth.

D   pronounced with retroflexion of the tongue. Turn the tongue back in the mouth, press the underside of it against the palate, and pronounce the *d* in *dog.*

R   also pronounced with retroflexion of the tongue.

Aspirated Consonants

Nepalis differentiate between aspirated and unaspirated consonants. This is quite difficult for native English speakers. Aspiration is indicated by an *h* following the consonant. Consciously avoid breathing hard or aspirating on the consonants that are not followed by an *h.*

The exception to the preceding rule in the transliteration scheme employed in this book applies to *ch* and *chh.* Only the latter is aspirated.

chh   press the blade of the tongue behind the upper teeth and try to say *ts.* At the same time, exert strong breath pressure so that when the tongue is released from the teeth, there is a loud emission of breath. Listen to a native Nepali speaker. It is like the *tch-h* in pi*tch* here.

ch   the unaspirated form as in *chalk, Chinese.*

Miscellaneous

k   like *c* in *cat.*

y   like *y* in *yeast.*

s   like *s* in *song.*

j   press the blade of the tongue against the upper teeth with the tip of the tongue pointed down and say *j* as in *January.* It is somewhat like *dz* and is especially found in words coming from Tibetan dialects.

ph   like *f* in *full.*

p   less aspiration than **ph** (more like **p** than **f**).

Other consonants should present little difficulty. When two consonants come together, be sure to pronounce them individually.

Questions

The basic form is to inflect at the end of the sentence; that is, raise the pitch of your voice on the ending word.

Asking the Way and Other Important Phrases

The following is a brief introduction to asking the way as you walk along trails, together with other essential phrases. Trekkers are advised to use other resources for further language study. The spacing for the gloss of the Nepali phrases may help you change the phrases to suit your needs as you gain facility with the language.

What is the name of this town?

yo   gAAU -ko naam ke   ho?
this town   of   name what is

Is this the road to Malemchighyang?

yo   malemchighang jaane   baa   To ho?
this Malemchighyang going   road is this

Where does this trail lead to?

yo   baaTo   kahAAsamma   jaanchha?
this trail   where up to   go

Which trail goes to Ringmo?

Ringmo   samma   kun baaTo   jaanchha?
Ringmo   up to   which trail goes

How many hours to Namche?

namche   -samma kati   ghanTaa
Namche   up to   how many   hours

laagchha?
does it take

Where can I get food?

khaanaa   kahAA   pAAIchha?
food   where   get

Where is there a hotel?

hoTel   kahAA   chha?
hotel   where   is

Can you cook food for us?

hami-laai khaanaa pakaaunu hunchha ki?
us   for   food   to cook   can you or

Where can I stay?

kahAA   basne?
where   stay

Are there people in Gopte now?

ahile   Gopte -maa manchhe chha?
now   Gopte   at   people   are there

May we (I) stay in your house?

tapAAIko ghar   -maa baas pAAIchha?
your   house   in   stay can get

Can I (we) stay here?

yahAA   baas   pAAIchha?
here   stay   can get

Can I get food here?

khaanaa   yahAA   pAAIchha?
food   here   can get

Please cook rice and lentils for me.

daal   bhaat   pakaaunos
lentils   rice   please cook

Please give me more rice.

bhaat   dinos
rice   please give

vegetables   **tarkaari**

That is enough.   **pugyo**
                   enough

Glossary of Nepali and Tibetan Words

beyul	hidden valley
bhaat	cooked rice
bhaTmaas	soybeans
bhaTTi	traditional Nepali inn
BhoTiya	Buddhist highlander of Nepal
chaarpi	latrine
chang	locally brewed beer
chAUmri or zopkio	a cross between a yak and a cow
chautaaraa	rectangular resting platform on a trail
chilim	clay pipe for smoking
chorten	Buddhist religious cubical structure
daal	lentil-like sauce poured over rice
daru or rakshi	a *Thakali* distilled spirit
dharmsala	rest house
Doko	conical basket for carrying loads
drokpa	Tibetan nomad
ghiu	clarified butter (*ghee* in India)
gomba	Tibetan Buddhist temple
goTh	shelter used by shepherds
himal	mountain
jAAR	locally brewed beer
juTho	socially unacceptable, or polluting
kata	ceremonial scarf of white cheesecloth
khola	river
la	pass (Tibetan for a high pass usually)
lekh	hill
lokta	bark of *daphne* plant used for making "rice" paper
loTaa	vessel for carrying water to clean oneself after defecating
maanaa	volume measure (20 oz, 2½ cups, or 0.7 l)
mani	prayer
naamlo	tumpline
namaskaar	traditional greeting (very polite and formal)
namaste	traditional greeting (less formal)
rakshi	distilled spirit

rupiyAA	smallest unit of money (about 2 cents, at 1996 U.S. exchange rate)
solja	Tibetan tea
taal	lake
thangka	Buddhist scroll painting
Topi	traditional men's hat of Nepal
tsampa	roasted barley flour, usually consumed by *BhoTiya*
Tudikhel	parade ground
yersa	a cluster of *goTh* in Khumbu, but also applies to other northern regions
zopkio or **chAUmri**	a cross between a yak and a cow

To speak a foreign language well . . . we must imitate and mimic the whole time. We must never imagine that our efforts will be laughed at. There are so many dialects . . . that speaking incorrectly does not sound so odd as it might in another country.

G. G. Rogers, *Colloquial Nepali*

Index

FIGURES

1. Nepal's protected areas and main physiographic zones 46
2. Map of the Himalaya showing the four tectonic zones 158
3. Crustal-scale cross-section of southern Tibet and eastern Nepal 158
4. North-south profile through central Nepal showing altitudinal forest distributions 159

MAPS

legend 19
locator 35
overall map of Nepal 35
1. North of Pokhara 165
2. Pokhara 166
3. To Solu-Khumbu and Rolwaling and toward the Arun Valley 214
4. Khumbu (Mount Everest Region) 224
5. Langtang, Gosainkund, and Helambu 249
6. Eastern Nepal (to Kangchenjunga Base Camp) 279
7. To Makalu Base Camp 310
8. Baglung and Beni to Dhorpatan 324
9. Dhorpatan to Jumla (via Southern Dolpa and Phoksumdo Tal) 333
10. Jumla and RaRa Lake 347

TABLES

Characteristics of the Physiographic Regions of Nepal: The Inhabited Areas 163
Climatological Data for Selected Trekking Towns 32
Equipment List 69–71
Essential Do's and Don'ts 103
Indicized and Tibeticized Polities 81
Summary of Treks 41–42
Trekking Peaks 30

TRAIL PROFILES

Besisahar to Muktinath via Thorung La 210
Birethanti to Muktinath 179
Birethanti to the Annapurna Sanctuary 192
Chomro to Suikhet 195
Dhunche to Tharepati via Gosainkunda 264
Dunai to Kaigaon via Tibrikot 345
Dunai to Phoksumdo Tal and Jumla, via Kaagmaara La 342
GhoRepani to Ghandruk 193
Ghunsa to Taplejung via Mirgin La 300
Jiri to Khumbu and Kala Pattar 230
Jumla to RaRa Lake 350
Namche Bazaar to Shyangboche to Gokyo Ri 235
Sundarijal to Tharepati to Malemchi Pul Bazaar via Shermathang 273
Syabrubensi to Kyangjin Gomba 255
Tumlingtar to Makalu Base Camp 315
Tumlingtar to Pangpema 294

GENERAL
bold signifies primary sources
acclimatization 116
agencies **20–25**
air travel **63–64**
altitude illness 107, 109, **115–23**
altitudes 146
amphibians 327
animals 160–61
Annapurna 34, 173, 180–85, 192–93, 196
Annapurna Conservation Area (ACAP) 34, 45, 59, 97, 166, 188–89
Annapurna Sanctuary 34, 45, 186–88
appendicitis 133
Arun III Dam 312

Baglung 325, 331
Baliphi 277
bamboo **169, 190,** 251
Bambu 250
Barabise 36, 245, 247
Barahachhetra 319
bargaining 85–86
Basantapur 37, 279–80, 284, 303, 315
bathing 85
batteries 54, 56, 97
Beding 242, 244–45
begging 89–90
Beni 185, 325
Besisahar 199
Bhandar 216
bhaTTi 73, 147–48
BhoTiya 162, **207,** 290, 344
Bhulbhule 200
Bigu Gomba **246**
Biratnagar 279–80
birds **160–61,** 182, 203, 228, 238, 241, 253, 256, 271, 319
Birethanti 167, 187
bites 128–29
blisters 123
Braga 205–06
Brahman 39, 266, **326**
brasswork 283
Buddhism **153,** 252
Bumlingtar 307, 312, 320
Bung 305
burns 130
buses 64–66, 213, 250, 275, 277, 302

camping 74–75
Chainpur 280, 282–83, 316

Chame 203
Chamkharka 320–21
Chandrakot 167
Chatra 318–19
Chautaaraa 277
chautaaraa 148
Chhetri 39, 266, **326**
Chhukhung 232
children 25, 77, 108–109
Cholang Pati 261
Chomro 189, 193–95
chorten 148
cicadas 311
climate 33
clothing 50–51, 83–84
compass 54
conditioning, physical 105
conservation 96–101
constipation 130
contact lenses 55, 132
cotton 305
cough 118, 130
customs 93–94

daal bhaat 57, **75,** 87, 96
Dana 171
DasAAI **282**
death 141
democracy 16
dental problems 134
depression 135
development 16–17, 302
Dhampus 178–79, 194
Dharan 37, 280, 283, 319
Dhaulagiri 38, 170, 176–77, 180–81, 323, 327
Dhorpatan 297, 323, 325, 330–32
Dhunche 248–50, 253, 260
diabetics 107
diapers 77
diarrhea 114
Dingboche 227, 231
directions (true right, left) **146**
disabilities 27
Diwali 286
Dobhaan 286–87
Dobhane 304
Dumre 195–96
Dunai 332, 336, 342

earthquakes 320
eating 86–87

economics 44, 102, 302, 321
economy 16
email 68
embassy 43, 92
emergency care 138–41
emotional problems 134–36
equipment 48–49, 69–71
Everest, Mount 36, 229–30, 284, 303, 315
eye problems 131–32

farming 163, 307, 341
festivals 247, 252, 318
fever 129
food 57–58, 72, 75–76, 87, 114
flowers 151, 269
footwear 49–50, 123
forests 156, 201, 260
frostbite 125–26
fuel 96
funerals 285

Gamow™ Bag 23, 111, **118–19**
Ganja La 256, 259, 271
geology 155, 317, 320
Ghandruk 188–89, 193
Ghasa 172
Ghora Tabela 252
GhoRepani 97, 169, 193
Ghunsa 290, 294, 300
Giardia lamblia 115
gifts 56, 87–89
Gokyo 223, 233–38
Gongtala 321
Gorak Shep 229
Gorkha 14, 39, 42, 346
Gosainkund 36, 259–69
goTh 75
Gudel 304
guides 21, **58–62**
Gupha Pokhari 284–85, 303
Gurkha 42, 218, 278, 307
Gurung 39, 84, 188, 204

habitats 159
HACE 122–23
HAPE 117, 119, 122
health care 138–139
heartburn 133
heat injury 126
Helambu 36, 248, 252, 265–76
helicopters 64, **139–41**

hemorrhoids 130
hemp 339
hepatitis 105
Hille 168, 316
Himalayan Rescue Association (HRA) 138–39, 207, 227
Hinduism **153**
history 14, 39, 42
hospitals 138–39
hotels 20–23, **72–74**, 147
hunting 100
hypothermia 124–25

immunizations 105
Indicization 81
infection 129–30
inflation 86
insects 55, 160, 241, 257, **288, 311**
insurance 108

Jaljala 328
Jangla 335
Jannu 284, 286, 291, 295–97
jewelry 66, 84, 91, 344
Jiri 36, 212–13
Jomosom 175
Jubing 218
Jumla 38, 41, 323, 336, 342, 346, 348, 353–54
Junbesi 216

Kaagmaara La 336, 340
Kagbeni 177
Kaigaon 340, 345
Kala Pattar 116, 229
Kali Gandaki 171
Kangchenjunga 37, 278, 284–87, 292–94, 297, 308, 323
Karikhola 37, 218
Kathmandu 265–66
Kekela 313
Kemba La 305, 306–307
kerosene 52, 73, 96
KhAADbari 280, 315–16
Kham Magar 330, 334
Khangsar 208
Khaptad National Park 46
Kharte 219, 305
Khembalung caves 321–22
Khudi 197
Khumbu 223–47
Khumjung 222–23, 232–33

Khutumsang 267–68
Kiranti 266, **307**
Kosi Tappu Wildlife Reserve 319
Kunde 223, 232
Kyangjin Gomba 255–56

Landruk 194
Langsisa 257
Langtang 36, 248–59
language 14, **82–83**, 369–73
Lapsang La 294–95
latrines 72, 99
leeches 128–29
Lete 172
Lhotse 37, 231, 284
Limbu **307**
Lobuche 228–29
lodges 20–23, **72–74**, 78, 147, 164
Lukla 36, 219
Lumle 167

Madi 316
Magar 39, 41, 218, **328**
mail 68
Makalu 37, 278, 306, 309, 314
Makalu–Barun National Park 37, 308,
    311, 320
malaria 107
Malemchi Pul Bazaar 264, 272, 273
Malemchighyang 264, 270
Malla Kingdom 346
mammals 161, 209–10, 218, 239
Manang 34, 195, 201, 206–08
Mangmaayaa Khola 317–18
Mani–rimdu 247
maps 47–48
marijuana 95, 136
Marpha 174
medical kit 52, **109–111**
meningitis 106
menstrual periods 132
Mirgin La 295
money 66–68, 89
monsoon **28–29**, 31, 33, 70–71
mountaineering 29–30
Muktinath 176, 178, 207, 210
music 39, 55, **121**
musk deer 218

Namche Bazaar 219–22
national parks 44, **45–47**, 73
Naya Pul 167

Nepalganj 38, 323
Nepali language 82, 369–73
nervous breakdown 135
nettle 308
New Year 318
Newar 161, **266**, 287
Num 312, 317
Nundhaki 284

Pairo 250
Pakhribaas 317
Panch Pokhari 265–77
Pangboche 226
Pangkongma La 219, 305
Pangpema 292
panic attacks 135
paper **183**, 307
Pati Bhanjyang 265–67, 276
pets 217
pheasants 173
Phedi 209, 264, 304
Pheriche 227
Phidim 280
phobias 126–27
Phoksumdo Tal 332, 335–36, 338–39,
    342
Phortse 231, 237–38
photography 56–57
physiographic regions 156–158
pilgrimage **176**, 262, 319
Pisang 205–206
Pokhara 34, 44, 164, 166, 323
police 154
pollution 86
porters 20–23, 58–63, 147
pregnancy 107, 111, 132
protected areas 45
Pungo Tenga 225
psychological problems 134–36

rabies 106, 128
rafting 30
Rai 36–37, **306, 307**
Ranas 14
RaRa Lake 38–9, 346, 348, 350, 352
religion 150, 153
renting equipment 48
reptiles 327
rhododendrons 168
Rimche 251, 259
Ringmo 217, 339
road accidents 65–66

robbery 90
Rolwaling 36, 240–41, 244–45, 247
Royal Bardia National Park 46
Royal Chitwan National Park 46
Royal Sukla Phanta Wildlife Reserve 47

Sagarmatha National Park 36, 59
Sagartara 335
Salpa Bhanjyang 304
Sangnasa 225
Sedua 312–13
sexual harassment 92
Shermathang 272, 276
Sherpas **220–21**, 233, 248, 284
Shershong 314
Shey Phoksumdo National Park 39, 337
Shivalaya 213
shivering 125
Shyangboche 223, 225, 232
Sing Gomba 260
Sinion La 295–96
Sinja 353–54
sinusitis 134
Sisuwatar 307
ski poles 54
skirts 50, 83
sleeping gear 51
snow blindness 130
Solu–Khumbu 36, 212
sprains 124
stoves 52
strains 124
stress 135
Suketar 300
Sundarijal 265
Surki La 306
swimming 85
Syabru 255, 260
Syabrubensi 249–51, 259
Syarpagaon 259

Tal 201
Talamarang 272–73, 275
Tamang 36, 252, **254**
Taplejung 278–80, 284, 286–87, 297, 299, 300
Tarai 14, 16
Tarke Ghyang 271–73
Tashigaon 37, 313

Tatopani 170, 185
telephone 68, 137–38
Tengboche 225
Thakali 34, **174–75**
Thami 238–41
Thamo 238–39
Tharepati 264, 270, 325
theft 90–91
Thodung 215
Thorung La 178, 195, 208–10, 323
Thubten Chholing 216
Tibetanization 81, 344
Tibrikot 342
ticks 129
Tihaar 282, **286**
Tilicho 176, 185, 208
tourism 9, 44, 102, 227
Tragdobuk 216
Tragsindho 218
Trashi Labsta 212, 240–43
travel times **145**, 164, 212, 248
trekking: agencies 22, 44, 356; peaks 30; permits 43–44; styles 20–24
Tribenighat 318
Tukche 173–74
Tumlingtar 278, 280, 303–305, 309, 311, 316–20
Tutula 314

urinary tract infections 134

vandalism 90
video cameras 56
visas 43–44
vomiting 115

waste disposal 97–100
water 98, 99, 112–13
weather 14, 28, 29, 31–33, 69
weddings 316
women's health problems 132–33
worms 133
wool 268

yak 150, 339
Yamphudin 298
yeti 233, **242**
Yolmo 248, 270

About the Author

Stephen Bezruchka first went to Nepal in 1969, drawn by his interest in climbing and a desire to get close to the world's highest summits. He spent a year there, between graduate studies in mathematics at Harvard University and the study of medicine at Stanford University, and wrote the first edition of this guide. His fascination with Nepal soon transcended its lofty mountains to focus on the social-cultural matrix that is a lifelong passion.

He returned to work in Nepal in the mid-1970s and in the mid-1980s. Initially he helped set up a community health project in western Nepal. Later he developed a remote district hospital as a teaching hospital for Nepali doctors and supervised the first physicians training there. Currently he is working with Nepali doctors to enable medical officers posted in remote district hospitals to carry out necessary surgery.

Stephen Bezruchka has trekked far and wide in Nepal. He has climbed in the far ranges of the earth, including the Yukon, Pakistan, and China and on Everest. He is the author of *Nepali for Trekkers, The Pocket Doctor: Your Ticket to Good Health while Traveling,* and *Altitude Illness: Prevention and Treatment.* Of Ukrainian descent, he traveled to the Ukraine and toured outdoor museums there that reminded him of the way life continues in Nepal today. He teaches at the School of Public Health and Community Medicine at the University of Washington and practices medicine in Seattle, but the lure of Nepal, the land and its people, keeps calling him back.

Chandra Pal Rai from Diding in SankhuwaSabha District has traveled with the author for the last ten years.

The Contributors

Carol Inskipp, who contributed the natural history information, is an ornithologist, nature conservationist, and writer with a special interest in the birds of Nepal. Since 1977 she has made many trips to the country studying birds with her husband, Tim. Together they wrote the standard work on the distribution of birds of Nepal. Carol has also written other books and articles on Nepali birds and their conservation.

Donald Messerschmidt, who contributed the material on the people of Nepal, is an anthropologist who advised me on trekking before I first came to the Himalaya and who has continued to provide information on Nepal for subsequent editions of this book. His first experience in Nepal was with the Peace Corps in 1963. He has worked in community development, taught in the American school in Kathmandu, studied the *Gurungs* of west-central Nepal for his Ph.D., led treks and study tours, conducted research, and participated in scientific forums on the Himalaya.

The section on jewelry comes from the studies of anthropologist **Bronwen Bledsoe**, whose interest in Nepal began on a college study tour led by Donald Messerschmidt; it has been updated by **Hannelore Gabriel**.

Daniel Schelling, who contributed the material on geology, has been actively involved in Himalayan geological research since 1983 and did his doctoral research on the geology of the Rolwaling and the eastern Nepal Himalaya. He is presently at the Energy and Geoscience Institute at the University of Utah, conducting research throughout the Himalaya.

माया नमार्नु होला

This message (*maayaa namaarnu holaa*), in Nepali script, was written by a Nepali innkeeper on a sign for trekkers seen north of Pokhara in 1978. Underneath it was written in English, "Come Back Again." The literal translation (or Nepali meaning) is "Don't let the love die."

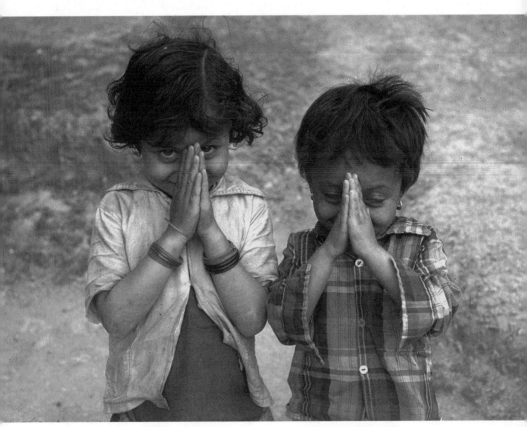

Children will delight in saying namaste *to you. (Mary Anne Mercer)*

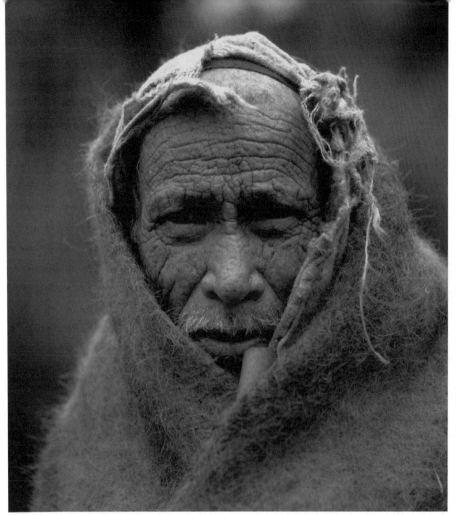

Postscript

As I write these last words, my thoughts return to you who were my comrades: the stubborn and indomitable peasants of Nepal. Once more I hear the laughter with which you greeted every hardship. Once more I see you in your bivouacs or about your fires, on forced march or in the trenches, now shivering with wet and cold, now scorched by a pitiless and burning sun. Uncomplaining, you endure hunger and thirst and wounds; and at last, your unwavering lines disappear into the smoke and wrath of battle. Bravest of the brave, most generous of the generous, never had country more faithful friends than you.

Ralph Lilley Turner, author of *Dictionary of the Nepali Language,* describing Gurkhas with whom he served in the British Army. He learned Nepali from these soldiers and wrote the definitive Nepali dictionary without ever having visited Nepal. Although colonial in scope, it captures the strength of the people.

THE MOUNTAINEERS, founded in 1906, is a nonprofit outdoor activity and conservation club, whose mission is "to explore, study, preserve, and enjoy the natural beauty of the outdoors. . . . " Based in Seattle, Washington, the club is now the third-largest such organization in the United States, with 15,000 members and five branches throughout Washington State.

The Mountaineers sponsors both classes and year-round outdoor activities in the Pacific Northwest, which include hiking, mountain climbing, ski-touring, snowshoeing, bicycling, camping, kayaking and canoeing, nature study, sailing, and adventure travel. The club's conservation division supports environmental causes through educational activities, sponsoring legislation, and presenting informational programs. All club activities are led by skilled, experienced volunteers, who are dedicated to promoting safe and responsible enjoyment and preservation of the outdoors.

If you would like to participate in these organized outdoor activities or the club's programs, consider a membership in The Mountaineers. For information and an application, write or call The Mountaineers, Club Headquarters, 300 Third Avenue West, Seattle, Washington 98119; (206) 284-6310.

The Mountaineers Books, an active, nonprofit publishing program of the club, produces guidebooks, instructional texts, historical works, natural history guides, and works on environmental conservation. All books produced by The Mountaineers are aimed at fulfilling the club's mission.

Send or call for our catalog of more than 300 outdoor titles:

The Mountaineers Books
1001 SW Klickitat Way, Suite 201
Seattle, WA 98134
800-553-4453
mbooks@mountaineers.org
www.mountaineersbooks.org